Lecture Notes in Computer Science   7753

Commenced Publication in 1973
Founding and Former Series Editors:
Gerhard Goos, Juris Hartmanis, and Jan van Leeuwen

T0224019

Chittaranjan Hota   Pradip K. Srimani (Eds.)

Distributed Computing and Internet Technology

9th International Conference, ICDCIT 2013
Bhubaneswar, India, February 5-8, 2013
Proceedings

 Springer

Volume Editors

Chittaranjan Hota
Birla Institute of Technology and Science, Pilani
Faculty Incharge, Information Processing and Business Intelligence Unit
Hyderabad Campus, Hyderabad, Andhra Pradesh 500078, India
E-mail: hota@bits-hyderabad.ac.in

Pradip K. Srimani
Clemson University, Department of Computer Science
Clemson, SC 29634, USA
E-mail: srimani@cs.clemson.edu

ISSN 0302-9743   e-ISSN 1611-3349
ISBN 978-3-642-36070-1   e-ISBN 978-3-642-36071-8
DOI 10.1007/978-3-642-36071-8
Springer Heidelberg Dordrecht London New York

Library of Congress Control Number: 2012955346

CR Subject Classification (1998): C.2.0, C.2.2, C.2.4-5, F.2.2, H.3.3-5, H.4.1, H.5.3, H.2.7-8, I.2.6, E.3, K.6.5, H.2.4

LNCS Sublibrary: SL 3 – Information Systems and Application, incl. Internet/Web and HCI

Typesetting: Camera-ready by author, data conversion by Scientific Publishing Services, Chennai, India

Printed on acid-free paper

Springer is part of Springer Science+Business Media (www.springer.com)

Preface

This volume contains the research papers presented at the 9th International Conference on Distributed Computing and Internet Technology (ICDCIT 2013) held during February 5–8, 2013, at Bhubaneswar, India. The conference was organized by the Kalinga Institute of Industrial Technology (KIIT) University, Bhubaneswar, India (www.kiit.ac.in). The research papers submitted were put through an intensive review process and out of 164 papers only 40 papers were selected for presentation on the basis of reviews and comments. Each paper was reviewed by at least one Program Committee member.

The conference had another three constituting events: the Third Students Research Symposium, the Third Industry Symposium, and the Second Project Innovation Contest. All these events were very successful in meeting their respective objectives. The volume also contains papers contributed by invited speakers: Amos Korman, Anwittaman Datta, Jukka K. Nurminen, Salil Kanhere, and Srini Ramaswamy. The contributions from these speakers were thankfully acknowledged.

Many contributed to the success of this conference. Achyuta Samanta, the Founder of KIIT University, is thanked for patronizing this conference series from its beginning. R.K. Shyamasundar, the General Chair, is also thanked for his support at various stages of the conference. He was instrumental for the success of this conference series. The support of the Advisory Committee was immense and their help is gratefully acknowledged. The services of the Program Committee members and reviewers is also thankfully acknowledged. Financial help, the infrastructural facility provided by KIIT, and the services of the Organizing Committee are again sincerely acknowledged. The students Bubli Sagar and Supriya Vaddi of the University of Hyderabad, who helped in the preparation of these proceedings, are gratefully appreciated. Our special thanks to Hrushikesha Mohanty and D.N. Dwivedy for making everything possible. Lastly, the editorial board would like to thank Springer for publishing these proceedings in its *Lecture Notes in Computer Science* series.

November 2012

Chittaranjan Hota
Pradip Srimani

Organization

Patron

Achyuta Samanta   KIIT, India

Advisory Committee

Maurice Herlihy   Brown University, USA
Gérard Huet   INRIA, France
Tomasz Janowski   UNU-IIST, Macao
P.P. Mathur   KIIT, India
H. Mohanty   University of Hyderabad, India
David Peleg   WIS, Israel

General Chair

R.K. Shyamasundar   TIFR, India

Program Co-chairs

Pradip K. Srimani   Clemson University, USA
Chittaranjan Hota   BITS Hyderabad, India

Conference Management Chair

Prachet Bhuyan   KIIT, India

Organizing Chair

Bhabani S.P. Mishra   KIIT, India

Finance Chair

Santosh Pani   KIIT, India

Publicity Chair

Arup Abhinna Acharya   KIIT, India

Registration Chair

Manoj Kumar Mishra   KIIT, India

Publications Chair

Nachiketa Tarasia   KIIT, India

Student Symposium Co-chair

Abhishek Thakur   BITS Pilani Hyderabad Campus, India
Jnyanaranjan Mohanty   KIIT Bhubaneswar, India

Industry Symposium Co-chairs

Srini Ramswamy   ABB R&D Bangalore, India
Madhur Khandelwal   Shopping Wish, Hyderabad

Program Committee

Shivali Agarwal   IBM Bangalore, India
Bharat Bhargava   Purdue University, USA
Debmalya Biswas   Nokia Research
Debabrata Das   IIIT, Bangalore, India
Manik Lal Das   DAIICT, Gandhinagar, India
Elsa Estevez   UNU/IIST
Ben Firner   Rutgers University, USA
Soumya K. Ghosh   IIT, Kharagpur, India
Veena Goswami   KIIT, Bhubaneswar, India
Indranil Gupta   UIUC Urbana-Champaign, USA
Maurice Herlihy   Brown University, USA
Chittaranjan Hota   BITS-Pilani Hyderabad Campus, India
Sarath Chandra Janga   IUPU, Indianapolis, USA
Salil Kanhere   The University of New South Wales
Kishore Kothapalli   IIIT Hyderabad, India
Neeraj Mittal   UT Dallas, USA
Durga Prasad Mohapatra   NIT Rourkela, India
G.B. Mund   KIIT Bhubaneswar, India
V. Krishna Nandivada   IIT, Chennai, India
Debi Prasad Pati   TCS Kolkata, India
Ron Perrott   University of Oxford, UK
Muttukrishnan Raj   City University, UK
Chitra T. Rajan   PSG Tech, Coimbatore, India
Srini Ramaswamy   ABB Corporate Research Bangalore, India
Tathagata Ray   BITS Pilani Hyderabad, India

Krishna S.   IIT Bombay, India
Pushpendra Singh   IIIT-Delhi, India
Pradip Srimani   Clemson University, USA
T.S.B. Sudarshan   Amrita University, Bangalore, India
Animesh Tripathy   KIIT Bhubaneswar, India
Siba Kumar Udgata   University of Hyderabad, India
James Wang   Clemson University, USA
Rajeev Wankar   University of Hyderabad, India

Additional Reviewers

Acharya, Arup Abhinna   Natarajan, Aravind
Agrawal, Sarita   Novales, Ramon
Amintoosi, Haleh   Parulekar, Tejal
Arjunan, Pandarasamy   Patra, Sarat
Babiceanu, Radu   Rathinasamy, Bhavanandan
Banerjee, Asim   Raval, Mehul
Bhargava, Bharat   Ray, Abhishek
Bhuyan, Prachet   Ray, Tathagata
Das, Ananda Swarup   S., Jithendrian
Ding, Yihua   Satheesh, Hariram
Guo, Yan   Song, Xuebo
Jetley, Raoul   Sudarsan, Sithu
Jinwala, Devesh   Vadivel, A.
Kumar, Pradeep   Vaidyanathan, Aparajithan
Lin, Weiwei   Vu, Hai
Mall, Rajib   Yoshigoe, Kenji
Martha, Venkata Swamy   Yu, Liguo
Mills, K. Alex   Zhang, Yuanyuan
Mishra, Manoj Kumar   Zhao, Yue
Mitra, Suman

Table of Contents

Theoretical Distributed Computing Meets Biology: A Review 1
  Ofer Feinerman and Amos Korman

Participatory Sensing: Crowdsourcing Data from Mobile Smartphones
in Urban Spaces 19
  Salil S. Kanhere

Energy Efficient Distributed Computing on Mobile Devices 27
  Jukka K. Nurminen

Data Insertion and Archiving in Erasure-Coding Based Large-Scale
Storage Systems 47
  Lluis Pamies-Juarez, Frédérique Oggier, and Anwitaman Datta

Medical Software – Issues and Best Practices 69
  Raoul Jetley, Sithu Sudarsan, Sampath R., and Srini Ramaswamy

Improved Interference in Wireless Sensor Networks 92
  Pragya Agrawal and Gautam K. Das

Trust Based Secure Gateway Discovery Mechanism for Integrated
Internet and MANET 103
  Mohammed Asrar Ahmed and Khaleel Ur Rahman Khan

Improving MapReduce Performance through Complexity
and Performance Based Data Placement in Heterogeneous
Hadoop Clusters 115
  Rajashekhar M. Arasanal and Daanish U. Rumani

Online Recommendation of Learning Path for an E-Learner under
Virtual University 126
  Prasenjit Basu, Suman Bhattacharya, and Samir Roy

A Parallel 2-Approximation NC-Algorithm for Range Assignment
Problem in Packet Radio Networks 137
  Bijaya Kishor Bhatta and D. Pushparaj Shetty

An Efficient Localization of Nodes in a Sensor Network Using Conflict
Minimization with Controlled Initialization 145
  Himangshu Ranjan Borah and Himkalyan Bordoloi

Abstract Interpretation of Recursive Queries 157
  Agostino Cortesi and Raju Halder

Verification of Message Sequence Structures 171
    Meenakshi D'Souza and Teodor Knapik

Neural Networks Training Based on Differential Evolution in Radial
Basis Function Networks for Classification of Web Logs 183
    Ch. Sanjeev Kumar Dash, Ajit Kumar Behera,
    Manoj Kumar Pandia, and Satchidananda Dehuri

Circle Formation by Asynchronous Transparent Fat Robots 195
    Suparno Datta, Ayan Dutta, Sruti Gan Chaudhuri, and
    Krishnendu Mukhopadhyaya

Controlling Packet Loss of Bursty and Correlated Traffics in a Variant
of Multiple Vacation Policy 208
    Abhijit Datta Banik and Sujit K. Samanta

Consistent Coordination Decoupling in Tuple Space Based Mobile
Middleware: Design and Formal Specifications 220
    Suddhasil De, Diganta Goswami, and Sukumar Nandi

Power Efficient Data Gathering for Sensor Network 232
    Anushua Dutta, Kunjal Thakkar, Sunirmal Khatua, and Rajib K. Das

Computing on Encrypted Character Strings in Clouds 244
    Günter Fahrnberger

Design of a New OFTM Algorithm towards Abort-Free Execution 255
    Ammlan Ghosh and Nabendu Chaki

GAR: An Energy Efficient GA-Based Routing for Wireless Sensor
Networks 267
    Suneet K. Gupta, Pratyay Kuila, and Prasanta K. Jana

Prediction of Processor Utilization for Real-Time Multimedia Stream
Processing Tasks.. 278
    Henryk Krawczyk, Jerzy Proficz, and Bartłomiej Daca

An Architecture for Dynamic Web Service Provisioning Using
Peer-to-Peer Networks.. 290
    Sujoy Mistry, Dibyanshu Jaiswal, Sagar Virani,
    Arijit Mukherjee, and Nandini Mukherjee

Network of Social Listeners.. 302
    Hrushikesha Mohanty

Computational Social Science: A Bird's Eye View 319
    Hrushikesha Mohanty

Localization Based on Two-Bound Reflected Signals in Wireless Sensor
Networks   334
    Kaushik Mondal, Arjun Talwar, Partha Sarathi Mandal, and
    Bhabani P. Sinha

Trading of Grade Based Incentives to Avoid Free Riding and Starvation
in P2P Network   347
    S. Moses Dian and B. Ramadoss

Supporting Location Information Privacy in Mobile Devices   361
    Deveeshree Nayak, M. Venkata Swamy, and Srini Ramaswamy

Adaptive Task Scheduling in Service Oriented Crowd Using SLURM . . .   373
    Vikram Nunia, Bhavesh Kakadiya, Chittaranjan Hota, and
    Muttukrishnan Rajarajan

An Efficient Method for Synchronizing Clocks of Networked ECUs
in Automotive Systems   386
    Kumar Padmanabh, Amit Gupta, and Purnendu Sinha

A Local Search Based Approximation Algorithm for Strong Minimum
Energy Topology Problem in Wireless Sensor Networks   398
    Bhawani S. Panda and D. Pushparaj Shetty

MSSA: A M-Level Sufferage-Based Scheduling Algorithm in Grid
Environment   410
    Sanjaya Kumar Panda and Pabitra Mohan Khilar

Privacy Preserving Distributed K-Means Clustering in Malicious Model
Using Zero Knowledge Proof   420
    Sankita Patel, Viren Patel, and Devesh Jinwala

Solving the 4QBF Problem in Polynomial Time by Using the
Biological-Inspired Mobility   432
    Bogdan Aman, Gabriel Ciobanu, and Shankara Narayanan Krishna

Slicing XML Documents Using Dependence Graph   444
    Madhusmita Sahu and Durga Prasad Mohapatra

Effective Web-Service Discovery Using K-Means Clustering   455
    A. Santhana Vijayan and S.R. Balasundaram

SPARSHA: A Low Cost Refreshable Braille for Deaf-Blind People
for Communication with Deaf-Blind and Non-disabled Persons   465
    Ruman Sarkar, Smita Das, and Sharmistha Roy

A New Approach to Design a Domain Specific Web Search Crawler
Using Multilevel Domain Classifier   476
    Sukanta Sinha, Rana Dattagupta, and Debajyoti Mukhopadhyay

An Efficient and Dynamic Concept Hierarchy Generation for Data
Anonymization 488
   Sri Krishna Adusumalli and V. Valli Kumari

Wikipedia Articles Representation with Matrix'u 500
   Julian Szymański

Recovery Protocols for Flash File Systems 511
   Ravi Tandon and Gautam Barua

Semantic Concurrency Control on Continuously Evolving OODBMS
Using Access Control Lists 523
   V. Geetha and N. Sreenath

Querying a Service from Repository of SMaps 535
   Supriya Vaddi and Hrushikesha Mohanty

Faster Query Execution for Partitioned RDF Data 547
   Sandeep Vasani, Mohit Pandey, Minal Bhise, and Trupti Padiya

A Selection Algorithm for Focused Crawlers Incorporating Semantic
Metadata 561
   Saurabh Wadwekar and Debajyoti Mukhopadhyay

Author Index 573

Theoretical Distributed Computing Meets Biology: A Review

Ofer Feinerman[1,*] and Amos Korman[2,**]

[1] The Weizmann Institute of Science, Israel
feinermanofer@gmail.com
[2] CNRS and University Paris Diderot, France
amos.korman@liafa.univ-paris-diderot.fr

Abstract. In recent years, several works have demonstrated how the study of biology can benefit from an algorithmic perspective. Since biological systems are often distributed in nature, this approach may be particularly useful in the context of distributed computing. As the study of algorithms is traditionally motivated by an engineering and technological point of view, the adaptation of ideas from theoretical distributed computing to biological systems is highly non-trivial and requires a delicate and careful treatment. In this review, we discuss some of the recent research within this framework and suggest several challenging future directions.

1 Introduction

1.1 Background and Motivation

Nature serves as inspiration for scientists in all disciplines and computer science is, certainly, no exception. The reverse direction, that of applying studies in computer science to improve our understanding of biological organisms, is currently dominated by the field of bioinformatics. A natural question to be asked is thus the following: how can we apply our knowledge in other aspects of computer science to enhance the study of biology? This direction of research may become particularly fruitful in the context of distributed computing, since indeed, biological systems are distributed in nature (e.g., cells are composed of proteins, organs of cells, populations of organisms and so on).

It is important to note that distributed computing is traditionally studied from an engineering and technological point of view where the focus is on the design of efficient algorithms to solve well defined problems. Analyzing algorithms as used in the biological world requires a different point of view, since the setting is usually unknown, as are the details of the algorithm and even the problem that it aims at solving. Hence, the adaptation of ideas from theoretical distributed computing to biological systems is highly non-trivial and requires

* Supported by the Israel Science Foundation (grant 1694/10) and by the Clore Foundation.
** Supported by the ANR projects DISPLEXITY and PROSE, and by the INRIA project GANG.

C. Hota and P.K. Srimani (Eds.): ICDCIT 2013, LNCS 7753, pp. 1–18, 2013.

a delicate and careful treatment. In many cases, such a study would require a collaboration between biologists that empirically investigate the phenomena, and computer science theoreticians who analyze it. The hope is that despite their enormous complexity, some aspects of biological systems can still be captured by relatively simple abstract models which can be analyzed using distributed computing techniques. In this case, the potential benefit of this direction of research would be huge, not only in terms of understanding large biological systems but also in enriching the scope of theoretical distributed computing.

The synergy between distributed computing and experimental biology is being tightened by methodological advances on both sides. On the distributed computing side, the last twenty years have been very fruitful in terms of advancing our fundamental understanding on topics such as dynamic networks, mobile agents, population protocols, and network computing in general. These advances may indicate that the field of distributed computing has reached the maturity level of being useful also for the context of understanding large biological systems. Since distributed computing addresses the relations between the single entity and the group from the theoretical perspective, experimentally, there is a need to simultaneously probe these two scales. Indeed, from the biological side, the main experimental challenge lies in being able to follow large numbers of identified individuals within behaving populations. The sheer size of these ensembles has, for many years, made this a formidable task. However several technological advances, and above all the huge increase in the availability of computing power, have brought this goal to within our reach.

1.2   Recent Technological Advances in Experimental Biology

Examples for the observation of large population are numerous and span various methodologies and biological systems. Fluorescence tagging methods provide detailed information of the internal state of cells in terms of both protein levels and fast phosphorylation dynamics. Coupled with microscopy or FACS measurements systems, fluorescence can be used to simultaneously and quantitatively measure ten or more such different internal variables over populations of millions of cells [27]. A second example comes from the field of neuroscience where there has been a growing emphasis on recording from large neuron populations of behaving animals. The relevant techniques include light-weight tetrodes and multi-electrode arrays [53] as well as the use of activity sensitive fluorescent proteins [10]. Cooperating biological individuals often engage in collective motions. The availability of high-resolution cameras and strong computers together with image processing analysis make these movements tractable. Here, too, examples are many ranging from immune cells moving within the body [29], cells within growing plants [45], birds in flocks [7], fish in schools, and ants within their colonies. Recent tagging technology has been applied to allow for long-term individual tracking of all members within a group (see Figure 1 and [42]). Another interesting example lies in the ability to measure and quantify population heterogeneity and specifically map the spread of behavioral thresholds of individuals to different stimuli [42,55].

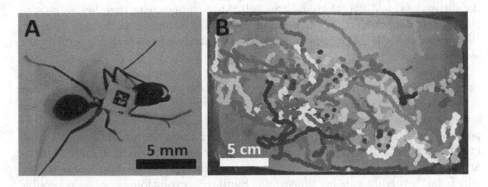

Fig. 1. A. a photo of a tagged carpenter ant worker. B. walking trajectories obtained from automatically tracking tagged ants.

Tracking all individuals within a group leads to the accumulation of huge data sets. On the one hand, this detailed provides us with the rich and detailed information that is required to test theoretical hypothesis. On the other hand, enormous datasets are difficult to manage towards the extraction of relevant information. This challenge has sparked the development of high-throughput automated ethonomics [8].

Experimental manipulations offer a great tool towards deciphering the data we collect and deciding between alternative hypotheses. Traditionally, such manipulations were administered at the level of the group. More recently, several methodologies for manipulating specific individuals within the group have been described. The most striking example is probability the ability to excite neurons by directed illumination which has opened up the field of opto-genetics [10] . Automated manipulation of the trajectories of specific individuals within groups have been demonstrated both in the context of fish and ant colonies [43].

1.3 Bringing the Two Disciplines Closer

Many fields have contributed to biology but we believe distributed computing can bring a new and fresh perspective. To elaborate more on that, we first discuss an interesting difference in the way the notion of a *model* is typically perceived by natural scientists and by computer scientists. In a sense, when it comes to settings that involve multiple individual entities (e.g., network processors, mobile agents, sensors, robots, etc.), computer scientists distinguish the *model* (sometimes called also *setting*), which includes a description of the environment and the restricted capabilities of the individuals, from the *algorithm*, which includes the course of actions which individuals follow. In a way, this corresponds to the distinction between *hardware* and *software*. For example, the topological space in which entities operate as well as their memory capacity are considered to be part of the model, and the particular way in which the entities utilize their memory is part of their algorithm. In contrast, researchers in the natural sciences typically do not make this distinction and treat all these components together as part of the model. We believe that the point of view which makes a distinction between the model and the algorithm can benefit the study of natural phenomena for several reasons.

Although life is highly plastic and evolvable one can still make distinctions between factors that constrain a living system and courses of actions that may be employed within such constrains. A simple example involves physical constraints such as quantum shot noise that defines a lower bound for any light perception be it biological [6] or artificial. Other examples are more subtle and include the distinction between the different time scales inherent to an evolutionary process. One can clearly classify slow evolving features as constraints within which fast evolving can be tuned [30]. Similarly, evolution is not a reversible process so that historical evolutionary decisions may constrain organisms for prolonged periods of times, this may even lead to evolutionary traps [44] which may be perilous for species survival. These internal "hardware" constraints together with environmental constraints are analogous to the computer scientific "model". Faster evolving parameters as well as actual cognitive, behavioral decisions are analogous to an "algorithm". We therefore believe that the distinction between these two terms promises a novel and relevant perspectives which can benefit the biological sciences. Theoretical computer science, and theoretical distributed computing in particular, can contribute in this direction.

Recently, several works have utilized methods from distributed computing to improve our understanding of biological systems . It is our belief, however, that all current achievements are very preliminary, and that this direction of research is still making its first steps. Indeed, one important issue to note in this respect, is that, currently, all corresponding works suffer from an (arguably inherent) *gap* between the analyzed setting and the "real setting", that is, the one apparent in nature. In each particular case, bridging this gap (or even just slightly reducing it), is a challenging task that must be a combined effort of both field biologists and theoreticians.

In this review, we describe four frameworks that aim to incorporate distributed computing with biological phenomena. In the following sections, we shall discuss the frameworks in detail, list current results, explain their potential impact on biology, and suggest future research directions. The four frameworks are divided according to the extent in which the model or the algorithm are assumed to be "known" (or "given"). That is, even though the biological setting is never, actually, known; assumptions regarding the model or algorithm can actually facilitate different lines of investigation.

1.4   The Four Frameworks

Before dwelling into the details, let us first list the frameworks and discuss them briefly. The frameworks are segregated using the distinction between model and algorithm as described above. At this point we would like to stress that our classification of papers into the four frameworks below is, to some extent, (as many other classifications) a matter of opinion, or interpretation.

1. **"Unknown" algorithm and "unknown" model.** Here, both the model and the algorithm are, mostly, absent, and two approaches have been considered to handle this complex situation.

   (a) **Surmising.** This classical approach aims at understanding some particular phenomena that has been empirically observed. The approach involves coming up with (somewhat informed) guesses regarding both the model and the algorithm, together with their analysis. The assumed model and algorithm typically do not claim to represent reality accurately, but rather to reflect some aspects of the real setting. The distributed computing experience would come handy for allowing the guessing of more involved and efficient algorithms and for enhancing their rigorous analysis. This type of study was conducted recently by Afek et al. [2] concerning the fly's brain, where the phenomena observed was that a variant of the Minimum Independent Set (MIS) problem is solved during the nervous system development of the fly.

   (b) **Finding dependencies between parameters.** This new framework aims at obtaining knowledge regarding the model by connecting it to the output of the algorithm, which is typically more accessible experimentally. The framework is composed of three stages. The first stage consists of finding an abstract setting that can be realizable in an experiment, parameterized by an unknown parameter a (e.g., the parameter can be the number of possible states that entities can possibly possess). The second stage involves analyzing the model and obtaining theoretical tradeoffs between the parameter a and the performance efficiency of the algorithm; the tradeoffs are obtained using techniques that are typically associated with distributed computing. Finally, the third stage consists of conducting suitable experiments and measuring the actual efficiency of the biological system. The idea is, that using the tradeoffs and the experimental results on the efficiency of the algorithm, one would be able to deduce information (e.g., bounds) regarding the parameter a. A first step to demonstrate this framework was recently made by the authors of this review [20], in the context of foraging strategies of ants.

2. **"Known" algorithm and "unknown" model.** This framework corresponds to the situation in which the algorithm is already fairly understood, and the challenge is to find a simple and abstract setting that, on the one hand, somehow captures some essence of the "real" setting, and, on the other hand, complies well with the given algorithm to explain some empirically observed phenomena. We are not aware of any work in the framework of biology where this framework was employed. However, the work of Kleinberg [31] on *small world* phenomena can serve as an example for this framework within the context of sociology.

3. **"Unknown" algorithm and "known" model.** In the context of large biological ensembles, this framework fixes an abstract model consisting of multiple processors (either mobile, passively mobile, or stationary) operating in a given setting. Two approaches are considered.

(a) **Complexity analysis.** Here, the complexity of the abstract model is analyzed, aiming at bounding the power of computation of the processors as a group. In all cases studied so far, the model seems to represent a very high level abstraction of reality, and the resulting computational power is typically very strong. Furthermore, known complexity results are obtained on models that seem too far from reality to be realized in experiments. Hence, this line of research currently not only does not involve experimental work, but also does not seem to be related to such experiments in the near future. As the focus of this review is on connections between theoretical work in distributed computing and experimental work in biology, we decided to only briefly discuss this line of research in this review.

(b) **Guessing an algorithm.** Here, again, the aim is to provide an explanation to some observed phenomena. The model is given to the researchers, and the goal is to come up with a simple algorithm whose analysis complies with the phenomena. For example, Bruckstein [9] aims at explaining the phenomena in which ant trails seem to be relatively straight. The paper relies on a fairly reasonable model, in which ants can see their nearest neighbors, all ants walk in one direction and in the same speed. Then the paper contributes by providing an algorithm whose outcome is straight lines.

4. **"Known" algorithm and "known" model.** This framework assumes a model and algorithm that have been substantiated to some extent by empirical findings. The efficiency of the algorithm is then theoretically analyzed, as is, with the goal of obtaining further insight into system function. The corresponding study is currently very limited: to the best of our knowledge, its merely contains works analyzing bird flocking algorithms.

1.5   Other Related Work

Computer science and biology have enjoyed a long and productive relationship for several decades. One aspect of this relationship concerns the field of *bioinformatics*, which utilizes computer science frameworks to retrieve and analyze biological data, such as nucleic acid and protein sequences. The field of *natural computing* is another aspect of this relationship; this field brings together nature and computing to encompass three classes of methods: (1) simulating natural patterns and behaviors in computers, (2) potentially designing novel types of computers, and (3) developing new problem-solving techniques. (For detailed reviews, see *e.g.,* [11,33,40].)

The motivation for the latter class of methods is to provide alternative solutions to problems that could not be (satisfactorily) resolved by other, more traditional, techniques. This direction of research is termed *bio-inspired computing* or *biologically motivated computing* [12,37], or *computing with biological metaphors* [50]. *Swarm intelligence*, for instance, refers to the design of algorithms or distributed problem-solving devices inspired by the collective behavior of social insects and other animal societies. This sort of work is inspired by biology but not bound by biology, that is, it doesn't have to remain true in the biology context. Examples of this approach can be found, *e.g.*, in the book by Dorigo and Stutzle [16] which describes computer algorithms inspired by ant behavior, and particularly, the ability to find what computer scientists would call shortest paths. Another example of this approach comes in the context of applications to robotics. *Swarm robotics*, for example, refers to the coordination of multi-robot systems consisting of large numbers of mostly simple physical robots [17].

The reverse direction, that of applying ideas from theoretical computer science to improve our understanding of biological phenomena, has received much less attention in the literature, but has started to emerge in recent years, from different perspectives. An example for such an attempt is the work of Valiant [51] that introduced a computational model of evolution and suggested that Darwinian evolution be studied in the framework of computational learning theory. Several other works (which are discussed in the following sections) took this direction by applying algorithmic ideas from the field of distributed computing to the context of large and complex biological ensembles.

At this point, we would like to note that in several works both directions of research co-exist. However, since the topic of this review focuses on implying ideas from distributed computing to biology, then, when discussing particular works, we shall focus our attention on this direction of research and typically ignore the bio-inspired one.

2 "Unknown" Model and "Unknown" Algorithm

This framework corresponds to the situation in which both model and algorithm are, to some extent, absent. Roughly speaking, two approaches have been considered to handle this complex situation. The first approach is classical in the context of science. It concerns the understanding of a particular phenomena that has been observed experimentally, and consists in guessing both a model and an algorithm to fit the given phenomena. The second approach aims at improving our understanding of the connections between model and/or algorithmic parameters, and to reduce the parameter space by finding dependencies between parameters. Furthermore, when coupled with suitable experiments, this approach can be used to obtain bounds on parameters; which may be very difficult to obtain otherwise. Let us first describe the more classical approach.

2.1 Surmising

This approach concerns a particular phenomena that has been observed empirically. After some preprocessing stage, consisting of high level observations and some data-analysis, the main goal is to come up with (informed) guesses for both a model and an algorithm to fit the given phenomena. In other words, the model and algorithm are tailored to the particular phenomena. Note that this guessing approach is hardly new in biology, and in fact, it is one of the more common ones. However, it is far less common to obtain such guesses using the types of reasoning that are typically associated with distributed computing. Indeed, the distributed computing experience would come handy here for two main reasons: (1) for allowing the guessing of more involved efficient algorithms and (2) for enhancing their rigorous analysis. This was the case in the recent study by Afek et al. [2] concerning the fly's brain, where the phenomena observed was that a variant of the Minimum Independent Set (MIS) problem is solved during the development of the nervous system of the fly.

MIS on the fly: Informally, the classical Maximal Independent Set (MIS) problem aims at electing a set of leaders in a graph such that all other nodes in the graph are connected to a member of the MIS and no two MIS members are connected to each other. This problem has been studied extensively for more than twenty years in the distributed computing community. Very recently, Afek et al. [2] observed that a variant of the distributed MIS problem is solved during the development of the fly's nervous system. More specifically, during this process, some cells in the pre-neural clusters become Sensory Organ Precursor (SOP) cells. The outcome of this process guarantees that each cell is either an SOP or directly connected to an SOP and no two SOPs are connected. This is similar to the requirements of MIS. However, the solution used by the fly appears to be quite different from previous algorithms suggested for this task. This may be due to the limited computational power of cells as compared to what is assumed for processors in traditional computer science solutions. In particular, in the "fly's solution", the cells could not rely on long and complex messages or on information regarding the number of neighbors they have.

Afek at al. suggested an abstract (relatively restrictive) model of computation that captures some essence of the setting in which flies solve the SOP selection problem. For this abstract model, the authors were able to develop a new MIS algorithm that does not use any knowledge about the number of neighbors a node has. Instead, with probability that increases exponentially over time, each node that has not already been connected to an MIS node proposes itself as an MIS node. While the original algorithm of Afek et al [2] requires that nodes know an upper bound on the total number of nodes in the network, a new version of this algorithm [1] removes this requirement.

The algorithms in [1,2] are motivated by applications to computer networks, and hence primeraly follow the bio-inspired approach. Nevertheless, it is interesting to note that some aspects of these algorithms are consistent with empirical observations. Indeed, in [2] the authors used microscopy experiments to follow SOP selection in developing flies, and discovered that a stochastic feedback process, in which selection probability increases as a function of time, provides a good match to the experimental results; such a stochastic feedback process is also evident in the corresponding algorithms. Hence, these works also follow the direction of research which is the topic of this review.

2.2 Finding Dependencies between Parameters

In contrast to the previous approach, this approach does not focus on understanding a particular phenomena, but instead aims at understanding the underlying connections between the model and/or algorithm ingredients. Indeed, a common problem, when studying a biological system is the complexity of the system and the huge number of parameters involved. Finding ways of reducing the parameter space is thus of great importance. One approach is to divide the parameter space into critical and non-critical directions where changes in non-critical parameters do not affect overall system behavior [22,26]. Another approach, which is typically utilized in physics, would be to define theoretical bounds on system performance and use them to find dependencies between different parameters. This approach may be particularly interesting in the case where tradeoffs are found between parameters that are relatively easy to measure experimentally and others that are not. Indeed, in this case, using such tradeoffs, relatively easy measurements of the "simple parameters" would allow us to obtain non-trivial bounds on the "difficult parameters". Note that such theoretical tradeoffs are expected to depend highly on the setting, which is by itself difficult to understand.

Very recently, a first step in the direction of applying this approach has been established by the authors of this review, based on ideas from theoretical distributed computing [20]. That work considers the context of central place foraging, such as performed by ants around their next. The particular theoretical setting, involving mobile probabilistic agents (e.g., ants) that search for food items about a source node (e.g., the nest) was introduced in [21] and has two important advantages. On the one hand, this setting (or, perhaps, a similar one) is natural enough to be experimentally captured, and on the other hand, it is sufficiently simple to be analyzed theoretically. Indeed, in [20] we establish tradeoffs between the time to perform the task and the amount of memory (or, alternatively, the number of internal states) used by agents to perform the task. Whereas the time to perform the task is relatively easy to measure, the number of internal states of ants (assuming they act similarly to robots) is very difficult to empirically evaluate directly.

As mentioned in [20], the natural candidates to test this framework on would be desert ants of the genus *Cataglyphys* and the honeybees *Apis mellifera*. These species seem to possess many of the individual skills required for the behavioral patterns that are utilized in the corresponding upper bounds in [20,21], and hence are expected to be time efficient.

It is important to note that it is not claimed that the setting proposed in [20] precisely captures the framework in which these species perform search (although it does constitute a good first approximation to it). Indeed, it is not unreasonable to assume that a careful inspection of these species in nature would reveal a somewhat different framework and would require the formulation of similar suitable theoretical memory bounds. Finding the "correct" framework and corresponding tradeoffs is left for future work. Once these are established, combining the memory lower bounds with experimental measurements of search speed with varying numbers of searchers would then provide quantitative evidence regarding the number of memory bits (or, alternatively, the number of states) used by ants. Furthermore, these memory bits must mainly be used by ants to assess their own group size prior to the search. Hence, such a result would provide insight regarding the ants' quorum sensing process inside the nest.

3   "Known" Algorithm and "Unknown" Model

This framework corresponds to the situation in which the algorithm is already fairly understood, and the challenge is to find a simple and abstract model that, on the one hand, somehow captures some essence of the "real" setting, and, on the other hand, complies well with the given algorithm to explain some empirically observed phenomena. Although this framework could be applied within the framework of biology we are not aware of any such work. Nevertheless, to clarify the usefulness of this framework, we describe works on *small world* phenomena and their applicability to sociology.

Small World Phenomena: It is long known that most people in social networks are linked by short chains of acquaintances. The famous "six degrees of separation" experiment by Milgram [38] implied not only that there are short chains between individuals, but also that people are good at finding those chains. Indeed, individuals operating with only local information are expected to find these chains by using the simple *greedy* algorithm. Kleinberg [31] investigated this *small world* phenomena from a distributed computing point of view, and came up with an extremely simple abstract model that, on the one hand, somehow captures some essence of the "real" setting, and, on the other hand, complies well with a greedy algorithm to explain the small world phenomena.

The model consists of a two-dimensional grid topology augmented with long-range connections, where the probability $\Pr(x, y)$ of a connecting node x with a node y is some (inverse proportional) function of their lattice distance $d(x, y)$, that is, $\Pr(x, y) \approx 1/d(x, y)^{\alpha}$, for some parameter α. This abstract model does seem to represent some essence of social networks, where it is reasonable to assume that each person has several immediate acquaintances and fewer "long range acquaintance", and that it is less likely to have a long range acquaintance if this acquaintance is "far away" (in some sense). Kleinberg [31] then studied distributed greedy algorithms that resemble the one used by Milgram: for transmitting a message, at each step, the holder of the message must pass it across one of its (either short or long range) connections, leading to one who minimizes the distance to the destination. Crucially, this current holder does not know the long range connections of other nodes. The algorithm is evaluated by its expected delivery time, which represents the expected number of steps needed to forward a message between a random source and target in a network generated according to the model. It turns out that when the long-range connections follow an inverse-square distribution, i.e., the case $\alpha = 2$, the expected time to deliver a message is small: polylogarithmic in the number of nodes. The setting was further analyzed proving that the exponent $\alpha = 2$ for the long range distribution is the only exponent at which any distributed algorithm on the grid can achieve a polylogarithmic time delivery.

Following [31], several other works investigated extensions of this model, in what has become a whole area of research (see [23] for a survey). In particular, Fraigniaud and Giakkoupis proved [24] that all networks are smallworldizable, in the sense that, for any network G, there is a natural way to augment G with long-range links, so that (a minor variant of) greedy routing performs in $2^{\sqrt{\log n}}$ steps. Before, [25] proved that this bound is essentially the best that you can expect in arbitrary networks. In addition, Chaintreau et al. [14] studied how the Kleinberg's harmonic distribution of the long-range links could emerge naturally from a decentralized process. It appears that if individuals move at random and tend to forget their contact along with time, then we end up with connections between individuals that are distributed harmonically, as in Kleinberg's paper.

4   "Unknown" Algorithm and "Known" Model

In the context of large biological ensembles, this framework fixes an abstract model consisting of multiple processors (either mobile, passively mobile, or stationary). Two approaches are considered. The first approach analyzes the computational power of such models, and the second suggests simple algorithms that can potentially operate within model constraints and explain known phenomena.

4.1   Computational Aspects

The fundamental question of what can be computed by biological systems is fascinating. One of the aspects of this question concerns, for example, the computational power of ants. It is quite evident that the computational abilities of the human brain are much more impressive than those of a typical ant colony, at least in some respects. A basic philosophical question is whether this computational gap is a consequence of the different physical settings (e.g., in the case of ants, this includes the physical organization of ants and their individual limitations), or because it was simply not developed by evolution as it wasn't necessary for survival. To put it more simply: is the reason that an ant colony is not as smart as a human brain because it *cannot* be or because it doesn't *need* to be?

While we are very far away from answering such a question, some very initial steps have been taken in this direction. Various abstract models which loosely represent certain settings in nature are suggested and their computational power is analyzed. Broadly speaking, in all such previous works, the analyzed model appears to be very strong, and is often compared to a Turing machine. It is important to note, however, that, as a generalization, the motivations for some of the suggested models in the literature come only partially from biology, and are affected equally by sensor networks and robotics applications. Indeed, in all cases studied so far, the model seems to represent a very high level abstraction of reality, and in particular, seems too far from reality to be realized in experiments.

Hence, this line of research currently not only does not involve experimental work, but also does not seem to be related to such experiments in the near future. As the focus of this review is on connections between theoretical work in distributed computing and experimental work in biology, we decided to only briefly discuss corresponding computational results.

Population Protocols: The abstract model of population protocols, introduced by Angluin et al. [3], was originally intending to capture abstract features of computations made by tiny processes such as sensors, but it was observed also that it may be useful for modeling the propagation of diseases and rumors in human populations as well as stochastically interacting molecules. The question of what can be computed by population protocols has been studied quite thoroughly. Specifically, perhaps the main result in the setting of population protocols is that the set of computable predicates under a "fair" adversary is either exactly equal to or closely related to the set of semilinear predicates [4]. The model was shown to be much more powerful under a (uniform) random scheduler, as it can simulate a register machine. For a good survey of population protocols, refer to [5].

A related model was studied by Lachmann and Sella [34], which is inspired by task switching of ants in a colony. The model consists of a system composed of identical agents, where each agent has a finite number of internal states. The agent's internal state may change either by interaction with the environment or by interaction with another agent. Analyzing the model's dynamics, the authors prove it to be computationally complete. A result in a similar flavor was obtained by Sole and Delgado [49].

Ant Robotics: Ant robotics is a special case of swarm robotics, in which the robots can communicate via markings [54]. This model is inspired by some species of ants that lay and follow pheromone trails. Recently, Shiloni at el. showed that a single ant robot (modeled as finite state machine) can simulate the execution of any arbitrary Turing machine [46]. This proved that a single ant robot, using pheromones, can execute arbitrarily complex single-robot algorithms. However, the result does not hold for N robots.

Hopfield Model: The celebrated Hopfield model [28] uses intuition from the field of statistical mechanics and neuroscience to provide intuition for associative memory in the brain. The model includes a learning stage at which a large number of distributed memories are imprinted onto a neuronal network. This is achieved by a very simple learning algorithm that fine tunes the connections (synapses) between the neurons. Once the memories are set, they can be retrieved by employing simple dynamics which is inspired by actual neuronal dynamics. Namely, neurons are modeled to be in one of two states as inspired by the all-or-none nature of action potentials; Second, neuronal dynamics are governed by local threshold computations as inspired by the actual physiological membrane thresholds. Formed memories are associative in the sense that partial memories are enough to reconstruct the full ones. The model was shown to be highly robust to failures such as connection, or neuronal deletions. Further, it has been proven, that this model for neuronal networks is computationally complete [47].

The Hopfield model is not only biologically inspired but also inspires biologists. It would be fair to say, that much of our intuition for distributed information storage and associative memories in the brain derives from this model. On the other hand, the Hopfield model is very far from being biologically accurate and as such it is not as useful as one might expect in the modeling of actual micro-circuits in the brain.

Distributed Computing on Fixed Networks with Simple Processors: Recently, Emek et al. [18] introduced a new relaxation of the Beeping model from [1,2], where the computational power of each processor is extremely weak and is based on thresholds. Despite the weak restrictions of the model, the authors show that some of the classical distributed computing problems (e.g., MIS, coloring, maximal matching) can still be solved somewhat efficiently. This shows that the power computation of such a model is high, at least by judging it from the point of view of tasks typically associated with computer networks.

4.2   Guessing an Algorithm

Here, again, the goal is to provide an explanation to some observed phenomena. The model is given to the researchers, and the goal is to come up with a simple algorithm whose analysis complies with the phenomena. For example, Bruckstein [9] aims at explaining the phenomena in which ant trails seem to be relatively straight. The paper relies on a fairly reasonable model, in which ants walking from their nest towards a food source initially follow a random, convoluted path laid by the first ant to find the food. The model further includes the reasonable assumption that an ant on the trail can see other ants in its proximity. The paper goes on to suggest a simple algorithm in which each ant continuously orients her direction toward the ant walking directly in front of her. It is shown that this algorithm results in a "corner-cutting" process by which the ant trail quickly converges to the shortest distance line connecting the nest and the food source.

5   "Known" Algorithm and "Known" Model

This framework concerns the analysis of specific algorithms operating in particular given models. The corresponding study currently includes works on *bird flocking* algorithms. In these cases, the specific algorithms and models studied are supported by some empirical evidence, although this evidence is, unfortunately, quite limited. The main objective of this framework is to have a better, more analytical, understanding of the algorithms used in nature. Nevertheless, potentially, this framework can also be used to give some feedback on the validity of the proposed algorithm. Indeed, on the one hand, some positive evidence is obtained if the (typically non-trivial) analysis finds the algorithm feasible and/or explaining a certain phenomena. On the other hand, proving its unfeasibility, e.g., that it requires unreasonable time to be effective, serves as a negative feedback, which may lead to disqualifying its candidature.

Bird Flocking Algorithms: The global behavior formed when a group of birds are foraging or in flight is called *flocking*. This behavior bares similarities with the swarming behavior of insects, the shoaling behavior of fish, and herd behavior of land animals. It is commonly assumed that flocking arises from simple rules that are followed by individuals and does not involve any central coordination. Such simple rules are, for example: (a) alignment - steer towards average heading of neighbors, (b) separation - avoid crowding neighbors, and (c) cohesion - steer towards average position of neighbors (long range attraction). With these three simple rules, as initially proposed by Reynolds [41], computer simulations show that the flock moves in a "realistic" way, creating complex motion and interaction. The basic flocking model has been extended in several different ways since [41]. Measurements of bird flocking have been established [19] using high-speed cameras, and a computer analysis has been made to test the simple rules of flocking mentioned above. Evidence was found that the rules generally hold true and that the long range attraction rule (cohesion) applies to the nearest 5-10 neighbors of the flocking bird and is independent of the distance of these neighbors from the bird.

Bird flocking has received considerable attention in the scientific and engineering literature, and was typically viewed through the lens of control theory and physics. Computer simulations support the intuitive belief that, by repeated averaging, each bird eventually converges to a fixed speed and heading. This has been proven theoretically, but how long it takes for the system to converge has remained an open question until the work of Chazelle [13]. Using tools typically associated with theoretical computer science, Chazelle analyzed two classical models that are highly representative of the many variants considered in the literature, namely: (a) the kinematic model, which is a variant of the classical Vicsek model [52], and (b) the dynamic model [15]. Chazelle proved an upper bound on the time to reach steady state, which is extremely high: a tower-of-twos of height linear in the number of birds. Furthermore, it turns out that this upper bound is in fact tight. That is, Chazelle proved that with a particular initial settings, the expected time to reach steady state is a tower-of-twos of height.

That lower bound is, of course, huge, and no (reasonably large) group of real birds can afford itself so much time. At first glance, it may seem as if this result already implies that real birds do not perform the considered algorithms. However, for such an argument to be more convincing, several assumptions need to modified to suit better the setting of real birds. The first issue concerns the notion of convergence. As defined in [13], reaching a steady state, means that the system no longer changes. Of course, birds are not expected to actually achieve this goal. It would be interesting in come up and investigate some relaxation to this notion of convergence, that would correspond better to reality. Second, it would be interesting to prove lower bounds assuming the "average initial setting", rather than the worst case one.

6   More Future Directions

Generally speaking, the direction of applying ideas from theoretical distributed computing to biology contexts is currently making its first baby steps. Hence, this direction is open to a large variety of research attempts. We have described several research frameworks to proceed in. Particular suggestions for future work using these frameworks can be found by inspecting some of the examples mentioned in the survey by Navlakha and Bar-Joseph [40] on bio-inspired computing. In particular, as mentioned in [40], two important examples of problems common to both biological and computational systems are distributed *consensus* [36] and *synchronization* [35,48]. In biology, consensus has an important role in coordinating populations. Fish, for instance, must be able to quickly react to the environment and make collective decisions while constantly being under the threat of predation. Synchronization is apparent in fireflies that simultaneously flash [39,56] and pacemaker cells in the heart [32]. We believe that the vast literature and advancements concerning synchronization and consensus in the context of theoretical distributed computing may also be used to enhance the understanding of corresponding biological phenomena.

References

1. Afek, Y., Alon, N., Bar-Joseph, Z., Cornejo, A., Haeupler, B., Kuhn, F.: Beeping a Maximal Independent Set. In: Peleg, D. (ed.) Distributed Computing. LNCS, vol. 6950, pp. 32–50. Springer, Heidelberg (2011)
2. Afek, Y., Alon, N., Barad, O., Hornstein, E., Barkai, N., Bar-Joseph, Z.: A biological solution to a fundamentaldistributed computing problem. Science 331(6014), 183–185 (2011)
3. Angluin, D., Aspnes, J., Diamadi, Z., Fischer, M.J., Peralta, R.: Computation in networks of passively mobile finite-state sensors. Distributed Computing 18(4), 235–253 (2006)
4. Angluin, D., Aspnes, J., Eisenstat, D., Ruppert, E.: The computational power of population protocols. Distributed Computing 20(4), 279–304 (2007)
5. Aspnes, J., Ruppert, E.: An introduction to population protocols. Bulletin of the European Association for Theoretical Computer Science, Distributed Computing Column 93, 98–117 (2007); An updated and extended version appears in Middleware for Network Eccentric and Mobile Applications. In: Garbinato, B., Miranda, H., Rodrigues, L. (eds.): pp. 97–120. Springer (2009)
6. Bialek, W.: Physical limits to sensation and perception. Annual Review of Biophysics and Biophysical Chemistry 16, 455–478 (1987)
7. Biallek, W., Cavagnab, A., Giardinab, I., Morad, T., Silvestrib, E., Vialeb, M., Walczake, A.M.: Statistical mechanics for natural flocks of birds. PNAS 109(13), 4786–4791 (2012)
8. Branson, K., Robie, A.A., Bender, J., Perona, P., Dickinson, M.H.: High-throughput ethomics in large groups of Drosophila. Nature Methods 6, 451–457 (2009)
9. Bruckstein, A.M.: Why the ant trails look so straight and nice. The Mathematical Intelligencer 15(2), 58–62 (1993)

10. Cardin, J.A., Carlén, M., Meletis, K., Knoblich, U., Zhang, F., Deisseroth, K., Tsai, L.H., Moore, C.I.: Targeted optogenetic stimulation and recording of neurons in vivo using cell-type-specific expression of Channelrhodopsin-2. Nature Protocols 5, 247–254 (2010)
11. de Castro, L.N.: Fundamentals of Natural Computing: Basic Concepts, Algorithms, and Applications. CRC Press (2006)
12. de Castro, L.N., Von Zuben, F.J.: Recent developments in biologically inspired computing. Idea Group Publishing (2004)
13. Chazelle, B.: Natural algorithms. In: Proc. 19th ACM-SIAM Symposium on Discrete Algorithms (SODA), pp. 422–431 (2009)
14. Chaintreau, A., Fraigniaud, P., Lebhar, E.: Networks Become Navigable as Nodes Move and Forget. In: Aceto, L., Damgård, I., Goldberg, L.A., Halldórsson, M.M., Ingólfsdóttir, A., Walukiewicz, I. (eds.) ICALP 2008, Part I. LNCS, vol. 5125, pp. 133–144. Springer, Heidelberg (2008)
15. Cucker, F., Smale, S.: Emergent behavior in flocks. IEEE Trans. Automatic Control 52, 852–862 (2007)
16. Dorigo, M., Stutzle, T.: Ant colony optimization. MIT Press (2004)
17. Dorigo, M., Sahin, E.: Swarm Robotics - Special Issue. Autonomous Robots 17, 111–113 (2004)
18. Emek, Y., Smula, J., Wattenhofer, R.: Stone Age Distributed Computing. Arxiv (2012)
19. Feder, T.: Statistical physics is for the birds. Physics Today 60(10), 28–30 (2007)
20. Feinerman, O., Korman, A.: Memory Lower Bounds for Randomized Collaborative Search and Implications for Biology. In: Aguilera, M.K. (ed.) DISC 2012. LNCS, vol. 7611, pp. 61–75. Springer, Heidelberg (2012)
21. Feinerman, O., Korman, A., Lotker, Z., Sereni, J.S.: Collaborative Search on the Plane without Communication. In: Proc. 31st Annual ACM SIGACT-SIGOPS Symposium on Principles of Distributed Computing (PODC), pp. 77–86 (2012)
22. Feinerman, O., Veiga, J., Dorfman, J.R., Germain, R.N., Altan-Bonnet, G.: Variability and robustness in T Cell activation from regulated heterogeneity in protein levels. Science 321(5892), 1081–1084 (2008)
23. Fraigniaud, P.: Small Worlds as Navigable Augmented Networks: Model, Analysis, and Validation. In: Arge, L., Hoffmann, M., Welzl, E. (eds.) ESA 2007. LNCS, vol. 4698, pp. 2–11. Springer, Heidelberg (2007)
24. Fraigniaud, P., Giakkoupis, G.: On the searchability of small-world networks with arbitrary underlying structure. In: Proc. 42th ACM Symposium on Theory of Computing (STOC), pp. 389–398 (2010)
25. Fraigniaud, P., Lebhar, E., Lotker, Z.: A Lower Bound for Network Navigability. SIAM J. Discrete Math. 24(1), 72–81 (2010)
26. Gutenkunst, R.N., Waterfall, J.J., Casey, F.P., Brown, K.S., Myers, C.R., Sethna, J.P.: Universally sloppy parameter sensitivities in systems biology models. PLOS Computational Biology 3(10), e189 (2007)
27. Herzenberg, L.A., De Rosa, S.C.: Monoclonal antibodies and the FACS: complementary tools for immunobiology and medicine. Immunology Today 21(8), 383–390 (2000)
28. Hopfield, J.J.: Neural networks and physical systems with emergent collective computational abilities. PNAS 79(8), 2554–2558 (1982)
29. Ishii, T., Ishii, M.: Intravital two-photon imaging: a versatile tool for dissecting the immune system. Ann. Rheum. Dis. 70, 113–115 (2011)
30. Jablonka, E., Lamb, M.J.: Evolution in four dimensions: Genetic, epigenetic, behavioral, and symbolic variation in the history of life. MIT Press (2005)

31. Kleinberg, J.M.: Navigation in a small world. Nature 406(6798), 845 (2000)
32. Kuramoto, T., Yamagishi, H.: Physiological anatomy, burst formation, and burst frequency of the cardiac ganglion of crustaceans. Physiol. Zool. 63, 102–116 (1990)
33. Olarius, S., Zomaya, A.Y.: Handbook of Bioinspired Algorithms and Applications. Chapman & Hall/CRC (2005)
34. Lachmann, M., Sella, G.: The Computationally Complete Ant Colony: Global Coordination in a System with No Hierarchy. In: Morán, F., Merelo, J.J., Moreno, A., Chacon, P. (eds.) ECAL 1995. LNCS, vol. 929, pp. 784–800. Springer, Heidelberg (1995)
35. Lenzen, C., Locher, T., Wattenhofer, R.: Tight bounds for clock synchronization. J. ACM 57(2) (2010)
36. Lynch, N.A.: Distributed Algorithms. Morgan Kaufmann Publishers Inc., San Francisco (1996)
37. Mange, D., Tomassini, M.: Bio-inspired computing machines: towards novel computational architecture. Presses Polytechniques et Universitaires Romandes (1998)
38. Milgram, S.: The small-world problem. Psychol. Today 1, 61–67 (1967)
39. Mirollo, R.E., Strogatz, S.H.: Synchronization of pulse-coupled biological oscillators. SIAM J. Applied Math 50, 1645–1662 (1990)
40. Navlakha, S., Bar-Joseph, Z.: Algorithms in nature: the convergence of systems biology and computational thinking. Nature-EMBO Molecular Systems Biology 7, 546 (2011)
41. Reynolds, C.: Flocks, herds and schools: A distributed behavioral model. In: SIGGRAPH 1987: Proceedings of the 14th Annual Conference on Computer Graphics and Interactive Techniques, pp. 25–34 (1987)
42. Robinson, E.J.H., Richardson, T.O., Sendova-Franks, A.B., Feinerman, O., Franks, N.R.: Radio tagging reveals the roles of corpulence, experience and social information in ant decision making. Behavioral Ecology and Sociobiology 63(5), 627–636 (2009)
43. Robinson, E.J.H., Feinerman, O., Franks, N.R.: Experience, corpulence and decision making in ant foraging. Journal of Experimental Biology 215, 2653–2659 (2012)
44. Schlaepfer, M.A., Runge, M.C., Sherman, P.W.: Ecological and evolutionary traps. Trends in Ecology and Evolution 17(10), 474–480 (2002)
45. Sena, G., Frentz, Z., Birnbaum, K.D., Leibler, S.: Quantitation of Cellular Dynamics in Growing Arabidopsis Roots with Light Sheet Microscopy. PLOS1 (2011)
46. Shiloni, A., Agmon, N., Kaminka, G.A.: Of Robot Ants and Elephants: A Computational Comparison. Theoretical Computer Science 412, 5771–5788 (2011)
47. Siegelmann, H.T., Sontag, E.D.: On the Computational Power of Neural Nets. Journal of Computer and System Sciences 50, 132–150 (1995)
48. Simeone, O., Spagnolini, U., Bar-Ness, Y., Strogatz, S.: Distributed synchronization in wireless networks. IEEE Signal Process. Mag. 25, 81–97 (2008)
49. Sole, R.V., Delgado, J.: Universal Computation in Fluid Neural Networks. Complexity 2(2), 49–56 (1996)
50. Paton, R.: Computing with biological metaphors. Chapman & Hall (1994)
51. Valiant, L.G.: Evolvability. J. ACM 56(1) (2009)
52. Vicsek, T., Czirok, A., Ben-Jacob, E., Cohen, I., Shochet, O.: Novel type of phase transition in a system of self-driven particles. Physical Review Letters 75, 1226–1229 (1995)

53. Viventi, J., Kim, D., Vigeland, L., Frechette, E.S., Blanco, J.A., Kim, Y., Avrin, A.E., Tiruvadi, V.R., Hwang, S., Vanleer, A.C., Wulsin, D.F., Davis, K., Gelber, C.E., Palmer, L., Spiegel, J., Wu, J., Xiao, J., Huang, Y., Contreras, D., Rogers, J.A., Litt, B.: Flexible, foldable, actively multiplexed, high-density electrode array for mapping brain activity in vivo. Nature Neuroscience 14, 1599–1605 (2011)
54. Wagner, I., Bruckstein, A.: Special Issue on Ant Robotics. Annals of Mathematics and Artificial Intelligence 31(1-4) (2001)
55. Westhus, C., Kleineidam, C.J., Roces, F., Weidenmuller, A.: Behavioural plasticity in the fanning response of bumblebee workers: impact of experience and rate of temperature change.Animal Behavior (in press, 2012)
56. Winfree, A.T.: Biological rhythms and the behavior of populations of coupled oscillators. J. Theor. Biololgy 16, 15–42 (1967)

Participatory Sensing: Crowdsourcing Data from Mobile Smartphones in Urban Spaces

Salil S. Kanhere

The University of New South Wales
Sydney, NSW, 2052, Australia
salilk@cse.unsw.edu.au

Abstract. The recent wave of sensor-rich, Internet-enabled, smart mobile devices such as the Apple iPhone has opened the door for a novel paradigm for monitoring the urban landscape known as participatory sensing. Using this paradigm, ordinary citizens can collect multi-modal data streams from the surrounding environment using their mobile devices and share the same using existing communication infrastructure (e.g., 3G service or WiFi access points). The data contributed from multiple participants can be combined to build a spatiotemporal view of the phenomenon of interest and also to extract important community statistics. Given the ubiquity of mobile phones and the high density of people in metropolitan areas, participatory sensing can achieve an unprecedented level of coverage in both space and time for observing events of interest in urban spaces. Several exciting participatory sensing applications have emerged in recent years. For example, GPS traces uploaded by drivers and passengers can be used to generate realtime traffic statistics. Similarly, street-level audio samples collected by pedestrians can be aggregated to create a citywide noise map. In this talk, we will provide a comprehensive overview of this new and exciting paradigm and outline the major research challenges.

Keywords: Participatory Sensing, Mobile Crowdsourcing, Urban Sensing.

1 Introduction

In recent times, mobile phones have been riding the wave of Moore's Law with rapid improvements in processing power, embedded sensors, storage capacities and network data rates. The mobile phones of today have evolved from merely being phones to full-fledged computing, sensing and communication devices. It is thus hardly surprising that over 5 billion people globally have access to mobile phones. These advances in mobile phone technology coupled with their ubiquity have paved the wave for an exciting new paradigm for accomplishing large-scale sensing, known in literature as *participatory sensing* [1], [2]. The key idea behind participatory sensing is to empower ordinary citizens to collect and share sensed data from their surrounding environments using their mobile phones.

C. Hota and P.K. Srimani (Eds.): ICDCIT 2013, LNCS 7753, pp. 19–26, 2013.

Mobile phones, though not built specifically for sensing, can in fact readily function as sophisticated sensors. The camera on mobile phones can be used as video and image sensors. The microphone on the mobile phone, when it is not used for voice conversations, can double up as an acoustic sensor. The embedded GPS receivers on the phone can provide location information. Other embedded sensors such as gyroscopes, accelerometers and proximity sensors can collectively be used to estimate useful contextual information (e.g., is the user walking or traveling on a bicycle). Further, additional sensors can be easily interfaced with the phone via Bluetooth or wired connections, e.g., air pollution or biometric sensors.

Participatory sensing offers a number of advantages over traditional sensor networks which entails deploying a large number of static wireless sensor devices, particularly in urban areas. First, since participatory sensing leverages existing sensing (mobile phones) and communication (cellular or WiFi) infrastructure, the deployment costs are virtually zero. Second, the inherent mobility of the phone carriers provides unprecedented spatiotemporal coverage and also makes it possible to observe unpredictable events (which may be excluded by static deployments). Third, using mobile phones as sensors intrinsically affords economies of scale. Fourth, the widespread availability of software development tools for mobile phone platforms and established distribution channels in the form of App stores makes application development and deployment relatively easy. Finally, by including people in the sensing loop, it is now possible to design applications that can dramatically improve the day-to-day lives of individuals and communities.

A typical participatory sensing application operates in a centralized fashion, i.e., the sensor data collected by the phones of volunteers are reported (using wireless data communications) to a central server for processing. The sensing tasks on the phones can be triggered manually, automatically or based on the current context. On the server, the data are analyzed and made available in various forms, such as graphical representations or maps showing the sensing results at individual and/or community scale. Simultaneously, the results may be displayed locally on the carriers' mobile phones or accessed by the larger public through web-portals depending on the application needs.

In this talk we will provide a comprehensive overview of this exciting and new paradigm. Section 2 will provide an overview of innovative participatory sensing applications that have been proposed in literature. Section 3 will provide a detailed discussion on the key research challenges posed by participatory sensing and focus on novel approaches to deal with the same. Finally, Section 4 will conclude the article.

2   Innovative Participatory Sensing Applications

The emergence of the participatory sensing paradigm has resulted in a broad range of novel sensing applications, which can be categorized as either *people-centric* or *environment-centric* sensing. People-centric applications mainly focus

on documenting activities (e.g., sport experiences) and understanding the behavior (e.g., eating disorders) of individuals. In contrast, environment-centric
sensing applications collect environmental parameters (e.g. air quality or noise
pollution). In this section, we present an overview of a few representative applications within each category.

2.1 People-Centric Sensing Applications

People-centric sensing uses the sensor devices integrated in mobile phones to
collect data about the user. In the following we present some examples.

Personal Health Monitoring. In personal health monitoring, mobile phones
are used to monitor the physiological state and health of patients/participants
using embedded or external sensors (e.g., wearable accelerometers, or air pollution sensors). For example, DietSense [3] assists participants who want to lose
weight by documenting their dietary choices through images and sound samples.
The mobile phones are worn around the neck of the participants and automatically take images of the dishes in front of the users. The images document the
participants' food selection and allow for an estimation of the food weight and
waste on the plates. Moreover, the mobile phones capture the participants' context during their meals by recording time of day, location, and sound samples to
infer potential relationships between the participants' behavior and their context
(e.g., having lunch in a restaurant or eating chips late at night on the sofa). All
captured data are uploaded to a personal repository, where the participants can
review them to select/discard the information to be shared with their doctors
and nutritionists.

Calculating Environmental Impact. PEIR (Personal Environmental Impact
Report) is a system that allows users to use their mobile phone to determine
their exposure to environmental pollutants [4]. A sensing module installed on
the phone determines the current location of the user as well as information
about the currently used mode of transportation (e.g., bus vs car), and transfers
this information to a central server. In return, the server provides the users with
information about the environmental impact of their traveling in terms of carbon and particle emissions. Additionally, the server estimates the participants'
exposure to particle emissions generated by other vehicles and fast food restaurants while commuting. The latter may be useful for health conscious users
who may want to avoid the temptation of stopping by such restaurants. The
mode of transport is inferred using accelerometer readings, while the route travelled is extracted from the captured location traces. Additional input parameters
and models are considered for determining the environmental factors, such as
weather conditions collected by weather stations, road traffic flow models, and
vehicle emission models.

Monitoring and Documenting Sport Experiences. BikeNet [5] presents a system for monitoring bicycling experiences of the participants. BikeNet draws a fine-grained portrait of the cyclist by measuring his current location, speed, burnt calories, and galvanic skin response. Multiple peripheral sensors are used to obtain this information: Microphone, magnetometer, pedal speed sensor, inclinometer, lateral tilt, GSR stress monitor, speedometer/odometer, and a sensor for CO_2 concentration. The peripheral sensors form a body area network and interact with the mobile phone over a wireless connection. The captured data can be reviewed by the cyclists themselves, but can also be merged with other participants' data or combined with additional parameters, such as air quality and traffic properties, in order to construct complete maps for the cycling community.

Enhancing Social Media. A large pool of applications utilizes data captured by sensors to enrich the contents shared in social media, such as blogs, social networks, or virtual worlds. CenceMe [6] integrates virtual representations of the participants' current state and context in social networks and virtual worlds. Based on multimodal information (acceleration, audio samples, pictures, neighboring devices, and location) captured by the mobile phone, context information is inferred in various dimensions, including the user's mood, location, and habits, as well as information about the currently performed activity and the environment. The inferred information is then posted as status message in social networks or translated into the virtual representation of participants in virtual worlds.

Price Auditing. PetrolWatch [7] presents a system for automatic collection of fuel prices using embedded cameras in phones. The mobile phone is mounted on the passenger seat of a car and faces the road to automatically photograph fuel price boards (using GPS and GIS) when the vehicle approaches service stations. The pictures are then uploaded to a central entity, which is responsible for image processing and price extraction. The brand of the service station is first inferred from the capture location in order to reduce the image processing complexity, as price boards of different brands differ in colors and dimensions. Assisted by this information, computer vision algorithms extract the fuel prices, and uploads them to the database. Users can query the system to determine the cheapest fuel that is available in their area of interest.

2.2   Environment-Centric Sensing Applications

In environment-centric scenarios, the mobile phones capture information via their embedded sensors and additional peripheral sensors about the surroundings of the participants. In contrast to most people-centric sensing scenarios, the captured data are mainly exploited at a community scale, e.g., to monitor the evolution of environmental parameters like air quality, noise, road and traffic conditions in cities, or to detect socially interesting events.

Air Quality Monitoring. In Haze Watch [8], mobile phones were interfaced to external pollution sensors, in order to measure the concentration of carbon monoxide, ozone, sulphur dioxide, and nitrogen dioxide concentration in the air. In comparison to meteorological stations, the mobile phones may collect less accurate measurements. However, their inherent mobility allows observing unpredictable events (e.g., accidental pollution), which cannot be detected by static stations and provide large spatial coverage. The mobile phones can thus complement static high-fidelity data captured by traditional meteorological stations by providing finer-grained readings. The timestamped and geotagged measurements are then uploaded to a server to build maps, which aggregate the readings of all participants and are accessible by the public. Individual measurements may also be displayed on the participant's mobile phone.

Monitoring Noise and Ambiance. Microphones in mobile phones can be configured to measure the surrounding noise level and give insights about the nature of contextual events. In EarPhone [9], the noise levels are used to monitor noise pollution, which can e.g. affect human hearing and behavior, and build representative pollution maps accessible to either specialists to understand e.g. the relationships between noise exposition and behavioral problems for the general public.

Monitoring Road and Traffic Conditions. The mobile phones can be exploited to document road and traffic condition. In Nericell [10], the embedded accelerometer, microphone, and positioning system (GPS or GSM radio) are used to detect and localize traffic conditions and road conditions, e.g., potholes, bumps, or braking and honking (which are both implicit indicators of traffic congestion). The application integrates the provided information about the surface roughness of the roads, the surrounding noise, and the traffic conditions into traffic maps, which are available to the public.

3   Key Research Challenges

Since participatory sensing relies on existing networking and sensing infrastructure, the key challenges are associated with handing the data, i.e., data analysis and processing, ensuring data quality, protecting privacy, etc. We now present a short overview of the key research challenges posed by this new and exciting paradigm. We also discuss some recent work in overcoming these challenges.

3.1   Dealing with Incomplete Samples

Since a participatory sensing system relies on volunteers contributing noise pollution measurements, these measurements can only come from the place and time where the volunteers are present. Furthermore, volunteers may prioritize the use of their mobile devices for other tasks. Or they may choose to collect data only when the phone has sufficient energy. Consequently, samples collected from mobile phones are typically randomly distributed in space and time, and are incomplete. The challenges thus is to recover the original spatiotemporal profile of the phenomenon being monitored from random and incomplete samples obtained via crowdsourcing. In [9], the authors have developed an innovative approach to deal with this issue using the technique of compressive sensing, in the context of a noise monitoring application.

3.2   Inferring User Context and Activities

Inferring the surrounding context (e.g., is the user in a party or a quiet room) and activities (is the user walking, running, traveling by car, etc) undertaken by the phone carrier is of interest in various participatory sensing applications (see for example Section 2.1). This is usually achieved using data collected by one or more embedded sensors in the phone which include accelerometers, microphone, GPS, etc. At the high-level, this is essentially a machine learning problem, since we want to the phones to be embedded with the smarts to recognise human activity. The typical approach adopted is to make use of supervised learning [6]. This involves the following three steps. The first step is to collect properly labelled sensor data for the various categories of interest (i.e. training). The second step involves identifying important features from this training data, which can uniquely identify each category (i.e. fingerprints). The final step is to choose an appropriate classification algorithm (e.g., support vector machines, neural networks, etc), which can be used to achieve accurate classification.

3.3   Preserving User Privacy

Current participatory sensing applications are primarily focused on the collection of data on a large scale. Without any suitable protection mechanism however, the mobile phones are transformed into miniature spies, possibly revealing private information about their owners. Possible intrusions into a user's privacy include the recording of intimate discussions, taking photographs of private scenes, or tracing a user's path and monitoring the locations he has visited. Many users are aware of the possible consequences, and may therefore be reluctant to contribute to the sensing campaigns. Since participatory sensing exclusively depends on user-provided data, a high number of participants is required. The users' reluctance to contribute would diminish the impact and relevance of sensing campaigns deployed at large scale, as well as limiting the benefits to the users. To encounter the risk that a user's privacy might be compromised, mechanisms to preserve user privacy are mandatory. The authors in [11] present a comprehensive application independent architecture for anonymous tasking and reporting. The infrastructure enables applications to task a mobile device using a new tasking language, anonymously distribute tasks to mobile devices and collect anonymous yet verifiable reports from the devices.

3.4   Evaluating Trustworthiness of Data

The success of participatory sensing applications hinges on high level of participation from voluntary users. Unfortunately, the very openness which allows anyone to contribute data, also exposes the applications to erroneous and malicious contributions. For instance, users may inadvertently position their devices such that incorrect measurements are recorded, e.g., storing the phone in a bag while being tasked to acquire urban noise information. Malicious users may deliberately pollute sensor data for their own benefits, e.g., a leasing agent may intentionally contribute fabricated low noise readings to promote the properties in a particular suburb. Without confidence in the contributions uploaded by volunteers, the resulting summary statistics will be of little use to the user community. Thus, it is imperative that the application server can evaluate the trustworthiness of contributing devices so that corrupted and malicious contributions are identified. Recent work [12] proposes a novel reputation system that employs the Gompertz function for computing device reputation score as a reflection of the trustworthiness of the contributed data.

3.5   Conserving Energy

Note that, the primary usage of mobile phones should be reserved for the users's regular activities such as making calls, Internet access, etc. Users will only volunteer to contribute data if this process does not use up significant battery so as to prevent them from accessing their usual services. Even though, most users charge their phones on a daily basis, it is thus important that participatory sensing applications do not introduce significant energy costs for users. Energy is consumed in all aspects of participatory applications ranging from sensing, processing and data transmission. In particular, some sensors such as GPS consume significantly more energy that others. As such, it is important for participatory applications to make use of these sensors in a conservative manner. In [13], the authors present an adaptive scheme for obtaining phone location by switching between the accurate but energy-expensive GPS probing to energy-efficient but less accurate WiFi/cellular localization. Similar approaches can be employed for duty-cycling other energy-hungry sensors.

4   Conclusion

In this talk, we introduced a novel paradigm called participatory sensing for achieving large-scale urban sensing by crowdsourcing sensing data from the mobile phones of ordinary citizens. We provided an overview of some of the exciting applications that have been proposed by the research community using this new idea. These range from collecting and sharing people-centric data to monitoring environmental parameters. We presented an overview of the key research challenges posed in implementing real-world participatory sensing systems and briefly discussed some of the existing solutions.

References

1. Burke, J., Estrin, D., Hansen, M., Parker, A., Ramanathan, N., Reddy, S., Srivastava, M.B.: Participatory Sensing. In: Proceedings of the World Sensor Web Workshop, in Conjunction with ACM SenSys 2006 (November 2006)
2. Campbell, A., Eisenman, S., Lane, N., Miluzzo, E., Peterson, R.: People-centric Urban Sensing. In: Proceedings of Second Annual International Wireless Internet Conference (WICON), pp. 2–5 (August 2006)
3. Reddy, S., Parker, A., Hyman, J., Burke, J., Estin, D., Hansen, M.: Image Browsing, Processing and Clustering for Participatory Sensing: Lessons from a DietSense Prototype. In: Proceedings of the Workshop on Embedded Networked Sensors (EmNetS), Cork, Ireland (June 2007)
4. Mun, M., Reddy, S., et al.: PEIR, the Personal Environmental Impact Report, as a Platform for Participatory Sensing Systems Research. In: Proceedings of ACM MobiSys, Krakow, Poland (June 2009)
5. Eisenman, S., Miluzzo, E., Lane, N., Peterson, R., Ahn, G., Campbell, A.: The Bikenet Mobile Sensing System for Cyclist Experience Mapping. In: Proceedings of ACM SenSys, Sydney, Australia (November 2007)
6. Miluzzo, E., Lane, N., Fodor, K., Peterson, R., Eisenman, S., Lu, H., Musolesi, M., Zheng, X., Campbell, A.: Sensing Meets Mobile Social Networks: The Design, Implementation and Evaluation of the CenceMe Application. In: Proceedings of ACM SenSys, Raleigh, NC, USA (November 2008)
7. Dong, Y., Kanhere, S.S., Chou, C.T., Bulusu, N.: Automatic Collection of Fuel Prices from a Network of Mobile Cameras. In: Proceedings of IEEE DCOSS 2008, Santorini, Greece (June 2008)
8. Carrapetta, J., Youdale, N., Chow, A., Sivaraman, V.: Haze Watch Project, http://www.pollution.ee.unsw.edu.au
9. Rana, R., Chou, C.T., Kanhere, S., Bulusu, N., Hu, W.: Ear-Phone: An End-to-End Participatory Urban Noise Mapping System. In: Proceedings of ACM/IEEE IPSN, Stockholm, Sweden (April 2010)
10. Mohan, P., Padmanabhan, V., Ramjee, R.: Nericell: Rich Monitoring of Road and Traffic Conditions using Mobile Smartphones. In: Proceedings of ACM SenSys, Raleigh, NC, USA (November 2008)
11. Kapadia, A., Triandopoulos, N., Cornelius, C., Peebles, D., Kotz, D.: AnonySense: Opportunistic and Privacy-Preserving Context Collection. In: Indulska, J., Patterson, D.J., Rodden, T., Ott, M. (eds.) PERVASIVE 2008. LNCS, vol. 5013, pp. 280–297. Springer, Heidelberg (2008)
12. Huang, K., Kanhere, S.S., Hu, W.: Are You Contributing Trustworthy Data? The Case for A Reputation Framework in Participatory Sensing. In: Proceedings of ACM MSWiM, Bodrum, Turkey (October 2010)
13. Gaonkar, S., Li, J., Choudhury, R.R.: Micro-Blog: Sharing and Querying Content Through Mobile Phones and Social Participation. In: Proceedings of ACM MobiSys, Breckenridge, CO, USA (June 2008)

Energy Efficient Distributed Computing on Mobile Devices

Jukka K. Nurminen

Aalto University, Helsinki, Finland
jukka.k.nurminen@aalto.fi

Abstract. Energy consumption is a critical aspect of mobile applications. Excessive drain of battery is one of the key complaints of handheld device users and a success bottleneck for many mobile applications. This paper looks at energy-efficiency from the application development point of view and reviews some answers to questions like what are the key principles in energy consumption in mobile applications and what kind of software solutions can be used to save energy? These issues are discussed in particular in the context of 3G cellular communication. Applications of the ideas are illustrated in energy efficient mobile peer-to-peer systems; BitTorrent and Kademlia DHT.

Keywords: energy-efficiency, peer-to-peer, mobile, communication, computing.

1 Introduction

Energy consumption is a critical aspect of mobile applications. Excessive drain of battery is one of the key complaints of handheld device users and a success bottleneck for many mobile applications. In the ICT field users and developers are used to rapidly increasing performance. While this is true, e.g. for CPU, Internet bandwidth, and hard disk size, the same does not apply to the battery capacity. Over the past decade the battery capacity growth has only been a few percentages per year. Therefore the demand and supply of battery power do not match. New applications and services increase energy spending and the battery technology is not able to keep up. Therefore new solutions to use the battery power in a smarter way are needed. Otherwise the energy spending starts to seriously limit the innovative possibilities to use the mobile devices.

Multiple approaches can be applied to handle the energy consumption problem. For instance, users would simply recharge their mobile devices more often. New, less intrusive recharging solutions, such as wireless charging, may help here but the problem is likely to still remain. Alternatively, because the battery power per a volume unit is not growing fast enough, the devices would use bigger batteries. For those devices that are bigger in physical size, such as tablet computers, this might be a valid option. However, people still seem to like small or slim devices limiting the room available for the battery. Periodically hopes also rise that some new battery technology, e.g. based on nano technology, would

C. Hota and P.K. Srimani (Eds.): ICDCIT 2013, LNCS 7753, pp. 27–46, 2013.

make a fundamental leap in battery performance. Unfortunately, nothing has really materialized on this area that would be widely available for the consumers. Finally the component technology in the devices is improving and new components spend considerable less energy for the same performance as older ones. This is definitely useful and benefits the end users. However, it alone may not be adequate for the increasing demand and therefore the smarter user of the available battery power is an important research direction to complement the hardware improvements.

In this paper the focus is on application level mechanisms. Most of the ideas can be implemented in the mobile applications, sometimes the ideas could also be implemented as middleware solutions on the mobile devices, as proxies at the network side, or as changes in the server behavior in data centers. According to our experience, in this way, it is possible to gain rather high energy savings, often several tens of percentages. The disadvantage of the application level mechanisms is that they only work for a certain application or a class of applications. Component level improvements, and other low-level changes, are often influencing a large set of applications, but typically the improvements are more modest.

Most of our observations apply to all kinds of handheld devices using different kinds of networks for their communication. However, in most cases our target and experimentation platform has been 3G cellular network. In this we differ from the bulk of prior research which has used WiFi. While both of these technologies are important we feel that the emphasizing cellular networking is important because it is the predominant network that mobile phones use ubiquitously. Moreover, its energy consumption presents a bit different kinds of problems than what is experienced with WiFi.

This paper is a rather personal view on energy-efficient distributed computing research. It draws most of its examples from the work I have been doing on energy efficiency first at Nokia Research Center and later at Aalto University. It does not attempt cover all the developments on this fast moving, expanding area but aims to highlight some of the key aspects that influence energy spending and show via examples how those can be taken advantage of when implementing energy-efficient distributed applications.

The example applications are mostly from peer-to-peer (P2P) solutions. P2P is a good playground to test these ideas because it highlight many of the problems present also in other distributed solutions. Moreover, with P2P it is sometimes possible to test the solutions as part of really huge systems. For instance, the Kademlia DHT (described more closely in Section 8) has allowed us to test the behavior of our mobile application in a setting with over one million peers.

The rest of this paper is divided into three main sections. First, we review some key principles of mobile energy consumption and briefly look at the empirical methodologies to study the area. In the following sections we show how these principles can be used to create energy efficient solutions first for BitTorrent-like content sharing solutions and then for distributed hash tables (DHTs). Finally, in the short conclusions section we summarize the key observations.

2 Principles of Energy Consumption

2.1 How to Measure Mobile Energy Consumption?

The research on energy efficient mobile applications has a strong empirical component. Of course, theoretical studies are possible but often the interactions and influencing factors are so complex that without experimentation it is hard to come up with any conclusive findings or improvements. Therefore, a key part of the research is measurements with different devices and with different solutions.

For the energy consumption measurements at least four approaches seem to be available:

1. The easiest approach is simply to utilize the phone battery indicator. Because this is a very crude way, in most cases, the measurement accuracy is not enough for relevant results.
2. A much better approach is to utilize a power metering application in a mobile device. The nice aspect of these is that you only need to install an application to the device, no additional hardware is needed. The most accurate results can be gained by a power metering app that measures the energy consumption directly from the energy and power management chipset that controls the battery operation. Nokia Energy Profiler [1] is the only application in this category. Unfortunately it only works with the older Symbian phones; for the current generation no such application exists. Because this kind of application requires access to the low-level hardware of the device it is very difficult, or impossible, to create such an application without the support of the phone manufacturer.
3. The other power metering application category is model based such as the PowerTutor for Android devices [2]. In these the application measures performance counters, such as CPU utilization or network use, and uses a model to derive from these primary measures an estimate for the power consumption. Unfortunately, the quality of the models limit the accuracy of this approach. Moreover, the resolution of this approach can be insufficient to study very rapid changes in energy consumption.
4. Finally, the widely available but a bit complicated approach is to use an external power meter. We, for instance, have used Monsoon power meter which is able to act both as a power source and at the same time record the spent power. This approach works nicely for devices with replaceable batteries. Unfortunately, the trend towards non-replaceable batteries, headed by Apple iPhone, is making this approach harder. Sometimes it is possible to physically open the device with special tools but this is clearly risky and requires further expertise.

2.2 Where Energy Is Spent in Mobile Devices?

When considering mobile device as a miniature computer the first assumption is that the CPU is an important consumer of electricity and major savings could be achieved by saving the amount of computation an application does. However, this assumption is false in general. An early analysis of mobile video streaming [3] showed that the communication spends almost half of the total energy, user interface has the the second biggest share and only less than 20% of energy is spent in the processing. More recent analysis, e.g. [4], indicate that close to 50% of the daily energy consumption is spent on GSM and the share of CPU is less than 20%. Of course the division between different components varies depending on the application. A stand-alone application would not spend much energy on communication but, on the other hand, most of the interesting, widely used mobile applications tend to do quite a lot of communication.

As a conclusion influencing the communication energy consumption seems to provide the biggest paybacks. In many applications it is not possible to influence the amount of data that has to be transferred but quite a bit of energy savings can be gained by organizing the communication in an energy-efficient fashion. A number of ways to do that are available, most of them relying on some kind of reshaping of the traffic. In many cases the reshaping in completely invisible to the end user. In other cases it may cause additional delays and it is up to user and application characteristics how much performance degradation is acceptable.

The trend towards larger display sizes and higher display resolutions is also likely to increase the energy consumption share of the user interface. However, influencing the user interface energy consumption at the application level is difficult. The solutions often depend on the display technology and require careful analysis how the user experiences them. In the rest of the paper we assume the user interface of the application will remain intact and we only focus on the communication and computation side.

2.3   The Higher the Bitrate the More Energy Efficient

An important observation in mobile phone power consumption is that a higher bitrate increases the energy-efficiency of a data transfer. Measurements in [5] show that especially for 3G cellular the power consumption of TCP data transfer is almost constant having only a weak dependency on the bitrate. Only when the bitrate drops to zero, meaning that there is no communication, the device is able to enter a sleep state with very low power consumption. An extensive set of measurements for WiFi power consumption [6] with three different mobile phone models shows very similar results for 802.11g WLAN.

Figure 1, based on the measurements data of [5] , illustrates how the energy consumption per bit varies as a function of communication speed. The shape of the curves clearly shows that the higher the bitrate the more energy-efficient the communication is. This suggests that in order to save battery we should try to arrange the data transfer activity in a way that the mobile device is able to experience as high bitrates as possible. Sample measurements, which naturally depend on the used device models and the test environment, show that as bit rate grows by 100 kB, the power consumption only increases by 0.3 W in WLAN and by 0.04 W in 3G cellular. An important exception to this linear dependency

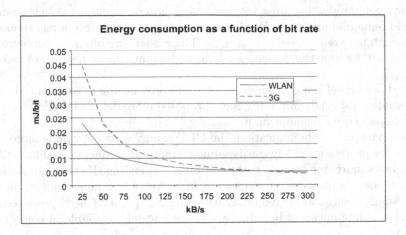

Fig. 1. Power consumption per bit as a function of communication speed

is the case when there is no communication which allows the wireless interface to enter an idle power-saving state.

$$E = t_{idle}P_{idle} + t_{active}P_{active} + E_{overhead} \tag{1}$$

Equation 1 shows a simple energy model where E is the overall energy consumption of a peer. P_{idle} and P_{active} are the idle and active state power consumptions, and t_{idle} and t_{active} are the times the peer spends in idle and active states. In the equation we assume that power consumption in active state is constant and not influenced by the bitrate (in reality the power consumption grows slightly as a function of bitrate and a more complicated model should take this into account). To give an indication of the magnitude of these values a measurement with Nokia N95 with 3G cellular gave the values $P_{active} = 1.3\,\mathrm{W}$ and $P_{idle} = 0.07\,\mathrm{W}$.

$E_{overhead}$ is the additional energy spent when transferring between idle and active states. As we see in section 2.5 this term can be very large in 3G cellular systems. In WiFi and the future cellular systems $E_{overhead}$ is far smaller but still a significant component. Therefore one important consideration is to avoid excessive changes between the states.

Equation (1) and the major power consumption difference between the active and idle states can be used to derive goals to minimize the energy consumption.

- The device should spend as little time as possible in active state.
- When in active state it should use the maximum bit rate for communication.
- To minimize $E_{overhead}$ the number of state changes should be minimized.

Clearly spending time in idle state is desirable for the energy consumption. However, in idle state there is no activity and no data transfer so in order to do useful work the device should be in active state. For energy-efficient behavior, the device should thus alternate between the two states. In active state, it should perform a communication burst with very high data rate, and between the bursts, it should remain in idle state. Furthermore, the communication bursts should be long enough to avoid excessive $E_{overhead}$. These goals are often contradicting. If we minimize the time the device spends in active state it can result into increase in $E_{overhead}$.

The above model is quite simple and focuses only on the most essential parts. Other studies, especially for WiFi, have proposed more detailed models for communication energy consumption [6].

In comparison to communication, the CPU energy consumption is more flexible. Modern processors widely use dynamic voltage and frequency scaling (DVFS) which allows more fine grained control of energy spending. If the computational needs are low the processor can execute in a slower but more energy efficient mode. Analoguous ideas for modulation scaling, e.g. [7], have been proposed also to wireless communication but they are not yet widely available in commercial products.

2.4 Parallel Data Transfers Saves Energy

When multiple services are running on the same mobile device, they typically schedule their activities independently without considering the other applications and services. Figure 2 shows an example of a case when the mobile phone is using email service, a photo upload service, and the user is making or receiving some phone calls. The active periods of different applications are marked with rectangles. Email service is an example of a periodic service. It checks periodically (with interval δ_{email}) if new mail has arrived. If new mail has arrived it is downloaded to the mobile phone. The length of the activity period varies as

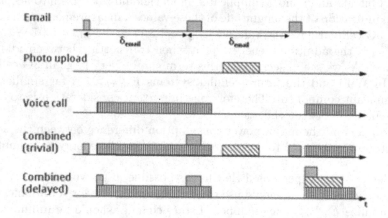

Fig. 2. Example sequence of events of three applications: email, photo upload, and voice call. Combined (trivial) shows the case where communication is started immediately for each application. Combined (delayed) shows the case where the communication is delayed to the time of the next voice call.

a function of the number and size of the email messages. Photo upload is an example of a user (or application) triggered activity. User takes a photo and the system uploads it to a photo sharing service. The uploading activity is started by a user action (shooting the picture or decision to store it). Finally, voice call activities are started at arbitrary time points either by the user or by calls coming in from the network.

When we analyze the combined effect of these three services as depicted on the line Combined (trivial) in Figure 2, we can see that when the starting times of these activities are chosen independently from each other, they occupy a large part of the time axis. This means that whenever any single application is active and transferring data, the radio of the mobile phone has to be powered on. As a result the energy consumption of the combined use case is high. However, if we have a possibility to delay the communication of the mobile services we can improve the situation. The line Combined (delayed) of Figure 2 shows the case when we delay the data transfer of non-urgent communications (email and photo upload activities in the example). Instead of following application specific schedules we put the data transfer needs into a wait-list and whenever a user makes or receives a voice call we activate the data transfers of the waiting services. As can be seen from Figure 2 the time when there are no ongoing data transfer activities is much longer when the delayed combination of different services is done.

Although the example shows the email and photo upload services as examples it should be easy to realize that there are a number of applications where such a combination makes sense. Other examples of non-urgent communications include calendar updates, software upgrades, twitter feeds, and backups. In fact, the more services the user is running on his device the higher the potential benefit from their smart combination. Building on the idea of Figure 2 it seems promising to schedule the data transfer of mobile services so that as much of the data transfer activities are taking place at the same time. A very simple mechanism to achieve this is to delay the data transfer of non-urgent services until a time when the user is having a phone call.

To evaluate the saving potential we experimented with downloading a 2 MB email attachment separately and during a voice call [5]. Figure 3 shows the chart of an example measurement with 3G. The x-axis of the chart shows the time and the y-axis the power consumption.

The chart shows the energy consumption in three different cases:

- The light gray/orange curve shows the energy consumption when only a voice call is active. In the early part 15-80 s the voice call is active and the display light is on. When the display light is switched off at 80s the energy consumption drops from 1.5 W to 1.2 W.
- The dark grey/blue curve shows the energy consumption when the phone is downloading content. As the figure shows the energy consumption is rather similar than in the case of voice call. When the display light is on the power consumption is around 1.5 W (20-90 s and 110-115 s). When the display light is off the power consumption is around 1.2 W

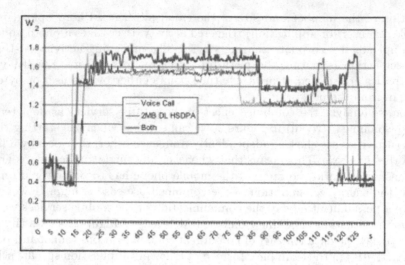

Fig. 3. Power consumption when a) a voice call is active, b) a data download is active, and c) both voice call and data download are active at the same time

- The thick gray/green curve shows a case when both voice call and data download are active simultaneously. The energy consumption is around 1.7 W and 1.4 W when the display light is on and off respectively.

We can see from the combined curve than when data download is performed during a voice call the power consumption is only slightly higher than what the voice call would anyhow require. In this measurement the extra power is only 10%. Likewise we can see that the data transfer time increases when done during voice call but the increase is not very big, only 12%. As a result if we do the data transfer during a voice call we are able to perform the same activity with only 23% of the energy that it would take without the voice call.

Transferring data during a cellular voice call is particularly energy efficient because voice requires a constant low bitrate data transfer both to and from the mobile phone. Because voice has to be sent continuously it is not a possible to power down the radio into an idle state. However, the radio interface of a mobile phone is able to handle a much larger bandwidth than what is needed for the voice. Whether this bandwidth is used or not does not have a major effect on the energy consumption. Therefore for the most energy efficient activity it makes sense to use as much of the available bandwidth as possible if the radio in any case is active.

2.5   The Head and Tail Energies Can Be Surprisingly Long

Another important observation related to mobile communication is that activation of the wireless interface before data can be transferred and its deactivation after the data transfer, require time and energy. The amount of these head and tail energies varies with different communication technologies. Especially the tail energies are large in cellular data networks. The exact values are controlled by the network operators and vary from operator to operator. One study in US found that in 3G it takes over 12 seconds before the radio interface returns to idle state after the end of data transfer (in comparison to 6 s in 2nd generation GSM, and less than 1 s in WiFi) [8]. This suggests that we should send the data in fewer and larger bursts to minimize the burst specific overheads.

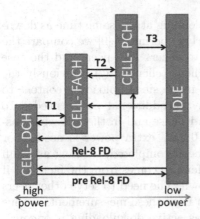

Fig. 4. 3G RRC state machine with CELL_DCH, CELL_FACH, CELL_PCH states

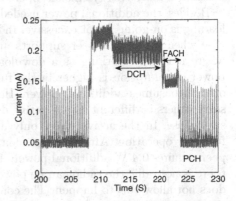

Fig. 5. Current consumption at different states and state transitions with Lumia 800

Figure 4 shows the different states in the 3G cellular radio resource controller state machine. Major data transfers are done in CELL_DCH state and once the last bit has been sent the T1 timer starts to run. Only after T1 and the following T2 timers have expired the mobile device is back in the IDLE state (or in terms of energy consumption similar CELL_PCH state). The energy consumption of these states is visible in Figure 5 indicating both a big difference in the power consumption in different states and the slow shift back to idle state.

3 BitTorrent Energy Consumption

BitTorrent is one of the prime content sharing mechanisms in P2P networks. In addition to its wide and dubious to download pirated content, the technology and its derivatives are increasing used also for commercial applications. When implementing BiTorrent on mobile phones (SymTorrent for Symbian and MobTorrent for J2ME phones[1]) it became clear that the capabilities of mobile phones are perfectly adequate for this kind of applications but, at the same time, the energy spending of the application turned out to be an important concern. In the following we discuss some ways how to improve the energy efficiency of BitTorrent on battery powered devices.

---

[1] Available as open source at http://amorg.aut.bme.hu

3.1 Being Selfish Is Bad for Energy Consumption

An obvious idea to increase the energy-efficiency of BitTorrent on a mobile device is to target a very selfish behavior. However, it turns out that this approach is not very useful. The tit-for-tat mechanism of BitTorrent rewards with high download speeds those peers who are actively uploading data to others. As explained in Section 2.3, a higher download speed is good for the energy-efficiency. Therefore peers which upload content to others experience higher download speeds and, as a result, a more energy-efficient operation.

Besides, the additional power needed for uploading at the same time as downloading is on-going is not excessive. In our early experiment [9] we compare the case when the mobile peer supports uploads to others (full peer) and the case where it is only working as a downloading client (client only). Obviously the power consumption is higher in the full peer mode since uploading content to others consumes additional power. However, the additional power needed to serve others is different in the active download phase and in the following passive phase. In the active phase only around 0.2 W extra power is needed for full peer operation. After the download has been completed, working as a full peer requires 0.4 W additional power. The difference comes from the fact that if there is no traffic the radio can be powered down. The need to serve other peers does not allow this to happen. The conclusion from these measurements is thus that acting as a full peer is feasible as long as active downloading is ongoing. Uploading to others requires only about 25% extra power but this is likely to be compensated by the faster download speed after which the phone can enter the energy-friendly idle state. Note that after the download is completed the phone should no longer serve others because this increases the power consumption by about 200%.

Naturally, the pressure to serve others is also good for the operation of the whole system (swarm in the BitTorrent terminology) because free-riders would otherwise damage the performance of all downloaders. If the swarm consists of both energy-sensitive peers (e.g. mobile devices) and regular peers (with access to power grid) it could be possible to offset the selfish behavior of energy-sensitive peers if their number is small enough. In some use cases, e.g. in music downloading the same content is reasonable both for mobile and regular peers and in this case the mobile peers could take advantage of the stronger power of regular peers. In other cases, e.g. video where the resolution needs of mobile and regular peers are likely to be very different, this is not likely to be the case because completely different files would be used. The mobile swarm would be almost fully consisting of energy-sensitive devices and therefore it is essential that they also contribute to the operation.

3.2 Bursty BitTorrent Communication

Section 2.3 highlighted the fact that energy can be saved by transferring the data faster because then the peers can spend more time in idle state. In this section we discuss how such thinking can be applied to BitTorrent.

Standard BitTorrent transfers content via a request-response mechanism: peers are constantly requesting pieces of the data from each other, and serving the requests whenever they have free upload slots. The peers that are currently served are selected by the tit-for-tat mechanism [10], which favors peers actively contributing to the swarm. In terms of energy efficiency, the main problem is that if the available upload bandwidth of the sender is lower than the download capacity of the receiver, the receiver may not be able download at full speed. This is especially true for recently connected peers, which will receive even less bandwidth because of the tit-for-tat mechanism. Mobile devices, which often cannot accept incoming connections and generally have slower network connections, are even more likely to be stuck at slow download speeds.

One idea to ensure that a mobile peer gets data fast is to create a schedule of data transfer intervals. In this way the mobile peers could alternate between high bitrate active states and completely idle states. This has to be done carefully so that the modified system does not penalize the operation of the regular peers and provide unfair advantage to the mobile peers. To experiment with this concept we developed a BurstTorrent protocol that treats the energy-limited and the regular peers in a different way [11].

The key requirements for the system can be summarized as follows:

- The energy consumption of energy-limited peers must be less compared with using standard BitTorrent. The download time for energy-limited peers can be longer.
- Regular peers must not be penalized; they must receive the content in about the same amount of time as with standard BitTorrent.
- Preserve compatibility with standard BitTorrent as much as possible. Peers not supporting the protocol and regular peers still use standard BitTorrent to transfer data between each other.

The proposed protocol uses the concept of scheduled transfers. An energy-limited peer, which is downloading content from a BitTorrent swarm, negotiates time intervals with regular peers when the regular peers would promise to use all the necessary resources to send content to the downloading peer with the agreed speed. This way it can be ensured that when an energy-limited device is in active state, it receives data at full speed.

Regular peers maintain an upload schedule in which they store points of time when data is needed to be sent to limited peers. Similarly to this, energy limited peers use a download schedule to calculate times when they can request new pieces of data. Scheduled transfers require regular peers to control and regulate their upload speed. They need to be able to reserve a portion of their bandwidth at certain times for the scheduled uploads. Nevertheless, this can be implemented relatively easily with a flow control mechanism, holding back packets to regular peers if the upload speed to energy limited peers is lower than required. If a regular peer cannot transfer at the agreed speed, the schedule can become corrupted, which can result in loss of energy, but it has only a temporary effect and does not ruin the whole transfer process.

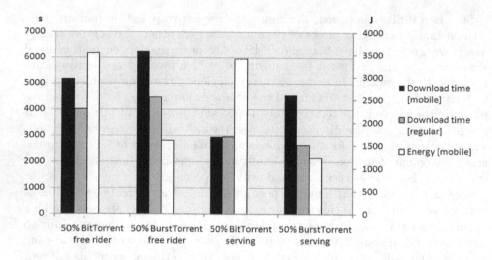

Fig. 6. Simulation results with 50% of the peers being energy-limited

We analyzed how BurstTorrent compares with normal BitTorrent using two different strategies for the energy-limited peers: energy-limited peers only downloaded content (free rider cases) and energy-limited peers also uploaded to regular peers during the active periods (serving cases).

The results depicted in Figure 6 show that the simple and obvious strategy where energy-limited peers are free-riders using standard BitTorrent is bad. In all measures they experienced worse performance than the energy-limited peers which were able to contribute by uploading.

As expected, in terms of energy consumption, BurstTorrent clearly outperformed standard BitTorrent. In the 50% energy-limited case, it achieved 64% less power consumption in the serving mode and 52% in the free rider mode. The downside of the energy saving was the download time that was 54% longer for serving peers and 50% longer for free-riders in comparison to standard BitTorrent.

With BurstTorrent the serving strategy was superior to the freeriding BurstTorrent in all attributes. This shows that the tit-for-tat mechanism works effectively with BurstTorrent as well. Even if the free-riding strategies are worse in comparison with serving strategies, we cannot ignore them since it can be that energy-limited devices are not able to upload because of the operator policies or other limitations. In those cases BurstTorrent is able to effectively reduce the energy consumption. However, the negative side-effect is that the download time of the regular peers increases dramatically.

Regarding the download time of regular peers, there was a 2% to 10% increase in the case of BurstTorrent free rider compared with standard BitTorrent free rider. However, if uploading was enabled, regular peers achieved shorter download times with BurstTorrent than with standard BitTorrent. This is mainly because energy-limited peers using BurstTorrent do not upload to each other but only to regular peers.

Table 1. Measurement results of downloading a 25MB torrent

Method	Energy (J)	Download time (S)	Avg. download speed (KB/s)
SymTorrent	672	465	58
CloudTorrent	248	189	189

Although this approach seems to work nicely in the simulated environment it has the main problem that it requires a change in the BitTorrent protocol. Therefore, it is not compatible with the existing BitTorrent communities and having enough incentives to change all existing BitTorrent client applications to support this kind of approach is prohibitively difficult. A much easier way from the deployment perspective is to develop energy-efficient solutions that only require local changes in a client. In the next section we discuss one such idea.

3.3   Using the Cloud

The cloud computing is easily seen as a way to reduce the load of the mobile devices, e.g. by offloading part of the work to the servers in the cloud. It is easy to understand that such approach makes sense in a CPU intensive calculation but could the similar approach also make sense in peer-to-peer content downloading. It turns out that is makes a lot of sense and reduces the energy consumption considerably [12].

In order to evaluate the concept of using a centralized proxy for providing energy-efficient access to content shared via BitTorrent to mobile devices, we created a cloud-based BitTorrent proxy and compared its performance with SymTorrent, a native BitTorrent client for Symbian-based mobile phones. The cloud-based BitTorrent proxy, referred to as CloudTorrent, consists of two main parts: a phone application communicating with the cloud and a server hosting the remote BitTorrent client. All communication between the server and the client is carried out via HTTP connections. On the server side, we use uTorrent, which is a popular free PC BitTorrent client with most of its functions available via an HTTP-based API.

Downloading content using CloudTorrent is performed in two steps. First the server side uses the BitTorrent protocol to download the content to the Cloud-Torrent server. Once the torrent download is completed, the content is transferred to the phone via an HTTP connection. We compared the performance of native BitTorrent client (SymTorrent) and the proxy-based approach (Cloud-Torrent) with a series of measurements. We used Nokia N82 phones, 3G data connection, and an Amazon EC2 instance with at least 10 Mb/s uplink capacity. In the test case, a 25 MB size torrent was downloaded to the phone using the two methods.

The measurements results are depicted in Table 1. The download time is the total time from the invocation of the download to the time the full content has arrived to the mobile. The average download speed, on the other hand, focuses only on the speed experienced by the mobile device: in the proxy case the HTTP file transfer from the server to mobile and in the SymTorrent case the aggregate download speed from different peers.

CloudTorrent outperformed SymTorrent both in terms of energy consumption and in download time. The difference in energy consumption can mainly be attributed to difference in download speeds; CloudTorrent was able to reach much higher, and thus more energy efficient, transfer speed than SymTorrent. In the CloudTorrent case, the server isolated the mobile client from the limitations and speed variations of the torrent download and provided a fast, dedicated connection to the mobile. SymTorrent, on the other hand, received data from several peers and suffered directly from the bandwidth limitations of the peers, Internet bottlenecks, and competition between multiple downloaders.

Moreover, since the BitTorrent client in the cloud is able to serve its peers with high upload speeds, the tit-for-tat mechanism increases the download speed of the torrent. If we compare the torrent download times only (and exclude the time transferring the file from the server to the mobile) we notice that CloudTorrent server was able to download the torrent 88% faster than SymTorrent.

Figure 7 depicts the energy consumption and downlink bitrate curves of the two test cases. The power consumption of using SymTorrent was almost constant with about 2 W average. The download bitrate for the torrent was only around 50 kB/s and there was noticeable variance in the experienced rate. In the case

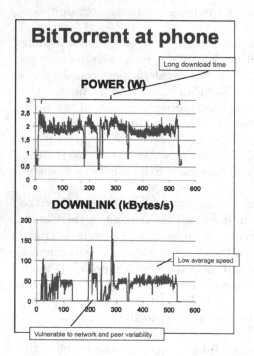
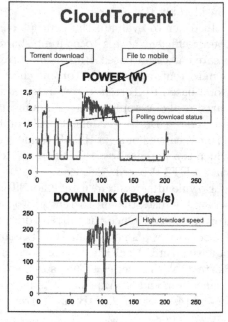

Fig. 7. Comparison of power consumption and downlink bitrate between SymTorrent vs. CloudTorrent

of CloudTorrent, there is very little communication at the beginning while the BitTorrent client in the cloud is downloading the content. During this period the phone is idle waiting for the content to be ready and periodically polls the server for the progress of the download activity. Once the BitTorrent client at the cloud has downloaded the full content (at around 75s) the server pushes the content to the phone. During the push activity the phone is able to receive the content with almost four times faster than what is possible with SymTorrent. This speed difference is the major source for the energy saving.

Figure 7 also shows how the large head energy of 3G cellular communication (discussed in Section 2.5) creates unnecessary energy consumption. In order to know when the cloud server has completed the download, the mobile client periodically polls its status via HTTP (the spikes at 25 s and 50 s time points) The query involves only a few bytes of data transfer, but the power consumption remains at a high level for around 10 s. Obviously, polling is not the best technology choice here and even more efficient operation could be achieved by some kind of push protocol that would eliminate the unnecessary polling.

We have also investigated alternative solutions to the cloud hosted server, for instance, hosting the proxy in a distributed fashion in broadband routers at homes [13].

4   DHT Energy Consumption

DHTs (Distributed Hash Tables) are peer-to-peer systems that enable the storage and retrieval of key-value pairs in a completely distributed and scalable way. DHTs can be used in distributed storage systems, file sharing, service discovery, and, generally, in any kind of system that requires lookup services. In principle, their operation is simple; users simply store and retrieve key-value -pairs. However, efficiently distributing this operation to peers that may join or leave the system frequently creates complexity. And, when mobile peers enter the picture, doing the operation in an energy-efficient way creates yet another dimension to deal with.

To study the load and energy consumption of being a member of a DHT we have performed measurements with a mobile DHT client developed for Symbian OS [14]. The application implements the Kademlia protocol [15] and connects to the Mainline BitTorrent DHT network, which usually has around two million concurrent users [16]. So this setting allows us to study the operation of a mobile device as part of a really huge community.

Figure 8 shows how the number of incoming messages and energy spending (in 15 min bins) as a function of the time since the node joined the DHT. The incoming traffic is gradually increasing as time passes. This is due to the mechanism Kademlia nodes use to populate their routing tables. The longer a node stays online, the more significant position it receives in its neighbors routing tables. Since Kademlia prefer long-living nodes to those that have been online for only a shorter period, the addresses of these are sent to other nodes more frequently. During the three-hour tests, more than two third of the message traffic was the result of incoming queries initiated by other nodes in the network.

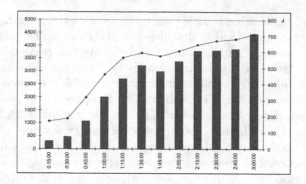

Fig. 8. Energy consumption and # of messages in each 15 min interval for a mobile peer in Mainline BitTorrent DHT (Kademlia) over 1 million users

In this setting a typical smart phone battery would be depleted in about 5 hours. This is clearly too short to consider serious applications, for instance, for using DHT to keep track of the mobile phone locations in a peer-to-peer SIP system [17].

4.1   Probabilistic Message Dropping

To reduce the energy spending on mobile nodes in a heterogeneous DHT we investigated the idea of selectively responding to queries coming from other DHT nodes. Processing incoming messages is the most significant factor that affects the energy consumption of a DHT node. The key idea that by dropping incoming request, the energy consumed by mobile nodes can be significantly reduced. Our proposed mechanism is simple: if an incoming request is received, it is dropped with a certain probability P_{drop}. The value of P_{drop} would depend on the battery status of the node. Dropping a request in this context means that no response is sent back to the initiator of the request. The energy saved by applying this method is the result of two factors:

- Mobile nodes do not completely parse incoming requests, and do not send responses.
- Due to the fact that most DHTs favor active, correctly behaving nodes, much less requests are sent to the mobile nodes.

The latter factor is the more significant, especially in DHTs that have high maintenance traffic, such as Kademlia. Since other nodes detect that the mobile node is not responding, it is demoted or even removed from the routing table.

Figure 9 shows the results of the energy measurements. Changing P_{drop} has a significant effect on the consumption: dropping 50% of the incoming requests can reduce the consumed energy by 55%. As noted before, this is mainly due to the lower number of requests sent to the mobile node. It can also be seen that there is no significant benefit of increasing P_{drop} above 0.7.

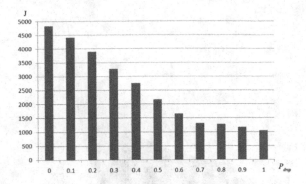

Fig. 9. Energy as a function of dropping probability

While this approach seems to be fine from the mobile peers energy point of view, it raises an obvious question of what happens to the overall operation of the DHT system if some peers start to behave in this way. To study this we divided the nodes on the DHT into two classes characterized by their message dropping parameter P_{drop}. Fixed nodes (having plentiful energy) follow the standard protocol behavior, and reply to all incoming requests ($P_{drop} = 0$). If we intend to connect to existing, deployed DHTs, we can assume that the majority of the nodes in the network are full peers. Mobile nodes have $P_{drop} > 0$.

Although the amount of energy saved is most significant in the $P_{drop} = 1$ case, this behavior is acceptable only if the number of mobile nodes is relatively small, compared to the number of fixed nodes. In a DHT where the ratio of mobile nodes exceeds a certain level, the performance of the DHT would be greatly reduced if all mobile nodes act as clients only. A solution for this problem is to enable mobile nodes to reply to some of the queries sent by other nodes, but not all of them. In this way, the mobile nodes still participate in the DHT to a certain degree, but they also keep energy consumption at a lower level by limiting the number of the responses. The open questions are how parameter P_{drop} affects the performance of the DHT and what the ideal value is for this parameter in a certain DHT setup. We analyzed this by simulating the behavior of a DHT.

Figure 10 shows a plot of the expected lookup latency, $E[W]$, as a function of the ratio of mobile nodes in the network, m, and the probability that a mobile node drops an incoming request, P_{drop}. The base lookup latency is 60 seconds (which was observed in the Mainline BitTorrent DHT). It can be seen in the graph that adding mobile nodes or increasing the dropping probability does not have a significant impact on lookup latency as long as there are enough fixed nodes in the network. When the ratio of mobile nodes does not exceed 30%, operating the mobiles in client-only mode ($P_{drop} = 1$) is even acceptable, since it does not cause significant increase in lookup latency. This is mainly the result of the fact that Kademlia uses parallel routing and multiple messages are sent out in each routing step, a dropped message increases the routing latency if all other requests fail in that particular routing step.

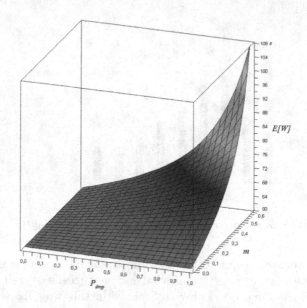

Fig. 10. Relationship between dropping probability (P_{drop}), ratio of mobile and normal peers (m), and expected delay E[W]

Comparing Figures 9 and 10 allows us to do some further observations. In particular, if we choose $P_{drop} = 0.7$) after which the energy saving in a mobile peer starts to slow down (see Figure 9) we can see that even if half of the peers in the DHT were mobiles the performance would still be reasonably fine.

Although this analysis is about Kademlia most of the findings can be applied to other DHTs as well. One requirement is that the DHT has multiple replicas for each stored value. This is important, because if a value is stored in only one node, and this node does not answer an incoming request, then the request would fail completely, which is unacceptable in a properly working DHT.

5   Conclusions

In this paper we have looked at the key principles of energy consumption of mobile devices from the communication and computing point of view. Our view has been on the software level and we have looked at solutions that can be implemented in mobile applications, proxies, or data centers. We can identify some characteristics that influence the energy consumption. These include

- Communication is a major energy consumer often spending 50% of energy. Reshaping the communication pattern often results into major energy savings.
- Higher bitrate improves energy efficiency of data transfer
- Delaying non-urgent data transfers and grouping them with voice calls allows highly energy efficient transfer of data

- Especially in 3G cellular networks the changes between idle and active states are very slow. Therefore transferring as much data as possible in a single burst is recommended

We have illustrated some solutions to reduce the energy consumption by looking at BitTorrent and Kademlia DHT systems. These peer-to-peer systems are useful for experimentation because they present many characteristics of distributed solutions, are widely used, and have big communities that can be taken advantage of in large scale tests. Some of the ideas we have discussed are

- The energy benefits of altruistic behavior in peer-to-peer systems
- Changing BitTorrent protocol to transfer data in a bursty fashion on mobile nodes
- Using the cloud to assist in content download
- Saving energy by selectively choosing which queries to react

With the increasing use of mobile, battery-powered devices the energy-efficient operation of applications and services is a highly relevant research field. It would be important also to spread the ideas to the developer communities because a smart design of an application can have an important influence.

Acknowledgements. I would like to extend my thanks to former colleagues at Nokia Research Center and research partners in Budapest University of Technology and Economics for many of the original studies covered in this paper. This work was partly supported by the Academy of Finland, grant number 253860.

References

1. Creus, G., Kuulusa, M.: Optimizing Mobile Software with Built-in Power Profiling. Springer (2007)
2. Zhang, L., Tiwana, B., Qian, Z., Wang, Z., Dick, R., Mao, Z., Yang, L.: Accurate online power estimation and automatic battery behavior based power model generation for smartphones. In: Proceedings of the Eighth IEEE/ACM/IFIP International Conference on Hardware/Software Codesign and System Synthesis, pp. 105–114. ACM (2010)
3. Neuvo, Y.: Cellular phones as embedded systems. In: 2004 IEEE International Solid-State Circuits Conference, Digest of Technical Papers, ISSCC 2004, pp. 32–37. IEEE (2004)
4. Carroll, A., Heiser, G.: An analysis of power consumption in a smartphone. In: Proceedings of the 2010 USENIX Conference on USENIX Annual Technical Conference, p. 21. USENIX Association (2010)
5. Nurminen, J.: Parallel connections and their effect on the battery consumption of a mobile phone. In: 2010 7th IEEE Consumer Communications and Networking Conference (CCNC), pp. 1–5 (2010)
6. Xiao, Y., Savolainen, P., Karppanen, A., Siekkinen, M., Ylä-Jääski, A.: Practical power modeling of data transmission over 802.11 g for wireless applications. In: Proceedings of the 1st International Conference on Energy-efficient Computing and Networking, pp. 75–84. ACM (2010)

7. Schurgers, C., Aberthorne, O., Srivastava, M.: Modulation scaling for energy aware communication systems. In: Proceedings of the 2001 International Symposium on Low Power Electronics and Design, pp. 96–99. ACM (2001)

8. Balasubramanian, N., Balasubramanian, A., Venkataramani, A.: Energy consumption in mobile phones: a measurement study and implications for network applications. In: Proceedings of the 9th ACM SIGCOMM Conference on Internet Measurement Conference, pp. 280–293. ACM (2009)

9. Nurminen, J., Noyranen, J.: Energy-consumption in mobile peer-to-peer-quantitative results from file sharing. In: 5th IEEE Consumer Communications and Networking Conference, CCNC 2008, pp. 729–733. IEEE (2008)

10. Cohen, B.: Incentives build robustness in bittorrent. In: Workshop on Economics of Peer-to-Peer systems, vol. 6, pp. 68–72 (2003)

11. Kelényi, I., Nurminen, J.K.: Bursty content sharing mechanism for energy-limited mobile devices. In: Proceedings of the 4th ACM Workshop on Performance Monitoring and Measurement of Heterogeneous Wireless and Wired Networks, PM2HW2N 2009, pp. 216–223. ACM, New York (2009)

12. Kelényi, I., Nurminen, J.: Cloudtorrent-energy-efficient bittorrent content sharing for mobile devices via cloud services. In: 2010 7th IEEE Consumer Communications and Networking Conference (CCNC), pp. 1–2. IEEE (2010)

13. Kelnyi, I., Ludanyi, Á., Nurminen, J.: Using home routers as proxies for energy-efficient bittorrent downloads to mobile phones. IEEE Communications Magazine 49, 142–147 (2011)

14. Kelényi, I., Nurminen, J.: Energy aspects of peer cooperation measurements with a mobile dht system. In: IEEE International Conference on Communications Workshops, ICC Workshops 2008, pp. 164–168. IEEE (2008)

15. Maymounkov, P., Mazières, D.: Kademlia: A Peer-to-Peer Information System Based on the XOR Metric. In: Druschel, P., Kaashoek, M.F., Rowstron, A. (eds.) IPTPS 2002. LNCS, vol. 2429, pp. 53–65. Springer, Heidelberg (2002)

16. Crosby, S., Wallach, D.: An analysis of bittorrents two kademlia-based dhts. Technical report, Technical Report TR07-04, Rice University (2007)

17. Kelényi, I., Nurminen, J., Matuszewski, M.: Dht performance for peer-to-peer sip-a mobile phone perspective. In: 2010 7th IEEE Consumer Communications and Networking Conference (CCNC), pp. 1–5. IEEE (2010)

Data Insertion and Archiving in Erasure-Coding Based Large-Scale Storage Systems

Lluis Pamies-Juarez[1], Frédérique Oggier[1], and Anwitaman Datta[2]

[1] School of Mathematical and Physical Sciences
[2] School of Computer Engineering
Nanyang Technological University, Singapore
{lpjuarez,frederique,anwitaman}@ntu.edu.sg

Abstract. Given the vast volume of data that needs to be stored reliably, many data-centers and large-scale file systems have started using erasure codes to achieve reliable storage while keeping the storage overhead low. This has invigorated the research on erasure codes tailor made to achieve different desirable storage system properties such as efficient redundancy replenishment mechanisms, resilience against data corruption, degraded reads, to name a few prominent ones. A problem that has mainly been overlooked until recently is that of how the storage system can be efficiently populated with erasure coded data to start with. In this paper, we will look at two distinct but related scenarios: (i) *migration to archival* - leveraging on existing replicated data to create an erasure encoded archive, and (ii) *data insertion* - new data being inserted in the system directly in erasure coded format. We will elaborate on coding techniques to achieve better throughput for data insertion and migration, and in doing so, explore the connection of these techniques with recently proposed locally repairable codes such as self-repairing codes.

1 Introduction

The ability to store securely and reliably the vast amount of data that is continuously being created by both individuals and institutions is a cornerstone of our digital society. A study sponsored by the information storage company *EMC* estimated that the world's data would have reached 1.8 zettabytes of data to be stored by the end of 2011.[1]

The massive volume of data involved means that it would be extremely expensive, if not impossible, to build a single piece of hardware with enough storage as well as I/O capabilities to meet the needs of most organizations and businesses. A practical alternative is to scale out (or horizontally): resources from multiple interconnected storage nodes are pooled together, and more such nodes can be organically added as and when the demand for storage resources grows. We call these systems *Networked Distributed Storage Systems* (NDSS). NDSS come in many flavors such as data centers and peer-to-peer (P2P) storage/backup systems, which have their unique characteristics, but also share several common

---

[1] http://www.emc.com/about/news/press/2011/20110628-01.htm

C. Hota and P.K. Srimani (Eds.): ICDCIT 2013, LNCS 7753, pp. 47–68, 2013.

properties. Given the system scale, failure of a significant subset of the constituent nodes, as well as other network components, is a norm rather than the exception. To enable a highly available overall service, it is thus essential to both tolerate short-term outages of some nodes and to provide resilience against permanent failures of individual components. Fault-tolerance is achieved using redundancy while long-term resilience relies on replenishment of lost redundancy over time. To that end, erasure codes have become popular to achieve system resilience while incurring low storage overhead. Recent years have accordingly witnessed the design of erasure codes tailor made to meet distributed storage system needs, more specifically, a lot of work has been done to improve the storage system's repairability. This line of work has been surveyed in [4, 6].

This article focuses on a different aspect of erasure code design. A relatively unexplored problem in the literature is, how does the erasure coded data come into being to start with?

In a replication based NDSS, when a new object needs to be stored, the first node receiving the same can forward it to another node to replicate the data, and so on. Such a pipelined approach allows quick data insertion and replication in the system, the load of data insertion is distributed among multiple nodes, and a single node is not overloaded with the task.

In contrast, in an erasure coding based NDSS, traditionally, one node has the burden to first encode the new object (after obtaining it if necessary), and then distribute the encoded pieces to other storage nodes. The computational and communication resources of this node thus become a bottleneck. In this paper we summarize some recent results delving into two distinct scenarios, where distributing the load to create erasure coded data improves the throughput of populating the NDSS with erasure coded data.

Note that in the following, we use the term 'source' to mean whichever node has a full copy of the data. It could be a gateway node that receives the data from an end-user who 'owns' and uploads the same to the NDSS, or it could be an NDSS node where the data is created locally by some application.

Migration to Archival. If the data is originally stored in the system in replicated format, but subsequently needs to be migrated into erasure coding based archive, then existing replicas of the data can be exploited to distribute the load of the erasure coding process. This scenario is typical since newly arrived objects are often stored as replicas, which ensures efficient reads and fault tolerance while the objects are being frequently manipulated. When accesses to the objects become rarer, they are archived using erasure coding, and the replicas are discarded.

Data Insertion. When new data is being inserted into the system, if such a data is to be stored in NDSS directly in erasure coded format, then the computational resources of the storage nodes can be utilized to reduce the amount of redundant data that the source needs to itself create and inject individually to the different storage nodes.

For these two distinct scenarios - migration to archival and data insertion - we have devised (so far unrelated) mechanisms [7–9] to improve the system's throughput. Before summarizing these approaches, we next provide a brief background of erasure codes for NDSS.

2   Background on Erasure Coding for Distributed Storage

We can formally define the erasure encoding process as follows. Let the vector $\mathbf{o} = (o_1, \ldots, o_k)$ denote a data object of $k \times q$ bits, that is, each symbol o_i, $i = 1, \ldots, k$ is a string of q bits. Operations are typically performed using finite field arithmetic, that is, the two bits $\{0, 1\}$ are seen as forming the finite field $\mathbb{F}_2$ of two elements, while o_i, $i = 1, \ldots, k$ then belong to the binary extension field $\mathbb{F}_{2^q}$ containing 2^q elements. The encoding of the object $\mathbf{o}$ is performed using an $(n \times k)$ generator matrix G such that $G \cdot \mathbf{o}^T = \mathbf{c}^T$, in order to obtain an n-dimensional codeword $\mathbf{c} = (c_1, \ldots, c_n)$ of size $n \times q$ bits.

When the generator matrix G has the form $G = [I_k, G']^T$ where I_k is the identity matrix and G' is a $k \times m$ matrix, $m = n - k$, the codeword $\mathbf{c}$ becomes $\mathbf{c} = [\mathbf{o}, \mathbf{p}]$ where $\mathbf{o}$ is the original object, and $\mathbf{p}$ is a parity vector containing $m \times q$ parity bits. The code is then said to be *systematic*, in which case the k parts of the original object remain unaltered after the coding process. The data can then still be reconstructed without requiring a decoding process by accessing these systematic pieces.

If any arbitrary k of the c_is can be used to reconstruct the original information $\mathbf{o} = (o_1, \ldots, o_k)$, then the code is said to be *maximum distance separable* (MDS). For any given choice of n and k, an MDS code provides the best fault-tolerance for up to $n - k$ arbitrary failures.

Systematic MDS codes have thus traditionally been preferred in storage systems, given the practical advantages they provide.

Other system considerations may however prompt for non-MDS and/or non-systematic codes as well. For instance, dependencies within small subsets of codewords may allow for better and faster repairs [5] - which is desirable for long-term resilience of the system, even if it marginally deteriorates the system's tolerance of the number of simultaneous faults. In fact, in the recent years, repairable erasure codes have been vigorously researched [4,6], and it continues to be an open-end and popular topic of study. Likewise, non-systematic codes may provide a basic level of confidentiality [3] of the stored content since an adversary with access to any one (or very small number of) storage node(s) will not be able to see the content.

3   Migration from Replication to Erasure Coded Archive

Often, when new data is introduced in a storage system, it is replicated (3-way replication is a popular approach) for fault-tolerance. Furthermore, such a replication strategy can be leveraged to support higher throughput of data access when different applications are trying to read the same data simultaneously, or by migrating computing tasks to a relatively less loaded subset of the replicas instead of moving the data around. Data is often accessed and manipulated

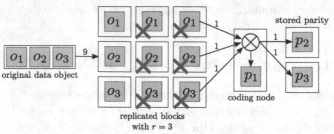

(a) Traditional archiving (e.g. as done in HDFS-RAID [2]).

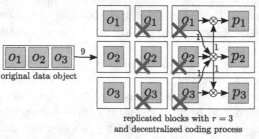

(b) Decentralized encoding.

Fig. 1. An example of migration of replicated data into an erasure coded archive. The squares represent storage nodes and the arrows across boxes denote data (labels indicate the actual amount) transferred over the network. We can see how (a) requires a total of *five* network transfers while (b) needs only *four* network transfers. The "X" symbol denotes the replicas that are discarded once the archival finishes, and the symbol $\otimes$ denotes an encoding operation.

frequently when it has been acquired recently, but over time, once the need to access it decreases, it is desirable to reduce the storage overhead by replacing the replicas and instead archive the data using erasure coding [2]. We propose to effectuate this migration via a decentralized encoding process, which, as we will see later, provides significant performance boosts.

3.1   Motivating Examples

We will use Figure 1 for an illustration of an abstracted toy example of migration of a replicated system into an erasure coded archival. Suppose that we have a data object comprising of three parts (o_1, o_2, o_3), and the parts o_i are stored at three different nodes each (i.e., using a 3-way replication). Traditionally, one node (the coding node) would require (o_1, o_2, o_3) to be collocated, based on which it can compute some parity coefficients (p_1, p_2, p_3), keeping p_1 for itself and then distributing p_2 and p_3. This will require a total of five network transfers including the communication cost of downloading the three original parts to start with. Alternatively, one of the nodes which already stores o_2 could download o_1 and o_3, from which it can compute the parity p_2, and then distributes p_2 to one of the nodes which stored o_1 (respectively o_3), each of which could compute parity pieces p_1 and p_3 respectively using p_2 and o_1 (respectively o_3). This process where the existing replicas are exploited costs only four network transfers. In both cases, the codeword $(c_1, \ldots, c_6) = (o_1, o_2, o_3, p_1, p_2, p_3)$ has been computed and distributed over six different nodes. The remaining pieces of the original data can be garbage collected subsequently. Also note that if each storage node had a communication bottleneck, such that it could only upload or download one piece in an unit time, then the centralized approach would have required five time units for data transfer, in addition to the computation time. If p_2 is pipelined to o_3 via o_1 (not shown in the figure) then the decentralized approach would take three time units for data transfer, in addition to the computation time at the three different nodes, some of which happens in parallel.

The above toy example illustrates that there is a potential benefit both in terms of reduced network traffic, and possibly also in terms of the time taken to carry out a single encoding, by decentralizing the process and leveraging on existing replicas. The example however does not reveal what the parity pieces p_is are, and what specific computations need to be carried out. In fact, as we will see next, different strategies can be devised, depending on how many replicas are present in the system when the migration to erasure coded archive starts, what is the original placement of these replicas, how is the encoding process distributed and what are the properties of the resulting codeword.

We will next give two explicit toy examples, to illustrate two types of decentralized encoding. The first one ends up in a non-systematic codeword, while the second yields a systematic codeword. The first one assumes that each piece of the object and its replica(s) are initially placed in different nodes. The latter assumes that some of these pieces are cleverly collocated, in order to achieve further savings in communication. Subsequently, we will elaborate on a more general theory of decentralized coding, along with some early results.

Example 1. Suppose that an object $\mathbf{o} = (o_1, o_2, o_3, o_4)$, $o_i \in \mathbb{F}_{2^q}$, of $k = 4$ blocks is stored over $n = 8$ nodes using two replicas of $\mathbf{o}$, which are initially scattered as follows:

$$\mathcal{N}_1 : o_1, \mathcal{N}_2 : o_2, \mathcal{N}_3 : o_3, \mathcal{N}_4 : o_4,$$
$$\mathcal{N}_5 : o_1, \mathcal{N}_6 : o_2, \mathcal{N}_7 : o_3, \mathcal{N}_8 : o_4.$$

Clearly, such a setup can guarantee fault-tolerance against only a single arbitrary failure, though some combinations of multiple failures may also be tolerated, if one copy of each piece survives in the system. Consider that it needs to be archived using a codeword $\mathbf{c} = (c_1, \ldots, c_8)$. In this example, the resulting erasure coded data coincidentally has the same storage overhead as the original replication scheme (though this is not necessary, as we will see latter when we generalize the ideas), but will have significantly higher fault tolerance.

Unlike in Figure 1 where one node distributes its data to two other storage nodes, in this example, since more nodes are involved, the coding process is done in a pipelined manner, namely node 1 forwards $o_1 \psi_1$, i.e. some multiple of o_1, to node 2, which computes a linear combination of the received data with o_2, and forwards it again to node 3, and so on. More generally, node i encodes the data it gets from the previous node together with the data it already has and forwards it to the next node. We denote the data forwarded from node i to its successor, node j, by $x_{i,j}$, which is defined as follows:

$$x_{1,2} = o_1\psi_1,$$
$$x_{2,3} = x_{1,2} + o_2\psi_2 = o_1\psi_1 + o_2\psi_2,$$
$$x_{3,4} = x_{2,3} + o_3\psi_3 = o_1\psi_1 + o_2\psi_2 + o_3\psi_3,$$
$$x_{4,5} = x_{3,4} + o_4\psi_4 = o_1\psi_1 + o_2\psi_2 + o_3\psi_3 + o_4\psi_4,$$
$$x_{5,6} = x_{4,5} + o_1\psi_5 = o_1(\psi_1 + \psi_5) + o_2\psi_2 + o_3\psi_3 + o_4\psi_4,$$
$$x_{6,7} = x_{5,6} + o_2\psi_6 = o_1(\psi_1 + \psi_5) + o_2(\psi_2 + \psi_6) + o_3\psi_3 + o_4\psi_4,$$
$$x_{7,8} = x_{6,7} + o_3\psi_7 = o_1(\psi_1 + \psi_5) + o_2(\psi_2 + \psi_6) + o_3(\psi_3 + \psi_7) + o_4\psi_4,$$

where $\psi_j \in \mathbb{F}_{2^q}$, $j = 1, \ldots, 7$, are some predetermined values. After the nodes have distributed their stored data, they are left to generate an element of the final codeword c_i by encoding the received data together with the locally available data as follows:

$$c_1 = o_1\xi_1,$$
$$c_2 = x_{1,2} + o_2\xi_2 = o_1\psi_1 + o_2\xi_2,$$
$$c_3 = x_{2,3} + o_3\xi_3 = o_1\psi_1 + o_2\psi_2 + o_3\xi_3,$$
$$c_4 = x_{3,4} + o_4\xi_4 = o_1\psi_1 + o_2\psi_2 + o_3\psi_3 + o_4\xi_4,$$
$$c_5 = x_{4,5} + o_1\xi_5 = o_1(\psi_1 + \xi_5) + o_2\psi_2 + o_3\psi_3 + o_4\psi_4,$$
$$c_6 = x_{5,6} + o_2\xi_6 = o_1(\psi_1 + \psi_5) + o_2(\psi_2 + \xi_6) + o_3\psi_3 + o_4\psi_4,$$
$$c_7 = x_{6,7} + o_3\xi_7 = o_1(\psi_1 + \psi_5) + o_2(\psi_2 + \psi_6) + o_3(\psi_3 + \xi_7) + o_4\psi_4,$$
$$c_8 = x_{7,8} + o_4\xi_8 = o_1(\psi_1 + \psi_5) + o_2(\psi_2 + \psi_6) + o_3(\psi_3 + \psi_7) + o_4(\psi_4 + \xi_8),$$

where $\xi_j \in \mathbb{F}_{2^q}$, $j = 1, \ldots, 8$, are also predetermined values.

Note that the coding process can be implemented in a pipelined manner, and both phases can be executed simultaneously: as soon as node i receives the first few bytes of $x_{i-1,i}$ it can start generating the first bytes of c_i, and concurrently forward $x_{i,i+1}$ to node $i+1$.

The end result is a non-systematic codeword $(c_1, \ldots, c_8)$ that has a high fault tolerance. By selecting values of ψ_i and ξ_i that do not introduce linear dependencies within the codeword, the original object **o** can be reconstructed from any combination of four codeword symbols except the combination $\{c_1, c_2, c_5, c_6\}$ [8]. In this specific case the symbols c_1, c_2, c_5 and c_6 are linearly dependent (this can be checked using symbolic computations) since:

$$c_1\left[(\psi_1\xi_6\xi_2^{-1} + \psi_5 + \xi_5)\xi_1^{-1}\right] + c_2\left[\xi_6\xi_2^{-1}\right] + c_5 + c_6 = 0,$$

recalling that $2 \equiv 0$ in $\mathbb{F}_{2^q}$. Then, this $(8,4)$ code has $\binom{8}{4} - 1 = 69$ possible 4-subsets of codeword symbols that suffice to reconstruct the original object **o**. It represents a negligible degradation with respect to the fault tolerance of an MDS code, where $\binom{8}{4} = 70$ such possible 4-subsets exist.

Example 2. The second example is that of a systematic (10,6) erasure code, which provides $m = 10 - 6 = 4$ blocks of redundancy (parity blocks). Consider a data object $\mathbf{o} = (o_1, o_2, \ldots, o_6)$ to be stored with a replica placement policy that stores $r = 3$ replicas of $\mathbf{o}$, that is, three replicas of every o_i, $i = 1, \ldots, 6$ (for a total of 18 data blocks). We assume that one of the replicas of $\mathbf{o}$ is stored in $k = 6$ different nodes, which will finally constitute the systematic part of the codeword, $c_1 = o_1, \ldots, c_k = o_k$. Of the $(r - 1)k = 12$ remaining replica pieces left, we select a subset of ℓ of them to be stored in the $m = 4$ coding nodes that will carry out the decentralized encoding process. The assignment of these ℓ replicas is as follows:

$$\mathcal{N}_1 = \{o_1, o_2, o_3\}\,;\ \mathcal{N}_2 = \{o_4, o_5, o_6\}\,;\ \mathcal{N}_3 = \{o_1, o_2\}\,;\ \mathcal{N}_4 = \{o_3, o_4\}\,,$$

where $\mathcal{N}_j$ denotes the set of blocks stored in node j. Note that only $\ell = 10$ out of the available $(r-1)k = 12$ blocks are replicated in the m coding nodes, while the remaining two can be flexibly stored in other nodes, e.g., to balance the amount of data stored per node. Such a collocation of multiple pieces reduces the amount of fault-tolerance enjoyed by the data while it is stored using replication.[2] Note also that no node stores any repeated block, since this would further reduce fault tolerance.

To describe the decentralized encoding process we use an iterative encoding process of $\nu = 7$ steps, in which every $\psi_i, \xi_j \in \mathbb{F}_{2^q}$ are predetermined values that define the actual code instance. During step 1, node 1 which has $\mathcal{N}_1$ generates

$$x_1 = o_1\psi_1 + o_2\psi_2 + o_3\psi_3$$

and sends it to node 2, which uses $\mathcal{N}_2$ and x_1 to compute

$$x_2 = o_4\psi_4 + o_5\psi_5 + o_6\psi_6 + x_1\psi_7$$

during step 2. After two more steps, we get:

$$x_3 = o_1\psi_8 + o_2\psi_9 + x_2\psi_{10}$$
$$x_4 = o_3\psi_{11} + o_4\psi_{12} + x_3\psi_{13},$$

and node 4 forwards x_4 to node 1, since $\nu = 7 > m = 4$, which creates

$$x_5 = o_1\psi_{14} + o_2\psi_{15} + o_3\psi_{16} + x_4\psi_{17}$$

before sending x_5 to node 2. For the last two iterations, both node 2 and node 3 use respectively $\mathcal{N}_2$, x_1 and x_5, and $\mathcal{N}_3$, x_2 and x_3 together, to compute

$$x_6 = o_4\psi_{18} + o_5\psi_{19} + o_6\psi_{20} + x_1\psi_{21} + x_5\psi_{22}$$
$$x_7 = o_1\psi_{23} + o_2\psi_{24} + x_2\psi_{25} + x_6\psi_{26}.$$

---

[2] By carrying out erasure coding of subset of pieces from different objects, one may be able to alleviate this problem of initial fault-tolerance, while still using precisely the same scheme.

After this phase, node 1 to 4 are locally storing:

$$\mathcal{N}_1 = \{o_1, o_2, o_3, x_4\}$$
$$\mathcal{N}_2 = \{o_4, o_5, o_6, x_1, x_5\}$$
$$\mathcal{N}_3 = \{o_1, o_2, x_2, x_6\}$$
$$\mathcal{N}_4 = \{o_3, o_4, x_3, x_7\}$$

from which they compute the final m parity blocks:

$$p_1 = o_1\xi_1 + o_2\xi_2 + o_3\xi_3 + x_4\xi_4$$
$$p_2 = o_4\xi_5 + o_5\xi_6 + o_6\xi_7 + x_1\xi_8 + x_5\xi_9$$
$$p_3 = o_1\xi_{10} + o_2\xi_{11} + x_2\xi_{12} + x_6\xi_{13}$$
$$p_4 = o_3\xi_{14} + o_4\xi_{15} + x_3\xi_{16} + x_7\xi_{17}.$$

As in Example 1, all values $\psi_i, \xi_i \in \mathbb{F}_{2^q}$ are also predetermined to optimize fault-tolerance.

The final codeword is $\mathbf{c} = [\mathbf{o}, \mathbf{p}] = (o_1, \ldots, o_6, p_1, \ldots, p_4)$. There is a total of ν blocks transmitted during the encoding process (those forwarded during the iterative phase). In this example, $\nu = 7$, and the encoding process requires two block transmissions less than the classic encoding process, which requires $n - 1 = 9$ blocks, thus achieving a 22% reduction of the traffic.

We will next elaborate the general theory of each of the two variations of the decentralized codes, along with summary of some results.

3.2   Generating a Non-systematic Erasure Code

Example 1 is a particular case of RapidRAID codes [8] for $k = 4$ and $n = 8$. We next present a general definition of RapidRAID codes [8] for any pair (n, k) of parameters, where $n \leq 2k$. We start by stating the requirements that RapidRAID imposes on how data must be stored:

- When $n < 2k$, two of the originally stored replicas should be overlapped between n storage nodes: a replica of $\mathbf{o}$ should be placed in nodes 1 to k, and a second replica of $\mathbf{o}$ in nodes from $n - k$ to n.
- The final n redundancy blocks forming $\mathbf{c}$ have to be generated (and finally stored) in nodes that were already storing a replica of the original data.

We then formally define the temporal redundant block that each node i in the pipelined chain sends to its successor as:

$$x_{i,i+1} = x_{i-1,i} + \sum_{o_j \in \text{node } i} o_j\psi_i, \quad 1 < i < n - 1, \tag{1}$$

with $x_{0,1} = 0$, while the final redundant block c_i generated/stored in each node i is:

$$c_i = x_{i-1,i} + \sum_{o_j \in \text{node } i} o_j\xi_i, \quad 1 < i < n, \tag{2}$$

where $\psi_i, \xi_i \in \mathbb{F}_{2^q}$ are static predetermined values specifically chosen to guarantee maximum fault tolerance.

3.3   Generating a Systematic Erasure Code

We will next assume that only $m = n - k$ nodes will participate in the encoding process (k nodes are storing the systematic pieces), as illustrated in Example 2. However, the proposed strategy also requires a carefully chosen collocation of several distinct replica pieces within the same node that participates in the decentralized encoding process.

Then, a total of ℓ different block replicas are allocated (collocated) among the m coding nodes, i.e., the content of the set $\mathcal{N}_j$ for each node j. For the sake of simplicity, we assume that the ℓ replicas are deterministically assigned in a sequential manner as illustrated in Example 2, trying to even out the number of blocks assigned to each node. A formal description of this allocation is provided in Algorithm 1.

Algorithm 1. Replica placement policy

1: $i \leftarrow 1$
2: **for** $j = 1, \ldots, m$ **do**
3:     $\alpha \leftarrow \lfloor \ell/m \rfloor$
4:     **if** $j \leq (\ell \bmod m)$ **then**
5:         $\alpha \leftarrow \alpha + 1$
6:     **end if**
7:     $\mathcal{N}_j = \{o_l : l = (j \bmod k), \ j = i, \ldots, i + \alpha\}$
8:     $i \leftarrow i + \alpha$
9: **end for**

This assignment policy imposes some restrictions on the location of the different replicated blocks (block collocation), which might require changes on the random assignment policy commonly used in NDSS. Furthermore, collocating block replicas in a same node reduces the fault tolerance of replicated data. This problem can be of special importance for the extreme case when $\ell = (r - 1)k$ (all replicas are stored within only m nodes), although for small values of ℓ the assignment policy provides some flexibility on where to assign the $(r-1)k - \ell$ remaining replicas. However, as we will show in Section 3.5, small ℓ values increase the chances of introducing linear dependencies during the distributed encoding process, reducing the resiliency of the encoded data. In this last case the negative effects of a small ℓ value can be counterbalanced by adopting larger ν values. There is then a trade-off between the values ℓ and ν, and the fault tolerance of the replicated and encoded data.

Remark 1. In the case of $\ell = k$, there is no replica assignment policy and a random placement can be used.

Given the replica assignment policy, the decentralized encoding process is split into two different phases: the *iterative encoding* and the *local encoding*.

The iterative encoding consists of ν sequential encoding steps, where at each step, each node generates and forwards a temporary redundant block. For each step i, where $i = 1, \ldots, \nu$, node $j = (i \bmod m)$ which stores the set of blocks $\mathcal{N}_j = \{z_1, z_2, \ldots\}$ locally computes a temporary block $x_i \in \mathbb{F}_{2^q}$ as follows:

$$x_i = z_1\psi_1 + z_2\psi_2 + \cdots + z_{|\mathcal{N}_j|}\psi_{|\mathcal{N}_j|}, \tag{3}$$

where $\psi_i \in \mathbb{F}_{2^q}$ are predetermined values. Once x_i is computed, node j sends x_i to the next node $l = (i + 1 \bmod m)$, which stores locally the new temporary block: $\mathcal{N}_l = \mathcal{N}_l \cup \{x_i\}$, after which, node l computes x_{i+1} as defined in (3) and forwards it to the next node. The iterative process is similarly repeated a total of ν times.

After this iterative encoding phase, each node $i = 1, \ldots, m$ executes a local encoding process where the stored blocks $\mathcal{N}_i$ (including the temporary blocks generated during the iterative encoding phase) are combined to generate the final parity block p_i (for predetermined values of $\xi_i \in \mathbb{F}_{2^q}$) as follows:

$$p_i = z_1\xi_1 + z_2\xi_2 + \cdots + z_{|\mathcal{N}_i|}\xi_{|\mathcal{N}_i|}. \tag{4}$$

Finally, we describe the overall distributed encoding algorithm (including the iterative encoding and the local encoding) in Algorithm 2. Note that values ψ_l and ξ_l (lines 7 and 17) are picked at random. In a sufficiently large field (e.g., when $q = 16$) this random choice will not introduce additional dependencies (w.h.p.) other than the ones introduced by the iterative encoding process itself [1].

Algorithm 2. Decentralized redundancy generation

1: $l \leftarrow 1$
2: $j \leftarrow 1$
3: $x \leftarrow 0$
4: **for** $i = 1, \ldots, \nu$ **do**   ▶ Generation of the ν temporary blocks.
5:      $x \leftarrow 0$
6:      **for** $z \in \mathcal{N}_j$ **do**   ▶ Coding operation as described in (3).
7:          $x \leftarrow x + \psi_l \cdot z$
8:          $l \leftarrow l + 1$
9:      **end for**
10:      $j \leftarrow (i + 1) \bmod m$
11:      $\mathcal{N}_j \leftarrow \mathcal{N}_j \cup \{x\}$ ▶ Each union ($\cup$) represents a block transfer.
12: **end for**
13: $l \leftarrow 1$
14: **for** $i = 1, \ldots, m$ **do**   ▶ Generation of the final m parity blocks.
15:      $p_i \leftarrow 0$
16:      **for** $x \in \mathcal{N}_i$ **do**   ▶ Coding operation as described in (4).
17:          $p_i \leftarrow p_i + \xi_l \cdot x$
18:          $l \leftarrow l + 1$
19:      **end for**
20: **end for**

3.4   General Distributed Encoding Framework

Both distributed encoding schemes follow the same approach: a set of n nodes, labelled from node 1 to node n, store an original configuration of data pieces. Then one node starts the encoding process by transmitting to the next node (next according to the labeling) a linear combination of the pieces it stores. The second node then keeps what it receives, what it owns, and sends a combination of both to the next node, and this is iterated until a codeword is computed.

- In the first case, the first node starts the process, which is repeated until reaching the nth node. The original configuration assumes, if $n = 2k$, that node 1 to node k each stores one piece of the data object, as does every node, from node $k + 1$ to node n. If $n < 2k$, the two copies of the original object are initially overlapped. This results in a non-systematic codeword.
- In the second case, to ensure that the codeword will be systematic, node 1 to node k store the k pieces of the original object, while nodes $k + 1$ to n store different configurations of the same. The iterative encoding only involves the $n - k$ latter nodes, which compute the parity coefficients. As a result, one round of this process (going from node $k + 1$ to node n) is typically not enough to ensure a good fault tolerance, and thus the encoding often necessitates several rounds.

3.5   Results

Encoding Times Analysis. One of the main advantages of distributing the erasure code redundancy generation across several nodes is that the required encoding times can be potentially reduced, providing more efficient ways of archiving replicated data. In this section we report performance results of an implementation of a (16,11)-RapidRAID [8] code (Section 3.2) which achieves significantly shorter encoding times in a testbed of 50 HP ThinClient computers, as compared to an efficient implementation of a (16,11) classical Cauchy Reed-Solomon erasure code.

Note however that the encoding speedup of RapidRAID is obtained at the expense of involving a total of $n = 16$ nodes in the encoding process, instead of the single node involved in classic encoding process. Thus, it is important to measure the encoding throughput of a classic erasure code involving the same number of nodes, i.e., when $n = 16$ classic encoding process are executed in parallel. Besides that, in practical scenarios storage nodes might be executing other tasks concurrently along with data archival processes, which might cause some nodes to experience overload or network congestions, which in turn might affect the coding times. Hence measuring the encoding times of both strategies (decentralized encoding vs. classic encoding) when some of the n nodes or networks are overloaded is another interesting aspect to study. In the experiments reported next, such bottlenecks are emulated in our testbed by reducing the network bandwidth of some nodes from 1GBps to 500MBps, and adding to these nodes a 100ms network latency (with a deviation of up to ±10ms).

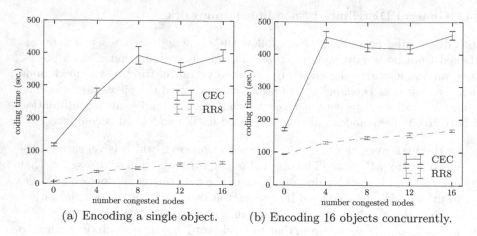

(a) Encoding a single object.   (b) Encoding 16 objects concurrently.

Fig. 2. Average time required to encode 16 concurrent objects using a (16,11) Cauchy Reed-Solomon code and a (16,11) RapidRaid code implemented using 8-bit finite-field operations. Nodes have 500Mbps connections with a latency of 100ms±10ms. Error bars depict the standard deviation value.

In Figure 2 we depict the encoding times of the (16,11) RapidRAID implementation (RR8) and the (16,11) Cauchy Reed Solomon Code (CEC). In Figure 2a we show the encoding times for a single data object and different number of congested nodes. In this case a single data object is encoded in a totally idle system. We see how when there are no congested nodes the RapidRAID implementations have of the order of 90% shorter coding times as compared to the classic erasure code implementation. Distributing the network and computing load of the encoding process across 16 different nodes reduces the encoding time significantly. In Figure 2b we depict the per-object encoding times obtained by executing 16 concurrent classic encoding processes and 16 concurrent RapidRAID encoding processes on a group of 16 nodes. According to further experiments on EC2 (not reported here, but details can be found in [8]), the two RapidRAID implementations achieve a reduction of the overall coding time by up to 20% when there are no congested nodes.

We further observe from Figure 2 that the coding times of RapidRAID codes have a quasi-linear behavior when the number of congested nodes increases. However, in the case of classic erasure codes, we observe that even a single congested node has major impact on the coding times. In general, these results show how RapidRAID codes significantly boost the performance of the encoding process over congested networks.

Fault Tolerance Analysis. As was illustrated in Example 1, RapidRAID codes offer a high fault tolerance. Some numerical analysis in [8] show how for short codes RapidRAID are MDS codes when $k \geq n - 3$, and that for practical values of k out of this range RapidRAID codes offer a fault tolerance comparable to that of MDS codes. One of the reasons for this high fault tolerance is that the encoding process is distributed across a large number of storage nodes (across n nodes), which due to the random nature of the encoding process, reduces the chances of introducing linear dependencies within the codeword symbols. However, in the case of the systematic erasure code presented in Section 3.3, the encoding process is distributed across a smaller set $m = n - k$ nodes, and then the chances to introduce linear dependencies within the codeword symbols increase.

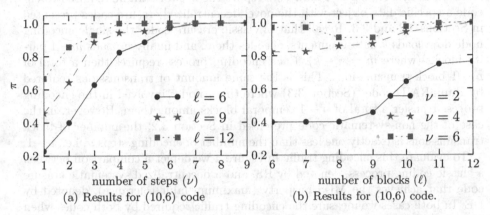

(a) Results for (10,6) code

(b) Results for (10,6) code.

Fig. 3. Fault tolerance achieved by our decentralized erasure coding process as a function of the number of encoding steps, ν, and the number of co-located block replicas, ℓ. The fault tolerance π is expressed as the proportion of k-subsets of the codeword $\mathbf{c}$ that do not contain linear dependencies. When this value is one, the code is MDS and has maximum fault tolerance.

In this latter case it is then important to evaluate the fault tolerance of the obtained code for different code parameters. We divide the fault tolerance analysis in two experiments, one aiming at evaluating the effects of the number of encoding steps ν, and another one at the effects of the collocated replicas ℓ.

In Figure 3a we show the fault tolerance π of the code (proportion of linearly independent k-subsets) as a function of the number of steps ν. For each of the three different codes we depict the effects of ν for three different values of ℓ. We can see how the proportion of linearly independent k-subsets increases as more encoding iterations are executed. Achieving the maximum fault tolerance (when the fraction of linearly independent k-subsets is one) requires less iterations for high replica collocation values ℓ.

Similarly, in Figure 3b, we display the fault tolerance as a function of the number of blocks stored within the m coding nodes ℓ. For each code we also present the results for three different values of ν, which aim at showing the fault tolerance (i) when only a few coding nodes execute the iterative encoding process, (ii) when all coding nodes execute it exactly once, and (iii) when some coding nodes execute it more than once. In general we can see how increasing the number of initially collocated replicas ℓ increases the fault tolerance of the code. However, for small values of ν there are cases where increasing ℓ might slightly reduce the fault tolerance. Finally, we want to note that in those cases where $\nu \leq m$ (only a few coding nodes execute the iterative encoding), the code produced by the decentralized coding can never achieve maximum fault tolerance. To achieve maximum fault tolerance, all the m coding nodes need to execute at least one coding step.

Network Traffic Analysis. Finally, we report the network traffic required to encode a specific data object with the novel decentralized erasure codes presented in Sections 3.2 and 3.3. Recall that in classic erasure codes the single encoding node downloads k data fragments, encodes them, and finally uploads $m - 1$ parity blocks (where $m = n - k$). Each encoding process requires then a total of $n - 1$ block transmissions. This is the same amount of transmissions required by RapidRAID codes (Section 3.3) where the n nodes involved in the encoding process transfer a total of $n - 1$ temporal blocks among them. However, in the case of the non-systematic code presented in Section 3.2, the number of block transmissions is exactly one less than the number of encoding steps ν, i.e., $\nu - 1$.

To evaluate this encoding traffic in Figure 4 we depict a comparison between a classic coding process, denoted by RS, and a decentralized systematic erasure code that achieves the MDS property (maximum fault tolerance), denoted by DE. In both cases we measure the encoding traffic required by both codes when $\ell = k$ and $\ell = 2k$, and in the case of DE, using the minimum value of ν required to achieve the MDS property. We show the comparison for three different code parameters. For the (6,3) code there are traffic savings only when the $m = 3$ coding nodes originally stored all the $(r - 1)k$ replicas. In this case the decentralized coding saves one block transfer. In the case of the (10,6) the decentralized coding process always requires less network traffic, even for low replica collocation levels, and these traffic savings are amplified for the (14,10) code. In this last case the savings range from a 24% in the case of the low replica collocation ($\ell = k$), up to 56% for high collocation values ($\ell = 2k$).

4   Encoding Data during the Insertion Process

In the previous section we presented two distributed erasure codes that allow to efficiently archive an object **o** that is originally replicated. In this section we will present a technique to directly store the object **o** in an encoded format without first (temporarily) creating replicas at all. For instance, if multimedia content is being stored it may as well be stored directly in erasure coded format, unlike data that is used for analytics, and is archived only after the processing is completed.

First we will introduce the concept of *locally repairable codes*, and then we will show how such codes can be exploited to encode data *on-the-fly* while being introduced in the system in order to improve data insertion throughput.

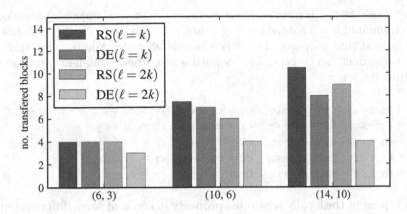

Fig. 4. Comparison of the number of transferred blocks during the encoding of a classical Reed-Solomon code (RS) and the decentralized coding (DE) for two different replica collocation values: $\ell = k$ and $\ell = 2k$. All DE codes are MDS codes optimized to minimize the number of coding steps ν.

4.1   Locally Repairable Erasure Codes

In classic erasure codes described in Section 2, the generation of each codeword symbol $c_i \in \mathbf{c}$ requires the access to the whole original data vector $\mathbf{o}$. When a storage node fails, repairing one missing codeword symbol $c_i \in \mathbf{c}$ requires to access k different codeword symbols and reconstruct $\mathbf{o}$, which entails a high I/O cost (accessing k different storage disks across the network). In contrast, locally repairable erasure codes allow to repair particular codeword symbols c_i by retrieving only d symbols, for small values of d, $d < k$, which can be as small as $d = 2$ [5]. Reducing the number of nodes needed to carry our a repair simplifies the repair mechanism, requires less I/O operations, and reduces the repair traffic with respect to classical erasure codes for a wide range of failure patterns, and can also speed-up the repair process.

Example 3. Let us present a simple locally repairable erasure code, specifically a (7,3)-code with the following generator matrix:

$$G^T = \begin{pmatrix} 1\,0\,0\,1\,1\,0\,1 \\ 0\,1\,0\,1\,0\,1\,1 \\ 0\,0\,1\,0\,1\,1\,1 \end{pmatrix}.$$

This code takes an object $\mathbf{o} = (o_1, o_2, o_3)$, $o_i \in \mathbb{F}_{2^q}$, and generates a codeword $\mathbf{c} = (c_1, \dots, c_7)$ that contains the three original symbols (i.e., systematic symbols) plus all their possible xor combinations:

$$\begin{aligned} c_1 &= o_1; & c_4 &= o_1 + o_2; & c_7 &= o_1 + o_2 + o_3; \\ c_2 &= o_2; & c_5 &= o_1 + o_3; \\ c_3 &= o_3; & c_6 &= o_2 + o_3. \end{aligned}$$

It is easy to see that it is possible to reconstruct the original object by downloading a minimum of $k = 3$ redundant fragments, e.g., c_5, c_6 and c_7, although not all k-subsets hold that property –i.e., it is a non-MDS code. Additionally, each redundant fragment can be generated by xoring two other redundant fragments in three different ways:

$$
\begin{array}{lllll}
c_1 = c_2 + c_4; & c_2 = c_5 + o_7; & c_4 = c_3 + c_7; & c_6 = c_1 + c_7; & c_7 = c_3 + c_4; \\
c_1 = c_3 + c_5; & c_3 = c_4 + c_7; & c_4 = c_5 + c_6; & c_6 = c_2 + c_3; & \\
c_1 = c_6 + c_7; & c_3 = c_1 + o_5; & c_5 = c_1 + c_3; & c_6 = c_4 + c_5; & \\
c_2 = c_1 + c_4; & c_3 = c_2 + c_6; & c_5 = c_2 + c_7; & c_7 = c_1 + c_6; & \\
c_2 = c_3 + o_6; & c_4 = c_1 + c_2; & c_5 = c_4 + c_6; & c_7 = c_2 + c_5. &
\end{array}
$$

We can represent the locally repairable property in terms of seven different repair groups $R = \{r_1, \ldots, r_7\}$, where:

$$
\begin{array}{llll}
r_1 = \{c_1, c_2, c_4\}; & r_2 = \{c_1, c_3, c_5\}; & r_3 = \{c_1, c_6, c_7\}; & r_4 = \{c_2, c_3, c_6\}; \\
r_5 = \{c_2, c_5, c_7\}; & r_6 = \{c_3, c_4, c_7\}; & r_7 = \{c_4, c_5, c_6\}.
\end{array}
$$

Each codeword symbol $c_i \in r_j$ can be repaired/generated by summing the other symbols in r_j, $c_i = \sum_{c_k \in r_j \setminus \{c_i\}} c_k$.

Locally Repairable Code. We can generically define a locally repairable code as an undirected bipartite graph $\mathcal{G} = (C \cup R, E)$, where the set of vertices U represents the set with all the codeword symbols $C = \{c_i : c_i \in \mathbf{c}\}$, the set of vertices R represented all the repair groups $R = \{r_i, \ldots, r_r\}$, and $c_i \in r_j \Longleftrightarrow (c_i, r_j) \in E$. Then, for any $c_i \in r_j$, the locally repairable property guarantees that

$$
c_i = \sum_{c_k \in r_j \setminus \{c_i\}} \psi_k c_k,
$$

for predetermined ψ_k values, $\psi_k \in \mathbb{F}_{2^q}$.

4.2   In-Network Redundancy Generation

As noted in the introduction, pipelining can be trivially used to create replication based redundancy. To do so, a source node sends the data to be stored to a first storage node, which stores it and simultaneously forwards it to a second storage node, and so on. However, as discussed in Section 2, erasure coding schemes do not allow to generate data redundancy of newly inserted data "on-the-fly", and often this process is carried out off-line in a batch process [2]. In this section we show how locally repairable codes are potentially amenable to be used in the on-line redundancy generation of newly inserted data. We will refer to this redundancy generation approach as an *in-network* redundancy generation process.

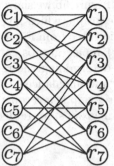
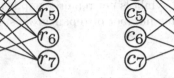
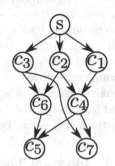

(a) Bipartite graph of the lo-   (b) Purging R to obtain the   (c) Redundancy gen-
cally repairable code.   redundancy generation graph.   eration graph.

Fig. 5. In-network redundancy generation using the (7,3)-code from Example 3

Example 4. Let us consider the same (7,3) locally repairable code described in
Example 3. In Figure 5c we show an in-network redundancy generation example
for this code. The source node receives an object $\mathbf{o} = (o_1, o_2, o_3)$ and uploads
each of these fragments to nodes from 1 to 3, which respectively store $c_1 = o_1$,
$c_2 = o_2$ and $c_3 = o_3$. Then, nodes 1 and 2 send their respective fragments, c_1
and c_2, to node 4, which computes and stores $c_4 = c_1 + c_2$. The rest of the nodes
compute the fragments $c_6 = c_2 + c_3$, $c_5 = c_4 + c_6$ and $c_7 = c_3 + c_4$ in a similar
manner.

Note that the creation of c_5 and c_7 depends on the previous generation of c_4
and c_6. Although at a first glance it might seem that symbols c_5 and c_7 can be
created only some time in the future after the generation of c_4 and c_6, practical
implementations can overcome this restriction by allowing nodes 4 and 6 to start
forwarding the first generated bytes of c_4 and c_6 to nodes 5 and 7 in a streamlined
way, similarly to the pipelined copy used in replication. By doing it, blocks c_4 to
c_7 can be generated quasi-simultaneously once nodes 1 to 3 received their blocks
from the source node. However, in those situations where data from the source
is being generated/received while it is being inserted, fragments o_1 to o_3 will
be sequentially uploaded, delaying the generation of symbols c_4 to c_7, and thus,
lengthening the overall redundancy generation process.

This example allow us to show how the local repairability groups can be
exploited to generate the in-network redundancy generation tree depicted in
Figure 5c. However, obtaining such a tree for any arbitrary locally repairable
code is not trivial. One possible way to obtain it is to consider the bipartite
graph representation of the (7,3) locally repairable code, which we depict in
Figure 5a. This graph contains all the codeword symbols c_i in the left-hand side
of the graph, and all the repair groups r_i in the right-hand side of the graph.
Then, since the original object $\mathbf{o}$ contains $k = 3$ symbols, the source node has
to mandatorily upload three symbols to three different nodes (left-hand side
vertices). The rest of the $n - k$ codeword symbols will be generated using $n - k$
different repair groups. It means that we can purge all except $n - k$ repair groups

from the right-hand side of the graph. In our example, in Figure 5b we show how we remove $|R| - (n - k)$ repair groups from the bipartite graph, which gives us the basic topology of the in-network redundancy generation tree from Figure 5c. Although in this case any combination of $|R| - (n - k)$ repair groups can be removed to obtain a valid redundancy generation tree, determining the repair groups to remove can be more complicated in asymmetric and unbalanced locally repairable codes, where the number of symbols per repair group is not constant, and not all symbols appear in the same number of repair groups. More details on these issues can be found in [7].

4.3   Insertion Times

Inserting a data object $\mathbf{o} = (o_1, \ldots, o_k)$, $o_i \in \mathbb{F}_{2^q}$, using an in-network redundancy generation process requires two different steps: (i) a source node initially generates and uploads k different codewords symbols to k different nodes, and (ii) these k nodes forward the symbols to the remaining $n - k$ nodes in a streamlined manner, allowing them to generate the remaining $n - k$ codeword symbols. Then, the overall time T required to encode and store an object $\mathbf{o}$ is bounded by $T \geq T_S + T_{net}$, where T_S is the time the source needs to upload k symbols, and T_{net} is the time the in-network redundancy generation needs to generate the rest of the $n - k$ symbols. It is important to note that, neglecting encoding times, T_S is proportional to the amount of data uploaded by the source, which is $q \times k$ bits, and T_{net} is proportional to the maximum number of successors a node in the in-network redundancy generation tree has, which is two for the nodes 2, 3 and 4 in the example depicted in Figure 5c. Then, in general, if this maximum number of successors is smaller than $n - k$, the overall insertion time T will be shorter than the insertion time of a classic erasure encoding process.

This simplistic analysis shows that an in-network redundancy generation can indeed increase the storage throughput of the classic erasure code insertion. However, this throughput can be further exacerbated when the source node and the set of storage nodes have additional (mismatched) temporal constraints on resources availability. For example, in datacenters storage nodes might be used for computation processes which require efficient access to local disks. Since inserting encoded data consumes large amounts of local disk I/O, system administrators might want to avoid to store while nodes are executing I/O intensive tasks – e.g., Mapreduce tasks.

To model this temporal constraints we will use the binary variable $a(i, t) \in \{0, 1\}$, which represents whether or not node i is available for sending/receiving data during time step t where each time step is of a duration of τ seconds. If we assume that the time step duration τ is equal to the time required to send/receive a symbol $c_i \in \mathbb{F}_{2^q}$, then, when all nodes are available, the source node can insert one full object $\mathbf{o}$ per time step. However, when some of the n nodes are not available, the source will have to wait until these nodes become available again, reducing the insertion throughput. To overcome this problem, the source node can group different objects $(\mathbf{o}_1, \mathbf{o}_2, \ldots)$ and store them altogether using the same in-network redundancy generation tree. By doing so the source will be able

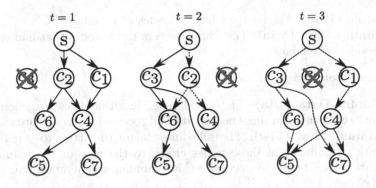

Fig. 6. The source S inserts two objects o_1 (depicted with continuous arrows) and o_2 (depicted with dashed arrows) in three time steps. At each time step there is one node that is not available for sending/receiving data.

to start inserting symbols from o_2 while it is still waiting for completing the insertion of o_1.

Example 4. Assume that a source node aims at storing two objects o_1 and o_2 using the in-network redundancy tree depicted in Figure 5c. Due to temporal constraints, node 3 is unavailable at $t = 1$, node 1 is unavailable at $t = 2$, and node 2 is unavailable at $t = 3$, as depicted in Figure 6. Under these circumstances, during $t = 1$ the source can send the symbols c_1 and c_2 of o_1 (depicted with continuous line arrows) to nodes 1 and 2, and then trigger the generation of c_4. However, c_5, c_6 and c_7 cannot be generated because they depend on c_3, whose corresponding node is unavailable. During $t = 2$, the source can then send the missing symbol c_3 of o_1, and finally trigger the generation of c_5, c_6 and c_7. However, during this very same step, the source can also start sending the symbol c_2 of o_2 (depicted with dashed line arrows). All remaining symbols of o_2 can be finally generated during the third time step $t = 3$.

This example shows a specific in-network redundancy generation scheduling that allows to insert two different objects in there time steps. In this case the in-network redundancy generation tree is the same for the three steps, however, in some cases it might also be possible to increase the insertion throughput by using different redundancy generation trees at each time step. Unfortunately, due to the vast scheduling possibilities that arise when nodes have temporal availability constraints, determining an optimal schedule given an arbitrary locally repairable code becomes a complex problem [7], even when the node availabilities $a(i, t)$ are known beforehand.

Instead of finding an optimal in-network redundancy generation schedule, different heuristics can be used to maximize the insertion throughput. In particular, we identify two questions that an heuristic scheduling algorithm can answer at each time step t: (i) Which set of nodes must the source send data to? (ii) Which repair groups are used to generate in-network redundancy? For the first question we propose two different answers:

1. **Random (Rnd)**: The source selects k nodes at random.
2. **Minimum Data (Min)**: The source selects the k nodes that had received less codeword symbols.

And for the second question:

1. **Minimum Data (Dta)**: The scheduling algorithm tries to generate in-network redundancy in those nodes that had received less codeword symbols.
2. **Maximum Flow (Flw)**: The scheduling algorithm tries to generate in-network redundancy in those nodes closer to the root of the redundancy generation tree, trying to maximize the redundancy generation flow.

Combining these four different approaches we can obtain four different redundancy generation scheduling algorithms, namely *RndFlw*, *RndDta*, *MinFlw* and *MinDta*. In the next section we will compare the insertion throughput of each of these.

4.4   Evaluation

In this section we evaluate the insertion performance of an in-network redundancy generation algorithm and we compare it with the naive erasure coding insertion process. The erasure code used in both the cases is the locally repairable code described in Example 3.

The reported results are obtained using a discrete-time simulator, where node availabilities $a(i, t)$ are modeled using real availability traces collected from a Google data center [3]. These traces contain the normalized I/O load of more than 12,000 servers monitored for a period of one month. Specifically, we consider that a server is available to upload/download data when its I/O load is under the p-percentile load. We consider three different percentiles, $p = 0.25, 0.5, 0.75$, giving us three different node availability constraints.

In Figure 7a we show the increment of the data insertion throughput achieved by the in-network redundancy generation process. This increment is higher when nodes have high availability, and thus it is more likely that all the nodes in a repair group are available.

In Figure 7b we show the increment on the required network traffic of the in-network redundancy generation strategy. The total traffic required for in-network redundancy generation can be up to 50% higher than what is needed by the classic insertion process. The network traffic increment is higher for high node availabilities, since the opportunities to use the local repairability property increase since generating a symbol using in-network redundancy requires twice as much traffic as generating it from the source.

This increase in traffic is approximately the same or even less than the boost in storage throughput, even for low availability scenarios. Thus the in-network redundancy generation scales well by achieving a better utilization of the available ephemeral network resources than the classical storage process.

---

[3] Publicly available at: http://code.google.com/p/googleclusterdata/

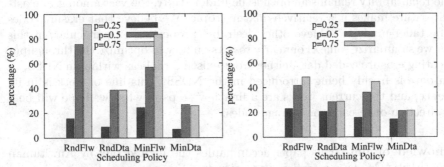

(a) Increment of the maximum amount of stored data (throughput).

(b) Increment of the required network traffic.

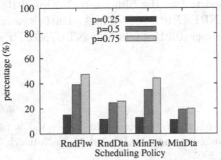

(c) Reduction of the data uploaded by the source.

Fig. 7. Performance of the in-network redundancy generation compared to the classic erasure encoding data insertion process

Finally, in Figure 7c we show the reduction of data uploaded by the source. In the classic insertion approach the source needs to upload $7/3 \simeq 2.33$ times the size of the actual data to be stored; $4/7 \simeq 57\%$ of this data is redundant. The in-network redundancy generation process allows to reduce the amount of data uploaded by the source. In this figure we can see how in the best case (*RndFlw* policy) our approach reduces the source's load by 40% (out of a possible 57%), yielding an 40-60% increment on the overall insertion throughput.

5   Conclusions

Storage technologies have continuously been undergoing a transformation for decades. While erasure coding techniques have long been explored in the context of large-scale systems (among other kind of storage environments), the explosive growth of storage needs in recent years has accelerated the research on and adoption of storage centric erasure codes. The issue of repairability of erasure codes [4,6] has particularly been a key avenue of investigation in the last years.

While repairability remains an open issue under study, the vast amount of existing literature makes it a relatively mature topic. We believe that erasure codes can be tailor-made to achieve other desirable properties. In particular, in this paper we summarize some of our early results on how to optimize the throughput of creating erasure coded data, either from existing replicas within an NDSS, or when data is freshly being introduced in the NDSS. This line of work is in its nascence, and the current works are a first few steps in what we hope will be a new direction of research on storage codes.

Acknowledgement. This paper accompanies the invited talk by Anwitaman Datta titled *"On data insertion and migration in erasure-coding based large-scale storage systems"* at ICDCIT 2013 conference. L. Pamies-Juarez and F. Oggier's research is supported by the Singapore National Research Foundation under Research Grant NRF-CRP2-2007-03. A. Datta's work is supported by A*Star TSRP grant number 1021580038 and NTU/MoE Tier-1 grant number RG 29/09.

References

1. Acedaski, S., Deb, S., Mdard, M., Koetter, R.: How good is random linear coding based distributed networked storage. In: Workshop on Network Coding, Theory, and Applications, NetCod (2005)
2. Apache.org. HDFS-RAI, http://wiki.apache.org/hadoop/HDFS-RAID
3. Cleversafe, http://www.cleversafe.com
4. Datta, A., Oggier, F.: An overview of codes tailor-made for networked distributed data storage. CoRR, abs/1109.2317 (2011)
5. Oggier, F., Datta, A.: Self-repairing homomorphic codes for distributed storage systems. In: The 30th IEEE Intl. Conference on Computer Communications, INFOCOM (2011)
6. Oggier, F., Datta, A.: Coding techniques for repairability in networked distributed storage systems (2012),
   http://sands.sce.ntu.edu.sg/CodingForNetworkedStorage/pdf/longsurvey.pdf
7. Pamies-Juarez, L., Datta, A., Oggier, F.: In-network redundancy generation for opportunistic speedup of backup. CoRR, abs/1111.4533 (2011)
8. Pamies-Juarez, L., Datta, A., Oggier, F.: RapidRAID: Pipelined Erasure Codes for Fast Data Archival in Distributed Storage Systems. In: The 32nd IEEE International Conference on Computer Communications (Infocom 2013) (2013)
9. Pamies-Juarez, L., Oggier, F., Datta, A.: Decentralized Erasure Coding for Efficient Data Archival in Distributed Storage Systems. In: Frey, D., Raynal, M., Sarkar, S., Shyamasundar, R.K., Sinha, P. (eds.) ICDCN 2013. LNCS, vol. 7730, pp. 42–56. Springer, Heidelberg (2013)

Medical Software – Issues and Best Practices

Raoul Jetley[1], Sithu Sudarsan[2], Sampath R.[3], and Srini Ramaswamy[1]

[1] Industrial Software Systems
ABB Corporate Research, Bangalore, India
[2] Device Security Assurance Center, India Development Center
ABB Corporate Research, Bangalore, India
[3] CEO, BeWo Technologies, Chennai, India
{Raoul.Jetley,sudarsan.sd}@in.abb.com, srini@ieee.org,
sampath@bewotechno.com

Keywords: Medical Software, Healthcare Systems, Software Development, Risk Management, Safety Standards, Interoperability, Security and Privacy, Human Factors, Usability.

1   Introduction

The design and functional complexity of medical software has increased during the past 50 years, evolving from the use of a metronome circuit for the initial cardiac pacemaker to functions that include electrocardiogram (EKG) analysis, laser surgery, and networked systems for monitoring patients across various healthcare environments. Software has become ubiquitous in healthcare applications, as is evident from its prevalent use for controlling medical devices, maintaining electronic patient health data, and enabling healthcare information technology (HIT) systems. As the software functionality becomes more intricate, concerns arise regarding efficacy, safety and reliability. It thus becomes imperative to adopt an approach or methodology based on best engineering practices to ensure that the possibility of any defect or malfunction in these devices is minimized.

Software developers are typically concerned with the functionality and security aspects. However, when it comes to medical software, safety issues become critical. In the case of medical devices, software needs to not only ensure that the device is functioning safely and reliably, but also that it should recover from an adverse event in a safe manner. Similarly, network accessible data needs to address privacy issues and allow access in accordance with the appropriate laws and regulations.

In this paper, we discuss best practices for development of medical software. Section 2 presents popular software development paradigms used for developing medical software, including the V-model, Model Based Development (MBD) and agile methods. The section also highlights some of the standards and safety assurance case for software certification.

Section 3 discusses approaches used to facilitate data transfer and interconnect devices in medical systems and HIT systems. The section outlines current standardization efforts for interoperable medical devices. Section 4 addresses issues pertaining to security and privacy concerns both at the device as well as system level. Section 4

C. Hota and P.K. Srimani (Eds.): ICDCIT 2013, LNCS 7753, pp. 69–91, 2013.
© Springer-Verlag Berlin Heidelberg 2013

outlines how human factors engineering (HFE) and usability guidelines can be used to implement effective and easy-to-use software for medical systems. Finally, Section 6 concludes the paper.

2   Development Paradigms for Medical Software

Manufacturers of medical products and healthcare software have adopted risk management techniques to help reduce the risks associated with software. Risk management is typically addressed as part of the software development life cycle (SDLC). The IEC 62304 (IEC, IEC 62304: 2006 Medical device software– software life cycle processes 2006) standard has emerged as a global benchmark for management of the SDLC. IEC 62304 is a standard for software design in medical products adopted by the European Union and the United States. Adhering to IEC 62304 ensures that quality software is produced by means of a defined and controlled process of software development. This process must contain a set of requirements based on the safety class of the software that is being developed.

The IEC 62304 standard expects the manufacturer to assign a safety class to the software system as a whole. The classification is based on the potential to create a hazard that could result in an injury to the user, the patient or other people.

The standard classifies software into three distinct classes, as follows:

— Class A: No injury or damage to health is possible
— Class B: Non-serious injury is possible
— Class C: Death or serious injury is possible

A brief summary of the effects of safety classification on the documentation and process is shown in Table 1. In practice any manufacturer developing medical software will carry out verification, integration and system testing on all software classes. However, the difference is that formal detailed documentation does not need to be generated for Class A code. Cross-referencing and verification of requirements also does not need to be formally proven for Class A software but are mandatory for Class C code.

Regardless of the safety class, safety is of foremost importance when developing medical software. The primary requirement for this software is that it should perform as intended and not fail in an unexpected manner, so as to endanger the lives of the patient or users.

At the most basic level, medical software is no different from any other type of software, and can be developed using any of the traditional software development techniques. However, to address the additional safety requirements, the software development paradigm is modified slightly for medical software.

Table 1. Summary of the IEC 62304 safety classification on the code development process

Software Documentation	Class A	Class B	Class C
Software Development Plan	A software development plan is required for all classes		
Software Requirements Specification	Software requirements specification is required for all classes		
Software Architecture	Not required	Software architecture documentation required; Refined to software unit level for Class C products	
Software Detailed Design	Not required	Not required	Detailed design required for all software units
Software Unit Implementation	All units need to be implemented, documented and source controlled		
Software Unit Verification	Not required	Verification required; Processes, test cases and acceptance need to be documented	Verification required; Processes, safety test cases and acceptance need to be documented
Software Integration and Integration Testing	Not required	Integration testing required	
Software System Testing	Not required	System testing required	
Software Release	Need to document software release version	Need to list unresolved software anomalies, annotated with impact on safety or effectiveness, including operator usage and human factors	

2.1   The V-Model for Software Development

A popular development paradigm for (safety-critical) medical software is based on the V-model (Davis 2000); itself a modification of the traditional waterfall model. The V-model of software development relates different stages of analyses to activities in the software process. For each stage in the software process, there is a related testing or analysis activity. Figure 1 depicts the major elements of a typical V-model for safety-critical systems.

According to this model, once requirements are gathered from the user, detailed hazards identification and risk assessment is performed to identify hazards and risks associated with the software's requirements. Requirements are formalized to come up with the system requirements, which in turn are used to develop the architectural and detailed designs. Once implemented, the software is tested at various levels. Unit testing and integration testing are carried out to assure the correctness of the various design modules. System verification is performed to test the architectural design, while validation is used for ensuring that all the specifications are correctly implemented. The last phase in the model is certification, during which the safety-critical system must be tested and evaluated by independent third parties (e.g., a certifying authority) against standardized criteria in order to obtain a certificate for release to service.

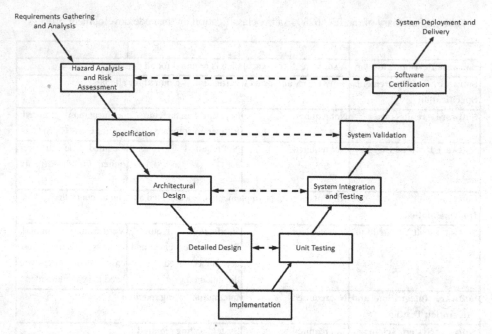

Fig. 1. The V-model for developing safety-critical software

2.2   Hazard Analysis and Risk Assessment

IEC 62304 stipulates that software must be developed using a risk management process compliant with ISO 14971. Effective software risk management consists of three activities – analysis of software contributing to hazardous situations, identifying risk control measures, and risk management of software changes.

Software risk analysis typically involves several processes that clarify the role of software in meeting the system's safety requirements. The risk analysis identifies how software failure can lead to compromised safety requirements and ultimately to patient or user hazards. Risk analysis is applied at different levels of detail throughout product development. Therefore, this analysis supports the formulation of a system-wide risk analysis to understand how all aspects of the system support the safety specification.

Initial Hazards analysis and risk assessment is typically performed during the definition phase. More detailed analysis is carried out during the design phase. The initial analysis is required to identify various software hazards, enumerating the significant causes linked to potential occurrence, an occurrence probability and the corresponding severity level. It should also include the minimum response necessary to mitigate the potential hazard.

Detailed risk analysis can be done three ways. First, a development team can develop a fault tree analysis (FTA) (Averett 1988), which is a top-down approach. A second, popular approach is to create a software failure modes and effects analysis (FMEA) (Stamatis 2003). An FMEA is a bottom-up analysis, starting with software faults and working up to the possible hazards. A third, hybrid approach employs the FMEA techniques to work from a software component fault up through a lower level and gate of the system-wide fault tree.

2.3   Software Certification

Many organizations use safety assurance cases as a means of documenting, comprehending, contracting, certifying and regulating the development of complex safety critical systems. Assurance cases have found application in the transportation sector (railway systems, aviation, etc.), energy sector (e.g., power plants), and defense systems sector. Regulatory agencies are increasingly using assurance cases as a tool to evaluate manufacturers' submissions in this regard.

An assurance case consists of a structured argument, supported by a body of evidence that provides a compelling, comprehensible and valid case that a system is safe for a given application in a given environment. Correspondingly, manufacturers of medical software can develop an assurance case for their software and use it to provide assurances of safety as required by regulators.

The main elements of an assurance case are:

Claim	Statement about a property of the system or some subsystem
Evidence	Data which is used as the basis of the assurance argument. This can be facts, (e.g. based on established scientific principles and prior research), assumptions, or sub-claims, derived from a lower-level sub-argument.
Argument	Logical construct that links the evidence to the claim,
Inference	Is the means for deducing the claim from the evidence; e.g., deterministic, probabilistic, or qualitative assertions.

The organization of these elements is illustrated in Figure 2.

The evidence itself can be a sub-claim that is a subsidiary assurance-case. This means that there can be a relatively simple top-level argument, supported by a hierarchy of subsidiary assurance cases. This structuring makes it easier to understand the main arguments and to partition the assurance case activities.

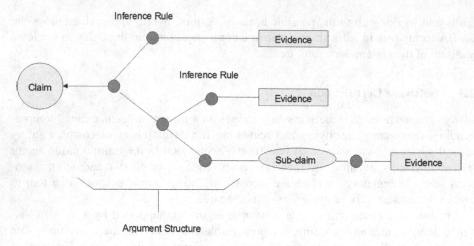

Fig. 2. An Assurance Case Structure

One way to structure the assurance case could be to have claims correspond to requirements from various standards and regulatory guidance documents. Arguments would reason that the system adequately addresses the different requirements. The evidence would then comprise of test reports and data representing that the system complies with the requirements and will always be in a known safe state.

2.4   Model-Based Development

Another development paradigm popular with developers and regulators is MBD (Ray 2010). MBD is a formal methods-based software development paradigm that uses the notion of executable models to design and verify software. Executable models allow for the explicit capture of data-flow (through system models) and control-flow (through states and transitions) thus enabling software developers to program using exclusively conceptual design-time artifacts. Moreover, unlike traditional design models, these can be simulated just like code (hence the word executable), and verified against safety requirements.

Figure 3 shows the MBD process applied to the V-model. As shown in the figure, formal specifications are defined and used to develop an executable model of the software, which can then be verified against the safety requirements using simulation and/or model checking techniques. The model can also be used to automatically derive the code for the system. The generated code is verified using static analysis and constraint solving to ensure that the safety requirements are not violated (and that the code conforms to the model). Finally, the system is validated before being sent for certification.

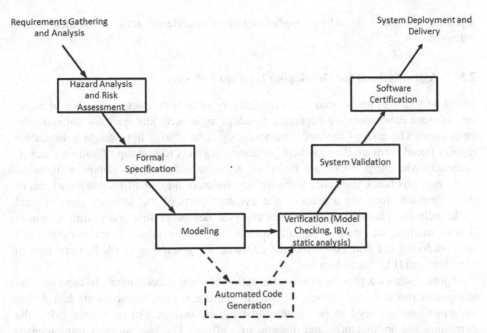

Fig. 3. A Process for Model based Development

An advantage of MBD is that the formal execution semantics of executable models allow for very precise definitions of how the software behaves. This makes it possible for researchers to develop theories, algorithms, and tools for automatically verifying designs. Using model-checking (E. M. Clarke 2000), for example, safety requirements can be formulated as mathematical formulae and the design model is then explored, using sophisticated graph traversal techniques, to check whether the design satisfies the requirements. Using instrumentation-based verification (IBV) (Ray 2010), requirements can be formulated as mini-models themselves and harnessed to the main design models. Tests are then exhaustively generated by an "intelligent" (automated) pessimistic tester which tries to execute the model in such a way that the requirements are violated. If the tester fails (i.e. does not succeed in "breaking" the model), then the requirements are satisfied.

By allowing engineers to develop executable designs for their systems, MBD can provide a framework for formal verification and validation. Executable models, while more abstract than programming languages, can be simulated, and used to automatically derive source code, thus promoting re-use. The models themselves can be behavioral (or function based), object-oriented, or defined as a state machine. Though much of the mathematical analysis has traditionally been used only in academic communities, of late a number of commercial tools that leverage the power of executable modeling have become available, e.g., Matlab® and Reactis®. This has made it feasible to use model-based development in a realistic medical device engineering environment.

MBD can also help in the formulation of the safety assurance case. Results of the design and code verification can serve as evidence to support assurance case claims and arguments, thus providing a higher degree of confidence in the correctness of the software.

2.5   Agile Methods for Developing Medical Software

Faced with shorter turnaround times for delivery of their products, a number of medical software developers are beginning to adopt agile methodologies for software development. The goal of the agile methodology is to offer a lightweight solution for rapidly paced software development processes. It refers to a group of software development methodologies that are based on iterative software development methods. Agile methods break the entire software development into small increments. Each of these iterations involves a team all the essential parts of the software development cycle including planning, requirements analysis, design, coding and testing. Completion of multiple iterations eventually results into final product. Some popular agile methodologies (Martin 2003) include eXtreme Programming (XP), Feature Driven Development (FDD) and Scrum.

Figure 4 shows a generic process for agile software development. In the agile development process, user stories are used to capture system requirements and define the functions that need to be implemented by the system. For each user story, the corresponding architectures and designs are defined. The user story is implemented and tested against system requirements. The story is integrated with other implementations and integration tests are carried out. Acceptance criterion for the tests is typically set to only 80%-90% code coverage. Once all the stories are implemented and tested individually, regression testing is performed on the entire system and the software is released.

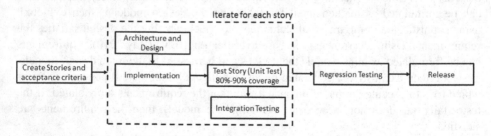

Fig. 4. The Basic Agile Process

When used to develop medical software, the agile process is modified to conform to requirements of IEC 62304. Figure 5 shows a modified version of the agile process, used for developing medical software. As is required for medical software, each step in the process is exhaustively documented. In order to assure that safety requirements are satisfied, the acceptance criterion for testing is increased to 100% coverage. The software system, once integrated is subject to final verification and validation, which is rigorously documented as well. Ensuring that each step is well documented satisfies regulatory and certification requirements.

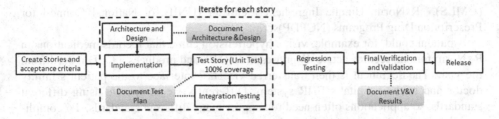

Fig. 5. Modified Agile Process for Medical Software

3   Interoperability

Modern medical systems are increasingly being integrated in order to allow systems to exchange data with each other and control individual device functions. There are two main aspects to this integration effort. The first addresses exchanging data from one patient record or hospital information system to another. A parallel effort is aimed at improving connectivity among medical devices to reduce medical errors and improve efficiency and effectiveness in high-acuity care areas. Major concerns exist in terms of data quality of the primary data as any lacunae would result in ripple effects becoming the weak link in the chain.

3.1   Integration of Electronic Health Records

With the change in usage of medical record systems from paper based to electronic record systems, there is an increased accessibility of information among healthcare providers. Because of this increased accessibility, healthcare providers have better informed decision making regarding patient's health. Electronic health records (EHRs) are thus beneficial to patients as well as to the health care institution and healthcare industry in general.

With the growing concern over the cost and quality of medical care, EHRs serve as the basis for quality assurance by health care organizations, insurance companies and other payers. This activity has taken on increasing importance with the growth of managed care, which requires that clinical decisions be scientifically justified as well as cost-effective.

The healthcare industry started using EHR systems a quarter of a century ago (Häyrinen 2008). When it was started, most systems were networked within their own healthcare institutions. With the advances and development of technology, many different health record systems have been developed throughout the world. However, due to the use of these disparate technologies and record systems, there are many standards for coding, formatting and exchanging healthcare data across HIT applications. Some of the prevalent formats for EHRs include the following array of standards (Houtchens 1995): Health Level 7 (v2.x or v3) (Dolin 2006), Accredited Standards Committee X12, Continuity of Care Record/Continuity of Care Document (CCR/CCD), International Classification of Diseases (v9 or v10) ICD9/ICD10, Systematized Nomenclature of Medicine (SNOMED), Unified Medical Language System

(UMLS), RxNorm, Unique Ingredient Identifier (UNII), or National Council for Prescription Drug Programs (NCPDP)script 10.x.

A patient could, for example, visit a hypertension clinic that records medications in RxNorm format, records active diagnoses in ICD10, and produces a CCD record from the visit. The document is then transferred via HL7 interface to the patient's family doctor and to the hospital's EHR system. Different systems operate using different standards, so applications often need to support many different standards. To complicate the matter, the standards themselves may be continually changing and evolving. A major challenge in modern healthcare is to provide an integrated, interoperable solution to EHR exchange.

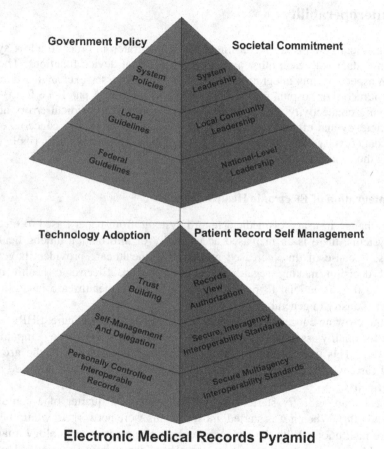

Electronic Medical Records Pyramid

Fig. 6. Multifaceted Issues for Achieving Interoperable, Electronic Health Records

EHRs include information as medical images, patients' histories, prescriptions, physician orders and other important information, spread across multiple departments and facilities. Many current systems for electronic patient record storage fragment their medical records by using incompatible means of acquiring, processing, storing and communicating relevant data. There is a distinct lack of a provision for data integrity in these systems with ad hoc adherences to publicly available standards, more so because these standards are themselves still evolving within the IT community.

Figure 6 identifies the requirements for an interoperable and portable electronic medical records system. The figure shows a pyramid model used for guidance and decision-making. The four distinct facets of the pyramid influence and guide the development of EHRs. The facets of the pyramid, as shown in Figure 6, include: government, society / community, technology and the patient itself. Each of these facets in turn consists of four specific resolution layers that culminate in the development and establishment of a viable portable, interoperable EHR system. At the base each resolution layer is the core philosophical value that is the basis for each (facet) dimensional aspect. The resolution of these facets is incremental. However, for the first three facets (government, society and technology) these layers are defined in an increasingly fine-grained manner. For the fourth (facet) dimension, the patient, however, it becomes more coarse-grained, in terms of establishing trust relationships and relinquishing control to allow more 'widespread' access of an individual's personal health records.

For an effective EHR system that can help support the needs of the practitioners and the health care system, appropriately addressing and effectively dealing with the issues identified along all these four dimensions is crucial and critical.

3.2 Medical Device Connectivity

An Institute of Medicine study estimates that preventable clinical errors lead to 50,000 to 90,000 deaths per year (IOM 1999). Although clinical devices are not directly responsible for these preventable deaths, computing and automation technology acting in an integrated system could provide a virtual safety buffer to protect patients from many of these errors.

A key functionality for this integration is providing a capability to monitor and control device operation. A mechanism needs to be in place to stream device data, integrate information from multiple devices into single customizable displays, and monitor alarms across groups of co-operating devices. In order to enable this, supervisory monitoring and control systems can be developed that enable interoperability across these co-ordinate communication between devices.

Medical device Interoperability can provide mechanisms to implement safety systems and enable rapid and innovative medical solutions. The importance of device interoperability is underscored in the US National Health Information Technology (NHIT) report (NHI04 2004) that establishes the need for development and implementation of an interoperable HIT infrastructure to improve the quality and efficiency of health care. The interoperable HIT infrastructure would:

1. Ensure that appropriate information to guide medical decisions is available at the time and place of care;
2. Improve health care quality, reduces medical errors and advances the delivery of appropriate evidence-based medical care;

3. Reduce health care costs resulting from inefficiency, medical errors, inappropriate care and incomplete information; and
4. Promote a more effective marketplace, greater competition and increased choice through the wider availability of accurate information on health care costs, quality and outcomes.

Achieving interoperability of medical devices requires a paradigm shift, as devices which previously have been end-products in the medical device marketplace — or vertically integrated into a system by a single manufacturer — may now become components in a larger multi-vendor system. Standards need to be put in place, not only to ensure seamless integration of disparate devices, but also to focus attention on key safety and effectiveness considerations.

There are two distinct, and closely related, facets of medical device interoperability that interoperability standards need to address:

— Data communication where data and device state are made available to other devices in the clinical care setting. For example, populating the EHR with data from bedside monitors, infusion pumps, ventilators, portable imaging systems and other hospital and home-based medical devices. Reliable data will support complete and accurate EHR and robust databases for continued quality improvement use.
— Medical device control where "stand-alone" devices can be used together to accomplish a task, possibly outside the capabilities of any of the component devices. Standards will permit the integration of medical devices to produce "error-resistant" systems with safety interlocks between medical devices to decrease use errors, closed-loop systems to regulate the delivery of medication and fluids and remote patient management to support health care efficiency and safety (e.g., remote intensive care unit, management of infected/contaminated casualties).

Standardization efforts are underway to address both these aspects of interoperability. A summary of the major standards is provided in the following section.

3.3   Interoperability Standards

There are a number of industry consortia and working groups that are working towards developing universal standards for medical device interoperability. The most notable of these, Continua Health Alliance is a global industry alliance that creates open interoperability specifications for personal connected health monitoring products and services. Continua has provided the Continua Design Guidelines (CDG) (Wartena 2009) that contain references to standards and specifications that Continua has selected for ensuring interoperability of devices.

The standards identified by Continua address both data communication and control aspects of medical device interoperability. Some of the major interoperability standards targeted specifically towards interoperability are discussed below.

ISO/IEEE 11073

CEN ISO/IEEE 11073 Health informatics – Medical / health device communication standards is a set of several standards that address various aspects of medical device connectivity and data exchange, including the physical and electrical connections and connector form factors, parameter nomenclature and units of measure, and variable semantics, to name a few. This standard began as the Medical Information Bus (MIB), and its successor, the IEEE 1073 standard. These gradually increased in scope and have now evolved into the ISO/IEEE 11073 set of standards. Commercial implementations of this standard in medical devices is limited at present, but is expected to increase in the future. Several other derivative standards utilize the IEEE 11073 standards both directly and indirectly (M. D. Clarke 2007) (Yao 2005). The standards are targeted at personal health and fitness devices (such as glucose monitors, pulse oximeters, weighing scales, medication dispensers and activity monitors) and at continuing and acute care devices (such as pulse oximeters, ventilators and infusion pumps). They comprise a family of standards that can be layered together to provide connectivity optimized for the specific devices being interfaced. The published standards in the family consist of the following parts:

— 11073-00101 Health informatics – Point-of-care medical device communication – Part 00101: Guide—Guidelines for the use of RF wireless technology
— 11073-10101:2004(E) Health informatics – Point-of-care medical device communication – Part 10101: Nomenclature
— 11073-10201:2004(E) Health informatics – Point-of-care medical device communication – Part 10201: Domain information model
— 11073-20101:2004(E) Health informatics – Point-of-care medical device communication – Part 20101: Application profile - Base standard
— 11073-30200:2004 Health informatics – Point-of-care medical device communication – Part 30200: Transport profile - Cable connected
— 11073-30300:2004(E) Health informatics – Point-of-care medical device communication – Part 30300: Transport profile - infrared wireless

Health Level 7

Health Level 7 (HL7) provides a framework (and related standards) for the exchange, integration, sharing, and retrieval of electronic health information. These standards define how information is packaged and communicated from one party to another, setting the language, structure and data types required for seamless integration between systems.

The HL7 standard is the most widely used data exchange format in healthcare, and has also been adopted as the most widely supported high level syntax for data transfer from medical devices or device gateways. There are currently two versions of HL7:

— HL7 Version 2.X. The 2.X versions of HL7 are the most commonly used versions in device connectivity data interchange. Most of these versions are reasonably backwards compatible with minor differences.

— HL7 Version 3.X. Although the version 3 of the HL7 standard supports more complex data semantics, and a Domain Object Model (DOM), it has not been utilized for device connectivity so far by any vendor.

The primary downside for vendors of using HL7 as the only standard for device data exchange is that HL7 only provides the syntax for the data exchange. There are no semantics to actually use this data without additional context or nomenclature information, in a portable manner. Also, by its very nature and design, the HL7 syntax is extremely verbose with a lot of repetitive fields and characters, partly in order to be human readable. This makes it an extremely inefficient format for medical devices that need to send out large volumes of data in a short amount of time. In spite of these drawbacks, HL7 has emerged as the industry standard for device data exchange.

IEC 80001

IEC 80001 standard is currently under development to address the complexity of medical devices and systems in network environments and when they are aggregated to form "systems of systems". This standard has been initiated to develop a framework for risk management of these complex infrastructures and their components. The intent of this standard is the application of risk management to enterprise networks incorporating medical devices. The standard applies risk management throughout the life cycle enterprise networks incorporating medical devices. The standard defines a process and defines responsibilities for each of the actors. The standard addresses the process of identification and management of hazards and risks caused by this networked aggregation that may not have been foreseen when the original products were developed. The intent is to use the standard to develop or implement safe and effective medical systems consisting of complex components in a distributed network environment.

The different parts of this standard include:

— Application of risk management for IT-networks incorporating medical devices – Part 1: Roles, responsibilities and activities
— Application of risk management for IT-networks incorporating medical devices – Part 2-3: Guidance for wireless networks
— Application of risk management for IT-networks incorporating medical devices – Part 2-2: Guidance for the communication of medical device security needs, risks and controls
— Application of risk management for IT-networks incorporating medical devices – Part 2-1: Step by Step Risk Management of Medical IT-Networks; Practical Applications and Examples

IHE–PCD Workgroup

The IHE-PCD (Integrating the Healthcare Enterprise–Patient Care Device) (John G. Rhoads 2010) is an initiative sponsored by the American College of Clinical Engineering (ACCE) and the Health Information Management Systems Society (HIMSS). IHE-PCD defines use case-bounded "Profiles" to describe clinical "transactions" that involve "actors" (e.g. entities like the sending device and the receiving CIS). The messaging syntax used primarily is HL7 version 2.6, with additional constraints and reduced optional fields, so that the messages are unambiguous, reproducible, and well defined between the sending and the receiving systems. This constraining of the underlying standards allows the semantics and the syntax of the messages to be rigorously defined and specified. In essence, the conversation between the sending device or system and the receiving system has been pre-defined to a high degree of detail. This allows systems that are independently developed, but adhere to the IHE-PCD "Profile", to interoperate without individual customized configuration. The section below elaborates the different IHE-PCD profiles that are currently in draft or final implementations.

The IHE-PCD initiative has seen widespread support from most of the major device vendors, and will be slowly appearing in commercially available systems as the IHE-PCD profiles are transitioning into their final implementation versions.

ASTM F2671

The ASTM ICE (Integrating the Clinical Environment) standard (ASTM F2671-2009) was chartered by the American Society for Testing and Materials (ASTM) and is co-sponsored by the American Society for Anesthesiology (ASA). The ICE standard defines a medical system designed to safely provide data acquisition and integration and control of a heterogeneous combination of medical devices and other equipment in a high-acuity patient environment and enable the creation of systems for innovation in patient safety, treatment efficacy, and workflow efficiency. ICE is a patient safety standard which requires biomedical device integration at the point-of-care.

The goal of the standard is to drive interoperability standards definition toward safety. The contention is that if there is not a bi-directional flow of data (technical closed loop without reliance on a human to close the loop), then safety is not being improved. Current activity involves a gap analysis of existing communication standards to support ICE in which six clinical scenarios are analyzed to identify action not covered by existing standards that would affect a safe function of the device in the clinical scenarios. The first standard being compared to the clinical requirements workflow is IEEE 11073. This work is being done in conjunction with the IHE-PCD group.

Interoperability is one of the biggest challenges in HIT today. A plethora of standards have emerged to address this issue, but the real challenge is in coming up with a technical solution to support information exchange, be it between different formats of medical records, or devices from different vendors.

4   Security and Privacy Issues in Healthcare

The growing dependence of healthcare systems on IT and the increasing number of threats resulting from distributed and decentralized implementations of EHR systems make them highly susceptible to security threats and privacy issues. As medical systems collect and exchange personal health data, assuring security for these systems becomes very important. Lack of security may not only lead to loss of patient privacy, but may also cause harm to the patient by allowing attackers to introduce bogus data or modify/suppress legitimate information. This could result in erroneous diagnosis or treatment.

One of the most vulnerable aspects of modern medical systems is their communication capability, especially when using a wireless interface. Vulnerabilities in the communication interface can allow attackers to monitor and alter the function of medical devices without even being in close proximity to the patient (Panescu 2008). Recent demonstrations of attacks on implantable cardiac defibrillators (D. Halperin 2008) have showed the possibility for attackers to surreptitiously read a patient's EKG data as well as administer an untimely shock. Securing all communication interfaces is therefore vitally important for medical software design.

Providing secure communication for medical systems software requires preventing attackers from joining devices around the patient as legitimate nodes and introducing bogus health data; accessing confidential health data collected or exchanged; and keeping some or all health data from being reported or modifying actual health data. Medical systems security depends on the maintenance of four basic properties:

1. Data Integrity: All information generated and exchanged in a system is accurate and complete without any alterations;
2. Data Confidentiality: All medical information generated is only disclosed to those who are authorized;
3. Authentication: All communicating devices know about all other entities with whom they are interacting; and
4. Physical/Administrative Security: All devices and associated equipment used by caregivers should be protected from tampering.

4.1   Attack Classes

Some of the main classes of attacks for medical systems include:

— Eavesdropping & Traffic Analysis: In this type of attack, the attacker (both passive and active) can overhear (using a hand-held device for example) the communication taking place within the system (e.g., between devices). This 'eavesdropping' can allow an attacker to learn about the devices connected to the patient, the capabilities of the device through the model type communicated during the handshaking process, instructions given to the devices by the caregiver, the settings to which individual devices are programmed, or patient health information. Using this information, an attacker can infer detailed information about the current status of the patient's ailments and track the patient throughout the healthcare facility.

— Man-in-the-Middle: An (active) attacker can mount Man-in-the-Middle (MIM) attacks by inserting itself between communicating devices and passing data between them, making them believe that they are communicating directly. In a wireless environment, for example, such an attack can be mounted by jamming the signal from a device, while providing a clear signal to medical devices on another channel. This allows an attacker to access patient data in an unauthorized manner, know the status of the patient's health, and manipulate any data being sent to the caregiver. It also enables attackers to manipulate commands issued by the caregiver through message insertion and modification that can result in wrong diagnosis, treatment, and device actuation. An important consequence of MIM attacks is that they can be easily extended to mount Denial of Service (DoS) attacks on the medical system. For example, the attacker between the communicating devices can easily overwhelm the system by simply discarding the patient health information it collects leading to continuous repeated retransmissions, or by ensuring that the disconnection command issued by the system controller is never sent to medical devices forcing them to be in operation longer than required.

— Spoofing: A more generic version of the MIM attack involves an active attacker posing as a legitimate entity (caregiver). This attack does not require the attacker to be in between any two entities and is therefore relatively easier to mount. Another important difference between MIM and spoofing is that an attacker performing spoofing for the first time may not have any information about the protocol used between the devices and has to learn these protocols. The most common technique used while spoofing is a replay attack. Replaying an old message exchanged between two legitimate entities can easily fool the receiver into believing the legitimacy of the attacker.

— Physical Attacks: One of the most potent forms of attack possible, a physical attack, may involve modifying the functions of the devices, introducing a new device into the patient-cart configuration, replacing existing devices with malicious versions, or modifying data logs making non-repudiation difficult. Each of these attack vectors allows the attacker to become a part of the patient monitoring infrastructure and engage in misinformation and DoS without even being detected.

4.2   Providing Security Solutions

These issues and threats are not unique to the medical domain. These problems have been looked in a number of areas, from financial services to internet shopping, and technical solutions exist which can be applied to health care to increase privacy and security in a multi-user setting. The approaches can be divided into three parts – secure channel establishment, physical security, and access control.

Establishment of a secure channel between the entities in a medical network can be achieved by distributing cryptographic keys between them. The presence of such a channel prevents eavesdropping and traffic analysis by providing confidentiality through encryption. Existing cryptographic security solutions for securing wireless communication can be easily adapted to a medical environment. One way for establishing a secure channel is to establish a unique pair-wise symmetric master key between the entities in the system. The master key can then be used to establish a secure (confidentiality and integrity protected) communication channel between the entities and thwart the attacks presented in the previous section. During the handshake phase, devices can verify the presence of the master key with each other and use it for secure communication during all the other phases of operation. Session keys can be established in an authenticated manner using asymmetric key cryptographic techniques such as Public Key Infrastructure (PKI). Here, instead of pre-deploying symmetric keys, a public/private key pair and a protocol such as RSA or Diffie-Hellman (and its variants) can be used to distribute the keys.

Physical security can be achieved by controlling physical access to equipment used around the patient, and tamper proofing. Controlling physical access is the simplest way to ensure that physical security is maintained. However, this may not always be possible. Tamper-proofing techniques could include the placement of seals on individual devices and caregiver equipment. If a tamper-proofed entity is compromised without authorization, it could be prohibited from communicating with other entities in the environment, and a suitable warning message issued.

An additional level of security can be provided by building authorization primitives based on role-based access control. A prominent example of an access control construct is Role-based Access Control (RBAC) (D. F. Ferraiolo 1999). RBAC executing on a device can specify what privileges (with respect to patient data and device access) caregivers may have. If needed, the access control model can be allowed to dynamically vary the privileges of caregivers to enable appropriate delivery of health care in the event of emergencies.

5   Human Factors Engineering and Usability

Software developers often develop systems without taking into account the ease of use for their users. In the case of medical systems, a poorly designed interface not only makes the system cumbersome and error-prone, but may also endanger the safety of the patient. It is critical, therefore, to incorporate HFE principles to design and implement not only an effective, but a usable system.

HFE needs to be used when designing systems, software, and tools to fit human capabilities and limitations. Whether designing hardware or software, human factors need to be considered during the planning stage and throughout the project. Too often, these issues are considered only at the end-stages of product design, which results in either costly changes or reluctance to change the design. Applying Human Factors early in the process allows one to make changes and increase the learning speed, efficiency and comfort level with a product, which translates into product acceptance and use.

5.1   Usability Guidelines

There are several publications listing guidelines for usability and human factors for designing interfaces for medical systems (J. T. Zhang 2003) (Sawyer 1996). Most of these lists share certain core ideas. Many of these rules focus on the principles of User-centered design (UCD) (J. Zhang 2005) and apply to general software design not just that for medical systems. Some of the key guidelines include:

— Simplicity. Clinical systems are complex as well as information dense. Therefore, it is essential for efficiency as well as patient safety that displays are easy to read, that important information stands out, and that function options are straightforward.

— Consistency. Consistency is important to the design of any application. The more consistent a system is, the more easily a user can apply prior experience to a new system. This reduces the user's learning curve, leading to more effective usage and fewer errors.

— Familiarity/Predictability. Healthcare software needs to map properly to the existing processes in place, and must not negatively affect or significantly change these. The system should not contradict the user's expectation. Rather, it should exploit their prior experience and make use of conventions related to language and symbols.

— User Awareness. The system should be targeted towards the end user, taking special care to account for non-traditional, but likely users. For example, a medical device is not always used by trained medical personnel; it may be used by patients in a home-care environment. Similarly, certain systems may be used by patients with special needs (e.g., physically challenged or elderly patients). To this end, the system should cater to all possible user demographics. Often, this is done by providing shortcuts for routine procedures, or by providing multiple interfaces to perform the same operation.

— Effective Use of Language. All language used in a medical system should be concise and unambiguous. Abbreviations and acronyms should only be displayed when they are commonly understood and unambiguous. The vocabulary must be efficient to navigate, presented in terms familiar to clinical practice and at the appropriate level of granularity.

— User Indications. The user must be guided and kept aware of the system state at all times during operation. Prompts and menus must be used to cue the user regarding important steps. Dedicated displays or display sectors must be used to indicate system status and critical information (such as alarm conditions or warnings).

— Readability. Clinical users must be able to scan information quickly with high comprehension. The pace and frequent interruptions in clinical workflow guarantee that decisions will sometimes be made based upon cursory screen review. Simplicity, naturalness, language use, density and color all contribute to readability.

— Preservation of Context. Preservation of context relates to keeping screen changes and visual interruptions to a minimum during completion of a particular operation. Visual interruptions include anything that forces the user to shift visual focus away from the area on the screen where they are currently reading and/or working to address something else, and then re-establish focus afterward. Such interruptions can distract the user and lead to usage errors.

— User Feedback. The healthcare system should provide immediate and clear feedback following user entries. Additionally, it should provide users recourse in the case of an error and provide conspicuous mechanisms for correction and troubleshooting guides. User feedback should help reduce user errors and provide graceful recovery when mistakes are made. Good feedback also reassures the user that their actions have had the desired effect.

— Recognition rather than recall. The system should minimize the user's memory load by making objects, actions, and options visible. The user should not have to remember information from one part of the dialogue to another. Instructions for use of the system should be visible or easily retrievable whenever appropriate.

5.2   Human Factors Standards for Medical Software

Based on the key usability features and requirements, standards have been defined for software used in medical products and healthcare software. These standards include key strategies that suggest how to design better and more efficient medical devices in order to reduce or even eliminate mistakes. The prominent standards for medical products include:

ANSI/AAMI HE74:2001 Human Factors Design Process for Medical Devices

The AAMI HFE Committee developed this process–oriented standard to provide manufacturers with a structured approach to user interface design, helping them develop safe and usable medical devices. The standard helps manufacturers respond to the increasing number of national and international human factors standards in the medical field and the promulgation of new governmental regulations (based on ISO 9001) pertaining to medical systems user interface design (ANS01 2001). This standard includes an overview of the HFE discipline, a discussion on the benefits of HFE, a review of the HFE process and associated analysis and design techniques and a discussion on implementation issues and relevant national and international standards and regulations.

IEC 62366:2007 Medical Devices–Application of Usability Engineering to Medical Devices

This standard was developed to help manufacturers improve the usability and safety of medical devices. The standard recognizes that the use of all medical devices has associated risks and provides an engineering process for identifying, assessing and mitigating those risks. IEC 62366 (IEC, Medical Devices–Medical Devices 2007) describes a process that addresses medical device use errors and divides those errors into categories to guide their analysis. This process can be used to assess and mitigate risks caused by the usability problems associated with the normal and abnormal use of a medical device. As shown in Figure 6, use errors can be first separated by whether there were intended or unintended user actions or inactions. All unintended actions, as well as intended actions that are categorized as either mistakes or correct use, are considered to be part of normal, and thus foreseeable, use. The manufacturer can only be responsible for normal use. Abnormal use errors are outside the scope of manufacturer responsibility, and they need to be controlled by the hospital.

If the designer complies with the usability engineering process detailed in this standard, the residual risk associated with device usability is presumed to be acceptable. Patient safety will improve as future medical devices are designed to comply with this standard.

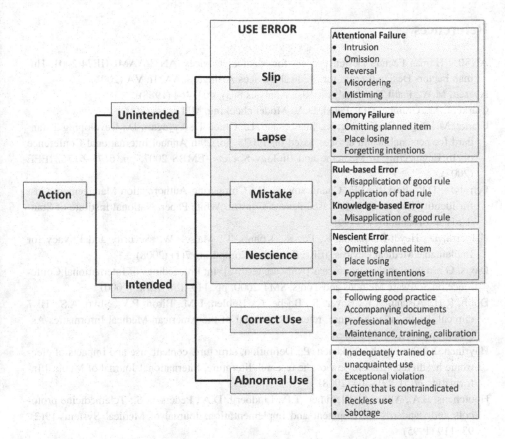

Fig. 7. Use Error Chart from IEC 62366:2007 (IEC, Medical Devices–Medical Devices 2007)

6 Conclusion

Healthcare systems are getting integrated increasingly and medical devices are communicating among themselves as well as with HIT systems. To address the resultant complexity, it is imperative to have the right set of engineering practices in place. Such engineering practices need to be standardized to ensure level playing field for all. In this paper, we have highlighted four aspects of medical software development, along with standards that are specific to healthcare domain. Our belief is that, if healthcare solution providers and medical software developers address (i) potential risks right from conception, while (ii) adhering to appropriate standards for interoperability (iii) without compromising security and privacy of the data and (iv) take into account ease of use for end users, we are confident of having a patient-centric healthcare solution that is safe, secure and reliable.

References

ANS01. Human Factors Design Process for Medical Devices. ANSI/AAMI HE74:2001, Human Factors Design Process for Medical Devices Arlington. AAMI, VA (2001)

Averett, M.W.: Fault Tree Analysis. Risk Analysis 8(3), 463–464 (1988)

Clarke, E.M., Grumberg, O., Peled, D.A.: Model checking. MIT press (2000)

Clarke, M., Bogia, D., Hassing, K., Steubesand, L., Chan, T., Ayyagari, D.: Developing a standard for personal health devices based on 11073. In: 29th Annual International Conference on In Engineering in Medicine and Biology Society, EMBS 2007, pp. 6174–6176. IEEE (2007)

Ferraiolo, D.F., Barkley, J.F., Chandramouli, R.: Comparing Authorization Management Cost for Identity-Based and Role-Based Access Control. White Paper. National Institute of Standards and Technology (1999)

Halperin, D., Heydt-Benjamin, T., Fu, K., Kohno, T., Maisel, W.: Security and Privacy for Implantable Medical Devices. IEEE Pervasive Computing 7(1) (2008)

Davis, G.: Managing the test process [software testing]. In: Proceedings of International Conference on Software Methods and Tools, SMT 2000, pp. 119–126. IEEE (2000)

Dolin, R.H., Alschuler, L., Boyer, S., Beebe, C., Behlen, F.M., Biron, P.V., Shvo, A.S.: HL7 clinical document architecture, release 2. Journal of the American Medical Informatics Association 13(1), 30–39 (2006)

Häyrinen, K., Saranto, K., Nykänen, P.: Definition, structure, content, use and impacts of electronic health records: a review of the research literature. International Journal of Medical Informatics 77(5), 291–304 (2008)

Houtchens, B.A., Allen, A., Clemmer, T.P., Lindberg, D.A., Pedersen, S.: Telemedicine protocols and standards: development and implementation. Journal of Medical Systems 19(2), 93–119 (1995)

IEC. IEC 62304: 2006 Medical device software – software life cycle processes. International Electrotechnical Commission, Geneva (2006)

IEC. Medical Devices–Medical Devices. IEC 62366:2007, Medical Devices–Medical Devices. IEC, Geneva (2007)

IOM, Institute of Medicine. To Err Is Human. Washington DC: National Academies Press (1999)

Rhoads, J.G., Cooper, T., Fuchs, K., Schluter, P., Zambuto, R.P. (2010), http://www.aami.org/publications/ITHorizons/2010/21-27_MDI_Rhoads (accessed November 7, 2012)

Martin, R.C.: Agile software development: principles, patterns, and practices. Prentice Hall PTR (2003)

NHI04. Incentives for the Use of Health Information Technology & Establishing the Position of the NHI IT Coordinator. Executive Order 13335. Office of Chief Information Officer, US NH (April 2004)

Panescu, D.: Emerging technologies [wireless communication systems for implantable medical devices. IEEE Engineering in Medicine and Biology Magazine 27(2), 96–101 (2008)

Ray, A., Jetley, R., Jones, P.L., Zhang, Y.: Model-Based Engineering for Medical-Device Software. Biomedical Instrumentation & Technology 44(6), 507–518 (2010)

Sawyer, D., Aziz, K.J., Backinger, C.L., Beers, E.T., Lowery, A., Sykes, S.M.: An Introduction to Human Factors in Medical Devices. US Department of Health and Human Services, Public Health Service, Food and Drug Administration, Center for Devices and Radiological Health (1996)

Stamatis, D.H.: Failure mode and effect analysis: FMEA from theory to execution. Asq Press (2003)

Wartena, F., Muskens, J., Schmitt, L.: Continua: The impact of a personal telehealth ecosystem. In: International Conference on eHealth, Telemedicine, and Social Medicine, eTELEMED 2009, pp. 13–18. IEEE (2009)

Yao, J., Warren, S.: Applying the ISO/IEEE 11073 standards to wearable home health monitoring systems. Journal of Clinical Monitoring and Computing 19(6), 427–436 (2005)

Zhang, J.: Guest editorial: human-centered computing in health information systems. Part 1: Analysis and design. Journal of Biomedical Informatics 38(1), 1–3 (2005)

Zhang, J., Johnson, T.R., Patel, V.L., Paige, D.L., Kubose, T.: Using usability heuristics to evaluate patient safety of medical devices. Journal of Biomedical Informatics 36(1), 23–30 (2003)

Improved Interference
in Wireless Sensor Networks

Pragya Agrawal[1] and Gautam K. Das[2]

[1] Department of Electronics and Communication Engineering
Visvesvaraya National Institute of Technology, Nagpur - 440011, India
[2] Department of Mathematics, Indian Institute of Technology Guwahati
Guwahati - 781039, India

Abstract. Given a set $\mathcal{V}$ of n sensor nodes distributed on a 2-dimensional plane and a source node $s \in \mathcal{V}$, the *interference problem* deals with assigning transmission range to each $v \in \mathcal{V}$ such that the members in $\mathcal{V}$ maintain connectivity predicate $\mathcal{P}$, and the maximum/total interference of the network is minimum. We propose algorithm for both *minimizing maximum interference* and *minimizing total interference* of the networks. For minimizing maximum interference we present optimum solution with running time $O((\mathcal{P}_n + n^2) \log n)$ for connectivity predicate $\mathcal{P}$ like strong connectivity, broadcast (s is the source), k-edge(vertex) connectivity, spanner, where $O(\mathcal{P}_n)$ is the time complexity for checking the connectivity predicate $\mathcal{P}$. The running time of the previous best known solution was $O(\mathcal{P}_n \times n^2)$ [3].

For minimizing total interference we propose optimum algorithm for the connectivity predicate broadcast. The running time of the propose algorithm is $O(n)$. For the same problem, the previous best known result was $2(1 + \ln(n - 1))$-factor approximation algorithm [3]. We also propose two heuristics for minimizing total interference in the case of strongly connected predicate and compare our results with the best result available in the literature. Experimental results demonstrate that our heuristic outperforms existing results.

Keywords: Wireless sensor networks, Interference.

1   Introduction

A sensor node is a small size, low-power device with limited computation and communication capabilities. A wireless sensor network (WSN) is a set of sensor nodes and each sensor of the network is able to measure certain physical phenomena like temperature, pressure, intensity of light or vibrations around it. Wireless networks of such sensor nodes have many potential applications, such as surveillance, environment monitoring and biological detection [1,7]. The objective of such network is to process some high-level sensing tasks and send the data to the application [5].

Since the sensor nodes are battery operated, so minimizing energy consumption is a critical issue for designing topology of wireless sensor networks to increase its lifetime. A message packet transmitted by a sensor device to another is

C. Hota and P.K. Srimani (Eds.): ICDCIT 2013, LNCS 7753, pp. 92–102, 2013.

often received by many nodes in the vicinity of the receiver node. This causes collision of signals and increased interference in its neighboring nodes, which leads to message packet loss. Due to packet loss the sender node needs to retransmit the message packets. Therefore, large interference of networks may result delays for delivering data packets and enhance the energy consumption of nodes in network. Thus interference reduction of nodes in a wireless sensor network is a crucial issue for minimizing (i) delays for delivering data packets and (ii) energy consumption of a wireless sensor network.

2   Network Model and Interference Related Problems

Definition 1. $\delta(u, v)$ *denotes the Euclidean distance between two sensor nodes* u *and* v. *A range assignment is* $\rho : \mathcal{V} \to \mathbb{R}$. *A communication graph* $G_\rho = (\mathcal{V}, E_\rho)$ *is a directed graph, where* $\mathcal{V}$ *is the set of sensor nodes and* $E_\rho = \{(u, v) | \rho(u) \geq \delta(u, v)\}$. G_ρ *is said to be strongly connected if there is a directed path between each pair of vertices* $u, v \in \mathcal{V}$ *in* G_ρ. G_ρ *is said to be an arborescence rooted at* $v \in \mathcal{V}$ *if there is a directed path from* v *to all other vertices* $u \in \mathcal{V}$ *in* G_ρ. *If* G_ρ *satisfy connectivity predicate* $\mathcal{P}$, *then we say that* $\mathcal{P} \in G_\rho$.

Different models have been proposed to minimize the interference in sensor networks [4,11,10]. In this paper, we focus on the following two widely accepted models:

- Sender Interference Model (SIM): The interference of a node $v \in \mathcal{V}$ is the cardinality of the set of nodes to whom it can send messages directly. The set of nodes interfered by v for the assigned range ρ is denoted by $I_S^v(\rho)$ and defined by $I_S^v(\rho) = \{v' \in \mathcal{V} \setminus \{v\} | \delta(v, v') \leq \rho(v)\}$, where $\rho(v)$ is the range of the node v. Therefore the interference value of node v is equal to $|I_S^v(\rho)|$ with respect to range assignment ρ.
- Receiver Interference Model (RIM): The interference of a node $v \in \mathcal{V}$ is the cardinality of the set of nodes from which it can receive messages directly. The set of nodes interfering v for the assigned range ρ is denoted by $I_R^v(\rho)$ and defined by $I_R^v(\rho) = \{v' \in \mathcal{V} \setminus \{v\} | \delta(v, v') \leq \rho(v')\}$, where $\rho(v')$ is the range of the node v'. Therefore the interference value of node v is equal to $|I_R^v(\rho)|$ with respect to range assignment ρ.

In the interference minimization problems, the goal is to minimize the following four objective functions:

(a) **MinMax SI (MMSI):** Given a set $\mathcal{V}$ of n sensor nodes, find a range assignment function ρ such that the communication graph G_ρ satisfy the connectivity predicate $\mathcal{P}$ and maximum sender interference of the sensor nodes in the network is minimum i.e.,

$$\min_{\rho | \mathcal{P} \in G_\rho} \max_{v \in \mathcal{V}} I_S^v(\rho)$$

(b) **Min Total SI (MTSI):** Given a set $\mathcal{V}$ of n sensor nodes, find a range assignment function ρ such that the communication graph G_ρ satisfy the connectivity predicate $\mathcal{P}$ and total sender interference of the entire sensor network is minimum i.e.,

$$\min_{\rho | \mathcal{P} \in G_\rho} \sum_{v \in \mathcal{V}} I_S^v(\rho)$$

(c) **MinMax RI (MMRI):** Given a set $\mathcal{V}$ of n sensor nodes, find a range assignment function ρ such that the communication graph G_ρ satisfy the connectivity predicate $\mathcal{P}$ and maximum receiver interference of the sensor nodes in the network is minimum i.e.,

$$\min_{\rho | \mathcal{P} \in G_\rho} \max_{v \in \mathcal{V}} I_R^v(\rho)$$

(d) **Min Total RI (MTRI):** Given a set $\mathcal{V}$ of n sensor nodes, find a range assignment function ρ such that the communication graph G_ρ satisfy the connectivity predicate $\mathcal{P}$ and total receiver interference of the entire sensor network is minimum i.e.,

$$\min_{\rho | \mathcal{P} \in G_\rho} \sum_{v \in \mathcal{V}} I_R^v(\rho)$$

In the communication graph corresponding to a range assignment ρ, the number of out-directed edges and in-directed edges are same, which leads to the following result:

Theorem 1. *For any range assignment ρ,* **MTSI = MTRI**.

2.1   Our Contribution

In this paper, we propose algorithm for *minimizing maximum interference* and *minimizing total interference* of a given wireless sensor network. For minimizing maximum interference we present optimum solution with running time $O((\mathcal{P}_n + n^2) \log n)$ for connectivity predicate $\mathcal{P}$ like strong connectivity, broadcast, k-edge(vertex) connectivity, spanner. Here $O(\mathcal{P}_n)$ is the time complexity for checking the connectivity predicate $\mathcal{P}$. The running time of the previous best known solution was $O(\mathcal{P}_n \times n^2)$ [3].

For minimizing total interference we propose optimum algorithm for the connectivity predicate broadcast. The running time of the propose algorithm is $O(n)$. For the same problem, the previous best known result was $2(1 + \ln(n-1))$-factor approximation algorithm [3]. We also propose two heuristics for minimizing total interference in the case of strongly connected predicate and compare our result with the best result available in the literature. Experimental results demonstrate that our heuristic outperforms existing results.

We organize remaining part of this paper as follows: In Section 3, we discuss existing results in the literature. The algorithm for the optimum solution of minimizing maximum interference for different connectivity predicate appears in Section 4. In Section 5, we present optimum algorithm to minimize total interference for the connectivity predicate broadcast. Heuristics for minimizing total interference for the strongly connected predicate appears in Section 6. Finally, we conclude the paper in Section 7.

3 Related Works

Tan et al. studied minimization of the average interference and the maximum interference for the highway model, where all the nodes are arbitrarily distributed on a line [12]. For the minimum average interference problem they proposed an exact algorithm, which runs in $O(n^3\Delta^3)$ time, where n is the number of nodes and Δ is the maximum node degree in the communication graph for the equal range assigned to each nodes equal to the maximum consecutive distance between two nodes. For the minimization of maximum interference problem, they proposed $O(n^3\Delta^{O(k)})$ time algorithm, where $k = O(\sqrt{\Delta})$. Lou et al. improves the time complexity to $O(n\Delta^2)$ for the minimization of average interference problem [6]. Rickenbach et al. proved that minimum value of maximum interference is bounded by $O(\sqrt{\Delta})$ and presented an $O(\sqrt[4]{\Delta})$-factor approximation algorithm, where Δ is the maximum node degree in the communication graph for some equal range ρ_{max} assigned to all the nodes [10].

For 2D networks, Buchin considered receiver interference model and proved that minimizing the maximum interference is NP-hard [2] whereas Bilò and Proietti considered sender interference model and proposed a polynomial time algorithm for minimizing the maximum interference [3]. Their algorithm works for many connectivity predicate like simple connectivity, strong connectivity, broadcast, k-edge(vertex) connectivity, spanner, and so on. They also proved that any polynomial time α-approximation algorithm for minimum total range assignment problem with connectivity predicate $\mathcal{P}$ can be used for designing a polynomial time α-approximation algorithm for minimum total interference problem for $\mathcal{P}$. Panda and Shetty considered 2D networks with sender centric model and proposed an optimal solution for minimizing the maximum interference and a 2-factor approximation algorithm for average interference [9]. Moscibroda and Wattenhofer proposed $O(\log n)$-factor greedy algorithm for minimizing average interference [8].

4 Minimization of Maximum Interference

In this section we consider sender centric interference model. Given a set $\mathcal{V} = \{v_1, v_2, \ldots, v_n\}$ of n sensor nodes distributed on a 2D plane, the objective is to find a range assignment $\rho : \mathcal{V} \to \mathbb{R}$ such that the corresponding communication graph G_ρ contains connectivity predicate $\mathcal{P}$ like strong connectivity, broadcast, k-edge(vertex) connectivity, spanner etc. Bilò and Proietti considered the same problem and proposed $O(\mathcal{P}_n \times n^2)$ time algorithm for optimum solution, where $\mathcal{P}_n$ is the time required to check predicate $\mathcal{P}$ for a given communication graph [3].

Here we propose an algorithm to solve the above problem optimally. The running time of our algorithm is $O((\mathcal{P}_n + n^2) \log n)$, which leads to a big improvement over [3].

4.1 Algorithm

In the network, the number of nodes is n, which means maximum possible interference of a node is $n-1$. The main idea of our algorithm is very simple: first we start range assignment to each of the node in such a way that the interference of each node is k $(1 \le k \le n-1)$. Next we test whether the communication graph contains the connectivity predicate $\mathcal{P}$ or not. If the answer is *yes*, then we try for lower values of k. Otherwise we try for higher values of k. The pseudo code for minimizing maximum sender interference (MMSI) algorithm is described in Algorithm 1.

In the algorithm we use a matrix M of size $n \times n - 1$ and $M(i,j) = \delta(v_i, u)$, where $u \in V$ such that if $\rho(v_i) = \delta(v_i, u)$, then $|I_S^{v_i}(\rho)| = j$ for all $i = 1, 2, \ldots n$ and $j = 1, 2, \ldots, n-1$. In other words, $M(i,j)$ contains a range $\rho(v_i)$ of v_i such that $|I_S^{v_i}(\rho)| = j$.

Algorithm 1. MMSI$(\mathcal{V}, \mathcal{P})$

1: **Input:** a set $\mathcal{V} = \{v_1, v_2, \ldots, v_n\}$ of n nodes and a connectivity predicate $\mathcal{P}$.
2: **Output:** a range assignment ρ such that $\mathcal{P} \in G_\rho$ and total interference.
3: Construct the matrix M as described above.
4: $\ell \leftarrow 0$, $r \leftarrow n - 1$
5: **while** $(\ell \ne r - 1)$ **do**
6:     **for** $(i = 1, 2, \ldots, n)$ **do**
7:        $\rho(v_i) = M(i, \lfloor \frac{\ell+r}{2} \rfloor)$
8:     **end for**
9:     Construct the communication graph G_ρ corresponding to ρ.
10:     Test whether G_ρ contains connectivity predicate $\mathcal{P}$ or not.
11:     **if** (answer of the above test is *yes*) **then**
12:        $r = \lfloor \frac{\ell+r}{2} \rfloor$ /* maximum interference is at most $\lfloor \frac{\ell+r}{2} \rfloor$ */
13:     **else**
14:        $\ell = \lfloor \frac{\ell+r}{2} \rfloor$ /* minimum interference is greater than $\lfloor \frac{\ell+r}{2} \rfloor$ */
15:     **end if**
16: **end while**
17: **for** $(i = 1, 2, \ldots, n)$ **do**
18:     $\rho(v_i) = M(i, r)$
19: **end for**
20: Return(ρ, r)

Theorem 2. *Algorithm 1 computes minimum of maximum sender interference (MMSI) optimally and its worst case running time is $O((\mathcal{P}_n + n^2) \log n)$.*

Proof. Let ρ (respectively, ρ') be the range assignment to the nodes in $\mathcal{V}$ when the sender interference of each node is ℓ (respectively, r). The correctness of the Algorithm 1 follows from the fact (i) the Algorithm 1 stops when $\ell = r - 1$ such that G_ρ does not contain connectivity predicate $\mathcal{P}$ whereas $G_{\rho'}$ contains connectivity predicate $\mathcal{P}$ and (ii) if $\rho'(u) > \rho(u)$, then $I_S^u(\rho') \ge I_S^u(\rho)$.

Construction of each row of the matrix M needs a sorting of $(n-1)$ elements. Therefore, construction time of matrix M (line number 3 of the Algorithm 1) takes $O(n^2 \log n)$ time in worst case. Construction of the communication graph G_ρ (line number 9 of the Algorithm 1) and testing connectivity predicate (line number 10 of the Algorithm 1) take $O(\mathcal{P}_n)$ time. Again, each execution of **while** loop in line number 5 reduce the value $(\ell - r)$ by half of its previous value. Therefore, Algorithm 1 calls the **while** loop $O(\log n)$ time. Thus, the time complexity results of the theorem follows.   □

5 Minimization of Total Interference

Given a set $\mathcal{V} = \{v_1, v_2, \ldots, v_n\}$ of n sensor nodes and a source node $s \in \mathcal{V}$ distributed on a 2D plane, the objective is to find a range assignment $\rho : \mathcal{V} \to \mathbb{R}$ such that the corresponding communication graph G_ρ contains an arborescence rooted at s (connectivity predicate is broadcast) and the total interference (sender/receiver) is minimum. Bilò and Proietti considered the same problem and proposed $2(1 + \ln(n-1))$-factor approximation algorithm [3]. Here we propose a very simple optimum algorithm. The running time of the algorithm is linear. The pseudo code for the minimum total sender interference (MTSI) algorithm is described in Algorithm 2. Though the propose algorithm is trivial, we are proposing it for completeness of the literature.

Lemma 1. *For any range assignment ρ, if the communication graph $G_\rho = (\mathcal{V}, E_\rho)$ contains arborescence rooted at any node u in the network of n nodes, then the minimum total sender interference of the networks is at least $n - 1$.*

Proof. Since the communication graph G_ρ contains an arborescence rooted at u, each node $v \in \mathcal{V} \setminus \{u\}$ has an incoming edge. Therefore, the total receiver interference is at least $n - 1$. Thus, the lemma follows from Theorem 1.   □

Algorithm 2. Optimum algorithm for minimizing maximum sender interference

1: **Input:** a set $\mathcal{V} = \{v_1, v_2, \ldots, v_n\}$ of n nodes and a source node $s \in \mathcal{V}$.
2: **Output:** a range assignment ρ such that communication graph G_ρ contains an arborescence rooted at s and total interference (MTSI).
3: **for each** $i = 1, 2, \ldots, n$ set $\rho(v_i) \leftarrow 0$
4: $\rho(s) = \delta(s, u)$, where $u \in \mathcal{V}$ is the farthest node from s.
5: Return$(\rho, n - 1)$ /* $\sum_{v \in \mathcal{V}} I_S^v(\rho) = n - 1$ */

Theorem 3. *Algorithm 2 produces the optimum result in $O(n)$ time.*

Proof. The correctness of the algorithm follows from (i) the fact that total interference produce by Algorithm 2 is $n - 1$ and (ii) Lemma 1. Time complexity follows from the **for** loop (line number 3) and line number 6 of the algorithm. □

6 Heuristics for Strongly Connected Predicate

In this section, we propose two heuristics for range assignment ρ to a given set $\mathcal{V} = \{v_1, v_2, \ldots, v_n\}$ of n sensor nodes distributed on a 2D plane such that the communication graph G_ρ is strongly connected (see Algorithm 3 and Algorithm 4). The objective of the range assignment is to minimize total sender interference (MTSI) of the entire network. Experimental results presented in the Subsection 6.1 demonstrate that our heuristics perform very well compare to existing result in the literature.

Algorithm 3. MTSI$(\mathcal{V}, \mathcal{P})$

1: **Input:** a set $\mathcal{V} = \{v_1, v_2, \ldots, v_n\}$ of n nodes.
2: **Output:** a range assignment ρ such that $\mathcal{P} \in G_\rho$ and total interference of the network, where $\mathcal{P}$ is strongly connected.
3: **for** $(i = 1, 2, \ldots, n)$ **do**
4:    $\rho(v_i) \leftarrow 0$ /* initial range assignment */
5:    $|I_S^{v_i}(\rho(v_i))| \leftarrow 0$ /* initial interference assignment */
6:    $T_I \leftarrow 0$ /* initial total interference */
7: **end for**
8: $\mathcal{U}_1 = \{v_i\}$ and $\mathcal{U}_2 = \mathcal{V} \setminus \{v_i\}$
9: **while** $(\mathcal{U}_2 \neq \emptyset)$ **do**
10:    Choose $u_1, u_1' \in \mathcal{U}_1$ and $u_2 \in \mathcal{U}_2$ such that if $\delta(u_1, u_2) > \rho(u_1)$ and $|I_S^{u_1}(\delta(u_1, u_2))| - |I_S^{u_1}(\rho(u_1))| + |I_S^{u_2}(\delta(u_2, u_1'))| \leq |I_S^{w_1}(\delta(w_1, w_2))| - |I_S^{w_1}(\rho(w_1))| + |I_S^{w_2}(\delta(w_2, w_1'))|$; otherwise $|I_S^{u_2}(\delta(u_2, u_1'))| \leq |I_S^{w_2}(\delta(w_2, w_1'))|$ for all $w_1, w_1' \in \mathcal{U}_1$ and $w_2 \in \mathcal{U}_2$.
11:    $T_I = T_I + |I_S^{u_1}(\delta(u_1, u_2))| - |I_S^{u_1}(\rho(u_1))| + |I_S^{u_2}(\delta(u_2, u_1'))|$ /*total interference*/
12:    $\rho(u_1) = \max(\rho(u_1), \delta(u_1, u_2))$ and $\rho(u_2) = \delta(u_2, u_1')$ /* new range assignments */
13:    $|I_S^{u_1}(\rho(u_1))| = |I_S^{u_1}(\delta(u_1, u_2))|$ and $|I_S^{u_2}(\rho(u_2))| = |I_S^{u_1}(\delta(u_2, u_1'))|$ /* new interference assignments */
14:    $\mathcal{U}_1 = \mathcal{U}_1 \cup \{u_2\}$ and $\mathcal{U}_2 = \mathcal{U}_2 \setminus \{u_2\}$
15: **end while**
16: Return(ρ, T_I)

Theorem 4. *The running time of the Algorithm 3 is polynomial in input size.*

Proof. The input size of the Algorithm 3 is n. In each execution of **While** loop (line number 9 of the Algorithm 3), the size of the set $\mathcal{U}_2$ is decreasing by 1. Choosing the vertices u_1, u_1', u_2 (line number 10 of the Algorithm 3) needs $O(n^3)$ time. Thus, the time complexity result of the theorem follows. □

The total interference return by the Algorithm 3 depends on the initial choice of node v_i in line number 8 of the heuristic. Consider an instance in the Fig. 1, where sensor nodes are $\{v_1, v_2, \ldots, v_7\}$ distributed on a line from left to right and Euclidean distance between two consecutive nodes v_i and v_{i+1} are given above the line segment joining the nodes v_i and v_{i+1}. In line number 8 of the

Algorithm 3, if $v_i = v_7$, then the range assignment of the nodes by the Algorithm 3 is as follows: $\rho(v_1) = 2, \rho(v_2) = 2, \rho(v_3) = 4, \rho(v_4) = 6, \rho(v_5) = 12, \rho(v_6) = 24$ and $\rho(v_7) = 24$ and the corresponding total interference of the network is 19, whereas if $v_i = v_1$, then the range assignment of the nodes by the Algorithm 3 is as follows: $\rho(v_1) = 2, \rho(v_2) = 48, \rho(v_3) = 2, \rho(v_4) = 4, \rho(v_5) = 6, \rho(v_6) = 12$ and $\rho(v_7) = 24$ and the corresponding total interference of the networks is 12. Based on this observation, we design an improved algorithm IMTSI (see Algorithm 4) for minimizing total sender interference for strongly connected predicate.

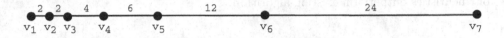

Fig. 1. Example of a network

Algorithm 4. IMTSI$(\mathcal{V}, \mathcal{P})$ /* $\mathcal{P}$ is strongly connected */

1: **Input:** a set $\mathcal{V} = \{v_1, v_2, \ldots, v_n\}$ of n nodes.
2: **Output:** a range assignment ρ such that $\mathcal{P} \in G_\rho$ and total interference.
3: $T_I' \leftarrow \infty$ /* initial total interference */
4: **Set** $\rho'(v_i) \leftarrow 0$ **for all** $i = 1, 2, \ldots, n$ /* initial range assignment */
5: **for** $(i = 1, 2, \ldots, n)$ **do**
6:    $T_I \leftarrow 0$
7:    **for** $(i = 1, 2, \ldots, n)$ **do**
8:       $\rho(v_i) \leftarrow 0$ /* initial range assignment for i-th iteration*/
9:       $|I_S^{v_i}(\rho(v_i))| \leftarrow 0$ /* initial interference assignment for i-th iteration */
10:    **end for**
11:    $\mathcal{U}_1 = \{v_i\}$ and $\mathcal{U}_2 = \mathcal{V} \setminus \{v_i\}$
12:    **while** $(\mathcal{U}_2 \neq \emptyset)$ **do**
13:       Choose $u_1, u_1' \in \mathcal{U}_1$ and $u_2 \in \mathcal{U}_2$ such that if $\delta(u_1, u_2) > \rho(u_1)$ and $|I_S^{u_1}(\delta(u_1, u_2))| - |I_S^{u_1}(\rho(u_1))| + |I_S^{u_2}(\delta(u_2, u_1'))| \leq |I_S^{w_1}(\delta(w_1, w_2))| - |I_S^{w_1}(\rho(w_1))| + |I_S^{w_2}(\delta(w_2, w_1'))|$; otherwise $|I_S^{u_2}(\delta(u_2, u_1'))| \leq |I_S^{w_2}(\delta(w_2, w_1'))|$ for all $w_1, w_1' \in \mathcal{U}_1$ and $w_2 \in \mathcal{U}_2$.
14:       $T_I = T_I + |I_S^{u_1}(\delta(u_1, u_2))| - |I_S^{u_1}(\rho(u_1))| + |I_S^{u_2}(\delta(u_2, u_1'))|$
15:       $\rho(u_1) = \max(\rho(u_1), \delta(u_1, u_2))$ and $\rho(u_2) = \delta(u_2, u_1')$
16:       $|I_S^{u_1}(\rho(u_1))| = |I_S^{u_1}(\delta(u_1, u_2))|$ and $|I_S^{u_2}(\rho(u_2))| = |I_S^{u_1}(\delta(u_2, u_1'))|$
17:       $\mathcal{U}_1 = \mathcal{U}_1 \cup \{u_2\}$ and $\mathcal{U}_2 = \mathcal{U}_2 \setminus \{u_2\}$
18:    **end while**
19:    **if** $T_I < T_I'$, **then** $T_I' = T_I$ and $\rho' = \rho$
20: **end for**
21: Return(ρ', T_I')

In Algorithm 4, we introduce one extra **for** loop in the line number 7 to the Algorithm 3. The running time of the Algorithm 3 is polynomial (see Theorem 4). Thus the following theorem follows for the Algorithm 4.

Theorem 5. *The running time of the Algorithm 4 is polynomial in input size.*

6.1   Experimental Results

The model consists of n sensor nodes randomly distributed in a 1000×1000 square grid. For different values of n, we execute our heuristic 100 times for different input instances. We have taken average value of the total interference. In Fig. 2, we have shown average interference of our heuristics and compare it with the best available algorithm improved SMIT [9]. In Table 1, we have shown the comparison of the total average interference between our heuristics and the algorithm proposed in [9]. These experimental results demonstrate that our heuristics outperform existing algorithm.

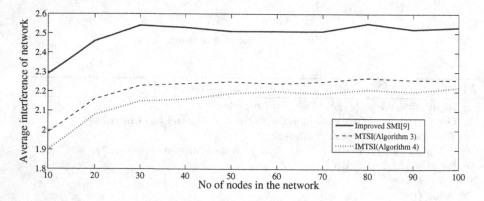

Fig. 2. Average node interference

Table 1. Simulation results for total interference

# of nodes (n)	Total Average Interference		
	MTSI (Algorithm 3)	IMTSI (Algorithm 4)	Improved SMIT [9]
10	1.99	1.90	2.29
20	2.16	2.08	2.46
30	2.23	2.15	2.54
40	2.24	2.16	2.53
50	2.25	2.19	2.51
60	2.24	2.20	2.51
70	2.25	2.19	2.51
80	2.27	2.21	2.55
90	2.26	2.20	2.52
100	2.26	2.22	2.53

7 Conclusion

In this paper we considered 2D networks i.e., the wireless nodes are distributed on a 2D plane. All the results presented in this paper are applicable in 3D networks also. Here we considered interference (sender interference model) minimization problem in wireless sensor networks. We proposed algorithm for *minimizing maximum interference* and *minimizing total interference* of a given network. For minimizing maximum interference we presented optimum solution with running time $O((\mathcal{P}_n + n^2)\log n)$ for connectivity predicate $\mathcal{P}$ like strong connectivity, broadcast, k-edge(vertex) connectivity, spanner, where n is the number of nodes in the network and $O(\mathcal{P}_n)$ is the time complexity for checking the connectivity predicate $\mathcal{P}$. The running time of the previous best known solution was $O(\mathcal{P}_n \times n^2)$ [3]. Therefore, our solution is a significant improvement over the best known solution with respect to time complexity.

For minimizing total interference we proposed optimum algorithm for connectivity predicate broadcast. The running time of the proposed algorithm is $O(n)$. For the same problem, the previous best known result was $2(1 + \ln(n - 1))$-factor approximation algorithm [3]. Therefore, our solution is a significant improvement over the existing solution in the literature. We also proposed two heuristics for minimizing total interference in the case of strongly connected predicate and compare our results with the best result available in the literature. Experimental results demonstrate that our heuristics outperform existing result.

References

1. Akyildiz, I.F., Su, W., Sankarasubramaniam, Y., Cayirci, E.: Wireless sensor networks: A survey. Computer Networks 38, 393–422 (2002)
2. Buchin, K.: Minimizing the maximum interfrence is hard (2008), http://arxiv.org/abs/0802.2134v2
3. Bilò, D., Proietti, G.: On the complexity of minimizing interference in ad-hoc and sensor networks. Theo. Comp. Sc. 402, 43–55 (2008)
4. Burkhat, M., Rickenbach, P., von Wattenhofer, R., Zollinger, A.: Does topology control reduce interference. In: 5th ACM International Symposium on Mobile Ad-Hoc Networking and Computing, pp. 9–19. ACM Press, New York (2004)
5. Funke, S., Kesselman, A., Kuhn, F., Lotker, Z., Segal, M.: Improved approximation algorithms for connected sensor cover. Wireless Networks 13, 153–164 (2007)
6. Lou, T., Tan, H., Wang, Y., Lau, F.C.M.: Minimizing Average Interference through Topology Control. In: Erlebach, T., Nikoletseas, S., Orponen, P. (eds.) ALGOSENSORS 2011. LNCS, vol. 7111, pp. 115–129. Springer, Heidelberg (2012)
7. Mainwaring, A., Polastre, J., Szewczyk, R., Culler, D., Anderson, J.: Wireless sensor networks for habitat monitoring. In: 1st ACM International Workshop on Wireless sensor networks and Applications, pp. 88–97. ACM Press, New York (2002)
8. Moscibroda, T., Wattenhofer, R.: Minimizing interference in ad hoc and sensor networks. In: ACM 2005 Joint Workshop on Foundations of Mobile Computing, pp. 24–33. ACM Press, New York (2005)
9. Panda, B.S., Shetty, D.P.: Strong Minimum Interference Topology for Wireless Sensor Networks. In: Thilagam, P.S., Pais, A.R., Chandrasekaran, K., Balakrishnan, N. (eds.) ADCONS 2011. LNCS, vol. 7135, pp. 366–374. Springer, Heidelberg (2012)

10. von Rickenbach, P., Schimid, S., Wattenhofer, R., Zollinger, A.: A robust interference model for wireless ad-hoc networks. In: 19th IEEE International Parallel and Distributed Processing Symposium, IPDPS (2005)
11. von Rickenbach, P., Wattenhofer, R., Zollinger, A.: Algorithmic models of interference in wireless ad hoc and sensor networks. IEEE/ACM Trans. on Net. 17, 172–185 (2009)
12. Tan, H., Lou, T., Lau, F.C.M., Wang, Y., Chen, S.: Minimizing Interference for the Highway Model in Wireless Ad-Hoc and Sensor Networks. In: Černá, I., Gyimóthy, T., Hromkovič, J., Jefferey, K., Královič, R., Vukolić, M., Wolf, S. (eds.) SOFSEM 2011. LNCS, vol. 6543, pp. 520–532. Springer, Heidelberg (2011)

Trust Based Secure Gateway Discovery Mechanism for Integrated Internet and MANET

Mohammed Asrar Ahmed[1] and Khaleel Ur Rahman Khan[2]

[1] MJCET, Hyderabad, AP
asrar7.ahmed@gmail.com
[2] ACEEC, Hyderabad, AP
khaleelrkhan@gmail.com

Abstract. The Integration of MANETs and infrastructure networks such as Internet, extends network coverage and increases the application domain of MANET. Several strategies exist for integration of two networks. Most of them presume that a non-adversarial environment prevails in the network. However such an ideal scenario is not always guaranteed. Nodes many behave maliciously due to scarcity of resources, congestion, or malicious intentions. In this paper a trust based, load aware, and secure gateway discovery for IIM is proposed. It employs the concept of mutual trust and authentication among nodes to prevent malicious activities. However a notable exception is that a node may experience packet-drop due to congestion on route or overflow in the interface queue of an intermediate node; this is not a malicious behaviour. In order to avoid such false malicious behaviours, we employ an effective and adaptive load balancing scheme to avoid congested routes. Thus it would be a novel strategy that ensures the routing in the Integrated Internet and MANET to be trustworthy, secure, efficient, and robust.

Keywords: MANET, IIM, Trust, Gateway, Malicious Nodes, Authentication.

1 Introduction

Mobile Ad hoc Networks (MANET) have been a challenging research area for last decade because of its versatility in routing, resource constraints, and security issues. Although a stand-alone MANET is easy to deploy and useful in many cases, MANET connected to Internet is more desirable than a stand-alone MANET. An Integrated MANET extends the area of coverage of network, avoids dead-zones in a network. But the integration of two networks is not straightforward due to topological differences, routing protocols, packet formats etc. Therefore an intermediate node called Gateway is neede to hide architectural differences. Any node desirous of Internet connectivity has to first discover route to Gateway and then register with it to avail connectivity. Several strategies have been proposed to integrate MANETs with Internet. A survey of these strategies can be found in [1].

Most existing strategies presume that a non-adversarial environment prevails in the network. But such an ideal scenario is always marred by unprecedented malicious behaviors of mobile nodes. Nodes may behave maliciously and gateway discovery is

C. Hota and P.K. Srimani (Eds.): ICDCIT 2013, LNCS 7753, pp. 103–114, 2013.

often vulnerable to variety of security threats. In study of related work we found that only a few strategies address prevention of malicious attacks on gateway discovery. We propose a trust based load-aware secure gateway discovery protocol. In the proposed approach of Manoharan et. al. [2], concept of trust, route load and hop count is used to discover trusted and less congested routes. This approach has been extended by introducing an inclusive computation of route trust which facilitates in better estimate of route's trustworthiness. In order to reduce the control overhead because of malicious nodes, congestion or mobility, proposed protocol maintains multiple routes between source node and the gateway. We also extend the routing security proposed by Bin Xie et. al. [3], implementing it in three tier and hybrid architectures [4]. Further we also modified the approach used in [3] by omitting the source route list used in routing messages and performing encryption on only few fields of gateway advertisement message. The registration process in [3] is made even simpler by allowing the route reply from gateway to be piggy bagged with advertisement message.

The remainder of the paper is organized as follows: Section 2 provides an overview of related work. Section 3 presents a brief discussion on the possible attacks on IIM. In Section 4 proposed strategy for secure gateway discovery is presented. Section 5 contains the simulation results and discussion. Finally section 6 concludes the paper.

2   Related Work

Integration of Internet and MANET has been extensively researched due to its usefulness. There are numerous strategies that cater to the integration of two networks. We have classified these strategies into three categories: Primitive Strategies, Performance Centric Strategies, and Security Centric Strategies. Primitive strategies can be found in references given in [4-8], Performance Centric Strategies can be found in references [10-12], and Security Centric Strategies can be found in [2-3]. These strategies have been studied and compared against common parameters.

2.1 Comparison Framework for Integration Strategies

The above strategies to integrate MANETs with Internet differ from each other in several aspects. These differences could arise due to the architecture being used, i.e. it may be two layered, three layered or hybrid. Different strategies might use different ad hoc routing protocols in MANET routing. Some strategies are based on Mobile IPv4 and others are based on Mobile IPv6. Similarly the gateway discovery in some strategies is reactive, proactive, or hybrid. Yet another dimension of difference is the provision for security and trust among mobile nodes to ensure the secure routing and gateway discovery. A comparison of these strategies based on above metrics is given in Table 2.

Table 1. Comparison of Strategeis

Integration Strategy	Ad hoc Routing Protocl	Gateway Discovery Technique	Architecture used for Integration	Trust among Mobile Nodes	Security in Ad hoc routing	Congestion Avoidance	Handoff Decision
MEWLANA	DSDV	Proactive	3 - Tier	No	No	No	Hop Count
ICFIAN	EDSDV	Reactive	3 - Tier	No	No	No	Infinite hop count
3THIRPIIM	CGSR	Hybrid	3 – Tier	No	No	No	Cluster Head Proximity
HAICMANET	Any on demand prtocol	Hybrid	2 – Tier	No	No	No	Using MMCS Cell switching Algorithm
HAIMFGMG	AODV	Reactive	Hybrid	No	No	No	Hop Count
PLAGDIC	AODV	Proactive	2 – Tier	No	No	Yes	Interface Queue length
EGDIIM	AODV	Proactive	3 – Tier	No	No	Yes	Path Load, Queue Length
ISAGDHM	AODV	Reactive	3 – Tier	No	No	Yes	Hop Count
TBGDIIM	AODV	Hybrid	3 – Tier	Yes	Partially	Yes	Route Selection Value
FIIANS	Any on demand protocol	Reactive	2 – Tier	Yes	Yes	No	Hop Count

3   Security in Integrated Internet and MANET

An integrated MANET is vulnerable to different types of attacks due to multihop routes. A node may appear to be a selfish node by refusing to forward the packet meant for its neighbor to preserve its battery. Nodes may selectively or blindly drop the packets. A survey of attacks on MANET can be found in [12]. Gateway discovery and registration is vulnerable to different attacks. Registration attacks are of three types: Registration Poisoning, Bogus Registration, and Replay Attacks [13]. As it is evident from the table 1, there are presently a very few strategies which address the security quotient in discovering gateways to connect to Internet. Therefore in this paper we propose a strategy to discover routes to gateway which are secure, trustworthy and less congested.

4   Proposed Protocol

As stated earlier, the majority of existing strategies presume that the integration of Internet and MANET takes place in a congenial environment. But such ideal scenarios are never guaranteed due to aforementioned scenarios. Hence a gateway discovery protocol is needed which not only selects the routes that are more trusted but also less congested. In the existing strategies we found that no single strategy takes into account these two important dimensions of routing efficiency. This motivates to devise a protocol which discovers routes between a node and gateway to be secure, trusted, less congested and robust. The robustness is ensured by maintaining multiple alternative routes between mobile node and gateway. The proposed protocol is based on trust among mobile nodes and adaptive load balancing technique. In [2] trustworthiness of routes is computed using a normalized metric called as RSV, Route Selection Value. In proposed strategy, computation of RSV has been modified to reflect the inclusive estimate of trust of a route rather than the trust of adjacent nodes en route as it is in [2]. RSV is computed based on Residual Route Load Capacity, Route Trust, and Hop Count using normalization of these parameters. Below we present the explanation of above parameters.

4.1   Residual Route Load Capacity

RRLC [2] is the minimum of available load capacity at any node inclusive of gateway and source nodeAssuming that a node, say m, has a maximum load capacity of μ, and the currently the node is handling a traffic of λ_m from s mobile sources each of packet size k_i and packet arrival rate r_i. Now the residual load capacity at node m is given as [14] using equation 1:

$$C_m = \mu - \lambda_m, \text{ where } \lambda_m = \sum_{i=1}^{s} r_i k_i \tag{1}$$

Each node computes its C_m using equation 1, and RRCL = minimum $\{C_{GW}, C_{IMN1}, C_{IMN2}, .. , C_{SMN}\}$, where subscripts denote the gateway, intermediate nodes and source node sequentially. Routes with largest RRLC are preferred.

4.2   Route Trust

Route Trust RT is used in the computation of normalized metric RSV. To compute Route Trust, RREP and RREQ packet formats have been extended to accommodate Advertised Trust Value ATV and Observed Trust Value OTV. A node claims is trustworthiness using ATV. When a node receives this value, it compares it against the actual observed value OTV, where OTV is computed based on neighbor's behavior such as number of packets it has forwarded, dropped on behalf of this node [2].

The computation of Route Trust has been modified in the proposed protocol to reflect the better estimate of actual trustworthiness of route. In [2], the route trust is computed from the perspective of only pairs of neighbor nodes. It does not give us a clear insight into the overall trust of the route. We propose to compute Route Trust as the minimum of all of node trusts along the path. The disadvantage in [2] is that the trust is computed for route between two immediate neighbors, because few nodes on route may be least trusted and remaining is highly trusted. Therefore such routes are likely to be more vulnerable due to least trusted nodes on routes. But if the trust of route is taken to be the smallest value of trust of nodes along the path, the bottleneck in trustworthiness of routes can be easily identified. Trust is computed as follows:

Initially RT: =0.5;

Gateway computes RT as RT:= ATV_G, Gateway unicasts RREP on reverse path to M_1

For each M_i Route Trust is computed as follows:

$RT(M_i)$: = min (OTV_G, ATV_i) for i: =1;
$RT(M_i)$: = min (OTV_j, ATV_i) for j: =i-1, and 2<=i<=n, (n is number of hops)

4.3   Computation of Route Selection Value

The source mobile node may receive multiple route replies RREP_Is from different neighbors. In such situation the node computes the metric called as Route Selection Value (RSV) [2]. In proposed protocol we modified this computation to just include the modified route trust as shown in equation 2. The α_1, α_2, and α_3 are predefined constants, and their values range from 0 to 1. Values of these constants are set based on node mobility, application type etc. RT_i is the route trust value observed by node i, and RT_{avg} is the average of route trusts of all received route replies. H_i and H_{avg} are the hop count and average hop count of all received routes respectively. C_r is the residual route load capacity of a route. Source node then selects the route to the gateway as the one which can be reached with maximum value for RSV.

$$RSV := \alpha_1 (RT_i / RT_{avg}) + \alpha_2 (H_i / H_{avg}) + \alpha_3 (Cr / C_{max}) \qquad (2)$$

4.4   Secure Gateway Discovery

In order to get connected to the Internet, a mobile node needs to discover and register with a gateway. As stated in section 3, intermediate nodes misguide the gateway discovery in various ways. In the proposed strategy we extend the routing security design proposed by Bin Xie [3]. In [3], the strategy is implemented in Two Tier architecture of IIM. We extend it to be used in Three Tier and Hybrid architectures [4]. In [3], the advertisement message is encrypted using the shared secret key. In our proposed strategy we encrypt only few pivotal fields of advertisement message as mobile nodes are resource constrained. We also omit the source route list used in [3] as construction of source route list is not needed in Ad hoc On Demand Distance Vector Routing Protocol AODV, since it uses reverse path. In order to ensure routing security, we presume that mobile nodes share a secret key with the foreign agent Diffie Hellman Key Exchange algorithm.

The figure 1 illustrates the proposed secure gateway discovery mechanism. The notations used in protocol are given in table 2. The flowchart for the algorithm is given in figure 2. A mobile station MS desirous of Internet connection broadcasts a gateway solicitation message GWSol to its neighbor A. This message is signed by private key of MN. When the neighbor node A receives the request, it checks its validity of it using public key, nonce, and timestamp. After validation it appends its own signature to the request and further broadcasts. This sequence of actions is done at each intermediate node. When a gateway node receives the request, it then forwards it to the foreign agent FA. The FA creates a mobility binding for the source node by creating a record of identifier and public key of source node and generates advertisement message containing timestamp and nonce fields.

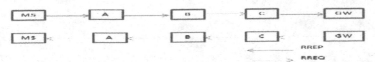

Fig. 1. A scenario of propagation of GWSol messages

The Gateway on receiving advertisement from FA, generates the route reply by embedding this advertisement and unicasts it on reverse path. Gateway node computes its Route Trust, CGW, and Hop information for the reply. Each intermediate node also performs similar computations before forwarding the reply to next node on reverse path. On receiving reply, source node issues a registration request after successfully decrypting the cipher text of nonce and timestamp using the same shared secret key. The novelty of this approach is that no other node can ever learn about the actual values of these fields as they don't have knowledge of shared secret key. Registration request is forwarded by intermediate nodes on established route till it reaches the gateway. The gateway unicasts this request to FA for verification of nonce and timestamp received by FA.

4.5   Provision for Multiple Routes

A node receives more than one route reply in response to a route request. In [2], the route with the highest RSV is retained and rest of them was discarded. But in the event of frequent route breakages the intermediate node has to start a route repair. Since this node is in the vicinity of overloaded or malicious nodes, a local route repair may not be a stable solution. Such a route may be prone to frequent breakages in future. The routing performance of the protocol can be improved if multiple routes to the gateway are preserved. When a node receives multiple replies, it preserves these replies in a route cache and selects the one with highest RSV. Hello packets of minimal size are used to keep alternate routes alive.

Table 2. Notations used in Protocol

Noation	Description
MS_{HM}	Mobile station Home address
HA_{id}, FA_{id}	HA and FA IP address as its identity
N_x	Nonce issued by X, e.g. HA or MS (a random no)
CA	Certification Authority
K_x, K_x^{-1}	Public and Private key of X
$[M] K_x^{-1}$	Digital signature of message M generated using private key of X
$Cert_X$	Certificate of X
T_{issue}, T_{expire}	Issuing and expiration time of certificate
t	Timestamp, current estimated time
S_{MS-HA}	Shared Secret key between MS and HA

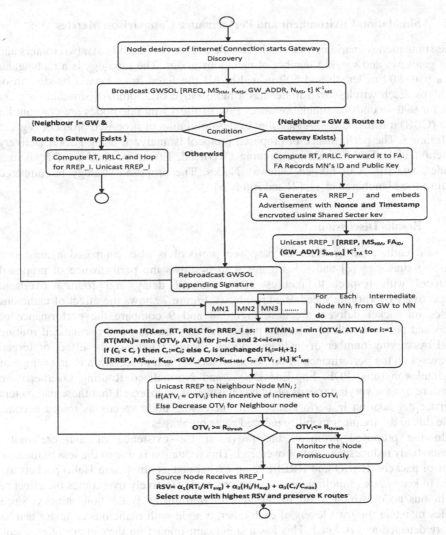

Fig. 2. Flowchart for Proposed Protocol

5   Simulation Results and Analysis

The proposed strategy is implemented using the network simulator ns-2.31. The simulations were run under different parameters as mentioned below by varying mobile node speeds, number of malicious nodes, and forged gateway nodes. The performance of the proposed strategy is compared with the Manoharan et al [2] and Bin Xie [3] reactive discovery approaches in similar simulation environment.

5.1   Simulation Environment and Performance Comparison Metrics

The simulation scenario consists of 15 mobile nodes, two fixed hosts, two routers and two gateways and varying number of malicious nodes. The topology is a rectangular area with 800 m length and 500 m width. All the fixed links have a bandwidth of 10Mbps. Each wireless transmitter has a radio range of 250m. All simulations were run for 900 seconds of simulation time. Five of the 15 mobile nodes are constant bit rate (CBR) traffic sources. A snapshot of the simulation of proposed protocol is given in figure 3. The performance of proposed protocol is analyzed using Packet Delivery Fraction PDF, End-End Delay, Routing Overhead, Effect of number of Malicious Nodes, and Effect of Forged Gateway Nodes. The proposed strategy is compared against the Manoharan et. al. [2] and Bin Xie [3].

5.2   Results Discussion

As said earlier, performance of proposed protocol is also compared against two existing strategies [2] and [3]. Figures 4 to 6 shows the performance of proposed protocol with respect to metrics PDF, end-end delay and routing overhead respectively by varying speed of ad hoc hosts. Figure 7 shows the effect of malicious nodes on packet delivery fraction. Figure 8 and 9 compare the performance of proposed protocol with [2, 3] using packet delivery fraction and normalized routing load by varying number of malicious nodes. Figure 10 shows the effect of forged gateways on the performance of proposed protocol. Each observation is an average of 3 simulation runs. PDF, End-End Delay, and Normalized Routing Overhead are measure against varying speeds of ad hoc hosts. It was observed that these parameters register degradation in performance with increasing node speeds as routes become stale due to the frequent mobility induced route breakages.

In the proposed protocol, the provision for existence of multiple routes substantially reduces the control overhead. This reduction is due to the less number of control packets (RREQ and RREP) being exchanged as small size Hello packets are used to keep track of multiple routes. The protocol effectively overcomes the effect of malicious nodes which resort to selective forwarding or Black hole attacks. Since nodes maintain the trust levels of each other, a node with malicious behavior can be easily detected and isolated. This has a significant impact on throughput of protocol. A set of nodes were randomly chosen as malicious nodes and simulations were run with varying number of such nodes. In simulation results we observed a significant improvement in PDF in presence of such nodes when compared to PDF in [2, 3]. This improvement is achieved mainly because of mutual trust and a constant watch on the trust level of route by means of exchange of hello packets containing the trust and load information in them.

The proposed protocol efficiently prevents the attacks on gateway discovery. The Forged gateway attack is prevented as the forged gateway does not have knowledge of shared secret key between node and foreign agent. Registration Replay attack is prevented using the nonce and timestamp being sent as cipher text. Since only mobile node and foreign agent have knowledge of shared secret key, no other node can ever learn about these two fields and hence duplication of such messages can be easily figured out. Impact of forged gateway attack is also curtailed with the help of shared secret keys and encryption of timestamps and nonce fields in advertisement. A forged gateway does not possess the shared secret keys shared between node and foreign agents. In presence of nodes resorting to Wormhole or Blackhole attacks, [2, 3] observe higher end-end delay and routing overhead as many local route repairs take place or altogether new routes are sought. In proposed strategy, due to the provision of multiple routes, route discovery related control packets need not be exchanged and hence result in a decline in end-end delay and routing overhead. However proposed protocol relies on small size Hello packets to be exchanged to keep routes alive. The number of control packets exchanged in presence forged gateways is same as in absence of such nodes. Registration with forged gateway is prevented because these forged gateways cannot proceed with encryption of advertisement fields using shared secret keys as they don't have any such keys shared with mobile nodes.

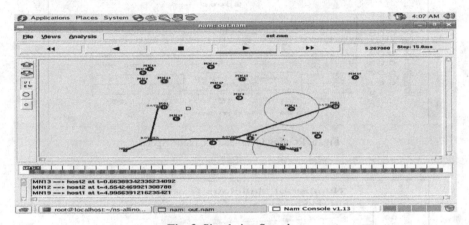

Fig. 3. Simulation Snapshot

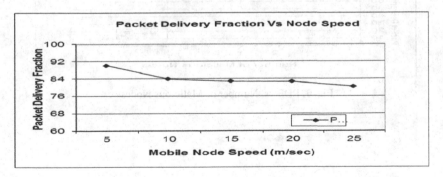

Fig. 4. Packet delivery fraction vs. Mobile node Speed

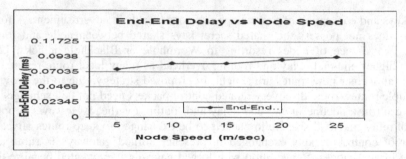

Fig. 5. End-End Delay vs Node Speed

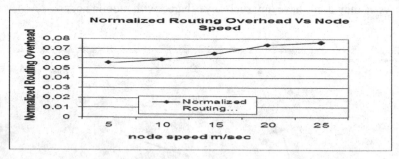

Fig. 6. Routing Overhead vs. Node Speed

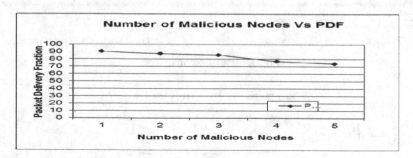

Fig. 7. PDF vs. Number of Malicious Nodes

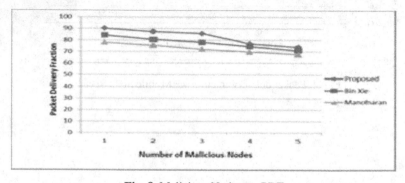

Fig. 8. Malicious Nodes vs. PDF

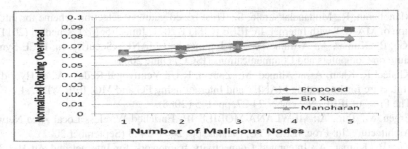

Fig. 9. Normalized Routing Overhead vs. Number of malicious Nodes

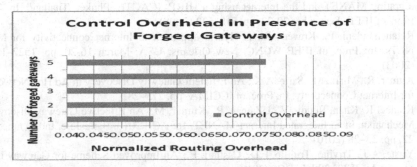

Fig. 10. Effect of Forged gateway on Routing Overhead

6   Conclusion

In this paper a protocol is presented which discovers trusted, secure and less congested routes to reach the gateway nodes offering connection to Internet nodes. A notable feature of this approach is that it not only prevents the malicious behaviors of mobile nodes but also dynamically adapts to the less congested routes. In order to ensure better connectivity, multiple routes are maintained between nodes and gateway. This results in significant decrease in routing overhead and end-end delay as less number of control packets need to be exchanged. It also registers an increase in throughput as a dynamic load balancing scheme is employed. Protocol always prefers a route that is highly trusted and less congested resulting in better performance when compared to other existing strategies as demonstrated in simulation results. At the expense of smaller Hello packets, a large number of control packets can be avoided by maintaining multiple routes between nodes and gateways.

References

[1]   Khaleel R. Khan, Zaman, R.U., Venugopal Reddy, A.: Integrating MANETs and the Internet: challenges and a review of strategies. In: COMSWARE (IEEE CNF), January 6-10, pp. 536–543 (2008)

[2] Manoharan, R., Mohanalakshmie, S.: Trust based gateway selection scheme for integration of MANET with Internet. In: IEEE ICRTIT 2011, June 3-5. MIT, Chennai (2011)

[3] Xie, B., Kumar, A.: A framework for Internet and MANET Security. In: IEEE Symposium on Computers and Communications (ISCC) (June 2004)

[4] Khaleel R. Khan, Asrar Ahmed, M., Zaman, R.U., Venugopal Reddy, A.: A Hybrid Architecture for Integrating MANET and Internet using FG and MG, IFIP WDIC, UAE. In: The Proc. of IEEE, November 24-27, pp. 1–5 (2008)

[5] Ergen, M., Puri, A.: MEWLANA-MOBILE IP: Enriched Wireless Local Area Network Architecture. In: Proc. IEEE VTC, Canada, pp. 2449–2453 (September 2002)

[6] Xie, B., Kumar, A.: Integrated Connectivity framework for Internet and Ad Hoc Networks. In: 2004 IEEE ICMASS, pp. 540–542 (2004)

[7] Khaleel R. Khan, Zaman, R.U., Venugopal Reddy, A.: A Three-Tier Architecture for Integrating MANET and the Internet using a HIRP, ICACTE, Phuket, Thailand. In: The Proc. of IEEE, December 20-22, pp. 518–522 (2008)

[8] Ratanchandani, P., Kravets, R.: A Hybrid approach to Internet connectivity for MANETs. In: Proc. of IEEE WCNC, New Orleans, USA, March 16-20, pp. 1522–1527 (2003)

[9] Kumar, R., Misra, M., Sarje, A.K.: An Efficient Gateway Discovery in Ad Hoc Networks for Internet Connectivity. In: Proc. of ICCIMA, pp. 275–281

[10] Khaleel R. Khan, Reddy, V., UZaman, R., Kumar, M.: An Effective Gateway Discovery Mechanism in an Integrated Internet-MANET. In: ACE 2010, Bangalore, India, June 21-22, pp. 24–28 (2010)

[11] Yuste, A.J., Triviño, Trujillo, F.D., Casilari, E.: An Improved Scheme for Gateway Discovery. In: IEEE 30th ICDCS (2010)

[12] Xiao, Y., Shen, X., Du, D.-Z.: Wireless Network Security. Springer (2007)

[13] Xie, B.: Heterogeneous Wireless Networks – Networking Protocol to Security. VDM Verlag Dr. Muller (2007)

[14] Safdar, et al.: Multiple End-to-End QoS Metrics Gateway Selection Scheme in MANETs. In: Proceedings of the ICET, pp. 446–451 (October 2009)

Improving MapReduce Performance through Complexity and Performance Based Data Placement in Heterogeneous Hadoop Clusters

Rajashekhar M. Arasanal and Daanish U. Rumani

{rajashekharma,daanish.rumani}@gmail.com

Abstract. MapReduce has emerged as an important programming model with clusters having tens of thousands of nodes. Hadoop, an open source implementation of MapReduce may contain various nodes which are heterogeneous in their computing capacity for various reasons. It is important for the data placement algorithms to partition the input and intermediate data based on the computing capacities of the nodes in the cluster. We propose several enhancements to data placing algorithms in Hadoop such that the load is distributed across the nodes evenly. In this work, we propose two techniques to measure the computing capacities of the nodes. Secondly, we propose improvements to the input data distribution algorithm based on the map and reduce function complexities and the measured heterogeneity of nodes. Finally, we evaluate the improvement of the MapReduce performance.

Keywords: Data processing, MapReduce, Heterogeneous cluster, Hadoop

1 Introduction

Map-reduce programming model was introduced by Google and is one of the most popular models in cloud computing to solve many data intensive problems on a distributed cluster [6]. Hadoop is an open source implementation of MapReduce developed initially by Yahoo! [7]. It has been popular among the researchers as well as commercial users like Facebook, LinkedIn, Adobe, etc. Using this programming model, large amounts of data can be processed in a parallel fashion using large clusters of interconnected nodes.

The MapReduce framework consists of two main phases – map and reduce. In map phase, a larger problem is divided into smaller sub problems and the sub-problems are processed in parallel to produce the results for the sub-problems. These intermediate results are then processed and combined during the reduce phase in parallel to form the final output for the job. Hadoop splits the input data into a number of small chunks and places the chunks on Hadoop Distributed File System (HDFS) such that the data distribution happens evenly across all the nodes. This helps distribute the load on all the nodes evenly and also increases the parallelism with respect to data read and write. Also, the data has to be stored close to the nodes performing the computation in the cluster such that the data transfer between the nodes in the cluster is minimal. So, jobs which consume data residing on the distributed file system have to

C. Hota and P.K. Srimani (Eds.): ICDCIT 2013, LNCS 7753, pp. 115–125, 2013.

be scheduled such that the tasks (sub-problems in a job) are provisioned close to the nodes having the data to exploit data locality [3].

In a cluster, we observe that all the nodes may not be equal in their computing performance. Hence, some nodes might finish their assigned work faster than others which results in imbalance of this data load distribution. This increases the overall time taken for the job to complete. One way to balance the load is to distribute the data based on the computing capacities of the nodes in the cluster. There has been research into this area of data placement [4] which attempts to improve the data distribution such that the nodes get a fair share of data to process based on their computing capacities and their processing times are almost equal.

We observe that calculating the computing capacity of each node in the cluster before a job starts is one of the important steps. This has to happen as early as possible. Currently Hadoop accepts these computing capacities (or ratio of performances of each node) as user configuration input. The user has to come up with the ratios and needs to supply them through the configuration file. The user might not have access to the internal details of the nodes on which the submitted job might run. Also, it is costly to experiment by running parts of jobs to calculate the computing ratios in terms of time, resources and money. Further the map and reduce steps might be of non-linear complexities with respect to the data size they process. When the nodes are heterogeneous, distributing data as per the computing ratios alone will not suffice.

1.1   Contributions

This paper proposes and evaluates the following enhancements to Hadoop:

- A mathematical model to estimate the computing ratios based on the hardware specifications like CPU speed, physical memory size, virtual memory size, current CPU usage, number of CPUs etc. available on the nodes in the cluster.
- A history based method to calculate the machine computing ratios after the job is complete.
- A tool for data distribution based on computing ratios.
- Evaluation of the improvements to the system based on the models discussed above both for linear and non-linear jobs.

The rest of the paper is organized as follows. In Section 2 we discuss two models to calculate the computing ratios - a mathematical model and a history based model. We then provide the implementation details of the models in Section 3. In Section 4, we discuss the experimentation results to show improvement in MapReduce performance. We finally discuss the related work and future work in Sections 5 and 6 respectively.

2   Proposed Enhancements

2.1   Methods to Calculate Computing Ratio

A Mathematical Model to Calculate Computing Ratios

We propose a model to calculate the computing ratios mathematically using the hardware resources which are available at disposal on each node during the job execution time. We have seen that the computing ratios are different for different applications, as their data processing footprint (the type of data the MapReduce job looks for and acts upon) is different and the complexities of the user-provided *map()* and *reduce()* functions might be different, though the amount of data being processed is the same and are run on the same nodes. Hadoop [4] expects users to provide the computing ratios as input through configuration files. So, users have to arrive at the computing ratios on their own before starting their job. This is difficult, as a user might not have access to the underlying nodes (in a cloud computing environment) and also has to rely on some early experimentation on the allocated nodes which consumes time and resources.

To overcome the challenges, we can mathematically calculate the ratios. In arriving at approximate computing ratios, we can look at the hardware resources that are available when a job is just about to get scheduled on the nodes and compare them with each other to arrive at a possible computing ratio for each of the nodes. The heartbeats from each data node to the name node are processed to fetch the hardware resource availability information. However, these ratios might not be optimal, but are definitely a good start and theoretically convey the computing ratios for linear *map()* and *reduce()*.

Before running a job on the cluster the user may manually run the computing ratio calculator tool to collect the available resources for the underlying nodes. The tool analyzed the heartbeats coming from each task tracker node to the job tracker. The heartbeats contain the current free resource information. In case of multi-tenancy, even though there are multiple jobs scheduled on the nodes the heartbeats provide a measurement of available resources at that point of time. Input data may now be distributed based on the new dynamically calculated computing ratios.

Job History Based Model to Calculate Computing Ratios

As discussed earlier, the mathematical model could have considerable error in calculating the computing ratio of a machine. Once a job is run on the cluster, we can collect the job history and analyze to measure the machine performances. In our work, we analyze total input bytes in the map phase for each node and the time taken by the *map()* to process the amount of data.

In theory, a powerful node would have processed more data in lesser time as compared to a weaker node. Based on this information for each node in the cluster, we compare the nodes with each other and arrive at the computing ratios.

2.2   Data Placement and Distribution

Complexity and Capacity Based Input Data Distribution for Map Step

We propose an enhancement over [4] to consider the algorithmic complexity of *map()* in addition to the computing ratio for making data placement decisions. The algorithmic complexity of *map()* plays a major role in making data placement decisions.

Let us illustrate with an example. Suppose that there are two machines, A and B, in the cluster. A is two times as powerful than B. In case of [4] data would be portioned such that A would need to process **2N** data blocks and B would have to process **N** data blocks with **3N** being the total number of data blocks to process. Obviously, [4] assumes linear complexity of *map()*. However if *map()* was of quadratic complexity then the data distribution would not be optimal. Machine A would take longer than machine B even though it is more powerful i.e. machine A would straggle.

The computing ratio gives a measure of the available capacity of the computing nodes whereas the functional complexity of *map()* would dictate the amount of data that should be placed on each computing nodes such that no stragglers are expected.

3   Implementation Details

3.1   Calculating Computing Ratios

Mathematical Model

The computing capacity of a machine is a function of several attributes like CPU speed, internal memory size, processor cache size, network speed, disk rotation speed, bus speed and many others. As an example, Table 1 shows a calculation based on the values with an arbitrary function $f_{capacity} = a*C + b*M + c*B + d*Cache + e*N$, with predetermined values for a, b, c... so on depending on the job type (IO bound or CPU bound).

The above function is just an illustration of how one can arrive at the computing ratios mathematically. The computing ratios denote that the node A is twice as fast as node B.

Table 1. An example of two nodes in a cluster with varying computing capacities and their computing ratios (CR) as per the capacity calculator function (higher the CR, slower the node)

Node	CPU Speed (Symbol - C)	L1 Cache (in KB) (Symbol - Cache)	Memory (Symbol - M)	Network speed (Symbol - N)	$f_{capacity}$ (with a = b = c = d = e = 1)	CR
A	2GHz	256	2GB RAM	2-port 1GigE	6.256	1
B	1GHz	128	1GB RAM	1-port 1GigE	3.128	2

CrCalculator Tool

In Hadoop, all the datanodes in the cluster regularly update the namenode about their current resource utilization information through heartbeat mechanism. A standalone utility called CrCalculator was developed to calculate the computing ratios mathematically. The utility first fetches datanode information from namenode and then calculates the computing ratios of the nodes in the cluster based on the available resources of the datanodes. Typically in a Hadoop cluster, a node acts as both datanode and a TaskTracker to reap the benefits of data locality while processing jobs.The utility outputs the mathematically calculated computing ratios in an XML file, which can be further used as a configuration file for many purposes.Based on the computing ratios, the CrCalculator also balances the data in the cluster such that the data is distributed as per the computing power of the nodes.

History Based Model

In Hadoop, the *TaskTrackers* send heartbeats to the *JobTracker* with the free resource information, job information, etc. The heartbeat messages from the task trackers provide information about each task that was run on the task tracker. This information can be used to calculate the computing ratio even while other jobs are running on the cluster. The heartbeats contain several useful counters like the total input bytes to the map phase, total output bytes of map, start time, end time, etc.

We make use of these counters to arrive at a score for each node:

$$Score = \sum_{task} \frac{(MapInputBytes)}{(Totaltimetakentoprocess)}$$

Once the score for each node is calculated, the scores are normalized such that the most powerful node gets a computing ratio 1.0. Higher the ratio, weaker is the machine.

3.2   Distributing Data

After we arrive at the computing ratios, we need to consider the algorithmic complexity of *map()* while making data placement decisions. We consider three machines A, B, and C such that A is twice as capable when compared to B and A is thrice as capable when compared to C. Thus the computing ratio is 1:2:3. Lower numbers represent faster or more capable machines. Consider that the *map()* of a particular program is of quadratic complexity i.e. $O(n^2)$. Thus we need to allocate appropriate number of data blocks to A, B, and C so that they would complete processing their share in almost the same time. This is required to ensure that there would be no stragglers.

Considering the computing ratios we can say that if A takes one second to complete a unit of work, then B would require 2 seconds and C would require 3 seconds to perform that same task as A. If N is the total number of blocks that need to be processed, then considering linear complexity, machine A should process **N/2** blocks, B should process **N/3** blocks and C should process **N/6** blocks. Thus if one data block required an equivalent processing of one second on machine A then, theoretically, all three machines would require **N/2** seconds to complete.

But recall that the algorithmic complexity of the *map()* task is quadratic with respect to the input size. Thus we would have to distribute data differently. Again let us consider that X data blocks would require X^2 seconds of equivalent processing on machine A. Therefore machine B would require $2X^2$ seconds and machine C would require $3X^2$ seconds for the same task. Let us place X_1 data blocks on machine A, X_2 data blocks on machine B and X_3 data blocks on machine C. We aim to make (approximately):

$$\boxed{(X_1)^2 = 2(X_2)^2 = 3(X_3)^2}$$ ... (Equation 1)

We know that:

$$\boxed{X_1 + X_2 + X_3 = N}$$ ... (Equation 2)

N is the total number of data blocks. Solving the two equations we can arrive at the optimal values for X_1, X_2, and X_3.

4   Experimentation Results

4.1   Cluster Setup

We used Amazon EC2 [11] instances as our test machines. We evaluated on two cluster setups. Table 2 lists the EC2 instances and their capabilities.

Table 2. An example of two nodes in a cluster with varying computing capacities and their computing ratios (CR) as per the capacity calculator function

Name	Type	CPU Cores	Memory
Micro1	Micro	Up to 2	613 MB
Micro2	Micro	Up to 2	613 MB
Small	Small	1	1.7 GB
Small2	Small	1	1.7 GB
Medium	Medium	2	3.7 GB
Medium2	Medium	2	3.7 GB
Large	High CPU – Medium	10	1.7 GB

The first cluster (Cluster A) consists of *hadoop-micro1, hadoop-micro2, hadoop-small, hadoop-medium*, and *hadoop-large*. The second cluster (Cluster B) consists of *hadoop-small, hadoop-small2, hadoop-medium, hadoop-medium2*, and *hadoop-large*. All the recordings used were repeated five times and their average was used.

4.2   Mathematical Computing Ratio Based Balancer

We balanced 1.6 GB data on the Cluster A using the mathematical computing ratios. Figure 1 shows the data distribution. The node with lowest computing ratio ("Large") gets the largest amount of data to process, and the slowest node ("Micro1") gets the lowest amount of data to process. Hadoop tries to schedule the tasks on or close to the nodes having the data to be processed.

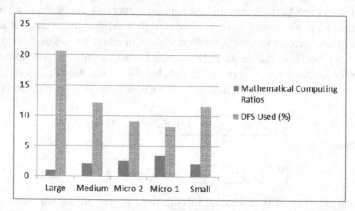

Fig. 1. Comparing the Mathematical Computing Ratios and HDFS disk space used

As the Large node stores more data, more tasks are proportionately scheduled on this node as compared to the other node. This helps in reducing the data transfer among the nodes. Also the node can process the local data faster. Now because the data processing happens in proportion to the computing power, all the tasks now finish around the same time, avoiding the staggering or longer waits for task completion.

We ran grep job over the data and saw an overall **11.4%** improvement by balancing the data as per the computing ratio among the nodes. A sample output of the CrCalculator xml configuration file is as below:

```xml
<?xml version="1.0" encoding="UTF-8" standa-
lone="no"?><configuration>
<property>
<name>calculatecrflag</name>
<value>false</value></property>
<property>
<name>10.10.219.1:50010</name>
<value>2.3274264</value></property>
<property>
<name>10.99.39.78:50010</name>
<value>2.0536118</value></property>
<property>
<name>10.118.246.141:50010</name>
<value>2.0536118</value></property>
<property>
<name>10.114.209.163:50010</name>
<value>2.0536118</value></property>
<property>
<name>10.195.7.105:50010</name>
<value>1.0</value></property>
</configuration>
```

The configuration file contains the hostname of the datanodes as property-names with the computing-ratio as values. The calculatecrflag tells the utility on whether to calculate the computing ratios again or to read the values in the file to balance the data.

4.3 Execution History Based Computing Ratio

In Fig. 2, we see a comparison of the mathematically calculated computing ratios versus the computing ratios measured based on execution history. For most of the cases, the values match, except for the "small" instance. This shows that mathematical model can sometimes be inaccurate and should only serve as a starting point to arrive at the ratios when no other reference is available. Since history based model depends on the actual job history, it gives accuracy and is more close to the actual performance of the nodes.

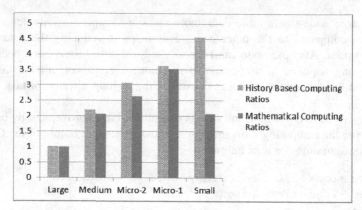

Fig. 2. Comparing two methods of calculating the computing ratios

4.4   Complexity Based Computing Ratio

Two representative programs were used to evaluate algorithmic complexity based computing ratio viz. LinearIncrement and QuadraticSort. These tests were performed on Cluster B.Both LinearIncrement and QuadraticSort are adaptations of the hadoop word-count example. Both process text files containing lines of space separated 1000 random numbers in the range [0, 10000].LinearIncrement adds 1 to each of the 1000 numbers in a line and writes it back to the output as text. QuadraticSort sorts the 1000 numbers using bubble sort ($O(n^2)$) and writes them back as text.Each file contains 3500 lines and we used 35 files as our test data.

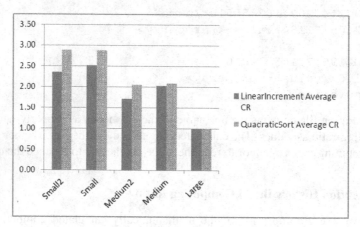

Fig. 3. Computing Linear and Quadratic computing ratios (based on history)

The graph in Fig. 3 shows the history based measurements for the two jobs. We can see that the ratio *Large:Small2* changes between the two jobs. Had the jobs not differed in their complexity, this ratio would have been constant as large and small2 would have taken resources proportionately. This shows that the ratios also depend on the algorithmic complexity of the different phases.

We can see that the average computing ratios for the linear job are closer to each other than the ones for the quadratic job. For non-linear jobs, the computing ratios of the nodes are not only proportional to the computing power, but they also rely on the complexity of the job.In case of quadratic job the heterogeneity will be exposed more, because of the time spent by each task on a node. Our job was not purely quadratic in the input size, but was only quadratic to an extent to sort the numbers in each row. Hence a slight increase in the ratios as compared to a linear *map()* function.

5   Related Work

M. Mustafa Rafique et.al.[1]exploit heterogeneity in large scale asymmetric multi-core clusters. They classify computing nodes into two types 1) Well provisioned nodes which have large amounts of memory and 2) Small memory nodes which have limited amounts of memory. They propose using asymmetric multi-core clusters for accelerating Map-Reduce programs in much the same way desktop games use the Graphical Processing Unit (GPU).

A well provisioned node that serves as a manager is connected to a large number of small memory nodes via high bandwidth I/O interconnects. Data meant for the small memory nodes is accumulated on the well provisioned manager node. This data is streamed to the small memory nodes as they require the data. The small memory compute nodes send their results to the manager which collects results from all the nodes and merges it before returning the final results.But, in a typical Hadoop cluster, the nodes are not well connected with high bandwidth interconnects. In such situations, the data prefetching and streaming would not work well. So, we are motivated towards minimizing the data transfers between the nodes.

S. Babu [2] proposes the concept of dynamically tuning job specific parameters based on the job submitted such that the resources are utilized efficiently. The authors propose several approaches to tune the parameters involving both history based and profiling models to adjust job specific parameters prior to or while the job is running on the cluster. However, MapReduce currently does not have any parameters related to heterogeneity which can be tuned dynamically. Hence, this model needs to be enhanced.

Quincy [3] introduces a fair scheduler that balances the priority of the tasks and data locality. It aims to schedule jobs close to where the data resides. It structures the scheduling problem as a *min-cost flow* problem where the nodes and edges of the graph are assigned weights and flow capacities. However, Quincy does not consider heterogeneity in computing capacities in the cluster and data distribution.

J. Xie et.al. [4]solve the data skew problem by distributing data such that faster nodes in the cluster process higher amounts of data as compared to the weaker nodes. The main idea is to measure the processing powers of the nodes in the cluster by running the same amount of job on each node and recording the response times. Based on the response times, the computing ratios are calculated.The ratiosare used to decide the amount of input dataeach node has to store and process. They also propose a data redistribution mechanism, which is required for moving the data due to changing data (say append/insertion or deletion of data which cause increase or reduction in data) and addition of new compute nodes to the cluster. They create two lists - one with over-utilized nodes and the other with under-utilized nodes. A data redistribution server decides how much data has to move, the source node and the destination node and repeatedly moves the data. This process repeats until all the nodes are loaded as per their compute ratio.

We observe that the method of measuring the computing ratios and supplying the ratios to Hadoop is not sufficient to address all the challenges. Initial processing of an equal amount of data and recording the response times would result in inefficient use of time and resources. There is a need to find a way to calculate the computing ratios either dynamically or based on a history of previous runs. Secondly, they do not consider the complexity of map and reduce functions. If the map and reduce steps are non-linear, distributing the data as per the black-box measurements will lead to wrong distributions.

B. Gufleret. al. [5]propose a *fine partitioning* technique to split the intermediate data containing the key-value tuples into "p" partitions which is more than the number of reducers. Once the data is split into partitions, the assignment happens based on a weight function which depends on the number of key-value tuples and the size of the key-value tuples in a cluster. They assign the partitions to the reducers based on a greedy heuristic to balance the load – assign the largest (as per the weight) unassigned partition to the least loaded reducer. The paper also proposes a *dynamic fragmentation* technique which is done by the mappers on the fly while they are generating the intermediate data.

However, the above algorithms do not consider the heterogeneity in the node capacities. If the *reduce()* function is non-linear (say quadratic or cubic), the data skew (even though the data is distributed as per the complexity) due to varying computing capacities becomes huge and affects the performance of the MapReduce jobs. The algorithms need to be tweaked such that the assignment of the partitions or fragments depends on the complexity as well as computing capacity.

6   Future Work

The mathematical model can be extended in a number of ways. The mathematical model calculations can be extracted into a new class exposed via an interface. This provides the ability to supply a configurable method of calculating the computing ratios. We have used a very simple method to arrive at the computing ratios mathematically. This method can be enhanced to take care of the other details like – network bandwidth usage, cost of VMs, etc. to distribute data more accurately based on the users' needs.

Secondly the computing ratios can be calculated before the start of every new job. If the currently calculated computing ratios are different from the previously calculated ones beyond a set threshold, balancing can be automatically triggered based on the freshly calculated ratios.Further, the computing ratios could be normalized across different program executions and used to distribute the input data based on these ratios. This would require that the computing ratios be persisted either in the configuration files or elsewhere. Qin et al in 4 have shown that the computing ratio is job specific.

The computing ratios calculated based on job execution history can also be persisted and can be used for balancing. This is in contrast to the current approach where the computing ratios do not change automatically after they are calculated unless the user manually updates them before running his/her jobs.

There is scope for adjusting the computing ratios based on the algorithmic complexities of *map()* and *reduce()* automatically. Based on user input involving the complexity of the *map()* or *reduce()*, Hadoop can adjust the global computing ratios automatically to suit the new job. Adjusting them involves solving equations to arrive at the complexity adjusted computing ratios. This calculation can be automated by using an equation solver. Further the adjusted computing ratios can be used to balance the HDFS cluster.

The computing ratios arrived by either of the models can be used by Hadoop schedulers to decide which TaskTracker to choose while assigning tasks. As mentioned in related work, these ratios can be used in max-flow network problems directly as weights such that more tasks are scheduled on powerful machines than on weaker machines.Another generic use of the ratios would be in various kinds of load balancers in clouds. These ratios can easily be used to predict a node's behavior in terms of performance.

References

1. Mustafa Rafique, M., Rose, B., Butt, A.R., Nikolopoulos, D.S.: Supporting MapReduce on Large-Scale Asymmetric Multi-Core Clusters
2. Babu, S.: Towards automatic optimization of MapReduce programs. In: Proc. SoCC, pp. 137–142 (2010)
3. Isard, M., Prabhakaran, V., Currey, J., Wieder, U., Talwar, K., Goldberg, A.: Quincy: Fair Scheduling for Distributed Computing Clusters
4. Xie, J., Yin, S., Ruan, X., Ding, Z., Tian, Y., Majors, J., Manzanares, A., Qin, X.: Improving MapReduce performance through data placement in heterogeneous Hadoop clusters. In: Proc. IPDPS Workshops, pp. 1–9 (2010)
5. Gufler, B., Augsten, N., Reiser, A., Kemper, A.: Handling Data Skew in MapReduce. In: Proc. CLOSER, pp. 574–583 (2011)
6. Dean, J., Ghemawat, S.: MapReduce: Simplified Data Processing on Large Clusters. In: OSDI 2004: Sixth Symposium on Operating System Design and Implementation, San Francisco, CA (December 2004)
7. Hadoop, http://hadoop.apache.org/
8. Hadoop Single Node Setup, http://hadoop.apache.org/common/docs/r1.0.1/single_node_setup.html
9. Hadoop Cluster Setup, http://hadoop.apache.org/common/docs/r1.0.1/cluster_setup.html
10. Configuring Eclipse for Hadoop Development (a screencast), http://www.cloudera.com/blog/2009/04/configuring-eclipse-for-hadoop-development-a-screencast/
11. Amazon AWS, https://console.aws.amazon.com/console/home

Online Recommendation of Learning Path for an E-Learner under Virtual University

Prasenjit Basu[1], Suman Bhattacharya[2], and Samir Roy[3]

[1] Future Institute of Engineering and Management,
Sonarpur, Kolkata - 150, India
basuprasen@yahoo.com
[2] Techno India College of Technology,
Rajarhat, Kolkata - 153, India
suman93_2004@yahoo.co.in
[3] NITTTR(Kolkata), Block FC, Sector-III, Saltlake, Kolkata, India
samir.cst@gmail.com

Abstract. This paper presents a system to recommend a learning path to an e-learner of a virtual university according to the assessment of linear combination of learner specific parameters and system specific parameters. An online virtual university offers various courses. But learners of this university often face problems due to several constraints of the course. Online recommendation of learning path is an important research issue for virtual learning systems because no fixed learning path will be appropriate for all learners. Generally, inappropriate courseware leads a learner to cognitive overload or disorientation during learning processes, thus it results in reducing learning performance. The developed system implements a simple approach to recommend a learning path to guide a learner from any point of the course. Experimental result also supports the system by manifesting desired output.

Keywords: Learning path, curriculum sequencing, e-learning, virtual university, online recommendation.

1 Introduction

All recent advancements in Information and Communication Technology (ICT) have produced a great impact on every aspect of civilized life including education and training [1][2]. It is now applicable to different modes of education, e.g. distance education, web-based education, virtual university etc[3]. Moreover, researchers have explored different ways to enhance learning experience of self-paced e-learners in non-contact mode so that the lack of guidance from human tutor is compensated [4].

Over the past decades, e-Learning and the development of virtual campuses have evolved and developed at such a rapid rate that they are commonly accepted as an increasingly popular alternative to traditional face-to-face education [5][6]. The demand for higher education is expanding throughout the world. Various

C. Hota and P.K. Srimani (Eds.): ICDCIT 2013, LNCS 7753, pp. 126–136, 2013.

academic programs are being offered by the universities through e-learning to cater to the need of students from a wide range of backgrounds and geographical locations. The virtual university is an example of ICT enabled higher education system [7][8][9]. The term virtual university, has been used to denote quite a varied number of activities and institutions, which can, at the same time, be considered as a metaphor for the electronic, teaching, learning and research environment [10].

Generating Learning Path is widely explored by many researchers. Different approaches are applied in this regard. Learning Path Graph [19], Concept Map [11],[16] and Ontology [14][16] based learning can be categorized under Domain Modeling. Learning modules sequences are defined in term of competencies in such a way that sequencing problem can be represented like a classical Constraint Satisfaction Problem (CSP) [15]. In that paper constraint are described as learning resources such as pre-requisite and post requisite of a course. Genetic programming and Swarm intelligence techniques have applied for constructing adaptive learning path or solving CSP [12][17][15][23]. Some other approaches are also used to generate learning path. Statistical methods such as Bayesian probability theory [13][18] is one of them. Besides, automatic generation of Learning Path Algorithm [21], Petri Nets Based Approach [20][22] are also used. However intelligent search algorithm, such as Genetic Algorithm, Particle Swarm Optimization, Ant Colony Optimization etc. are highly computation intensive. These intelligent algorithms are best suited in NP complete or NP hard problems. Since the problem of curriculum sequencing or learning path generation is yet to be proved as a NP complete or NP hard problem, it is expected that efficient methods to tackle the said problem exists and can be found out. Therefore a method is needed which will be efficient and at the same time computationally not intensive. In this paper we present such an efficient method to solve the problem of curriculum sequencing.

This paper presents a system to provide customized learning path for an e-learner of a virtual university to help them achieve their learning objectives. In our approach, learners provide some personal choices or preferences to the system for a semester. Global data source also provides information related to an existing learner. The system computes Learning Path Indicator depending on those parameters. Ultimately it finds the recommended learning path for individual learner by employing the Learning Path Indicator. Rest of the paper is organized as follows. Section II describes methodology that has been used to describe the system. Section III proposes the system. Section IV furnishes implementation details. Finally, Section V concludes the paper.

2   Methodology

The paper presents a system that generates customized learning path for an e-learner of a virtual university. An e-learner being self-paced lacks human guidance to set his learning path that properly directs him towards the completion of the course.

The system considers a virtual university, which offers several courses. Each course contains different major and minor subjects and a minimum credit value. Major subjects are those, which are strongly related with the course objective and have been decided by the administrators of the course. Minor subjects, on the other hand, may not have any direct relations or associations with the course. Each subject of a course has a credit value and minimum effort time. There is a constraint for a learner regarding the earning of credit point. The constraint demands a minimum credit limit to be earned in the minor subjects and at the same time at the end of the course total credit must be greater or equal to the minimum credit required for the course. In the proposed system learner may also provide his preference list for some selected subjects.

The above stated considerations can be formulated by the following expressions

$$\sum_{i=1}^{n_{mjr}+n_{mnr}} C_{ri} \geq C_{grd} \tag{1}$$

Where,

n_{mjr} = number of major subjects opted by the learner
n_{mnr} = number of minor subjects opted by the learner
c_{ri} = credit point associated with each subject s_i
c_{grd} = Total credit point required for the whole course

If α and β are the minimum and maximum credit value to be earned by the major and minor subjects respectively then the expressions (2) and (3) show that major and minor subjects earn minimum and maximum credit points

$$\sum_{i=1}^{n_{mjr}} C_{ri} \geq \alpha \tag{2}$$

$$\sum_{i=1}^{n_{mnr}} C_{ri} \geq \beta \tag{3}$$

A subject of a course can have one or more prerequisites. It is necessary to clear all prerequisites of a subject before attempting it or sit for the examinations by choosing the subject. Now if a subject is a prerequisite for more than one subjects then by clearing the subject all dependent subjects become available for attempting. Therefore the numbers of dependent subjects imply that if a learner clears the subject then that many numbers (p_i) of dependent subjects may become available for the coming semesters.

Estimated effort time (T_i) is the time which is minimum requirement for general learner and has been set by the administrator. Similarly each subject has credit value, which has also been set by the administrator.

The proposed system formulates a function $f(i)$ for not cleared subjects that comprises all three parameters as shown in (4).

$$f(i) = p_i + T_i + c_{ri} \tag{4}$$

The above said function is applicable to each unclear subject. All the three parameters initial values are same for all learners and the system here introduces a learning path indicator (LPI) that is initially populated by the solutions generated by the function of the expression (4).

There are some other constraints whose value may vary from learner to learner, i.e. those constraints being different may be learner-specific. A learner being self-paced may not be able to give time properly or as much required for getting the required minimum duration. Again a previously attempted subject may also be in his choice. Moreover a learner may have his own preference list of subjects.

Learner dependent constraints constitute a fitness function $fit(i)$. According to the value of fitness function subjects show their appropriateness in the LPI listing. To compute fitness of a subject the fitness function requires values from three parameters. First one is affordable time (t_i) of a learner. Second parameter needs estimation of attempted subject, i.e. if the subject was previously attempted it gets a weightage in the fitness computation. Similarly if the subject is in preference list of the learner, it also gets a weightage. To compute these two values we define two more functions that return values if the subject was attempted earlier or the subject is in preference list.

$$f_{attmpt}(i) = \begin{cases} 0 & \text{if it is not attempted} \\ 1 & \text{if it is attempted} \end{cases} \tag{5}$$

$$f_{pref}(i) = \begin{cases} 0 & \text{if it is not in preference list} \\ 1 & \text{if it is in preference list} \end{cases} \tag{6}$$

The fitness function is calculated in the following way for subject s_i:

$$fit(i) = t_i + f_{atmpt}(i) + f_{pref}(i) \tag{7}$$

The function defined in (7) is calculated in every semester for each learner for all unclear subjects. Higher value in fitness function indicates that the subject is more appropriate to choose. Learning Path Indicator (LPI) is a linear combination of $f(i) and fit(i)$. It act as a controller that illustrates the position of the subject in the learning path and the calculation of LPI is done according to the following algorithm with order of complexity O(n):

1: Initialize p_i, T_i and C_{ri} for all unclear subjects
2: Repeat
3: calculate $f(i)$ according to (4)
4: compute $f_{atmpt}(i)$ and $f_{pref}(i)$ for the subject according to (5) and (6)
5: Evaluate fitness function fit (i) according to (7)
6: compute $LPI(i) := f(i) + fit(i)$

7: i := i + 1
8: Until i = Total Unclear Subjects

LPI(i) is used to generate the possible learning for the learner. According to the fitness value LPI(i) will be different for each subject si. The fitness value varies from learner to learner since it is dependent on constraints specific to a learner, but function f(i) is independent upon a learners choice. Better fitness value produces larger LPI value. Larger LPI indicates that the subject si associated with the LPI would be preferred at the top of the learning path, i.e. the learner will visit that node first.

2.1   Learning Path Generation

In order to select LPI, we adopted Forward Greedy Algorithm. There are two ways to use this algorithm. If the algorithm is used to improve an arbitrary prediction method then it is referred to as boosting and if it is applied to select relevant features then is referred to as forward feature selection[24][25]. Although a number of variations exist, they all share the basic form of greedily picking an additional feature at every step to aggressively reduce the squared error. This particular algorithm performs a full optimization using the selected basis function at each step, and is often referred to as Orthogonal Matching Pursuit or OMP. Incorporation of this algorithm helps us to deliver appropriate learning path.

3   Proposed System

The proposed system works for an individual learner appearing in a certain semester of course. The system also considers that the learner may not appear in certain semester or may use the system in every semester. There are two major components present in the proposed system: LPI generating component and Learning Path Generating (LPG) component. Moreover LPI generating component has three sub components. The job of those components is to generate LPI for each subject by incorporating system parameters and user given parameters. Number of dependent subjects, time required, credit value associated with the subject, the subject previously attempted or not are treated as system parameters and time affordable, subject in preference list are considered as user given parameters. Name of sub components are *BasicValueComputer, FitnessValue Computer* and *LPI ValueGenerator*. Information related to learner is stored in a global storage space. Global storage space that means the storage space is utilized by other departments like placement department, administration department etc. for accessing various learners information. Figure 1 represents basic building block of the system. The details of the components are described in the following paragraphs.

3.1 LPI Generating Component

This component accepts different learner specific and system specific parameters from learner and system respectively and provides output to LPG component. Here learner specific parameters are those parameters which vary from learner to learner but can be generated from system according to the System Global data of a learner. Again learner can also provide values for some parameters. For example, if a subject is in preference list of a learner then information will be provided by the learner, but information for previously attempted subjects will come from system, i.e. from global data store. The details of subcomponents are as follows.

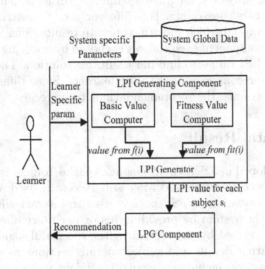

Fig. 1. Building Blocks of the Proposed System

1. *BasicValueComputer*:This component computes the value for function f(i) for each subject si according to the expression (4). The parameters that have been used here are system specific. Before generating the value of f(i) it calculates number of dependent subjects pi for the subject under consideration. To calculate p_i, it needs information for dependent subjects from system global data source. Similarly to include estimated effort time T_i for the subject and associated credit value cri for the same ,it requires the same data source. The system, before starting computation, first checks whether the subject is cleared or not. The computation is only carried out if the subject is not cleared. For the beginners thecomputation is done for all the subjects.

2. *FitnessValueComputer*: This component finds fitness value for each subject. It applies expression (7) for computing. It accepts three user specific parameters:1) t_i , 2) value generating from the expression (6) and 3) value approaching from expression (7). The parameter t_i denotes affordable time for the subject by

the learner. Expression (6) returns 0 if the subject is not in the preference list and expression (5) returns 0 if the subject is first time attempted.

3. *LPIGenerator*: LPI is generated by the basic values and fitness values. Minimum value that is populated to LPI for each subject is the basic value, i.e. when learner does not provide any information regarding affordable time or preference and when the subject is not attempted earlier. The output of LPI goes to LPG component to formulate learning path for individual learner.

3.2   LPG Component

The LPI generator component generates different indicator values from the function LPI(i) for each subject si for different unclear subjects. The values of LPI depend on the learners constraints. For different set of constraints the fitness value will be different and which in turn, generate results different set of LPI(i) values. In the LPG component each subject is chosen by applying forward greedy algorithm on those LPI values to find most suitable solution. The list of subject is then presented as recommendation to the learners. Since different users have different set of constraints, the recommendations to be received are different.

4   Experimental Result

The system is developed in J2EE environment. Apache Tomcat is used as virtual server to simulate web interface and Microsoft Access is used as the database to store learners information. A JSP page is used to interact with the learners. A learner accesses the system by providing his or her username and password. The information is verified by the system. After successful login learner gets a screen notifying learner details and subject details sections as shown in figure 2. Learner details section includes student id, student name, course name and semester id for which the learner is currently registered him. Subject details section includes information about those papers which are already cleared and information about those papers which are previously attempted.

Next screen is for accepting learners choice (figure 3). It allows a learner to choose subjects and to provide his affordable time. The list box only shows listing of unclear subject codes. A javascript code prevents a list box for displaying subject code(s) which are already selected. Moreover learner also provides his preference of subjects, if any. The whole information is submitted to the server and next screen appears to display learning path (figure 4).

The recommendation comes in tabular format. The subjects are listed in an order by maintaining serial numbers. Higher serial number indicates higher precedence. The subjects appear at the top of the list demand priority in clearance according to our recommendation.

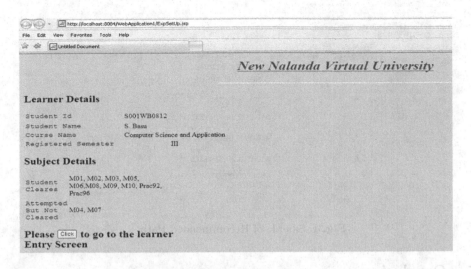

Fig. 2. Subject and Learner Information

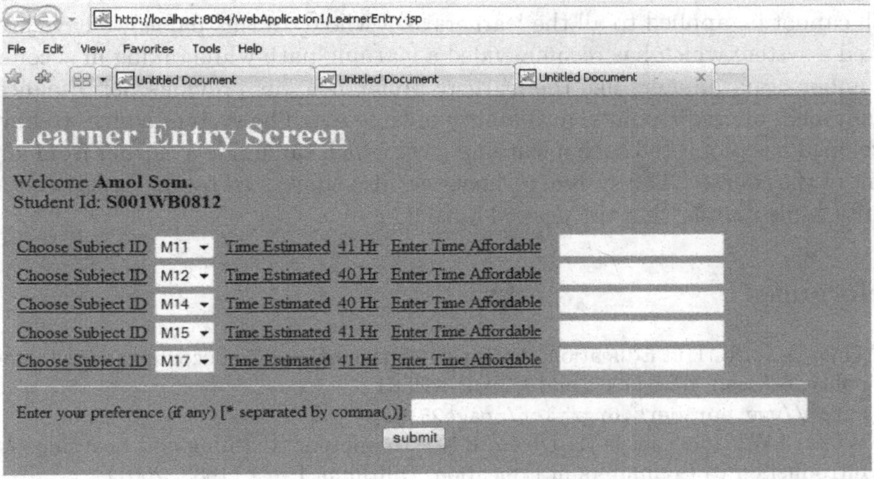

Fig. 3. Learner Entry Screen

Recommended Learning Path for **Amol Som**.
Student Id: **S001WB0812**.

Sl No	Suject Code	Subject Name	Credit Point	Estmated Time
1	M04	STATISTICE AND NUMERICALS	5	40
2	M07	COMPUTER ORGANISATION	5	40
3	M14	COMMUNICATION AND NETWORKING	6	45
4	M11	DATABASE MANAGEMENT SYSTEM	6	45
5	M12	AUTOMATA THEORY	5	40
6	M13	ARTIFICIAL INTELLIGENCE	5	40
7	M16	OBJECT ORIENTED PROGRAMMING AND UML	5	42

Fig. 4. Sample of Recommended Path

5   Conclusion

The urgency of virtual education is coming up in a rapid rate as it shows the prospect of removing the limitation of learning time, and space by providing a plethora of opportunities. But an online virtual university despite offering various courses may lead learners to confront several constraints often resulting in cognitive overload or disorientation during learning process. Online recommendation of learning path is, therefore a significant issue since any specific learning path cannot be applied to all the learners as a whole. In this paper we have presented a system which has recommended a learning path while taking in account a number of parameters like the learners preference, his previous performance, requirement of credit points, availability of time etc. The system which we have developed has pioneered such a learning path which can guide a learner from any point of the courses. The system is, however, also supported by the experimental results while manifesting the desired output.

References

1. Tinio, V.L.: ICT in Education. e-primers for the information economy, society and polity, e-Asean Task Force and UNDP-APDIP,
   http://www.eprimers.org/~ict/~page25.asp
2. Willis, J.W., Johnson, D.L., Dixon, P.N.: Computers, Teaching and Learning: An Introduction to Computers in Education. Dilithium Press (1983, 2001)
3. Kennewell, S.: Using Affordances and Constraints to Evaluate the use of Information Technology in Teaching and Learning. J. of Information Technology for Teacher Education 10(1 and 2), 101–116
4. Sleeman, D.J., Brown, J. (eds.): Introduction: Intelligent Tutoring System, in Intelligent Tutoring systems, pp. 1–11. Academic Press (1982)

5. Connolly, T.M., MacArthur, E., Stansfield, M.H., McLellan, E.: A quasi-experimental study of three online learning courses in computing. Computers and Education 49, 345–359 (2007)
6. Gunawardena, C.N., McIsaac, M.S.: Distance education. In: Jonassen, D.H. (ed.) Handbook of Research for Educational Communications and Technology, 2nd edn., pp. 355–396. LEA, Mahwah (2004)
7. The university: current challenges and opportunities Robin Mason. The Virtual University: Models and Messages Lessons from Case Studies, UNESCO 2006, pp. 49-70, ISBN 978-92-3-104026-9
8. Naidoo, V.: The changing venues for learning. In: Farrell, G. (ed.) The Changing Faces of Virtual Education, pp. 11–28. The Commonwealth of Learning, Vancouver (2001)
9. Sagna, O.: Les technologies de linformation et de la communication et le dveloppement social au Sngal: un tat des lieux. Paper PP TBS 1. Geneva: United Nations Research Institute for Social Development, Technology and Society Programme, pp. 13 (2001)
10. Van Dusen, W.D., et al.: A Manual for Conducting Student Attrition Studies, National Center for Higher Education Management Systems (1979)
11. Chen, C.-M., Peng, C.-J.: Personalized E-learning System based on Ontology-based Concept Map Generation Scheme. In: Seventh IEEE International Conference on Advanced Learning Technologies (ICALT 2007) (2007)
12. Hong, C.-M., Chen, C.-M., Chang, M.-H., Chen, S.-C.: Intelligent Web-based Tutoring system with Personalized Learning Path Guidance. In: 7th International Conference on Advanced Learning Technologies, ICALT 2007 (2007)
13. Marquez, J.M., Ortega, J.A., Gonzalez-Abril, L., Velasco, F.: Creating adaptive learning paths using Ant Colony Optimization and Bayesian Networks
14. Gascuena, J.M., Caballero, A.F., Gonzalez, P.: Domain Ontology for Personalized E- Learning in Educational Systems. In: Sixth IEEE International Conference on Advanced Learning Technologies , ICALT 2006 (2006)
15. de Marcos, L., Pages, C., Martnez, J.J., Gutierrez, J.A.L.: Competency-based Learning Object Sequencing using Particle Swarms. In: 19th IEEE International Conference on Tools with Artificial Intelligence (2007)
16. Chang, M., Chang, A., Heh, J.-S., Liu, T.-C.: Contextaware Learning Path planner 7(4) (April 2008)
17. Huang, M.-J., Huang, H.-S., Chen, M.-Y.: Constructing a personalized e-learning system based on genetic algorithm and casebased reasoning approach. Expert Systems with Applications 33, 551–564 (2007)
18. Anh, N.V., Ha, N.V., Dam, H.S.: Constructinga Bayesian Belief Network to Generate Learning Path in Adaptive Hypermedia System T.24, S.1 (2008)
19. Karampiperis, P., Sampson., D.: Adaptive Learning Resources Sequencing in Educational Hypermedia Systems. Educational Technologies and Society 8(40), 128–147
20. Gao, S., Zhang, Z.I., Hawryszkiewycz, I.: Supporting Adaptive Learning in Hypertext Environment: A High Level Timed Petri Net Based Approach. In: 5th IEEE International Conference on Advanced Learning Technologies 2005, pp. 735–739 (2005)
21. Carchiolo, V., Longheu, A., Malgeri, M., Mangioni, G.: Automatic generation of learning paths. In: Proceedings of the 10th International Conference IEEE on Electronic, Circuits and Systems, vol. 3, pp. 1236–1239 (2003)

22. Lin, W.H., Shih, T.K., Chang, W.-C., Yang, C.-H.: A Petri Nets-based Approach to Modeling SCORM Sequence. In: IEEE International Conference on Multimedia and Expo, ICME 2004, vol. 2, pp. 1247–1250 (2004)
23. Yang, Y.J., Wu, C.: An attributes based ant colony system for adaptive learning object recommendation. Expert Systems with Application 36, 3034–3047 (2009)
24. Zhang, T.: Adaptive Forward-Backward Greedy Algorithm for Sparse Learning with Linear Models. IEEE Transactions on Information Theory 57(7), 4689–4708
25. Tropp., J.A.: Greed is good: Algorithmic results for sparse approximation. IEEE Trans. Info. Theory 50(10), 2231–2242 (2004)

A Parallel 2-Approximation NC-Algorithm for Range Assignment Problem in Packet Radio Networks

Bijaya Kishor Bhatta[1] and D. Pushparaj Shetty[2]

[1] School of Math.-Stat-Computer Science,
Utkal University, Bhubaneswar 751004, India
[2] Computer Science and Application Group
Department of Mathematics
Indian Institute of Technology Delhi, Hauz Khas
New Delhi 110016, India
bijaya.kishor@gmail.com, prajshetty@maths.iitd.ac.in

Abstract. Given a set of sensors in a plane or in higher dimension, the strong minimum energy topology problem is to assign transmission range to each of the sensor nodes, so as to minimize the total power consumption. Here the constraint is that the network must be strongly connected. This problem is known to be NP-hard. As this problem has lot of practical application, several approximation algorithms and heuristics has been proposed. There exist a MST based 2-approximation algorithm for this problem having running time complexity of $O(n^2 \log n)$. In this paper we propose a simple parallel version of the 2-approximation algorithm. We prove that this parallel algorithm is a NC-algorithm and is also cost optimal for a dense graph. We prove that the algorithm has a time complexity $O(\log n)$ and work complexity $O(n^2)$ when the number of processor used is $O(n^2)$.

Keywords: Wireless Sensor Networks, Minimum Spanning Tree, Approximation algorithm, NC-algorithm, Multihop Packet Radio Network.

1 Introduction

A *multi-hop* Packet Radio Network is a set of radio stations located on a geographical region that are able to communicate by transmitting and receiving radio signals. Its importance has been increased due to the fact that there exist situations where the installation of the traditional wired network is impossible and in some cases even if possible but requires high cost. Many application and important features of wireless sensor networks can be found in an excellent survey paper [2]. Several variations of routing, broadcasting, and scheduling problem on radio network are discussed in [1,3,15]. A radio network is a finite collection of radio stations R located on a geographical area which can communicate between each other using their transmitting and receiving signal power. The range

C. Hota and P.K. Srimani (Eds.): ICDCIT 2013, LNCS 7753, pp. 137–144, 2013.
© Springer-Verlag Berlin Heidelberg 2013

assigned for each radio station $r \in R$ is given by $range(r)$, which is a positive real number. A signal transmitted from source s with power P_s is attenuated by a factor

$$P_r = \frac{P_s}{dist(s,t)^\alpha}$$

where $dist(s,t)$ is the Euclidean distance between the nodes s and t [7], and α is the *distance-power gradient*, which may vary from 1 to 6 depending on the various environmental factor. The message can be correctly decoded only when $P_r \geq \gamma$. Here constant $\gamma \geq 1$ is the *transmission quality parameter*. In this paper we assume the ideal case where $\alpha = 2$ and $\gamma = 1$. A sensor node can communicate directly with the nodes which are located within its transmission range. It uses *multi-hop* communication, to reach nodes outside its transmission range. Here intermediate nodes are used to relay the transmission until the destination node is reached.

1.1 Preliminaries and Problem Statement

Let $S = s_1, s_2, \ldots, s_n$ be a set of n radio stations placed in a Euclidean plane. Here $d(x,y)$ is the Euclidean distance from node x to node y. Let R be the range assignment for the set of nodes in S be written as $R = r(s_1), r(s_2), \ldots, r(s_n)$ where $r(s_i)$ is the range assigned to the radio station $s_i \in S$ Given a range assignment R,the following two kinds of graphs are defined.

- ▸ $\overrightarrow{G_R} = (S, A_R)$ is a directed graph, for range assignment R where the radio stations present in S represents the vertices and A_R represents the edge set, where $E_R = \{(s_i, s_j) | d(s_i, s_j)^2 \leq r(s_i)\}$. In other words, a directed edge (x, y) indicates that y is within the range of x.
- ▸ $G_R = (S, E_R)$ is a directed graph, for range assignment R where the radio stations present in S represents the vertices and E_R represents the edge set, where an edge $(u, v) \in E_R$ iff node u can send date to node v and v can send to u. i.e. $\{u, v\} \in E_R \iff \min\{R_u, R_v\} \geq d(u, v)^2$. In other words G_R contains only bidirectional edges.

The problem of finding a subgraph for a given network communication graph such that some specific network properties are satisfied is called *Topology Control Problem* in wireless sensor networks. The specific network property could be connectivity, minimum degree, minimum interference etc. The topology control problem is studied in detail (see [9,15]). One of foremost goals of topology control problem is to minimize the power consumption of the wireless network. So range assignment problem falls under the domain of topology control problem.

Depending upon the connectivity predicate the following range assignment problems are defined [8].

- ▸ Simple Connectivity or symmetric all-to-all communication: G_R must be connected.
- ▸ Strong Connectivity or all-to-all communication: $\overrightarrow{G_R}$ must be strongly connected.

▸ Broadcast or one-to-all communication: Given a source node $s \in V, \overrightarrow{G_R}$ must contain a directed spanning tree rooted at s.

It may be observed that the above ordering is in the decreasing order of strength. A range assignment is said to be complete if and only if $\overrightarrow{G_R}$ is strongly connected [12] as explained in strong connectivity predicate above. Bidirectional edges are preferred in wireless sensor networks mainly because the messages sent over a link are to be acknowledged [4]. The Strong Minimum Energy Topology (SMET) problem is an important topology control problem studied in [4,12] which follows the simple connectivity predicate defined above. The *SMET problem* in wireless sensor networks is to find an assignment of transmit powers to each sensor node such that the power consumption is minimum and the resulting topology is connected with only bidirectional links. A MST based heuristic for this problem is given by Kirousis *et al.* [12]. Let T be a spanning tree from a given network communication graph $G = (V, E, w)$, where w is the cost function. Let $P_T(v) = \max\{w(uv)|uv \in E(T)\}$ and $P(T) = \sum_{v \in V} P_T(v)$. Now the SMET problem reduces to finding MST T of $G = (V, E, w)$ such that $P(T)$ is minimum.

Chen *et al.* [4] gave a incremental power greedy heuristic and showed by simulation that their heuristic outperforms the MST based algorithm. Panda and Shetty [16] gave a Kruskal-incremental based heuristic and showed that this heuristic works better compared to both MST based algorithm and Prim-incremental heuristics.

NC-Algorithm: The class NC is the set of languages decidable in parallel time $T(n, p(n)) = O(log^{O(1)}n)$ with $p(n) = O(n^{O(1)})$ processors.

In this paper we give a parallel algorithm to the SMET problem. We have analyzed our algorithm and found that it is a NC- algorithm. We prove that it is also cost optimal for a dense graph. The rest of the paper is organized as follows. In section 2, we propose our parallel algorithm. In Section 3, the complexity analysis of the algorithm is discussed. Section 4 contains the summary conclusion and scope for future studies.

2   Algorithm

In this section we propose our parallel algorithm for the SMET problem which is given in [4]. The *FindMax* is the main module which computes the maximum adjacent edge to any given vertex. The corresponding algorithm is given in Algorithm 2.

2.1   Explanation

Before discussing to the main algorithm let us discuss the *FindMax* algorithm. This algorithm takes all the adjacent nodes of a given node u as input and returns the cost corresponding to the maximum incident edge on node u. Here we are using the sequence reduction approach [11]. During construction of the node we take n number of adjacent nodes where n is divisible by two, (if number

Input : A multi-hop mobile radio network in two or in higher dimension.
Output: A spanning tree having with minimum total energy consumption.
1 **for** *each i = 0 to n − 1 parallel* **do**
2   **for** *each j = 0 to n parallel* **do**
3        $P_{ij} = d[i][j]$

4 Compute the MST T using parallel approach.
5 **for** *each i = 0 to n − 1 parallel* **do**
6   max $= FindMax(i, adj(i))$
7   range(i)=max
8 Output $P_T(v) \forall v$ and $P(T)$

Algorithm 1: SMET-parallel

Input : A node u and all $adj(u)$
Output: cost c such that $c = \max(uv) \forall v \in adj(u)$
1 Initialization : $P[1 \ldots n] = \emptyset$
2 **for** *each i = 1 to n parallel* **do**
3     $P_i = u_i$
4 **for** *each h = 1 to* $\log n$ **do**
5   **for** *each i = 1 to* $n/2^h$ *parallel* **do**
6        $P_i = max(P_{2*i}, P_{2*i-1})$

7 Output $max = P_1$

Algorithm 2: $FindMax(u, adj(u))$

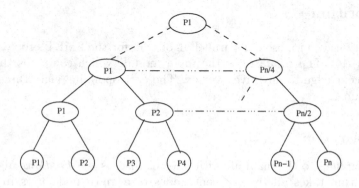

Fig. 1. Construction of tree for the FindMax Algorithm

of adjacent nodes is odd, then we add a dummy node so as to make it divisible by two). Now assign each of these nodes to processors as shown in Fig 1.

The processor P_i is used to store the distance from the node u to the adjacent node v_i, that is $P_i = d(u, v_i) \forall 1 \leq i \leq n$. The maximum among processors P_{2i} and P_{2i-1} for $1 \leq i \leq n/2$ is computed and stored in the processor P_i in upper layer. This steps are performed in a hierarchical manner, in every step there is a reduction of processors by a factor of two. This procedure continues until one node exists. In the final step the processor P_1 holds the maximum element, so the $FindMax$ method return the value present in the final step at the processor P_1. The Figure 1 captures this idea.

We can clearly see that the $FindMax$ algorithm time complexity is nothing but the height of the tree (only step 4 is responsible for the time complexity since step 5 is done in parallel). Let h be the height of the tree, then the time complexity for this $FindMax$ algorithm is $O(h) = O(\log n)$ since we are using n number of processors.

Now let us go for the main algorithm, this algorithm takes multi-hop mobile radio networks where nodes are placed either in two or in higher dimension. The purpose of this algorithm is to assign the range to all the nodes in such a manner that the network should be fully connected and the energy consumption by this network should be minimized. In this algorithm we first model the given network as a complete weighted graph where the vertices represent the sensors and link uv is present if u and v are within the communication range of each other. From the steps 1-3 of Algorithm 1 it is clear that the number of processor required is n^2 The Table 1 shows the assignment of distance to the processors.

Table 1. Initialization of the n^2 processors

$P_{00} = d[0,0]$	$P_{01} = d[0,1]$	...	...	$P_{0n} = d[0,n]$
$P_{10} = d[1,0]$	$P_{11} = d[1,1]$	...	...	$P_{1n} = d[1,n]$
...	...	...	...	...
...	...	...	...	...
$P_{n0} = d[n,0]$	$P_{n1} = d[n,1]$	...	...	$P_{nn} = d[n,n]$

Here the processor P_{ij} stores the distance between the node i and j that is P_{ij} = $d[i,j]$ for all i and j between 0 to n. Now find the MST from the given complete graph using the method given in [5]. The time complexity of this parallel MST algorithm is $O(\log n)$. After finding the MST, we assign the range to each node by using the $FindMax$ Algorithm , which returns the maximum distance node from the given node and we assign that distance as the range of the node. In similar manner we can assign the range for all the nodes parallel.

3   Analysis of Algorithm

In this section we analyze the time complexity, work complexity and the number of processor used in our algorithm. Let us calculate the Time complexity first:

3.1   Time Complexity

In the given Algorithm 1, the steps 1-3 are responsible for constructing a complete graph from the given nodes that is assigning the distance between two nodes to one processor. The assignment takes $O(1)$ time and all the assignments are done in parallel. Hence in Algorithm 1 steps 1-3 takes $O(1)$ time. In step 4 we find the MST from the constructed complete graph. Here we use the parallel approach for finding the MST. It is proved in [5] that the construction of the MST using parallel approach takes $O(\log n)$ time. Hence step 4 takes $O(\log n)$ time. Now in steps 5-7 we find the range for all the nodes using $FindMax$ algorithm. We have already seen that $FindMax$ algorithm returns the range of a node in $O(\log n)$ time. Since all the nodes can call the $FindMax$ in parallel, the time complexity for the steps 5-7 takes $O(\log n)$ time. Hence the total time complexity of the algorithm is

$$T(n) = O(1) + O(\log n) + O(\log n)$$

$$T(n) = O(\log n)$$

From above equations it is clear that the total time complexity of Algorithm 1 is $O(\log n)$. Since the time complexity is in $O(\log n)$ so we can conclude that our algorithm is a NC-algorithm.

3.2   Work Complexity

In our Algorithm 1, the step 1 has the work complexity $O(n)$, as here the number of iterations is n. The step 2 also takes $O(n)$ iterations. So the work complexity of steps 1-3 is $O(n^2)$. In step 4 we compute MST using the parallel MST algorithm. We can find from [5] that the number of operation for parallel MST is $O((m + n)(\log n))$ for EREW PRAM algorithm where n is the number of vertices in the graph and m is the number of edges in the given graph. The CRCW PRAM algorithm has $O((m + n) \log \log n)$ number of operations. But for dense graph the number of operation is $O(n^2)$. Now we can easily say that the number of operation for the Algorithm 2, that is $FindMax$ is $O(n)$. Hence the number of operations performed in steps 5-7 is $O(n^2)$. Now the total number of operations required for dense graphs is given by :

$$W(n) = O(n^2) + O(n^2) + O(n^2)$$

$$W(n) = O(n^2)$$

We have seen for a dense graph our algorithm is cost optimal since the best sequential algorithm time complexity till now is $O(n^2)$. Hence it is cost optimal for dense graph.

3.3   Number of Processor

When we analyze Algorithm 1, we can clearly see that it takes $O(n^2)$ number of processor, as steps 1-3 takes n^2 number of processors. For computation of the MST it takes $O(n^2)$ number of processors for a dense graph. And we can see that the $FindMax$ algorithm takes maximum n number of processors. Hence steps 5-7 take $O(n^2)$ number of processors. Hence the number of processor required for this algorithm is $O(n^2)$.

4   Conclusion and Future Work

In this paper, we proposed the parallel algorithm of the complete range assignment problem in two or higher dimension. Here we have proved that our algorithm is cost optimal as well as a NC-algorithm. The Algorithm 1 is a 2-approximation algorithm as the corresponding sequential algorithm is proved to be a 2-approximation algorithm [12]. The algorithm uses $O(n^2)$ number of processors. A further in depth analysis may reduce the number of processor and can achieve the same NC as well as cost optimal parallel algorithm for the given problem . There is also a scope to improve the approximation ratio by careful analysis. In this paper we only focus on the two or higher dimension range assignment problem but parallel algorithm for a one-dimensional linear radio network where the sensors nodes are located along a straight line can also be studied.

References

1. Arikan, E.: Some Complexity Result about Packet Radio Network. IEEE Transactions on Information Theory IT-30, 681–685 (1984)
2. Akyildiz, I.F., Su, W., Sankarasubramaniam, Y., Cayirci, E.: Wireless sensor networks: a survey. Computer Networks 38(4), 393–422 (2002)
3. Alon, N., Bar-Noy, A., Linial, N., Peleg, D.: A lower bound for radio broadcast. Journal of Computer and System Science 43, 290–298 (1991)
4. Cheng, X., Narahari, B., Simha, R., Cheng, M., Liu, D.: Strong minimum energy topology in wireless sensor networks:NP-Completeness and Heuristics. IEEE Transactions on Mobile Computing 2(3), 248–256 (2003)
5. Chong, K.W., Han, Y., Igarashi, Y., Lam, T.W.: Improving the efficiency of parallel minimum spanning tree algorithms. Discrete Applied Mathematics 126, 33–54 (2003)
6. Chong, K.W.: Finding minimum spanning trees on the EREW PRAM. In: Proceedings of the 1996 International Computer Symposium (ICS 1996), Taiwan, pp. 7–14 (1996)
7. Clementi, A.E.F., Penna, P., Silvestri, R.: On the Power Assignment Problem in Radio Networks. Mobile Networks and Applications 9, 125–140 (2000)
8. Fuchs, B.: On The Hardness Of Range Assignment Problems. Electronic Colloquium On Complexity, Report No. 113 (2005)
9. Gonzales, T. (ed.): Handbook of Approximation Algorithms and Metaheuristics, ch. 67. Chapman and Hall CRC (2007)

10. Goto, H., Hasegawa, Y., Tanaka, M.: Efficient Scheduling Focusing on the Duality of MPL Representatives. In: Proc. IEEE Symp. Computational Intelligence in Scheduling (SCIS 2007), pp. 57–64. IEEE Press (December 2007), doi:10.1109/SCIS.2007.357670
11. Grama, A., Karypis, G., Kumar, V., Gupta, A.: Introduction to Parallel Computing, 2nd edn. Pearson, Addison Wesley (2003)
12. Kirousis, L.M., Kranakis, E., Krizane, D., Pele, A.: Power consumption in packet radio networks. Theoretical Computer Science 243, 289–305 (2000)
13. Lloyd, E.L., Liu, R., Marathe, M.V., Ramanathan, R., Ravi, S.S.: Algorithmic aspects of topology control problems for Ad Hoc Networks. Mobile Networks and Applications 10, 19–34 (2005)
14. Santi, P.: Topology Control in wireless ad hoc and sensor Networks. ACM Computing Surveys 37(2), 164–194 (2005)
15. Santi, P.: Topology Control in wireless ad hoc and sensor Networks. Wiley Inter Science, Chichester (2005)
16. Panda, B.S., Pushparaj Shetty, D.: An Incremental Power Greedy Heuristic for Strong Minimum Energy Topology in Wireless Sensor Networks. In: Natarajan, R., Ojo, A. (eds.) ICDCIT 2011. LNCS, vol. 6536, pp. 187–196. Springer, Heidelberg (2011)

An Efficient Localization of Nodes
in a Sensor Network Using Conflict Minimization
with Controlled Initialization

Himangshu Ranjan Borah and Himkalyan Bordoloi

Department of Computer Science and Engineering
National Institute of Technology, Silchar
Silchar, India
{himangshu.nits,himkalyan89}@gmail.com

Abstract. Node localization in Wireless Sensor Networks has been a crucial problem in its domain. It refers to finding the absolute co-ordinates of the nodes in a network using some available information. In this paper we present a novel approach to solve the localization problem using controlled initial placement of nodes followed by conflict minimization. We use the actual location of certain nodes in the deployment field (anchor nodes), along with the neighborhood information of all the nodes to calculate the unknown locations. First we select a subset of nodes with healthy no. of anchors in neighborhood. These are then initialized at the mean locations of their neighboring anchors. Finally we apply conflict minimization (guided by a cost function) on these initial estimates to get their most probable actual locations. The process is executed iteratively, with placed nodes being considered as anchor nodes. The proposed scheme is tested using simulation on a sensor network of 400 nodes showing that it gives accurate and consistent location estimates of the nodes, and mitigates some of the basic shortcomings of previous approaches. It has a no. of advantages among which scalability, high convergence probability towards solution and less time complexity are most notable.

Keywords: Anchor Nodes, Conflict Minimization, Simulated Annealing, Neighborhood Information, Centralized Localization, Distributed Localization, Anchor Neighborhood.

1   Introduction

The tremendous advances of micro electromechanical systems (MEMS), computing and communication technology have favored the emergence of massively distributed, wireless sensor networks (WSN) consisting of hundreds and thousands of nodes. Each node is able to sense the environment, perform simple computations and communicate with each other or to the central unit. In a practical sensor network, there will be a large number of sensor nodes densely deployed at positions which may not be predetermined. In most sensor network applications, the information gathered by these micro-sensors will be meaningless unless the location from where the information is

C. Hota and P.K. Srimani (Eds.): ICDCIT 2013, LNCS 7753, pp. 145–156, 2013.

obtained is known. But to keep track of the location of thousands of nodes is almost impractical. Also, we can't afford to use GPS (Global Positioning System) because of high power consumption and other problems like reachability. All these factors make automatic localization capabilities highly desirable in sensor networks. Most of the localization techniques are centered on the concept of Anchor-nodes or Beacon-nodes [1]. These are the nodes in the networks whose absolute positions are known at any time (Using GPS kind of technique or its pre-determined). The other nodes use this information along with their neighborhood information to locate their own coordinates.

Since most applications depend on a successful localization, i.e. to compute their positions in some fixed coordinate system, it is of great importance to design efficient localization algorithms. In large scale ad hoc networks, node localization can assist in routing [1]. It can also be used in hospital environments to keep track of equipment, patients, doctors and nurses [1].

This paper presents a new approach of solving the localization problem by modeling it as a constraint based optimization problem. Our work is similar to the line of research done on the same problem by using Simulated Annealing technique [2][6][10]. We present a distant variant of the aforementioned optimization paradigm that has highly satisfactory results, at the same time removing some of the basic problems of the previous approaches, along with some added advantages.

The rest of the paper is organized as follows. The section 2 describes the related work and a quick overview of our model. Section 3 explains the conflict minimization approach used here. Section 4 illustrates the algorithm in details. The rest of the section is dedicated to results of the experiments and conclusion of the paper.

2   Related Work

The localization problem has been one of the very basic problems in the field of Wireless Sensor Networks and is under recent research topics. We can find a survey on the existing localization techniques in [1]. The trivial approaches include hyperbolic trilateration, triangulation, maximum likelihood estimation etc. [1] where we use the known locations of the anchor nodes to locate the unknown points by some geometrical analysis. Basically, the research on localization in wireless sensor networks can be classified into two broad categories, namely **centralized localization** and **distributed localization**. Centralized localization is based on migration of inter-node ranging and connectivity data to a sufficiently powerful central base station and then the migration of resulting locations back to respective nodes. The advantage of centralized algorithms are that it eliminates the problem of computation in each node, at the same time the limitations lie in the communication cost of moving data back to the base station. As representative proposals in this category [5], [6], [7] are explained in greater detail.   In [5] the authors present a centralized algorithm called MDS-MAP which is one of the most popular ones. In [6] the authors propose an innovative approach based on **Simulated Annealing** to localize the sensor nodes in a centralized manner. They modeled the placement of the nodes in terms of a cost function. The non-anchor nodes are given an arbitrary imaginary location first and then distance mismatches with original distance are removed with the help of cost function minimization using simulated annealing. But one very dangerous error appeared in their approach which is known as *flip ambiguity* as explained in [12] [16]. They also provided a method for the removal of *flip ambiguity*. Other papers like [10] [11] etc. presents some refined versions of the simulated annealing approach. Among the other optimization based approaches, authors in [13] approached the problem using convex optimization based on semi-definite programming. The connectivity of the network was represented as a set of convex localizing constraints for the optimization problem. Ref. [14] extended this technique by taking the non-convex inequality constraints and relaxed the problem to a semi-definite program. Tzu-Chen Liang improved the method described in [14] further by using a gradient-based local search method [15].

On the other hand, Beacon-based distributed algorithms, Relaxation-based distributed algorithms [3] [4], Coordinate system stitching based distributed algorithms [8] [9] are some of the most popular **distributed approaches**. In case of this approach, all the computational part is performed in the nodes itself which naturally increases the overhead on the nodes. It may be observed that most of the successful algorithms of this problem are basically distance based approaches where each non-anchor node has to know the distance from its neighbors. Here we define the neighborhood in terms of the transmission range **R**. The **neighborhood information** we are talking about is nothing but the true distances between the nodes which can be obtained by using any of the available techniques like Received Signal Strength Indicator (RSSI), Time based methods (ToA, TDoA), Angle-of-Arrival (AoA) etc. as discussed in [1]. This neighborhood information is the heart of the localization algorithms.

Simulated Annealing has been applied in many of the centralized algorithms. The idea of applying this technique in sensor localization problem for the first time was introduced in [6] and due to its desirable results in comparison with other centralized techniques, it was more acceptable. Despite its advantages over other solutions, there are some disadvantages. The most important disadvantage of this algorithm is the time-consuming calculations that grow with the size of network and consequently the localization process takes more time as well. Another disadvantage that we found was that it eliminated some of the nodes in the field as non-localizable because of the absence of sufficient anchor nodes in their neighborhood. Moreover, if we use random initial placement like the one used in [6] and other related publications, there is a certain probability that the algorithm will never converge to a solution.

In our paper, we present an architecture based on the optimization modeling. We start with a no. of nodes with some as initial **anchor nodes** (whose real coordinates are known beforehand). Then we prepare the neighborhood information of all the nodes with the help of the distance measuring techniques mentioned above. Initially, we find out the **anchor neighborhood** (no. of anchors present in the neighborhood) of all the non-anchor nodes. Then we select out the nodes with **anchor neighborhood** greater than a certain **threshold**. Those nodes are then placed in some hypothetical locations determined by the taking **mean** of the neighboring anchor locations. This controlled initial placement helps in ensuring the convergence of the algorithm within a very small no. of iterations. Those selected nodes form the **list** of nodes to be processed in the current pass (called *select nodes*). Then we use a conflict minimization approach similar to simulated annealing to determine the position of the selected non-anchor nodes. Starting with a list of initial anchor nodes, we gradually add the newly placed nodes to this list and repeat the process for the rest of the nodes. Thus we can even reach the nodes which are not in the neighborhood of any of the initial anchor nodes which is the main flavor of our approach. Finally we achieve a configuration which almost correctly mimics the true positions of the nodes. The main advantages of our approach over already implemented approaches are...

- Time complexity is less than that of simulated annealing based techniques.
- The approach is highly scalable because it uses one by one processing of the nodes while placing unlike a whole board approach of simulated annealing.
- No node needs to be eliminated before processing as non-localizable nodes because of the iterative update of the anchor nodes' list. This was a severe drawback that we observed in one of the similar earlier approach reported in [6].
- Controlled initial placement of the nodes helps in ensuring the convergence of the algorithm.

Since the algorithm is centralized, it enjoys the access to estimated locations and neighborhood information of all localizable nodes in the system.

3   Localization Based on Conflict Minimization

The conflict minimization using randomized search is a very effective and emerging methodology for solving the constraint based optimization problems. It has been applied in many fields where the problems may be modeled in an optimization platform. One good example of using conflict minimization in solving constraint based optimization can be found in [17] where the authors use it to solve the famous N-Queens problem. The idea is to start at an initial configuration of the problem and randomly perturbing the configuration to achieve local or global minima of the associated cost function. The cost function here means the condition depending on which we will be gradually moving towards the solution. The conflict minimization is very much effective in the problems where an exhaustive parsing through the solution space is either intractable or infeasible, both in terms of memory and space. It differs from normal gradient based search in the way it used randomization concept. This technique outpaces the performance of other related methods like simulated annealing, especially with regard to scalability.

The theory of conflict minimization can be well applied to the problem of node localization. We first define a cost function that depends on the neighborhood information of each node. The neighborhood information here is the distances between the nodes as stated already. Then we start with an initial configuration of the nodes (in a controlled manner as described above) and try to perturb the configuration randomly by processing each of the unplaced nodes at a time. We move in the direction of the decreasing cost function up to a certain no. of iterations and finally settle the node in a position with minimum cost. We also use an iterative anchor nodes update policy that helps to position the non-anchor nodes that are not in direct contact of the initial anchor nodes.

Let us consider a sensor network of total n nodes, m anchor nodes with known locations and n-m non-anchor nodes with unknown locations. For simplicity, let the nodes lie on a plane such that node i has location (xi, yi). All the nodes have the ability to measure the distances between them and their one hop neighbors which may be used to find out the actual cost adjacency matrix of the nodes (measured distances,). This matrix is the only information that we have along with coordinates of the anchor nodes, which acts as the neighboring information. Again for a particular placement of the nodes in the board, we will have another cost adjacency matrix calculated from those estimated coordinates (estimated distances). These two distances may be used to formulate a cost function [6] to use with the localization problem. The cost function is given below in (1).

$$\text{Cost Function, CF} = \sum_{i=m+1}^{n} \sum_{j \in N_i} (D_{ij} - d_{ij})^2 \tag{1}$$

Where N_i is the set of all the anchor nodes present in the neighborhood of the node i, d_{ij} is the measured distance between node j and j, and $D_{ij} = \sqrt{(X_i - X_j)^2 - (Y_i - Y_j)^2}$ is the estimated distance based on the current estimated coordinates of the nodes i and j, i.e. (X_i, Y_i) and (X_j, Y_j). Here in the case of estimated distance, (X_j, Y_j) always corresponds to some anchor node and hence its values are accurately known. The cost function (1) provides a quantitative measure of the goodness of a coordinate estimate. Our aim is to process node by node for all the non-anchor nodes and find the local minima of the cost function for each using the conflict minimization scheme described above. We save the location estimate giving the minimal value of the cost function in each case as the final location of that node.

4   The Algorithm

In an abstract view, the algorithm may be divided into two subroutines, which are called from a main program to get the results. They are described below:

4.1   Subroutine 1: *makeNextInitialConfig()*:

Below we describe the first subroutine named *makeNextInitialConfig()*. The data structure *finalLocs* contains the locations of the placed nodes. Initially it contains the locations of the anchor nodes and all other nodes are set to zero. *tempAnchor* is the list containing the anchor nodes at a particular pass. It is initialized with initial anchor nodes and keeps on growing as new locations are determined. The output *initialConfig* contains the initial placement of the selected nodes as calculated by the algorithm. The program basically find out the anchor neighborhood rich points and places them in somewhat nearby positions (i.e. the estimated locations) to their actual locations so that the next phase of the algorithm can correct the remaining ambiguity of placement.

```
FUNCTION makeNextInitialConfig ()

INPUTS: finalLocs, tempAnchor, neighbours, size, thresh
old
OUTPUTS: selNodes, initialConfig

FOR I = 1: size

IF (node i is anchor node)
CONTINUE;
ELSE
Find the number of anchor nodes present in the neighbor-
hood of i(anchor neighborhood)
END IF

Enter nodes i into the list selNodes if it's anchor
neighborhood is greater than threshold.
END FOR

IF (selNodes is empty)
Reduce the threshold by one and make a recursive call.
END IF

Initialize the initialConfig to all zeros.
Copy the anchor locations to the initialConfig from fi-
nalLocs.

FOR i=1: size

IF (node i is in the selNodes)

Find out the coordinates of the anchor points in its
neighborhood.

Select a fix no. of anchors among them so that the list
contains maximum possible initial anchor nodes. (The list
is called anchorSubset)

Estimate the location of node i by averaging the coordi-
nates of the selected anchor nodes.

Enter the estimated location to initialConfig.
END IF
END FOR
END FUNCTION
```

4.2   Subroutine 2: *conflictMinimised()*:

In this section, we describe the pseudo code of the second subroutine. This calculates the final estimates of the location of the non-anchor nodes. It processes each node in the *selNodes* data structure and finds the probable estimate of their true location using the conflict minimization approach. Starting from the initial placement of the node, it successively disturbs its location in random directions to see whether any improvement in the cost function is attained. Finally it settles down to a coordinate estimate which gives the minimum local value of the cost function (CF) within P iterations. Finally it stores the newly calculated location into the *finalLocs* data structure. The matrix named *costAdjacencyMat* is the neighborhood distance containing matrix (actual distances calculated using distance measuring techniques). During the process we keep on decrementing the value of D so as to increase the probability of converging into the solution.

```
FUNCTION conflictMinimised()

INPUTS: costAdjacencyMat, initialConfig, D, beta,P,size,
neighbours, tempAnchor, selNodes, finalLocs
OUTPUTS: finalLocs

SET Cost Function (CFold) =INFINITY;

FOR each node in the selNodes

SET D to initial value.

FOR I = 1: P

Perturb the estimated location of the node (as found in
initialConfig) in any random direction within a range of
D.
Calculate the cost function (CF) for the new estimated
location with respect to a subset of neighboring anchors
(same anchorSubset that was calculated during the initial
placement in the first subroutine.).

IF (CFnew <= CFold)

Keep the current perturbation.
CFold = CFnew;
D = beta*D;

ELSE
Revert the changes.
END IF
```

```
END FOR
Update the locations of the just processed node in the
matrix finalLocs.

END FOR
END FUNCTION
```

Finally, we combine the above two subroutines as shown below in the main program. After the execution of main (), we find the *finalLocs* containing all the estimated locations of the nodes, which is the required output of the whole algorithm. The success of the algorithm lies centrally in the idea of controlled initial placement of the nodes, unlike the haphazard random initialization of the previous approaches. Though some of the authors like [10] used controlled trilateration based initial placement, it was computationally expensive because it needed rigorous floating point calculations involving square and square root finding. In our simple averaging concept, those disadvantages are almost eliminated.

```
FUNCTION main ()
WHILE (All the nodes are not anchor nodes)

Calculate the neighborhood of the nodes from the cost ad-
jacency matrices determined through distance measuring
techniques. (The transmission range R specifies the
neighborhood)

CALL makeNextInitialConfig();
CALL conflictMinimised();

Append the selNodes of the current pass to the tempAnchor
list.

END WHILE
END FUNCTION
```

5   Experiments and Simulation Results

In order to evaluate the performance of the proposed algorithm, we simulated the various phases of the approach in MATLAB. A sensor network of total 400 nodes was created by deploying the nodes randomly in a 100 by 100squareregion. Among them we selected out 10% and 15% anchor nodes randomly for our experiments. The values of P, beta and D are set to 100, 0.85 and 2 respectively as they are found to give optimal results using extensive experimentation. The most important factor that has a direct impact on the final results is the transmission range R of the nodes which defines the neighborhood of a node. This affects the anchor neighborhood of the nodes in different passes. Below we show the final placement scenario of the nodes for 10% and 15% anchors in Fig. 1 and Fig. 2 respectively. We measure the performance of the algorithm in terms of the error function as defined in many literature like [6][10] etc. The measure is defined as...

$$\text{Location Error} = \frac{1}{n} * \frac{\sum_{i=1}^{n}(x_i - X_i)^2 + (y_i - Y_i)^2}{R^2} * 100\% \tag{2}$$

Where 'n' is the total number of nodes taken into consideration and R is the transmission range of each node. Here (X_i, Y_i) is the estimated location of sensor node and (x_i, y_i) is the true location of sensor node. The error value is reported in percentage, normalized by the transmission range.

We show below the plot of the error values with respect to the transmission range R for the two cases of 10% and 15% anchor points in Fig. 3. We also show a comparison of the location errors with the previous results obtained by using a modified simulated annealing technique described in [10]. We can see that the error decreases to a much greater extent in case of 15% anchors. Thus we have got almost comparable results with the previous researchers by using a technique that eliminates many existing shortcomings.

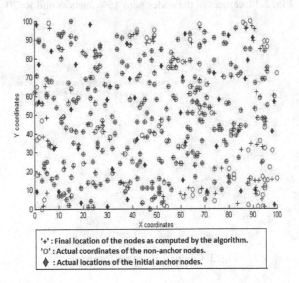

'+' : Final location of the nodes as computed by the algorithm.
'O' : Actual coordinates of the non-anchor nodes.
◆ : Actual locations of the initial anchor nodes.

Fig. 1. Placement of the nodes with 10% anchors and R=20

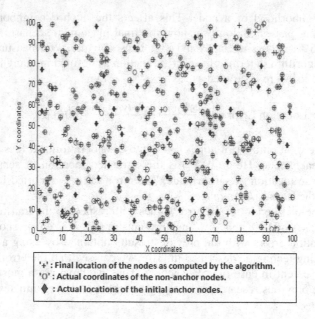

'+' : Final location of the nodes as computed by the algorithm.
'O' : Actual coordinates of the non-anchor nodes.
◆ : Actual locations of the initial anchor nodes.

Fig. 2. Placement of the nodes with 15% anchors and R=20

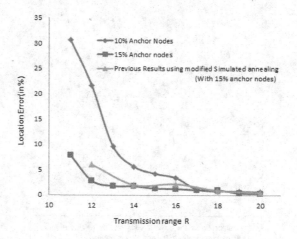

Fig. 3. Comparison of performances

6   Conclusions and Future Work

In this paper we have presented a conflict minimization based approach to find out the location of the non-anchor nodes distributed in an application field. Using the neighborhood information, i.e. the actual cost adjacency matrix calculated by using the distance measuring techniques, we successively find out the locations of the unknown nodes and make them anchor nodes. While dealing with a non-anchor node, we calculate the anchor neighborhood of the node. If the anchor neighborhood is greater than a particular threshold, then it's selected for processing. We find a fix no. of anchors that are present in the neighborhood of that node (*anchorSubset*) and use them to estimate an initial location of the node. Then, using the above mentioned neighborhood information; we apply the conflict minimization algorithm to find the true estimate of the node. The main advantage of the algorithm is that it does the processing of the nodes one by one which makes it highly scalable and the performance becomes independent on the no. of nodes. However increasing the initial no. of anchor nodes boosts up the accuracy to a certain extent. Another important advantage that we have here is that our algorithm has an extremely low probability of getting diverged from the solution because of the controlled initial placement of the nodes unlike the previous simulated annealing based approaches. This also helps reducing the processing time.

One possible shortcoming of the approach is that if the no. of initial anchor points is extremely small or clustered into a very narrow region, then the cumulative propagated error may be high. This problem can be eliminated by ensuring a somewhat uniformly distributed anchor nodes. Moreover, the problem of flip-ambiguity [12] [16] is another area of concern that should be taken into consideration. Although in our experiments we did not encounter any instance of flip-ambiguity, the theoretical possibility has not been totally eliminated. These issues may be taken into consideration in further studies.

References

1. Pal, A.: Localization Algorithms in Wireless Sensor Networks: Current Approaches and Future Challenges. Network Protocols and Algorithms 2(1), 45–74 (2010)
2. Kirkpatrick, S., Gelatt, C.D., Vecchi, M.P.: Optimization by Simulated Annealing. Science 220(4598), 671–680 (1983)
3. Priyantha, N., Balakrishnan, H., Demaine, E., Teller, S.: Anchor-free Distributed Docalization in Sensor Networks. MIT Laboratory for Computer Science, Technical Report TR-892 (April 2003)
4. Savarese, C., Rabaey, J., Beutel, J.: Locationing in Distributed Ad-Hoc Wireless Sensor Networks. In: Proceedings of IEEE International Conference on Acoustics, Speech, and Signal Processing (ICASSP 2001), Salt Lake City, Utah, USA, vol. 4, pp. 2037–2040 (May 2001)
5. Shang, Y., Ruml, W., Zhang, Y., Fromherz, M.: Localization From Mere Connectivity. In: Proceedings of ACM Symposium on Mobile Ad Hoc Networking and Computing (MobiHoc 2003), Annapolis, Maryland, USA, pp. 201–212 (June 2003)
6. Kannan, A.A., Mao, G., Vucetic, B.: Simulated Annealing Based Wireless Sensor Network Localization. Journal of Computers 1(2), 15–22 (2006)
7. Alippi, C., Vanini, G.: A RSSI-Based and Calibrated Centralized Localization Technique or Wireless Sensor Networks. In: Proceedings of Fourth IEEE International Conference on Pervasive Computing and Communications Workshops (PERCOMW 2006), Pisa, Italy, pp. 301–305 (March 2006)

8. Moore, D., Leonard, J., Rus, D., Teller, S.: Robust Distributed Network Localization with Noisy Range Measurements. In: Proceedings of the Second ACM Conference on Embedded Networked Sensor Systems (SenSys 2004), Baltimore, MD, pp. 50–61 (November 2004)

9. Meertens, L., Fitzpatrick, S.: The Distributed Construction of a Global Coordinate System in a Network of Static Computational Nodes from Inter-Node Distances, Kestrel Institute Technical Report KES.U.04.04, Kestrel Institute, Palo Alto (2004)

10. Shahrokhzadeha, M., Haghighata, A.T., Mahmoudia, F., Hrokhzadeh, B.: A Heuristic Method for Wireless Sensor Network Localization. In: International Symposium on Intelligent Systems Techniques for Ad hoc and Wireless Sensor Networks, pp. 813–819 (2011)

11. Li, Y., Xing, J., Yang, Q., Shi, H.: Localization Research Based on Improved Simulated Annealing Algorithm in WSN. In: The 5th International Conference on Wireless Communications, Networking and Mobile Computing (WiCOM 2009), pp. 1–4 (2009)

12. Kannan, A.A., Fidan, B., Mao, G.: Analysis of Flip Ambiguities for Robust Sensor Network Localization. IEEE Transactions on Vehicular Technology 59(4), 2057–2070 (2010)

13. Doherty, L., Pister, K., El Ghaoui, L.: Convex Position Estimation in Wireless Sensor Networks. In: IEEE INFOCOM 2001, vol. 3, pp. 1655–1663 (2001)

14. Biswas, P., Ye, Y.: Semidefinite Programming for Ad Hoc Wireless Sensor Network Localization. In: Information Processing in Sensor Networks, IPSN 2004, pp. 46–54 (2004)

15. Liang, T.C., Wang, T.C., Ye, Y.: A Gradient Search Method to Round the Semidefinite Programming Relaxation Solution for Ad Hoc Wireless Sensor Network Localization. Sanford University, formal report 5 (2004)

16. Severi, S., Abreu, G., Destino, G., Dardari, D.: Efficient and Accurate Localization in Multihop Networks. In: Proc. Asilomar Conf. Signals, Systems, and Computers (November 2009)

17. RokSosic, J.G.: Efficient Local Search with Conflict Minimization: A Case Study of the N-Queen Problem. IEEE Trans. Knowledge and Data Engineering 6(5), 661–668 (1994)

Abstract Interpretation of Recursive Queries

Agostino Cortesi[1] and Raju Halder[2]

[1] DAIS, Università Ca' Foscari Venezia, Italy
cortesi@unive.it
[2] Dept. of Comp. Sc. & Engg., Indian Institute of Technology Patna, India

Abstract. In this paper, we extend recent works on concrete and abstract semantics of structured query languages by considering recursive queries too. We show that combining abstraction of data and widening operators that guarantee the convergence of the computation may be useful not only for static analysis purposes, but also as a sound and effective tool for query language transformations.

Keywords: Abstract Interpretation, Widening Operators, Recursive Queries, Databases.

1 Introduction

Abstract Interpretation [9] is a general theory for designing approximate semantics of programs which can be used to gather information about programs in order to provide sound answers to questions about their run-time behaviors.

Although the Abstract Interpretation is routinely used to cope with infinite state systems, it can effectively be applied to database systems which are in general finite [13,14]. In fact, due to exponentially increasing amount of data, the database systems are facing serious challenges while managing, processing, analyzing, or understanding large volume of data in restricted environments. As a result, performance of the systems in terms of optimization issues are really under big threat. The Abstract Interpretation formulation of database systems serves as a formal foundation of many interesting real-life applications, for instance, (i) to address security properties, like watermarking and access control [11,15]; (ii) to provide a novel cooperative query answering schema [12]; (iii) to serve as static analysis framework for transactions to optimize integrity constraint checking [14]; (iv) to perform abstract slicing of applications accessing or manipulating databases [16], etc. In this paper, we address a challenging feature of database query languages: the treatment of recursive queries.

Recursive queries have been introduced into the SQL languages according to ANSI SQL-99 standard in order to facilitate the access of hierarchical data, leading to more elegant and better performing applications [21]. This can be implemented by defining either a Recursive Common Table Expression (RCTE) or a Recursive View. For instance, given an initial table "flight" containing direct flight information, the following recursive query uses recursive common table expression "destinations" and returns all the destinations reachable from

C. Hota and P.K. Srimani (Eds.): ICDCIT 2013, LNCS 7753, pp. 157–170, 2013.

"Marcopolo (VCE)" along with the number of connections (including the direct ones from "flight") and total cost to arrive at that final destination:

```
WITH destinations (departure, arrival, connects, cost ) AS (
% anchor member......
        SELECT f.departure,f.arrival, 0, ticket
        FROM flights f WHERE f.departure = 'Marcopolo (VCE)'
    UNION ALL
% recursive member......
        SELECT r.departure, b.arrival, r.connects + 1, r.cost + b.ticket
        FROM destinations r, flights b WHERE r.arrival = b.departure)
SELECT DISTINCT departure, arrival, connects, cost FROM destinations;
```

Observe that the anchor member of the query is an initialization full-select that seeds the recursion, whereas the recursive member is an iterative full-select that contains a direct reference to itself in the FROM clause. Examples of some applications where recursive queries play important roles, are bill-of-material, reservation, trip planner, networking planning system, etc.

Over last four decades, relational algebra and relational calculus by E. F. Codd [6,7] are extensively used as a formal semantic description of query languages for relational databases. However, these models do not support the semantics of recursive queries. Later, Aho and Ulman [2] increased the expressive power of relational query languages by introducing least fix-point operator for recursive queries. Various proposals focussing on optimization of recursive queries can be found in [1,4,5,19,20].

The size and nature of database content may affect recursive query executions: for instance, a cyclic nature of data in a database may put any recursive query computation into an infinite loop. Therefore, when issuing recursive queries, it is important to the database-users to fully understand database schema and underlying database content, and to formulate recursive queries accordingly in order to avoid the possible errors which may occur during execution. For instance, if a user wants the infinite cycle to stop, she can specify the NOCYCLE keyword on the CONNECT BY clause (so that no error is issued for cyclic data) or can specify a limit on the number of iterations that a recursive query is allowed to perform.

To remedy such shortcomings and to enhance the efficiency and effectiveness of the information retrieval system, in this paper we extend our previous works on concrete and abstract semantics of database query languages [14] to the case of recursive queries too. In particular,

- We define an overapproximation of the fix-point semantics of recursive queries that replaces the possibly infinite number of concrete program executions, which might not be fully computed in practice, by an abstract execution that is guaranteed to be executable.

– We show that through a suitable choice of a widening operator [8,10], an abstract computation of recursive queries can lead to effective results, by enforcing and accelerating the convergence of fixpoint computations.

The structure of the paper is organized as follows: Section 2 illustrates a motivating example. Section 3 recalls some basics on fix-point trace semantics of programs. Section 4 describes the concrete and abstract semantics of programs embedding SQL statements that cover recursive queries too. In section 5, we define a widening operator for abstract databases that guarantees the convergence of abstract fixpoint computations. Finally, in section 6, we conclude our work.

2   A Motivating Example

Consider a database containing flight information depicted in Table 1. Recall

Table 1. Database "flight"

flight no.	source	destination	cost ($)
F001	Fiumicino (FCO)	Zurich (ZRH)	410.57
F002	Marcopolo (VCE)	Orly (ORY)	325.30
F003	Orly (ORY)	Zurich (ZRH)	200.00
F004	Orly (ORY)	Fiumicino (FCO)	428.28
F005	Zurich (ZRH)	Marcopolo (VCE)	250.15

the recursive query mentioned in the introduction part that returns all the flight destinations reachable from "Marcopolo (VCE)" along with the number of connections and total cost to arrive at that final destination. The anchor member of the query returns the base result set that contains initial destinations having direct flight from "Marcopolo (VCE)" as shown below:

departure	arrival	connects	cost
Marcopolo (VCE)	Orly (ORY)	0	325.30

In the first iteration the recursive member adds the following result set:

departure	arrival	connects	cost
Marcopolo (VCE)	Zurich (ZRH)	1	525.30
Marcopolo (VCE)	Fiumicino (FCO)	1	753.58

Continuing this way, after only three iterations, the result set returned by the running query is:

departure	arrival	connects	cost
Marcopolo (VCE)	Orly (ORY)	0	325.30
Marcopolo (VCE)	Zurich (ZRH)	1	525.30
Marcopolo (VCE)	Fiumicino (FCO)	1	753.58
Marcopolo (VCE)	Marcopolo (VCE)	2	775.45
Marcopolo (VCE)	Madrid-Barajas (MAD)	2	1164.15
Marcopolo (VCE)	Orly (ORY)	3	1100.75
Marcopolo (VCE)	Marcopolo (VCE)	3	1414.30

Observe that several pairs (departure, arrival) are repeated with different connectivity and cost. The recursive computation is, therefore, infinite due to the cyclic nature of the data in the database and can never reach to a fixpoint.

This yields the system to fail the execution and generates an "error" or "warning" message without providing any result to the end users, which might be interested only on the reachability between two airports on minimum number of connections and on the best price.

As a way to overcome such situation, in section 5 we will describe how to use an abstract version of this computation and how to get a computable sound overapproximation of all the concrete tuples generated by the concrete recursive query through a suitable widening operator.

3   Preliminaries

A fix-point of a function $f \in \mathcal{D} \to \mathcal{D}$ is an element $x \in \mathcal{D}$ such that $f(x) = x$. If f is defined over a partial order $\langle \mathcal{D}, \sqsubseteq \rangle$, then the least fix-point lfp$f$ of f is the unique $x \in \mathcal{D}$ such that $f(x) = x$ and $\forall y \in \mathcal{D}. \ y = f(y) \implies x \sqsubseteq y$. Given a function f defined over a poset $\langle \mathcal{D}, \sqsubseteq \rangle$ and an element $z \in \mathcal{D}$, we denote with lfp$_z^{\sqsubseteq} f$, the least fix-point of f w.r.t. the order $\sqsubseteq$ larger than z, if it exists. Sometimes, when the order and the element are clear from the context, we will simply write lfp$f$. The dual notion is that of greatest fix-point gfp$f$.

Theorem 1 (Tarski's fixpoint Theorem [3]). *Let $\langle \mathcal{D}, \sqsubseteq, \bot, \top, \sqcup, \sqcap \rangle$ be a complete lattice. Let $f \in \mathcal{D} \to \mathcal{D}$ be a monotonic function. Then the set $\mathcal{L} = \{x \in \mathcal{D} \mid f(x) = x\}$ is a non-empty complete lattice w.r.t the order $\sqsubseteq$ with infimum lfp $f = \sqcap \{x \in \mathcal{D} \mid f(x) \sqsubseteq x\}$ and supremum gfp $f = \sqcup \{x \in \mathcal{D} \mid f(x) \sqsupseteq x\}$.*

3.1   Traces

Program executions are recorded in finite or infinite sequences of states, called traces, over a given set of commands. Given a (possibly infinite) set Σ of states, we consider the following sets:

$$\tau^n = [0, n-1] \mapsto \Sigma \qquad \text{is the set of finite sequences } \sigma = \sigma_0 \ldots \sigma_{n-1} \text{ of length } |\sigma| = n \in \mathbb{N} \text{ over } \Sigma.$$

$$\tau^+ = \bigcup_{n>0} \tau^n \qquad \text{is the set of non-empty finite sequences over } \Sigma.$$

$$\tau^* = \tau^+ \cup \{\epsilon\} \qquad \text{is the set of finite sequences over } \Sigma \text{ where } \{\epsilon\} \text{ is an empty sequence.}$$

$$\tau^\omega = \mathbb{N} \mapsto \Sigma \qquad \text{is the set of infinite sequences } \sigma = \sigma_0 \ldots \sigma_n \ldots \text{ of length } |\sigma| = \omega.$$

$$\tau^\infty = \tau^+ \cup \tau^\omega \qquad \text{is the set of non-empty sequences over } \Sigma.$$

$$\tau^\propto = \tau^\infty \cup \{\epsilon\} \qquad \text{is the set of all sequences over } \Sigma.$$

The semantics of a program P can be expressed by a fixpoint operator as follows:

Theorem 2 (Fixpoint partial trace semantics [18]). *Let Σ be a set of states, $\xrightarrow{P} \subseteq \Sigma \times \Sigma$ be the transition relation associated with a program P, $\mathcal{I}_0 \subseteq \Sigma$ be a set of initial states and $\mathcal{F} \in \wp(\Sigma) \mapsto \wp(\tau^*) \mapsto \wp(\tau^*)$ be*

$$\mathcal{F}(\mathcal{I}) = \lambda X . \mathcal{I} \cup \{\sigma_0 \to \ldots \sigma_n \to \sigma_{n+1} \mid \sigma_0 \to \ldots \sigma_n \in X, \sigma_n \xrightarrow{P} \sigma_{n+1}\}.$$

Then, the partial trace semantics of P, $\mathscr{T}[\![P]\!] \in \wp(\Sigma) \mapsto \wp(\tau^*)$ is

$$\mathscr{T}[\![P]\!](\mathcal{I}_0) = lfp_{\emptyset}^{\subseteq} \mathcal{F}(\mathcal{I}_0) = \bigcup_{i \leq \omega} \mathcal{F}^i(\mathcal{I}_0)$$

4 Programs Embedding SQL Statements

In this section, we recall some basics of [14], where we introduced a concrete and abstract semantics of database query languages, and we extend it to consider also recursive queries.

An application embedding SQL statements basically interacts with two worlds: *user world* and *database world*. Corresponding to these two worlds there exist two sets of variables: database variables $\mathbb{V}_d$ and application variables $\mathbb{V}_a$. Variables from $\mathbb{V}_d$ are involved only in the SQL statements, whereas variables in $\mathbb{V}_a$ may occur in all types of instructions of the application. Any SQL statement Q is denoted by a tuple $Q = \langle A, \phi \rangle$ where A and ϕ refer to *action part* and *pre-condition part* of Q respectively. A SQL statement Q first identifies an active data set from the database using the pre-condition ϕ, and then performs the appropriate operations on that data set using the SQL action A. The pre-condition ϕ appears in SQL statements as a well-formed formula in first-order logic. Table 2 depicts the syntactic sets and the abstract syntax of programs embedding SQL statements. For more details, the reader may refer to [13,14].

4.1 Program Environments

The SQL embedded program P acts on a set of constants $const(P) \in \wp(\mathbb{C})$ and set of variables $var(P) \in \wp(\mathbb{V})$, where $\mathbb{V} \triangleq \mathbb{V}_d \cup \mathbb{V}_a$. These variables take their values from semantic domain $\mathfrak{D}_{\mho}$, where $\mathfrak{D}_{\mho} = \{\mathfrak{D} \cup \{\mho\}\}$ and $\mho$ represents the undefined value.

Now we define two environments $\mathfrak{E}_d$ and $\mathfrak{E}_a$ corresponding to the database and application variable sets $\mathbb{V}_d$ and $\mathbb{V}_a$ respectively.

Definition 1 (Application Environment). *An application environment $\rho_a \in \mathfrak{E}_a$ maps a variable $v \in dom(\rho_a) \subseteq \mathbb{V}_a$ to its value $\rho_a(v)$. So, $\mathfrak{E}_a \triangleq \mathbb{V}_a \longmapsto \mathfrak{D}_{\mho}$.*

Definition 2 (Database Environment). *We consider a database as a set of indexed tables $\{t_i \mid i \in I_x\}$ for a given set of indexes I_x. We define database environment by a function ρ_d whose domain is I_x, such that for $i \in I_x$, $\rho_d(i) = t_i$.*

Table 2. Abstract Syntax of programs embedding SQL statements

Syntactic Sets:	
$n : \mathbb{Z}$ (Integer)	$b : \mathbb{B}$ (Boolean Expressions)
$k : \mathbb{S}$ (String)	$A : \mathbb{A}$ (Action)
$c : \mathbb{C}$ (Constants)	$\tau : \mathbb{T}$ (Terms)
$v_a : \mathbb{V}_a$ (Application Variables)	$a_f : \mathbb{A}_f$ (Atomic Formulas)
$v_d : \mathbb{V}_d$ (Database Variables)	$\phi : \mathbb{W}$ (Pre-condition)
$v : \mathbb{V} \triangleq \mathbb{V}_d \cup \mathbb{V}_a$ (Variables)	$Q : \mathbb{Q}$ (SQL statements)
$e : \mathbb{E}$ (Arithmetic Expressions)	$I : \mathbb{I}$ (Program statements)

Abstract Syntax:

$c ::= n \mid k$
$e ::= c \mid v_d \mid v_a \mid op_u\, e \mid e_1\, op_b\, e_2$, where $op_u \in \{+, -\}$ and $op_b \in \{+, -, *, /, \ldots\ldots\}$
$b ::= e_1\, op_r\, e_2 | \neg b | b_1 \vee b_2 | b_1 \wedge b_2 | true | false$, where $op_r \in \{=, \geq, \leq, <, >, \neq, \ldots\}$
$\tau ::= c \mid v_a \mid v_d \mid f_n(\tau_1, \tau_2, ..., \tau_n)$, where f_n is an n-ary function.
$a_f ::= R_n(\tau_1, \tau_2, ..., \tau_n) \mid \tau_1 = \tau_2$, where $R_n(\tau_1, \tau_2, ..., \tau_n) \in \{true, false\}$
$\phi ::= a_f \mid \neg\phi_1 \mid \phi_1 \vee \phi_2 \mid \phi_1 \wedge \phi_2 \mid \forall x_i\, \phi \mid \exists x_i\, \phi$
$g(e) ::= \text{GROUP BY}(e) \mid id$
$r ::= \text{DISTINCT} \mid \text{ALL}$
$s ::= \text{AVG} \mid \text{SUM} \mid \text{MAX} \mid \text{MIN} \mid \text{COUNT}$
$h(e) ::= s \circ r(e) \mid \text{DISTINCT}(e) \mid id$
$h(*) ::= \text{COUNT}(*)$
$\boldsymbol{h}(\boldsymbol{x}) ::= \langle h_1(x_1), ..., h_n(x_n) \rangle$, where $\boldsymbol{h} = \langle h_1, ..., h_n \rangle$ and $\boldsymbol{x} = \langle x_1, ..., x_n \rangle$
$f(e) ::= \text{ORDER BY ASC}(e) \mid \text{ORDER BY DESC}(e) \mid id$
$A ::= select(v_a, f(e'), r(\boldsymbol{h}(\boldsymbol{x})), \phi, g(e)) \mid update(\boldsymbol{v_d}, e) \mid insert(\boldsymbol{v_d}, e) \mid delete(v_d)$
$Q ::= \langle A, \phi \rangle \mid Q' \text{ UNION } Q'' \mid Q' \text{ INTERSECT } Q'' \mid Q' \text{ MINUS } Q''$
$I ::= skip \mid v_a := e \mid v_a :=? \mid Q \mid if\, b\, then\, I_1\, else\, I_2 \mid while\, b\, do\, I \mid I_1; I_2$

Definition 3 (Table Environment). *Given a database environment ρ_d and a table $t \in d$. We define $attr(t) = \{a_1, a_2, ..., a_k\}$. So, $t \subseteq D_1 \times D_2 \times .... \times D_k$ where, a_i is the attribute corresponding to the typed domain D_i . A table environment ρ_t for a table t is defined as a function such that for any attribute $a_i \in attr(t)$,*

$$\rho_t(a_i) = \langle \pi_i(l_j) \mid l_j \in t \rangle$$

Where π is the projection operator, i.e. $\pi_i(l_j)$ is the ith element of the l_j-th row. In other words, ρ_t maps a_i to the ordered set of values over the rows of the table t.

4.2 Small-Steps Operational Semantics of Programs Embedding SQL

Let Σ be a set of states defined by $\Sigma \triangleq \mathfrak{E}_d \times \mathfrak{E}_a$, where $\mathfrak{E}_d$ and $\mathfrak{E}_a$ denote the set of all database environments and the set of all application environments respectively. That is, a state $\sigma \in \Sigma$ is denoted by a tuple $\langle \rho_d, \rho_a \rangle$ where $\rho_d \in \mathfrak{E}_d$ and $\rho_a \in \mathfrak{E}_a$ are the database environment and application environment respectively. The set of states of P is, thus, defined as $\Sigma[\![P]\!] \triangleq \mathfrak{E}_d[\![P]\!] \times \mathfrak{E}_a[\![P]\!]$ where $\mathfrak{E}_d[\![P]\!]$ and $\mathfrak{E}_a[\![P]\!]$ are the set of database and application environments of the program P whose domain is the set of program variables.

The transition relation $S \in (\mathbb{I} \times \Sigma) \mapsto \wp(\Sigma)$ specifies which successor states $\langle \rho'_d, \rho'_a \rangle \in \Sigma$ can follow when a statement $I \in \mathbb{I}$ executes on state $\langle \rho_d, \rho_a \rangle \in \Sigma$.

Therefore, the transitional semantics $S[\![P]\!] \in (P \times \Sigma[\![P]\!]) \mapsto \wp(\Sigma[\![P]\!])$ of a program $P \in \mathbb{P}$ restricts the transition relation to program instructions, $i.e.$

$$S[\![P]\!](\langle \rho_d, \rho_a \rangle) = \{\langle \rho'_d, \rho'_a \rangle \mid \langle \rho_d, \rho_a \rangle, \langle \rho'_d, \rho'_a \rangle \in \Sigma[\![P]\!] \wedge \langle \rho'_d, \rho'_a \rangle \in S[\![I]\!](\rho_d, \rho_a) \wedge I \in P\}$$

4.3   Partial Trace Semantics of Programs Embedding SQL

Let us consider a set of states in the form of $\Sigma_{\mathcal{L}} = \mathcal{L} \times \Sigma$ where $\mathcal{L}$ is the set of labels. Let $\mathcal{I}_0 = \{(l_0, \rho_0) \mid \rho_0 = \langle \rho_d, \rho_a \rangle \in \Sigma[\![P]\!]\} \subseteq \Sigma_{\mathcal{L}}[\![P]\!]$ be the set of initial states of P where l_0 is the entry label of P. According to Theorem 2, the partial trace semantics of P can be defined as

$$\mathscr{T}[\![P]\!](\mathcal{I}_0) = \text{lfp}_{\emptyset}^{\subseteq} \mathcal{F}(\mathcal{I}_0) = \bigcup_{i \le \omega} \mathcal{F}^i(\mathcal{I}_0)$$

where

$$\mathcal{F}(\mathcal{I}) = \lambda \mathcal{T}. \ \mathcal{I} \cup \{(l_0, \rho_0) \to \ldots (l_n, \rho_n) \to (l_{n+1}, \rho_{n+1}) \mid (l_0, \rho_0) \to \ldots (l_n, \rho_n) \in \mathcal{T}$$
$$\wedge l_n = \mathcal{L}[\![I]\!] \wedge \rho_{n+1} \in S[\![I]\!](\rho_n) \wedge l_{n+1} \in \text{succ}(l_n)\}$$

and the function $\text{succ}(l)$ returns the set of program labels which are successors of l.

Partial Trace Semantics of Recursive Queries. Let us now turn our attention to recursive queries. Let $Q = \langle {}^{l_0}Q_a, {}^{l_1}Q_r \rangle$ be a recursive query where ${}^{l_0}Q_a$ and ${}^{l_1}Q_r$ denote the anchor member and the recursive member in Q at program labels l_0 and l_1 respectively. Suppose $\mathcal{I}_0 = \{\langle l_0, \rho_0 \rangle \mid \rho_0 = \langle \rho_d, \rho_a \rangle \in \Sigma[\![Q]\!]\}$ is the set of initial states of Q such that the recursive common table expression is $\emptyset$. Let $S[\![Q_a]\!](\langle l_0, \rho_0 \rangle) = \langle l_1, \rho_1 \rangle$. By specializing the definition above, the partial trace semantics of Q can be defined by

$$\mathscr{T}[\![Q]\!](\mathcal{I}_0) = \text{lfp}_{\emptyset}^{\subseteq} \mathcal{F}(\mathcal{I}_0) = \bigcup_{i \le \omega} \mathcal{F}^i(\mathcal{I}_0)$$

where

$$\mathcal{F}(\mathcal{I}) = \lambda \mathcal{T}. \ \mathcal{I} \cup \{(l_0, \rho_0) \to (l_1, \rho_1) \to \ldots (l_1, \rho_n) \to (l_1, \rho_{n+1}) \mid$$
$$((l_0, \rho_0) \to (l_1, \rho_1) \to \ldots (l_1, \rho_n)) \in \mathcal{T} \wedge \rho_{n+1} \in S[\![Q_r]\!](\rho_n)\}$$

Approximation of Fix-Point Semantics. As stated in [10], when considering an abstraction of the semantic domain, an overapproximation of the fix-point semantics depicted so far can be efficiently computed.

Let $\mathcal{D}$ be the semantic domain. Let $\text{lfp}_{\perp} \mathcal{F}$ where $\mathcal{F} \in \mathcal{D} \mapsto \mathcal{D}$ be the semantics of a given program P. Assume the Galois Connection $\langle (\mathcal{D}, \mathcal{F}, \perp), \alpha, \gamma, (\widetilde{\mathcal{D}}, \widetilde{\mathcal{F}}, \widetilde{\perp}) \rangle$ where α and γ are abstraction and concretization functions respectively, such that $\text{lfp}_{\widetilde{\perp}}(\widetilde{\mathcal{F}})$ is not computable iteratively in finitely many steps. Suppose $\widetilde{\mathcal{A}}$ is an upper approximation of $\text{lfp}_{\widetilde{\perp}}(\widetilde{\mathcal{F}})$ which is effectively computed using widening [8,10]. Since $\text{lfp}_{\perp} \mathcal{F} \sqsubseteq \text{lfp}_{\widetilde{\perp}}(\widetilde{\mathcal{F}})$ and $\text{lfp}_{\widetilde{\perp}}(\widetilde{\mathcal{F}}) \sqsubseteq \widetilde{\mathcal{A}}$, so by monotonicity and transitivity, we get $\text{lfp}_{\perp} \mathcal{F} \sqsubseteq \widetilde{\mathcal{A}}$.

4.4   Lifting the Semantics to Abstract Domains

We lift the concrete semantics of programs embedding SQL statements to an abstract setting by introducing the notion of abstract databases in which some information are disregarded and concrete values are possibly represented by suitable abstractions.

Definition 4 (Abstract Databases). *Let dB be a database. A database $\widetilde{dB} = \alpha(dB)$ where α is the abstraction function, is said to be an abstract version of dB if there exist a representation function γ, called concretization function such that for all tuple $\langle x_1, x_2, \ldots, x_n \rangle \in dB$ there exist a tuple $\langle \widetilde{y}_1, \widetilde{y}_2, \ldots, \widetilde{y}_n \rangle \in \widetilde{dB}$ such that $\forall i \in [1 \ldots n]$ $(x_i \in id(\widetilde{y}_i) \vee x_i \in \gamma(\widetilde{y}_i))$, where id represents identity function.*

Example 1. Consider the table *"emp"* depicted in Table 3 that provides information about employees of a company. We assume that ages, salaries, and number of children of employees lie between 5 to 100, between 500 to 10000 and between 0 to 10 respectively. Considering an abstraction where ages and salaries of employees are abstracted by elements from the domain of intervals, and number of children in the attribute '*Child-no*' are abstracted by abstract values from the abstract domain $D^{abs}_{Child-no} = \{\bot, \text{Zero, Few, Medium, Many}, \top\}$ where $\top$ represents *"any"* and $\bot$ represents *"undefined"*. The abstract table *"$\widetilde{emp}$"* corresponding to *"emp"* w.r.t. these abstractions is shown in Table 4.   The

Table 3. Employee table *"emp"*

eID	Name	Age	Dno	Pno	Sal	Child − no
1	Matteo	30	2	1	2000	4
2	Alice	22	1	2	1500	2
3	Joy	50	2	3	2300	3
4	luca	10	1	2	1700	1
5	Deba	40	3	4	3000	5
6	Andrea	70	1	2	1900	2
7	Alberto	18	3	4	800	1
8	Bob	14	2	3	4000	3

Table 4. Abstract table *"$\widetilde{emp}$"* corresponding to *"emp"*

$\widetilde{eID}$	Name	$\widetilde{Age}$	$\widetilde{Dno}$	$\widetilde{Pno}$	$\widetilde{Sal}$	Child − no
1	Matteo	[25,59]	2	1	[1500,2499]	Medium
2	Alice	[12,24]	1	2	[1500,2499]	Few
3	Joy	[25,59]	2	3	[1500,2499]	Medium
4	luca	[5,11]	1	2	[1500,2499]	Few
5	Deba	[25,59]	3	4	[2500,10000]	Many
6	Andrea	[60,100]	1	2	[1500,2499]	Few
7	Alberto	[12,24]	3	4	[500,1499]	Few
8	Bob	[12,24]	2	3	[2500,10000]	Medium

correspondence between concrete and abstract values of the attribute, for instance '*Child-no*' can be formally expressed by the abstraction and concretization functions $\alpha_{child-no}$ and $\gamma_{child-no}$ respectively as follows:

$$\alpha_{child-no}(X) \triangleq \begin{cases} \bot & \text{if } X = \emptyset \\ \text{Zero} & \text{if } X = \{0\} \\ \text{Few} & \text{if } \forall x \in X : 1 \leq x \leq 2 \\ \text{Medium} & \text{if } \forall x \in X : 3 \leq x \leq 4 \\ \text{many} & \text{if } \forall x \in X : 5 \leq x \leq 10 \\ \top & \text{otherwise} \end{cases}$$

$$\gamma_{child-no}(y) \triangleq \begin{cases} \emptyset & \text{if } y = \bot \\ \{0\} & \text{if } y = \text{Zero} \\ \{x : 1 \leq x \leq 2\} & \text{if } y = \text{Few} \\ \{x : 3 \leq x \leq 4\} & \text{if } y = \text{Medium} \\ \{x : 5 \leq x \leq 10\} & \text{if } y = \text{Many} \\ \{x : 0 \leq x \leq 10\} & \text{if } y = \top \end{cases}$$

We can similarly define the abstraction-concretization functions for other attributes as well. Observe that the abstraction-concretization functions for the attributes 'eID', 'Dno' and 'Pno' are identity function id.

The abstract versions corresponding to all concrete functions such as Group By, Order By, Aggregate Functions, Set Operations, etc are defined in such a way so as to preserve the soundness condition. For more details, see [13,14].

5 Widening Operators for Abstract Databases

In section 4.3, we saw that widening operator is crucial to make the abstract semantics computable. In this section, we instantiate a widening operator to the case of abstract databases to suitably deal with convergence of abstract recursive query computations.

In the literature [8,10], a widening operator is defined as follows:

Definition 5 (Widening). *Let* $\langle \mathcal{D}, \sqsubseteq, \bot, \top, \sqcup, \sqcap \rangle$ *be a lattice. The partial operator* $\nabla : \mathcal{D} \times \mathcal{D} \mapsto \mathcal{D}$ *is a widening if*

- *for each* $x, y \in \mathcal{D}$: $x \sqsubseteq x \nabla y$ *and* $y \sqsubseteq x \nabla y$.
- *for each increasing chain* $x_0 \sqsubseteq x_1 \sqsubseteq \ldots$, *the increasing chain defined by* $y_0 = x_0$, $y_{n+1} = y_n \nabla x_{n+1}$ *for* $n \in \mathbb{N}$, *is not strictly increasing.*

Theorem 3 (Convergence [9]). *Given a sequence* $\{x_0, x_1, x_2, \ldots \ldots\}$, *the increasing chain* $\langle y_k, k \in \mathbb{N} \rangle$ *defined by* $y_0 = x_0$ *and*

$$y_{n+1} := \begin{cases} y_n & \text{if } \exists l \leq n : x_{n+1} \sqsubseteq y_l \\ \\ y_n \nabla x_{n+1}, & \text{otherwise} \end{cases}$$

is strictly increasing up to a least $l \in \mathbb{N}$ *such that* $x_l \sqsubseteq y_l$ *and the sequence is stationary at* l *onwards.*

The following example defines a widening operator for the domain of intervals.

Example 2 (Widening for intervals). Consider a lattice of intervals $\mathcal{D} = \{\bot\} \cup \{[l, u] \mid l \in \mathbb{Z} \cup \{-\infty\}, \ u \in \mathbb{Z} \cup \{+\infty\}\}$ ordered by $\forall x \in \mathcal{D}, \ \bot \leq x$ and $[l_0, u_0] \leq [l_1, u_1]$ if $l_1 \leq l_0$ and $u_0 \leq u_1$. Let k be a fixed positive integer constant, and I be any set of indices. The following defines a threshold widening operator defined on $\mathcal{D}$ by

$$\nabla^k(\{\bot\}) = \bot$$

$$\nabla^k(\{\bot\} \cup S) = \nabla^k(S)$$

$$\nabla^k(\{[l_i, u_i] : i \in I\}) = [h_1, h_2]$$

where

$$h_1 = min\{l_i : i \in I\} \ \text{if} \ min\{l_i : i \in I\} > -k \ \text{else} \ -\infty$$

$$h_2 = max\{u_i : i \in I\} \ \text{if} \ max\{u_i : i \in I\} < k \ \text{else} \ +\infty$$

As a partial order between abstract databases $\tilde{d}_1, \tilde{d}_2 \in \tilde{D}$ (denoted $\tilde{d}_1 \sqsubseteq \tilde{d}_2$) we consider the following:

Definition 6 (Partial order between abstract databases). *Given two abstract databases $\tilde{d}_1, \tilde{d}_2 \in \tilde{D}$. The partial order between $\tilde{d}_1$ and $\tilde{d}_2$ (denoted $\tilde{d}_1 \sqsubseteq \tilde{d}_2$) can be defined as follows:*

- *$\tilde{d}_1 \sqsubseteq \tilde{d}_2$ if $\forall \tilde{t}_i \in \tilde{d}_1, \exists \tilde{t}_j \in \tilde{d}_2 : \tilde{t}_i \leq \tilde{t}_j$.*
- *$\tilde{t}_i \leq \tilde{t}_j$ if $attr(\tilde{t}_i) \subseteq attr(\tilde{t}_j)$ and $\forall \tilde{r} \in \tilde{t}_i, \exists \tilde{r}' \in \tilde{t}_j : \gamma(\tilde{r}.\tilde{a}) \subseteq \gamma(\tilde{r}'.\tilde{a})$ for all $\tilde{a} \in attr(\tilde{t}_i)$.*

Let us consider recursive queries now. The convergence of recursive queries on an initial database depends on:

- the volume of the data in the initial database,
- the absence of cyclic data.

Note that we assume the initial database always finite as databases are finite (though unbounded in their sizes).

Let $Q : \mathcal{D} \mapsto \mathcal{D}$ be a recursive query which is monotone over the database domain $\mathcal{D}$. Consider a Galois Connection $(\langle \mathcal{D}, Q, d_0 \rangle, \alpha, \gamma, \langle \tilde{D}, \tilde{Q}, \tilde{d}_0 \rangle)$, where d_0 is the initial database in which recursive common table expression is $\emptyset$ and

$$\alpha : \mathcal{D} \rightarrow \tilde{D} \text{ - Abstraction mapping function.}$$
$$\gamma : \tilde{D} \rightarrow \mathcal{D} \text{ - Concretization mapping function.}$$
$$\langle \mathcal{D}, Q, d_0 \rangle \text{ - Concrete specifications.}$$
$$\langle \tilde{D}, \tilde{Q}, \tilde{d}_0 \rangle \text{ - Abstract specification.}$$

In case of abstract least fix-point computation $\text{lfp}^{\sqsubseteq}_{\tilde{d}_0}$ where $\sqsubseteq$ is a partial order over $\tilde{D}$, of recursive queries, either one of the following conditions is sufficient to guarantee the convergence:

- The abstraction function α removes the cyclic nature of the data when abstracting d_0 into $\widetilde{d_0}$.
- The abstract database domain $\widetilde{\mathcal{D}}$ is of finite height.

If none of the conditions is satisfied, then in order to enforce and accelerate the convergence of abstract computations of recursive queries, we are forced to instantiate a suitable widening operator.

Widening Construction. Given an abstract database domain $\widetilde{\mathcal{D}}$ over a set of attributes $\{\widetilde{a_i} \in \widetilde{A_i} \ : \ i \in \mathbb{I}\}$, where $\mathbb{I}$ is a finite set and $\widetilde{A_i}$ is the abstract attribute domain for $\widetilde{a_i}$. Let $\mathbb{J} \subseteq \mathbb{I}$ be a set of attributes such that $|\widetilde{A_j}|$ is finite for all $j \in \mathbb{J}$.

Let $\widetilde{d_1} \sqsubseteq \widetilde{d_2} \sqsubseteq \cdots \sqsubseteq \widetilde{d_n}$ be an increasing chain in $\widetilde{\mathcal{D}}$. Let ∇_i be the widening operator defined over $\widetilde{A_i}$ with $i \in \mathbb{I}\backslash\mathbb{J}$.

A generic widening operator ∇_d over the whole database domain is defined as follows: Let $\widetilde{d_1} = \{\widetilde{t_1^1}, \widetilde{t_2^1}, \ldots, \widetilde{t_n^1}\}$ and $\widetilde{d_2} = \{\widetilde{t_2^1}, \widetilde{t_2^2}, \ldots, \widetilde{t_m^2}\}$.

$$\widetilde{d_1} \nabla_d \widetilde{d_2} = ((((\widetilde{d_1} \nabla_t \widetilde{t_1^2}) \nabla_t \widetilde{t_2^2})\ldots) \nabla_t \widetilde{t_m^2}) \tag{1}$$

where

$$\widetilde{d} \nabla_t \widetilde{t} = \begin{cases} \text{if } \exists \widetilde{t'} \in \widetilde{d} \ : \ attr(\widetilde{t'}) = attr(\widetilde{t}) \\ (\widetilde{d}\backslash\widetilde{t'}) \cup (\widetilde{t'} \oplus \widetilde{t}) \\ \\ \widetilde{d} \cup \{\widetilde{t}\} \quad \text{otherwise} \end{cases}$$

Consider two abstract tables $\widetilde{t}$ and $\widetilde{t'}$ where $attr(\widetilde{t}) = attr(\widetilde{t'})$. Let $\widetilde{t} = \{\widetilde{r_1}, \widetilde{r_2}, \ldots, \widetilde{r_p}\}$ and $\widetilde{t'} = \{\widetilde{r_1'}, \widetilde{r_2'}, \ldots, \widetilde{r_q'}\}$. The operation $\widetilde{t^*} = \widetilde{t} \oplus \widetilde{t'}$ is defined as follows: $\forall \widetilde{r_l'} \in \widetilde{t'}$,

$$\begin{cases} \text{if } \exists \widetilde{r_k} \in \widetilde{t} \ : \ \forall \widetilde{a} \in (\{\widetilde{a_j} \mid j \in \mathbb{J}\} \cap \{attr(\widetilde{t})\}) \ \ \widetilde{r_k}.\widetilde{a} = \widetilde{r_l'}.\widetilde{a} \\ \widetilde{t^*} = (\widetilde{t}\backslash\widetilde{r_k}) \cup \{\widetilde{r_k} \diamond \widetilde{r_l}\} \\ \\ \widetilde{t^*} = \widetilde{t} \cup \{\widetilde{r_l'}\} \quad \text{otherwise} \end{cases}$$

Consider two records of the same table, *i.e.* two abstract tuples $\widetilde{r}$ and $\widetilde{r'}$ such that for all $h \in \mathbb{J} \ : \ \widetilde{r}.\widetilde{a_h} = \widetilde{r'}.\widetilde{a_h}$ (where $\widetilde{a_h}$ is an attribute of that table). The operation $\widetilde{r^*} = \widetilde{r} \diamond \widetilde{r'}$ is defined as follows:

$$\widetilde{r^*}.\widetilde{a_k} = \begin{cases} \widetilde{r}.\widetilde{a_k} \ \nabla_k \ \widetilde{r'}.\widetilde{a_k} \quad \text{if } k \notin \mathbb{J} \\ \\ \widetilde{r}.\widetilde{a_k} \quad \text{otherwise} \end{cases} \tag{2}$$

where ∇_k is the widening operator on the domain $\widetilde{A_k}$ satisfying the standard conditions of definition 5.

Let us illustrate the widening operator defined above using our running example.

Example 3. Consider the running example of section 2. Consider the domain of intervals as an abstract domain for the attribute "cost". The abstract database "$\widetilde{flight}$" corresponding to "flight" is depicted in Table 5. In this example, the

Table 5. Abstract Database "$\widetilde{flight}$"

flight no.	source	dest	cost
F001	Fiumicino (FCO)	Zurich (ZRH)	[410.57, 410.57]
F002	Marcopolo (VCE)	Orly (ORY)	[325.30, 325.30]
F003	Orly (ORY)	Zurich (ZRH)	[200.00, 200.00]
F004	Orly (ORY)	Fiumicino (FCO)	[428.28, 428.28]
F005	Zurich (ZRH)	Marcopolo (VCE)	[250.15, 250.15]

indexed set $\mathbb{J}$ corresponds to the attributes $\widetilde{flight\ no.}$, $\widetilde{source}$ and $\widetilde{dest}$: observe that for these attributes the abstraction function is just the identity. For the other attributes $\widetilde{connects}$ and $\widetilde{cost}$, corresponding to the indexed set $\mathbb{I} \setminus \mathbb{J}$, we consider the widening operator for the domain of intervals introduced in Example 2. The application of this widening operator results into a fast convergence of the fixpoint computation of the running query, yielding to the following approximate result after $(k_1 * k_2)$ iterations, where k_1 and k_2 represent the threshold for the widening operators in case of the two interval domains corresponding to the attributes $\widetilde{connects}$ and $\widetilde{cost}$ respectively:

departure	arrival	connects	cost
Marcopolo (VCE)	Orly (ORY)	[0, ∞]	[325.30, ∞]
Marcopolo (VCE)	Zurich (ZRH)	[1, ∞]	[525.30, ∞]
Marcopolo (VCE)	Fiumicino (FCO)	[1, ∞]	[753.58, ∞]
Marcopolo (VCE)	Marcopolo (VCE)	[2, ∞]	[775.45, ∞]

Observe that although users are not able to get the exact details, they still get a precise information on the minimum number of connections and on the best price for all reachable destinations. A more sophisticated widening operator might also be used to get more precise information, by allowing the multiple occurrences of the same pair ($\widetilde{departure}$, $\widetilde{arrival}$) up to a threshold number of cases.

Convergence. It can be observed from equations 1 and 2 that ∇_d is defined in terms of widening operators that satisfy the standard conditions of Definition 5. Therefore, by Theorem 3, we can prove that the upward iteration sequence starting at the initial abstract database $\widetilde{d_0}$ and such that

$$\widetilde{d_{i+1}} := \begin{cases} \widetilde{d_i} & \text{if } \widetilde{Q}(\widetilde{d_i}) \sqsubseteq \widetilde{d_i} \\ \widetilde{d_i} \; \nabla_d \; \widetilde{Q}(\widetilde{d_i}), & \text{otherwise} \end{cases}$$

where $\widetilde{Q} : \widetilde{\mathcal{D}} \mapsto \widetilde{\mathcal{D}}$ is an abstract recursive query which is monotonic function, converges after a finite number $l \in \mathbb{N}$ of iterations and gives a sound approximation of $\mathrm{lfp}^{\sqsubseteq}_{\widetilde{d_0}} \widetilde{Q}$.

6   Conclusions

In this work, we dealt with a fast convergence of recursive queries independent of the database content. We discussed how the application of widening operators in the context of Abstract Interpretation make the system more effective and efficient in case of recursive query executions, in particular when the presence of large volume of data or the presence of cyclic nature of data in a database affect recursive execution and result into a convergence after finitely many steps or result into an infinite loop.

Acknowledgement. Work partially supported by PRIN 2010-11 project "Security Horizons".

References

1. Agrawal, R., Devanbu, P.: Moving selections into linear least fixpoint queries. IEEE Transactions on Knowledge and Data Engineering 1(4), 424–432 (1989)
2. Aho, A.V., Ullman, J.D.: Universality of data retrieval languages. In: Proceedings of the POPL 1979, pp. 110–119. ACM Press (1979)
3. Alfred, T.: A lattice-theoretical fixpoint theorem and its applications. Pacific J. Math. 5(2), 285–309 (1955)
4. Burzańska, M., Stencel, K., Wiśniewski, P.: Pushing Predicates into Recursive SQL Common Table Expressions. In: Grundspenkis, J., Morzy, T., Vossen, G. (eds.) ADBIS 2009. LNCS, vol. 5739, pp. 194–205. Springer, Heidelberg (2009)
5. Chakravarthy, U.S., Grant, J., Minker, J.: Logic-based approach to semantic query optimization. ACM Transactions on Database Systems 15(2), 162–207 (1990)
6. Codd, E.F.: Relational completeness of database subanguages. In: Database Systems, pp. 65–98 (1972)
7. Codd, E.F.: A relational model of data for large shared data banks. Communications of the ACM 25th Anniversary Issue 26(1), 64–69 (1983)
8. Cortesi, A., Zanioli, M.: Widening and narrowing operators for abstract interpretation. Computer Languages, Systems & Structures 37, 24–42 (2011)
9. Cousot, P., Cousot, R.: Abstract interpretation: a unified lattice model for static analysis of programs by construction or approximation of fixpoints. In: Proceedings of the POPL 1977, pp. 238–252. ACM Press (1977)
10. Cousot, P., Cousot, R.: Comparing the Galois Connection and Widening/Narrowing Approaches to Abstract Interpretation. In: Bruynooghe, M., Wirsing, M. (eds.) PLILP 1992. LNCS, vol. 631, pp. 269–295. Springer, Heidelberg (1992)
11. Halder, R., Cortesi, A.: A Persistent Public Watermarking of Relational Databases. In: Jha, S., Mathuria, A. (eds.) ICISS 2010. LNCS, vol. 6503, pp. 216–230. Springer, Heidelberg (2010)
12. Halder, R., Cortesi, A.: Cooperative Query Answering by Abstract Interpretation. In: Černá, I., Gyimóthy, T., Hromkovič, J., Jefferey, K., Králović, R., Vukolić, M., Wolf, S. (eds.) SOFSEM 2011. LNCS, vol. 6543, pp. 284–296. Springer, Heidelberg (2011)
13. Halder, R.: Extending Abstract Interpretation to New Applicative Scenarios. Ph.D. thesis, Università Ca' Foscari Venezia (2012)

14. Halder, R., Cortesi, A.: Abstract interpretation of database query languages. Computer Languages, Systems & Structures 38, 123–157 (2012)
15. Halder, R., Cortesi, A.: Fine Grained Access Control for Relational Databases by Abstract Interpretation. In: Pedrosa, V. (ed.) ICSOFT 2010. CCIS, vol. 170, pp. 235–249. Springer, Heidelberg (2012)
16. Halder, R., Cortesi, A.: Abstract program slicing of database query languages. In: Proceedings of the the 28th Symposium On Applied Computing - Special Track on Database Theory, Technology, and Applications. ACM Press, Coimbra (2013)
17. Halder, R., Pal, S., Cortesi, A.: Watermarking techniques for relational databases: Survey, classification and comparison. Journal of Universal Computer Science 16(21), 3164–3190 (2010)
18. Logozzo, F.: Class invariants as abstract interpretation of trace semantics. Computer Languages, Systems & Structures 35, 100–142 (2009)
19. Ordonez, C.: Optimization of linear recursive queries in sql. IEEE Transactions on Knowledge and Data Engineering 22(2), 264–277 (2010)
20. Pieciukiewicz, T., Stencel, K., Subieta, K.: Usable Recursive Queries. In: Eder, J., Haav, H.-M., Kalja, A., Penjam, J. (eds.) ADBIS 2005. LNCS, vol. 3631, pp. 17–28. Springer, Heidelberg (2005)
21. Przymus, P., Boniewicz, A., Burzańska, M., Stencel, K.: Recursive Query Facilities in Relational Databases: A Survey. In: Zhang, Y., Cuzzocrea, A., Ma, J., Chung, K.-i., Arslan, T., Song, X. (eds.) DTA and BSBT 2010. CCIS, vol. 118, pp. 89–99. Springer, Heidelberg (2010)

Verification of Message Sequence Structures

Meenakshi D'Souza[1] and Teodor Knapik[2]

[1] IIIT-Bangalore, India
meenakshi@iiitb.ac.in
[2] ERIM, Université de la Nouvelle Calédonie
knapik@univ-nc.nc

Introduction

We study the problem of using monadic second order (MSO) logic to reason about certain distributed infinite state systems that communicate by exchanging messages. The success of MONA [6] and similar tools shows that a non-elementary worst-case complexity of MSO logic is not relevant in the practice of model checking. Indeed, MSO logic enjoys a satisfactory expressive power for many applications since it subsumes many temporal and program logics. Towards obtaining decidable MSO theory, we consider systems that are not explicitly product-based but, still have an underlying component-based structure. One such model is that of Message Sequence Charts (MSCs). MSCs are an ITU–standardized notation widely used in early stages of design of communication protocols [11]. An MSC depicts the exchange of messages between processes and corresponds to a single partially ordered execution of the system. Message Sequence Graphs (MSGs) provide a mechanism to specify collections of MSCs. MSGs are defined as finite graphs whose vertices are labelled with finite MSCs. They allow MSCs to be combined using the operations of choice, concatenation and repetition. Note however that in the present paper MSGs need not be finite.

CMSGs [5] are finite graphs like MSGs but the vertices are labelled with Compositional MSCs (CMSCs). A CMSC is an MSC with *unmatched* send or receive events (in addition to the normal send and receive events). These are send (receive) events whose corresponding receive (send) events do not occur within the MSC. While defining the language represented by the CMSG as concatenation of CMSCs along a path, these unmatched send (receive) events are matched up with their corresponding receive (send) events.

The main aim of this paper is to consider infinite MSC–like structures and to obtain the decidability of MSO theories of these structures. We consider arbitrary (possibly infinite) graphs labelled by a finite set of MSCs. The semantics of such an *infinite MSG* is given by its corresponding *message sequence structure (MSS)*. Given an infinite MSG, its MSS is obtained by replacing each vertex with the MSC labelling it and by asynchronously concatenating the MSCs labelling adjacent vertices. We construct an MSO–transduction [2] between an MSG and its corresponding MSS. It follows that the MSO theory of the resulting MSS is decidable whenever the MSO theory of the given MSG is so. We extend these results to CMSSs corresponding to unfoldings of possibly infinite CMSGs which

C. Hota and P.K. Srimani (Eds.): ICDCIT 2013, LNCS 7753, pp. 171–182, 2013.
© Springer-Verlag Berlin Heidelberg 2013

are bounded in the sense of [10]. In this way we obtain a wide range of infinite MSSs (resp. CMSSs) the MSO theory of which is decidable.

Most of work about model checking in this context has been focused on linearizations. [7] provides a survey of several results, with special emphasis on regular MSC languages. Here we follow the approach of [9] where the model checking problem for finite MSGs or its unfoldings against specifications written in MSO logic which are interpreted directly on MSSs (and not on their linearizations) is shown to be decidable. For unfoldings of bounded finite CMSGs this problem is shown to be decidable in [10].

1   Message Sequence (Charts, Graphs and Structures)

Let us fix a finite set of processes $\mathcal{P}$ for the rest of the paper and let p, q range over $\mathcal{P}$. Let us also fix a finite set of messages Γ and a finite set of local actions Λ. Let $\Sigma_p = \{(p!q, a), (p?q, a), (p, l) \mid q \in \mathcal{P}, p \neq q, a \in \Gamma, l \in \Lambda\}$ denote the set of actions that p participates in. The action $(p!q, a)$ should be read as "p sends the message a to q" while the action $(p?q, a)$ means "p receives the message a from q". The pair (p, l) represents p doing a local action l. Let $\Sigma = \bigcup_{p \in \mathcal{P}} \Sigma_p$ denote the set of all actions.

Definition 1.1. *A Message Sequence Chart (MSC) over $\mathcal{P}$ is a tuple $M = (E, \{\leq_p\}_{p \in \mathcal{P}}, \lambda, \eta)$ where*

- *E is a finite set of events.*
- *$\lambda : E \to \Sigma$ is the labelling function which identifies for each event an action. Let $E_p = \{e \in E \mid \lambda(e) \in \Sigma_p\}$ denote the set of events of E which p participates in. Also, let $E_! = \{e \in E \mid \lambda(e) = (p!q, a)$ for some $p, q \in \mathcal{P}, a \in \Gamma\}$ denote the set of send events and $E_? = \{e \in E \mid \lambda(e) = (p?q, a)$ for some $p, q \in \mathcal{P}, a \in \Gamma\}$ denote the set of receive events of E.*
- *$\eta : E_! \to E_?$ is the matching function which associates with each send event, its corresponding receive event. We require η to be bijective and, for every $e, e' \in E$, if $\eta(e) = e'$, then $\lambda(e) = (p!q, a)$ and $\lambda(e') = (q?p, a)$ for some $p, q \in \mathcal{P}, a \in \Gamma$.*
- *$\leq_p$ is a total order on E_p for each $p \in \mathcal{P}$. Let $\widehat{\leq} = (\bigcup_{p \in \mathcal{P}} \leq_p) \cup \{(e, e') \mid e, e' \in E$ and $\eta(e) = e'\}$. Let $\leq = (\widehat{\leq})^*$ be the reflexive–transitive closure of $\widehat{\leq}$. Then $\leq$ denotes the causal ordering of events in the CMSC and we require it to be a partial order on E.*

The assumption of FIFO communication channels between processes is not necessary here for an MSC. It may be expressed by an MSO sentence to check.

An MSC $M = (E, \{\leq_p\}_{p \in \mathcal{P}}, \lambda, \eta)$ can be thought of as a relational structure in the following obvious way: $M = (E, \{\leq_p\}_{p \in \mathcal{P}}, \{c\}_{c \in \Sigma}, \eta)$ where $\eta(x_1, y_2) \wedge \eta(x_2, y_1)$, E and $\{\leq_p\}_{p \in \mathcal{P}}$ are as above, $\eta(e_1, e_2)$ holds iff $\eta(e_1) = e_2$, for $c \in \Sigma$, $c(e)$ holds iff $\lambda(e) = c$.

A *message sequence graph (MSG)* is an $\mathcal{M}$–labelled graph $G = (V_G, r_G, \xrightarrow[G]{}, \sigma_G)$ where V_G is at most countable set of vertices, $r_G \in V_G$ is the root of the graph, $\xrightarrow[G]{}$ is the edge relation, $\sigma_G \colon V_G \to \mathcal{M}$ is the labelling map into a finite set $\mathcal{M} = \{M_1, \ldots, M_n\}$ of MSCs over $\mathcal{P}$.

The semantics of an MSG is described by its corresponding MSS. Consider an $\mathcal{M}$–labelled graph $G = (V_G, r_G, \xrightarrow[G]{}, \sigma_G)$. For each $v \in V_G$, let $\sigma_G(v) = (E^v, \{\leq_p^v\}_{p \in \mathcal{P}}, \lambda^v, \eta^v)$ denote the MSC labelling the vertex v. The *message sequence structure (MSS)* corresponding to G is $\mathsf{MSS}(G) := (E, \{s_p\}_{p \in \mathcal{P}}, \{\iota_p\}_{p \in \mathcal{P}}, \{c\}_{c \in \Sigma}, \eta)$ where

- $E := \bigcup_{v \in V_G} \{v\} \times E^v$,
- $s_p := \big\{ ((v_0, e), (v_t, e')) \mid v_0, v_t \in V_G, \ t \geq 1,$
  e is the maximum p–event (wrt. $\leq^{v_0}$) in $\sigma_G(v_0)$,
  e' is the minimum p–event (wrt. $\leq^{v_t}$) in $\sigma_G(v_t)$,
  $\exists (v_i)_{i \in [t-1]}$ s.t. $v_0 \xrightarrow[G]{} v_1 \xrightarrow[G]{} \cdots \xrightarrow[G]{} v_t$
  and $E_p^{v_i} = \varnothing$ for $i \in [t-1] \big\}$
  $\cup \big\{ ((v, e), (v, e')) \mid v \in V_G, \ e'$ is an immediate $\leq_p^v$ successor of $e, \big\}$
- $\iota_p := \{ (r_G, e) \mid e$ is the minimum p–event (wrt. $\leq_p^v$) in $\sigma_G(r_G) \}$
- $c := \{ (v, e) \in E \mid \lambda^v(e) = c \}$,
- $\eta := \{ ((v, e), (v, e')) \mid v \in V_G, (e, e') \in \eta^v \}$.

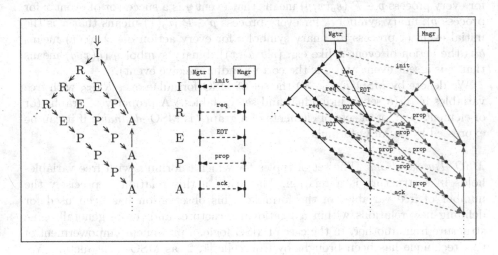

Fig. 1. An infinite MSG (left) and its corresponding MSS (right)

Since an MSS may have circuits, we use a successor relation in the above definition instead of its reflexive-transitive closure as the latter is not necessarily an order. The MSS corresponding to an MSG is yet another graph and represents the behavior corresponding to messages exchanged between processes, as per the structure of the underlying graph. Later, we will define structures corresponding to paths in the MSG and these structures will be infinite deterministic MSS.

An example of an infinite MSG and its corresponding MSS is given in Fig. 1. It is a simplified view of a transaction between two processes `Negotiator` and `Manager`. `Negotiator` forwards to `Manager` customers' requests for resource allocation. Allocation is done "by slots". Several requests for a slot are sent, ended by an `EOT` message indicating the end of requests for the next slot. Then `Manager` makes a proposal of resource allocation in response to every request and sends back every proposal to `Negotiator` in charge of routing it to the corresponding customer. Every customer either accepts or rejects the proposal. Customer acceptance/rejection is forwarded by `Negotiator` to `Manager` as an acknowledgement. Our simplified view of Fig. 1 does not represent customers.

2   Monadic Second–Order Logic Applied to MSC-Related Structures

We recall that *Monadic Second–order logic* is first–order logic augmented with (uppercase) variables denoting subsets of the domain of the considered structure, and new atomic formulae of the form $x \in X$ expressing the membership of x in a set X in addition to first–order atomic formulae. To express properties of scenarios specified by an MSG and represented by the corresponding MSS, first-order atomic formula use symbols from $\mathcal{R}_{\text{MSS}}$ which consist of binary symbol s_p for every process $p \in \mathcal{P}$ ($s_p(x, y)$ means that event y is a successor of event x for process p), unary symbol ι_p for every process $p \in \mathcal{P}$ ($\iota_p(x)$ means that x is the initial event of process p), unary symbol c for every action $c \in \Sigma$ ($c(x)$ means c is the action of event x like e.g. $(p!q, a)(x)$), binary symbol η ($\eta(x, y)$ means that x is a sent event and y is the corresponding receive event).

We denote by $\text{MSO}(\mathcal{R}_{\text{MSS}}, \mathcal{X})$ the set of MSO formulae over $\mathcal{R}_{\text{MSS}}$ with free variables in $\mathcal{X}$ (a set of individual and set variables.) A property of graphs (or of elements and/or of sets of elements of a graph) is MSO–*definable* if it can be expressed by an MSO formula.

MSO–Transductions. The set of tuples for which a formula with free variables holds in a structure is a relation. The arity of this relation is precisely the number of free variables of the formula. This observation has been used for defining new relations within a relational structure, and, more generally, one structure from another. In the case of MSO logic, a prominent empowerment of this technique has been brought by Courcelle [1, 2] as MSO-transduction. We consider a particular case of parameterless MSO-transduction.

Given set $\mathcal{R}$ and $\mathcal{R}'$ of ranked relation symbols, a *(parameterless) MSO–transduction* is a function f from the class of $\mathcal{R}$-structures into the class of $\mathcal{R}'$-structures defined, from $k \in \mathbb{N}$ and MSO formulae α in $\text{MSO}(\mathcal{R}, \varnothing)$, $\delta_1, \ldots, \delta_k$ in $\text{MSO}(\mathcal{R}, \{x\})$, $\theta_{r,i_1,\ldots,i_n}$ in $\text{MSO}(\mathcal{R}, \{x_1, \ldots, x_n\})$, for $r \in \mathcal{R}', n = \rho(r), 1 \leq i_1, \ldots, i_n \leq k$, as follows, for an $\mathcal{R}$-structure S:

1. $f(S)$ is undefined iff $S \nvDash \alpha$.
2. Assuming $S \models \alpha$, then $f(S) = T$ where T is constructed as follows:

- the domain D_T of T is given by $D_T = D_1 \times \{1\} \cup \ldots \cup D_k \times \{k\} \subseteq D_S \times [k]$; each D_i is $\{x \in D_S \mid S \models \delta_i(x)\}$;
- each relation r_T, for $r \in \mathcal{R}'$ is defined on T as the union of sets of tuples of the form $\{((x_1, i_1), \ldots, (x_n, i_n)) \mid S \models \theta_{r,i_1,\ldots,i_n}(x_1, \ldots, x_n), \ x_1 \in D_{i_1}, \ldots x_n \in D_{i_n}\}$, for all $i_1, \ldots, i_n \in [k]$.

The tuple $\Delta = \langle \alpha, \delta_1, \ldots, \delta_k, \{\theta_{r,i_1,\ldots,i_{\rho(r)}}\}_{r \in \mathcal{R}, 1 \leq i_1,\ldots,i_{\rho(r)} \leq k} \rangle$ is called a *definition scheme*. Since T is uniquely associated with S and Δ whenever it is defined, we can denote T by $\mathrm{def}_\Delta(S)$. The transduction f is then defined by $f(S) = T = \mathrm{def}_\Delta(S)$. An MSO–transduction is k–*copying*, if $k > 1$.

We say that a function f from the class of $\mathcal{R}$-structures into the class of $\mathcal{R}'$-structures is *MSO–compatible* [3] if there exists a total recursive mapping $f^\#\colon \mathrm{MSO}(\mathcal{R}', \varnothing) \to \mathrm{MSO}(\mathcal{R}, \varnothing)$ such that $S \models f^\#(\varphi)$ iff $f(S) \models \varphi$. We call $f^\#(\varphi)$ the *backwards translation* of φ relative to f.

Theorem 2.1 (Courcelle 91). *Every MSO-transduction is MSO–compatible.*

The construction of the backwards translation underlying the proof of this theorem is our main tool for transferring decidability of the MSO theory of an MSG into the corresponding MSS. Another tool is the unfolding.

Unfolding. Let Π denote a finite alphabet. A rooted Π–labelled graph is a tuple $G = (V_G, r_G, \underset{G}{\longrightarrow}, \sigma_G)$ where V_G denotes the set of vertices, $r_G \in V_G$ is a distinguished vertex called *the root of* G, $\underset{G}{\longrightarrow} \subseteq (V_G \times V_G)$ is the edge relation of G and $\sigma_G\colon V_G \to \Pi$ is the labelling function which associates a label from Π to every vertex in V_G. The *unfolding of* G, written $\mathrm{Un}(G)$, is the tree $T :=$ $(V_T, r_T, \underset{T}{\longrightarrow}, \sigma_T)$ defined by $V_T = \{r_G v_1 \ldots v_n \mid r_G \underset{G}{\longrightarrow} v_1 \underset{G}{\longrightarrow} \cdots \underset{G}{\longrightarrow} v_n\}$, $r_T = r_G$, $\underset{T}{\longrightarrow} = \{(r_G v_1 \ldots v_{n-1}, r_G v_1 \ldots v_n) \mid r_G \underset{G}{\longrightarrow} v_1 \underset{G}{\longrightarrow} \cdots \underset{G}{\longrightarrow} v_n\}$, and $\sigma_T(r_G v_1 \ldots v_n) = \sigma_G(v_n)$. The following is an adaptation of Theorem 22 of [3].

Theorem 2.2 (Courcelle, Walukiewicz 98). *The unfolding is MSO–compatible.*

3 MSO Transduction from MSGs to MSSs

In this section, we will show that there exists an MSO–transduction which maps every MSG to the corresponding MSS.

Let us fix a finite set of MSCs $\mathcal{M} = \{M_1, M_2, \ldots M_n\}$ with $M_l = (E^l, \{\leq_p^l\}_{p \in \mathcal{P}}, \lambda^l, \eta^l)$, for $l \in [n]$ and an MSG $G = (V_G, r_G, \underset{G}{\longrightarrow}, \sigma_G)$. The definition scheme uses symbols from $\mathcal{R}_{\mathrm{MSG}}$ which consists of unary symbol r ($r(x)$ means that x is the root of the graph), unary symbols of $\mathcal{M} = \{M_1, M_2, \ldots M_n\}$ ($M_l(x)$ means that vertex x is labelled by MSC M_l), binary symbol $\to$ ($x \to y$ means that there is an edge from x to y).

We denote by $\mathcal{M}_p^\varnothing$ the subset of MSCs from $\mathcal{M}$ which have no event for process p: $\mathcal{M}_p^\varnothing := \{M_l \in \mathcal{M} \mid E_p^l = \varnothing\}$. Without loss of generality, we may assume that $E^1, E^2, \ldots E^n$ are disjoint subsets of $\mathbb{N}$ such that $\bigcup_{l=1}^n E^l = [k]$ for some $k \in \mathbb{N}$. For a regular expression R, we denote by $\mathsf{path}_R(x, y)$ an MSO formula saying that there is a path with a label in a rational set R between two vertices is MSO definable (see e.g. [2]).

We define a k–copying transduction $\mathcal{T}\mathsf{MSC} \colon G \mapsto \mathsf{MSS}(G)$ that replaces every vertex in G with its MSC (as given by σ_G) and in addition, it "locally concatenates" the MSCs corresponding to adjacent vertices.

Definition scheme Δ associated with $\mathcal{T}\mathsf{MSC}$ is given by $\Delta = (\mathsf{true}, \delta_i, \{\theta_{(s_p,i,j)}\}_{p \in \mathcal{P}}, \{\theta_{(\iota_p,i)}\}_{p \in \mathcal{P}}, \{\theta_{(c,i)}\}_{c \in \Sigma}, \theta_{(\eta,i,j)} \mid i, j \in [k])$, where

- Formula δ_i is $M_l(x)$, where l is such that $i \in E^l$. It means that the vertices of the i–th copy are precisely those labelled by MSC M_l such that i is an event of M_l.
- For each $p \in \mathcal{P}$, the formula $\theta_{(s_p,i,j)}(x, y)$ is a disjunction $\varphi \vee \psi$ where φ is defined by $\mathsf{path}_{M_l(\mathcal{M}_p^{\varnothing})^* M_m}(x, y)$ if $\max_p(E^l) = i$, and $\min_p(E^m) = j$ otherwise. ψ is defined by $M_l(x) \wedge x = y$, if $i, j \in E^l$ and j is an immediate successor of i w.r.t. $\leq_p^l$, false, otherwise.
- For each $p \in \mathcal{P}$, the formula $\theta_{(\iota_p,i)}(x)$ is defined by $r(x) \wedge M_l(x)$, if $\min_p(E^l) = i$, false, otherwise.
- For each $c \in \Sigma$, the formula $\theta_{(c,i)}(x)$ is defined by $M_l(x)$, if $\lambda^l(i) = c$, false, otherwise.
- $\theta_{(\eta,i,j)}(x, y)$ is defined by $M_l(x) \wedge x = y$, if $(i, j) \in \eta^l$, false, otherwise.

By adding dummy events with internal actions, we can transform set $\mathcal{M}$ of MSC labels so that $\mathcal{M}_p^{\varnothing} = \varnothing$ for every process p. Then φ is simply $x \to y$ or false depending on i and j of $\theta_{(s_p,i,j)}(x, y)$: $x \to y$, if $\max_p(E^l) = i$ and $\min_p(E^m) = j$, false, otherwise. Under this simplification, definition scheme Δ consists of first order quantifier free formulae with at most two atomic formulae and at most two variables. Consequently only polynomial overhead results from corresponding backwards translation for model–checking.

Proposition 3.1. $\mathsf{def}_\Delta(G) = H$ *iff G is a MSG and H is its corresponding MSS.*

Since Δ mimics the definition of the MSS associated to an MSG, this proposition follows by construction. The next corollary follows from Theorem 2.1 and Proposition 3.1.

Corollary 3.2. *For every MSG G, the MSO theory of $\mathcal{T}\mathsf{MSC}(G)$ is decidable if the MSO theory of G is so.*

4 Properties of a Language of MSCs

We now consider maximal paths in an MSG and consider MSSs obtained by asynchronous concatenation of MSC labelling the vertices of the MSG. These structures are nothing but infinite MSCs, as considered in [8] for example.

Consider an MSG G. We denote the collection of MSCs obtained by concatenating MSCs labelling the vertices of maximal paths in G by $\mathsf{PMSC}(G)$:

$\text{PMSC}(G) := \{\mathcal{JMSC}(\varrho) \mid \varrho$ is a maximal possibly infinite path starting from $r_G\}$. The following proposition is used to check whether an MSO sentence holds for every MSC of $\text{PMSC}(G)$.

Proposition 4.1. *For every MSG G and for every MSO sentence φ one can construct an MSO sentence ψ such that $\text{PMSC}(G) \models \varphi$ iff $\text{Un}(G) \models \psi$, where $\text{Un}(G)$ stands for the unfolding of G from its root.*

The following corollary follows from the above proposition and Theorem 2.2.

Corollary 4.2. *For every MSG G the MSO theory of $\text{PMSC}(G)$ is decidable if the MSO theory of G is so.*

Although we consider maximal (possibly infinite) paths, we can obtain analogous results for a language of MSSs corresponding to all finite paths of an MSG. The above corollary establishes a generic result concerning the decidability of the MSO-theory of MSCs generated by (maximal) paths in structures labelled by MSCs.

5   CMSC–Labelled Graphs

Definition 5.1. A Compositional Message Sequence Chart *(CMSC)* over $\mathcal{P}$ is a tuple $M = (E, \{\leq_p\}_{p \in \mathcal{P}}, \lambda, \eta)$ where $E, \leq_p, \lambda$ are as defined in an MSC and η is a partial matching function which associates with a send event, its corresponding receive event. Unlike in an MSC, η is only an injective function. We say that $e \in E_!$ is an unmatched send event if η is not defined on e and $e \in E_?$ is an unmatched receive event if $e \notin \eta(E_!)$.

In this section, we consider graphs labelled with compositional MSCs. Similar to MSGs, the semantics of CMSC–labelled graphs will be obtained by *concatenating* the CMSCs labelling adjacent vertices in the graph. Concatenation of two CMSCs is done by (asynchronously) concatenating the events of each process, and by matching up some unmatched sends of the resulting CMSC with corresponding unmatched receives.

Definition 5.2. Let $M_i = (E^i, \{\leq_p^i\}_{p \in \mathcal{P}}, \lambda^i, \eta^i)$, $i = 1, 2$ be two CMSCs, with $E^1 \cap E^2 = \varnothing$. Also, let M_1 have no unmatched receives. Then the concatenation of M_1 and M_2, written $M_1 M_2$ is a CMSC $(E, \{\leq_p\}_{p \in \mathcal{P}}, \lambda, \eta)$ where $E = E^1 \cup E^2$, $\lambda = \lambda^1 \cup \lambda^2$, $\leq_p = \leq_p^1 \cup \leq_p^2 \cup \{(e_1, e_2) \mid e_1 \in E_p^1, e_2 \in E_p^2\}$ and η is defined as follows:

- If $e \in E_!^i$ and $\eta^i(e)$ is defined, where $i \in [2]$, then $\eta(e) = \eta^i(e)$.
- Let $e_1 \in E_!^1$, η^1 be undefined on e_1, and $\lambda(e_1) = (p!q, a)$. If there is an event $e_2 \in E_?^2 \setminus \eta^2(E_!^2)$ such that $\lambda(e_2) = (q?p, a)$ and
$$|\{f \in E \mid f \leq_p e_1 \wedge \lambda(f) = (p!q, a) \wedge f \notin \mathcal{D}om(\eta^1)\}| =$$
$$= |\{f' \in E \mid f' \leq_q e_2 \wedge \lambda(f') = (q?p, a) \wedge f' \notin \eta^2(E_p)\}|,$$
then we set $\eta(e_1) = e_2$. Clearly, if such an e_2 exists, it is unique.
- η is undefined on all other events of $E_!$.

Note that concatenation of two CMSCs is not an MSC in general. The result of the concatenation may still have some unmatched send events. It may also have unmatched receive events but then we disallow it be used as the left member of another concatenation. Requiring the first member of a concatenation has no unmatched receive events makes it a partial operation. When we write a series of concatenations $N_1 N_2 \cdots$ we always mean a left–to–right application, i.e. the term $((N_1 N_2) N_3) \cdots$. Note that concatenation is not associative and is sensitive to the order in which it is made.

We define a CMSG just like a CMSC–labelled graph. A *compositional message sequence graph (CMSG)* is given by a tuple $G = (V_G, r_G, \xrightarrow{G}, \sigma_G)$ where V_G is at most countable set of vertices, $r_G \in V_G$ is the root of the graph, $\xrightarrow{G}$ is the edge relation, $\sigma_G \colon V_G \to \mathcal{M}$ is the labelling map into a finite set $\mathcal{M} = \{M_1, \ldots, M_n\}$ of CMSCs over $\mathcal{P}$.

Like an MSG, CMSG represents a variety of scenarios defined by concatenation of individual CMSCs labelling a path in the graph. However, defining a CMSS analogous to the notion of an MSS is meaningless in general. Indeed, given a sequence of labels $N_1 N_2 \cdots N_k \ldots N_{k+m} \cdots$ corresponding to a path of a CMSG, the matching between sends of N_k and receives of N_{k+m} depends not only on MSCs occurring between N_k and N_{k+m} but also on the prefix $N_1 N_2 \cdots N_{k-1}$. Hopefully, this matching is unambiguous in cases when CMSG is a word or a tree. Moreover, provided an additional restriction, it may be defined by means of an MSO–transduction. An essential ingredient of this transduction is an automaton accepting sequences of CMSCs satisfying this restriction.

6   Bounded Sequences of CMSCs

We start this section by pointing out that a counter automaton can be simulated by a finite CMSG. The number of processes we need for this simulation is twice the number of counters. Each counter corresponds to an ordered pair of processes (p, q). Its value is encoded by the number of unmatched send events from p to q. Then the increment (resp. decrement) is realised by a CMSC say $I_{(p,q)}$ (resp. $D_{p,q}$) with only one event labelled $(p!q, a)$ (resp. $(q?p, a)$) and non-zero test of the counter is realised by $D_{p,q}$ followed by $I_{(p,q)}$.[1]

As consequence of this fact, we need to restrict the expressive power of CMSGs by bounding the number of unmatched send events. Given the set of all sequences of CMSCs corresponding to maximal paths of a CMSG and $b \in \mathbb{N}$, we wish to construct an automaton that accepts all those paths whose sequences of CMSCs have the following property: for every finite prefix ϱ of an accepted path, consider the CMSC M_ϱ obtained by concatenating the CMSCs along ϱ. Then, M_ϱ is such that for every pair of processes $p, q \in \mathcal{P}$ and each message $a \in \Gamma$ the number of unmatched sends of a from p to q is at most b. We make this precise below.

Consider a CMSC $M = (E, \{\leq_p\}_{p \in \mathcal{P}}, \lambda, \eta)$. For each pair of processes $p, q \in \mathcal{P}$ such that $p \neq q$, we define two sequences over E: the sequence of unmatched

---

[1] As for multi-counter automata with zero test, it is straightforward to establish that multi-counter automata with non-zero test are again Turing–complete.

sends of message a from p to q, written $U_{(p!q,a)}(M)$, and the sequence of un-matched receives by q from p of message a, written $U_{(q?p,a)}(M)$.

Definition 6.1. *A sequence of CMSCs $N_1, N_2, \ldots$ is said to be b–bounded, for $b \in \mathbb{N}$, if for every prefix $\varrho = N_1, N_2, \ldots N_i$ of the sequence, the CMSC $N_\varrho = N_1 N_2 \ldots N_i$ obtained by concatenating the CMSCs along ϱ, we have $|U_{(p!q,a)}(N_\varrho)| \leq b$ for all $p, q \in \mathcal{P}$ and $a \in \Gamma$. We say that a CMSG G is b–bounded if every maximal path starting from the root of G is so.*

Note that our notion of boundedness is similar to [10] but differs from the one of [4] where it depends on linearizations. Moreover it should not be confused with analogous notion for message passing automata. Unlike other approaches, we do not address channel capacity related questions here. According to our definition, every sequence of MSCs $M_1 M_2 \ldots$ is 0-bounded. Consequently our notion is meaningful for sequences of CMSCs (but not for sequences of MSCs) and is used for transforming such sequences into their concatenations.

In order to define an MSO–transduction, which, given $N_1, N_2, \ldots N_i, \ldots$ yields the CMSC obtained as concatenation $N_1 N_2 \ldots N_i \ldots$, we first construct a finite automaton $\mathcal{A}_{b,\mathcal{M}}$ which accepts all b–bounded sequences of CMSCs for which the concatenation is defined.

6.1   An Automaton for Checking b–Boundedness

The states of automaton $\mathcal{A}_{b,\mathcal{M}}$ record the number of unmatched sends of each message between every pair of processes. As for MSGs, we fix a finite set of CMSCs $\mathcal{M} := \{M_i \mid i \in [n]\}$ with $M_i = (E^i, \{\leq_p^i\}_{p \in \mathcal{P}}, \lambda^i, \eta^i)$.

The automaton is given by $\mathcal{A}_{b,\mathcal{M}} = (Q_{\mathcal{A}_{b,\mathcal{M}}}, \xrightarrow{\mathcal{A}_{b,\mathcal{M}}}, I_{\mathcal{A}_{b,\mathcal{M}}}, F_{\mathcal{A}_{b,\mathcal{M}}})$ where $Q_{\mathcal{A}_{b,\mathcal{M}}} := \{\chi \mid \chi \colon ((\mathcal{P} \times \mathcal{P}) \setminus \mathrm{Id}_\mathcal{P}) \times \Gamma \to [b]\}$ where $\mathrm{Id}_\mathcal{P}$ is the identity relation on $\mathcal{P}$, $I_{\mathcal{A}_{b,\mathcal{M}}} := \{\chi_0 \mid \chi_0(p, q, a) = 0, \text{ for all } a \in \Gamma, p, q \in \mathcal{P}, p \neq q\}$, $F_{\mathcal{A}_{b,\mathcal{M}}} := Q_{\mathcal{A}_{b,\mathcal{M}}}$, $\chi \xrightarrow{M}_{\mathcal{A}_{b,\mathcal{M}}} \chi' \in (Q \times \mathcal{M} \times Q)$ is a transition of $\mathcal{A}_{b,\mathcal{M}}$ whenever $\chi(p, q, a) - |U_{(q?p,a)}(M)| \geq 0$ and $\chi'(p, q, a) = \chi(p, q, a) - |U_{(q?p,a)}(M)| + |U_{(p!q,a)}(M)|$.

Note that $\mathcal{A}_{b,\mathcal{M}}$ is deterministic and that $Q_{\mathcal{A}_{b,\mathcal{M}}}$ is a set of functions χ where for every pair of processes $p, q \in \mathcal{P}$ and message $a \in \Gamma$, $\chi(p, q, a)$ is a number of unmatched sends of a from p to q taking a value $\leq b$.

Observe that $\mathcal{A}_{b,\mathcal{M}}$ may be considered as a Büchi automaton or as an automaton on finite words. Indeed, a finite or infinite word on the alphabet $\mathcal{M}$ is b–bounded iff every prefix of the word satisfies the property required by Definition 6.1. We have therefore the following.

Proposition 6.2. *$\mathcal{A}_{b,\mathcal{M}}$ is a Büchi automaton (resp. finite automaton) which accepts exactly all b–bounded (resp. finite b–bounded) sequences over $\mathcal{M}$.*

Since one can define in MSO that every path of a CMSG G starting at its root belongs to a language accepted by a Büchi automaton (resp. finite automaton), we have the following.

Corollary 6.3. *Given a CMSG G having a decidable MSO theory and a bound $b \in \mathbb{N}$, one can decide whether G is b–bounded.*

Note that this corollary contrasts with analogous undecidability results for communicating automata and CMSGs based on a different notion of boundedness [4]. Note also that the simulation of a counter machine by a finite CMSG opening this section shows that the question whether there exists $b \in \mathbb{N}$ such that a finite CMSG is b–bounded is, of course, undecidable.

6.2 Matching Automata

Based on automaton $\mathcal{A}_{b,\mathcal{M}}$, we now define a family of automata that will be useful for matching up the unmatched send events with their corresponding receive events: $\{\mathcal{A}_{\chi,e} \mid \exists$ a reachable state χ' of $\mathcal{A}_{b,\mathcal{M}}$,

$$\exists \text{ a transition } \chi' \xrightarrow[\mathcal{A}_{b,\mathcal{M}}]{M} \chi \text{ s.t. } e \text{ is an unmatched send event of } M\}.$$

Let $M \in \mathcal{M}$, let $e := U_{(p!q,a)}(M)(j)$ be the j-th unmatched send event of M with $\lambda(e) = (p!q, a)$ for some $p, q \in \mathcal{P}$ and $a \in \Gamma$, and let $\chi \in Q_{\mathcal{A}_{b,\mathcal{M}}}$ be a state of $\mathcal{A}_{b,\mathcal{M}}$ such that $\chi' \xrightarrow[\mathcal{A}_{b,\mathcal{M}}]{M} \chi$ for some reachable $\chi' \in Q_{\mathcal{A}_{b,\mathcal{M}}}$.

We define an automaton $\mathcal{A}_{\chi,e} := (Q_{\mathcal{A}_{\chi,e}}, \xrightarrow[\mathcal{A}_{\chi,e}]{}, I_{\mathcal{A}_{\chi,e}}, F_{\mathcal{A}_{\chi,e}})$ where $Q_{\mathcal{A}_{\chi,e}} :=$ [b] $I_{\mathcal{A}_{\chi,e}} := \chi'(p, q, a) - |U_{(q?p,a)}(M)| + j$, $F_{\mathcal{A}_{\chi,e}} := 0$, $r \xrightarrow[\mathcal{A}_{\chi,e}]{N} s$ iff $r \neq 0$ and $s = r - |U_{(q?p,a)}(N)|$ and $s > 0$, or $r - |U_{(q?p,a)}(N)| \leq 0$ and $s = 0$. The states of $\mathcal{A}_{\chi,e}$ record the number of unmatched send events of message a from p to q up to occurrence e of M. When the final state is reached through a transition $r \xrightarrow[\mathcal{A}_{\chi,e}]{N} 0$, then e is matched up with a receive event $e' := U_{(q?p,a)}(N)(r)$.
The next lemma follows from the construction of $\mathcal{A}_{b,\mathcal{M}}$ and $\mathcal{A}_{\chi,e}$.

Lemma 6.4. *Let $\chi_0 \xrightarrow[\mathcal{A}_{b,\mathcal{M}}]{N_1} \chi_1 \xrightarrow[\mathcal{A}_{b,\mathcal{M}}]{N_2} \cdots \xrightarrow[\mathcal{A}_{b,\mathcal{M}}]{N_n} \chi_n$ for some $b \in \mathbb{N}$, let $e \in U_{(p!q,a)}(N_n)$ and let $q_0 \xrightarrow[\mathcal{A}_{\chi_n,e}]{N_{n+1}} q_1 \xrightarrow[\mathcal{A}_{\chi_n,e}]{N_{n+2}} \cdots \xrightarrow[\mathcal{A}_{\chi_n,e}]{N_{n+m}} q_m$, where q_0 is the initial and q_m is the final state of $\mathcal{A}_{\chi_n,e}$. Then the occurrence of $e' := U_{(q?p,a)}(N_{n+m})(q_{m-1})$ is the one that matches up the occurrence of e within N_n provided that $N_1 \cdots N_{n+m}$ is defined.*

Note that the above lemma does not claim that $N_1 \cdots N_{n+m}$ is b–bounded. Consequently, one has to consider an appropriate product of the two automata in order to simultaneously check for b–boundedness of the input sequence and look for the matching event. More precisely, let $\mathcal{A}_{b,\mathcal{M},\chi}$ be defined as $\mathcal{A}_{b,\mathcal{M}}$, except for the initial state: $I_{\mathcal{A}_{b,\mathcal{M},\chi}} := \{\chi\}$. We denote by $\mathcal{B}_{\chi,e}$, the product of $\mathcal{A}_{b,\mathcal{M},\chi}$ and $\mathcal{A}_{\chi,e}$.

6.3 Bounded Concatenation Is MSO–Compatible

We now define an MSO transduction $\mathfrak{JCMSC}_b$ which given a b–bounded sequence $W = N_1, N_2, N_3 \ldots$ of CMSCs, yields the CMSC, CMSC-word(W), resulting from the concatenation $N_1 N_2 N_3 \ldots$. It is represented like an MSS, CMSC-word$(W) = (E, \{s_p\}_{p \in \mathcal{P}}, \{c\}_{c \in \Sigma}, \eta)$ except that relation η is a partial bijection.

Our assumptions for this transduction are the same as for $\mathcal{J}$MSC (see Sect. 3) except that $\mathcal{M} = \{M_1, M_2, \ldots, M_n\}$ is a set of finite CMSCs and that $\mathcal{J}$CMSC$_b$ applies on b–bounded CMSGs of the form $\overset{N_1}{\bullet} \longrightarrow \overset{N_2}{\bullet} \longrightarrow \overset{N_3}{\bullet} \longrightarrow \cdots$. Recall that $M_i = (E^i, \{\leq_p^i\}_{p \in \mathcal{P}}, \lambda^i, \eta^i)$ and $\bigcup_{i=1}^n E^i = [k]$ for some $k \in \mathbb{N}$. The definition scheme associated with $\mathcal{J}$CMSC$_b$, written Δ' uses Δ. It is given by

$$\Delta' := (\alpha, \delta_1, \delta_2, \ldots, \delta_k, \{\theta_{(s_p, i, j)}\}_{p \in \mathcal{P}}, \{\theta_{(\iota_p, i)}\}_{p \in \mathcal{P}}, \{\theta_{(c, i)}\}_{c \in \Sigma}, \theta'_{(\eta, i, j)}),$$

where $\delta_1, \delta_2, \ldots, \delta_k, \{\theta_{(s_p, i, j)}\}_{p \in \mathcal{P}}, \{\theta_{(\iota_p, i)}\}_{p \in \mathcal{P}}, \{\theta_{(c, i)}\}_{c \in \Sigma}$ are as for Δ and

- $\alpha := \alpha_{\text{chain}} \wedge \alpha_{\mathcal{A}_{b, \mathcal{M}}}$ where α_{chain} says that the input graph is a linear chain, $\alpha_{\mathcal{A}_{b, \mathcal{M}}}$ says that $\mathcal{A}_{b, \mathcal{M}}$ has an accepting run on $\overset{N_1}{\bullet} \longrightarrow \overset{N_2}{\bullet} \longrightarrow \overset{N_3}{\bullet} \longrightarrow \cdots$,
- $\theta'_{(\eta, i, j)}(x, y)$ is defined by $M_l(x) \wedge x = y$, if $(i, j) \in \eta^l$ and $\bigvee_{\chi \in Q_{\mathcal{A}_{b, \mathcal{M}}}} (\beta_\chi(x) \wedge \exists z (x \longrightarrow z \wedge \gamma_{\chi, i, j}(z, y)))$, otherwise. where $\beta_\chi(x)$ says that starting at the root of a CMSG, automaton $\mathcal{A}_{b, \mathcal{M}}$ reaches vertex x in state χ. Formula $\gamma_{\chi, i, j}(z, y)$ says that starting at vertex z, after transition $(\chi', q) \xrightarrow[B_{\chi, i}]{N} (\chi'', 0)$ automaton $B_{\chi, i}$ reaches vertex y such that $N(y)$ holds with $U_{(q?p, a)}(N)(q) = j$ and $\lambda(i) = (p!q, a)$.

It is well known that the existence of an accepting run of an automaton on a (finite or infinite) word may be expressed by an MSO sentence. Thus, formula $\alpha_{\mathcal{A}_{b, \mathcal{M}}}$ may look like the one given in page 397 of [12]. Formulae $\beta_\chi(x)$ and $\gamma_{\chi, i, j}(z, y)$ are similar.

Proposition 6.5. $\text{def}_{\Delta'}(G) = H$ iff G is a b–bounded sequence of CMSCs represented by a CMSG and H a CMSC resulting from the concatenation of the sequence.

Corollary 6.6. If a b–bounded sequence $N_1, N_2, \ldots$ of CMSCs has a decidable MSO theory then the CMSC resulting from the concatenation $N_1 N_2 \ldots$ has a decidable MSO theory.

We may use $\mathcal{J}$CMSC$_b$ in the case of b–bounded CMSG G, in order to check whether an MSO sentence holds for every CMSC resulting from the concatenation along each maximal path starting from the root. More precisely, we consider

$$\text{PCMSC}(G) := \{\mathcal{J}\text{CMSC}_b(\varrho) \mid \varrho \text{ is a maximal path of } G \text{ starting from } r_G\}.$$

The following proposition is established similarly to Proposition 4.1.

Proposition 6.7. For every b–bounded CMSG and for every MSO sentence φ, one may construct an MSO sentence ψ such that $\text{PCMSC}(G) \models \varphi$ iff $\text{Un}(G) \models \psi$, where $\text{Un}(G)$ stands for the unfolding of G from its root.

Corollary 6.8. For every b–bounded CMSG G the MSO theory of $\text{PCMSC}(G)$ is decidable if the MSO theory of G is so.

With slight modifications we obtain analogous results for a language of CMSCs corresponding to all finite paths of a bounded CMSG.

7 Conclusion

We have shown that the truth of an MSO sentence on an infinite MSSs reduces to the truth of an MSO sentence on the underlying MSGs. Since there are many interesting classes of infinite graphs with decidable MSO theory, we obtain the decidability of corresponding MSSs. The result has been extended to infinite CMSGs provided they are bounded and past independent.

We also have shown, for given bound $b \in \mathbb{N}$ and a finite set of CMSCs, the construction of a Büchi automaton which accepts exactly all b-bounded sequences of CMSCs. Consequently, the b-boundedness of a CMSG with a decidable MSO theory is also decidable.

The core of our decidability proofs are constructions of MSO–transductions. This is different from [9] and [10] where a more elementary proof for unfoldings of finite MSGs is based on a construction of an automaton corresponding to an MSO formula.

References

[1] Courcelle, B.: Monadic second–order definable graph transductions: a survey. Theoretical Comput. Sci. 126, 53–75 (1994)
[2] Courcelle, B., Engelfriet, J.: Graph structure and Monadic Second-Order Logic, a Language Theoretic Approach. Cambridge University Press (2012)
[3] Courcelle, B., Walukiewicz, I.: Monadic second–order logic, graph coverings and unfoldings of transition systems. Annals of Pure and Applied Logic 92, 35–62 (1998)
[4] Genest, B., Kuske, D., Muscholl, A.: On communicating automata with bounded channels. Fundam. Inform. 80(1-3), 147–167 (2007)
[5] Gunter, E.L., Muscholl, A., Peled, D.A.: Compositional Message Sequence Charts. In: Margaria, T., Yi, W. (eds.) TACAS 2001. LNCS, vol. 2031, pp. 496–511. Springer, Heidelberg (2001)
[6] Klarlund, N., Møller, A., Schwartzbach, M.I.: MONA implementation secrets. Int. J. Found. Comput. Sci. 13(4), 571–586 (2002)
[7] Kumar, K.N.: The theory of MSC languages. In: D'Souza, D., Shankar, P. (eds.) Modern Applications of Automata Theory. IISc Research Monograph Series, vol. 2, World Scientific (2012)
[8] Kuske, D.: Regular sets of infinite message sequence charts. Inf. Comput. 187(1), 80–109 (2003)
[9] Madhusudan, P.: Reasoning about Sequential and Branching Behaviours of Message Sequence Graphs. In: Yu, Y., Spirakis, P.G., van Leeuwen, J. (eds.) ICALP 2001. LNCS, vol. 2076, pp. 809–820. Springer, Heidelberg (2001)
[10] Madhusudan, P., Meenakshi, B.: Beyond Message Sequence Graphs. In: Hariharan, R., Mukund, M., Vinay, V. (eds.) FSTTCS 2001. LNCS, vol. 2245, pp. 256–267. Springer, Heidelberg (2001)
[11] Rudolph, E., Graubmann, P., Grabowski, J.: Tutorial on message sequence charts. Computer Networks and ISDN Systems 28(12), 1629–1641 (1996)
[12] Thomas, W.: Languages, automata and logic. In: Rozenberg, G., Salomaa, A. (eds.) Beyond Words. Handbook of Formal Languages, vol. 3, pp. 389–455. Springer, Heidelberg (1997)

Neural Networks Training Based on Differential Evolution in Radial Basis Function Networks for Classification of Web Logs

Ch. Sanjeev Kumar Dash[1], Ajit Kumar Behera[2],
Manoj Kumar Pandia[2], and Satchidananda Dehuri[3]

[1] Department of Computer Science,
[2] Department of Computer Application,
Silicon Institute of Technology, Silicon Hills, Patia, Bhubaneswar, 751024
{sanjeev_dash,manoj_pandia}@yahoo.com, ajit_behera@hotmail.com
[3] Department of Systems Engineering, Ajou University,
San 5, Woncheon-dong, Yeongtong-gu, Suwon-443-749, South Korea
satchi@ajou.ac.kr

Abstract. With the fastest growth of World Wide Web it is quite difficult to track and understand users' need for the owners of a website. Hence, an intelligent analyzer is proposed to find out the browsing patterns of a user. Moreover the pattern, which is revealed from this deluge of web access logs must be interesting, useful, and understandable. In this paper, a two phases learning algorithm with a modified kernel for radial basis function neural networks is proposed to classify the web pages on time of access and region of access. In phase one a meta-heuristic approach known as differential evolution is used to reveal the parameters of the modified kernel. The second phase focus on optimization of weights for learning the networks. The simulation result shows that the proposed learning mechanism is evidently producing better classification accuracy vis-à-vis radial basis function neural networks.

Keywords: Differential evolution, Radial basis function neural networks, Classification, Web log.

1 Introduction

Over the last decade, the proliferation of information on the World Wide Web (WWW) in short called web has resulted a large repository of web documents stored in multiple websites. This plethora and diversity of resources has promoted the need for developing a semi-automatic mining technique on the WWW, thereby giving rise to the term web mining [15].

Every website contains multiple web pages. Every web page has: 1) contents which can be in any form e.g. text, graphics, multimedia etc; 2) links from one page to another; and 3) users accessing the web pages. According to this the area web mining can be categorized as in Figure 1.

C. Hota and P.K. Srimani (Eds.): ICDCIT 2013, LNCS 7753, pp. 183–194, 2013.

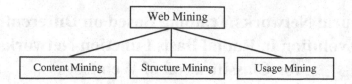

Fig. 1. Web mining categorization

Mining the contents of web pages is called "Content Mining". Mining the links between web pages is called "Structure Mining". Mining the web access logs is called "Web Usage Mining".

Web servers record and mount up data about user interactions whenever request for resources are received. Analyzing the web access logs of different web sites can help understand the user behavior and the web structure, thereby improving the design of this colossal collection of resources. To proceed towards a semi-automatic intelligent web an analyzer, obviating the need for human intervention, we need to incorporate and embed computational or artificial intelligence into web analyzing tools. The necessity of creating server side and client side intelligent systems that can effectively mine for knowledge both across the internet and in particular web localities is drawing the attention of researchers from the domains of information retrieval, knowledge discovery, machine learning, artificial intelligence, and computational intelligence, among others.

However, the problem of developing semi-automated tools in order to find, extract, filter, and evaluate the users desired information from unlabeled, distributed, and heterogeneous web access logs data is far from being solved. To handle these characteristics and overcome some of the limitations of existing methodologies radial basis function neural network (RBFN) [14] a member of computational intelligence family seems to be a good candidate. However, the problem of appropriate number of basis functions remains a critical issue for RBF network. Because too few basis functions can not fit the training data adequately, also too many basis functions yield poor generalization ability. Differential Evolution (DE) [21], an emerging evolutionary computation technique was used to fix the structure of the network in advance according to the prior knowledge. In this paper, DE algorithm is adopted to auto configure the structure of RBF network to design a classifier for web access logs classification. Zhichao et al.[17] and Chen et al.[18] works of RBFN for classification of web usage data are the source of motivation to carry out this work, among others.

Over the last several decades multilayer perceptron (MLP) network and RBFN is the popular network architectures used in most of the applications. In MLP, the weighted sum of the inputs and bias term are passed to activation level through a transfer function to produce the output, and the units are arranged in a layered feed-forward topology called Feed Forward Neural Network (FFNN). In particular, MLP using back-propagation learning algorithm has been successfully applied to many applications. However, the training speed of MLP is typically much slower than those of feed-forward neural network comprising of single layer. Moreover, the problems such as local minima trapping, saturation, weight interference, initial weight dependence, and over-fitting make MLP training difficult [20]. Additionally, it is also very difficult to fix the parameters like number of neurons in a layer, and number of hidden layers in a network, thereby deciding a proper architecture is not easy. These issues create another source of motivation to choose RBFN.

Radial basis function neural network is based on supervised learning. RBFN networks are also good at modeling nonlinear data and can be trained in one stage rather than using an iterative process as in MLP. Radial basis function networks [1, 2, 3] have been studied in many disciplines like pattern recognition [4], medicine [5], multi-media applications [6], computational finance [7], software engineering [9], etc. It is emerged as a variant in late 1980's, however its root entrenched in much older pattern recognition, numerical analysis and other related fields [8]. The basic architectural framework of RBFN and details is discussed in Section 2.

2   A Framework of RBFNs in Web Access Logs

Figure 2 describes overall framework of our research. Subsection 2.1 describes the web usage mining and steps required for preprocessing the dataset highlighted in the framework. Subsection 2.4 briefly describes RBFN and 2.5 describe about the DE for classification of web access logs.

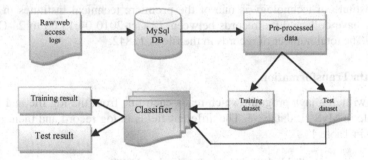

Fig. 2. Block diagram of web log classification

2.1   Web Usage Mining and Preprocessing

While visiting a website user navigates through multiple web pages. Each access to a web page is stored as a record in log files. These log files are managed by web servers. The format of log files varies from server to server. Apache web server maintains two different log file format namely 1) Common Log Format, 2) Combined Log Format. The general format of an access log file in Apache web server is given below.

```
Common Log Format - LogFormat "%h %l %u %t \"%r\" %>s %b"
common
Example - 122.163.111.210 - - [22/Oct/2010:04:15:03 -
0400] "GET /index.html HTTP/1.1" 404 494
Combined Log Format - LogFormat "%h %l %u %t \"%r\" %>s
%b \"%{Referer}i\" \"%{User-agent}i\""
```

Example - 127.0.0.1 - frank [10/Oct/2000:13:55:36 -0700]
"GET /apache_pb.gif HTTP/1.0" 200 2326
"http://www.example.com/start.html"   "Mozilla/4.08   [en]
(Win98; I ;Nav)"

The raw data from access log file are not in a state to be used for mining. These records must be pre-processed first. Pre-processing [16] involves 1) Data cleaning, 2) User identification, 3) Session identification. After pre-processing these records can be used as training and test data set for classification.

For pre-processing work we have followed the database approach where all the raw records are inserted in to a table and the pre-processing tasks such as data cleaning, user identification and session identification are done using SQL queries. This approach gives better flexibility and faster execution.

First the raw web access log records are scanned from log files and inserted into a table which is designed in MySQL database. As we know query execution is easy and also the time taken for query execution is very less in comparison to file processing. Once all records are inserted successfully, then the steps of preprocessing can be executed.

In this paper, we have used the web access log data from www.silicon.ac.in. Silicon institute of technology is one of the premiere technical institutes in Odisha, India. We have collected the records between 22-Oct-2010 04:15:00 to 24-Oct-2010 04:05:48. The total number of records in the file is 12842.

2.2   Data Transformation

We have written a java program which reads each line from the log file and insert in to the table in MySQL database. The different fields in log record and their value are described in Table 1.

Table 1. Field name & value of a HTTP request

Value	Field Name
122.163.111.210	IP Address
-	Client ID
-	User ID
[22/Oct/2010:04:15:00 -0400]	Request Date & Time
"GET /sitsbp/index.html HTTP/1.1"	Request Method, URL, Protocol
200	Response Status
4520	Bytes Sent
"http://www.google.co.in/search?hl=en&rlz=1R2ADFA_e nIN388&q=silicon+institute+of+technology&btnG=Searc h&meta=&aq=f&aqi=&aql=&oq=&gs_rfai="	Referrer
"Mozilla/4.0 (compatible; MSIE 6.0; Windows NT 5.1; GTB0.0; SV1; .NET CLR 2.0.50727; .NET CLR 3.0.04506.30; .NET CLR 3.0.4506.2152; .NET CLR 3.5.30729; RediffIE8)"	User Agent

The pseudo code of data transformation is given below

```
While not EOF
    Read each line
    Split the line into words separated by " " (blank
space)
    IP = first word
    clientID = second word
    userID = third word
    begin = indexof('[')
    end = indexof(']')
    accessDateTime = charbetween(begin,end)
    rest = substring(end,length(line)-end)
    scan each character of the rest string
    requestedURL = characters between first pair of " "
    referrer = characters between second pair of " "
    userAgent = characters between third pair of " "
End While
```

First split the line into words separated by blank space. After this we get the clientIP, clientID, nad userID. As the request date and time is written in pair of square brackets [] so we find the index of '[' and ']' and then get the characters between these index by using getChars() method. Then the rest part is stored in another variable and using another loop and searching character by character we retrieve the requested URL, request status, method, user agent etc.

2.3   Data Cleaning

For data cleaning we need to remove all the records which contain the request for files like jpg, gif, css, js etc. For this we execute the delete query.

Before the data cleaning the total number of records were 12842. After the data cleaning now it contains 1749 records, which are the actual page access records. Every unique page is assigned a PageID. The total number of unique web pages is found to be 97.

2.4   Radial Basis Function Neural Networks

The multi-layered feed forward network (MFN) is the most widely used neural network model for pattern classification. The basic architecture of a three-layered network is shown in Figure 3. A RBFN has three layers including input layer, hidden layer and output layer. The input layer is composed of input data. The hidden layer transforms the data from the input space to the hidden space using a non liner function. The output layer, which is linear, yields the response to the network. Its training procedure is usually divided in to two stages. First, the centers and widths of the hidden layer are determined by various ways like clustering algorithms such as k-means [10], vector quantization [11], decision trees [12], or self-organizing future maps [13]. In this paper random initialization of centers and width is considered and then fine tuned over iterations. Second the weights connecting the hidden layer with the output are determined by singular value decomposition (SVD) or least mean square (LMS) algorithm. Here SVD is used for optimizing the weights. The number of basis functions controls the complexity and the generalization ability of RBF network.

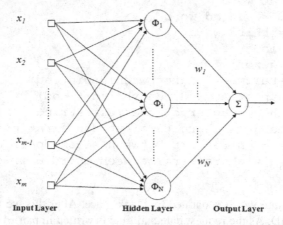

Fig. 3. Architecture of a radial basis function network

The argument of the activation function of each hidden unit in an RBFN computes the Euclidean distance between an input vector and the center of the unit.

$$\Phi_i(x) = \exp\left(-\frac{\|x - \mu_i\|^2}{2\sigma_i^2}\right) \tag{1}$$

where $\|...\|$ represents Euclidean norm, μ_i, σ_i and Φ_i are center, width and the output of the ith hidden unit. The output layer, a set of summation units, supplies the response of the network.

The commonly used radial basis functions are enumerated in Table 2 as follows:

Table 2. Different kernel functions used in RBF network

Name of the Kernel	Mathematical Formula
Gaussian Functions	$\Phi(x) = \exp\left(-\dfrac{x^2}{2\sigma^2}\right)$ width parameter $\sigma > 0$
Generalized Multi-Quadric Functions	$\Phi(x) = \left(x^2 + \sigma^2\right)^{\beta}$, parameter $\sigma > 0, 1 > \beta > 0$
Generalized Inverse Multi Quadric Functions	$\Phi(x) = \left(x^2 + \sigma^2\right)^{-\alpha}, \sigma > 0, \alpha > 0$
Cubic Function	$\Phi(x) = x^3$

2.5   Differential Evolution

Differential Evolution (DE) [21, 22, 23, 24, 28], is a population based stochastic search algorithm which typically operates on real valued chromosome encodings. Like GAs, DE maintains a population of potential solution encodings which are then perturbed in an effort to uncover yet better solutions to a problem in hand. In GAs [25] the basic steps are selection, crossover and mutation. However in DE, individuals are represented as real-valued vectors, and the perturbation of solution vectors is based on the scaled difference of two randomly chosen individuals of the current population. One of the advantages of this approach is that the resulting 'step' size and orientation during the perturbation process automatically adapts to the fitness function landscape.

Although several DE algorithms available in literature Das et al. [22, 29] we primarily describe a version of the algorithm based on the DE/rand/1/bin scheme [21]. The different variants of the DE algorithm are described using the shorthand DE/x/y/z, where x specifies how the base vector is chosen, y is the number of difference vectors used, and z denotes the crossover scheme.

A notable feature of the mutation step in DE is that it is self-scaling. The size/rate of mutation along each dimension stems solely from the location of the individuals in the current population. The mutation step self-adapts as the population converges leading to a finer-grained search. In contrast, the mutation process in GA [26] is typically based on (or draws from) a fixed probability density function.

Rationale for an DE-RBF Integration: There are a number of reasons to support that an evolutionary methodology, particularly DE coupled with a RBF can prove fruitful in the classification tasks. In classification of web logs, it is a challenging job to approximate an arbitrary boundary of complex phenomenon. Hence, combining DE with the universal approximation qualities of a RBF produces a powerful modeling methodology.

Learning Procedure: As mentioned there are two phases within the learning procedure. In phase one differential evolution is employed to reveal the centers and spread of the RBFNS. Although centers, spread and weights can be evolved using DE, but here we restrict ourselves with evolving only centers and spreads. This ensures efficient representation of an individual of DE [27]. If we encode all the parameters such as centers, spread and weights into an individual chromosome, the chromosome length is too long and the search space becomes too large, which results in a very slow convergence rate. Since the performance of the RBFNs mainly depends on center and spread of the kernel, we just encode the centers and spread into a individual chromosome for stochastic search.

Suppose the maximum number of kernels is set to K_{max}, then the structure of the individual is represented in Figure 4.

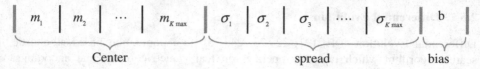

$$\underbrace{\left|\quad m_1 \quad\left|\quad m_2 \quad\right|\quad \cdots \quad\right|\quad m_{K\max}\right.}_{\text{Center}}\quad \underbrace{\sigma_1\quad\left|\quad \sigma_2 \quad\right|\quad \sigma_3 \quad\right|\quad \cdots\cdots \quad\left|\quad \sigma_{K\max}\right.}_{\text{spread}}\quad \underbrace{\left|\quad b \quad\right|}_{\text{bias}}$$

Fig. 4. Structure of an individual

In other words each individual has three constituent parts such as center, spread and bias. The length of an individual is $2K_{\max}+1$.

The algorithmic framework of DE-RBF is described as follows: Initially, a set of n_p individuals (i.e., n_p is the size of the population) pertaining to networks centers spread and bias are initialized randomly, the individuals have the form:

$$x_i^{(t)} = \left\langle x_{i1}^{(t)}, x_{i2}^{(t)}, ..., x_{id}^{(t)} \right\rangle \qquad i = 1, 2, ..., n_p \tag{2}$$

where $d = 2 \cdot k_{\max} + 1$ and t is the iteration number.

In each iteration, e.g., iteration t, for individual $x_i^{(t)}$ undergoes mutation, crossover and selection as follows:

Mutation: For vector $x_i^{(t)}$ a perturbed vector $V_i^{(t+1)}$ called donor vector is generated according to equation (3).

$$V_i^{(t+1)} = x_{r1}^{(t)} + m_f \cdot \left(x_{r2}^{(t)} - x_{r3}^{(t)} \right), \tag{3}$$

where m_f is the mutation factor, lies in the interval (0,2], the indices r_1, r_2 and r_3 are selected randomly from $\{1,2,3,...,n_p\}$, such that $r_1 \neq r_2 \neq r_3 \neq i$.

Crossover: The trial vector is generated as given in equation (4).

$$u_{ij}^{(t+1)} = \begin{cases} v_{ij}^{(t+1)} & if \; rand \leq c_r \; or \; i = rand\,(1,2,...,d) \\ x_{ij}^{(t)} & if \; rand > c_r \; and \; i \neq rand\,(1,2,...,d) \end{cases} \tag{4}$$

where $j=1..d$, *rand* is random number generated in the range (0,1), c_r is the user specified crossover constant from the range (0,1) and *rand* (1,2,...,d) is a random integer from [1,2,...,d].

Finally, we use selection operation and obtain the target vector $x_i^{(t+1)}$ as given in equation (5).

$$x_i^{(t+1)} = \begin{cases} u_i^{(t+1)} & if \; f\left(x_i^{(t+1)} \right) \leq f\left(x_i^{(t)} \right) \\ x_i^{(t)}, & otherwise \end{cases}, \quad i=1,2,...,d. \tag{5}$$

The fitness function which is used to guide the search process is defined in equation (6).

$$f(x) = \frac{1}{N} \sum_{1}^{N} \left(t_n - \hat{\Phi}\left(\vec{x_i}\right) \right)^2 \qquad (6)$$

where N is the total number of training sample, t_n is the actual output and $\Phi(x_i)$ is the estimated output of RBFNs. Once the centers and spreads are fixed, the task of determining weights in second phase of learning reduces to solving a simple linear system. In this work the pseudo inverse method is adopted to find out a set of optimal weights.

The pseudo-code for computing spread, center and bias using DE, as follows:

```
Begin
      t=1;
      initialize a set of nₚ individuals
```
$$x_i^{(t)} = < x_{i1}^{(t)}, x_{i2}^{(t)}, ..., x_{id}^{(t)} > , \quad i = 1, 2, ..., n_p \quad \text{randomly;}$$
```
      For t=1 to maxG do
          For i=1 to nₚ do
```
Mutation step: for each vector $v_i^{(t)}$ a perturbed

vector $v_i^{(t+1)}$ called the donor vector is generated according to equation (3).

Crossover step: the trial vector $u_i^{(t+1)}$ is generated according to equation (4).

Compute fitness function according to equation (6) and train dataset.

Selection step: get the target vector $x_i^{(t+1)}$ according to equation (5)
```
          End for
          t=t+1
      End for
End
```
After getting center, spread and bias from the above pseudo-code now the weights of the network can be computed by pseudo-inverse method as described in equation (7).

$$Y = W\Phi$$
$$W = \left(\Phi^T \Phi \right)^{-1} \Phi^T Y \qquad (7)$$

Pseudo code of DE-RBF:

```
Begin
        Compute the center, spread, and bias according to
        the above pseudo-code;
        Calculate the basis function(Φ) ;
        Compute the weight according to equation (7);
        Calculate the output as Y=WΦ ;
```

        Calculate the accuracy by comparing actual output
        with desired output;
End

3   Experimental Study

3.1   Description of Dataset and Parameters

For classification purpose we have categorized the access time into 2 categories, i.e. from 00:00 hours to 12:00 hours 1 and 12:00 to 24:00 as 2. Similarly we have grouped all the region of access into 2, i.e. IP addresses accessing from within India as 1 and IP addresses accessing from outside India as 2. To find the region from IP address we have used the website www.ip2location.com [19].

    Our class attribute is frequent. For this we have considered two values i.e. 1 for not frequent and 2 for frequent. This dataset includes 237 instances and each having 4 attributes e.g. ID, request count, timeid, locationid.

    The instances are classified into 2 classes (i.e., every instance either belongs to class 1 or 2). Class 1 has 129 instances, and class 2 contains 108. None of the attributes contain any missing values.

3.2   Results and Analysis

In this experimental set up a learning algorithms (i.e., RBFNs) and considered for a comparative study with the proposed method DE-RBF.

    The results obtained from our experimental study are enumerated in Table 3. In our work two training algorithms were compared. In DE-RBF the parameter were set as follows : mutation factor m_f=0.2 and crossing factor c_r=0.5. Corresponding to different kernels like Gaussian functions, multi-quadratic functions, inverse multi-quadratic function, and cubic function, it is observed that Cubic kernels in DE-RBF gives better result as compared to other kernels of RBF and DE-RBF networks for web log dataset.

Table 3. Classification accuracy obtained from simulation of Gaussian function, Multi – quadratic function, Inverse multi-quadratic function, Cubic function

Name of the Kernel	RBF			DE-RBF		
	No of Hidden units	Training	Testing	No of Hidden units	Training	Testing
Gaussian	5	81.3953	79.0698	9	88.453	84.769
Multi – quadric	5	86.8217	77.5194	9	86.4217	84.194
Inverse multi-quadric	5	75.9690	76.722	9	88.3454	82.446
Cubic	5	77.5194	74.5736	9	88.4924	84.924

4   Conclusion and Future Work

In this paper, DE algorithm a population-based iterative global optimization has been used to train a RBF networks for classification on web log data. The method of encoding a RBF network into an individual is given, where only the centers and the spread of the hidden units are encoded. Here, we have considered the attributes like region and time of the dataset in the process of classification; however, this can be extended to some more attributes like user agent and referrer of the dataset. Experimental result shows that DE algorithm based RBFN is performing better than RBFN irrespective of kernels considered in this paper. Further, it is observed that by taking different basis functions we get varying accuracy levels.

References

1. Powell, M.J.D.: Radial Basis Functions for Multi-variable Interpolation: A Review. In: IMA Conference on Algorithms for the Approximations of Functions and Data, RMOS Shrivenham, UK (1985)
2. Broomhead, D.S., Lowe, D.: Multivariable Functional Interpolation and Adaptive networks. Complex Systems 2, 321–355 (1988)
3. Buhmann, M.D.: Radial Basis Function Networks. Encyclopedia of Machine Learning, pp.823–827 (2010)
4. Theodoridis, S., Koutroumbas, K.: Pattern Recognition. Academic Press, San Diego (1998)
5. Subashini, T.S., Ramalingam, V., Palanivel, S.: Breast Mass Classification Based on Cytological Patterns Using RBFNN and SVM. Expert Systems with Applications 36(3(2)), 6069–6076 (2009)
6. Dhanalakshmi, P., Palanivel, S., Ramalingam, V.: Classification of Audio Signals Using SVM and RBFNN. Expert Systems with Applications 36(3(1)), 5284–5290 (2009)
7. Sheta, A.F., De Jong, K.: Time Series Forecasting Using GA Tuned Radial Basis Functions. Information Sciences 133, 221–228 (2001)
8. Park, J., Sandberg, J.W.: Universal Approximation Using Radial Basis Function Networks. Neural Computation 3, 246–257 (1991)
9. Idri, A., Zakrani, A., Zahi, A.: Design of Radial Basis function Neural Networks for Software Effort Estimation. International Journal of Computer Science Issues 7(4), 11–17 (2010)
10. Broomhead, D.S., Lowe, D.: Multivariable functional interpolation and Adaptive networks. Complex Systems 2, 321–355 (1988)
11. Moody, J., Darken, C.J.: Fast Learning Networks of Locally-Tuned Processing Units. Neural Computation 6(4), 281–294 (1989)
12. Falcao, A.O., Langlois, T., Wichert, A.: Flexible Kernels for RBF Networks. Neuro Computing 69, 2356–2359 (2006)
13. Ghodsi, A., Schuurmans, D.: Automatic Basis Selection Techniques for RBF Networks. Neural Networks 16, 809–816 (2003)
14. Bishop, C.M.: Neural Networks for Pattern Recognition. Oxford University Press, New York (1995)
15. Chen, H., Zong, X., Lee, C.-W., Yeh, J.-H.: World Wide Web Usage Mining Systems and Technologies. Journal of Systemics, Cybernetics and Informatics 1(4), 53–59 (2003)

16. Srivastava, J., Cooley, R., Deshpande, M., Tan, P.: Web Usage Mining: Discovery and Applications of Usage Patterns from Web Data. SIGKDD Explorations 1(2), 1–12 (2000)
17. Li, Z., He, P., Lei, M.: Applying RBF Network to Web Classification Mining. Journal of Communication and Computer 2(9) (2005) ISSN 1548-7709
18. Junjie, C., Rongbing, H.: Research of Web classification mining based on RBF neural network. In: Proceedings of Control, Automation, Robotics and Vision Conference, vol. 2, pp. 1365–1367 (2004)
19. http://www.ip2location.com
20. Dehuri, S., Cho, S.B.: A Comprehensive Survey on Functional Link Neural Networks and an Adaptive PSO-BP Learning for CFLNN. Neural Computing and Applications 19(2), 187–205 (2010)
21. Stron, R., Price, K.: Differential Evolution-A Simple and Efficient Adaptive Scheme for Global Optimization over Continuous Spaces. Technical Report TR-05-012: International Computer Science Institute, Berkely (1995)
22. Price, K., Storn, R., Lampinen, J.: Differential Evolution: A Practical Approach to Global Optimization. Springer (2005)
23. Stron, R.: System Design by Constraint Adaption and Differential Evolution. IEEE Transactions on Evolutionary Computation 3, 22–34 (1999)
24. Naveen, N., Ravi, V., Rao, C.R., Chauhan, N.: Differential Evolution Trained Radial Basis Function Network: Application to Bankruptcy Prediction in Banks. IJBIC 2(3/4), 222–232 (2010)
25. Naveen, N., Ravi, V., Rao, C.R.: Rule Extraction from Differential Evolution Trained Radial Basis Function Network Using Genetic Algorithms. In: CASE 2009, pp.152–157 (2009)
26. Zhao, W., Huang, D.S.: The Structure Optimization of Radial Basis Probabilistic Neural Networks Based on Genetic Algorithms. In: Proceedings of the IJCNN 2002, Honolulu HI, USA, pp. 1086–1091 (2002)
27. Yu, B., He, X.: Training Radial Basis Function Networks with Differential Evolution. World Academy of Science, Engineering and Technology 11, 337–340 (2005)
28. Stron, R., Price, K.: Differential Evolution-Simple and Efficient Heuristic for Global Optimization over Continuous Spaces. Journal of Global Optimization 11, 341–359 (1997)
29. Das, S., Suganthan, P.N.: Differential Evolution: A Survey of the State-of-the-Art. IEEE Transactions on Evolutionary Computation 15(1), 4–31 (2011)

Circle Formation
by Asynchronous Transparent Fat Robots

Suparno Datta[1], Ayan Dutta[2],
Sruti Gan Chaudhuri[3], and Krishnendu Mukhopadhyaya[3]

[1] Department of Computer Science, RWTH Aachen, Germany
[2] Computer Science Department, University of Nebraska at Omaha
[3] ACM Unit, Indian Statistical Institute, Kolkata
suparno.datta@rwth-aachen.de, adutta@unomaha.edu,
{sruti_r,krishnendu}@isical.ac.in

Abstract. This paper proposes a distributed algorithm for circle formation by a system of mobile robots. Each robot observes the positions of other robots and moves to a new position. Eventually they form a circle. The robots do not store past actions. They are anonymous and cannot be distinguished by their appearance and do not have a common coordinate system (origin and axis) and chirality (common handedness). Most of the earlier works assume the robots to be dimensionless (points). In this paper a robot is represented as a unit disc (*fat robot*). The robots are assumed to be transparent in order to achieve full visibility. However, a robot is considered as a physical obstacle for another robot. The robots execute the algorithm asynchronously.

Keywords: Asynchronous, Transparent Fat Robots, Circle Formation.

1 Introduction

The field of cooperative mobile robotics has received a lot of attention from various research groups in institutes as well as in industries. A focus of these research and development activities is the distributed motion coordination which allows the robots to form certain patterns [9]. Motion planning algorithms for robotic systems are very challenging due to severe limitations, such as in communication between the robots, hardware constraints, obstacles etc. The significance of positioning the robots based on some given patterns is useful for various tasks, such as operations in hazardous environments, space mission, military operations, tumor excision[7] etc. In addition, formation of patterns and flocking of a group of mobile robots is also useful for providing communication in ad-hoc mobile networks. Pattern formation by cooperative mobile robots involves many geometric issues [9]. This paper addresses one such geometric problem, circle formation. The robots are free to move on the 2D plane. They are anonymous. They do not have a common coordinate system and are unable to remember past actions. Furthermore, the robots are incapable of communicating directly and can only interact by observing each others position. Based on this model, we

C. Hota and P.K. Srimani (Eds.): ICDCIT 2013, LNCS 7753, pp. 195–207, 2013.

study the problem of the mobile robots positioning themselves to form a circle.
The robots are represented as unit discs (*fat robots* [1]). The robots are assumed
to be transparent in order to ensure full visibility. But they act as physical obstruction for another robots. The formation of a circle provides a way for robots
to agree on a common origin point and a common unit distance. The main idea
is to let each robot execute a simple algorithm and plan its motion adaptively
based on the observed movement of other robots, so that the robots as a group
will manage to form a given pattern (a circle in this case).

2   Related Works

A large body of research work exists in the context of multiple autonomous mobile robots exhibiting cooperative behavior. The aim of such research is to study
the issues such as group architecture, resource conflict, origin of cooperation,
learning and geometric problems [11]. The computational model popular in literature for mobile robot is called the *weak model* [5]. Under this model robots are
considered to be points which move on the plane. The robots have no identity,
no memory of past actions (oblivious), no common sense of direction and distance. The robots execute cycles consisting of three phases, *look-compute-move*
described below:

- *Look*: Determine the current configuration by identifying the locations of all
  visible robots and marking them on the robot's (the one that is executing
  the cycle) private coordinate system.
- *Compute*: Based on the locations of all the visible robots, compute a location
  T, where this robots should move now.
- *Move*: Travel towards the point T in straight line.

The robots may execute the cycles synchronously or asynchronously or semi-
synchronously. The definitions of the models are as follows:

- *Fully−synchronous* (*FSYNC*) model: The robots are driven by an identical
  clock and hence operate according to the same cycles, and are active in every
  cycle.
- *Semi − synchronous* (*SSYNC*) model: The robots operate according to
  the same cycles, but need not be active in every cycle. A fairness constraint
  guarantees that each robot will eventually be active (infinitely many times)
  in any infinite execution.
- *Asynchronous* (*ASYNC*) model: The robots operate on independent cycles
  of variable length. Formally, this can be modeled by starting each cycle with
  a "Wait" step of arbitrary variable length.

Formation of circle by multiple autonomous mobile robots is defined as follows-
*A set of robots is given. The robots are asked to position themselves on the cir-
cumference of a circle in finite time.* Sugihara and Suzuki [9] proposed a simple
heuristic algorithm for the formation of an approximation of a circle under limited visibility. However, the algorithm does not guarantee that the formed circle

will be uniform. Sometimes it may bring the robots to form a Reuleaux triangle [1] instead of a circle. Suzuki and Yamashita[10] proposed a regular polygon formation algorithm for non-oblivious robots. Défago and Konogaya [2] came up with an improved algorithm by which a group of oblivious robots eventually form a circle. The algorithm consists of two sub-algorithms. The first part brings the system towards a configuration in which all robots are located on the boundary of the circle. The second part converges towards a homogeneous distribution of the robots along the circumference of the circle. All of these solutions assume semi-synchronous (SSM)[10] model in which the cycles of all robots are synchronized and their actions are atomic. Katreniak [6] used an asynchronous CORDA [8] model to form a biangular circle [2]. Défago and Souissi [3] presented an algorithm where a group of mobile robots, starting from any arbitrary configuration, can be self-organized to form a circle. This algorithm has the useful property that it allows robots to be added, removed or relocated during its execution. The robots share neither knowledge of the coordinate systems of the other robots nor of a global one. However, robots agree on the chirality of the system (i.e., clockwise/counterclockwise orientation).

All of these algorithms assume that a robot is a point which neither creates any visual obstruction nor acts as an obstacle in the path of other robots. Czyzowicz et al.,[1] extend the traditional *weak model* [5] of robots by replacing the point robots with unit disc robots (*fat robots*). Dutta et. al. [4] proposed a circle formation algorithm for *fat robots* assuming common origin and axes for the robots. Here the robots are assumed to be transparent in order to avoid visibility block. However, a robot acts as an physical obstacle if it falls in the path of other robots. The visibility range/radius of the robots is assumed to be limited. Many of the earlier circle formation algorithms required the system to be synchronous which is also an ideal situation. Dutta et. al. [4] assumed asynchronous system. In this paper we propose a circle formation algorithm for asynchronous, transparent *fat robots* with no agreement on common origin and axes.

3 Circle Formation by Multiple Transparent Fat Robots

We first describe the computation robot model used in this paper and present an overview of the problem. Then we move to the solution approach and present the algorithms with the proofs of their correctness.

3.1 Underlying Computation Model of Robots

Let $R = r_1, r_2, \ldots, r_n$ be a set of points on the plane representing a set of fat robots. A robot is represented by its center, i.e., by r_i we mean a robot whose center is r_i. We use the basic structure of *weak model* [5]. The following assumptions describe the system of robots deployed on the 2D plane:

---

[1] A Reuleaux triangle is a curve of constant width constructed by drawing arcs from each polygon vertex of an equilateral triangle between the other two vertices[12].

[2] In a biangular circle, there is a center and two non zero angles α and β such that the center between each two adjacent points is either α or β and these angles alternate.

- The robots are autonomous.
- The robots execute their cycles (*Look-Compute-Wait-Move*) asynchronously.
- The robots are anonymous and homogeneous in the sense that they are unable to uniquely identify themselves, neither with a unique identification number nor with some external distinctive mark (e.g. color, flag, etc.).
- A robot can sense all other robots irrespective of their configuration.
- Each robot is represented as a unit disc (*fat robots*).
- The robots are assumed to be transparent to achieve full visibility.
- CORDA [8] model is assumed for robots' movement. Under this model the movement of the robots is not instantaneous. While in motion, a robot may be observed by other robots.
- The robots have no common orientation or scale. Each robot uses its own local coordinate system (origin, orientation and distance) and has no particular knowledge about the coordinate system of any other robot or of a global coordinate system.
- The robots can not communicate explicitly. Each robot has a device which takes picture or senses over 360 degrees. The robots communicate only by means of observing other robots using the camera or sensor. The robots are able to compute the coordinates (w.r.t. its own coordinate system) of other robots by observing through the camera or sensor.
- The robots have infinite visibility range.
- The robots are oblivious. They do not remember the data from the previous cycles.
- Initially all robots are stationary.

3.2   Overview of the Problem

Let R be a set of stationary transparent *fat robots*, under the computation model described in section 3.1 is given. The objective is to move the robots in R in order to form a circle. First, the robots compute the Smallest Enclosing Circle (SEC) with R. Let P be the center of the SEC. The aim of each robot is to find a destination on the circumference of the SEC and move to that destination. The robot nearest to the circumference of the SEC, (i.e., farthest from P) is the one which moves towards the circumference of the SEC. During this period, all other robots remain in their positions. However, there may be multiple robots nearest to the circumference of the SEC. This means that these robots are equidistant from P and they lie on a circle centered at P. Let $C(1)$ be the set of robots nearest to P. We call this set, the robots at 1st level of distances. Similarly $C(2)$ is the set of robots 2nd nearest to P. We call this set, the robots at 2nd level of distances. Let there be m such levels of distances. The robots which are at i^{th} level of distance from P constitute the set $C(i)$ ($1 \leq i \leq m$). The robots in $C(m)$ are actually on the SEC. We can visualize the configuration of robots as m concentric circles whose center is P (Fig.1.). If any robot is at the center then it is considered to be on a circle with radius zero and denoted by $C(0)$. This set of circles is arranged according to their distances from P as $C = \{C(0), C(1), C(2), \ldots, C(m)\}$. Since the SEC is unique, the set C is also unambiguous. Each robot computes this sequence C. The robots in $C(m-1)$ are considered for moving and they move to $C(m)$. All robots always move outwards from P. Finally all robots in R are on SEC.

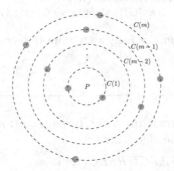

Fig. 1. An example of a set of robots and their multiple levels of distances

3.3   Expanding the Smallest Enclosing Circle

Before a robot computes its destination it executes a preprocessing algorithm for expanding the SEC. In this algorithm robots check following conditions.

1. If SEC is not large enough to accommodate all robots, then SEC is expanded.
2. It may be the case when a robot from $C(m-1)$ finds its destination on $C(m)$ for moving, but its path towards the destination is either intersected by the path of other robots or some other robots lie on its path. In this situation, the SEC is expanded.
3. If the robots initially are in *lock* configuration (discussed in section 3.5) then the SEC is expanded.

In order to expand SEC the robots on the SEC move a certain distance (depending on the number of robots) radially away from the center of SEC. We now introduce some definitions which will be used in the algorithm SEC_Expansion(r).

- $RECSEC(R)$ - The minimum perimeter of a circle required to accommodate all the robots in R. This is proportional to the number of robots in R.
- $CURSEC(R)$ - The perimeter of the present SEC i.e., circumference of $C(m)$.
- $DIS(r) = (RECSEC(R) - CURSEC(R))/2\pi$: The distance, robots in $C(m)$ move radially outward in order to make radius of SEC into $RECSEC(R)$ from $CURSEC(R)$.

Note that, this is an asynchronous system; so all the robots on $C(m)$ may not execute this algorithm at the same time. This algorithm may be executed more than once and the center of the new SEC may not remain same as the one before expansion. However, once the terminating condition is achieved i.e. when $CURSEC(R) \geq RECSEC(R)$ then this algorithm stops.

Algorithm 1. SEC_Expansion(r)

Input: (i) The set of robots R;(ii) A robot $r \in R$.
Output: $RECSEC(R)$: An expanded SEC of R.
Compute $CURSEC(R)$ and $RECSEC(R)$;
if *(CURSEC(R) < RECSEC(R)) $\vee$ (r is on C(m))* **then**
  | Computes $DIS(r)$;
  | Move r $DIS(r)$ distance radially away from the centre of
  | $CURSEC(R)$;
else
  | r does not move ;

Correctness of the Algorithm *SEC_Expansion(r)*: The following lemmas prove the correctness of the algorithm.

Lemma 1. *The radius of the $CURSEC(R)$ is never decreased by the execution of SEC_Expansion(r).*

Proof. According to the algorithm *SEC_Expansion(r)*, a robot either moves away from the center of the current SEC or stay still. Hence, the radius of the circle either increases or remains same.   □

Lemma 2. *SEC_Expansion(r) stops after a finite number of steps.*

Proof. After every execution of *SEC_Expansion(r)*, $CURSEC(R)$ increases (lemma 1). Once $CURSEC(R) \geq RECSEC(R)$ is true, the algorithm stops. Since, the number of robots is finite, $RECSEC(R)$ is finite and $CURSEC(R) \geq RECSEC(R)$ becomes true after a finite time. Hence, the result follows.   □

3.4 Computing the Destinations of the Robots

Let us introduce some notations and definition which will be used later.

- $|A|$: Number of elements in set A.
- $Dist(A, B)$: The euclidean distance between two points A and B.
- T_r: Computed destination for r.
- $LN(r, i)$: i^{th} left (clockwise w.r.t. r) neighbor of the robot r on the circumference of the circle on which r lies.
- $RN(r, i)$: i^{th} right (anti clockwise w.r.t. r) neighbor of the robot r on the circumference of the circle on which r lies.
- $Poly(C(k))$: The convex polygon formed by the robots on the circumference of the circle $C(k) \in \mathcal{C}$.
- $Maxe(Poly(C(k)))$: The unique longest edge of $Poly(C(k))$. (If there are more than one longest edge, then the next maximum length is found until we get a single edge of maximum length.) If R is not in symmetric configuration (described in section 3.5), then a longest unique edge is positively found.
- $Projpt(r, C(k))$: The projected (radially inward or outward) point of the robot position r on the concentric circle $C(k) \in \mathcal{C}$.
- $SER(R)$: SEC computed by a robot $r \in R$. $SEC(R) > RECSEC(R)$.

Definition 1. *If the circular area of radius 2 and centered at point t does not contain the center of any other robot, then t is called a vacant point.*

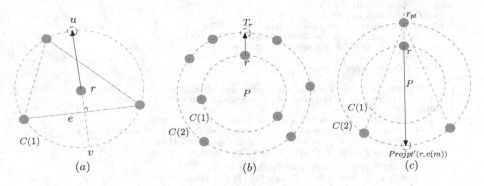

Fig. 2. Examples of *Compute_destination(r)* for a robot r for $m = 1$ and $m = 2$

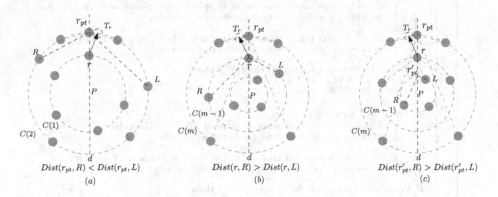

Fig. 3. Example of *Compute_destination(r)* for a robot r for $m \geq 2$

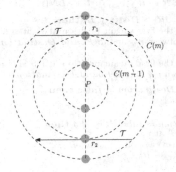

Fig. 4. Example of Compute_destination(r) for a collinear robot r

---

Algorithm 2. Compute_destination(r)

Input: (i) A set of robots R, such that $SEC(R) > RECSEC(R)$. (ii) A robot r in $C(m-1)$.
Output: The destination for r, T_r.
$Found\_Destination \leftarrow false$;
if $(Found\_Destination == false) \vee ((m = 1) \wedge (|C(0)| = 1))$ *(Fig. 2(a).)* **then**
     Compute $Poly(C(m))$; $e \leftarrow Maxe(Poly(C(m)))$; $l \leftarrow$ bisector of e;
     $u \leftarrow$ intersection point of l and $C(m)$ at that side of e where r lies;
     $T_r \leftarrow u$;
     $Found\_Destination \leftarrow true$;
else
     if $Projpt(r, C(m))$ *is a vacant point (Fig. 2(b).)* **then**
         $T_r \leftarrow Projpt(r, C(m))$; $Found\_Destination \leftarrow true$;
     else
         // $Projpt(r, C(m))$ is not a vacant point.
         if $(m = 2) \wedge (|C(1)| = 1) \wedge (Projpt'(r, C(m)))$ *(the point diametrically opposite*
         to $Projpt(r, C(m)))$ is a vacant point (Fig. 2(c).) **then**
            $T_r \leftarrow Projpt'(r, C(m))$; $Found\_Destination \leftarrow true$;
         $r_{pt} \leftarrow Projpt(r, C(m))$; $d \leftarrow Projpt'(r, C(m))$;
         if $Found\_Destination = false$ *(Fig. 3(a).)* **then**
            $i \leftarrow 1$; $R \leftarrow RN(r_{pt}, i)$; $L \leftarrow LN(r_{pt}, i)$;
            while $Dist(r_{pt}, R) = Dist(r_{pt}, L)$ **do**
                $i + +$; $R \leftarrow RN(r_{pt}, i)$; $L \leftarrow LN(r_{pt}, i)$;
            if $Dist(r_{pt}, R) > Dist(r_{pt}, L)$ **then**
                $T_r \leftarrow$ the first vacant position at right side (anti clockwise w.r.t. r) of r_{pt}
                between r_{pt} and d; $Found\_Destination \leftarrow true$;
            else
                $T_r \leftarrow$ the first vacant position at left side (clockwise w.r.t. r) of r_{pt}
                between r_{pt} and d; $Found\_Destination \leftarrow true$;

         if $Found\_Destination = false$ *(Fig. 3(b).)* **then**
            $i \leftarrow 1$; $R \leftarrow RN(r, i)$; $L \leftarrow LN(r, i)$;
            while $Dist(r, R) = Dist(r, L)$ **do**
                $i + +$; $R \leftarrow RN(r, i)$; $L \leftarrow LN(r, i)$;
            if $Dist(r, R) > Dist(r, L)$ **then**
                $T_r \leftarrow$ the first vacant position at right side (anti clockwise w.r.t. r) of r_{pt}
                between r_{pt} and d; $Found\_Destination \leftarrow true$;
            else
                $T_r \leftarrow$ the first vacant position at left side (clockwise w.r.t. r) of r_{pt}
                between r_{pt} and d; $Found\_Destination \leftarrow true$;

         if $Found\_Destination = false$ *(Fig. 3(c).)* **then**
            $k \leftarrow 1$;
            while $(Found\_Destination = false) \wedge (k < m)$ **do**
                $r'_{pt} \leftarrow Projpt(r, C(m-k))$; $i \leftarrow 2$; $R \leftarrow RN(r'_{pt}, i)$; $L \leftarrow LN(r'_{pt}, i)$;
                while $Dist(r'_{pt}, R) = Dist(r'_{pt}, L)$ **do**
                    $i + +$; $R \leftarrow RN(r'_{pt}, i)$; $L \leftarrow LN(r'_{pt}, i)$;
                if $Dist(r'_{pt}, R) > Dist(r'_{pt}, L)$ **then**
                    $T_r \leftarrow$ the first vacant position at right side (anti clockwise w.r.t. r) of
                    r_{pt} between r_{pt} and d; $Found\_Destination \leftarrow true$;
                else
                    $T_r \leftarrow$ the first vacant position at left side (clockwise w.r.t. r) of r_{pt}
                    between r_{pt} and d; $Found\_Destination \leftarrow true$;
                if $Found\_Destination = false$ **then**
                    $k + +$;

     if $Found\_Destination = false$ *(Fig. 4.)* **then**
         Draw tangent $\mathcal{T}$ at r;
         $\mathcal{T}$ intersects $C(m)$ at point L_p and R_p;
         $T_r \leftarrow L_p$; or $T_r \leftarrow R_p$;

Return T_r;

The algorithm *Compute_destination(r)* assumes that no *lock* configuration is encountered either at initial stage or at intermediate stage.

Definition 2. *A robot is called an eligible robot, if it finds a unique[3] destination (using Compute_destination(r)) on the circumference of SEC.*

Correctness of the Algorithm *Compute_destination(r)*: Following lemmas prove the correctness of the algorithm Compute_destination(r).

Lemma 3. *Every robot in R is an eligible robot.*

Proof. The proof follows from the fact that $SEC(R) > RECSEC(R)$.   □

Lemma 4. *The path of each robot is obstacle free.*

Proof. Only the robots on $C(m-1)$ are selected for moving and $SEC(R) > RECSEC(R)$. The robots always move outwards. Hence, the result follows.   □

3.5 Characterizing Lock Configurations

Definition 3. *A straight line $\mathcal{L}$ is called a line of symmetry for R if $\mathcal{L}$ divides R (excepting those robots which lie on $\mathcal{L}$) into two parts, such that one part is a mirror image of the other (Fig. 5.).*

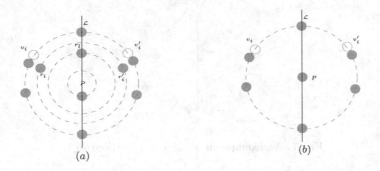

Fig. 5. Examples showing a set of robots in Symmetric Configuration ($\emptyset_S$)

Note that if all the robots are collinear, the line containing all the robots is a line of symmetry.

Definition 4. *R is said to be in symmetric configuration $\emptyset_S$, if R has a line of straight symmetry (Fig. 5.).*

Let r be a robot on the circle $C(m-i)$ $(1 \leq i \leq m-1)$. r is projected (radially outward) on the circle $C(m)$. Let r' be the projected point. Let us denote the rectangular area with length $l = Dist(r, r')$ and width 2 as shown in Fig. 6., as $rect(rr')$.

---

[3] No two robots will have same destination.

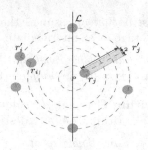

Fig. 6. An example of free robots and locked robots

Definition 5. *r is said to be a free robot if rect(rr′) does not contain any part of other robot. A robot which is not free is called locked robot.*

In Fig. 6., r_i is a locked robot but r_j is a free robot.

Definition 6. *If (a) m = 2; and (b) the number of vacant points on C(m) = the number of robots in C(m − 1); and (c) ∀r_i ∈ C(m − 1), r_i is not a free robot; and (d) R is in Ø_S ; then R is in lock configuration (denoted by Ø_L (Fig. 7)).*

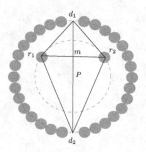

Fig. 7. An example of a *lock* configuration$(Ø_L)$

Observation 1. *If the number of vacant points on C(m) > the number of robots in C(m − 1) then any r_i in C(m − 1) eventually finds its unique destination on C(m) using Compute_destination(r_i).*

Lemma 5. *If R is not in Ø_L , then ∀r_i ∈ R, r_i is an eligible robot.*

Proof. Follows from observation 1.   □

3.6   Detection of Lock Configurations

The circle formation algorithm presented in this paper assures that no *lock* configuration is formed due to the execution of the algorithm. The function Check_lock(r, T_r) is used by robots to check whether a *lock* configuration occurs when r reaches its computed (using Compute_destination(r)) destination T_r.

3.7   Circle Formation Algorithm

Finally the algorithm Circle_form(r) forms the circle. Each robot in R computes the SEC of R and the sequence of concentric circles $\mathcal{C}$ (as described in section 3.2). Each robot from $C(m-1)$ finds its destination on $C(m)$, using algorithm Compute_destination(r) and moves towards it. However, r does not move if any following cases occurs.

- **Case 1.** If r is not in $C(m-1)$, then r does not move.
- **Case 2.** If r is on the SEC i.e., on $C(m)$ then r does not move.
- **Case 3.** Using Check_lock(r, T_r), r checks whether the configuration is in $\emptyset_L$, when r reaches to T_r. If the next configuration is going to be in $\emptyset_L$, then r does not move.
- **Case 4.** If the line joining r and T_r intersects $C(m-1)$ or contains any part of other robots or intersects the path of other robots, then r does not move.

Case 3 and 4 are eliminated using SEC_Expansion(r) algorithm.

Algorithm 3. Circle_form(r)

Input: (i) The set of robots R;(ii) A robot $r \in R$.
Output: The SEC of R such that all robots in R lie on SEC of R.
if *r is in case* 1 *or* 2 **then**
 | r does not move;
else
 | $T_r \leftarrow$ Compute_destination(r);
 | **if** *r is in case* 3 *or* 4 **then**
 | | SEC_Expansion(r);
 | **else**
 | | $T_r \leftarrow$ Compute_destination(r);
 | | r moves to T_r;

Correctness of the Algorithm Circle_form(r): Following lemma, observation and theorem prove the correctness of the algorithm.

Lemma 6. *Lock configuration is successfully removed by SEC_Expansion(r) algorithm.*

Proof. Follows from the proof of correctness of the algorithm SEC_Expansion(r). □

Observation 2. *Circle_form(r) does not create any lock configuration.*

Theorem 1. *Circle_form(r) forms a circle after a finite time.*

Proof. If initially R is in $\emptyset_L$, SEC_Expansion(r) removes the *lock* configuration (lemma 6). Moreover, Circle_form(r) algorithm does not create any *lock* configuration observation 2. From lemma 5, if R is not in $\emptyset_L$, Compute_destination(r) successfully computes a deterministic destination for r. Hence, the result follows.   □

4   Conclusion

In this paper, a distributed algorithm is presented for circle formation by autonomous, oblivious, homogeneous, non communicative, asynchronous, transparent *fat robots* having individual coordinate systems. The algorithm ensures that multiple mobile robots will form a circle in finite time. The robots are considered to be transparent in order to achieve full visibility. However, a robot is considered as a physical obstacle for another robot. The algorithm presented in this paper also assures that there is no collision among the robots. The work will be extended further for solid *fat robots* which obstruct the visibility of the other robots.

Acknowledgement

- Sruti Gan Chaudhuri would like to acknowledge the Council of Scientific and Industrial Research, Govt. of India, for their assistance.
- Krishnendu Mukhopadhyaya would like to acknowledge the Department of Science and Technology, Govt. of India, for their assistance.

References

1. Czyzowicz, J., Gasieniec, L., Pelc, A.: Gathering Few Fat Mobile Robots in the Plane. Theoretical Computer Science 410, 481–499 (2009)
2. Défago, X., Konagaya, A.: Circle Formation for Oblivious Anonymous Mobile Robots with no Common Sense of Orientation. In: Proc. 2nd International Annual Workshop on Principles of Mobile Computing, pp. 97–104 (2002)
3. Défago, X., Souissi, S.: Non Uniform Circle Formation Algorithm for Oblivious Mobile Robots with Convergence Towards Uniformity. Theoretical Computer Science 396(1-3), 97–112
4. Dutta, A., Gan Chaudhuri, S., Datta, S., Mukhopadhyaya, K.: Circle Formation by Asynchronous Fat Robots with Limited Visibility. In: Ramanujam, R., Ramaswamy, S. (eds.) ICDCIT 2012. LNCS, vol. 7154, pp. 83–93. Springer, Heidelberg (2012)
5. Efrima, A., Peleg, D.: Distributed Algorithms for Partitioning a Swarm of Autonomous Mobile Robots. Theoretical Computer Science 410, 1355–1368 (2009)
6. Katreniak, B.: Biangular Circle Formation by Asynchronous Mobile Robots. In: Pelc, A., Raynal, M. (eds.) SIROCCO 2005. LNCS, vol. 3499, pp. 185–199. Springer, Heidelberg (2005)
7. Payton, D., Estkowski, R., Howard, M.: Pheromone Robotics and the Logic of Virtual Pheromones. In: Şahin, E., Spears, W.M. (eds.) Swarm Robotics 2004. LNCS, vol. 3342, pp. 45–57. Springer, Heidelberg (2005)
8. Prencipe, G.: *InstantaneousActions* vs. *FullAsynchronicity*: Controlling and Coordinating a Set of Autonomous Mobile Robots. In: Restivo, A., Ronchi Della Rocca, S., Roversi, L. (eds.) ICTCS 2001. LNCS, vol. 2202, pp. 154–171. Springer, Heidelberg (2001)
9. Sugihara, K., Suzuki, I.: Distributed Motion Coordination of Multiple Mobile Robots. In: Proc. IEEE International Symposium on Intelligent Control, pp. 138–143 (1990)

10. Suzuki, I., Yamashita, M.: Distributed Anonymous Mobile Robots: Formation of Geometric Patterns. SIAM Journal of Computing 28(4), 1347–1363 (1999)
11. Uny Cao, Y., Fukunaga, A.S., Kahng, A.B.: Cooperative Mobile Robotics: Antecedents and Directions. Autonomous Robots 4, 1–23 (1997)
12. Weisstein, E.W.: Reuleaux Triangle, From MathWorld- A Wolfram Web Resource, http://mathworld.com/ReuleauxTriangle.html

Controlling Packet Loss of Bursty
and Correlated Traffics in a Variant
of Multiple Vacation Policy

Abhijit Datta Banik[1,*] and Sujit K. Samanta[2]

[1] School of Basic Sciences, Indian Institute of Technology
Samantapuri, Nandan Kanan Road, Bhubaneswar-751013, India
[2] Department of Mathematics, National Institute of Science and Technology
Palur Hills, Berhampur - 761008, India
banikad@gmail.com, adattabanik@iitbbs.ac.in,
sujit.samanta@rediffmail.com

Abstract. This paper presents a finite-buffer single server queue where
packets arrive according to a batch Markovian arrival process (BMAP).
Partial batch acceptance strategy has been analyzed in which the incoming packets of a batch are allowed to enter the buffer as long as there is
space. When the buffer is full, remaining packets of a batch are discarded.
The server serves till system is emptied and after that it takes a maximum H number of vacations until it either finds at least one packet in the
queue or the server has exhaustively taken all the vacations. We obtain
some important performance measures such as probability of blocking
for the first-, an arbitrary- and the last-packet of a batch, mean queue
lengths and mean waiting time of packet. The burstiness of the correlated traffic influences the probability of packet loss which makes buffer
management to satisfy the Quality of Service (QoS) requirements.

Keywords: Buffer management, correlated arrivals, variant of multiple
vacation policy, packet loss probability.

1 Introduction

The performance analysis of various communication network is gaining increasing importance nowadays. The performance analysis of statistical multiplexer
whose input consists of a superposition of several packetized sources have been
done through some analytically tractable arrival process, viz., Markovian arrival
process (MAP), see Lucantoni et al. [9]. Later Lucantoni [7] introduced batch
Markovian arrival process ($BMAP$) which is a convenient representation of the
versatile Markovian point process, see Neuts [11].

Queueing systems with vacations are considered to be an effective instrument
in modelling and analysis of communication networks and several other engineering systems in which single server is entitled to serve more than one queue, for
detail, see Tian and Zhang [15] and references therein. Queueing systems with

---

*Corresponding author.

C. Hota and P.K. Srimani (Eds.): ICDCIT 2013, LNCS 7753, pp. 208–219, 2013.

server's vacations and MAP or $BMAP$ as input process, i.e., $MAP/G/1/\infty$ and $BMAP/G/1/\infty$ queue have been analyzed by Lucantoni et al. [9] and Lucantoni [7], respectively. Queueing analysis of finite systems are more realistic than infinite systems. The study of finite capacity vacation model with $BMAP$ arrival, that is, finite-capacity $BMAP/G/1$ queue has been done by Dudin et al. [4] where they have presented analysis for partial batch acceptance-, total batch acceptance- as well as total batch rejection-strategies. More detail study of $BMAP/G/1/N$ queue with vacation(s) under exhaustive service discipline was performed by Niu et al. [13]. Recently, Banik [2] investigated $BMAP/G/1/\infty$ queue with a variant of multiple vacation policy. In this paper, we consider a $BMAP/G/1/N/VMV$ queue with VMV stands for variant of multiple vacation policy. This means that the server will go for a vacation if the system becomes empty after a service. The server is allowed to take maximum H consecutive vacations if the system remains empty after the end of a vacation. The vacation schedule is exactly similar to that of Ke [6]. Similar model with single as well as multiple vacations were previously analyzed in [13] for the case of partial- and total-batch rejection strategies. We analyzed the model for the case of partial batch rejection strategy.

The model presented in this paper may be useful for the performance evaluation of an energy-aware medium access control (MAC)/physical (PHY) layer protocol in view of bursty traffic arrival patterns (modeled as BMAP). The MAC/PHY layer in a node is modeled as a server and a vacation queueing model is utilized to represent the sleep and wakeup mechanism of the server. Energy efficiency is a major concern in traditional wireless networks due to the limited battery power of the nodes, see Azad [1], Miao et al. [10] and references therein for details. In one direction to save energy in such a network is to bring into play an efficient sleep and wakeup mechanism to turn off the radio transceiver irregularly in order that the desired trade-off between the node energy savings and the network performance can be achieved.

2   Description of the Model

We analyze the $BMAP/G/1/N/VMV$ queue with variant of multiple vacation policy, where N is the capacity of the queue excluding the one in service. When the server finishes servicing a customer and finds the queue empty, the server leaves for a vacation. The server takes vacations consecutively until either the server finds a customer at a vacation completion instant or the server has taken a maximum number, denoted by H (> 0), of vacations. In case of arrivals occurred during a vacation, the server resumes service immediately at that vacation completion instant. In case of no arrivals occurred during the period of H consecutive vacations have completed, the server stays idle and waits to serve the next arrival. Customers are assumed to arrive at the queueing system according to an m-state batch Markovian arrival process $(BMAP)$. The arrival process is characterized by $m \times m$ matrices $\mathbf{D}_k$, $k \geq 0$, where (i, j)-th $(1 \leq i, j \leq m)$ element of $\mathbf{D}_0$, is the state transition rate from state i to state j in the underlying Markov chain without an arrival, and (i, j)-th element of $\mathbf{D}_k$, $k \geq 1$, is the state transition rate from state i to state j in the underlying Markov chain with an arrival of batch size k. The matrix $\mathbf{D}_0$ has nonnegative off-diagonal and negative diagonal elements, and the matrix $\mathbf{D}_k$, $k \geq 1$, has nonnegative elements. Let $Y(t)$ denote the number of arrivals in $(0, t]$ and $J(t)$ be the state of the underlying Markov chain at time t with state space $\{i : 1 \leq i \leq m\}$. Then $\{Y(t), J(t)\}$ is a two-dimensional Markov process of $BMAP$ with state space $\{(n, i) : n \geq 0, 1 \leq i \leq m\}$. The infinitesimal generator of $BMAP$ is given by

$$\mathbf{Q} = \begin{pmatrix} \mathbf{D}_0 & \mathbf{D}_1 & \mathbf{D}_2 & \mathbf{D}_3 & \cdots \\ 0 & \mathbf{D}_0 & \mathbf{D}_1 & \mathbf{D}_2 & \cdots \\ 0 & 0 & \mathbf{D}_0 & \mathbf{D}_1 & \cdots \\ \vdots & \vdots & \vdots & \vdots & \ddots \end{pmatrix}.$$

As $\mathbf{Q}$ is the infinitesimal generator of the $BMAP$, we have $\sum_{k=0}^{\infty} \mathbf{D}_k \mathbf{e} = \mathbf{0}$, where $\mathbf{e}$ is an $m \times 1$ vector with all its elements equal to 1. Further, since $\mathbf{D} = \sum_{k=0}^{\infty} \mathbf{D}_k$ is the infinitesimal generator of the underlying Markov chain $\{J(t)\}$, there exists a stationary probability vector $\overline{\pi}$ such that $\overline{\pi}\mathbf{D} = \mathbf{0}$ and $\overline{\pi}\mathbf{e} = 1$. Then the average arrival rate (λ^*) and average batch arrival rate (λ_g) of the stationary $BMAP$ are given by $\lambda^* = \overline{\pi} \sum_{k=1}^{\infty} k\mathbf{D}_k \mathbf{e}$ and $\lambda_g = \overline{\pi}\widetilde{\mathbf{D}}_1 \mathbf{e}$, respectively, where $\widetilde{\mathbf{D}}_n = \sum_{k=n}^{\infty} \mathbf{D}_k$, $n \geq 1$. Let us define $\{\mathbf{P}^{(k)}(n, t), 0 \leq k \leq N, 0 \leq n \leq k, t \geq 0\}$ as $m \times m$ matrix whose (i, j)-th element is the probability to admit n customers in the queue during the time interval $(0, t]$ and to have the state j of the underlying Markov chain of the $BMAP$ at the epoch t conditional that the state of this process was i at the epoch 0 and at most k customers can be admitted during the interval $(0, t]$. Since we deal with finite-buffer queue with batch arrival, we consider following batch acceptance/rejection strategies as follows.

Partial batch rejection: An arriving batch finds not enough space in the buffer and some of the customers of that batch are accepted and rests are rejected. The matrices $\mathbf{P}^{(k)}(n, t)$ then satisfy the following difference-differential equations:

$$\frac{d}{dt}\mathbf{P}^{(k)}(n, t) = \sum_{r=0}^{n} \mathbf{P}^{(k)}(r, t)\mathbf{D}_{n-r}, \quad 0 \leq k \leq N, \ 0 \leq n < k, \tag{1}$$

$$\frac{d}{dt}\mathbf{P}^{(k)}(n, t) = \sum_{r=0}^{n} \mathbf{P}^{(k)}(r, t)\widetilde{\mathbf{D}}_{n-r}, \quad 0 \leq k \leq N, \ n = k. \tag{2}$$

Let $S(x)\{s(x)\}$ be the distribution function (DF) {probability density function (pdf)} of the service time S of a typical customer. Let the consecutive vacations taken by the server are denoted by the random variables V_i $(i = 1, 2, \ldots, H)$ with $V_i(x)\{v_i(x)\}$ be the DF {pdf}. The mean service [vacation] time is $E(S)$ $[E(V_i)]$. The service-, each vacation-times are assumed to be independent and identically distributed (i.i.d.) random variables (r.vs.), and they are independent of the arrival process. The traffic intensity is given by $\rho = \lambda^* E(S)$. Further, let ρ' be the probability that the server is busy.

3   Queue Length Distribution at Different Epochs

Consider the system at service completion and vacation termination epochs. Let t_0, t_1, t_2, ... be the time epochs at which service completion or vacation termination occurs. Let t_k^+ denote the time epoch just after a service completion or vacation termination. The state of the system at t_k^+ is defined as $\zeta_k = \{N_q(t_k^+), \ J(t_k^+), \ \xi(t_k^+)\}$, $k \geq 0$, where $N_q(t_k^+)$ is the number of customers in the queue and $J(t_k^+)$ is the state of the underlying Markov chain of $BMAP$. If t_k^+ is a service completion epoch, then $\xi(t_k^+) = B$, where 'B' stands for busy state of the server; $\xi(t_k^+) = l$ if t_k^+ is the l-th vacation termination epoch. Then $\{\zeta_k, \ k \geq 0\}$ forms an embedded Markov chain which is irreducible, aperiodic, and therefore the Markov chain is ergodic. Thus, the limiting probabilities are defined as

$$\pi_i^+(n) = \lim_{k \to \infty} P\{N_q(t_k^+) = n, \ J(t_k^+) = i, \ \xi(t_k^+) = B\}, \quad 1 \leq i \leq m,$$

$$\omega_{i,l}^+(n) = \lim_{k \to \infty} P\{N_q(t_k^+) = n, \ J(t_k^+) = i, \ \xi(t_k^+) = l\}, \quad 1 \leq i \leq m, \ 1 \leq l \leq H.$$

Let $\boldsymbol{\pi}^+(n) \ [\boldsymbol{\omega}_k^+(n)]$ be the $1 \times m$ vector whose i-th component $\pi_i^+(n) \ [\omega_{i,k}^+(n)]$ is the probability that there are n customers in the queue at service completion [k-th vacation termination] epoch and batch arrival process in phase i.

In order to obtain the queue length distributions at various epochs, we define the $m \times m$ matrices $\mathbf{A}_n^{(r)}$ and $\mathbf{V}_{n,k}^{(r)}$ ($0 \leq r \leq N$, $0 \leq n \leq r$, $1 \leq k \leq H$) as follows. The (i,j)-th element $[A_n^{(r)}]_{ij}$ of $\mathbf{A}_n^{(r)}$ is the conditional probability that given a departure of a customer which left at least one customer in the queue and the batch arrival process in phase i, the next departure occurs with the batch arrival process in phase j and during this service there were n ($0 \leq n \leq r$) arrivals accepted in the system whereas at most r ($0 \leq r \leq N$) customers can be admitted during the service. Similarly, the (i,j)-th element $[V_{n,k}^{(r)}]_{ij}$ of $\mathbf{V}_{n,k}^{(r)}$ denotes the conditional probability that given a departure or $(k-1)$-th (> 0) vacation termination which leaves the system empty, and k-th vacation begins with the arrival process in phase i, the end of the vacation occurs with the arrival process in phase j, and during that vacation there were n ($0 \leq n \leq r$) arrivals whereas at most r ($0 \leq r \leq N$) customers can be admitted during the vacation. Therefore, for $0 \leq r \leq N$, $0 \leq n \leq r$, we have

$$\mathbf{A}_n^{(r)} = \int_0^\infty \mathbf{P}^{(r)}(n,t) \, dS(t), \tag{3}$$

$$\mathbf{V}_{n,k}^{(r)} = \int_0^\infty \mathbf{P}^{(r)}(n,t) \, dV_k(t), \quad 1 \leq k \leq H. \tag{4}$$

Observing the system at two consecutive embedded Markov points, we obtain the transition probability matrix (TPM) $\mathcal{P}$ with four block matrices of the form:

$$\mathcal{P} = \begin{bmatrix} \boldsymbol{\Xi}_{(N+1)m \times (N+1)m} & \boldsymbol{\Psi}_{(N+1)m \times (N+1)Hm} \\ \boldsymbol{\Delta}_{(N+1)Hm \times (N+1)m} & \boldsymbol{\Phi}_{(N+1)Hm \times (N+1)Hm} \end{bmatrix}_{(N+1)(H+1)m \times (N+1)(H+1)m,}$$

where $\Xi_{(N+1)m \times (N+1)m}$ describes the probability of transitions among the service completion epochs. The elements of this block can be expressed in the form:

$$\Xi_{(i,B),(j,B)} = \begin{cases} \mathbf{A}_{j-i+1}^{(N-i+1)} & 1 \leq i \leq N, \ i-1 \leq j \leq N, \\ \mathbf{0}_m & \text{otherwise}, \end{cases}$$

where $\mathbf{0}_m$ is null matrix of order $m \times m$. Second block of the TPM gives the probability of transitions from any service completion epoch to the next vacation termination epochs. The structure of this block denoted by $\mathbf{\Psi}_{(N+1)m \times (N+1)Hm}$ is given by

$$\mathbf{\Psi}_{(i,B)(j,k)} = \begin{cases} \mathbf{V}_{j,1}^{(N)} & i=0, \ 0 \leq j \leq N, \ k=1, \\ \mathbf{0}_m & \text{otherwise}. \end{cases}$$

Third block of the TPM describes the probability of transition from every vacation termination epoch to the next service completion epochs. The structure of this block denoted by $\mathbf{\Delta}_{(N+1)Hm \times (N+1)m}$ is given by

$$\mathbf{\Delta}_{(i,k)(j,B)} = \begin{cases} \overline{\mathbf{D}}_1 \mathbf{A}_0^{(N)} & i=0, \ j=0, \ k=H, \\ \sum_{r=1}^{j+1} \overline{\mathbf{D}}_r \mathbf{A}_{j-r+1}^{(N-r+1)} & i=0, \ 1 \leq j \leq N-1, \ k=H, \\ \sum_{r=1}^{N} \overline{\mathbf{D}}_r \mathbf{A}_{j-r+1}^{(N-r+1)} & i=0, \ j=N, \ k=H, \\ \mathbf{A}_{j-i+1}^{(N-i+1)} & 1 \leq i \leq N, \ i \leq j \leq N, \ 1 \leq k \leq H, \\ \mathbf{0}_m & \text{otherwise}, \end{cases}$$

where $\overline{\mathbf{D}}_k = (-\mathbf{D}_0)^{-1}\mathbf{D}_k$, $1 \leq k \leq N-1$, and $\overline{\mathbf{D}}_N = (-\mathbf{D}_0)^{-1}[\widetilde{\mathbf{D}}_N]$ represent the phase transition matrix during an inter-batch arrival time, i.e., the (i,j)-th $(1 \leq i,j \leq m)$ entry of the matrix $\overline{\mathbf{D}}_k$ is the conditional probability that an idle or dormant period ends with an arrival of a batch of size k and the arrival process is in state j, given that the idle period began with the arrival process in phase i. The fourth block of the TPM describes the transition from each vacation termination epoch to the next vacation termination epoch. The elements of this block $\mathbf{\Phi}$ are given by

$$\mathbf{\Phi}_{(i,k)(j,r)} = \begin{cases} \mathbf{V}_{j,r}^{(N)} & i=0, \ 0 \leq j \leq N, \ 1 \leq k \leq H-1, \ r=k+1, \\ \mathbf{0}_m, & \text{otherwise}. \end{cases}$$

One may note here that in the case of single vacation policy, i.e, when H is fixed to 1 then at the end of a vacation if there are no customers in the system then the server is not allowed to go for another vacation rather it remains in dormant state. Therefore, $\mathbf{\Phi}$ is the null matrix of the appropriate order.

The evaluation of the matrices $\mathbf{A}_n^{(r)}$ ($\mathbf{V}_{n,k}^{(r)}$), in general, for arbitrary service (vacation) time distribution requires numerical integration or infinite summation and it can be carried out along the lines proposed by Lucantoni [7] for $BMAP$ arrival. However, when the service time distributions are of phase type (PH-distribution), these matrices can be evaluated without any numerical integration, see Neuts [12, 67-70]. It may be noted here that various service time distributions arising in practical applications can be approximated by PH-distribution.

The unknown probability vectors $\pi^+(n)$ and $\omega_k^+(n)$ can be obtained by solving the system of equations: $\left(\pi^+, \omega^+\right) = \left(\pi^+, \omega^+\right)\mathcal{P}$, where $\pi^+ = [\pi^+(0), \pi^+(1),$ $\ldots, \pi^+(N)]$ and $\omega^+ = [\omega_1^+(0), \omega_2^+(0), \ldots, \omega_H^+(0), \omega_1^+(1), \omega_2^+(1), \ldots, \omega_H^+(1), \ldots,$ $\omega_1^+(N), \omega_2^+(N), \ldots, \omega_H^+(N)]$ using GTH algorithm, see Grassmann et al. [5].

Considering a departure of a customer from the system as an embedded point one can also construct a Markov chain like previous section without considering vacation termination instant. In this case departure epoch probabilities can be obtained through the proportionality relations between distributions of number of customers in the queue at service completion and departure epochs. Let $\mathbf{p}^+(n)$, $0 \leq n \leq N$, denote the row vector whose i-th element is the probability that there are n customers in the queue and phase of the arrival process is i at departure epoch of a customer. Since $\mathbf{p}^+(n)$ is proportional to $\pi^+(n)$ and $\sum_{n=0}^{N} \mathbf{p}^+(n)\mathbf{e} = 1$, one can easily establish that

$$\mathbf{p}^+(n) = \frac{\pi^+(n)}{\sum_{k=0}^{N} \pi^+(k)\mathbf{e}}, \quad 0 \leq n \leq N. \tag{5}$$

Lemma 1. *The expression for ρ' is given by*

$$\rho' = \frac{E(S) \sum_{n=0}^{N} \pi^+(n)\mathbf{e}}{T}, \tag{6}$$

where $T = \sum_{n=0}^{N}\sum_{k=1}^{H} E(V_k)\omega_k^+(n)\mathbf{e} + E(S)\sum_{n=0}^{N} \pi^+(n)\mathbf{e} + \omega_H^+(0)(-\mathbf{D}_0)^{-1}\mathbf{e}$.
Proof: *Here,* $\sum_{n=0}^{N}\sum_{k=1}^{H} \omega_k^+(n)\mathbf{e}$ *is the probability that an arbitrary Markov point is a vacation completion instant. On the other hand,* $\sum_{n=0}^{N} \pi^+(n)\mathbf{e}$ *is the probability of Markov point being a service completion instant. Thus, the mean interval T between two successive Markov points is equal to $E(S)$ with probability* $\sum_{n=0}^{N} \pi^+(n)\mathbf{e}$ *and $E(V_k)$ with probability* $\sum_{n=0}^{N} \omega_k^+(n)\mathbf{e}$, $1 \leq k \leq H$, *which is given above, where $\omega_H^+(0)(-\mathbf{D}_0)^{-1}\mathbf{e}$ is the term due to mean inter-batch arrival time of customers when the server is idle. This can be verified as shown below. Let $\mathbf{U}$ denote an $m \times m$ matrix whose (i,j)-th element U_{ij} is the mean sojourn time of the system in an idle period with phase j, provided at the initial instant of the idle period the phase was i. With the help of equation (1), it can be written as*

$$\mathbf{U} = \int_0^\infty \mathbf{P}^{(N)}(0, t)dt = \int_0^\infty e^{\mathbf{D}_0 t}dt = (-\mathbf{D}_0)^{-1}. \tag{7}$$

Therefore, the carried load ρ' follows Equation (6) from the standard probability argument that ρ' should be equal to $E(S)$ is multiplied by the mean rate of departure of customers.

To obtain queue length distribution at arbitrary epoch we develop relations among the number of customers in the queue at embedded Markov points (service completion, vacation termination and arbitrary) using the argument of Markov renewal theory and semi-Markov process.

Let $\boldsymbol{\pi}(n)$ $[\boldsymbol{\omega}_k(n)]$, $1 \leq k \leq H$, be the row vectors of order $1 \times m$ whose i-th component $\pi_i(n)$ $[w_{i,k}(n)]$ denotes the probability of n customers in the queue and the batch arrival process in phase i, when the server is busy [on k-th vacation] at arbitrary epoch. The i-th component $\nu_i(0)$ of $\boldsymbol{\nu}(0)$ represents the probability that the server is in dormant state and the batch arrival process in phase i at arbitrary epoch.

In order to obtain the queue length distribution, we introduce the $m \times m$ matrices $\widehat{\mathbf{A}}_n^{(r)}$ and $\widehat{\mathbf{V}}_{n,k}^{(r)}$ ($0 \leq r \leq N$, $0 \leq n \leq r$, $1 \leq k \leq H$) whose (i,j)-th element is defined as follows. The element $[\widehat{A}_n^{(r)}]_{ij}$ denotes the limiting probability that n customers are arrived during an elapsed service time with phase of the arrival process j, provided at the initial instant of previous departure epoch the arrival process was in phase i and during the service at most r ($0 \leq r \leq N$) customers can be admitted in the system. Similarly, $[\widehat{V}_{n,k}^{(r)}]_{ij}$ denotes the limiting probability that n customers are arrived during the elapsed time of k-th vacation with phase of the arrival process j, provided at the initial instant of previous departure epoch or $(k-1)$-th vacation termination epoch the phase of the arrival process is i and during the k-th vacation at most r ($0 \leq r \leq N$) customers can be admitted in the system. Therefore, for $0 \leq r \leq N$, $0 \leq n \leq r$, we have

$$\widehat{\mathbf{A}}_n^{(r)} = \frac{1}{E(S)} \int_0^\infty \mathbf{P}^{(r)}(n,x)(1 - S(x))\, dx \qquad (8)$$

$$\widehat{\mathbf{V}}_{n,k}^{(r)} = \frac{1}{E(V_k)} \int_0^\infty \mathbf{P}^{(r)}(n,x)(1 - V_k(x))\, dx, \quad 1 \leq k \leq H. \qquad (9)$$

The matrices $\widehat{\mathbf{A}}_n^{(r)}(\widehat{\mathbf{V}}_{n,k}^{(r)})$ can be expressed in terms of $\mathbf{A}_n^{(r)}(\mathbf{V}_{n,k}^{(r)})$ which are given for one of them as follows:

$$\widehat{\mathbf{A}}_0^{(r)} = \frac{1}{E(S)} \left(\mathbf{I}_m - \mathbf{A}_0^{(r)} \right)(-\mathbf{D}_0)^{-1}, \quad 0 \leq r \leq N,$$

$$\widehat{\mathbf{A}}_n^{(r)} = \left(\sum_{k=0}^{n-1} \widehat{\mathbf{A}}_k^{(r)} \mathbf{D}_{n-k} - \frac{1}{E(S)} \mathbf{A}_n^{(r)} \right)(-\mathbf{D}_0)^{-1}, \quad 0 \leq r \leq N, \ 0 \leq n < r,$$

$$\widehat{\mathbf{A}}_r^{(r)} = \left(\sum_{k=0}^{r-1} \widehat{\mathbf{A}}_k^{(r)} \widetilde{\mathbf{D}}_{r-k} - \frac{1}{E(S)} \mathbf{A}_r^{(r)} \right)(-\mathbf{D}_0)^{-1}, \quad 0 < r \leq N,$$

where $\mathbf{I}_m$ is an identity matrix of order $m \times m$.

Now using similar results of Markov renewal theory and semi-Markov process, see e.g., Çinlar [3], we obtain

$$\boldsymbol{\nu}(0) = \frac{1}{T}\boldsymbol{\omega}_H^+(0) \int_0^\infty \mathbf{P}^{(N)}(0,t)dt = \frac{1}{T}\boldsymbol{\omega}_H^+(0)(-\mathbf{D}_0)^{-1},$$

$$\boldsymbol{\pi}(n) = \frac{E(S)}{T} \sum_{r=1}^{n+1} \left(\boldsymbol{\pi}^+(r) + \boldsymbol{\omega}_H^+(0)\overline{\mathbf{D}}_r + \sum_{k=1}^{H} \boldsymbol{\omega}_k^+(r) \right) \widehat{\mathbf{A}}_{n-r+1}^{(N-r+1)}, \quad 0 \leq n \leq N-2,$$

$$\boldsymbol{\pi}(N-1) = \frac{E(S)}{T} \sum_{r=1}^{N-1} \left(\boldsymbol{\pi}^+(r) + \boldsymbol{\omega}_H^+(0)\overline{\mathbf{D}}_r + \sum_{k=1}^{H} \boldsymbol{\omega}_k^+(r) \right) \widehat{\mathbf{A}}_{N-r}^{N-r+1}$$

$$+\frac{E(S)}{T}\left(\omega_H^+(0)\overline{\mathbf{D}}_N + \sum_{k=1}^{H}\omega_k^+(N) + \boldsymbol{\pi}^+(N)\right)\widehat{\mathbf{A}}_0^{(1)},$$

$$\boldsymbol{\pi}(N) = \frac{E(S)}{T}\sum_{r=1}^{N-1}\left(\boldsymbol{\pi}^+(r) + \omega_H^+(0)\overline{\mathbf{D}}_r + \sum_{k=1}^{H}\omega_k^+(r)\right)\widehat{\mathbf{A}}_{N-r+1}^{(N-r+1)}$$

$$+\frac{E(S)}{T}\left(\omega_H^+(0)\overline{\mathbf{D}}_N + \sum_{k=1}^{H}\omega_k^+(N) + \boldsymbol{\pi}^+(N)\right)\widehat{\mathbf{A}}_1^{(1)},$$

$$\boldsymbol{\omega}_1(n) = \frac{E(V_1)}{T}\boldsymbol{\pi}^+(0)\widehat{\mathbf{V}}_{n,1}^{(N)}, \quad 0 \le n \le N-1,$$

$$\boldsymbol{\omega}_k(n) = \frac{E(V_k)}{T}\omega_{k-1}^+(0)\widehat{\mathbf{V}}_{n,k}^{(N)}, \quad 2 \le k \le H, 0 \le n \le N-1,$$

$$\boldsymbol{\omega}_1(N) = \frac{E(V_1)}{T}\boldsymbol{\pi}^+(0)\widehat{\mathbf{V}}_{N,1}^{(N)},$$

$$\boldsymbol{\omega}_k(N) = \frac{E(V_k)}{T}\omega_{k-1}^+(0)\widehat{\mathbf{V}}_{N,k}^{(N)}, \quad 2 \le k \le H,$$

where T is derived in Lemma 1. Let $\mathbf{p}(n)$ be the $1 \times m$ vector whose i-th component represents the probability that there are n $(0 \le n \le N)$ customers in the queue at an arbitrary epoch and state of the arrival process is in phase i at arbitrary epoch. Then, in vector notation, we have

$$\mathbf{p}(0) = \boldsymbol{\nu}(0) + \boldsymbol{\pi}(0) + \sum_{k=1}^{H}\boldsymbol{\omega}_k(0), \ \ \mathbf{p}(n) = \boldsymbol{\pi}(n) + \sum_{k=1}^{H}\boldsymbol{\omega}_k(n), \ 1 \le n \le N. \quad (10)$$

Let $\mathbf{p}^-(n)$ be the $1 \times m$ vector whose i-th component represents the probability that a batch arrival finds n $(0 \le n \le N)$ customers in the queue and the arrival process is in state i at an arrival epoch. Then, in vector notation, we have

$$\mathbf{p}^-(n) = \frac{1}{\lambda_g}\mathbf{p}(n)\sum_{k=1}^{\infty}\mathbf{D}_k, \quad 0 \le n \le N. \quad (11)$$

Remark 3.1: One may note that the expression of ρ' obtained in equation (6) can be a valid check with the result $\rho' = \sum_{n=0}^{N}\boldsymbol{\pi}(n)\mathbf{e}$ which gives the same expression as in (6) using embedded Markov point equations at service completion and vacation termination epoch. Similarly, $\sum_{n=0}^{N}\sum_{k=1}^{H}\boldsymbol{\omega}_k(n)\mathbf{e} + \boldsymbol{\nu}(0)\mathbf{e}$ gives $(1 - \rho')$ which can verify the results.

4 Performance Measures

The average number of customers in the queue at an arbitrary epoch is $Lq = \sum_{n=1}^{N}n\mathbf{p}(n)\mathbf{e}$, the average number of customers in the queue when the server is busy is $Lq_1 = \sum_{n=1}^{N}n\boldsymbol{\pi}(n)\mathbf{e}$, and the average number of customers in the queue when the server is on vacation is $Lq_2 = \sum_{n=1}^{N}n\sum_{k=1}^{H}\boldsymbol{\omega}_k(n)\mathbf{e}$.

Blocking Probability: The first customer in a batch (and therefore the whole batch) is lost if there is no waiting space for an arriving batch, i.e., if an arriving batch finds N customers in the queue. Since pre-arrival epoch probabilities are known, the blocking probability of the first customer of a batch is given by

$$PBL_f \equiv \mathbf{p}^-(N)\mathbf{e} = \frac{1}{\lambda_g}\mathbf{p}(N)\sum_{k=1}^{\infty}\mathbf{D}_k\mathbf{e}. \tag{12}$$

An arbitrary customer in a batch is lost if he finds n $(0 \leq n \leq N)$ customers in the queue upon arrival and his position in his batch is $k \geq N+1-n$. Hence, the blocking probability of an arbitrary customer is given by

$$PBL_a = \sum_{n=0}^{N}\mathbf{p}(n)\sum_{k=N+1-n}^{\infty}\mathbf{G}_k\mathbf{e}, \text{ where } \mathbf{G}_k = \frac{1}{\lambda^*}\sum_{n=k}^{\infty}\mathbf{D}_n, \quad k = 1,2,3,\ldots \tag{13}$$

is a matrix of order $m \times m$ whose (i,j)-th element represents the probability that the position of an arbitrary customer in an arriving batch is k with phase changes from state i to j; for details, see Samanta et al. [14].

The last customer in a batch is lost if he finds n $(0 \leq n \leq N)$ customers in the queue upon arrival and his batch size is $k \geq N+1-n$. Thus, the blocking probability of the last customer of a batch is given by

$$PBL_l = \frac{1}{\lambda_g}\sum_{n=0}^{N}\mathbf{p}(n)\sum_{k=N+1-n}^{\infty}\mathbf{D}_k\mathbf{e}. \tag{14}$$

Mean waiting time w_a (in queue) of an arbitrary customer can be obtained using Little's rule and it is given by $w_a = Lq/\lambda'$, where $\lambda' = \lambda^*(1 - PBL_a)$ is the effective arrival rate. One may note that λ' can also be obtained from Lemma 1 through equating steady-state effective arrival rate to the steady-state effective departure rate as follows.

$$\lambda' = \frac{\sum_{n=0}^{N}\boldsymbol{\pi}^+(n)\mathbf{e}}{T}. \tag{15}$$

Thus value of λ' can be a valid check while performing numerical results.

Optimal Policy: Here we develop the total expected cost function per unit time for $BMAP/G/1/N/VMV$ queueing system in which N is a decision variable. We construct a similar cost structure that has been widely used in many works, see Lee and Srinivasan [8]. For this we need explicit expressions for θ_1 and θ_2 defined as expected length of busy and idle periods, respectively. From the definition of the carried load ρ' (the fraction of time that the server is busy), it can be written as

$$\frac{\theta_1}{\theta_2} = \frac{\rho'}{1 - \rho'}. \tag{16}$$

We first discuss the expected busy period which is comparatively easy to evaluate. Let $N_q(t)$ denote the number of customers in the queue at time t and $\xi_q(t)$ be the state of the server, i.e., busy $(= 1)$ or idle $(= 0)$. Then $\{N_q(t), \xi_q(t)\}$ enters the set of busy states, $\varUpsilon \equiv \{(0, 1), (1, 1), (2, 1), \ldots, (N, 1)\}$ at the termination of an idle period. The conditional probability that $\{N_q(t), \xi_q(t)\}$ enters any state, given that $\{N_q(t), \xi_q(t)\}$ enters $(0, 0)$, is therefore $C\mathbf{p}^+(n)\mathbf{e}$, $0 \leq n \leq N$, where $C = \frac{1}{\mathbf{p}^+(0)\mathbf{e}}$. Now $\{N_q(t), \xi_q(t)\}$ enters $(n, 1)$, $0 \leq n \leq N$, irrespective of customers' arrival during a service time, which may happen in expected time $E(S)$. Thus, we have

$$\theta_1 = \frac{E(S)\sum_{n=0}^{N}\mathbf{p}^+(n)\mathbf{e}}{\mathbf{p}^+(0)\mathbf{e}} = \frac{E(S)}{\mathbf{p}^+(0)\mathbf{e}}. \tag{17}$$

Using (17) in (16), we obtain

$$\theta_2 = \left(\frac{1 - \rho'}{\rho'}\right)\frac{E(S)}{\mathbf{p}^+(0)\mathbf{e}}. \tag{18}$$

Total Expected Cost Function: Our objective here is to determine the optimum value of the control parameter, say N^*, so as to minimize the cost function given below. Let us define the following costs per unit of time. $C_h =$ holding cost per unit time per customer present in the queue; $C_v =$ cost incurred per unit time for keeping the server on vacation; $C_b =$ cost incurred per unit time for keeping the server busy; $C_u =$ start-up cost per unit time for turning the server on; $C_d =$ shut-down cost per unit time for turning the server off; $C_l =$ a fixed cost incurred per unit time for every lost customer. Using the definitions of each cost element listed above, the total expected cost function per unit time is given by

$$F(N) = C_h L_q + C_v(1 - \rho') + (C_b + C_d + C_u)\rho' + \lambda^* C_l PBL_a. \tag{19}$$

We determine the optimal value of the control parameter through minimizing the value of the total expected cost derived in (19). For each selection of the optimum value of N, N^* is determined by satisfying the following inequality

$$F(N^* + 1) \geq F(N^*) \leq F(N^* - 1). \tag{20}$$

One may be interested to obtain the optimal value H^* of H given N in the similar manner.

5   Numerical Results

To get some practical idea of the systems we provide some numerical examples. It would be helpful for the engineers and practitioners to know how system performance measures behave with the corresponding change of critical model parameters. Numerical works have been carried out in LINUX environment using C++ language.

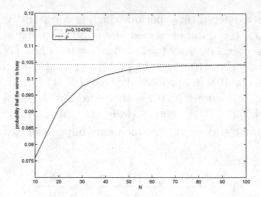

Fig. 1. N versus probability that the server is busy

For $BMAP/PH/1/N$ queue with vacation, we have taken the following parameters. The $BMAP$ representation is taken as $\mathbf{D_0} = \begin{bmatrix} -6.937500 & 0.937500 \\ 0.062500 & -0.195800 \end{bmatrix}$,
$\mathbf{D_1} = \begin{bmatrix} 1.200000 & 0.000000 \\ 0.000000 & 0.026660 \end{bmatrix}$, $\mathbf{D_2} = \begin{bmatrix} 1.800000 & 0.000000 \\ 0.000000 & 0.039990 \end{bmatrix}$,
$\mathbf{D_5} = \begin{bmatrix} 1.800000 & 0.000000 \\ 0.000000 & 0.039990 \end{bmatrix}$ and $\mathbf{D_8} = \begin{bmatrix} 1.200000 & 0.000000 \\ 0.000000 & 0.026660 \end{bmatrix}$. The PH-type
of service time is taken as $\beta = \begin{bmatrix} 0.4 & 0.6 \end{bmatrix}$, $\mathbf{S} = \begin{bmatrix} -23.683 & 0.453 \\ 0.367 & -16.866 \end{bmatrix}$ with
$E(S) = 0.053491$. The PH-type of vacation time is taken as $\alpha = \begin{bmatrix} 0.3 & 0.7 \end{bmatrix}$,
$\mathbf{T} = \begin{bmatrix} -2.098 & 1.899 \\ 0.071 & -2.832 \end{bmatrix}$ with $E(V) = 0.505898$. For this model, we have $H = 4$,
$\lambda^* = 1.949878$, and $\rho = 0.104302$. In Figure 1, we have plotted the probability that the server is busy (ρ') against buffer capacity (N), where N varies from 10 to 100. Since offered load $\rho = 0.104302 < 1$ is low and therefore as buffer space increases the model behaves as infinite buffer queue. Consequently ρ' asymptotically approaches towards ρ. We have used our approach described in Section 3 to evaluate service completion and vacation termination epoch probabilities for $BMAP/PH/1/N$ model. After that we have evaluated the quantity $\rho' = 0.104264$ which closely matches with ρ (upto four decimal places) when $N = 100$. Next we obtain arbitrary epoch probabilities according to Section 3. It is found that $\sum_{n=0}^{N} \boldsymbol{\pi}(n)\mathbf{e} = 0.104264$ also matches with above ρ' for $N = 100$. We have verified the fact $\sum_{n=0}^{N} \boldsymbol{\pi}(n)\mathbf{e} = \rho'$ in other numerical experiment except $N = 100$. The above fact is one of the checks of our analytical as well as numerical results. However, due to lack of space several other results are not presented here.

6   Conclusions

In this paper, we have analyzed the $BMAP/G/1/N$ queue with a variant of multiple vacation policy under partial batch acceptance strategy. Several other batch acceptance/rejection strategies (e.g., total batch rejection, total batch acceptance etc.) can be done on this queueing system. This queueing model can be extended to multiple adaptive vacations, or state dependent vacations/service, or the Bernoulli vacation schedule, etc. These problems are left for future investigations.

Acknowledgements. The first author acknowledges partial financial support from the seed money project of Indian Institute of Technology, Bhubaneswar, India. The second author was supported partially by National Institute of Science and Technology, Berhampur, Orissa, India.

References

1. Azad, A.P.: Analysis and Optimization of Sleeping Mode in WiMAX via Stochastic Decomposition Techniques. IEEE Journal on Selected Areas in Communications 29, 1630–1640 (2011)
2. Banik, A.D.: The infinite-buffer single server queue with a variant of multiple vacation policy and batch Markovian arrival process. Applied Mathematical Modelling 33, 3025–3039 (2009)
3. Çinlar, E.: Introduction to stochastic process. Printice Hall, N.J. (1975)
4. Dudin, A.N., Shaban, A.A., Klimenok, V.I.: Analysis of a queue in the $BMAP/G/1/N$ system. International Journal of Simulation 6, 13–23 (2005)
5. Grassmann, W.K., Taksar, M.I., Heyman, D.P.: Regenerative analysis and steady state distributions for Markov chains. Operations Research 33, 1107–1116 (1985)
6. Ke, J.C.: Operating Characteristic analysis on the $M^{[X]}/G/1$ system with a variant vacation policy and balking. Applied Mathematical Modelling 31, 1321–1337 (2007)
7. Lucantoni, D.M.: New results on the single server queue with a batch Markovian arrival process. Stochactic Models 7, 1–46 (1991)
8. Lee, H.S., Srinivasan, M.M.: Control policies for the $M^X/G/1$ queueing system. Management Science 35, 708–721 (1989)
9. Lucantoni, D.M., Meier-Hellstern, K.S., Neuts, M.F.: A single-server queue with server vacations and a class of non-renewal arrival process. Advances in Applied Probability 22, 676–705 (1990)
10. Miao, G., Himayat, N., Li, Y., Swami, A.: Cross-layer optimization for energy-efficient wireless communications: a survey. Wireless Communications Mobile Computing 9, 529–542 (2009)
11. Neuts, M.F.: A versatile Markovian point process. Journal of Applied Probability 16, 764–779 (1979)
12. Neuts, M.F.: Matrix-Geometric Solutions in Stochastic Models: An Algorithmic Approach. Johns Hopkins Univ. Press, Baltimore (1981)
13. Niu, Z., Shu, T., Takahashi, Y.: A vacation queue with set up and close-down times and batch Markovian arrival processes. Performance Evaluation 54, 225–248 (2003)
14. Samanta, S.K., Gupta, U.C., Sharma, R.K.: Analyzing discrete-time D-$BMAP/G/1/N$ queue with single and multiple vacations. European Journal of Operational Research 182(1), 321–339 (2007)
15. Tian, N., Zhang, Z.G.: Vacation queueing models: Theory and applications. International Series in Operations Research and Management Science. Springer, New York (2006)

Consistent Coordination Decoupling in Tuple Space Based Mobile Middleware: Design and Formal Specifications

Suddhasil De, Diganta Goswami, and Sukumar Nandi

Department of Computer Science and Engineering,
Indian Institute of Technology Guwahati, Assam 781039, India
{suddhasil,dgoswami,sukumar}@iitg.ernet.in

Abstract. Tuple Space based Mobile Middleware (TSMM), with tuple space as its coordination medium, provides multiple decoupled behaviors for coordinating interactions between different agents of supported applications. However, maintaining consistency in TSMM is a challenging problem, considering its underlying infrastructure with unpredictable host mobility, sporadic network dynamics, and unreliability in communication links. Existing TSMM maintains consistency by coupling interacting agents, which in turn reduces decoupling abilities of TSMM, thereby restricting development of robust and flexible applications. This paper addresses consistency problems while decoupling agent interactions in TSMM, which renders complete decoupling of interactions. It proposes mechanisms to resolve consistency problems in a fully-decoupled TSMM. Both OUT-consistency and IN-consistency problems are handled in proposed mechanisms. This paper also suggests an approach for formalizing proposed consistency mechanisms in TSMM in order to appropriately analyze reliability and robustness of TSMM as coordination platform for mobile applications. Formalization is carried out using Mobile UNITY.

Keywords. Mobile middleware, coordination, tuple space, reactivity, consistency, Mobile UNITY.

1 Introduction

Mobile middleware originates to support execution of distributed applications in presence of mobility and dynamics in underlying infrastructure. It incorporates a suitable *coordination medium* for managing asynchronous interactions between different active components of an application, called *agents*, whose execution is supported by computing environments called *hosts*. Suitability of different coordination media for agent interaction depends on their abilities to support asynchronous communication and dynamic context. Tuple space [1] supports multiple inherent decoupled behaviors, and as such is a potential coordination medium for mobile middleware [2], which is then called Tuple Space based Mobile Middleware (TSMM) [3]. In TSMM, *tuple* is considered as basic unit of information exchanged during interaction of the agents via a shared repository

C. Hota and P.K. Srimani (Eds.): ICDCIT 2013, LNCS 7753, pp. 220–231, 2013.

called *tuple space*, while *antituple* is considered as basic unit of search key to identify some specific tuples residing in tuple space.

Each tuple is a set of several heterogeneously-typed fields having values (called *actual*). During interaction between any pair of agents (initiator of interaction is *reference agent* and destination becomes *target agent*), reference agent is interested in one/more *sought tuples* that are related to its interaction. It uses antituple to identify these sought tuples. Each antituple is also a set of heterogeneously-typed fields, with some fields being *actual*, while others having placeholders for *actual* (called *formal*). While searching for sought tuples, antituple fields are compared with tuple fields following 'type-value', 'exact value' and 'polymorphic' matching conditions. Only fields of sought tuples match positively with fields of given antituple. Different primitives are defined to carry out writing, reading and withdrawing tuples from tuple space [1], some of which are *single*, while others are *bulk*. *Tuple-producing* primitives (e.g. out, outg) write tuples in tuple space, while *tuple-reading* primitives (e.g. rd, rdp, rdg, rdgp) and *tuple-consuming* primitives (e.g. in, inp, ing and ingp) read and withdraw sought tuples respectively from tuple space, once they are looked up in tuple space using given antituple.

In tuple space, consistency problem has been studied since tuple spaces are geographically scattered in different locations and user still gets the idea of logically shared common tuple space. In such cases of decentralized tuple space implementations, two facets of consistency problem has been identified, viz. *OUT-consistency* and *IN-consistency* [4]. OUT-consistency refers to the situation where an antituple of a single tuple-consuming primitive (viz. in or inp) matches more than one tuple from tuple spaces of different target agents, and only one tuple is actually withdrawn as sought tuple, while other tuples are to be retained in their respective tuple spaces. On the other hand, IN-consistency refers to the situation where a newly written tuple matches multiple pending tuple-consuming primitives, and only one of them actually withdraws that tuple as sought tuple, while others are still kept blocked. It is to be noted that OUT-consistency problem is not an issue for bulk tuple-consuming operations (viz. ing or ingp), whereas tuple-producing and -reading primitives never create a consistency problem. Furthermore, IN-consistency problem is limited within a particular tuple space, and as such it can be handled easily compared to OUT-consistency problem. Different mechanisms exist in literature to handle OUT-consistency problem in decentralized implementations, viz. *strict/exclusive*, *nonexclusive* and *weak* approaches of executing tuple-consuming primitives [5]. Their degree of weakness vary in decreasing order. In contrast, IN-consistency problem is resolved by simply imposing *strict/exclusive* way of executing different primitives.

Consistency problems are equally prevalent in recent tuple space implementations too, including TSMM. Its prominence has been further increased after TSMM achieves synchronization decoupling (i.e. decoupling between reference agent and its invoked primitives) by incorporating *reactivity* in tuple space. Existing TSMM, like TuCSoN [6], MARS [7], LIME [8], TOTA [9], LIMONE [10], EgoSpaces [11] etc., supports reactivity in either rudimentary or refined forms.

In these TSMM, when a reaction fires at tuple space of target agent, it responds to reference agent synchronously, for which availability of reference agent is a necessity. As such, OUT-consistency problem has been handled by allowing sought tuple from a target agent, which responds first, to fulfill requirement of reference agent. However, underlying infrastructure of TSMM has unpredictable host mobility, sporadic network dynamics, and unreliability in wireless communication links. Reference agent executing over such a dynamic infrastructure can hardly manage to keep itself available for receiving responses from target agents. Also, this coupled behavior of reactions reduces decoupling abilities of existing TSMM, and incurs additional overheads by sending responses repeatedly till successful receipt. Moreover, applications tend to loose robustness and flexibility, as responses are not guaranteed to be delivered to reference agent.

This paper addresses consistency problems in a fully-decoupled TSMM, which has enhanced reactivity in its tuple space rendering total decoupling of agent interactions [12]. Contribution of this paper is twofold. Firstly, it proposes mechanisms to resolve consistency problems in coordinating interactions in fully-decoupled TSMM. Proposed mechanisms handle both OUT-consistency and IN-consistency problems. Secondly, this paper also suggests an approach of formally specifying proposed consistency mechanisms using Mobile UNITY [13], to define its precise semantics and lay the foundation for its integration into formal specification of entire TSMM [14]. Favoring Mobile UNITY over other formal tools is due to its suitability for modeling inherently nonterminating programs (like mobile middleware), reasoning about agents temporal behavior using its proof rules, and following stepwise modeling and refining. Authors believe that formalization of consistency-resolving mechanisms, particularly in TSMM, has not yet been presented in literature. However, formal specification of other functionalities of TSMM, viz. decoupled reactivity in tuple space [12], discovery and communication mechanisms in TSMM [15] etc., has been recently expressed. Rest of the paper is organized as follows. Section 2 presents proposed consistency mechanisms applicable to TSMM, which is next formalized using Mobile UNITY in section 3. Finally, section 4 concludes the paper.

2   Proposed Consistency Mechanisms in TSMM

2.1   Preliminaries

A fully-decoupled TSMM assumes that connectivity of underlying network can be *dynamic* and *unreliable*, whereas coordination between its two interacting agents can be *asymmetric*. Former assumption is essential to deal with host mobility and wireless connectivity of underlying network. In latter assumption, an agent interacting asymmetrically can accept/deny interactions with other available agents depending on context, like users' choice, link capacity, security.

Tuple Space Model. In fully-decoupled TSMM, tuples and antituples are considered as *unordered* sequence of heterogeneously typed elements, as presented in [16]. Tuple space is partitioned into *preamble* and *tuple store* for identifying *apposite tuples*, as shown in [17]. Preamble holds all index tables corresponding to different constituent fields of all tuples present in tuple space, while tuple store is the actual storehouse of those tuples. Content of each index table indicates locations of different apposite tuples in tuple store for given antituple. Moreover, tuple-consuming primitives, after withdrawing one/more sought tuples, update all relevant index tables in preamble. On the other hand, tuple-producing primitives first write given tuple(s) in tuple store, and update indices of written tuple(s) in all required index tables. Both local and remote tuple-producing, tuple-reading and tuple-consuming primitives are included. Remote primitives can be blocking or nonblocking, whereas local primitives are solely nonblocking.

Reactivity Model. Reference agent is completely decoupled from target agent by *decoupled reactivity* [12]. In this reactivity model, an additional layer of decoupling medium is introduced to store responses from actions (of reactions) till reference agent becomes available. It removes the need for both reference and target agents to be available at same time once reactions fire, thus enabling application designers to build robust applications. This decoupling medium is a special tuple space, which is housed at each host and termed as *host tuple space* (HTS), to differentiate from *agent tuple space* (ATS) of each agent. Two special primitives, inject and eject, are provided for storing and withdrawing special tuples (viz. *reaction tuple* and *response tuple*) respectively from HTS. Both reaction tuple and response tuple are unordered tuples [16], as their arity and nature of constituent fields can vary with nature of invoked remote primitives.

Reaction tuple is generated for shipping parameters of any remote primitive invoked by reference agent to target agents. It comprises of all parameters required for successful execution of remote primitive in target agent. It is next inserted into HTS of reference host using inject primitive. On availability of target host, this reaction tuple is withdrawn from reference host's HTS using eject, passed over communication links to reach target host, and subsequently inserted into its HTS. Eventually, reaction tuple is withdrawn from target host's HTS, once desired target agent becomes available. It is processed next to extract parameters of invoked primitive, and execution of invoked remote primitive starts at target agent. In case of reading/withdrawing operations, target agent is responsible for shipping results of execution (viz. sought tuple(s) from ATS of target agent) to reference agent. It generates response tuple to pack the results and other necessary parameters. Following previous approach, this response tuple eventually reaches reference agent, and sought tuple(s) are extracted from it.

Architecture. Fully-decoupled TSMM provides agent interactions that are totally decoupled. Its architecture, shown in Figure 1, presents a tuple space distribution among hosts and agents, which is unlikely in existing TSMM. In this distribution, each agent holds ATS for coordination purpose, whereas each host holds HTS for storing reaction/response tuples (collectively referred as RT) to be transferred to destination agents/hosts. Host Server, a primary component of each host in this TSMM, holds HTS and is responsible to manage transfer of RT using Communication Manager and Discovery Manager. Reference agent encapsulates its

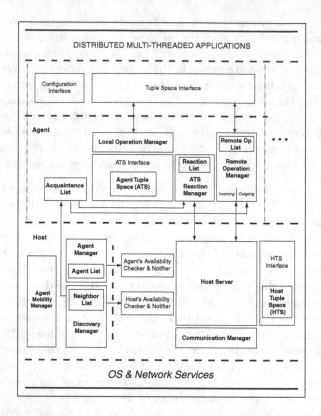

Fig. 1. Architecture of a fully-decoupled TSMM

interacting data within tuples/antituples, and converts them to reaction tuples before handing over to Host Server for transfer to target agent(s). Each target agent also encapsulates its interacting data within tuples, converts them to response tuples, and passes to Host Server for transmitting back to reference agent. During inter-host transfer, Host Server periodically checks NeighborList of Discovery Manager for host availability, and hands over different RT that are destined to available hosts, to Communication Manager. Also, it stores received RT from Communication Manager in its HTS before delivering them to its respective agents.

Additional Supporting Components. TSMM requires support of TSMM-specific Discovery Manager and Communication Manager for its working. Discovery Manager furnishes an updated knowledge of available agents (along with their hosts) that are reachable from (i.e. neighbors of) source host. This knowledge is utilized by other components of TSMM, including Host Server and Communication Manager. Up-to-date information of availability is attained by exchanging a special tuple called Beacon, and preserving them in NeighborList.

Primary emphasis of Communication Manager is to reliably transfer RT from one host to another, using TSMM-specific acknowledgement mechanism. However, acknowledgement is not required for hosts communicating using wired network interfaces; it is required when hosts are communicating via wireless network interfaces. RT, handed over by Host Server, are converted to RT messages before being transferred to destination host. Information about target agents are present in RT itself. During communication via wireless network interface, each host additionally preserves a copy of RT message in a special data structure, CommStash before passing it to transport service. At destination side, each host directly hands over RT from RT message, received via wired interface, to Host Server for further processing. However, on receiving RT message via wireless interface, each host acknowledges its receipt before giving RT to Host Server.

2.2 Proposed Consistency Mechanisms

A fully-decoupled TSMM has a extensive repertoire of tuple space primitives for supporting coordination of wide variety of applications. So, mechanisms for handling both OUT-consistency and IN-consistency problems are proposed. In case of invoke of single remote tuple-reading and -consuming primitives, OUT-consistency is to be maintained by first accumulating all responses from other target agents at reference agent, and later, a single sought tuple is nondeterministically chosen from them. This approach is essential, considering that agent interaction has been fully-decoupled in this TSMM. Once a sought tuple is selected, single tuple-reading and -consuming primitives behave differently. Since OUT-inconsistency is not caused by tuple-reading primitives, all other tuples, which are received as responses for invoked single tuple-reading primitives (like, rd and rdp) and are finally not selected, are subsequently discarded by reference agent. However, for single tuple-consuming primitives (like, in and inp), reference agent maintains OUT-consistency by sending positive and negative acknowledgements to those target agents, whoever has responded. Positive acknowledgement (sent as ACK tuple) is sent back to that target agent, whose tuple is chosen nondeterministically, and negative acknowledgements (sent as NACK tuples) are sent to all other remaining target agents who have responded.

Target agent, on receiving NACK tuple, reinserts its responded tuple, which is not selected and sent back by reference agent via NACK tuple, in its respective ATS using a tuple-producing primitive. Target agent, which receives ACK tuple, need not to carry out any tuple reinsertion. Effectively, that target agent actually performs tuple-withdrawal operation on its ATS. For bulk tuple-reading and -consuming primitives, all responses from different target agents are kept as sought tuples by reference agent. Hence, only ACK tuples are sent back to all target agents, whoever has responded. Figure 2(a) and Figure 2(b) show how a pair of interacting agents behave during tuple-reading and -consuming primitives respectively in intra-host interactions, whereas Figure 3(a) and Figure 3(b) show same behavior in inter-host interactions. ACK tuples and NACK tuples are considered as special system tuples, and accordingly, they are converted to response tuples while being shipped from one agent to another via Host Server.

Resolving IN-consistency problem in this TSMM is comparatively easy. Since IN-consistency problem is restricted to a particular ATS, it is proposed to be solved by imposing a predefined ordering scheme in that tuple space, and by

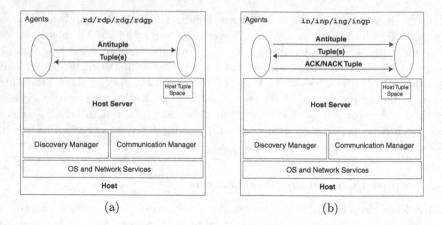

Fig. 2. OUT-consistency of remote (a) tuple-reading and (b) tuple-consuming primitives in intra-host agent interaction

enforcing each operation to happen in a strict/exclusive way. For instance, if execution of all tuple space primitives, including pending reactions of blocked tuple-reading and -consuming primitives, are scheduled in a particular order (say, first-in-first-out or FIFO order), IN-consistency problem will not arise. In TSMM, each blocked primitive registers a reaction for continuing lookup on its behalf. While inserting a particular tuple in ATS, tuple-producing primitive first acquires access of that ATS, writes given tuple, and subsequently releases that access. Once insertion is over, all registered reactions are served one-by-one (according to pre-defined order) by following same approach of acquiring and releasing access of ATS. Both pre-defined ordering and strict/exclusive way of accessing ATS together resolves IN-consistency problem in fully-decoupled TSMM.

3   Formalization of Proposed Consistency Mechanisms

This section presents an approach of formally specifying proposed consistency mechanisms for fully-decoupled TSMM, and includes integration of these specifications in formalization of entire TSMM [14]. In this formal system, which comprises of a set of formal programs representing different hosts and agents, i-th host is specified by **Program** $host(i)$, whereas k-th agent is represented by **Program** $agent(k)$. Functionalities of different components of host, including Transport Interface, Discovery Manager, Communication Manager, Host Server, Agent Manager etc., are contained in **Program** $host(i)$. Similarly, agent behavior, including functionalities of ATS, Local Operation Manager, Remote Operation Manager, ATS Reaction Manager etc. are contained in **Program** $agent(k)$. While formalizing $host(i)$, underlying network infrastructure of TSMM is assumed to be Infrastructure Basic Service Set (iBSS) (i.e. Wireless LAN). However, in above formal system, many aspects of TSMM, inter alia Agent Mobility Manager, are not directly formalized, to keep it simple.

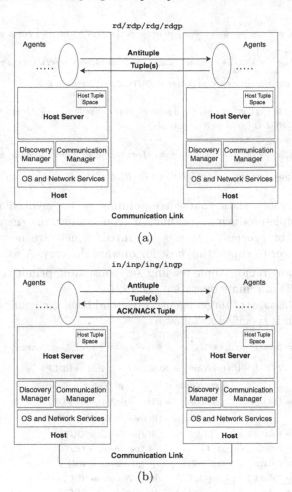

Fig. 3. OUT-consistency of remote (a) tuple-reading and (b) tuple-consuming primitives in inter-host agent interaction

3.1   Formalizing Proposed Consistency Mechanisms

Proposed consistency mechanisms for TSMM, as presented in section 2.2, operates at the agent-level, and consequently, formalization of these consistency mechanisms has to be included within **Program** $agent(k)$. Remote Operation Manager of reference agent, shown in Figure 1, is responsible for ensuring OUT-consistency. It initiates any remote tuple space operation that reference agent intends to execute on specified target agent(s), as shown next:

$$\langle \quad t, tuple, prType := tuple, \varepsilon, \varepsilon \parallel prid := \texttt{getPrID}(prName) \parallel rform := 1$$
$$\parallel \langle \parallel a : 1 \leq a \leq TAs$$
$$:: \mathcal{Q}_{T_{a_k}^S} := \mathcal{Q}_{T_{a_k}^S} \bullet \texttt{createRTuple}_r(rform, prid, prName, t, mode, aid, taids[a]))$$
$$\rangle \quad \text{if } ((prType = remote) \wedge (prName = \mathsf{OUT}) \wedge \neg(tuple = \varepsilon)) \tag{1}$$

$\langle$ $\mathbf{t}, tuples, prType := tuples, \emptyset, \varepsilon \parallel prid := \mathtt{getPrID}(prName) \parallel rform := 1$

$\parallel \langle\parallel a : 1 \leq a \leq TAs$

$\qquad :: \mathcal{Q}_{T_{a_k}^S} := \mathcal{Q}_{T_{a_k}^S} \bullet \mathtt{createRTuple}_r(rform, prid, prName, \mathbf{t}, mode, aid, taids[a])\rangle$

$\rangle$ if $((prType = remote) \wedge (prName = \mathsf{OUTG}) \wedge \neg(tuples = \emptyset))$ $\qquad\qquad$ (2)

$\langle$ $a, atuple, prType := atuple, \varepsilon, \varepsilon \parallel prid := \mathtt{getPrID}(prName) \parallel rform := 1$

$\parallel ROL := ROL \cup \{prid, prName, taids\}$

$\parallel \langle\parallel a : 1 \leq a \leq TAs$

$\qquad :: \mathcal{Q}_{T_{a_k}^S} := \mathcal{Q}_{T_{a_k}^S} \bullet \mathtt{createRTuple}_r(rform, prid, prName, a, mode, aid, taids[a])\rangle$

$\rangle$ if $((prType = remote) \wedge (prRdIn = TRUE) \wedge \neg(atuple = \varepsilon))$ $\qquad\qquad$ (3)

Above specifications show that corresponding to an invoked remote primitive (whether tuple-producing, -reading, or -consuming), one/more reaction tuples (expressed as $rform := 1$) are generated, which are next enqueued in $\mathcal{Q}_{T_{a_k}^S}$ for hand over to supporting host for onward delivery. Also, $agent(k)$ notes down invoke of any remote tuple-reading, or -consuming primitive (expressed as $prRdIn = TRUE$) in remote operation list ROL.

ATS Reaction Manager of target agent(s) respond back the result of that remote operation, which is specified as follows:

$\langle$ $r, \mathcal{Q}_{T_{a_k}^R} := \mathtt{head}(\mathcal{Q}_{T_{a_k}^R}), \mathtt{tail}(\mathcal{Q}_{T_{a_k}^R}) \parallel prid := r \uparrow \mathrm{prid} \parallel prName := r \uparrow \mathrm{pName}$

$\parallel prBulk := TRUE$ if $((prName = \mathsf{RDG}) \vee (prName = \mathsf{RDGP})$

$\qquad\qquad\qquad\qquad \vee (prName = \mathsf{ING}) \vee (prName = \mathsf{INGP}))$

$\sim$ $:= FALSE$ if $((prName = \mathsf{RD}) \vee (prName = \mathsf{RDP})$

$\qquad\qquad\qquad\qquad \vee (prName = \mathsf{IN}) \vee (prName = \mathsf{INP}))$

$\parallel \langle$ $\langle t := r \uparrow \mathrm{data} \parallel \mathtt{out}(\mathbf{t}, \mathbf{T}) \rangle$ $\qquad$ if $(prName = \mathsf{OUT})$

$\quad \parallel \langle \mathbf{t} := r \uparrow \mathrm{data} \parallel \mathtt{outg}(\mathbf{t}, \mathbf{T}) \rangle$ $\qquad$ if $(prName = \mathsf{OUTG})$

$\quad \parallel \langle a := r \uparrow \mathrm{data} \parallel \mathbf{t} := \mathtt{rd}(a, \mathbf{T}) \rangle$ $\quad$ if $(prName = \mathsf{RD})$

$\quad \parallel \langle a := r \uparrow \mathrm{data} \parallel \mathbf{t} := \mathtt{rdg}(a, \mathbf{T}) \rangle$ $\quad$ if $(prName = \mathsf{RDG})$

$\quad \parallel \langle a := r \uparrow \mathrm{data} \parallel \mathbf{t} := \mathtt{rdp}(a, \mathbf{T}) \rangle$ $\quad$ if $(prName = \mathsf{RDP})$

$\quad \parallel \langle a := r \uparrow \mathrm{data} \parallel \mathbf{t} := \mathtt{rdgp}(a, \mathbf{T}) \rangle$ $\quad$ if $(prName = \mathsf{RDGP})$

$\quad \parallel \langle a := r \uparrow \mathrm{data} \parallel \mathbf{t} := \mathtt{in}(a, \mathbf{T}) \rangle$ $\quad$ if $(prName = \mathsf{IN})$

$\quad \parallel \langle a := r \uparrow \mathrm{data} \parallel \mathbf{t} := \mathtt{ing}(a, \mathbf{T}) \rangle$ $\quad$ if $(prName = \mathsf{ING})$

$\quad \parallel \langle a := r \uparrow \mathrm{data} \parallel \mathbf{t} := \mathtt{inp}(a, \mathbf{T}) \rangle$ $\quad$ if $(prName = \mathsf{INP})$

$\quad \parallel \langle a := r \uparrow \mathrm{data} \parallel \mathbf{t} := \mathtt{ingp}(a, \mathbf{T}) \rangle$ if $(prName = \mathsf{INGP})$

$\quad \parallel rform := 2$

$\quad \parallel \mathcal{Q}_{T_{a_k}^S} := \mathcal{Q}_{T_{a_k}^S} \bullet \mathtt{createRTuple}_{r'}(rform, prid, prName, t, aid, r \uparrow \mathrm{rAid})$

$\qquad\qquad\qquad\qquad\qquad\qquad\qquad\qquad\qquad\qquad$ if $(prBulk = FALSE)$

$\quad \parallel \mathcal{Q}_{T_{a_k}^S} := \mathcal{Q}_{T_{a_k}^S} \bullet \mathtt{createRTuple}_{r'}(rform, prid, prName, \mathbf{t}, aid, r \uparrow \mathrm{rAid})$

$\qquad\qquad\qquad\qquad\qquad\qquad\qquad\qquad\qquad\qquad$ if $(prBulk = TRUE)$

$\quad \rangle$ if $(r \uparrow \mathrm{tAid} = aid)$

$\rangle$ if $(\neg(\mathcal{Q}_{T_{a_k}^R} = \perp) \wedge (\mathtt{head}(\mathcal{Q}_{T_{a_k}^R}) \uparrow \mathrm{rform} = 1))$ $\qquad\qquad$ (4)

Above specifications depict that, at target agent, parameters of invoked primitive are extracted to carry out the desired operation, and outcome of that operation (particularly, tuple-reading or -consuming operation) are packed into response tuple (expressed as $rform := 2$) and enqueued in $\mathcal{Q}_{T^S_{a_k}}$ for delivery.

On receiving multiple responses, Remote Operation Manager of reference agent undertakes proposed OUT-consistency mechanism, which is shown next:

$$
\langle \quad r, \mathcal{Q}_{T^R_{a_k}} := \text{head}(\mathcal{Q}_{T^R_{a_k}}), \text{tail}(\mathcal{Q}_{T^R_{a_k}}) \quad \| \quad prid := r \uparrow \text{prid}
$$
$$
\| \langle \quad \mathbb{T}_{prid} := \mathbb{T}_{prid} \cup \{r \uparrow \text{tAid}, r \uparrow \text{data}\}
$$
$$
\| \langle \exists e : (e \in ROL) \wedge (e \uparrow 1 = prid) :: e \uparrow 3 := e \uparrow 3 \setminus r \uparrow \text{tAid} \rangle
$$
$$
\rangle \quad \text{if} \ ((r \uparrow \text{rAid} = aid) \wedge \text{isPresent}_{\text{in} ROL}(prid, r \uparrow \text{tAid}))
$$
$$
\rangle \quad \text{if} \ (\neg(\mathcal{Q}_{T^R_{a_k}} = \perp) \wedge (\text{head}(\mathcal{Q}_{T^R_{a_k}}) \uparrow \text{rform} = 2)) \tag{5}
$$

$$
\langle \| e : (e \in ROL) \wedge (e \uparrow 3 = \emptyset)
$$
$$
:: \quad prid, prName := e \uparrow 1, e \uparrow 2 \| ROL := ROL \setminus e
$$
$$
\| \langle \ \langle \| e : e \in \mathbb{T}_{prid} :: \mathbf{t} := \mathbf{t} \cup e \uparrow \text{tuples} \rangle \| \text{retTuples2Usr}(\mathbf{t})
$$
$$
\| \langle \| e : e \in \mathbb{T}_{prid} \wedge ((prName = \text{ING}) \vee (prName = \text{INGP})) :: rform := 3
$$
$$
\| \mathcal{Q}_{T^S_{a_k}} := \mathcal{Q}_{T^S_{a_k}} \bullet \text{createRTuple}_{r'}(rform, prid, prName, aid, e \uparrow \text{tAid}) \rangle
$$
$$
\rangle \quad \text{if} \ ((prName = \text{RDG}) \vee (prName = \text{RDGP}) \vee (prName = \text{ING}) \vee (prName = \text{INGP}))
$$
$$
\| \langle \ \langle \| e : e = e'.(e' \in \mathbb{T}_{prid}) :: t, taid := e \uparrow \text{tuple}, e \uparrow \text{tAid} \rangle \| \text{retTuple2Usr}(t)
$$
$$
\| \langle rform := 3 \| \mathcal{Q}_{T^S_{a_k}} := \mathcal{Q}_{T^S_{a_k}} \bullet \text{createRTuple}_{r'}(rform, prid, prName, aid, taid) \rangle
$$
$$
\text{if} \ ((prName = \text{IN}) \vee (prName = \text{INP}))
$$
$$
\| \langle \| e : e \in \mathbb{T}_{prid} \wedge \neg(e \uparrow \text{tAid} = taid) \wedge ((prName = \text{IN}) \vee (prName = \text{INP}))
$$
$$
:: \quad rform := 4
$$
$$
\| \mathcal{Q}_{T^S_{a_k}} := \mathcal{Q}_{T^S_{a_k}} \bullet \text{createRTuple}_{r'}(rform, prid, prName, e \uparrow \text{tuple}, aid, e \uparrow \text{tAid}) \rangle
$$
$$
\rangle \quad \text{if} \ ((prName = \text{RD}) \vee (prName = \text{RDP}) \vee (prName = \text{IN}) \vee (prName = \text{INP}))
$$
$$
\rangle \tag{6}
$$

Above specifications describe that, reference agent stores multiple results from different target agent(s) in a temporary space (viz. $\mathbb{T}_{prid}$) till all results have been received, after which tuple or tuples from received results are returned back to user application according to single or bulk invoked primitive respectively. At the same time, positive as well as negative acknowledgements of received results are packed into ACK tuples (expressed as $rform := 3$) and NACK tuples (expressed as $rform := 4$) respectively and enqueued in $\mathcal{Q}_{T^S_{a_k}}$ for onward delivery to responded target agent(s).

ATS Reaction Manager of target agent, on receiving ACK/NACK tuple, performs rest of proposed OUT-consistency mechanism, which is shown next:

$$
\langle \quad r, \mathcal{Q}_{T^R_{a_k}} := \text{head}(\mathcal{Q}_{T^R_{a_k}}), \text{tail}(\mathcal{Q}_{T^R_{a_k}})
$$
$$
\| \langle t := r \uparrow \text{data} \| \text{out}(t, \mathbf{T}) \rangle \quad \text{if} \ ((r \uparrow \text{tAid} = aid) \wedge (r \uparrow \text{rform} = 4))
$$
$$
\rangle \quad \text{if} \ (\neg(\mathcal{Q}_{T^R_{a_k}} = \perp) \wedge ((\text{head}(\mathcal{Q}_{T^R_{a_k}}) \uparrow \text{rform} = 3) \vee (\text{head}(\mathcal{Q}_{T^R_{a_k}}) \uparrow \text{rform} = 4))) \tag{7}
$$

Above specifications show that, on receiving NACK tuple, it is extracted and data tuple is inserted back into ATS of target agent. However, no action is taken on receipt of ACK tuple.

Proposed IN-consistency mechanism is integrated within each invoked primitive and also within reactions generated corresponding to these primitives.

Consequently, specifications of these primitives and their reactions cover representation of proposed IN-consistency mechanism [12]. Reactions are specified as reactive statements in this formalization approach, and accordingly they access tuple space once its state changes. In each such occasion of accessing tuple space in some order, tuple space is first locked, and subsequently the operation is performed to completion before releasing the lock. Combining Equation (1) to Equation (7) specifies behavior of proposed consistency mechanisms, which has to be included in **Program** $agent(k)$ to derive formalization of entire TSMM.

4   Conclusion

This paper has proposed mechanisms to resolve both OUT-consistency as well as IN-consistency problems in a fully-decoupled TSMM that facilitates complete decoupling of agent interactions. The paper has also suggested an approach of formally specifying proposed consistency mechanisms using Mobile UNITY, which can be subsequently integrated in formalization of entire TSMM for analysis of its reliability and robustness as coordination middleware.

References

1. Gelernter, D.: Generative Communication in Linda. Transactions on Programming Languages and Systems 7(1), 80–112 (1985)
2. Cabri, G., Ferrari, L., Leonardi, L., Mamei, M., Zambonelli, F.: Uncoupling Coordination: Tuple-Based Models for Mobility. In: Bellavista, P., Corradi, A. (eds.) The Handbook of Mobile Middleware, pp. 229–255. Auerbach Pub. (2007)
3. De, S., Nandi, S., Goswami, D.: Architectures of Mobile Middleware: A Taxonomic Perspective. In: Proc. 2nd IEEE Intl. Conf. on Parallel, Distributed and Grid Computing (PDGC 2012) (December 2012)
4. Feng, M.D., Gao, Y.Q., Yuen, C.K.: Distributed Linda Tuplespace Algorithms and Implementations. In: Buchberger, B., Volkert, J. (eds.) CONPAR 1994 and VAPP 1994. LNCS, vol. 854, pp. 581–592. Springer, Heidelberg (1994)
5. Chiba, S., Kato, K., Masuda, T.: Exploiting a Weak Consistency to Implement Distributed Tuple Space. In: Proc. 12th Intl. Conf. on Distributed Computing Systems (ICDCS 1992), pp. 416–423 (June 1992)
6. Omicini, A., Zambonelli, F.: Coordination for Internet Application Development. Autonomous Agents and Multi-Agent Systems 2, 251–269 (1999)
7. Cabri, G., Leonardi, L., Zambonelli, F.: MARS: A Programmable Coordination Architecture for Mobile Agents. Internet Computing 4(4), 26–35 (2000)
8. Murphy, A.L., Picco, G.P., Roman, G.C.: Lime: A Coordination Model and Middleware supporting Mobility of Hosts and Agents. Transactions on Software Engineering and Methodology 15(3), 279–328 (2006)
9. Mamei, M., Zambonelli, F., Leonardi, L.: Tuples On The Air: a Middleware for Context-Aware Computing in Dynamic Networks. In: Proc. 23rd Conf. on Distributed Computing Systems Workshops (ICDCSW 2003), pp. 342–347 (May 2003)
10. Fok, C.L., Roman, G.C., Hackmann, G.: A Lightweight Coordination Middleware for Mobile Computing. In: De Nicola, R., Ferrari, G.-L., Meredith, G. (eds.) COORDINATION 2004. LNCS, vol. 2949, pp. 135–151. Springer, Heidelberg (2004)

11. Julien, C., Roman, G.C.: EgoSpaces: Facilitating Rapid Development of Context-Aware Mobile Applications. Transactions on Software Engineering 32(5), 281–298 (2006)
12. De, S., Nandi, S., Goswami, D.: Modeling an Enhanced Tuple Space based Mobile Middleware in UNITY. In: Proc. 11th IEEE Intl. Conf. on Ubiquitous Computing and Communications (IUCC 2012), pp. 1684–1691 (June 2012)
13. Roman, G.C., McCann, P.J., Plun, J.Y.: Mobile UNITY: Reasoning and Specification in Mobile Computing. Transactions on Software Engineering and Methodology 6(3), 250–282 (1997)
14. De, S., Goswami, D., Nandi, S., Chakraborty, S.: Formalization of a Fully-Decoupled Reactive Tuple Space model for Mobile Middleware. In: Proc. 5th Intl. Conf. on MOBILe Wireless MiddleWARE, Operating Systems, and Applications (MOBILWARE 2012) (November 2012)
15. De, S., Chakraborty, S., Goswami, D., Nandi, S.: Formalization of Discovery and Communication Mechanisms of Tuple Space Based Mobile Middleware for Underlying Unreliable Infrastructure. In: Proc. 2nd IEEE Intl. Conf. on Parallel, Distributed and Grid Computing (PDGC 2012) (December 2012)
16. De, S., Nandi, S., Goswami, D.: On Performance Improvement Issues in Unordered Tuple Space based Mobile Middleware. In: Proc. 2010 Annual IEEE India Conference (INDICON 2010) (December 2010)
17. De, S., Goswami, D., Nandi, S.: A New Tuple Space Structure for Tuple Space based Mobile Middleware Platforms. In: Proc. 2012 Annual IEEE India Conference (INDICON 2012) (December 2012)

Power Efficient Data Gathering
for Sensor Network

Anushua Dutta[1], Kunjal Thakkar[1], Sunirmal Khatua,[2] and Rajib K. Das[2]

[1] Tata Consultancy Service
[2] University of Calcutta, Kokata-700009, WB, India

Abstract. In this paper we have presented an algorithm to construct a rooted tree with base station as root connecting all the sensor nodes. The tree is constructed with the aim of maximizing the network life-time. It is assumed that all the nodes have same initial energy, but they can adjust their transmission range and thus the amount of energy needed for transmission may vary. The cost of a node is the amount of energy spent by it in each data gathering round. While determining the lifetime of a node, the energy lost in the process of constructing the tree is also considered. Thus the lifetime of a node is its residual energy (initial energy minus energy spent in exchanging messages for construction) divided by its cost. The lifetime of the network is the minimum of the lifetimes of all the nodes in the sensor network. It is also assumed the sensed data is aggregated so that nodes send a fixed sized message to its parent in each data gathering round. The algorithm works in two phases: In the first phase, an initial tree is constructed where the path from a sensor node to the base station consists of least possible number of hops. In the second phase (called fine-tuning) nodes may change their parents if that lead to a reduction in maximum cost of the three nodes involved (the node, its present parent, its future parent). The algorithms for both the phases (initial tree construction and fine-tuning) are distributed where nodes take decision Bbased on the status of its neighbors. Experimental results show that fine-tuning leads to considerable improvement in lifetime of the network. The lifetime computed is significantly higher than those obtained by other well-known algorithms for data gathering.

1 Introduction

In wireless sensor networks, a base station (sometimes called a sink node) sends commands to and receives data from the sensor nodes. The base station is a powerful node that serves as the interface between the users and the physical system under observation. The aim of this work is, given a sensor network, to find energy efficient paths for transmission of data from each node in the network to the base station so as to maximize the network lifetime. The lifetime of a network is defined to be the time during which the base station can gather data from each and every sensor. The energy of a sensor node is mainly drained by transmission and reception of data packets. By conventional communication model, the power for reception is assumed to be constant, whereas the transmission power depends

C. Hota and P.K. Srimani (Eds.): ICDCIT 2013, LNCS 7753, pp. 232–243, 2013.

on the Euclidean distance between the two nodes. A data gathering schedule specifies how the data packets from all sensor nodes are collected and routed to the base station in each round. Given the locations of the sensors and the base station, and the energy level at each sensor, the problem of finding an efficient data gathering and aggregation algorithm that maximizes the lifetime is called Maximum Lifetime Data Aggregation problem.

Extensive research has been done so far on this issue [4], [5], [6], [7], [8],[9]. In most of these works, the objective is to construct a rooted tree with base station as the root. Cost of each node is the transmission energy spent in sending a packet to its parent plus the receiving energy spent in receiving data from its children. In most of the works [3], [11], [10], the lifetime is found by dividing the initial energy by maximum node cost. In our work, the cost of a node is determined in the same way, but lifetime computation is little bit different. The energy drained in the process of construction of tree is subtracted from the initial energy and that is called the *residual energy*. The lifetime of a node in terms of rounds is given by its residual energy when tree construction is over divided by its cost. The minimum of the lifetime of all the nodes is considered as the lifetime of the sensor network.

The organization of the paper is as follows. Section 2 defines the problem and the cost model assumed and related work in this area. The next two sections describe the distributed algorithm used to construct and fine-tune the tree for data gathering. Section 5 gives the experimental results and performance analysis and Section 6 concludes the paper.

2 Problem Definition and Cost Model

The system initializes with a set of n sensor nodes randomly placed over a wide region along with a fixed base station. The base station has comparably more energy, computational power and memory than the sensor nodes. The senor nodes are considered to be of very limited energy, computational power and other resources. Each sensor node has the same initial energy and capable of broadcasting within a limited range R. Two nodes are adjacent (one hop neighbor) only if the Euclidean distance between them is less than or equal to R. The problem is to find a tree rooted at base station spanning all the sensor nodes so as to maximize the lifetime of the network in terms of rounds. In each round, each sensor collects data from its children (if any), combines them with its own sensed data, and sends that to its parent. The data are combined according to certain aggregation function so that packet sizes remain the same. A round is complete when the data reaches the Base station.

2.1 Cost Model

We assume the model presented in [2], where, a sensor node dissipates $E_{\mathrm{elec}} = 50nJ$/bit to run the transmitter or receiver circuitry and $E_{\mathrm{amp}} = 100pJ$/bit/m^2 for the transmitter amplifier. The radios have power control and can expend the minimum required energy to reach the intended recipients. The radios can be turned off to avoid receiving unintended transmissions.

Transmitting : Let $ET_x(k, d)$ be the transmission cost of sending a k bit message over distance d.

$$ET_x(k, d) = E_{\text{elec}} * k + E_{\text{amp}} * d^2 * k \qquad (1)$$

Receiving : Let $ER_x(k)$ be the cost of receiving a k bit message.

$$ER_x(k) = E_{\text{elec}} * k \qquad (2)$$

Like in [3], we assume $k = 2000$ and initial energy for each sensor $= 0.25J$. The total node cost for each node v with m children in the tree is given by:

$$C_x(v) = m * ER_x(k) + ET_x(k, d(v, u)) \qquad (3)$$

where u is the parent of v and $d(v, u)$ is the distance between v and u. From now on we denote by $T_x(u, v)$ the transmission cost $ET_x(k, d(u, v))$.

2.2 Related Works

There has been substantial research carried out in this are. In [4], it has been shown that data aggregation can reduce power consumption and thus increase lifetime. Several researchers [5], [6], [7] have focused on finding the amount of time (or number of rounds) each of the trees in a set of pre-calculated candidate trees should be used in order to maximize the total lifetime. The set of pre-calculated candidate trees is usually the set of all possible trees rooted at the base station. The problem with this approach is that the number of all possible spanning trees rooted at the base station is huge for a large sensor network and their enumeration is computationally prohibitive. The works in [8], [9] try to construct a tree without relying on a set of pre-calculated candidate trees. In this approach, it is not necessary to enumerate all possible spanning trees. This approach can be further enhanced by constructing new trees at appropriate time instants. The PEDAP protocol proposed in [8] computes a minimum spanning tree where cost of an edge (u, v) is the total energy expenditure in sending a packet from u to v. The PEDAP-PA (Power Aware) protocol proposed in [8], takes the remaining energy of each node into account. The MNL algorithm proposed in [9] constructs a spanning tree that maximizes the minimum residual energy among the nodes. The MNL algorithm starts with the base station as the initial tree. A node is chosen to be included in the current tree if it maximizes the minimum residual energy among the tree nodes including itself. The nodes are included in the current tree one at a time until all nodes are included. The work in [3], referred to as MULTIHOP, also takes the approach of adding one node at a time starting with Base Station. But here that node is added to the tree which minimizes the maximum cost of all the tree nodes after addition. Here each tree node finds among its tree nodes a candidate node for possible inclusion and sends that information to BS. The BS selecets the best candidate and convey that information to the specific node. Even though the experimental results show that MULTIHOP gives much better lifetime than obtained using minimum spanning tree or shortest path tree, it has the drawback of taking a very long time to construct the complete tree for large networks.

The works [11], [10] are in similar line. In [10], it is considered that all sensors have fixed and the same transmission power level but may have varying initial energy. They proved that finding a tree that yeilds the maximum lifetime is an NP complete problem. A lower bound on the inverse lifetime of the optimal data gathering tree was derived. An approximate algorithm was developed to find a data gathering tree whose lifetime is worse than that of the optimal tree by a small margin. They have used a greedy approach to construct an initial tree. Then there are a sequence of steps to modify the tree to move towards the optimal. Each step involving adding an edge to form a cycle and then deleting another edge to break the cycle. This leads to change in cost of the nodes involved. But as the transmission energy of the nodes are same, the change in cost is only due to change in the number of children. In [11], the nodes are considered to have heterogeneous and adjustable transmission range. In computing the cost of a node, the transmission cost of a node corresponds to the maximum transmission energy needed to send a k bit message to reach all its neighbor node in the data gathering tree. Here also an initial tree is modified by creating a cycle and breaking the cycle. In the process the child parent relation of the nodes on the cycle can be reversed but the assumed transmission cost model ensures that only the cost of the nodes to(from) which edges are added(deleted) undergo changes. This process is iterated until no improvements in lifetime is possible. The algorithm for modification is run centrally on BS. But the information needed for this computation has to be collected at the BS, and after computation the relevant information has to be sent to respective nodes. There is no discussion about how this can be done while keeping the energy lost in message exchanges as low as possible.

We take the same cost model as MULTIHOP [3]. The transmission cost of a node is the maximum energy needed to send a k bit message to its parent and receiving cost is proportional to the number of children. We start from the base station and construct the tree allowing multiple additions to the tree simultaneously. First all one-hop neighbors of BS are added to the tree, then all two-hop neighbors and so on. After tree construction by this greedy approach is over, a phase of fine-tuning is carried out. During this phase, through a distributed algorithm nodes change parents or adopt new children. We also consider the drainage of battery energy during both initial tree construction and fine-tuning.

3   ALGORITHM for HOPEG and Fine Tuning

Following steps are performed in order to construct the tree

- Compute the neighboring nodes of each sensor and base station by exchanging hello messages.

- Construct an initial tree network taking into consideration energy constraints consisting of the existing sensor nodes and base station. This algorithm is termed as HOPEG (**Hop** Count based **E**fficient Data **G**athering)
- Perform fine tuning, that is, dynamically change parent for some selected nodes in the tree for better performance and achieving more energy efficiency in the data gathering process.

3.1   Initial Tree Construction by HOPEG

The algorithm HOPEG involves exchange of 4 types of messages

1. COST(*id, cost, hc*) message : *id* is the id of the node sending the message, *cost* is the node's cost, and *hc* is the node's hop count from base station.
2. CONFIRM(s, r) message : sent by node s to node r.
3. MAXHOP(s, r, hc) message : sent by node s to node r.
4. FINAL-HOP-COUNT(s) message : broadcast by node s.

At first, BS broadcasts COST messages with *cost* zero, and *hc* zero. All the one-hop neighbors respond with CONFIRM messages, sets their *cost* values and *hc* values appropriately.

Nodes at level i, send COST messages which are received by their neighbors. A node u, which is not already part of the tree upon receiving COST message(s) from a set of node $S(u)$, selects one of $S(u)$, say p, as its parent based on the following condition

$$\max(T_x(u,p), (C_x(p) + R_x)) \le \max(T_x(u,k), (C_x(k) + R_x)) \forall k \in S(u) \quad \text{(A)}.$$

All one hop neighbors of BS get COST message from only the BS, and set their parent as BS.

We describe the distributed algorithm HOPEG as what every node u does on receipt of different types of message.
On receipt of
COST message : sends CONFIRM (u, p) message based on condition (A); sets its cost as $T_x(u, p)$; broadcasts COST messages

CONFIRM(s, p) message : adds s to its children; updates its cost as $C_x(p) \leftarrow C_x(p) + R_x$.

When a node does not receive any CONFIRM message in response to its COST message, it considers itself as a leaf node and initiate the phase to determine the maximum hop count of the tree as follows:

- A leaf node sends a MAXHOP message to its parent
- A node n, on receiving MAXHOP messages from all its children finds the maximum hc values received and sends that maximum in a MAXHOP message to its parent.
- Base station on receiving MAXHOP messages from all its children knows that tree construction is over, finds the maximum hop count h_{max} of the tree and then broadcasts the maximum hop count h_{max} to its children by FINAL-HOP-COUNT message.

– Any non-leaf node on receiving FINAL-HOP-COUNT message from its parent broadcasts it.

4   Fine Tuning

After HOPEG, the fine-tuning phase starts. The fine-tuning phase is carried out for h_{max} number of rounds by all nodes. In each round, a node may change its parent or adopt a new child, if that leads to lower the cost. After one round of fine-tuning the levels of the nodes are recomputed. This is necessary because a node u, can select another node v as its new parent only if level of v is less than or equal to level of u.

Fine tuning is a distributed algorithm which is to be performed concurrently at each sensor node(belonging to the initial tree) to see if the cost could be further reduced by changing its parent node. This change results in a dynamic tree formation.

Before giving the algorithm for fine tuning we present the following definition which is the focal point of this algorithm.

Definition 1. *Triple-max(n, p) for the pair of nodes n and p where n is the computing node and p is its neighbor contesting for becoming its new parent, is defined as the maximum of $C_x(n)$, $C_x(p)$, and $C_x(r)$ where r is the current parent of n. Old-triple-max(n, p) is the maximum value of the above 3 values in the current state (i.e while node r is node n's current parent). New triple-max(n, p) also denoted by Cmax(n, p) is the maximum of the above 3 values in the state if the change was to be made(i.e if link between node r and n is broken and node p is made n's parent). The change in the 3 values would be the following:*

$$New\ C_x(n) \leftarrow C_x(n) - T_x(n, r) + T_x(n, p)$$
$$New\ C_x(p) \leftarrow C_x(p) + R_x$$
$$New\ C_x(r) \leftarrow C_x(r) - R_x$$
$$Cmax(n, p) = \max(NewC_x(n), NewC_x(p), NewC_x(r)).$$

If $Cmax(n, p)$ is less than Old-triple-max(n, p), it is advantageous to change n's parent. Each such change guarantees that the maximum cost of the network will not increase, but does not guarantee that maximum cost of network will decrease. We can only hope that the node with highest cost will change its parent at some stage and thus maximum node cost of the network will be reduced. Experimental results show that maximum node cost does decrease and network life time does increase as a result of fine tuning

4.1   Messages Exchanged for Fine Tuning

Fine-tuning involves exchange of four kinds of message: COST, REQUEST for adoption, RESPONSE to adoption and BREAKUP. A round consists of 4 phases and after that another round starts.

- COST$(m, C_x(m), \text{level}(m))$ message: This message is broadcast by node m in phase 1 of each round of fine tuning. In the first round all nodes broadcast COST messages, but after that only those nodes whose costs or levels are changed in a given round need to broadcast COST messages in the next round.
- REQUEST $(n, m, Cmax(n, m))$ for adoption message: This message is sent in phase 2, by a node n to node m to indicate that node n wants node m to be its parent. Here, $Cmax(n, m)$ is as defined in 1.
- RESPONSE (m, n) to adoption: This message is sent in phase 3 by a node m to n to indicate that m is agreed to adopt n as child.
- BREAKUP (n, p) : This message is sent in phase 4, by a node n to its current parent p. The node p interprets it to break link between n and p. The new parent takes it as a confirmation that a new child n is adopted as a result of its RESPONSE.

REQUEST Message. A node gets the cost of its neighbors and then selects a subset of these nodes suitable for sending REQUEST message based on the following conditions

1. $\text{level}(p) \leq \text{level}(n)$
2. $Cmax(n, p)$ is less than Old-triple-max(n, p)
3. n has not received a REQUEST message from p

We will show later that the first and third condition helps in avoiding cycles in the resulting graph.

Given a set of nodes P which satisfy the above condition, REQUEST message is sent to a node $p \in P$ such that $Cmax(n, p)$ is minimum.

On Receipt of REQUEST Message. On receipt of REQUEST messages from a set of nodes Q, a node p may do different things depending on the following cases:

Case 1: It has not sent a REQUEST or not yet received a RESPONSE message to its own REQUEST:

Find node m such that $Cmax(m, p) \leq Cmax(k, p)$ for all $k \in Q$, Locks itself, and then send RESPONSE message to m.

Case 2: It is not locked and has received a RESPONSE message from a node q: It does not send any RESPONSE message but sends a BREAKUP message to its current parent r which is also heard by q. Whenever a node sends BREAKUP message it updates its cost. In this case its new cost will be $C_x(p) \leftarrow C_x(p) - T_x(p, r) + T_x(p, q)$. The node sets q as its new parent.

Case 3: It is locked (sent RESPONSE to m) and received RESPONSE from q. In this case, p checks whether it will go for double update (double update means its cost will change both due to change of its parent and addition of a new child). Let $C'_x(p)$ be the new cost of p, if q is made the parent of p. If $C'_x(p) + R_x \leq Cmax(m, p)$, it will send BREAKUP message to its current parent and q. Otherwise, only a single update will be allowed, and no BREAKUP message will be sent.

BREAKUP Message. A node r on receiving BREAKUP message from one of its children m, removes m from its children and updates its cost as
$C_x(r) \leftarrow C_x(r) - R_x$

A node p after sending RESPONSE to adoption message to a node n waits for the BREAKUP message from n to its old parent. Only then it adds n to its children and updates its cost as $C_x \leftarrow C_x + R_x$

If a node locks itself, the lock remains valid only in the current round.

4.2   Set Level of Each Node in the Tree

This step is not required during initial tree construction as the level and hop-count of each node is being set as they are being included to the tree. But later on the level of nodes change and each round of fine-tuning is followed by a level computation step.

The base station's level is fixed at 0. The base station broadcasts a SET-LEVEL message which includes the level of the node broadcasting it(in this case the base station), which is received by only its children nodes The children nodes then set their level to 1 more than the level in the message. All non-leaf nodes on receiving SET-LEVEL message from their parents broadcast SET-LEVEL messages to their children. In this way the messages are broadcast till the leaf nodes of the tree are reached.

The decision to run Fine-tuning for $h_{\max}$ rounds has been arrived at empirically. It was observed that running fine-tuning longer than that does not lead to reduction in costs of the nodes. Since h_{max} is known to all the nodes after construction of initial tree, each node can decide on its own when to terminate the fine-tuning process without requiring further message exchanges.

4.3   Correctness of Fine-Tune Algorithm

It is necessary to show that the distributed algorithm for fine-tuning does not break the initial tree into disconneceted components. Here, we present the following lemma.

Lemma 1. *If the initial tree after HOPEG consists of n number of nodes, the graph obtained after any rounds of fine-tuning is also a tree consisting of n number of nodes.*

Proof. Since in fine-tuning a subset of the nodes change their parent i.e., break the connection with earlier parent and selects a new parent, the total number of links in the resulting graph after any rounds of fine-tuning remains the same. Since the initial tree consists of $n - 1$ edges, the resultant graph also contains $n - 1$ edges. So, we only need to show that the resultant graph does not contain any cycle, to prove that it is a tree with n nodes.

Suppose for the sake of contradiction that the graph after fine tuning has at least one cycle. Suppose, r be the first round of fine-tuning which generates a cycle. Suppose the cycle consists of k nodes $v_0, v_1, \ldots v_{k-1}$ where $v_{(i+1) \bmod k}$ is

Table 1. Before Fine-Tuning when Range=40m

# of Nodes	HOPEG-COST	HOPEG-Life	MULTIHOP-Cost	MULTIHOP-Life
70	0.67	370	0.59	359
80	0.71	351	0.56	357
90	0.68	368	0.56	361
100	0.71	352	0.55	332

Table 2. After Fine-Tuning when Range=40m

# of Nodes	HOPEG-COST	HOPEG-Life	MULTIHOP-Cost	MULTIHOP-Life
70	0.59	417	0.56	363
80	0.54	454	0.54	355
90	0.52	467	0.52	373
100	0.52	468	0.51	325

the parent of v_i, for $0 \leq i \leq k - 1$. We first show that all the edges of the cycle must be added in round r.

Let $l(v)$ denote the level of v at the start of round r. At the start of round r the graph is still a tree and hence levels of nodes are well defined. Suppose some of the edges of the cycle were present after round $r - 1$. For every such edge $(v_i, v_{(i+1) \bmod k})$ $l(v_i) > l(v_{(i+1) \bmod k})$. Since a node can send request message to only nodes at level same or lower than itself, for all other edges $l(v_j) \geq l(v_{(j+1) \bmod k})$. Hence we arrive at a contradiction. So, the only possibility is that all the edges of the cycle were added in round r and all the nodes of the cycle were at the same level at the start of round r. In round r every node v_i has received RESPONSE from $v_{(i+1) \bmod k}$ and sent RESPONSE to $v_{(i-1) \bmod k}$. Now according to algorithm for fine-tuning, if a node receives RESPONSE to its own request before sending RESPONSE message, it does not send RESPONSE message. So, every node v_i must have sent RESPONSE message to $v_{(i-1) \bmod k}$ before receiving RESPONSE message from $v_{(i+1) \bmod k}$. This again leads to a contradiction.

5   Simulation Study

We have simulated the HOPEG and Fine-tuning algorithm and compared its performance with the algorithm presented in [3] which have used the same cost model and parameters. We have not compared with the works in [11] and [10] as they use different cost models and diferent restrictions. Also, they use centralized algorithm to modify the tree whereas ours is a distributed algorithm. All the works so far in this area only considered the cost of nodes and thus the maximum cost of the nodes determined the lifetime of the network. But the drainage of energy due to message passing in constructing the tree though small, cannot be ignored completely. That the drainage of energy plays a part in determining the

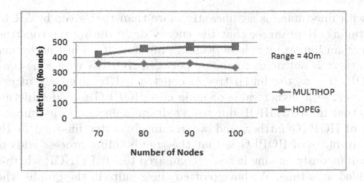

Fig. 1. Graph for Range 40m

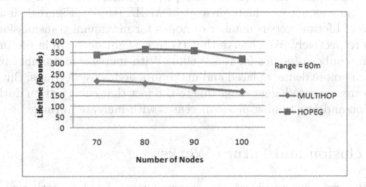

Fig. 2. Graph for Range 60m

lifetime is evident when we analyses and compare our work with [3] (referred to as MULTIHOP from here on). For simulation purpose, a number of sensor nodes are placed randomly in a 300 m× 300m area and the number of nodes varied from 60 to 100. The maximum transmission range of sensor nodes are varied from 40m to 70m. To make a fair comparison the maximum node cost and lifetime is determined for the same placement of sensor nodes and same parameters. For a given number of sensor nodes, and given maximum transmission range, we have considered 20 such random configurations of sensor nodes and computed the averages. The simulation is done using java on an windows platform.

We have constructed the tree using both HOPEG and MULTIHOP. The initial energy for each node is taken to be 0.25mj. For each message exchange during HOPEG and Fine-tuning the drainage of energy is considered. After termination of the algorithm life-time of each node is computed by dividing its residual energy by its cost. The minimum of the life-times of all the nodes gives the lifetime of the network. We have tabulated the results for maximum transmission range 40m, the maximum node cost and lifetime for HOPEG and MULTIHOP. Here the maximum node cost is expressed in mJ. The tables 1 and 2 shows that on applying fine tuning, maximum node cost decreases significantly for HOPEG but only a little for MULTIHOP. As a result the maximum lifetime given by

HOPEG with fine-tuning is significantly more than that given by MULTIHOP with fine-tuning. Here we see that the energy drain during the construction of the tree play an important role in deciding lifetime. If we just go by maximum node cost, there is not much to choose between HOPEG with Fine-tuning and MULTIHOP. But as the initial tree is constructed by a greedy algorithm in HOPEG, even with higher value of node cost HOPEG provides lifetime comparable to that in MULTIHOP due to less drain of energy. Fine-tuning reduces node cost of HOPEG farther, and we get much better life-time in HOPEG. Another advantage of HOPEG is that the tree building process adds multiple nodes simultaneously making it faster compared to MULTIHOP where a single node is added at a time. We have plotted the results in the graphs where lifetime given by HOPEG with fine-tuning is placed along with lifetime given by Multihop without fine-tuning (Fine-tuning as a technique has been developed in this work and was not originally present in MULTIHOP). Figure 1 and 2 give the graphs of lifetime versus number of nodes for maximum transmission range 40 and 60 respectively. We observe that there is slight decrease in lifetime with increase in number of nodes for range 60m. With increase in mumber of nodes the nodes are more densely placed and maximum node cost decrases. But overall lifetime decreases with higher range due to the fact that energy drain during tree construction and fine tuining phase increases with increase in range.

6   Conclusion and Future Works

In this paper we have considered the construction of a data gathering tree so that lifetime of the network is maximized. We consider that each sensor nodes start with same initial energy, but the transmission range of the sensor nodes are adjustable. We have presented a greedy algorithm to construct an initial tree and then an algorithm to fine-tune the tree to reduce cost. Fine-tuning involves h_{max} rounds and in each round a subset of nodes change their parents or adopt new children. The earlier works in this area did not consider the drainage of energy in message passing while the tree is built. We have considered that, and found it to be a significant factor. Even though lifetime depends both on cost and residual energy, while fine-tuning, we have only considered the cost. This is because the tree giving minimum cost only depends on the nodes position and fine-tuning process is more likely to converge to an optimal tree if cost is the only consideration.

Any distributed algorithm for tree construction for data gathering should also try to minimize the number of message exchanged in the process. The other alternative is to compute the tree by a centralized algorithm at Base station. But gathering the data needed for computation, and then disseminating the relevant information to the sensor nodes will also drain energy. Since, the transmission energy depends on message size, transferring the required information keeping the message size small would be an important issue.

Fine tuning as a technique can be applied on any initial tree. As a direction for future research, we can think of applying this idea to provide fault-tolerance.

Any time a node finds its parent faulty or drained of energy, it can send request for adoption to another node. But here, in addition to the cost of neighbor nodes, their residual energies have to be considered.

References

1. Lindsey, S., Raghavendra, C., Sivalingam, K.: Data Gathering in Sensor Networks using Energy*Delay metric. IEEE TPDS 19(3), 924–935 (2002)
2. Lindsey, S., Raghavendra, C.: PEGASIS: Power Efficient Gathering in Sensor Information Systems. In: Proc. of the IEEE Aerospace Conf., pp. 1–6 (2002)
3. Bhattacharya, S., Das, N.: Distributed Data Gathering Scheduling in Multihop Wireless Sensor Networks for Improved Lifetime. In: ICCTA 2007, pp. 46–50 (2007)
4. Madden, S., Szewczyk, R., Franklin, M.J., Culler, D.: Supporting Aggregate Queries Over Ad-Hoc Wireless Sensor Networks. In: Proceedings of 4th IEEE Workshop on Mobile Computing and Systems Applications, pp. 49–58 (2002)
5. Kalpakis, K., Dasgupta, K., Namjoshi, P.: Efficient algorithms for maximum lifetime data gathering and aggregation in wireless sensor networks. Computer Networks 42(6), 697–716 (2003)
6. Xue, Y., Cui, Y., Nahrstedt, K.: Maximizing lifetime for data aggregation in wireless sensor networks. Mobile Networks and Applications 10(6), 853–864 (2005)
7. Kalpakis, K., Tang, S.: A combinatorial algorithm for the Maximum Lifetime Data Gathering and Aggregation problem in sensor networks. In: Proceedings of the International Symposium on a World of Wireless, Mobile and Multimedia Networks (WoWMoM), pp. 1–8 (2008)
8. Tan, H.O., Korpeoglu, I.: Power Efficient Data Gathering and Aggregation in Wireless Sensor Networks. ACM SIGMOD Record 32(4), 66–71 (2003)
9. Liang, W., Liu, Y.: Online Data Gathering for Maximizing Network Lifetime in Sensor Networks. IEEE Transaction on Mobile Computing 1(2), 2–11 (2007)
10. Wu, Y., Fahmy, S., Shroff, N.B.: On the Construction of a Maximum Lifetime Data Gathering Tree in Sensor Networks: NP-Completeness and Approximation Algorithm. In: Proceedings of the IEEE INFOCOM, pp. 356–360 (2008)
11. Lin, H.-C., Li, F.-J., Wang, K.-Y.: Constructing Maximum-lifetime Data Gathering Trees in Sensor Networks with Data Aggregation. In: Proc. IEEE ICC (2010)

Computing on Encrypted Character Strings in Clouds

Günter Fahrnberger

FernUniversität in Hagen, Department of Communication Networks,
Universitätsstraße 1, 58097 Hagen, Germany
guenter.fahrnberger@fernuni-hagen.de

Abstract. Many organizations today are turning towards the contemporary concept of Cloud Computing, which entails the transfer of their applications (processing both sensitive and non-sensitive data) into online repositories or clouds. Encryption schemes based on homomorphic functions can provide the technology required to protect the confidentiality of this data. Their limitation, however, lies in their ability to process numeric values only. This paper, therefore, is focused on proposing a new encryption scheme relying on character string splitting and ciphering with additional components on the user and cloud side to support querying and modifying character string functions. Ultimately, what eventuates is an environment where a cloud is unaware of the contents of any input character strings, and of the output data during processing.

Keywords: blind computing, character string, character string function, cloud, cloud computing, secure computing, selective encryption, selective string encryption, string function.

1 Introduction

If a cloud is used purely for the storage of data (excluding any option to query or modify that data), then cryptography offers numerous options to not only secure the transfer of information to and from the cloud, but also to house it within. Since the invention of the public-key cryptosystem RSA in 1978, there have been constant enquiries to access and modify encrypted data directly. Direct operations on encrypted data must generate encrypted output, which can be decrypted to desired useful results.

Promising solutions for such enquiries based on homomorphic encryption schemes have been offered, where, for an arithmetical function, a corresponding homomorphic function in the cloud is sought, which delivers the same result [3], [4], [11], [13]. If such a homomorphic function can be found, then the problem is resolved, and the cloud can apply it to the data without deciphering it or its meaning.

While homomorphic encryption schemes will play an important role in future, they do not support calculations on encrypted character strings. Character strings are sequences of symbols from an alphabet Σ (otherwise known as a character set). Although character strings can be represented by positive binary, octal, decimal or hexadecimal numbers, a string function $h(y): \Sigma^* \to \Sigma^*$ can neither be substituted by an arithmetic function $f(x): \text{IN} \to \text{IN}$, nor by a homomorphic function $g(E(x)): \text{IN} \to \text{IN}$

C. Hota and P.K. Srimani (Eds.): ICDCIT 2013, LNCS 7753, pp. 244–254, 2013.
© Springer-Verlag Berlin Heidelberg 2013

due to the fact that representative codings of strings can only be used for identification. Their numerical values do not designate any rank or quantity.

Alternative approaches (which will be discussed in further detail in chapter 2) are based on proposing a framework enabling "equality-queries" and "similarity-queries" over encrypted character strings in databases despite omitting methods of how to cut out specific parts of a ciphered input character string. Figure 1 highlights known solutions in black-colored SQL-notation [10]. The red-colored ones in Java-notation are unknown [6].

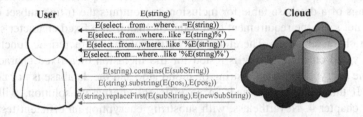

Fig. 1. Computing on encrypted character strings in databases

This paper is focused on proposing a solution for this shortcoming by introducing a new encryption scheme which is based on character string splitting and makes an attempt to process the encrypted character strings as well (as shown by the red-tagged strings functions above).

Chapter 3 proposes a solution requiring minimal encryption and decryption efforts by the user application. It does this by incorporating functions in the cloud application that focus on quick and simple search, compare and replace operations instead of mathematical ones. This is achieved using pre-encrypted values of a repository in the cloud. Additionally a short overview about the security of the proposed solution is given.

Chapter 4 examines the results of an experiment investigating the proposed solution. Efficiency in terms of time and space are analyzed and compared with other approaches.

Chapter 5 summarizes and concludes this study.

2   Related Work

As mentioned in the introduction, some research has already delved into methods to enable queries over encrypted character strings in relational databases contained within untrustworthy environments (like clouds) [2], [8], [9], [14], [15], [16]. Equally, research literature also documents alternative approaches of dealing with the issue by using many end-to-end security proposals like EndSec [7].

Both types of approaches make databases and distributed applications safer in untrustworthy environments, but they lack functions, which can search for substrings in encrypted character strings, and modify them through cutting or replacing.

These different approaches are not suitable for modifying character string functions for several reasons.

Database approaches save encrypted character strings and the output of their characteristic functions as indexes. This excludes modifying functions onto them in an encrypted environment. End-to-end approaches use conventional block encryption, which prevents any operations from being made on the aforementioned character strings, and therefore excludes them from any further discussion in this chapter. Substring encryption allows modifications on encrypted strings without losing confidentiality.

Each database approach searches with a given matching pattern in all existing character strings of a database table for inclusion and outputs the fitting subset of them. This does not meet the requirement to test the inclusion of a fixed character substring in a given character string. Therefore, the output of the characteristic function of a given encrypted character string is tested for the inclusion of a fixed character substring in the encrypted character string on cloud side and the database is not necessary anymore. If this modification ends in an efficient alternative solution, will be examined in chapter 4. Nevertheless, with substring encryption an efficient test for the inclusion of an encrypted character substring (matching the pattern in an encrypted character string) is included.

Database approaches always encrypt a character string en bloc. This supports only the exchange of a whole character string in the database table. However, a function is required to keep or exclude certain parts of a character string. Substring encryption achieves this requirement.

3   Substring Encryption

3.1   Architecture of Substring Encryption

Figure 2 gives a broad overview about the basic architecture of the proposed encryption scheme. An existing user application, which wants a cloud to take over the evaluation of certain string functions, needs to be supplemented by the three components: Confidential string splitting/concatenation, string cryptography and transport cryptography. The corresponding node in the cloud also consists of three components: Transport cryptography, the cloud application/rules table and a substring repository.

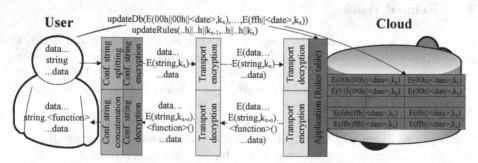

Fig. 2. Architecture of substring encryption

User. The functionality on the user-side works as follows: The component "confidential string splitting" detects confidential character strings and shapes them to useful substrings. It then enriches each of the substrings with structural information and passes them to the component "confidential string encryption", where they are encrypted piece by piece. The component "confidential string decryption" later deciphers the scrambled output of confidential string functions and passes them on for "confidential string concatenation", where the output is reassembled. All of these components let non-confidential data pass unchanged during dataflow.

Transport. Transport encryption is applied to all data (including data already containing ciphered confidential character strings) thereby providing basic protection against any threats on the transmission path.

Cloud. The parameters of functions, which shall be applied to incoming confidential character strings, can be transferred together with the input data, can be a part of the program code or can be contained within a rules table, whose rules are applied sequentially. The cloud application can execute all string functions on unencrypted character strings and supports the functions contains(), substring() and replaceFirst() for encrypted character strings by binding special implementations dynamically.

3.2   Details of Substring Encryption

Confidential String Splitting and Concatenation. This component decides if and how it splits given confidential plaintext strings. According to the use case, the number and lengths of the individual substring may be fixed or variable. It is supposed that as many bytes of a confidential string as possible shall be maintained and encrypted together as a substring to generate optimum secrecy. Splitting shall be done only if necessary because otherwise it reduces the secrecy of the individual substrings. The sizes of the unencrypted portions do not need to be equal. In the best case scenario, the whole character string can be maintained en bloc, provided that parts are not processed by string operations in the cloud, e.g. if just the comparison with other strings is tested. In the worst-case scenario, the character string must be split byte by byte, e.g. to measure the string length correctly. If each individual character is encrypted separately in the next component, then the process is reduced to character encryption.

For example, an international ITU-T E.164 telephone number consists of CC (Country Code), NDC (National Destination Code) and SN (Subscriber Number) [5]. Just for storage purposes all three parts can be kept together to obtain the highest secrecy. For international routing, the number would be split into CC and NDC+SN. For national transition the three parts CC, NDC, SN; or the two parts CC+NDC and SN are imaginable. For Operator routing decisions, the separation of the SN could become necessary.

After splitting a character string into useful portions, each portion is enriched with the string position index of its first symbol and an optional variable like the current date stamp (see definition 1). Therefore, each piece starts with one string fragment, followed by a delimiter and the string position. Optionally, one more delimiter together with the variable is appended. At least, the first delimiter is necessary, because the substring size can vary. The second delimiter can be omitted, if the position field always has a predefined size. If the position field has a fixed size and the optional variable is not needed, then even the first delimiter might be omitted. Delimiters that could be considered would be characters that are not used anywhere else in the portion, e.g. one of the four separators with a decimal code between 28 and 31 in character set ISO/IEC 8859-1.

Definition 1 (Confidential string splitting). Let $p = p_1...p_m \in \Sigma^*$ be a string over alphabet Σ, comprised of concatenated substrings $p_i \in \Sigma^*$, where $i = 1,...,m$, let $pos_i \in \Sigma^*$ be the position index of the beginning of p_i in p, let $x \in \Sigma^*$ be an optional variable and $\| \in \Sigma$ be a delimiter symbol. Then the string p is split into m portions

$$q_i = p_i\|pos_i\|x, \text{ where } i = 1,...,m. \tag{1}$$

The integrated locations in the individual pieces allow for transferring them out of sequence between the user and cloud environment, and avoid cipher text repetitions inside one portion. This makes it more difficult for cryptanalysis to break them. The optional incorporated variable is exchanged periodically and helps to hamper replay attacks without the need to exchange the secret key.

Confidential string concatenation means the reversion of confidential string splitting and is done for decrypted results from the cloud (see definition 2).

Definition 2 (Confidential string concatenation). If $q_1,...,q_m$, where $q_i = p_i\|pos_i\|x$ for i $= 1,...,m$, is the set of the decrypted substrings of a string p (see definition 4), whose elements can be delivered out of sequence by the cloud application, then the reconstruction of the plaintext string p is done by arranging the positions in ascending order, i.e. $pos_{ji} < pos_{ji+1}$, and concatenating $p = p_{j1},...,p_{jm}$.

Confidential String Cryptography. Only strings with confidential contents shall be processed encrypted, which meets Shannon's third criterion regarding a valuable secrecy system [12], which demands that enciphering and deciphering be kept as simple as possible to save efforts. Therefore, the enriched substrings of definition 1 are encrypted piece by piece (see definition 3). For the ciphered results of the character string functions received from the cloud, decryption is performed piece by piece as well (see definition 4). No other party other than the cloud user knows the secret key and can decrypt the confidential contents. For strings, which deserve protection, a modern symmetric cryptosystem like AES (Advanced Encryption Standard) is assumed, purely because it offers a higher encryption/decryption bandwidth and needs shorter keys than an asymmetric one at the same level of security [1]. This fulfils Shannon's second secrecy requirement regarding keeping the size of keys as small as possible [12]. The underlying cryptosystem must be easily replaceable. It should be unquestionably exchanged if its vulnerability exceeds any observable modern security norms.

Definition 3 (Confidential string encryption). Let $q_1,...,q_m$ be the enriched substrings of a string p according to Def. 1, let K be a set of secret keys, and let E: $\Sigma^* \times K \rightarrow \Sigma^*$ be a symmetric encryption function, where $k_x \in K$ is a user's secret key. Then the q_i are encrypted individually in ECB (electronic codebook) mode by

$$p_i' = E(q_i, k_x), \text{ where } i = 1,...,m \qquad (2)$$

$p_1', p_2', ... p_{m-1}'$ and p_m' are assembled randomly (which is submitted to the cloud), whereby the encrypted portions are brought out of sequence.

Definition 4 (Confidential string decryption). Let $p_1',...,p_m'$ be the encrypted substrings of a string p according to Def. 3, let K be a set of secret keys, and let D: $\Sigma^* \times K \rightarrow \Sigma^*$ be a symmetric decryption function, where $k_x \in K$ is a user's secret key. Then the p_i' are decrypted individually in ECB mode by

$$q_i = D(p_i', k_x), \text{ where } i = 1,...,m \qquad (3)$$

If for any $i = 1,...,m$, the decrypted portion q_i is not of the form $p_i||pos_i||x$, then deciphering is retried for the concerned cipher text p_i' with the older keys k_{x-o}, where o = $1,...,o_{max}$, until $q_i = D(p_i', k_{x-o})$ is of the required form. Otherwise, no key succeeds and the affected result is invalid and must therefore be discarded.

The lifetime of a used secret key k_x is limited similar to the optional variable, which forces periodic key replacements [1]. Before each periodic key replacement all pre-encrypted values for the substring repository and the application/rules table in the cloud must be recalculated and updated by the functions updateDb() and update-Rules() atomically within the change. In many encryption schemes, "used" secret keys are discarded after their lifetime to render replay attacks useless. Distributed applications (which imply store and forward mechanisms) must keep a well-defined number of historical keys k_{x-o}, where x-o is the oth from last optional variable on the client side to allow for the decryption of older strings as well. In the event that older keys are permitted, the cloud's user application needs to take the responsibility of monitoring for replay attacks by initiating automatic checks (including threshold alarming) on the usage frequency of old keys.

Transport Cryptography. During the transmission of sensitive and non-sensitive data, transport encryption is desired as a foundation to impede cipher text only attacks against encrypted confidential character strings. After removal of this basic protection, all information (except confidential character strings) is available in plaintext. As for confidential string cryptography, a modern symmetric cryptosystem like AES is assumed. The periodic key exchange cannot be performed by the user side alone, because the cloud must also know the key to release and engage transport encryption. Diffie-Hellman's key exchange offers a good possibility here.

Confidential String Evaluation. In the code of the cloud application/rules table, character string functions of the types contains(), substring() and replaceFirst() may be called for plaintext or encrypted character strings. The attached parameters must either be plaintext or encrypted as well. Consequently, for encrypted character strings, a new data type SecureString may be defined with special implementations for these three methods.

The method contains() tests the inclusion of an encrypted character substring in an encrypted input character string and is fed with the matching pattern string on all possible positions. This allows running this test for specific string positions only or for the complete input character string. contains() is implemented in a way, where each of the encrypted character substrings of a given encrypted character string is compared to all matching pattern strings. Definition 5 shows that even one match in all comparisons causes the function result "true" immediately, if there is no match at all, then contains() returns "false".

Definition 5 (contains): Let $p_1', \ldots, p_m'$ be the encrypted substrings of a queried string p according to Def. 3, and let $q_{1,j}, \ldots, q_{n,j}$ be the encrypted substrings of a matching pattern string q according to Def. 3, where one of the substrings has the lowest position j, then p is queried by

$$\text{contains}(\{p_1', \ldots, p_m'\}, \{\{q_{1,1}', \ldots, q_{n,1}'\}, \ldots, \{q_{1,y}', \ldots, q_{n,y}'\}\}) = \text{true, if } \exists j \ \forall l \in \{1, \ldots, n\} \ \exists i \ p_i = q_{l,j}, \text{ and false otherwise} \tag{4}$$

The function replaceFirst() not only does the same as contains(), but additionally replaces the first occurrence of the specified matching pattern string with another specified character string (see definition 6). Therefore replaceFirst() is called with the matching pattern string on specific, or all possible positions, plus the replacement string on specific or all possible positions. The replacement can be the empty string ε as well. For one search position only, the implementation of replaceFirst() demands two arguments - one encrypted character substring as matching pattern and another one as replacement. For multiple search position indexes, replaceFirst() must be called with two arrays of encrypted character strings that have the same number of elements. One of them contains the matching patterns strings and the other one the replacement strings. If a matching pattern at position j can be tested positive as part of the given encrypted character string, then its replacement must be located at position j of the replacement array.

Definition 6 (replace): Let $p_1', \ldots, p_m'$ be the encrypted substrings of a processed string p according to Def. 3, let $q_{1,j}, \ldots, q_{n,j}$ be the encrypted substrings of a matching pattern string q according to Def. 3, where one of the substrings has the lowest position j, and let $r_{1,j}, \ldots, q_{t,j}$ be the encrypted substrings of a replacement string r according to Def. 3, where one of the substrings has the lowest position j, then p is replaced by

$$\text{replace}(\{p_1', \ldots, p_m'\}, \{\{q_{1,1}', \ldots, q_{n,1}'\}, \ldots, \{q_{1,y}', \ldots, q_{n,y}'\}\}, \{\{r_{1,1}', \ldots, r_{t,1}'\}, \ldots, \{r_{1,y}', \ldots, r_{t,y}'\}\}) = (\{p_1', \ldots, p_m'\} \setminus \{q_{1,j}', \ldots, q_{n,j}'\}) \cup \{r_{1,j}', \ldots, r_{t,j}'\} \text{ with lowest possible j, if } \exists j \ \forall l \in \{1, \ldots, n\} \ \exists i \ p_i = q_{l,j}, \text{ and } \{p_1', \ldots, p_m'\} \text{ otherwise} \tag{5}$$

The operation substring() returns the substrings, which begin at the given string positions (see definition 7). It is called with all or only specific beginning positions between a start and an end index.

Definition 7 (substring): Let $p_1',...,p_m'$ be the encrypted substrings of a processed string p according to Def. 3, let $pos_i \in \Sigma^*$ be specified beginning positions, let $x \in \Sigma^*$ be an optional variable, let $\| \in \Sigma$ be a delimiter symbol, let K be a set of secret keys, let $E: \Sigma^* \times K \rightarrow \Sigma^*$ be a symmetric encryption function, where $k_x \in K$ is a user's secret key, and let $pos_i' = E(pos_i\|x, k_x)$, where $i = 1,...,j$, then p is cut by

$$substring(\{p_1',...,p_m'\}, \{pos_1',...,pos_j'\}) = P' \subseteq \{p_1',...,p_m'\}, \text{ where } p_i' \in P' \tag{6}$$
$$\text{and } \exists y \; p_i' = E(p_i\|pos_y\|x, k_x)$$

If $p_j \in \Sigma^n$, where n > 1, then the surplus characters of resulting string must be trimmed in the user application.

Therefore, access to an appropriate substring repository in the cloud is needed. The repository contains the relations between all possible encrypted substrings $E(c\|pos_c\|x, k_x)$, where $c \in \Sigma^*$ and x = optional variable (up to a specified maximum length, and up to a maximum position index) and their encrypted beginning positions $E(pos_c\|x, k_x)$, where $c \in \Sigma^*$ and x = optional variable. The size of the substring repository is specified in definition 8. The implementation of substring() expects one encrypted beginning position or an array of encrypted beginning positions as argument. Each encrypted character substring of a given encrypted character string is checked, if it has a relation to one of the specified encrypted beginning positions in the repository. If there is a link, then it is added to the function result.

Definition 8 (Substring repository size). Let $|\Sigma|$ denote the cardinality of alphabet Σ, n_{min} the minimum substring length, n_{max} the maximum substring length, pos_{min} the minimum position index and pos_{max} the maximum position index, then the substring repository size is

$$|db| := \sum_{n=n_{min}}^{n_{max}} |\Sigma|^n * (pos_{max} - pos_{min} - n + 2) \tag{7}$$

The occurrences of encrypted character (sub)strings and positions must be exchanged in the cloud application/rules table by the routine updateRules(). Also in the substring repository by the method updateDb() at each renewal of the optional variable or of the symmetric key k_x atomically. To manage these exchange transactions quickly the old (sub)strings and positions in the program code, rules table and substring repository of the cloud stay active until the transfer of the new ones is finished.

3.3   Security of Substring Encryption

If an attacker compromises the cloud user's computer, then he gets knowledge of all processed and unprocessed confidential plaintext character strings easily. In case the user's computer is protected, which attacks are possible against the cloud application?

The cloud application receives an encrypted character string as an object containing its substrings out of sequence. The simplest but least promising chance to find out the secret key is a brute force attack with all possible keys against an encrypted substring until one key delivers a useful result. Another possibility to infer a plaintext substring is a statistical analysis how often an encrypted substring occurs in several encrypted strings. The random sequence of the substrings and block ciphering, where the encrypted substring length hides the plaintext substring length, make this attack more complicated.

4   The Experiment and the Analysis

The purpose of the experiment is to show the validity of the proposed substring or character encryption scheme and to compare its space and time performance with four other approaches for four different string operations in a simulated tier-2-architecture. For substring encryption, strings are divided into the least possible number of substrings, each with a maximum size of four characters. Beside the introduced substring or character encryption scheme, the following approaches are considered during the tests: No encryption, only transport encryption, end-to-end encryption and the mentioned derivate of the database approach in chapter 2 (in which the database on the cloud side is replaced by the matching pattern). The encryption algorithm of all schemes, except one (which has no encryption), is AES-128. Therefore, the length of the secret key is 128 bits. To implement the encryption schemes, the programming language is Java 7. All tests are conducted on a HP DL380 G5 machine with 8 2,5GHz cores, 32GB RAM and Fedora Core 16 64 bit Linux as the operating system.

Firstly, the space performance of all six mentioned approaches is tested by varying the character string length and measuring the occupied Java heap space of one encrypted string in bytes. Observing the approach without any incorporated encryption, the space usage of a plaintext string is evaluated. Figure 3(a) shows that the required memory increases linearly with the string length. The overhead for the three approaches that allow computations on encrypted character strings is 10 times that for any of the others. The usage of character encryption leads to about a 30% lower memory consumption compared to the database approach (p=0,000 with K-S test). The space usage of substring encryption is about 70% lower compared with that of the database approach (p=0,000 with K-S test).

Secondly, the inclusion of a four characters long substring problem is tested for 1,000,000 random string samples per each string length. This is evaluated in nanoseconds per operation. According to figure 3(b), any involved encryption increases time usage by a factor of 1.000. The improved performance of character (p=0,336 with K-S test) and substring encryption (p=0,000 with K-S test) over the database approach can be easily observed as well.

Thirdly, the previous four characters long substring problem is replaced by another one in 1,000,000 random string samples for each string length. Again, this is measured in nanoseconds per operation. Figure 3(c) displays that similar behavior as for the previous operation contains() can be observed. However, in this instance, the time demand of plaintext strings is ten times greater, and encryption schemes display 50% higher. Reference values for the database approach are omitted here, because it does not support the operation replaceFirst().

Finally, a substring up to four characters long is cut out of 1,000,000 random string samples for each string length by the operation substring(). Yet again, (for consistency) the measurement is taken in nanoseconds per operation. Figure 3(d) displays that character and substring encryption do not perform as well as transport encryption only, but do provide security within the cloud application.

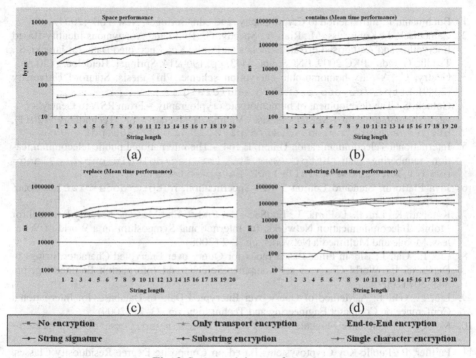

(a)

(b)

(c)

(d)

| -■- No encryption | -*- Only transport encryption | End-to-End encryption |
| -+- String signature | -+- Substring encryption | -+- Single character encryption |

Fig. 3. Space and time performance

5   Conclusion

An encryption scheme based on introducing the concept of substring or character encryption was proposed to enable querying and modifying functions on encrypted character strings in untrustworthy environments (like clouds). The recommended solution contains additional components in a user application to identify the logical parts of a confidential string (which is going to be processed in the cloud). It involves the process of splitting them, encrypting them separately removing the encryption of the resulting fragments and finally reassembling them.

The supplement in the cloud application processes character strings by querying them and removing the relevant parts of them or adding pre-encrypted substrings from an appropriate substring repository. The suggested approach is intended for distributed applications with high security demands (not only during transmission but also during computation and detention) in an unconfident cloud.

In conclusion, the analysis confirmed that substring and character encryption, which can be considered as the first selective encryption schemes that offer either more supported string functions under encryption or more space and time performance or both when compared to other similar approaches.

References

1. Buchmann, J.: Introduction to Cryptography, 2nd edn. Springer, New York (2004)
2. Camenisch, J., Kohlweiss, M., Rial, A., Sheedy, C.: Blind and Anonymous Identity-Based Encryption and Authorised Private Searches on Public Key Encrypted Data. In: Jarecki, S., Tsudik, G. (eds.) PKC 2009. LNCS, vol. 5443, pp. 196–214. Springer, Heidelberg (2009)
3. Gentry, C.: A fully homomorphic encryption scheme. PhD thesis, Stanford University (2009), http://crypto.stanford.edu/craig
4. Goluch, S.: The development of homomorphic cryptography – From RSA to Gentry's privacy homomorphism. Master thesis, Vienna University of Technology (2011), http://www.ub.tuwien.ac.at/dipl/2011/AC07811660.pdf
5. International Telecommunication Union: E.164 – The international public telecommunication numbering plan, http://www.itu.int/rec/dologin_pub.asp?lang=e&id=T-REC-E.164-201011-IPDF-E&type=items
6. Java Platform, Standard Edition 7 API Specification, http://docs.oracle.com/javase/7/docs/api
7. Kotapati, K., Liu, P., LaPorta, T.: EndSec – An End-to-End Message Security Protocol for Mobile Telecommunication Networks. In: International Symposium on a World of Wireless, Mobile and Multimedia Networks, pp. 1–7 (2008)
8. Liu, L., Gai, J.: Bloom Filter Based Index for Query over Encrypted Character Strings in Database. In: World Congress on Computer Science and Information Engineering, pp. 303–307 (2009)
9. Liu, L., Gai, J.: A Method of Query over Encrypted Data in Database. In: International Conference on Computer Engineering and Technology, pp. 23–27 (2009)
10. MySQL 5.5 Reference Manual, http://downloads.mysql.com/docs/refman-5.5-en.a4.pdf
11. Paillier, P.: Public-Key Cryptosystems Based on Composite Degree Residuosity Classes. In: Stern, J. (ed.) EUROCRYPT 1999. LNCS, vol. 1592, pp. 223–238. Springer, Heidelberg (1999)
12. Shannon, C.E.: Communication Theory of Secrecy Systems. Bell System Technical Journal 28(4), 656–715 (1949), http://netlab.cs.ucla.edu/wiki/files/shannon1949.pdf
13. Rivest, R.L., Shamir, A., Adleman, L.: A method for obtaining digital signatures and public-key cryptosystems. Communications of the ACM 21(2), 120–126 (1978)
14. Wang, Z.-F., Dai, J., Wang, W., Shi, B.-L.: Fast Query Over Encrypted Character Data in Database. Communications In Information and Systems 4(4), 289–300 (2004)
15. Wang, Z.-F., Wang, W., Shi, B.-L.: Storage and Query over Encrypted Character and Numerical Data in Database. In: The Fifth International Conference on Computer and Information Technology, Shanghai, pp. 591–595 (2005)
16. Zhu, H., Cheng, J., Jin, R.: Executing Query over Encrypted Character Strings in Databases. Frontier of Computer Science and Technology, pp. 90–97 (2007)

Design of a New OFTM Algorithm
towards Abort-Free Execution

Ammlan Ghosh[1] and Nabendu Chaki[2]

[1] Department of Computer Science and Engineering
Siliguri Institute of Technology, Siliguri, West Bengal, India
ammlan.ghosh@gmail.com
[2] Department of Computer Science and Engineering
University of Calcutta, Kolkata, India
nabendu@ieee.org

Abstract. The Software Transactional Memory (STM) is a promising alternative to lock based concurrency control. Three well studied progress conditions for implementing STM are, wait-freedom, lock-freedom and obstruction-freedom. The wait-freedom is the strongest progress property. It rules out the occurrence of deadlock and starvation but impose too much implementation overhead. The obstruction freedom property is weaker than wait-freedom and lock-freedom. Obstruction Free Transactional Memory (OFTM) is simpler to implement, rules out the occurrence of deadlock and has faster performance in absence of contention. A transaction T_k that opens an object, say X, for updating may be in the active state even after completion of update operation on X. Hence, object X cannot be accessed by any other transaction as the current transaction T_k is still active. At this point, if another transaction T_m wants to acquire object X at this point (for read/write), either T_k needs to be aborted or T_m must wait till T_k finishes. Both of these approaches are detrimental for the performance of the system. Besides, OFTM does not allow T_m to wait for the completion of T_k. In this paper, a new OFTM implementation methodology has been proposed to allow the second transaction T_m to proceed immediately without affecting the execution of the first transaction T_k. The proposed approach yields higher throughput as compared to existing OFTM approaches that calls for aborting transactions.

Keywords: Lock, Software Transactional Memory (STM), Obstruction-free Transactional Memory (OFTM), Abort-Free, Throughput.

1 Introduction

Writing scalable concurrent programs with traditional locking techniques for multi-core processor is a challenging task for the programmers. The locks are prone to several well known problems such as deadlock, priority inversion, convoying and lack of fault tolerance. The course-grained locks are even less scalable and as a result, threads might block each other even when there is no interference. While fine-grained locks are good for such scenario, issues like deadlock becomes even more complex

C. Hota and P.K. Srimani (Eds.): ICDCIT 2013, LNCS 7753, pp. 255–266, 2013.
© Springer-Verlag Berlin Heidelberg 2013

and crucial with decreasing granularity of locks. Besides, fine-grain locks are more prone to error.

Software Transactional Memory (STM) systems have been proposed to overcome such drawbacks [1, 2, 4, 6]. STMs employ atomic primitives like compare-and-swap (CAS) and load-linked/store-conditional (LL/SC). These are widely supported by multi-core processors and have several advantages like low time and space complexity, reduced performance overhead, etc. Simple implementation mechanisms are embedded into the compilers for languages like Java and C# etc. to aid in implementation of STM. The term STM was first coined by Shavit and Touitou in 1995 to describe software implementation of transactional memory for a multi-word synchronization on a static set of data using LL/SC. Herlihy et. al. proposed the first STM to manage dynamic set of data (DSTM) using obstruction free non-blocking synchronization technique [2].

The term "obstruction freedom" had been used in [2] aiming that the progress for any thread eventually executes in isolation and hence does not affect execution of another thread. Since then different obstruction free STM implementation (OFTM) has been proposed including ASTM [4], RSTM [5] and NZTM [6]. All these techniques tried to minimize the overhead of the transaction processing. Guerraoui and Kapalka [5] presented a formal definition of OFTM and have established power and limitations of OFTM.

In this paper, a new OFTM implementation methodology has been proposed to allow a transaction to proceed immediately without affecting the execution of the conflicting transaction that has an exclusive ownership of the object. In Section 2, the background on non-blocking techniques of STM has been presented. Section 3, describes the basic design space of currently available OFTM techniques. Section 4 presents the proposed algorithm. In section 5, the performance of the proposed algorithm has been evaluated. The paper ends with concluding remarks in section 6.

2   Background

A transaction is typically defined as a sequence of operations executed by a single process on a set of data items shared with other transactions [8]. Transactions include the read and write operations by which data sets are accessed and try-commit and try-abort operations by which a transaction requests are committed or aborted.

A Software Transactional Memory [1], abbreviated as STM, is the data representation for transactions using base objects and primitive operations. The primitive operations for STM can be read and write or may be more sophisticated operations like CAS (Compare and Swap) or DCAS (Double-word Compare and Swap). The CAS is used to read from a memory location and to write the modified value by ensuring that the location has not been altered meanwhile. The DCAS effectively executes two CAS operations simultaneously and both the memory locations are updated if values have not been altered.

STM implementation can also be considered as a generic non-blocking synchronization technique that allows sequential objects to be converted into concurrent objects [1]. When a transaction wants to update any concurrent object, it declares its intention so that other transactions recognize this. Subsequently, it acquires the ownership of that particular concurrent object. After making the intended updates, the transaction releases the ownership of that concurrent object. The process of acquiring and releasing ownership of concurrent objects is done automatically in a non-blocking synchronization technique. This is to guarantee consistent updates using compare-and-swap (CAS) and load-linked/store-conditional (LL/SC).

In non-blocking synchronization technique, whenever contention arises, the processes need not wait to get access to a concurrent object. Instead, either it aborts its own atomic operation or aborts the atomic operation of process with which the contention is created. Non-blocking synchronizations have been classified into three main categories as follows [9]:

- **Wait Freedom:** An STM implementation is wait-free if every transaction is guaranteed to commit in a finite number of steps. The wait-freedom is the strongest property of a non-blocking synchronization in terms of the progress guarantees. The basic definition of wait-free property rules out the occurrences of deadlock and starvation.
- **Lock-Freedom:** An STM implementation is lock free if some transactions are guaranteed to commit in a finite number of steps. Lock-freedom is a weaker progress guarantee property of a non-blocking synchronization and does not guarantee that every transaction will commit. Lock-freedom rules out the occurrences of deadlocks but suffers from starvation.
- **Obstruction-Freedom:** An STM implementation is obstruction free [3] if every transaction is guaranteed to commit in absence of contention. Obstruction – freedom is the weakest progress guarantee property of a non-blocking synchronization and does not guarantee whether transaction will commit if more than one transaction takes steps. Obstruction-freedom rules out the occurrence of deadlocks but may suffers from live-locks if a group of processes keep preempting or aborting each other's atomic operations

Though wait-freedom and lock-freedom guarantee stronger progress property, they are usually complicated and expensive. The obstruction-free, non-blocking progress condition requires progress guarantees only in the absence of interference from other operations. This weaker requirement allows simpler implementation of STM that performs better in the common un-contended case. As stated above the obstruction-freedom does not guarantee progress under contention; it is combined with contention managers to facilitate progress. The contention manager determines which transaction may proceed and which transaction may wait or abort. The contention management comprises of notification method for various events along with request methods that ask manager to make a decision. The notifications include beginning of a transaction, successful/unsuccessful commit, acquire of an object etc. The request method asks contention manager to decide whether to restart the transaction or to abort competing transactions [10]. The contention management methods are called in response to obstruction free operation and hence they must be non-blocking and always eventually abort a competing transaction to avoid deadlock. There are various types of contention management policies. In [11], these have been classified as into the following three categories:

- **Incremental:** The priority of a transaction is built for incremental policies during its execution.

- **Non-Progressive:** It is assumed here that conflicting transactions will eventually complete, even if live-locks may occur.
- **Progressive:** This ensures a system-wide progress guarantee where at least one transaction will proceed to commit.

A structured categorization of different contention management policies identifying the common characteristics of each category would ease the task of the studying CM by a long way. However, that's beyond the scope of this paper primarily due to limited space.

3   OFTM Design Space

An obstruction-free STM, i.e., OFTM means that a thread is guaranteed to make progress when all other threads are suspended. Herlihy et al. [3] have given a generic definition of obstruction freedom as: 'A synchronization technique is obstruction-free if it guarantees progress for any thread that eventually executes in isolation'. As stated earlier; obstruction-freedom implements non-blocking synchronization with help of contention management policy, it is important to employ a good contention management policy to achieve an excellent performance. In [2], the first obstruction-free STM implementation is proposed called DSTM. DSTM introduces early release and invisible reads that doesn't require multiword CAS at commit time. It uses TMObject, a dynamic Transactional Memory Object, which encapsulates an object which is accessed by the transaction. The TMObject contains a pointer to a locator object. The locator object points to a descriptor of the most recent write transaction and old & new version of the data object. A transaction locator may be in Active, Committed or Aborted state. The write and read operation of DSTM uses the following logic.

   Transaction wants to update an object X using OFTM Synchronization: A transaction T_k acquires an exclusive but revocable ownership of an object X. This object can now point to the transaction descriptor of T_k and get information own by T_k. If another transaction T_m wants to update X before T_k has committed; the contention manager will decide whether to tell T_m to back off for a random duration or to abort T_k as T_m is always able to abort T_k and acquire X.

   Transaction wants to read an object Y using OFTM Synchronization: If T_k wants to read an object Y and found another transaction T_m is updating Y *then* T_k may eventually abort T_m. Otherwise if T_k finds that no other transaction is updating Y then T_k reads the current state of Y and later when T_k tries to commit, it checks for the consistent state of Y. Transaction T_k commits only if it finds a consistent state.

   When a transaction T_k acquires some object for read/write operation it makes the status field as 'Active'. When T_k tries to commit, if commit is successful then T_k changes its status field as 'Committed'. Otherwise, if T_k is aborted by other transaction, T_k changes its status field as 'Aborted'. Since Herlihy et al. obstruction-free STM implementation [2] several other obstruction-free STM have been proposed including ASTM [4], NZTM [6]. All of them have common basic high-level principle but different in implementation and optimization techniques.

4   Towards Abort-Free Execution

As shown in section 3, in OFTM approach, one transaction can eventually abort other transaction in case of conflict. While this would definitely affect the throughput, it may also lead to a live lock situation. The task of contention manager becomes critical here. In this section, a new OFTM algorithm has been presented that aims to avoid aborting any transaction while allowing execution in presence of contention. The basic concept of the proposed algorithm is discussed in section 4.1. Subsequently, the required data structure is presented.

4.1   Basic Concept

A transaction T_k may be in the active state even after completion of update operation in case transaction T_k opens an object X for updating. Hence, in a traditional lock-based approach, X cannot be accessed by any other transaction as the current transaction T_k is still active. However, at this point, if another transaction T_m tries to acquire X for read or write operation, the proposed algorithm allows T_m to access X rather than allowing T_m to abort T_k. The read operation of the proposed algorithm is similar to ASTM [4].   However, at the time of read operation the read transaction does not acquire a TMObject, rather it maintains a private read list and guarantees data consistency by re-validating the object data. The basic principles behind the write and read operation of the proposed algorithm are stated here.

Transaction wants to read an object Y: If T_k finds that no other transaction is updating Y then T_k reads the current state of Y and later when T_k tries to commit, it checks for the consistent state of Y; if it finds a consistent sate then only it commits.

If T_k wants to read an object Y and finds another transaction T_m is updating Y; then also T_k will read the current state of Y without aborting T_m. At the commit point T_m will checks for the consistent state of Y and if it is then commit else re-executes its steps with the current value of Y.

Transaction wants to update an object X: A transaction T_k acquires an exclusive ownership of an object X. This object can now points to the transaction descriptor of T_k and get information own by T_k. If another transaction T_m wants to access X, *for* update, before T_k has committed; T_m will be allowed to access X.

At this point T_m knows that T_k is active and X can be updated any time by T_k. So it would be T_m's responsibility to check the data consistency before commit. To facilitate this abort-free execution, T_m accesses X and stores the current value of X into its old data and updated value into the new data field. At the commit point T_m will check whether T_k has committed and the X's value is consistent, T_m will commit otherwise re-execute its steps with the current X's value.

4.2   Data Structure

The data Structure of the proposed model is similar to but not identical with that for DSTM and ASTM. Fig. 1.a depicts a transactional data structure, which contains only a Status field. A transaction has three states, ACTIVE, ABORTED or COMMITTED, which determine the most recent valid version of data objects. If the transaction is in ACTIVE or ABORTED state then the most recent valid version of the data object is the old version referred by the locator. If the transaction is in COMMITTED state, the most recent valid version of the data object is the new version referred by the locator.

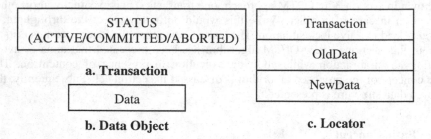

a. Transaction

b. Data Object

c. Locator

Fig. 1. a. Transaction Data Structure, b. Data Object, c. Locator Object

Figure 1.b depicts **Data Object** that contains the recent committed data object value and Figure 1.c depicts the **Locator Object**, which contains the three fields: Transaction points to the transaction that creates the locator; OldData is a copy of Data Object's recent committed value and NewData is the last updated value, which will be saved in the Data Object value by the transaction at commit time.

Transactional Memory Object (TMObject) structure as illustrated in Figure 2 encapsulates a program object that can be accessed by the transaction. TMObject has three fields. These are as follows:

a. ***WriterTransaction:** It points to the transaction, which has opened the object for write operation with an exclusive ownership on the object. This field is also works a start pointer.

b. ***WriterList:** This field points to the transaction that has accessed an object, which is exclusively own by other transaction for write operation. Using this field TMObject allows a conflicting transaction to access the object without aborting the owner transaction.

c. ***Data:** This field points to the Data object.

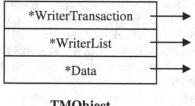

TMObject

Fig. 2. The TMObject Structure

4.3   Proposed Abort-Free OFTM Design

4.3.1   Read Operation

As stated earlier that read operation of the proposed algorithm is similar to ASTM though ours uses different TmObject structure. The Data filed of TM Object directly points to the Data object. However, at the time of read operation the read transaction does not acquire a TMObject, rather it maintains a private read list and guarantees data consistency by re-validating the object data. As mentioned earlier this read list private to the transaction and invisible to other transaction.

4.3.2 Write Operation

The write operation would be different in the presence and absence of a contention manager.

Write operation in absence of contention: When a Transaction wants to acquire some object for write operation it initiates a new locator and checks TMObject's WriterTransaction field. If this field is NULL or points to an Aborted or Committed Transaction's locator, it implies that there is no contention present. Hence, the transaction follows the steps described below to execute the write transaction. These steps are illustrated in Figure 3.

Case 1.1: Transaction T_m wants to access object X for write operation. T_m reads the TMObject's WriterTransaction field. If it points to T_m's transaction locator, it implies that the object has already opened by T_m for writing. Thus, T_m simply returns a pointer to the data field.

Case 1.2: If WriterTransaction returns NULL value or points to aborted or committed transaction – means there is no conflict with write transaction. So T_m changes the WriterTransaction filed to point to its Transaction. T_m uses CAS (Compare & Swap) to ensure meantime changes and perform the following steps:

— **Step 1:** T_m performs the write operation.
— **Step 2:** At the commit time T_m updates Object Data with its NewData value.
— Step 3: Tm changes its Transaction Data Structure Status field as Committed.

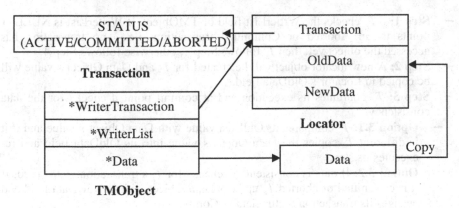

Fig. 3. Write Operation in absence of contention

Write Operation in Present of Contention: When a writer transaction T_m tries to acquire an active transaction's locator, say T_k, in the TMObject, as per the current OFTM implementation; T_m consult with contention manager and either it will aborts Tk or backs off for certain time.   As per the proposed algorithm neither T_m will abort T_k nor back-off for certain time; rather T_m will access the data object.

In order to implement this abort-free technique the algorithm uses *WriterList filed to create a new locator object for T_m and points it through *WriterList. The write operation is illustrated in Figure 4 and described in the following steps.

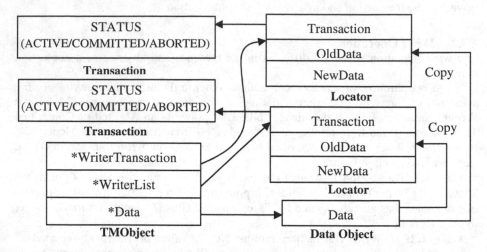

Fig. 4. Abort-free write operation in presence of contention

Case 2.1: Transaction T_m wants to access object X for write operation. T_m reads the TMObject's WriterTransaction field and finds that WriterTransaction points to an Active transaction T_k. Transaction T_m performs the following steps to access the object in abort-free way:

— **Step 1:** T_m checks the WrtierList field of TMObject. If WriterList is NULL or points to an Aborted or Committed transaction, i.e., no transaction has accessed the object yet; then T_m follows Step 2, otherwise follows Step 4.
— **Step 2:** A new locator object will be created for T_m and Data Object's value will be copied in Locator's OldData field.
— **Step 3:** T_m continues its execution and at commit point it checks for the data consistency.
  — **Option 3.1:** T_m compares its OldData value with Data Object's value and if it is different T_m copies the Data Object's value into its OldData field and re-executes its step.
  — **Option 3.2:** If data is consistent, T_m checks for T_k's transaction status filed. If it is committed or aborted T_m updates Data Object with is NewData field and changes its transaction Status field as Committed.
  — **Option 3.3** If T_m finds data is consistent and T_k's transaction status filed points to an Active transaction – means T_m has reached to its commit point but T_k has not yet committed; then T_m will consult with Contention Manager and either backs off   for some times or abort itself. However, in no case T_m will abort T_k.
— **Step 4:**   (Redirected from Case 2.1, Step 1). If T_m finds that WriterList points to a Transaction Locator T_x , i.e., T_x has already acquired the object that is exclusively owned by T_k. In this case T_m consults the contention manager (CM). CM will decide whether T_m will back off for some time or abort itself.

It is important to mention here that like any other OFTM implementation the proposed algorithm is also required a good contention management policy to achieve an excellent performance. The performance of the proposed mechanism has been discussed in the next section for various scenarios.

5   Performance Evaluation

The efficiency and performance improvement of the proposed method over the conventional OFTM [2] depends a lot on the size of the transactions in terms of their average execution time. This has been analyzed here in four different categories. However, towards the end of this section, it would be established that the bottom-line for the proposed approach would guarantee at least equivalent throughput as compared to the existing approaches [2].

Initially, only two transactions sharing a common resource is being considered. It is assumed that transaction T_k is in active state when transaction T_m is initiated and both the transactions need to acquire resource X. The first transaction T_k would update the resource X, while transaction T_m may either read or write on X. Let, $Size(T_x)$ denote the size of a transaction T_x in terms of its average execution time.

5.1   Case I: $Size(T_k) \approx Size(T_m)$

In this case, the first transaction T_k and the second transaction T_m are of equivalent size. Thus, even if T_k is active when T_m starts its execution, it is expected that transaction T_k would complete soon. Consequently, the chances that transaction T_k has already updated common resource X before T_m starts would be higher. In such a situation, transaction T_m would find that the value of X with which it started is same as the after T_k finishes. Even if T_k has updated the value of X after T_m is initiated, it may update X and finishes execution before T_m attempts to access it. According to *Case 2.1, Step 2,* of the proposed algorithm, transaction T_m would update the old-value of X at this point. In both of the situations stated, neither of the transactions T_k or T_m would be aborted. Thus unlike the existing OFTM solutions [2], the throughput of the system would not be affected.

However, if transaction T_k updates X after it is accessed in the second transaction T_m, then according to *Case 2.1, Step3, Option 3.1* of the proposed algorithm, transaction T_m is to be re-executed. Thus, depending on the time of actual update on X by T_k and the order of completion of T_k and access of X in T_m, either the second transaction needs to be re-executed or not. It may be safely inferred that for case I, the proposed OFTM implementation is expected to actually increase system throughput as it may not require any process to abort.

5.2   Case II: $Size(T_k) \ll Size(T_m)$

In this case, T_m must have been fired soon after T_k commenced and that could be the only possible explanation that even if T_k is very small, it remains in active state when T_m commences. As the size of T_k is much smaller as compared to that for T_m, it can be estimated in a quite realistic way that transaction T_k would be completed much before T_m reaches its commit point. In fact, T_k is not expected to remain active till T_m actually uses the common resource X. It may be inferred, that even if it is possible that T_m could be re-executed when transactions are of equivalent sizes [case I], the chances of such occurrence is quite unrealistic when Size(T_k) << Size(T_m). In a conservative assessment, the proposed OFTM implementation is expected to increase the system throughput for case II, as chances of aborting any process either small or large is less.

5.3   Case III: Size(T_k) >> Size(T_m)

In this case, there exists higher probability that the second transaction T_m spends maximum idle time D at its commit point and yet transaction T_k is in active state. This is the worst possible situation for the proposed algorithm. According to *Case 2.1, Step 3, Option 3.3* of the proposed algorithm, transition T_m requires to abort itself. However, even in this case, the proposed OFTM implementation would be better than [4]. Aborting the bigger transaction T_k for the sake of obstruction-free execution of T_m leads to redoing transaction T_k again from the beginning. This implies loss of throughput for the overall system. However, in the proposed approach, instead of T_k the second transaction T_m would be aborted. Transaction T_m with average execution time smaller than that for T_k, therefore, would not affect the throughput of the system as much of as re-execution of T_k would do.

Table 1. Impact of the Proposed Algorithm on Throughput

Sl. No.	Size (T_k)	Update Time for X in T_k	Size (T_m)	Start Time for T_m	Access time for X in T_m	Restarting T_m	Throughput using [2]	Throughput for proposed method
1	30	22	10	20	05	No	0.0400	0.0667
2	30	22	10	24	05	No	0.0370	0.0588
3	30	22	10	16	05	Yes	0.0435	0.0645
4	20	12	10	14	05	No	0.0588	0.0833
5	20	12	10	08	05	No	0.0714	0.0741
6	20	12	10	06	05	Yes	0.0769	0.1000
7	12	07	10	02	05	No	0.1429	0.1667
8	12	07	10	10	05	No	0.0909	0.1000
9	12	07	10	01	05	Yes	0.0952	0.1000
10	05	03	10	04	05	No	0.1333	0.1429
11	05	03	10	02	05	No	0.1333	0.1667

Table 1 lists some representative cases to study the efficiency of the proposed algorithm. Similar to what is followed in the rest of this paper, the two transactions T_k and T_m stand for the first and the following transactions respectively. The lengths of the transactions for rows 7, 8 and 9 correspond to case I, where Size(T_k) • Size(T_m). It is found that for two out of three cases, the throughput increases when the proposed method is used. The improvement in average throughput is 11.46% for the data set in rows 7 through 9 of Table 1.

On an average, the throughput using the proposed abort-free algorithm for case I is 10% higher than that for DSTM. The first six rows in Table 1 are examples for case III, when Size(T_k) >> Size(T_m). The proposed algorithm is best suitable for such cases. The improvement in average throughput is 36.57%. Fig. 5 illustrates the scenario for the data set in the first six rows of Table 1. The last two rows in Table 1 are examples when $Size(T_k) \ll Size(T_m)$ as mentioned in case II. The improvement in average throughput for the test cases is 16.13%.

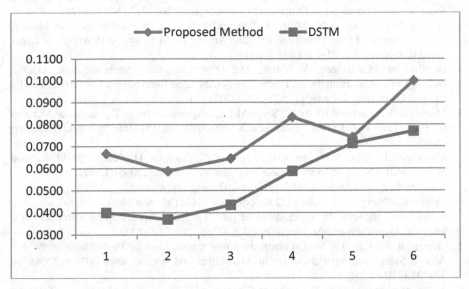

Fig. 5. Improvement in Throughput using Proposed OFTM vs. DSTM for $Size(T_k) \gg Size(T_m)$

6   Concluding Remarks

In this paper we have presented a new approach of OFTM implementation that aims to achieve abort-free operation. In all other proposed OFTM implementation; a transaction is allowed to abort a conflicting transaction i.e. if a transaction T_m finds a conflict with another transaction T_k then T_m can eventually abort T_k. This situation drastically reduces the throughput especially in absence of an efficient contention manager.

The proposed algorithm makes a strong argument to oppose the conventional obstruction freedom concept and never aborts an active transaction with the exclusive ownership of an object. In its present-form, if it is really required to abort a transaction the younger transaction will abort itself to avoid contention. The different possible scenarios are analyzed and it is found that a higher throughput is achieved where an active transaction with exclusive ownership of a shared object, is greater than or equal to a new transaction that wants to access the same object.

It may also be observed that when a data consistency problem occurs, the new transaction need not abort itself completely. Instead, a check-point may be set at the position where it has to access the shared object and the re-execution may start from that check-point. This however requires operating at an appropriate level of granularity. The current implementation is also been extended by the authors to study abort-freedom for multiple cascading transactions by making a linked list of them and pointing them through WrtierList filed of TMObject.

References

1. Shavit, N., Touitou, D.: Software transactional memory. In: ACM SIGACT-SIGOPS Symposium on Principles of Distributed Computing, pp. 204–213. ACM (1995)
2. Herlihy, M., Luchangco, V., Moir, M., Scherer III, W.N.: Software Transactional Memory for Dynamic-sized Data Structures. In: 22nd Annual ACM Symp. on Principles of Distributed Computing, pp. 92–101 (July 2003)
3. Herlihy, M., Luchangco, V., Moir, M.: Obstruction-free synchronization: Double-endedqueues as an example. In: Proceedings of the 23rd International Conference on Distributed Computing Systems, pp. 522–529 (2003)
4. Maranthe, V.J., Scherer III, W.N., Scott, M.L.: Adaptive Software Transactional Memory. In: Fraigniaud, P. (ed.) DISC 2005. LNCS, vol. 3724, pp. 354–368. Springer, Heidelberg (2005)
5. Marathe, V.J., Spear, M.F., Heriot, C., Acharya, A., Eisenstat, D., Scherer III, W.N., Scott, M.L.: The Rochester software transactional memory runtime (2006), http://www.cs.rochester.edu/research/synchronization/rstm/
6. Tabba, F., Wang, C., Goodman, J.R., Moir, M.: NZTM: non-blocking zero-indirection transactional memory. In: Proceedings of the 21st ACM Annual Symposium on Parallelism in Algorithms and Architectures (SPAA), pp. 204–213 (2009)
7. Guerraoui, R., Kapalka, M.: On obstruction-free transactions. In: Proceedings of the 20th Annual Symposium on Parallelism in Algorithms and Architectures (SPAA 2008), pp. 304–313 (2008)
8. Attiya, H.: Invited Paper: The Inherent Complexity of Transactional Memory and What to Do about It. In: Aguilera, M.K., Yu, H., Vaidya, N.H., Srinivasan, V., Choudhury, R.R. (eds.) ICDCN 2011. LNCS, vol. 6522, pp. 1–11. Springer, Heidelberg (2011)
9. Marathe, V.J., Scott, M.L.: A Qualitative Survey of Modern Software Transactional Memory Systems. Technical Report Nr. TR 839. University of Rochester Computer Science Dept. (2004)
10. Scherer III, W.N., Scott, M.L.: Advanced contention management for dynamic software transactional memory. In: PODC 2005: Proceedings of the Twenty-Fourth Annual ACM Symposium on Principles of Distributed Computing, NY, USA, pp. 240–248 (2005)
11. Saad, M.M., Ravindran, B.: RMI-DSTM: Control Flow Distributed Software Transactional Memory: Technical Report, ECE Dept., Virginia Tech. (2011)

GAR: An Energy Efficient GA-Based Routing
for Wireless Sensor Networks

Suneet K. Gupta, Pratyay Kuila, and Prasanta K. Jana

Department of Computer Science and Engineering
Indian School of Mines, Dhanbad-826 004, India
suneet.banda@gmail.com, {pratyay_kuila,prasantajana}@yahoo.com

Abstract. Routing with energy consideration has paid enormous attention in the field of Wireless Sensor Networks (WSNs). In Some WSNs, some high energy sensors called relay nodes are responsible to route the data towards a base station. Reducing energy consumption of these relay nodes allow us to prolong the lifetime and coverage of the WSN. In this paper, we present a Genetic algorithm based routing scheme called GAR (Genetic Algorithm-based Routing) that considers the energy consumption issues by minimizing the total distance travelled by the data in every round. Our GA based approach can quickly compute a new routing schedule based on the current network state. The scheme uses the advantage of computational efficiency of GA to quickly find out a solution to the problem. The experimental results demonstrate that the proposed algorithm is better than the existing techniques in terms of network life time, energy consumption and the total distance covered in each round.

Keywords: Wireless sensor networks, routing, genetic algorithm, network lifetime.

1   Introduction

Wireless Sensor Networks (WSNs) have been proven to be an effective technology for their wide range of applications, such as disaster warning systems, environment monitoring, health care, safety and strategic areas such as defense reconnaissance, surveillance, intruder detection etc. [1], [2]. However, the main task of WSNs in such application is to route the sensed data from randomly deployed sensor nodes to a remote Base Station (BS) called sink [3], [4]. Clustering of sensor nodes is an effective means to collect and route the sensed data using multi-hop communication usually in two-layer architecture. In the first layer, sensed data are locally aggregated by a special node called cluster head (CH) and then these aggregated data are routed to the base station through other CHs in the second layer [5], [6], [7]. By this way, the energy of the sensor nodes is conserved, the network lifetime of the WSN is prolonged and the scalability of the WSN can be increased.

However, the main constraints of the WSNs for such operation is the limited and irreplaceable power sources of the sensor nodes and in many scenarios it is difficult to replace the sensor nodes after complete depletion of their energy. Therefore, energy

C. Hota and P.K. Srimani (Eds.): ICDCIT 2013, LNCS 7753, pp. 267–277, 2013.
© Springer-Verlag Berlin Heidelberg 2013

consumption for the sensor nodes is the most challenging issue for the long time operation of WSNs [8], [9], [10]. Moreover, in many WSNs the cluster heads are usually selected amongst the normal sensor nodes which can die quickly due to extra work load for data aggregation and data forwarding with their limited energy. In this context, many researchers [5], [11], [12], [13] have proposed the use of relay nodes, which are provisioned with extra energy. These relay nodes are treated as the cluster heads and responsible for local data collection, their aggregation and communication of the aggregated data to the sink via other relay nodes. The functionality of a two tier WSNs with the relay nodes is shown in Fig. 1.

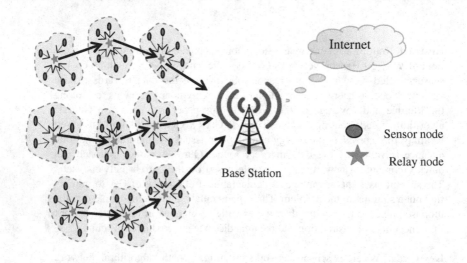

Fig. 1. An example of two-tiered wireless sensor network

Although the relay nodes are given extra energy, they are also battery operated and hence power constrained. Life time of the relay nodes is very crucial as the network life time of the WSN and the coverage fully depends on it. Therefore, energy efficient routing of the data through relay nodes is extremely important for reducing their energy consumption. It is noteworthy that for a WSN, with n relay nodes, each having an average of d valid one-hop neighbor relay nodes, the number of valid routes is d^n. This implies that the computational complexity of finding the best route for a large scale WSN is very high by a brute force approach. In order to select an energy efficient routing scheme from such a large solution space, a heuristic approach like Genetic Algorithm (GA) is extremely useful.

In this paper, we address the problem of routing the aggregated data from all the relay nodes to the sink via other relay nodes and propose a GA based routing scheme called GAR (Genetic Algorithm-based Routing) which considers the energy efficiency of the relay nodes. The GAR finds out the route from all the relay nodes to the BS by minimizing their overall distances with the view that the consumed energy to transmit the diffused data is proportional to the square of the distance between sender and receiver. Our approach can quickly compute a new routing schedule based on the current network state. We perform simulation run of the proposed method and evaluate with several metrics, namely network lifetime, energy consumption and distance covered in each round. The results are also compared with MHRM [14] as is done in [5]. The experimental results demonstrate the effectiveness of the proposed algorithm.

The paper is organized as follows. The related work is presented in Section 2. An overview of GA is given in section 3. The Network model and the terminologies are described in Section 4. The proposed algorithm and the experimental results are presented in Section 5 and 6 respectively, followed by the conclusion in Section 7.

2   Related Work

A number of routing protocols have been developed for WSN which can be found in [15], [16], [17] and their references. However, quite a few routing algorithms have been reported which are GA based. We review only those research works as they are related to our proposed algorithm. In [18], Huruiala et al. presented a GA based clustering and routing algorithm using a multi-objective function by choosing the optimal cluster-head and minimizing the transmission distance. Chakraborty [19] et al. developed a GA based protocol called GROUP in which a chain is formed to communicate with base station. The network lifetime is increased by allowing individual sensor nodes to transmit the message to the base station in non-periodical manner depending on their residual energy and location. Thus, this approach avoids forming greedy chains. In [20], L. Badia et al. presented a model by using a signal-to-interference ratio for scheduling and routing. Their results show that the model performs well for both small and large topologies. In [5], Ataul Bari et al. proposed a GA based algorithm for data routing using relay nodes in a two-tire wireless sensor networks. The main three operations namely selection, crossover and mutation used in their approach are as follows. Selection of individuals is carried out using the Roulette-wheel selection method and the fitness function is defined by network lifetime in terms of rounds. For mutation operation, they select a critical node from the relay nodes, which dissipates the maximum energy due to receiving and/or transmitting data. Mutation is done by either replacing the next-hop node of this critical node by a new next-hop relay node or by diverting some incoming flow towards that critical node to other relay node. The proposed work is also based on GA. However, it is different from [5] in respect of the following issues. 1) For selection of individuals, we use Tournament selection in contrast to Roulette-wheel selection. 2) Fitness function is defined in terms of total distance covered in a round rather than network life time in rounds. 3) In mutation, we select relay node, which uses maximum distance to transmit the data to its neighbour in contrast to a critical node defined in [5].

3   Overview of Genetic Algorithm

Genetic Algorithms (GAs) are adaptive methods that can be used in solving optimization problems. Their basic principles in the context of mathematical optimization have been rigorously described by John Holland [21]. GA begins with a set of randomly generated possible solutions, known as initial population. An individual solution is represented by a simple string or an array of genes and termed as a chromosome. The length of each chromosome in a population is same. Once an individual is generated, a fitness function is employed to evaluate its performance as a solution to the problem. This fitness function is based on how close an individual is to the optimal solution. Once the initial population of chromosomes is generated, two randomly selected chromosomes (parents) can produce two child chromosomes by a process called crossover in which the parent chromosomes exchange their genetic information. To produce a better solution, the child chromosomes undergo another process called mutation, in which the lost genetic values of the chromosomes are restored. Whenever the crossover and mutation are completed, the fitness function of the child chromosomes is evaluated and their fitness values are compared with that of all the chromosomes of the previous generation. In order to confirm that the current generation produces better result, two chromosomes of previous generation with poorest fitness values are replaced with the newly generated child chromosomes. The various steps of simple GA used in our proposed work are depicted in Fig. 2.

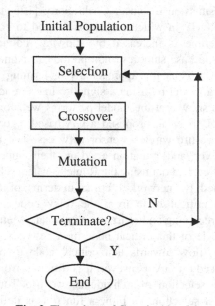

Fig. 2. Flow chart of Genetic Algorithm

4   Network Model and Terminologies

Here, we assume a WSN model, where all the sensor nodes along with some relay nodes are deployed randomly and they are stationary after deployment. The sensor nodes collect the local data and send it to their corresponding relay nodes. On receiving the data, the relay nodes aggregate them to reduce the redundant data within their cluster. Being a centralized approach, our algorithm assumes the exact location of the relay nodes which are known a priori through some location finding system such as GPS [22]. The relay nodes then route their aggregated data to the BS directly or via other relay nodes. Therefore, as per as data routing is concerned, all the relay nodes act as source or intermediate nodes treating the BS as the destination. It is obvious to note that for multi-hop communication, each relay node has to select a neighbor relay node in single-hop distance. Our algorithm deals with the selection of the best neighbour relay node to find the optimal route with respect to energy consumption. Each period of full data gathering and transmission of aggregated data from all the relay nodes to the BS is referred as a round [4]. The life time of the network is measured in terms of number of rounds until the first relay node dies. All communication is over wireless link. A wireless link is established between two nodes only if they are within communication range of each other. We use the following terminologies in the proposed algorithm.

- $V = \{C_1, C_2, ..., C_N\}$: The set of relay nodes including BS.
- $Dist\,(C_i, C_j)$: The distance between two relay nodes C_i and C_j.
- $Com\,(C_i)$: The set of all those relay nodes, which are within communication range of C_i. The BS may be a member of $Com(C_i)$.
- $Next\_Hops(C_i)$: The set of all relay nodes which can be selected as a next hop of C_i such that the next hop relay node must be towards the BS. In other words,

$$Next\_Hop(C_i) = \{C_j \mid C_j \in Com(C_i)\, and\, Dist(C_j, BS) < Dist(C_i, BS)\}$$

5   Proposed Algorithm

Now, we present our proposed algorithm. However, as the basic steps of the GA are repeated until the termination criterion is met, we present all basic steps, namely crossover and mutation along with the chromosome representation, creation of initial population, determining fitness function and the selection process as follows.

5.1   Chromosome Representation

We represent the chromosome as a string of relay nodes. The length of each chromosome is always equal to the number of relay nodes. A chromosome represents the route from each relay node to the BS. A routing schedule for a sub graph network along with the corresponding chromosome of eight relay nodes and one BS is shown in Fig. 3.

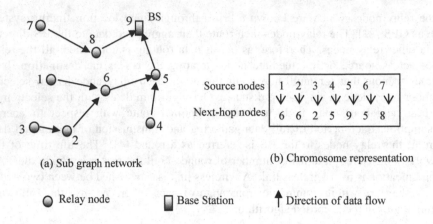

Source nodes	1	2	3	4	5	6	7
	↓	↓	↓	↓	↓	↓	↓
Next-hop nodes	6	6	2	5	9	5	8

(a) Sub graph network   (b) Chromosome representation

⬤ Relay node   ▯ Base Station   ↑ Direction of data flow

Fig. 3. Sub graph network of WSN and the corresponding Chromosome Representation

This is a directed acyclic graph $G(V,E)$, where E represents the edges $(C_i \rightarrow C_j)$, C_i is a relay node and C_j is either a relay node or BS such that C_j is closer to BS than C_i and C_j is within communication range of C_i. Fig. 3(b) is the corresponding chromosome. In this example, the value of the gene in position 1 is 6, indicating that node 1 selects the node 6 for data transmission. The value at 6 is 5 indicates that 5 is the next selected relay node and the value at 5 is 9 indicating the next relay node which is the BS (destination). Therefore the route is expressed as the path $1 \rightarrow 6 \rightarrow 5 \rightarrow 9$.

5.2   Initial Population, Fitness Function and Selection

The initial population is a collection of randomly generated chromosomes which correspond to a valid routing schedule. The valid chromosomes are generated in such a way that the value say j of the gene at position i is randomly selected such that $C_j \in Next\_Hop(C_i)$. As an example, the value at gene position 4, may select 6 or 5 in Fig.3 (a). However, it is shown to select 5 in Fig.3 (b). It is noteworthy that our GA based approach does not depend on any particular algorithm for generating the initial population. Moreover, it neither attempts to find a best route nor it considers the energy consumption of any relay node at the stage of initial population.

Now, we construct a fitness function to evaluate the individuals of the initial population. This helps us for the next step computation of GA, i.e., selection. We note that the total transmission distance covered by all source relay nodes to transmit the aggregated data to the BS is the main factor which we need to minimize. Therefore, our proposed work constructs the fitness function in such a way that the overall distance covered by the relay nodes is minimized in each round. The shorter the total transmission distance, the higher is the fitness value. Thus, each individual is evaluated by the following fitness function

$$Fitness(k) = \frac{1}{\sum_{i=0}^{N-1} Dist(C_i, Crom(k,i))}$$

where, *Fitness* (k) denotes the fitness value of the kth chromosome and $Crom(k,i)$ represents the value of the gene at i^{th} position in the kth chromosome. It is important to note that $Crom(k,i)$ actually represents the next hop neighbour relay node of C_i in the kth chromosome.

For the selection process, we select some valid chromosomes with higher fitness value. In our proposed method, we use tournament selection for selecting the chromosomes with best fitness values from the initial population. All selected chromosomes are used as parents to produce new child chromosomes (offspring) with the help of crossover operation discussed in the following section.

5.3 Crossover

To produce the new offspring from the selected parents, we use 1-point crossover. The crossover operation takes place between two randomly selected chromosomes. Parts of the selected chromosomes are exchanged at some crossover point which is randomly selected. The whole process is shown in Fig.4.

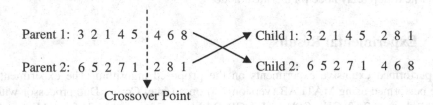

Fig. 4. Crossover Operation

***Lemma* 5.1:** The two child chromosomes produced by the above crossover operation is valid.

Proof: A chromosome is treated valid if it corresponds to a proper routing schedule that indicates a path from every relay node to the BS without any cycle. As mentioned in section 5.1, the chromosomes are generated in such a way that the value j of the ith gene is randomly selected such that $C_j \in Next\_Hop(C_i)$. Therefore, each next-hop relay node is valid. Moreover, there must be at least one relay node which can directly communicate with the BS so that each chromosome must have a route up to the BS. At the time of crossover, GAR just alters two parent chromosomes such that the value of each chromosome at a single gene position only is interchanged. As all parents are valid, therefore, new offspring must also be valid.

5.4   Mutation

We apply mutation at a selected gene rather than randomly selected gene. We select that gene which contributes maximum distance in a round and we call it critical node. We replace the critical node with other node in such a way that the new node must lead to BS covering minimum distance. The replacement of node is occurred as follows. Let i^{th} gene contributes maximum distance, i.e., the distance from C_i to the next-hop relay node is the largest. In that case, our approach searches for any other relay node C_r as next-hop node of C_i such that C_r is closer to C_i. This implies that $Dist (C_i, C_r)$ should be minimum. We also require that the total energy consumption via new relay node should be lesser than any other relay nodes, which implies that $\{(Dist(C_i, C_r))^2 + (Dist(C_r, BS))^2\}$ should be smallest. Combining these two, C_r is selected as the new next-hop relay node, if

$$Dist(C_i, C_r) * \{(Dist(C_i, C_r))^2 + (Dist(C_r, BS))^2\} \text{ is minimum.}$$

Lemma **5.2:** The new chromosome after the above mutation process is valid.

Proof: At the time of mutation, GAR just selects a critical node and replaces a new next hop relay node. Since all valid offspring are generated in crossover operation, we can say that mutation does not hamper the validity of these offspring by replacing a proper next-hop relay node for a critical node.

6   Experimental Results

We performed extensive experiments on the proposed algorithm. The experiments were performed using MATLAB (version 7.5) on an Intel Core 2 Duo processor with T9400 chipset, 2.53 GHz CPU and 2 GB RAM running on the platform Microsoft Windows Vista. For the experiments, we considered a WSN scenario assuming that the relay nodes are deployed in 200×200 square meter area and the position of the sink is (215,100). We use the same energy model and the corresponding typical parameters as have been used in LEACH [4]. We considered an initial population of 300 chromosomes. For crossover operation, we selected the best 5% chromosomes using tournament selection procedure. The proposed algorithm was run for 150 iterations. However, it started showing high-quality results after 30 epochs. We ran it by varying the relay nodes from 4 to 40. For the comparison purpose, we also ran the MHRM [14] algorithm as also done in [5], keeping the experimental parameters same as that of the proposed algorithm. The simulated results of both the algorithms are compared in terms of in terms of number rounds (i.e., network life time) and energy consumption, as shown in Fig. 5.

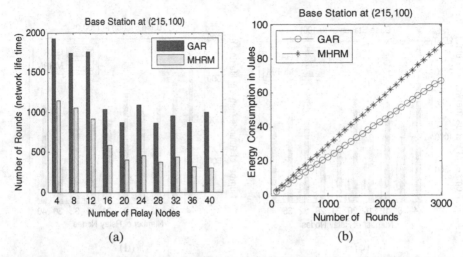

Fig. 5. Performance Comparison between GAR and MHRM in (a) Number of rounds (network life time) (b) Energy consumption in Jules

We also compare both the algorithms with respect to the total distance covered in each round. This can be observed from Fig. 6(a) that GAR covers significantly less distance than MHRM in a single round. We also ran GAR and MHRM after changing the position of the BS at several points i.e., (0, 0), (0, 100) and (200, 0) and compared results as shown in Fig. 6(b-d). It demonstrates that GAR outperforms the MHRM in network life time for all these cases.

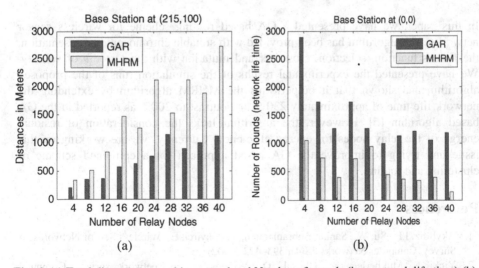

Fig. 6. (a) Total distance covered in a round and Number of rounds (i.e., network life time) (b) BS at (0, 0), (c) BS at (0, 100) and (d) BS at (200, 0)

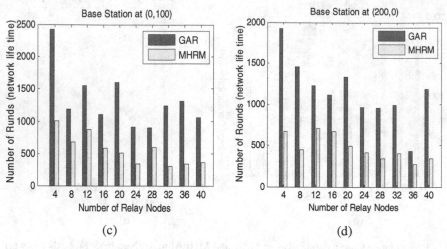

Fig. 6. (*Continued*)

It is clear from all these figures that the proposed algorithm can significantly extend the network life time in terms of rounds by approximately 230% compared to MHRM and hence is an improvement over the algorithm by the GA based algorithm by Ataul Bari et al. [5].

7   Conclusions

In this paper, we have presented a GA based routing scheme for wireless sensor networks. The algorithm has been provided with suitable chromosome representation, the fitness function, selection, crossover and mutation with their proofs of validity. We have presented the experimental results of the simulation runs of the proposed algorithm and shown that it outperforms the MHRM algorithm by extending the network life time of approximately 230 % in contrast to 200% as reported in the GA based algorithm [5]. However, the algorithm lacks the consideration of residual energy of the relay nodes for energy efficiency. Currently, we are working on this issue and trying to improve the GA based approach for a combined scheme of clustering and routing.

References

1. Akyildiz, I.F., Su, W., Sankarasubramaniam, Y., Cayirci, E.: Wireless Sensor Networks: A Survey. Computer Networks 38(4), 393–422 (2002)
2. Yick, J., Mukherjee, B., Ghosal, D.: Wireless sensor network survey. Computer Networks 52, 2292–2330 (2008)
3. Chong, C.-Y., Kumar, S.P.: Sensor networks: evolution, opportunities, and challenges. Proceedings of the IEEE 91(8), 1247–1256 (2003)

4. Heinzelman, W., Chandrakasan, A., Balakrishnan, H.: Energy efficient communication protocol for wireless micro-sensor networks. In: Proceedings of the 33rd HICSS, pp. 3005–3014 (2000)
5. Bari, A., Wazed, S., Jaekel, A., Bandyopadhyay, S.: A genetic algorithm based approach for energy efficient routing in two-tiered sensor networks. Ad Hoc Networks 7(4), 665–676 (2009) ISSN: 1570-8705
6. Hamed Abbasi, A., Younis, M.: A Survey on clustering algorithms for wireless sensor networks. Computer Communications 30, 2826–2841 (2007)
7. Boyinbode, O., et al.: A Survey on Clustering Algorithms for Wireless Sensor Networks. In: 13th International Conference on Network-Based Information Systems, pp. 358–364. IEEE (2010)
8. Anastasi, G., et al.: Energy conservation in wireless sensor networks: A survey. Ad Hoc Networks 7, 537–568 (2009)
9. Kim, K.T., et al.: An Energy Efficient Routing Protocol in Wireless Sensor Networks. In: Proc. of Int. Conf. on Comp. Sc. and Engg., pp. 132–139. IEEE (2009)
10. Lattanzi, E., et al.: Energetic sustainability of routing algorithms for energy-harvesting wireless sensor networks. Computer Communication 30, 2976–2986 (2007)
11. Tang, J., Hao, B., Sen, A.: Relay node placement in large scale wireless sensor networks. Computer Communications 4(29), 490–501 (2006)
12. Kuila, P., Jana, P.K.: Improved Load Balanced Clustering Algorithm for Wireless Sensor Networks. In: Thilagam, P.S., Pais, A.R., Chandrasekaran, K., Balakrishnan, N. (eds.) ADCONS 2011. LNCS, vol. 7135, pp. 399–404. Springer, Heidelberg (2012)
13. Gupta, G., Younis, M.: Load-balanced clustering of wireless sensor networks. In: ICC 2003. IEEE International Conference, vol. 3, pp. 1848–1852 (2003)
14. Chiang, S.-S., Huang, C.-H., Chang, K.-C.: A Minimum Hop routing Protocol for Home Security Systems Using Wireless Sensor Networks. IEEE Transactions on Consumer Electronics 53(4), 1483–1489 (2007)
15. Akkaya, K., Younis, M.: A survey on routing protocols for wireless sensor networks. Ad Hoc Networks 3, 325–349 (2005)
16. Saleem, M., Di Caro, G.A., Farooq, M.: Swarm intelligence based routing protocol for wireless sensor networks: Survey and future directions. Information Sciences 181, 4597–4624 (2011)
17. Boselin Prabhu, S.R., et al.: A Survey of Adaptive Distributed Clustering Algorithms for Wireless Sensor Networks. International Journal of Computer Science & Engineering Survey (IJCSES) 2(4), 165–176 (2011)
18. Huruiala, P.C., Urzica, A., Gheorghe, L.: Hierarchical Routing Protocol based on Evolutionary Algorithms for Wireless Sensor Networks. In: Roedunet International Conference, RoEduNet (2010)
19. Chakraborty, A., Mitra, S.K., Naskar, M.K.: A Genetic Algorithm inspired Routing Protocol for Wireless Sensor Networks. Int. J. of Computational Intelligence Theory and Practice 6(1) (2011)
20. Badia, L., Botta, A., Lenzini, L.: A genetic approach to joint routing and link scheduling for wireless mesh networks. Journal Ad Hoc Networks (2009)
21. Goldberg, D.E.: Genetic Algorithms: Search Optimization and Machine Learning. Addison Wesley, Massachusetts
22. Han, A., Liu, Y.: Research on Routing Algorithm Based on the ZigBee-GPRS Technology and the Hypergraph Model. Journal of Computational Information Systems 8(9), 3895–3902 (2012)

Prediction of Processor Utilization
for Real-Time Multimedia Stream Processing Tasks*

Henryk Krawczyk, Jerzy Proficz, and Bartłomiej Daca

Gdansk University of Technology, Narutowicza 11/12,
80-233 Gdansk, Poland
hkrawk@pg.gda.pl, {jerp,bdaca}@task.gda.pl

Abstract. Utilization of MPUs in a computing cluster node for multimedia stream processing is considered. Non-linear increase of processor utilization is described and a related class of algorithms for multimedia real-time processing tasks is defined. For such conditions, experiments measuring the processor utilization and output data loss were proposed and their results presented. A new formula for prediction of utilization was proposed and its verification for a representative set of tasks was performed.

Keywords: processor utilization prediction, real-time, multimedia, KASKADA platform.

1   Introduction

Various types of processing tasks cause different types of load: computation, memory, network etc. One of the most underestimated types is load appearing between RAM (Random Access Memory) and a processor cache memory. Fig. 1 presents an example of a typical architecture of a computation node used in a computation cluster. A multi-core processing unit (MPU) contains its own fast memory which is easily accessible, with high clock frequency, by its computation cores. On the other hand, the RAM is connected using much lower frequency as well as with a limited number of channels, what causes the possibility of performance bottleneck when some cores cannot get requested data from the RAM.

In this paper we focus on real-time multimedia related tasks execution by an MPU node. Our main aim is to find a model to predict processor utilization of a given computational node for a specific set of tasks realizing algorithms processing multimedia streams. Such model was necessary to implement the KASKADA platform (Polish abbreviation of Context Analysis of Camera Data Streams for Alert Defining Applications) built and utilized within the MAYDAY EURO 2012 project realized in Academic Computer Centre (TASK) of Gdansk University of Technology [1].

---

* The work was realized as a part of MAYDAY EURO 2012 project, Operational Program Innovative Economy 2007--2013, Priority 2 „Infrastructure area R&D".

C. Hota and P.K. Srimani (Eds.): ICDCIT 2013, LNCS 7753, pp. 278–289, 2013.

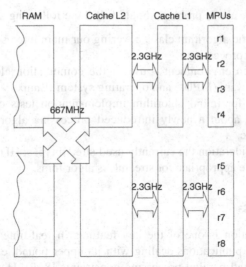

Fig. 1. A typical architecture of a computation node

1.1   Motivation

Multimedia processing is an essential part of the KASKADA platform, a soft real-time system dedicated for development and execution of the stream analysis algorithms, implemented as computation tasks and exposed to the user applications through web services. The main mechanisms and architecture of the platform including its main software and hardware components were described in [2,3].

The platform places only one stream type per node, where the stream type is defined by the same frequency and bandwidth of the processed streams. In such a case ,i.e. for streams with the same frequency, the theoretical utilization bound is 100%, even for the hard real-time constraints, where any data loss is unacceptable [4]. Moreover the total processor utilization for a node with a set of tasks executed concurrently is expected to be the sum of their processor utilizations, measured for each of them when running on the same node exclusively.

Thus the task allocation on the particular nodes in the whole cluster is assumed to be performed according to a specific heuristic solving the bin packing problem [5], based on the Best-Fit-Descending algorithm, to deal with variable sizes of the executed tasks and finite number of available computational nodes [6].

Initial utilization and output data loss measurements showed a non-linear increase of processor utilization for increasing task number. Moreover, for high node's processors utilization the amount of output data differed significantly. For such a case we found a lot of data stream elements missing, and the data loss depended on the stream type, task algorithm complexity and tasks number. This behavior seems to be caused by higher RAM-to-cache data exchange, when more tasks are executed concurrently.

The solution for the above problem should fulfill the following assumptions:

- it concerns a specific algorithm class, covering our main interests including typical multimedia stream processing,
- it reflects the given environment – use of the computation cluster environment, with a typical hardware (MPUs) and operating system (Linux),
- only a low effort for initial algorithm implementation tests can be accepted, *a priori* information about a newly introduced processing algorithm should be as minimal as possible,
- it takes under consideration the currently used stream types: HD, PAL and AUDIO as well as should be appropriate for streamless algorithms.

1.2   Related Works

The processor utilization is one of the key features in real-time systems' analysis. There are myriads of publications dealing with its upper bound, e.g. [7,4], related to scheduler heuristics and parallel processing constraints [8, 9]. However, all of them consider task utilization being simply additive without taking into account the memory bandwidth influence, which is not the case as we could notice non-linearity in its increase.

On the other hand, analysis of memory (RAM) falling behind the processors (including its cache memory) with the faster and faster clock speeds causes the occurrence of the so-called 'memory wall' [10]. It can be especially laborious for tasks processing massive streams of data, e.g. uncompressed multimedia content.

The idea of performance modeling and prediction including memory bandwidth is proposed in [11]. The procedure consists of the following steps: 1) benchmarking the machine, 2) collecting application characteristics, 3) system tuning and 4) application improvement. The specific set of tools was developed to support the steps, however the procedure needed to be executed manually.

In [12] a genetic algorithm extending the above approach was proposed. It enables automatic memory bandwidth modeling, which enables the prediction of the performance of an HPC application. The idea of the algorithm is to teach the bandwidth as a function of cache hit rates with the Multi MAPS benchmark as the fitness test.

An interesting model combining memory bandwidth and computational power of a processor was proposed by Williams et al. in [13]. They introduced additional application performance metric called "operational intensity", which indicates the number of floating point operations per one byte read from RAM memory (in FLOPS/byte).Thus, for the benchmarked application and the given MPU, the maximum used computational power can be predicted.

Alas, the above models are only useful for memory traffic prediction in the case of executing one application per one or more nodes. Hence we need to provide our own approach dealing with multiple independent tasks executed concurrently on the same node.

1.3   Contribution

Our contributions described in this article are summarized below:
- a definition of the multimedia stream processing algorithm class (section 2.1),
- an evaluation of the Intel Xeon E5345 processor for execution of sets of tasks realizing the algorithms belonging to the described class (section 3),
- a formula for prediction of processor utilization for the computational node by the tasks realizing algorithms of the defined class, depending solely on the specific hardware and stream type, but not on a specific algorithm (section 4.1).

The next section describes the considered algorithm class, providing its definition and proposing implementation details. The third section presents the evaluation experiments including a description of the test procedure and environment, benchmark algorithms and the results. The fourth section provides our estimation of processor utilization with the proposed formula, correction function and its empirical verification. The last section provides final remarks containing the conclusions and future works.

2   The Class of Multimedia Processing Algorithms

2.1   The Definition

In our considerations we assume a specific algorithm class. All tasks processing the streams are going to work according to the control-flow diagram presented in Fig. 2. In general an algorithm works in a loop which consists of the following steps:
- reception of an input data element – a chunk of data, e.g. a video frame or a bunch of audio samples, is received, unmarshaled and placed in the RAM memory, these actions require intensive RAM-to-cache communication,
- processing of the element – only this step depends on the specific algorithm, we assume that the computations are performed here,
- sending the processed element – the processed element is marshaled and sent to its destination, i.e. the next task in the pipeline or a streaming server providing the results to the user.

The above loop is preceded and followed by standard steps, executed only once during the processing lifetime:
- initialization of communication, when the connections to the input and output data streams are established and appropriate resources are allocated,
- finalization of communication, when the connections to the input and output data streams are closed, and related resources are released.

Our assumption is that a typical task for a specific stream type has a constant part of communication between processor, RAM and cache memory (RAM-to-cache), see Fig. 3. For this concern the typical algorithm should avoid memory copying and memory allocation for large objects, because it can significantly affect the node's processors utilization.

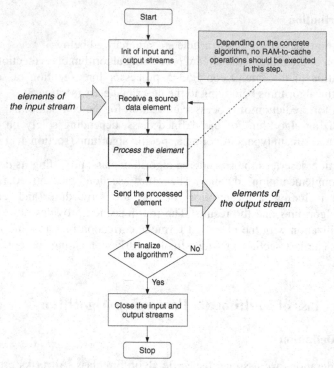

Fig. 2. A control flow diagram of the multimedia stream processing algorithm class

2.2   The Implementation

Algorithms of the described class are developed and executed in the multimedia processing system called the KASKADA platform. The platform is a middleware solution facilitating heavy multimedia processing in a supercomputer environment. It wraps the tasks implementing the algorithms into the web services, supporting SOAP and Active MQ protocols [2].

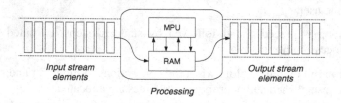

Fig. 3. Stream elements flow in the computational node

The described class is very broad and can be used for many types of multimedia analysis and processing, e.g. face recognition, background mask, crowd measurements, etc. However all these algorithms are built according to the same template and perform similar tasks. Moreover, the algorithms managed by the platform need to behave according to certain rules in order to keep stable environment for other executed computational tasks.

KASKADA framework is such a template. It is a C++ library with the classes and methods to support multimedia algorithms. Its main functionality covers audio/video stream decoding and encoding, C++ object serialization and inter-algorithm delivery, multimedia streams handling, dynamic tasks launching and basic life-cycle management support.

3   Evaluation Experiments

3.1   Benchmarks Algorithms, Procedure and Environment

We can perceive a single node as a computer containing two Intel Xeon E5345processors with four processing cores each ($P=8$), 8GB of operational memory, an InfiniBand20Gb/s network interface, and a small 165GB hard disk. The node works under a Debian Linux ver. 2.6.22.19 operating system.

The typical processing for the KASKADA platform copes with multimedia streams analysis and modification. The set of tasks, implementing the algorithms of the specified class (see sec. 2.1), used for the evaluations including the following executables:

- *relayer* – an implementation of an empty algorithm, forwarding the incoming input stream to the output, without any processing;
- *clock* – an implementation of a simple algorithm receiving a video stream, tagging it with the current time and passing the results as the output stream;
- *face detector* – an implementation of an algorithm recognizing faces in the incoming video stream every n-th frame and drawing a frame around the detected object, the marked images are transmitted as the output stream; implemented using the *Viola-Jones* object detection framework[14];
- *contours detection* – an implementation of an algorithm detecting contours on a video frame and drawing it on the image; implemented using *Canny* contour detection algorithm[15];
- *video merger* – an implementation of an algorithm merging two low resolution video streams into one, scaling its size and forwarding it to the output.

The above algorithms were implemented with support of the *OpenCV* library, which is the de facto standard for image analysis and modification[16].

Table 1 presents combinations of the above algorithms with the available data streams. For the given node only algorithms with low complexity can be used for video HD streams, otherwise the data loss is too high to be accepted by the user. PAL testing video stream's resolution was 704x576px and its frame rate – 20fps. Stream denoted by HD has resolution 1920x1080px and 30fps frame rate.

During the experiments we decided to record the following metrics:

- processor utilization – reflecting performance of the node, the high utilization level means weaker performance of the analyzed algorithm,
- output data loss – related to reliability, low loss of data elements in comparison to the ones generated by the algorithm means better reliability.

Table 1. The considered taskconfigurations

Task Configuration	Computation Complexity	Tested video stream type	
		PAL	HD
Relayer	None	+	+
Clock	Low	+	+
Face detection every 32nd frame	Medium	+	-
Face detection every 16th frame	Medium	+	-
Face detection every 4th frame	High	+	-
Contours detection	Medium	+	-
Video merger	Medium	+	-

In Linux, the average utilization can be easily measured using system standard tools like *top* or *ps*. The output data loss depends on the specific task algorithm and is determined by counting the number of the output data stream elements. The other measurements cover such factors like network load and memory usage.

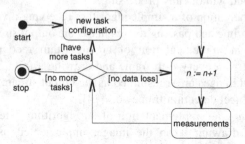

Fig. 4. The measurement procedure

We arbitrarily assume the output data loss to be acceptable as long as it is 1% or lower. Therefore our measuring procedure, presented in Fig. 4, iterates through the increasing stream number $n=1, 2...$ until the data loss is above the threshold, when the next task configuration is executed, or the whole procedure ends. Table 1 shows the task configurations prepared for the scalability tests. Note that at any given moment, only one task configuration is tested against multiple data streams.

The infrastructure used for the speedup measurements is presented in Fig. 5. The source streams archived in the mass storage are read by the decoding nodes, unpacked and transferred to the tested node, where the tasks are executed according to the assumed configuration (Table 1) and the measurements are performed. Afterwards, the processed streams are forwarded to the encoding nodes, packed and stored. Finally, the archived streams are checked for data loss.

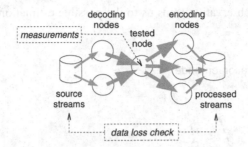

Fig. 5. The considered cluster infrastructure for single node evaluation

3.2   The Experimental Results

The results of the experiments are summarized in Table 2. In accordance with the assumed configurations (Table 1), 7 configurations processing PAL streams and 2 configurations processing HD streams were tested. The HD configurations could be executed only exclusively on the node, i.e. more than 1 HD task on 1 node causes unacceptable (over 1%) output data loss.

For PAL configurations, there is a possibility to execute more tasks on a single node, however the increase of the measured utilization is disproportional to the number of the deployed tasks, e.g. a Relayer task utilizes 0.68% of the node MPUs, working exclusively on the node and the same task utilizes 2.38% of the node MPUs with other tasks working concurrently.

Table 2. The results of the experiments. y– utilization of the node for 1 task exclusively, n_{max} – the maximum task number on the node with low data loss ($\leq 1\%$), y_{max}– utilization of the node for maximal number of tasks, y_{max}/n_{max}– utilization per 1 task for the maximal number of tasks.

Task Configuration	Y	n_{max}	Y_{max}	Y_{max}/n_{max}
Relayer (PAL)	0.68%	20	47.55%	2.38%
Clock (PAL)	1.87%	14	48.19%	3.44%
Face detection every 32nd frame (PAL)	7.55%	10	89.59%	8.96%
Face detection every 16th frame (PAL)	8.77%	8	81.00%	10.13%
Face detection every 4th frame (PAL)	28.65%	3	92.86%	30.95%
Video merger (PAL)	4.15%	9	68.99%	7.67%
Contours detection (PAL)	5.05%	11	99.22%	9.02%
Relayer (HD)	9.48%	1	9.48%	9.48%
Clock (HD)	14.87%	1	14.87%	14.87%

The PAL results are presented in a chart form in Fig. 6. It is characteristic that the non-linearity is less visible for more complex algorithms, where the computations are more intensive. This observation leads us to the possible estimation formula for node utilization prediction.

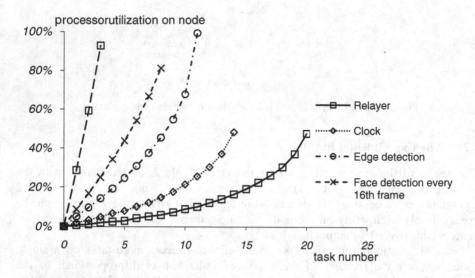

Fig. 6. The visualization of the experiments results for tasks processing PAL streams

4   Estimation for Utilization

4.1   The Formula of the Estimated Utilization

Let's assume that a set of tasks executed on a computation node c of a homogenous cluster C is denoted by T, an i-th element (task) of this set is described as follow:

$$t_i = (a_i, SI_i, SO_i, \gamma_i) \tag{1}$$

where a_i is the task algorithm, SI_i is the set of input streams, SO_i is the set of output streams and γ_i is the load which the t_i causes on the computation node, being executed exclusively.

Having a constant RAM-to-cache part of an algorithm, we argue that the increase of the node MPUs utilization is different for every additional stream processing task started at the node, even if it utilizes the same algorithm and data. Moreover, the increase depends on the number of concurrently processed streams at the node, i.e. the utilization is estimated according to the following equation:

$$\gamma(c, T) \approx \eta_h(\textstyle\sum_{i=1}^{|T|} |SI_i|) \sum_{i=1}^{|T|} \gamma_i \tag{2}$$

where the η_h is so-called correction function, representing a deviation from the linear utilization increase.

The experimental results show the increase of the node utilization by a task in case it is executed concurrently with other tasks. However, this observation is visible for

PAL configurations only. All tasks processing HD stream could be executed only exclusively on a node. Any attempt to start even only 2 tasks of the simplest algorithm caused unacceptable level of output data loss (>1%).

The correction function can be determined using the equation (3) – transformed formula (2):

$$\eta_{pal}(n) = \frac{\gamma(c, T_n)}{n\,\gamma} \tag{3}$$

where η_{pal} is the correction function, $\gamma(c, T_n)$ is the measured utilization for a given cluster node c and a set of n tasks: $T_n = \{t_1 = t,\ t_2 = t,\ \dots\ t_n = t\}$ and $t = (a, \{si\}, \{so\}, \gamma)$, where a is the measured algorithm, having a PAL input stream si and PAL output stream so, and γ is the load which t causes on the computation node c, being executed exclusively.

According to the formula(2), we can use the measured utilization of an arbitrary chosen task configuration, however we can notice the higher influence of external factors like the node operating system or network traffic in the case of lower measures. Thus for low task numbers we decided to use more complex algorithms: *face detection every 32nd and 16th frame*, and for higher task numbers: *relayer* and *clock*.

Fig. 7.presents the correction function chart. It shows that up to 6 processed streams, the utilization increase is almost linear (~1.0), but afterwards it grows in a much faster pace.

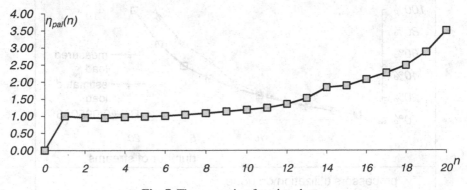

Fig. 7. The correction function chart

4.2   Verification of the Estimation Formula

To confirm the determined function we used the three measured algorithms: *face detection every 4th frame, video streams merging* and *contours detection in the video stream*. The results of the verification are presented in Fig. 8.We can observe that the predicted utilization is close to the real one, measured in the experiments, and the calculated square of Pearson correlation coefficient(R^2) values are over 0.95. The best results were achieved for lower tasks numbers (12 and less for *video merger* and 10 and less for *contours detector*). *Face detector*'s maximum number of tasks was predicted correctly, in the *video merger* algorithm case tasks number was underestimated by 1 and number of *contours detection* tasks was overestimated by 1.

5   Final Remarks

We proposed a new method for prediction of node MPUs utilization for a specific class of algorithms. The presented experiment results show that the method is correct for the tested hardware and the given implementation. It was used for allocation purposes within a cluster environment – the KASKADA platform.

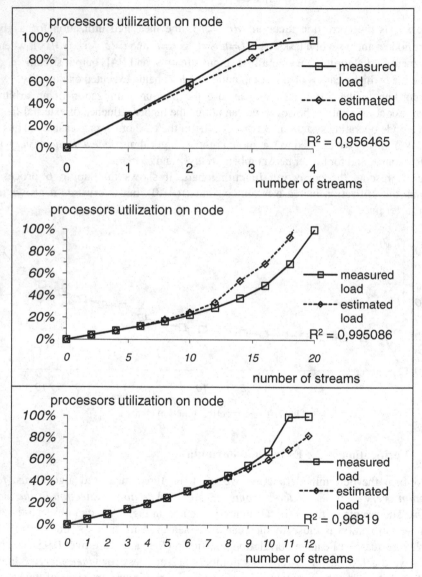

Fig. 8. Node utilization generated by tasks: face detection every 16th frame, video merger, contours detection(respectively).

The future works are going to be focused on the verification of the method in more advanced hardware/system environment and more efficient, optimized implementation of the framework for implementing algorithms. Furthermore, we plan to introduce direct hardware monitoring for memory bandwidth, enabling direct control of the memory traffic between MPUs and RAM.

References

1. Academic Computer Centre in Gdansk – TASK, http://www.task.gda.pl
2. Krawczyk, H., Knopa, R., Proficz, J.: Basic management strategies on KASKADA platform. In: EUROCON (2011)
3. Krawczyk, H., Proficz, J.: Real-Time Multimedia Stream Data Processing. In: Supercomputer Environment, Interactive Multimedia, pp. 289–312. InTech (2012)
4. Chen, D., Mok, A.K., Kuo, T.-W.: Utilization bound revisited. IEEE Transactions on Computers 52(3), 351–361 (2003)
5. Garey, M.R., Johnson, D.S.: Computers and Intractability: A Guide to the Theory of NP-Completeness. Series of Books in the Mathematical Sciences. W.H. Freeman, New York (1979)
6. Krawczyk, H., Proficz, J.: The task graph assignment for KASKADA platform. In: Proceedings of the International Conference on Software and Data Technologies, ICSOFT (2010)
7. Liu, C.L., Layland, J.W.: Scheduling Algorithms for Multiprogramming in a Hard Real-Time Environment. Journal of the Association for Computing Machinery 20(1), 46–61 (1973)
8. Lopez, J.M., Diaz, J.L., Garcia, D.F.: Utilization bounds for EDF Scheduling on Real-Time Multiprocessor Systems. Real-Time Systems 28(1), 39–68 (2004)
9. Qi, X., Zhu, D., Aydin, H.: Cluster scheduling for real-time systems: utilization bounds and run-time overhead. Real-Time Systems 47(3), 253–284 (2011)
10. Wulf, W.A., McKee Sally, A.: Hitting the Memory Wall: Implications of the Obvious. ACM SIGARCH Computer Architecture News 23(1), 20–24 (1995)
11. Snavely, A., Carrington, L., Wolter, N., Labarta, J., Badia, R., Purkayastha, A.: A Framework for Application Performance Modeling and Prediction, Baltimore MD (2002)
12. Tikir, M., Carrington, L., Strohmaier, E., Snavely, A.: A Genetic Algorithms Approach to Modeling the Performance of Memory-bound Computations. In: Proceedings of SC 2007, Reno, NV (2007)
13. Williams, S., Waterman, A., Patterson, D.: Roofilne: an insightful visual performance model for multicore architectures. Communications of the ACM 52(4), 65–76 (2009)
14. Viola, P., Jones, M.: Robust Real-time Object Detection. International Journal of Computer Vision (2001)
15. Canny, J.: A Computational Approach To Edge Detection. IEEE Trans. Pattern Analysis and Machine Intelligence 8(6), 679–698 (1986)
16. Pulli, K., Baksheev, A., Kornyakov, K., Eruhimov, V.: Real-time computer vision with OpenCV. Communications of the ACM 55(6), 61–69 (2012)

An Architecture for Dynamic Web Service Provisioning Using Peer-to-Peer Networks

Sujoy Mistry[1], Dibyanshu Jaiswal[2], Sagar Virani[2],
Arijit Mukherjee[3], and Nandini Mukherjee[2]

[1] School of Mobile Computing and Communications, Jadavpur University
[2] Dept. of Computer Science and Engineering, Jadavpur University
[3] Innovation Labs, Tata Consultancy Services, Kolkata

Abstract. Grid computing has made it possible for users to create complex applications by combining globally distributed data and analysis components and deploy them on geographically distributed resources for execution. Introduction of ad-hoc Virtual Organizations based on on-demand service provisioning further enhances this architectural concept. Job-based paradigms or reliance on relatively static UDDI lead to a failure in offering the complete dynamism of a heterogeneous distributed Grid. A possible alternative is the use of dynamic peer-to-peer (P2P) techniques within a Web Service based Grid to introduce the ability of the network to adapt to resource volatility already established in P2P-based content-delivery models. In this paper, we present the architecture of a demand-driven Web Service deployment framework that allows sharing of data and computing capacity using P2P technology as its backbone. We focus on various issues such as resource availability, scalability and abstraction. Demand-driven resource allocation is based on request parameters and availability of the resources to create the basis for a fully dynamic virtual market place of computational resources.

Keywords: Peer-to-Peer, UDDI, SOA, Web Services, Grid Computing, Virtual Organization, Virtual Market Place.

1 Introduction

Ad-hoc collaboration between different geographically distributed organizations increased rapidly because of recent major improvements in distributed systems which led to newer challenges such as heterogeneity, scalability and availability in distributed computing. Service Oriented Architectures(SOA)[1] and Grid computing[3] are some of the major innovative technologies which has been recently used by several organizations to provide solutions to distributed computing challenges. The fast expansion of inter-networking has created a situation where service or resource discovery and service deployment are amongst the major challenges for distributed computing. Grid and P2P are the most important technologies which break the nature of conventional distributed computing for sharing resources among the remotely distributed nodes. The emergence of the service-oriented model and Web Services paved the way for development

C. Hota and P.K. Srimani (Eds.): ICDCIT 2013, LNCS 7753, pp. 290–301, 2013.

of several Grid and Cloud computing platforms with a new approach for creating loosely-coupled dynamic distributed systems. To facilitate the evolution of these frameworks, several standards like the WS-Resource Framework (WS-RF)[6], WS- Interoperability Framework (WS-I) have been put forward by research groups and have been adopted by the standards bodies like W3C[4].

Some of the major challenges in research on SOA-centric distributed systems are resource/service discovery and on-demand deployment of computational entities (jobs or services) on dynamically acquired resources. The commonly available job-oriented frameworks such as Condor[7] is capable of acquiring idle resources from a pool by matching the requirements of a job in the queue and the resource characteristics. However, dynamic job-based frameworks has one constraint and i.e. after the execution of the job, it is removed from the queue, and for each subsequent invocation, the execution code and data must be resubmitted. As a contrast, dynamic deployment of services has amongst others, one major advantage: once the service is deployed, it stays on the resource until explicitly removed and the initial cost of deployment can be shared across multiple invocations. Projects like DynaSOAr[12] offer infrastructures to dynamically deploy services as and when required on a set of available resources with a clear separation between Web Service Providers who offer services to the consumers, and Host Providers, who offer computational resources on which the services are deployed. DynaSOAr, however suffers from issues related to dynamic service metadata and volatile resources, as it uses UDDI[9] as its registry, and fails to offer complete dynamism over a changing set of resources. With the advent of the Web Services model, UDDI became the standard technology for Web service discovery. It provides a centralized keyword based mechanism for service publication and discovery and thus the major drawback is the existence of a single point failure. Further, UDDI is primarily static in nature and fails to consider the inherent volatility of Grid resources, the effect of which is observed in DynaSOAr.

In this context, we are developing a fully distributed SOA-oriented framework which offers loose coupling, robustness, scalability, availability and extensibility for large-scale grid systems. In this paper the proposed distributed architecture acts as the basis of a service-oriented grid using P2P as its communication backbone, thus allowing more flexibility and dynamism when compared to previous approaches used for dynamic service deployment in grid environment. The main goals of the new architecture as mentioned below:

o To provide a distributed environment to overcome issues associated with centralized registry based architectures.
o To allow clients and service Providers mention specific requirements for a service in order to achieve desired quality of service for clients.
o To provide scalability by load-balancing of deployed instances and re-deploying on demand using a P2P communication model.

The paper is organized as follows: Section 2 gives the related work prior and alike to our architecture. Section 3 describes the actual concept and architecture of newly developed framework, as well as the implementation of the system.

Results of the developed system is given in Section 4 and discussion and future work in Section 5.

2   Background and Related Work

The popularization of Internet has made it possible for users to consume globally distributed services, which has also increased the use of internet resources and is symbolized by the advent of Grid/Cloud computing. Distributed applications have undergone a lot of changes after the introduction of service-orientation and Web Services within the Grid environment using standards like WSDL[10] for service description and SOAP[11] for message communication. Although a lot of work exists for resource discovery in grid, only few narrow down towards dynamic service deployment.

Dynamic deployment refers to demand-driven installation of the analysis code at run-time in such a way that the host computational node or the web server need not be restarted. In essence, the dynamic deployment referred here is equivalent to remote evaluation available in job scheduling systems, where the execution code from a consumer is sent to a remote resource for execution. One advantage of dynamic service deployment over a job based framework (like Condor or Globus) is that once the service is deployed, the deployed cost can be shared over many invocations of the service till the service is explicitly removed, whereas, in case of jobs, once the execution is over, it is removed from the job queue, and each subsequent execution requires the execution code and data to be resubmitted to the cluster. Some of the well known project like DynaSOAr, WSpeer[13], HAND[14], P2P Web Service Oriented Architecture works on this approach[15].

Among these frameworks, *DynaSOAr* can be differentiated by its unique architectural concept of separating the Web Service Provider from the Host Provider. The authors argue that a service provider may not always possess the resources for actual execution and may involve another organization for this purpose, creating ad-hoc virtual organizations. With the advent of different paradigms in Cloud Computing, we note that this concept is actually true in practice. The main advantages of this architecture are: (i) complete service orientation, (ii) one-time deployment of services and (iii) separation of service provisioning and resource provisioning. It was also claimed that in real-life scenarios, the service may have been advertised, but not deployed at the time of the consumer request, or the actual deployment endpoint may be overloaded at that point of time. DynaSOAr offered a framework where a consumer request for a service would be processed by a host most suited for the requirements specified by the consumer. If there were no existing deployments, an automatic deployment of the service will be triggered within the framework in a way transparent to the consumer. However, one of the major disadvantages of DynaSOAr was its reliance on a relatively static UDDI registry service known as Grimoires [17] which because of the static nature, failed to consider the volatility of resources within a Grid environment.

WSPeer provides a framework for deploying and invoking Web Services in dynamic manner. It offers two implementation for dynamic service invocation - (i) UDDI based which uses a centralized registry similar to DynaSOAr and (ii) P2PS based[16], which uses a pluggable architecture of peers communicating via abstract channels called pipes along with a tree of interfaces. It aims for each node to act as a complete interface to both publishing and invoking services, enabling applications to expose themselves as service oriented peers placing it self in between the layers of the application. Though devoid of service deployments, service requests are fetched solely on the basis of direct communication between the peers via Pipes.

HAND also provides dynamic Web Service Deployment using Globus Toolkit v4 container. HAND-C provides container-level dynamic deployment, i.e. during dynamic deployment the whole container is redeployed. Alternatively, HAND-S provides service deployment, where instead of whole container being deployed only the required service needs to be deployed.

Although these architectures support dynamic deployment, none of them offer full dynamism over a changing set of resources. Our aim is to find a perfect blend of the Web Services technologies as well as the distributed/grid and P2P environment of the resources for faster access and less failure at lower costs while serving the consumers.

3 Dynamic Service Provisioning in P2P Networks

3.1 Concepts

A static UDDI registry is one of the main bottlenecks in the service discovery mechanism of a distributed Web Service architecture. After the advent of the peer-to-peer (P2P) architecture, which is by far one of the most decentralized and distributed architectures, a combination of the peer-to-peer concepts with those of Web Services appears as the most promising model for a dynamic Web Service deployment framework. The decentralization concepts of a P2P network and its ability to handle a volatile set of resources combined with the capability of dynamic service deployment based on consumer demand will create a framework where the resources will be able to fulfill the need of virtual organizations(VO) and virtual marketplaces in terms of computation.

Our architecture is based on the concepts of P2P computing to enable dynamic on-demand service discovery and deployment on networked entities. In this approach we try to use the idle resources in the network via service deployments among those distributed resources on the basis of their capability and load factors. The concept of separating Service Provider and Resource Provider within this distributed environment also enhances the performance of data intensive jobs. In the real life scientific research fields, many research problems require lot of resources to analyze high volume of data. In most cases, the research organizations try to pool the computing resources from all over the world, and a P2P-oriented on-demand service deployment framework is likely to suit such requirements.

3.2 Proposed Architecture

Our architecture provides on-demand service deployment features over a network of computing resources using the peer-to-peer concepts. In this framework, although all the nodes are connected to each other, there is a clear distinction between them - some of the nodes act as provider of Web Services, whereas some are provider of computational resources. The key features of this architecture (shown in Figure 1) are:

a) Complete segregation of provider of services and provider of resources.
b) All the nodes act as peers to each other providing P2P based service publication, discovery, deployment and management.
c) Resource discovery and allocation in a heterogeneous environment as per resource availability and metric of the Web Service.
d) Scheduling of consumer requests following some basic scheduling algorithms like round-robin (RR) and least recently used (LRU).

The architecture is composed of three distinct layers: (i) The Consumer, who can request for any service available, from anywhere at any point of time; (ii) The Web Service Provider (WSP), who provide services to the consumer and takes care of all the collaboration with hosts; and (iii) The Host Provider (HP), who provides resources and platform for service execution.

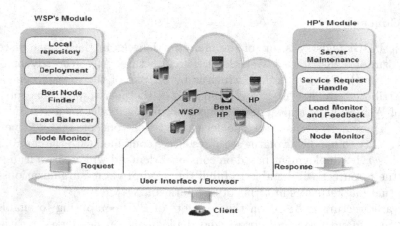

Fig. 1. Basic Architecture

The nodes willing to join the network register by providing its detailed information such as the node category (WSP or HP), host operating system, and other necessary information such as processor frequency, remaining physical memory. The WSP acts as the intermediary between consumers and computing hosts, to process service request while keeping the process completely transparent to the consumer. A WSP is responsible for managing service publication, handling consumer requests, choosing the best suited host for service deployment and/or request processing. During the request processing, WSP fetches every service request form the Deployed nodes according to the present load of the host. The WSP maintains a local repository of Web Services and a list of hosts on which services are deployed in order to serve the consumer requests. The consumers are provided with a user interface, maintained by the WSP with all the services it can provide along with their current status (shown in Figure 2).

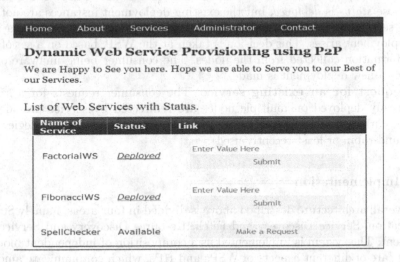

Fig. 2. Web Service Provider Interface

Each Web Service is accompanied with some information and service criteria like the *service name, current status* denoting whether it is deployed or not, as well as a set of *minimum requirements* with respect to the supported processor, required memory and operating systems for optimum performance. A Services can have either of the two *status*:

a) Available: The service is ready, but has not been deployed yet in the system. In such a case, the consumer can request for the service which will then be deployed on an available resource for processing the request.

b) Deployed: If the service has one or more ready deployments in the system, then the service URI of those instances will be provided.

Consumer requests are all made to the WSP. The WSP accepts the request and finds the most suitable HP to serve it. The Host Providers control the computational resources on which services can be deployed and requests from consumers be processed. The WSP monitors the HPs on the basis of their current CPU loads, collected dynamically after a certain interval of time.

3.3 Dynamic Deployment

When a service request is received at the WSP, there can be three interaction patterns depending on whether the service was deployed or not:

- ○ **First time deployment**: At the initial stage of the processing, for the first consumer request of a given service, i.e. the *status* of the service is *available*, the WSP uses some criteria to select the best HP to process the request. This HP will be directed by the WSP to download the corresponding service code from the repository and deploy it. The service *status* is then changed to *deployed*.
- ○ **Fresh deployment when current instances are busy**: For a service whose *status* is *deployed*, but the existing deployment instances are not able to serve the request (the nodes may be overloaded), the need for a fresh deployment arises. This decision is taken at the WSP, based on a set of load information collected from the nodes. The consumer being unaware of the fact a new deployment is made.
- ○ **Request for an existing service**: The consumer requests for a service already deployed on multiple nodes are redirected by service provider, to the currently selected best node, based on some scheduling strategies (like round-robin or least-recently-used).

3.4   Implementation

The overall architecture described above is divided in four areas, namely Service Publication, Service Discovery and Fetch, Resource Discovery and Service Deployment. The system is implemented as a composition of independent modules taking care of different aspects of WSPs and HPs, which communicate amongst each other to meet some common goal. Each of these nodes are distinguished by a set of *node properties* such as *node name*, *node category* - i.e. whether the corresponding node is a WSP or HP, and other static information such as *host operating system*, *processor frequency* and *physical memory*, all maintained within a *configuration file*. The nodes taking part in the architecture as WSP or HP are connected to each other in a P2P fashion by using JmDNS[18] and the *node properties* are known to each other. Following this, each phase of our system has it's functioning based on different modules like *ServiceMonitor, NodeCommunicatior, BestNodeFinder*. The *NodeCommunicatior* module establishes inter and intra-node communication of events. The *ServiceMonitor* component is responsible for publishing the service and making it discoverable based on its *status*. The *BestNodeFinder* component monitors all the nodes on the basis of their properties, runtime CPU and memory utilization to select one HP for new deployments and/or processing consumer requests.

Service Publication and Discovery - WSPs publish services by providing the corresponding service in the form of a WAR (web archive) file. Each service is characterized by a set of *service configurations* and *ServiceList* defined in files. Both these files are metadata files corresponding to each service, with identifiers such as *service name, service state - available or deployed, minimum deployment requirements* and *list of deployed nodes* etc. all maintained by *ServiceMonitor*. Each new service made available to the system make their attributes known with the state set as *available*. Consumers are the end users of the application and can interface with the application using a simple web browser making service requests to the system. The requests are made specifically to the WS providers currently available in the system, which are then further handled by the WSP in order to meet the consumer requirements. For the first request of the service encountered the service state is changed to *deployed* after which the all the consumer requests can be fetched and handled efficiently by the *BestNodeFinder*. A change in the configuration of a given service is acknowledged as an *ServiceConfigChangeEvent* and processed as *ServiceChangeEvent* based on the processing logic in Algorithm 1.

Algorithm 1: Algorithm for ServiceChangeEvent

```
 1  begin
 2  |   serviceName ← getServiceName();
 3  |   switch ServiceChangeEvent.getType() do
 4  |   |   case ADDED:
 5  |   |   |   // add or update service;
 6  |   |   |   status ← addService(serviceName);
 7  |   |   case CHANGED:
 8  |   |   |   // update service;
 9  |   |   |   status ← updateService(serviceName);
10  |   |   case REMOVED:
11  |   |   |   // undeploy service from node and remove from repository;
12  |   |   |   status ← undeployAndRemoveService(serviceName);
13  |   |   case DEPLOYED/REDEPLOYED:
14  |   |   |   // get service name and deploy service on a selected host;
15  |   |   |   node ← selectNode(nodeArray);
16  |   |   |   status ← deployService(serviceName, node);
17  |   |   case UNDEPLOY:
18  |   |   |   // undeploy service from node;
19  |   |   |   status ← undeployService(serviceName, node);
```

Among the listed events, the ADDED and CHANGED events drive the deployment process within the system and hence invoke the rest of the events as when required. On an occurrence of these events, a check is performed on the node to determine its category (WSP or HP) and the event is delegated in a proper direction if necessary. A WSP will never deploy the service within itself and will utilize the BestNodeFinder module to find the best suited node and deploy the service on the corresponding node. An HP will process the DEPLOYED or UNDEPLOYED events based on the status of the corresponding service.

Resource Discovery - Nodes acting as Host Providers play an equally important role in the performance of the architecture along with the WSP. Since we aim to serve our consumers in best possible way, a correct choice of the HP is required which meet the service requirements. The WSP uses the *BestNodeFinder* to search for a suitable node with enough resources among the available HP's to deploy the service.

Dynamic Deployment - A service is deployed when a request for it is received by the WSP and the service is *available*. The corresponding *ServiceChangeEvent* is acknowledged by the WSP which initiates the deployment process after performing a matchmaking over *node properties* of the available resources and the *minimum requirements* of the corresponding service with the help of BestNodeFinder. After the deployment all the service requests are then redirected to the node on which the service is deployed. It may so happen, that the current deployments get too busy with incoming requests and a specified *load threshold* is exceeded. This situation triggers a new deployment, and the BestNodeFinder component again performs a matchmaking to select another node and the service is deployed on the newly selected node. Incoming requests are routed to particular instances of a service based on some basic scheduling strategies such as Round Robin Reloaded (RRR)(Algorithm 2) and Least Recently Used Reloaded (LRUR)(Algorithm 3). The main motive underlying the use of the scheduling strategy is to increase the service availability and provide faster response times, while maximizing the resource utilization.

Algorithm 2: Algorithm for Round Robin Reloaded

```
 1 begin
 2     foreach ServiceList ∈ ServiceListMap do
 3         NodeFound ← FALSE;
 4         Marker ← ServiceList.getPointer();
 5         while not found suitable node do
 6             ServiceList.incrementPointer();
 7             tempNode ← DeployNodes.get(ServiceList.getPointer());
 8             if LoadThreshold(tempNode) == TRUE then
 9                 if Marker == ServiceList.getPointer() then
10                     // all nodes loaded
11                     NewDeploymentRequired();
12                     NodeFound ← TRUE;
13                 else
14                     ServiceList.setBestNode();
15                     NodeFound ← TRUE;
16             // update ServiceListMap with new ServiceList
17             UpdateServiceListMap(ServiceList);
```

---

4   Experimental Results

In this section we present the results of dynamically deploying web services to serve a large number of consumer requests made simultaneously. These tests were conducted using a simple web service for calculating the Nth Fibonacci term, with one WSP and many HPs. We start with making requests for a service which is not deployed initially, calculating response time for each request, keeping the load factors as 50% of CPU usage and a minimum free memory of 50 MB. The physical nodes used in the experiments were Intel Core 2 Duo with 1.86GHz frequency, 1GB RAM with Windows 7/Windows XP and Linux (Ubuntu) installed. In the

---

Algorithm 3: Algorithm for Least Recently Used Reloaded

```
1  begin
2     foreach ServiceList ∈ ServiceListMap do
3        NodeFound ← FALSE;
4        Marker ← ServiceList.getPointer();
5        while not found suitable node do
6           tempNode ← DeployNodes.get(ServiceList.getPointer());
7           if LoadThreshold(tempNode) == TRUE then
8              ServiceList.incrementPointer();
9              if Marker == ServiceList.getPointer() then
10                // all nodes loaded
11                NewDeploymentRequired();
12                NodeFound ← TRUE;
13           else
14              ServiceList.setBestNode();
15              NodeFound ← TRUE;

16           // update ServiceListMap with new ServiceList
17           UpdateServiceListMap(ServiceList);
```

---

graphs shown in Figure 3 we show the plots of 5000 consumer requests made to the corresponding service and the per service response time in seconds for the different scheduling strategies used.

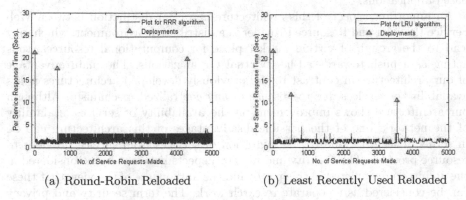

(a) Round-Robin Reloaded   (b) Least Recently Used Reloaded

Fig. 3. Experimental results for RRR and LRUR

The significant feature prominent in both the graphs is the time taken by the very first request to be served which is quite high as compared to the subsequent requests. The high response for the first request is caused by overhead of a new service deployment. One the service is deployed; subsequent requests are processed within a short duration till the instance becomes overloaded when a new deployment is triggered. When the new instances are deployed, the response time again increases for those particular requests for which the deployment was triggered. On the whole, the " deploy once, use many times " philosophy of web services is well observed in the experiment. As the service requests use the computational resources scheduled to them, the CPU load on the nodes may increase leading to higher response times - and such situations lead to fresh deployments to avoid the CPU loading on the resources. Based on the experiments conducted with different parameters, and comparing the results, we find the cumulative response time for LRUR is less than that of RRR with same parameter set. As the BestNodeFinder schedules the service requests to the HP with lowest load factor, we get lower response time but this leaves the other deployed HPs less used. In contrast the observation in RRR is just opposite as in this case the BestNodeFinder schedules the service requests evenly among all the HPs which may lead to higher response time if the HPs have a load factor just below the threshold.

5 Discussion and Future Work

In this paper we presented an architecture which depicts a new framework towards dynamic Web Service deployment in a distributed Grid environment. We have introduced the concept of P2P decentralization to our framework which offers full dynamism over grid based Web Service framework. We also bring the dynamic load balancing (although at a very basic level), dynamic demand driven service deployment, and resource allocation on the basis of minimum service Request parameters so that we can meet the demands of the newly available web based applications.

An important aspect of this architecture is a clear distinction between Web Service Provider and Resource Provider in a distributed environment, which may lead to the growth of virtual market place for computational resources, thus acting as a push towards ad-hoc Virtual Organizations. The main advantage of our architecture in contrast to the previously developed architectures is it's availability of services due to absence of any centralized mechanism. Although our architecture shows improvement on the availability of services, scalability of the network, one of the possible disadvantages of this architecture can be in terms of security, due to the migration of services from service provider to resource provider. The security and privacy aspects have not been considered in the architecture depicted in this paper and the authors are of the view that these can be considered as a separate research work. The term security and privacy here are subjective in nature with respect to whom and what information about the services are made available and accessible among the peer nodes. We believe that security and privacy related modules can be plugged into this architecture at a later stage.

We acknowledge that this architecture requires a lot of improvements to be made. Till now we have performed a dynamic load balancing (at a very basic level) which in future will be replaced by a more profound dynamic load balancing policy. Although we have offered service execution and fetching from host to consumer in P2P fashion, we aim to use P2P file sharing (BitTorrent like) based concepts for service deployments. Further, we shall try to achieve dynamic service deployment based Consumer-Level SLA as our final goal.

References

1. Sprott, D., Wilkes, L.: Understanding Service-Oriented Architecture. Microsoft Architect Journal (November 2004),
   http://msdn.microsoft.com/en-us/library/aa480021.aspx
2. Web Services Architecture, http://www.w3.org/TR/ws-arch/
3. Foster, I., Kesselman, C.: The Grid: Blueprint for a New Computing Infrastructure. Morgan Kaufmann, San Francisco (1999)
4. World Wide Web Consortium, http://www.w3.org/
5. Foster, I., Kesselman, C., Tuecke, S.: The Anatomy of the Grid: Enabling Scalable Virtual Organizations. International Jounral of Supercomputer Applications 15(3) (2001)
6. OASIS WebService Resource Framework(WSRF) TC,
   http://www.oasis-open.org/committees/tc_home.php?wg_abbrev=wsrf
7. Tannenbaum, T., Wright, D., Miller, K., Livny, M.: Condor - A Distributed Job Scheduler. In: Beowulf Cluster Computing with Linux. The MIT Press (2002)
8. The Globus Toolkit, http://www.globus.org/toolkit
9. Universal Description, Discovery and Integration(UDDI) v3.0.2,
   http://uddi.org/pubs/uddi-v3.0.2-20041019.htm
10. Web Services Description Language (WSDL) 1.1, W3C Note, March 15 (2001),
    http://www.w3.org/TR/wsdl
11. Simple Object Access Protocol (SOAP) 1.1, W3C Note, May 08 (2000),
    http://www.w3.org/TR/2000/NOTE-SOAP-20000508
12. Watson, P., Fowler, C., Kubicek, C., et al.: Dynamically Deploying Web Services on a Grid using DynaSOAr. In: Proc. International Symposium on Object and Component-Oriented Real-Time Distributed Computing, ISORC (2006)
13. Harrison, A., Taylor, I.: An Interface to WebService Hosting and Invocation. In: Proc. HIPS Joint Workshop on High-Performance Grid Computing and High-Level Parallel Programming Models (2005)
14. Qi, L., Jin, H., Foster, I., Gawor, J.: HAND: highly available dynamic deployment infrastructure for globus toolkit4,
    http://www.globus.org/alliance/publications/papers/HAND-Submitted.pdf.
15. Mondejar, R., Garcia, P., Pairot, C., Gomez Skarmeta, A.F.: Enabling Wide-Area Service Oriented Architecture through the p2pWeb Model. In: WETICE, pp. 89–94 (2006)
16. Mesaros, V., Carton, B., Van Roy, P.: P2PS: Peer-to-Peer Development Platform for Mozart. In: Van Roy, P. (ed.) MOZ 2004. LNCS, vol. 3389, pp. 125–136. Springer, Heidelberg (2005)
17. GRIMOIRES, http://www.omii.ac.uk/wiki/Grimoires
18. jmDNS, http://jmdns.sourceforge.net/

Network of Social Listeners

Hrushikesha Mohanty

Department of Computer and Information Sciences
University of Hyderabad
India
mohanty.hcu@gmail.com

Abstract. People in a society in some context lend an ear to their respective world members and so form a network of listening that is passively embedded in the society. This paper defines a model of listening that explains spread of a message creating listen pathways to reach people in the network. A metric listen weight, measures the message relevance perceived by a listener. And accumulation of this weight to a message while traversing a network projects the emergent relevance and intensity of the message spread. We propose a method to engineer listening process to make a society inclusive of listening.

Keywords: Social communication, Listeners Pathways, Computational Social Science.

1 Introduction

Communication among people has long been studied by sociologists and psychologists considering its importance in performing transactions of mutual interests. More, communication is considered as a signature of a culture. The sophistication in social communication indicates social aristocracy and maturity. So, is the importance of communication in history of mankind. In the world of computers and in distributed problem solving multi-agent systems have used communication as a tool to control and monitor agents' roles in solving problems [9]. At another end, both computing and communication together now offer a different world with cyber society where people communicate on cyber infrastructure being physically far away from each other. Information flow and structure formation in social networks have been a hot research topic [1] [3] [5]. In real world, goal specific communication particularly in business domain is studied to formulate marketing policy. Some of these models are reviewed in [11]. Also, there are works studying information flow in structured organisations [5]. But, there has been hardly any study on computational model to understand social communication in real world.

In reality, human society is a heterogeneous network of people connecting to each other in certain context. And this network with random structure changes dynamically unlike organisational structures that has fixed topology for conducting smooth organisational transactions. Ofcourse, a range of gossip algorithms

C. Hota and P.K. Srimani (Eds.): ICDCIT 2013, LNCS 7753, pp. 302–318, 2013.

for communication on randomly evolving networks like sensor networks have been studied [2]. These techniques in right way are not helpful to study real world social communication because characteristically people network is different from networks of computers. Hence, our interest here is to model social communication considering habitats of people in society.

We view communication includes both telling and listening. Readers may note the significance of characterising communication into two action-forms - telling and listening, as the former depends on perceptions of tellers whereas the later that of listeners. This work is based on the following basic and reasonable assumptions:: An individual

- listens to its acquaintances for information it needs.
- passes on information to acquaintances based on perception on their needs.

A person, unlike a node in a computer network, listening a message means, it collects and reasons on the usability of the message before passing on it to a neighbour. A person in society usually listens to another believing the later may pass some information of formers interest (on a context). Thus, a listen network of people across a society on some context gets defined. We view, for every society, implicitly on different contexts different listen social networks exist.

Utilization of implicitly defined networks needs investigation for making of a knowledge as well as inclusive society. It will also be useful for business promotions and governance. The immense usages it has particularly for people of developing countries include spread of healthcare message, information on livelihood management, education and governance notifications.

In this paper, we have taken up a study on listen network. First, we define a world of acquaintances of a person and then define an operator *listenTo* and its properties to show the role of the operator in making of a listen network. Multi-casting a message from a source to all in a population is implemented by flow of the message on pathways that are formed connecting people (needing the message) in a society. And while a message flows from one person to another i.e listened, then the flow of the message assumes a value based on habitat difference between the two. The more the value the more is the spread of a message in a population. A listen weight metric is defined to reason on a spread. Spread continues as long as a flow assumes a value more than the the threshold value at a visiting person. Else, the flow stops at a person and this means the message at the person has lost relevance. And so it decides against forwarding it. But, this may result some persons in network unreachable to the message. We define these people as *deaf* to the message. We have proposed measures like scheduling of flow through a population, providing bridges to deaf points in listen network for making a society inclusive of listening.

This paper in seven sections presents our idea on listening. The next section defines worlds of individuals and their context specific neighbourhoods such that they make a distributed representation of a network that's implicitly present in a society. The network is used for spread of a message from a source person possibly to all in society. Spread caused by one listening to another is specified by an operator *listenTo* in 3rd section. The 4th section talks of process of listening defined as a flow of a message making listen pathways on passive listen network that is implicitly defined on a society. A spread on traversing a pathway assumes a weight at a listener and it passes on if a spread has the required threshold value. The spread stops otherwise. The next section talks engineering of a listening process to make a society inclusive of listening. In 6th section, in absence of directly relevant works, we review some works that have certain similarity to our problem. The paper concludes with a remark in the last section.

2 Worlds of Listeners

A person being social has its world and makes goal specific communications among its world members. For example, a person may acquire information from its family members, colleagues and people it comes across and media at large. We would like to build a comprehensive structure around a person p with worlds comprising of own-world (ow), small-world (sw) and wide-world (ww). The people around a person is due to its three worlds as

$$p^w = ow^p \cup sw^p \cup ww^p$$

For example, own-world of a person is comprised of family members (people in living space) whereas its small-world includes people from its work spaces e.g. office, school, business and etc. And wide world includes media like television, Internet and printed media. A person wishing to acquire information usually listens to its world members. Readers are urged to make a note on small world definition made here.

The context of an interaction has definite bearing on modus operandi of a social communication. For example, on family matter or on a matter where a family has a stake, a person would like to listen to its family members. Whereas, on another context a person may choose to ask to members of its small world who it considers well conversant with. But in context like a political issue, one may like to listen to media, its wider world. Thus, the context of communication influences a person to choose whom it should listen to. Other than context, the personality has also a say on communication. A reclusive person feels convenient to listen to its own world while a cautious person prefers to listen to acquaintances i.e members of its small-world. A gregarious person, sometimes, chooses to ride on waves allowing itself to listen to its wide world (media) as in case of electioneering.

But, here in this paper we restrict to purposive interaction keeping ends-means into our purview. That is, a person r (*listener*) listens to another s (*listenee*) thinking the former will get relevant information from later. The relevance is defined with respect to a goal a person has i.e. how useful a piece of information is to achieve its goal. That is the message could be directly or indirectly useful to meet ones need. Another important assumption here we make is bidirectional world membership i.e if $r \in s^w$ then $s \in r^w$. The assumption is in tune with general social convention though there an otherwise situation is also possible.

In an earlier work,[6] I have discussed on needs of a person being in its habitat $< K, Q, R, L >$ defined by knowledge, goals, resources, and physical location. A person being in a three dimensional habitat (K, R, L) tries to achieve Q. We have defined operators to assess needs of a person with respect to its goals. A person always looks for a piece of information relevant to its needs. In a society there could be several people needing information m and so each of them listens to its world members from whom it may get the message. That is r listens to e on context m while $r \in e^w$ is specified by an operator $listenTo(r, e, m)$. For a population P there exists a passive listen network PLN that tells of possible listening pathways existing among people. Having a repository of population P one can derive PLN with the algorithm $findPLN$.

Algorithm findPLN takes input of each habitat $< k, q, r, l >$ of a person p present in society P. Functionality of the algorithm is primarily depends on $selectNhbr(p, m)$ that checks the habitats of all the members of p's neighbourhood i.e $ow^p \cup sw^p$. We assume p has an idea on neighbours' goals. The function test the relevance of message m to the goal of p's neighbourhood members. Though justifying relevance is subjective still one can implement by making each of population publishing a checklist of its goals and corresponding qualifiers. The algorithm finds the network that's implicit in a population.

Algorithm 1. findPLN

```
// Input: P = {< k, q, r, l >} Ouput: {sw_p^m}
begin
    for each p ∈ P do
    begin
        sw_p^m = nil;
        ∀ n ∈ sw_p do
        begin
            sw_p^m = sw_p^m ∪ selectNhbr(p, m);
        end
    end
end
```

Having such a network is not enough for making people listen. We need to study the dynamic behaviour of people on listening. The behaviour is based on two basic presumptions: 1. people with a message (information) wishes to pass it out to members of its own world. But the priority it takes for a member to pass the information adds to the velocity of the message at which it spreads out. 2. The spread of a message also depends on the way listener perceives a listenee i.e. its habitat. The degree of difference in their habitats contributes to slow spread of message in a network. We will further formalize this aspect of listening late just after formalizing listening, with an operator $listenTo$.

3   On Listening To

The operator $ListenTo(p, q, m)$ specifies - on context m, p listens to q. Sometimes, we also write simply $ListenTo(p, q)$ in the midst of discussion where the context of discussion remains unchanged. Some of the properties for the operators are as follows:

- Non-commutative: $listenTo(p, q) \not\Rightarrow listenTo(q, p)$
- Transitive: $listenTo(p, q), listenTo(q, r) \Rightarrow listenTo(p, r)$
- Distributive: i. $listenTo(p, (q + r)) \Rightarrow listenTo(p, q), listenTo(p, r)$
  ii. $listenTo(q + r), p) \Rightarrow listenTo(q, p), listenTo(r, p)$

The first rule says one listens to other does not mean the vice versa is true for all the times. The second rule on transitivity shows a set of people can form a chain of listeners making a pathway of listeners. The rule 3.i says a person in process of consultation may listen to a group of people q and r e.g. $(q + r)$. The rule 3.ii says of group of people listening to a person. For both the cases, the actions by individuals are syntactically separated by (,) a comma. However, while specifying its dynamic behaviour, individuals in a group either can choose to listen in sequence or parallel or even following mixed strategy. The way the group operation of $listenTo$ works has a bearing on speed of information flow among participants. These properties of $listenTo$ operator helps to model and analyze listen pathways in a population P. In next section we will take up the process of listening to make ground for discussion on listen pathways.

4   Process of *listenTo*

A person keeps its ears open to listen to a message from its neighbourhood. It looks for messages that are useful to it for achieving its goal. We have already discussed it. A person who listens is called *listener* and to whom it listens is called *listenee*. In general a person p listens to many of its world members on message m is specified as $listenTo(p, (p^w))$. Considering such listen links, we get passive listen network PLN defined over P a population. How does this network work? How does a person in network behave to make a message listened in its population? This is what we are going to discuss in this section.

Assume a person in network has message m. It knows who are its world members in need of m and pushes this message to them. Readers may note that the person here behaves like a router guiding flow of messages as per its world members' requirements. It's also to be noted that a person in the middle is a passive one engaged in just passing on a message. In order to be more specific, we make a difference between just passing on to telling a message. Because, telling a message (by a person) may add or delete to the original it has received. Here, passing on does not have that aspect. It just passes on a carbon copy of a received message upon adding a weight to the message. While passing on a message is instructional, telling a message is intentional. Ascribing weight to a message by a person reflects the importance the person perceives.

A weight ascribed to a message while passing it on, depends on listenee perception on listener. Such a weight is derived from degree of similarity of their habitats. In a way it talks of sociability of two involved in listening. So,a listenee e while passing on a message m to a listener r ascribes a weight called $ng^m_{(r,e)}$ neighbour gain defined as:

$$ng^m_{(e,r)} \quad = \quad \frac{<k,q,r,l> \; \cap \; <k',q',r',l'>}{<k,q,r,l>} \qquad = \quad \frac{|(H_e \cap H'_r)|}{|H_e|}$$

where $ng^m_{(e,r)}$ - e assigns neighbour gain weight to message m just before passing on to r. $< k,q,r,l >$ - H_e habitat of e and $< k',q',r',l' >$ - H_r habitat of r as perceived by e.

Now we will talk of listening at a person in middle of network. A person while listening to its neighbour tends to take note of the message as much as it takes the neighbour serious of the purpose. Usually, a message looses its weight (for not being able to convincingly useful to receiver) at each transmission. We reason out the cause for such loss is due to difference in habitats of the entities r, e. Let H_r be the habitat of r and that of e perceived by r be H'_e. Now, the loss of weight of a message m being listened by r after being passed out from e is known as neighbour loss and computed as:

$$nl^m_{(r,e)} \quad = \quad \frac{|(H_r - H'_e)|}{|H_r|}$$

We have presented two aspects of weights - one is due to listenee and the other is due to listener. Let us assume a message is charged with an initial message weight mw^m_o for a message m at origin o. Origin o is a person in a population from whom the message m starts flowing out. With these three types of weights we define listen weight for a message :

$$lw^m_o \quad = \quad mw^m_o$$
$$lw^m(r,e) \quad = \quad lw^m_e + ng^m_{(e,r)} - nl^m_{(r,e)}$$

At a person p, the weight a message m assumes is labelled as lw^m_p. $lw^m_{(r,e)}$ is a weight ascribed at r on receiving m from e. This is composed of listen weight of message at e i.e.lw^m_e and an added weight assigned by e for r i.e. neighbour gain weight $ng_{(e,r)}$ and a decrement by r on receiving from e i.e. neighbour loss weight $nl^m_{(r,e)}$. So, on a listening say at r, listen weight $lw^m(r,e)$ has two components $lwg^m_{(r,e)}$: listen weight gain at r on listening m from e, and similarly $lwl^m_{(r,e)}$: listen weight loss. So:

$$lwg^m_{(r,e)} \quad = \quad lw^m_e + ng^m_{(e,r)}$$
$$lwl^m_{(r,e)} \quad = \quad nl^m_{(r,e)}$$

Now, we say when a message is listened by a person, there is a gain as well as a loss of listen weight. In sequel to listening, a message may gain or loose its weight at persons it passes through.

Below we present an algorithm $calculateLW$ for calculating listen weight at listener p on listening to a message from listenee q. The algorithm also marks edges of a listen graph lg_m for message m. After defining listen weight mathematically, we would like to state the use of listen weight in the process of listening. One can view listen weight as a momentum at which a message is being listened. If a message looses momentum that is, when it achieves a value less than a stipulated threshold of a person, then the message does not emerge out of it i.e is not passed over to any of its neighbour. This aspect of variations in listen weight brings out further interesting questions and usages. Before going to deal with those we will spend a bit on analysis of listening process with respect to its variations in listen weight during listening.

Algorithm 2. calculateLW(o,m,P)

// Input: origin:o, population:P, message: m; and Ouput: lw_p^m
begin
Do at o {
   $lw_o^m = msgIWT$ // $msgIWT$ initial weight given to a message.
   $TellNhbr(o)$ // Tells to neigbours.
}
   for each $r \in P \wedge r \neq o$ do {
    On listening to $< m, lwg_{(e,r)}^m, e, r >$ do
    begin
     $nl_{(r,e)}^m = findListenLwt(m,e,r)$ // find weight loss in listening by e from r.
     $lw_{(r,e)}^m = lwg_{(e,r)m} - nl_{(r,e)}^m$ // e finds net weight on listening r.
     $lw_p^m = lw_{(r,e)}^m \circledast lw_p^m$ //e finds net weight on listening m.
     $TellNhbr(r)$
    end
   $TellNhbr(p)$
    for each $n \in sw_p^m$
    do {
    $ng_{(p,n)}^m = findNhbrGwt(m,p,n)$; //find weight gain by neighbour n.
    $lwg_{(p,n)}^m = lw_p^m + ng_{(p,n)}^m$ // p calculates weight at n message may gain.
    if $(lwg_{(p,n)}^m > mpwT_p^m)$ then
    //p passes on message to n if the message assumes a weight greater to threshold
      $message < m, lwg_{(p,n)}^m, p, n >$ // listened by p's world members.
    //$mpwT_p^m$ - the weight that depends on the person's choice.
    }
   end
 }
end

Analysis on Listening::   Algorithm *calculateLW* exhibits three cases on analysis of role of habitat and social perception in computation of listen weights. The cases are:

- *Case* 1 : listen weight gain ($ng_{(e,r)}^m > nl_{(r,e)}^m$)
- *Case* 2 : listen weight loss ($ng_{(e,r)}^m < nl_{(r,e)}^m$)
- *Case* 3 : listen weight unchanged ($ng_{(e,r)}^m = nl_{(r,e)}^m$)

It is to be noted here that social perception as well as habitat assume major roles in fixing neighbour weight loss and gain values. The two functions *findListenLwt* and *findNhbrGwt* used in algorithm respectively accounts for determining loss and gain for a neighbour of a person. Initially, let's assume a person uses a reference chart on its neighbours for fixing loss and gain in listen weight. One can think of automating the process considering it a prediction problem. Looking at the process of listening a social activity we bring out three categories as:

- $(ng_{(e,r)}^m = 1, nl_{(r,e)}^m = 0)$
- $(ng_{(e,r)}^m = 0, nl_{(r,e)}^m = 1)$
- $(0 < ng_{(e,r)}^m < 1, 0 < nl_{(r,e)}^m < 1)$

The first case talks about a situation where both listener as well as listenee have equivalent habitats $H_e \equiv H_r$ and they are socially homogeneous so that $H_e = H_e'$ and $H_r = H_r'$. The second case is just opposite that both have totally different habitats $\mid H_e \cap H_r \mid = 0$ and are socially isolated i.e $\mid H_e' \mid = 0$ and $\mid H_r' \mid = 0$. The last one talks about case when both have partially similarity in habitats and socially conversant to each other to some extent. Here $\mid H_e \cap H_r \mid \neq 0$, $H_r' \subset H_r$ and $H_e' \subset H_e$. The first one talks about a well knit community whereas the second case represents people of two indifferent heterogeneous community e.g. one is very rich and another is very poor. The third one talks of a common case. But the degree of homogeneity and social consciousness among people differ and so it is for assigning listen weights to a listening among such people. Further, in order to assess listen weight to a message during its listening across a population we need to understand how the patterns of listening of *ListenTo* operator has an impact. And such an observation follows in the next section.

4.1   Listen Patterns and Weights

ListenTo operator is used for four basic patterns of listening viz. *bi-directional listening, chain listening, multicast listening and repeat listening*. Listen weight computation for each pattern is of interest to analyze for their roles in spread of a message in a *PLN*. This spread activates the edges of the *PLN* leading to the people participating in a message spread.

Bi-directional listening does not necessarily negate the non-commutative property of *listenTo* operator for each can assign unequal listen weights to the same message at respective ends. So, it may lead us to a situation for unending repetitive message passings between two, resulting to unnatural increase in listen weights. For practical purpose assigning a direction to listening helps in analysis of a message spread. Later, we discuss on implications due to bi-directional message passings resulting to undesirable effects of a rumour-monger.

Chain listening pattern represents a situation of one listening to other in sequence. According to the Case 1, for people of a homogeneous community chain listening makes steady increase in listen weight. Where as just opposite happens for listening among people in a highly disparate community. Whereas, uneven changes to listen weight may happen for listening to a heterogeneous community. Multi-cast listening happens when many listen to one i.e $listenTo((s+t), u)$ and the repeat listening happens when one listens to many $listenTo(u, (s+t))$. For former, listen weight at s and t is computed as per the convention. In general, $lw^m_{(s,u)}$ and $lw^m_{(t,u)}$ will be different even though they have listened to the same listenee u. It's so for difference in their habitats. The case of listening to many for $listenTo(u, (s + t))$ is interesting for its impact on resulting listen weight at u. Let's modify computation of listen weight for repeated listening of the same message at listener u as::

$$lw^m_u = (\circledast)(lw^m_{(u,s)}, lw^m_{(u,t)})$$

A person on listening the same message from different people may compute weight to the message as shown above applying chosen operator $\circledast$ - can be max/min function. While the former reflects *easy-influenced* tendency of listener, the later talks of a *cautious* personality.

Passing of message at a person in reality is not one-time activity. A person in society, listens the same message at different times from its different world members. And similarly, it passes over the message to its world members (excluding the one who supplied the message) provided the change of listen weight values is is more than a stipulated value $mpwT^m_u$ (message passing threshold for a person u for message context m) . Ofcourse, fixing of this value is context as well as person specifics. Now, having defined a process of listening we will identify next, some of its characteristics.

4.2   On *listenTo* Process

Observation-1:For a person, assigning listen weight (of a message) is revisited for repeated listening to its world members.

The proposition follows directly from algorithm *calculateLW*. Listening process is a distributed algorithm being executed at each person in a population.A person on receiving a message calculates listen weight for the message. As the listening is asynchronous the person listens the same message at different times and so revises listen weight of the message.

Observation-2: Eventually, a connected person r assumes a listen weight lw^m_r for a message m.

Let us assume o is the origin from whom listening has started. A person r is connected means it has a path to reach o in PLN for message m on population P. By algorithm *calculateLW*, neighbours of o listens m from o and the process continues. By chain listening, we can say that a person r is in chain that starts from o, eventually listens m. Further by proposition-1, we say r receives m from each of its neighbours, provided it is in a chain emanating from o. In other words, for graph PLN if there are more than one path from o to r then the former receives m message ,more than once. And from repeat listening principle we conclude that at r a listen weight is calculated based on the chosen criteria (like max/min). Thus a connected person assumes a listen weight.

Proposition-1: In a population there could be some people deaf to a message m. In algorithm *calculateLW*, the decision making on message passing for listening by world members depends on $"if \quad (lwg^m_{(p,n)} > mpwT^m_p)$ then message $<$ $m, lwg^m_{(p,n)}), p, n > listened$ by $p^w"$. We know $lwg^m_{(p,n)}$ at p for a world member $n \in p^{\bar{w}}$ depends on habitat characteristics of p and n. Again, making world members listening depends on $mpwT^m_p$. As discussed in analysis of listening, loss of weights occur due to difference in communicating habitats. And if this loss continues for chain listening, then there could be a case for which condition of telling neighbour does not hold good at a person, so its world members don't listen m. If the same situation repeats for all the world members of a person p then it can not listen to m and so remains deaf to m in the population P.

Proposition-2: Listening a message m may be a non-terminating process for a population P.

Let's assume certain people of population P are connected for message m and have made PLN. And o be the first listenee. By Observation-2, all connected persons receive the message and assume a listen weight. Considering, each listening takes unit time and passing out message is instantaneous, we can say that message reaches at the farthest z (from o) person at distance d i.e. diameter of the PLN. Imagine, in P a message gains weight at each person of the path $(o \rightarrow z)$ for $(ng^m_{(e,r)} = 1, nl^m_{(r,e)} = 0)$ i.e the people on the path make a homogeneous community. Then $lw^m_o < lw^m_z$. According to the algorithm $calculateLW$, z again can make its neighbour n listen the message when $(lwg^m_{(z,n)} > mpwT^m_p)$. In practice it means because of increase in message weight z feels to reiterate the message to its neighbours to signal importance of the message. Once, this happens the message may retrace chain paths in PLN to reach a farthest path from z. Ironically, o may listen the same message for which it is the origin listenee. That says, *why a message sent to a population comes back to the origin again*. The case amplifies when second time from o message spreads out to the population. The process repeats as every time listen weight is increased and value of $mpwT^m_p$ is not raised. This explains a classic phenomena how a message goes around a population and people listen it again and again with increasing weights only if the population does not have an adaptive method to raise the threshold $mpwT^m_p$. Probably, that is the reason a population with static threshold (without dynamic change in its belief system) is prone to create rumour that intensifies in each round. Typically, this phenomena of repeated listening to a message is observed during communal disturbances.

5   Engineering Social Listening

We have modelled a context based listening population to a network called PLN and have presented an algorithm $calculateLW$ to compute listen weight for the message to show how actively the message is being received by individuals in population P.Listen weight is a concept showing how strong a message traverses across a cross section of people in a society. Naturally, we want to maximize listen weight of a message during its traversal so that it can reach out as many people as possible. While analysing listening process we have identified the relation between characteristics of human habitats and changes in listen weights when a message traverses from one variety of habitat to another. Making use of this notion, we are interested in scheduling of listening among members of a population for increasing listen weights so that, longer listening paths can be traversed by a message. That means more in P listens the message. Being specific in our purpose we intend to find answers for the following queries:

1. Can we engineer a listen pathway for a person maximizing path's listen weight?
2. Can a society be structured to maximize listen weights for a given message?
3. How to make a society inclusive of listening?

Engineering a Listen Pathway: Suppose, we are interested in finding a listen pathway from a person o to a person p in a society P for a message m so that the pathway has the best possible listen weight. The search in PLN starts from o till it reaches p. The strategy followed at each person r is to search for a listening neighbour n that has the maximum lwg_n^m. In order to reduce loss of weight due to listening, the person r looks for a listener n with habitat that is the most similar (among other neigbours' habitats) to its habitat. In case, a person does not find a neighbour than it looks for a person from the society P who can pass on the information from it to its neighbour. Let's call it *person-bridge* and its selection is done at function *getBridge*. (The function could be used recursively to find a person-bridge to another making a chain of persons bridging and so facilitating a deaf to listen m). If a person neither finds a neighbour nor finds a person-bridge, than the the finding of path unsuccessfully terminates. Otherwise, the algorithm returns a path from o to p with the best possible listen weight. Here, we want to reiterate our assumption that each could perceive habitats of its world members. *Algorithm3 : ListenPathway* presents an algorithm that finds a path from o to p with the best possible weight.

Scheduling Social Listening: For a society, making a message listening to the most, could be a useful purpose particularly in case of spreading welfare messages across. The problem here is to schedule people for listening so that the message possibly maximise its listen weight. This is required to assure spread of a message thorough society reaching as many people as possible. The heuristic to make it possible includes:

- Group population on habitat homogeneity : $Pg = findGrps(P)$
- Choose groups who require the message : $Pg' = chosGrps(Pg, m)$
- Choose a group possibly at centre of the population :$Cg = chosCntr(Pg')$
- Schedule the groups for message transmission : $scdlGrps(Pg')$

The above steps are to be carried out at social directory [7] having individuals habitat as well as their worlds information. With a threshold of difference between two habitats that is $\Delta(H_p, H_q) \leq \delta$ the habitats are considered similar. The function $findGrps(P)$ clusters people having similar habitats and produces a set of groups { $Pg = findGrps(P) \mid \forall\ pg \in Pg\ (if\ (|pg| > 1)\ then\ (\Delta(H_q, H_r) \leq \delta)\forall q, r \in pg)$ }.

Algorithm 3. listenPathway(q,p,m)

// at start $q = o$

begin

$s = getBest(sw_q^m, m) \wedge$

if $(s = nil)$ then terminate //no pathway to listener p

else if $(s \neq p)$ listenPathway(s, p, m)

end

$getBest(sw_q^m, m)$

begin

$r = nil$

if $\{\exists r' \in sw_q^m \mid ((lwg_{(q,r')}^m \geq lwg_{(q,r'')}^m) \wedge$

    $min(\Delta(H_r', H_r''))) \forall r'' \in sw_q^m\}$ then $(r = r')$

if $(r = nil)$ $r = getBridge(q, m)$

return(r)

end

$getBridge(q, m)$

begin

$b = nil$

if $\{(\exists b' \in P) \wedge (\exists r \in sw_q^m) \mid$

    $(\Delta(H_q', H_b) \leqslant \delta) \wedge (\Delta(H_b, H_r) \leqslant \delta)\}$

then $(b = b')$

return(b)

Groups who need a message m are identified by $chosGrps(Pg, m)$ i.e Pg'. A *need* of a message is defined when information contained in the message i.e. $inf(m)$ is a piece of knowledge required to achieve a goal q. Now, q could be a common goal to a set of groups. We find those groups as Pg' such that $\{Pg' = chosGrps(Pg, m) \mid \exists ((q \in g.q) \wedge (preK(inf(m), q)) \forall g \in Pg\}$ where $preK$ tests whether $inf(m)$ is a pre-condition to achieve a goal q and $g.q$ is the goal the group g has. Now, with the chosen groups Pg' we find out the maximum habitat distance the groups have. Let $maxHD$ is the maximum distance among the groups in Pg' then $\{\nexists g, g' \in Pg' \mid \Delta(H_g, H_g') > maxHD\}$. Now function $chosCntr(Pg')$ returns (a) group Cg that is almost middle among the groups i.e. $\forall g \in Pg'$, $\Delta(H_g, H_{Cg}) \leq \frac{maxHD}{2}$. Now having the chosen centre group Cg as a start point, we need to have a schedule of groups for listening so that an evolving listen pathway can have increasing listen weight. Increasing of listen weight of a message is useful for making it spread to the most possible extent in a society. We have seen, a homogeneous group has an additive contribution to the listen weight of a message on spread. And this contribution is directly proportional to the size of the group. So, for listening we schedule the chosen groups from centre group Cg based on two criteria i.e. group size as well as habitat homogeneity. The most populous and homogeneous groups are chosen first and then the next best and so on the schedule continues till all the groups are scheduled. At each stage the number of groups considered for listening depends on the number of boundary-members for a group (of the previous stage) exists. Readers may note that the term *boundary-member* for a group means the people having world members belong to other groups. The schedule generates an n-ary listen schedule tree rooted at Cg with nodes representing groups from Pg'. Assuming each group having the minimum d number of boundary-members, the height of the schedule tree will be $log_d^{|Pg'|}$. On finding the minimum group size we can have a conservative estimate on listen weight. Making a tree schedule also helps in parallel listening of the message reducing message listen time. Again, scheduling larger groups listen first, helps in increasing listen weight at the beginning so that unfavourable groups can ill afford to ignore the message for its gathered momentum. A detailed study on tree schedule is not taken up for obliging to the said page limitation.

Making Listening Socially Inclusive: We have already studied the process of listening in a society. There our interest is to discover listen pathways to people with possibly maximum listen weight. We have seen more the difference in habitats the more is loss in listen weight. When a listening process does not progress beyond a listen weight then it ceases there. If in case of an ongoing listening of a message, there is a person for whom the process ceases to progress at its world members then the person never gets the message. This makes a *deaf-point* in society. Making an information available for everybody in a society is an essential requirement for the making of an inclusive society. The very purpose motivates to engineer a society for elimination of its deaf-points. The process includes the following steps:

- Finding deaf-points
- Fixing bridge-persons

Exploring deaf-points starts with listing the vulnerables. Persons surrounded by heterogeneous habitats are considered here vulnerable for high possibility of being blocked for listening. On finding those we can get their vulnerability tested on calculating listen weight for its world members. Now, for each world member of a vulnerable, we compute listen weight *calculateLW* with respect to a given message m originating from a start point o . If for each neighbour of a vulnerable, listen weight is less than a threshold value then the vulnerable is marked as a deaf-point. And further for deaf-points, bridge-persons are found. The idea is presented in algorithm *getDeafsIn*. The algorithm uses functions: $?markedDeaf(vp)$, $markDeaf(vp)$ $getBridge(vp, m)$ and $assignBridge(vp, P)$ for querying to know whether a person is a deaf-point or not, marking deaf-points, getting and assigning a bridge person respectively. The function $getBridge(vp, m)$ recommends a bridge person for a vulnerable person so that it can receive a message m from the former. In case of unavailability of such person in P, we have assumed a bridge person can be assigned to the vulnerable may be by a designated agency. Thus the algorithm works for making a society inclusive of listening to a message.

Algorithm 4. getDeafsIn(o,m,P)

// at start $q = o$
begin
  Input: origin:o, population: P, message: m; *Output*: b: bridge person
  begin
    calculateLW(o,m,P)
    $vP = nil$; // vP: set of vulnerable persons
    $\forall p \in P \ do$
    $if \ \nexists \ n \in p^w \ | \ \Delta(H_n, H_p) < \delta$
    $then \ vP = vP \cup p \ \ od$ // found possible vulnerables
    $\forall vp \in vP \ do$
    $if \ \nexists \ n \in vp^w \in ow_p^m \ | \ lw_n^m > mpwT_n^m$
    $then \ markDeaf(vp) \ \ od$ // marked deaf points
    $\forall vp \in vP \ do$
    $if \ ?markedDeaf(vp) \ then \ b = getBridge(vp,m);$
    $if \ b = nil \ then \ assignBridge(vp,P) \ \ od$
  end

---

6   Related Works

Research in communication among entities on grid network and social network
(on Internet) focus on usage of social issues for host of purposes like mining relations and discovering structures among participants. We'll review some papers
to show the trend of research hoping the issues these papers address may help in
understanding process of dissemination of information in a society. Because, the
problem we have studied here is alike to network information flow problem studied in [10]. First we review a work on socio-cognitive grids [1] that includes communication among human and artificial processes. This type of communication
is found generally in P2P applications having issues in digital rights management, mass user support and customer-to-customer interaction. Purpose of this
study is to understand emergent structures in personal relations and their roles
in managing issues. Social structures such as reciprocity, social exchange and social networking are studied on the basis of classical sociological theory. In a work
[4] authors study a problem of information flow in an organisation and prescribes
the loss of communication for a hierarchical organisation can be mitigated by
side links accepting the possibility of some remain isolated of information because providing additional communication links for fail safe communication is
not practical at the absence of an optimised solution. Another interesting work
[3] reports a distance measure between two communicating on Internet by email
or on social networking. This measure is conceived in the line of vector clocks
studied for distributed algorithms. A temporal notion of distance is used to find
out a back bone of a social network. On processing on-line data, it's seen that a
back bone is a sparse graph with links that have potential to make information
flow in quickest time. It also has long-range bridges to give wide spread of a
social network. This finding casts new light on relationship between tie strength
and connectivity in social networks. Communication in a social network is al-

ways interesting particularly for its dynamic evolution. This phenomena is found in a society where new relations appear and old relations take different intensities making real world society complex. Study in [5] proposes a structure called community tree that records the structures emerging from the current status of a social network. Researchers have used the PageRank algorithm and random walks on graph to derive the community trees from social networks.

Communication among agents is a major means for collective problem solving. In [9] authors propose a communication framework for agents that is influenced by sociological systems-theory with the semantics of communicative actions that are empirical, rational, constructivist and consequentialist in nature. Authors have analyzed the implications of the proposed model on social reasoning both from an agent and the systemic perspectives. The proposed framework for an agent works on its expectations and cognitive social views. The paper views, the proposed approach helps in understanding Socionics.

Interactions particularly in business domain has taken prime role for business advancement. Because, it helps people to make a choice on and to promote business interests. We will, here position a review paper [11] that studies social interactions to assess impacts of marketing interactions. First it categorises interactions to passive and active types. The later follows principle of feedback to assess impacts of interactions. Based on impacts, social interactions are further categorised to social spillover and social multiplier. While the former allows information passes through a social network, the later due to feedback carries back the impact to people already visited in interaction network. Following different models it is shown that these two approaches of interactions has a bearing on designing of a marketing policy. The reviewed models include linear models of social interactions,discrete choice models and models with forward-looking consumer model, epidemiology/disease spreading model and spatial model. The paper finds that spillover effect among passive interaction helps to spread business information among mass and active interaction with feedback loop helps to magnify the effects.

Here in this paper we hypothesize, every society has context based listen network spreading listen pathways among people. A message spread follows these pathways to reach people. Spread i.e use of these pathways depend upon the message (context) and people (requirements). We have modelled a listening process and studied its use in re-engineering of social structure for making it an inclusive society for listening a message. Applications of this proposed method include designing a strategy for spreading information on social welfare, business promotion and political campaigns.

7   Conclusion

The paper has presented a concept called social listening and discussed different aspects of the concept. The idea of generating passive listen network PLN on a context m for a population P provides a means to explore possible pathways connecting people in a context. We propose listen weight metric, that a message

assumes at each person on a listen pathway. The weight is a measure of importance a person ascribes to a message. A person passes on a message to its world
members only when listen weight of the message is greater than a threshold value
called 'message passing weight' mpw it has put.

The paper provides a mathematical frame work explaining how a message
listened in a society and why after some time the message fades away from
the society. In the process some people may remain isolated of the message
because no listen pathway extends to them from origin. Model explains this
phenomenon and shows its possible occurrences due to heterogeneity of people
habitats. A solution is proposed to this social problem by finding groups on
habitat homogeneity , scheduling these groups for listening, identifying origin
of a schedule, identifying listen vulnerable persons and finding bridge persons
for them. An utility of the proposed idea can be explained with an example as::
Suppose a welfare agency wants to propagate a message among society. And for
so, it wants to study the population and make a schedule so that all in society
will be able to listen to the message. We would like to simulate for generating
a schedule of people listening the message. Inputs to simulation include initial
message weight, habitats and world members of each in the population.

The outputs include a listen network, listen weight of each in network for
the message, listen pathways from origin to each in population, bridge persons
and their locations in network. Simulation can be repeated to study listening
phenomenon for different parametric values (message passing weight threshold)
to see the relation between grouping and bridging of society.

Further study on this idea is interesting for some fundamental questions::
does grouping of finer granularity have any relation with the required number
of bridge persons? How does grouping with course granularity have an impact
on fixing of massage passing threshold value? Further questions - how do people
having multiple goals respond to listening of a particular message? Can we model
'listen highway' among people for making them listening on multiple contexts ?
These are the several stimulating questions left to be answered in future works.

References

1. Ramirez-Cano, D., Pitt, J.: Emergent Structures of Social Exchange in Socio-
   cognitive Grids. In: Moro, G., Bergamaschi, S., Aberer, K. (eds.) AP2PC 2004.
   LNCS (LNAI), vol. 3601, pp. 74–85. Springer, Heidelberg (2005)
2. Shah, D.: Gossip Algorithms. Foundations and Trends in Networking 3(1), 1–125
   (2008)
3. Kossinets, G., Kleinberg, J., Watts, D.: The Structure of Information Pathways in
   a Social Communication Network. In: KDD 2008, pp. 435–443 (2008)
4. Dirk, H., Ammosera, H., Kuhnerta, C.: Information flows in hierarchical networks
   and the capability of organizations to successfully respond to failures, crises, and
   disasters. Physica A 363, 141–150 (2006)
5. Qiu, J., Lin, Z., Tang, C., Qiao, S.: Discovering Organizational Structure in Dynamic Social Network. In: 2009 Ninth IEEE International Conference on Data
   Mining, pp. 932–957 (2009)

6. Mohanty, H.: Person habitat and migration modeling. In: 2011 Annual IEEE India Conference (INDICON), pp. 1–6 (2011)
7. Mohanty, H.: Modeling social directory- A formal approach. In: Recent Advances in Information Technology IEEE Proc. of RAIT, pp. 867–872 (2012)
8. Yang, H., Callan, J.: Learning the Distance Metric in a Personal Ontology. In: CIKM 2008, pp. 26–30 (2008)
9. Nickles, M., Rovatsos, M., Brauer, W., Weiss, G.: Communication Systems: A Unified Model of Socially Intelligent Systems. In: Fischer, K., Florian, M., Malsch, T. (eds.) Socionics. LNCS (LNAI), vol. 3413, pp. 289–313. Springer, Heidelberg (2005)
10. Ahlswede, R., Cai, N., Li, S.-Y.R.: Network Information Flow. IEEE Tr. Information Theory 46(4), 1204–1216 (2000)
11. Hartmann, W.R., Manchanda, P., Nair, H., Bothner, M., Dodds, P., Godes, D., Hosanagar, K., Tucker, C.: Modelling social interactions: Identification, empirical methods and policy implications. Market Lett. 19, 287–304 (2008)

Computational Social Science:
A Bird's Eye View

Hrushikesha Mohanty

Department of Computer and Information Sciences
University of Hyderabad
India
mohanty.hcu@gmail.com

Abstract. Social Systems and Computational Social Science - the terms often used interchangeably for the same concept speaks on emergence of a new area of research for both social and computing scientists with a hope of better understanding of social phenomena and using the same for delivering services to society. Further, the area assumes larger research interest for exploring behavior of netizens. This paper makes an attempt to follow the contours of research in this area with a proposal on designing of social systems.

Keywords: Social systems, Social networking, Computational social science.

1 Introduction

Here this study intends to understand social systems and their design principles. Ideally, a system made for society should be of the people, for the people addressing not only needs of today but also having provisions for future. The question of interest here is - what do we mean by *social systems*? Many have used the term in many ways. i. Some mean to multi-agent systems that use social theory for solving problems. *ii.* Currently many mean to Systems that support social networking in cyber world. *iii.* On the other hand information systems implementing social applications like e-governance, health care etc. are also termed as social systems. *iv.* Some investigators mean to systems that model and simulate social phenomena believing this understanding will help in designing systems of other three types.

In the process of understanding any natural phenomenon, researchers looked for formalism that could help to model the world under consideration. Later it's found, such phenomena goes beyond formalism with non-linearity that is required to incorporate in model; and that is achieved introducing chaos and complexity theory. Again, it's found unconvincing to think the world moves by chances and probabilistic choices. Thus realism has taken its position to explain world behaviour using genetic algorithm, bee colony algorithm etc. These techniques follow the reality i.e. patterns available in nature to solve problems. Again it's noticed that both observer and observed are not in consultation to

C. Hota and P.K. Srimani (Eds.): ICDCIT 2013, LNCS 7753, pp. 319–333, 2013.

explain themselves. Social systems needs a discourse among individuals and society. Both complement to each other in finding solution. Now, both computing power and techniques are at our disposal to realise such discourses required to find both quantitative and qualitative solutions to impending social problems.

This study aims to map and get an understanding of social systems. At first we list the levels of systems in general, and then seek to find a place for social systems. Section 2 presents on system categorisation. Third section highlights on complexity of social systems. Whereas fourth section lists the features social systems should have. A review on state-of-art of this area of study is presented in fifth section. Sixth section has a proposal on engineering approach of social systems. The paper concludes in seventh section. In any extent of imagination, I don't want to claim that the paper has made a tour covering all aspects of social systems. Still, the attempt has been made to understand the scope of the research in this area. The area in fledgling even strives for a unique title being identified by different names i.e. *Computational social science* and Social systems, as the case for Computational Biology and System Biology. In this paper I use both the terms finding the use appropriate in context. Next, the term Computational Social Science and its scope are explored.

1.1 Computational Social Science

Computational social science is an emerging field that leverages the capacity of information systems in dispensing services to society in a way guided by social practices and sensitivities reflected in prevailing society. Researchers in [4] discusses on issues that computational social science should intend to answer. It talks of two basic questions : what this branch would offer to community and what are the obstacles it faces now. For example, by collecting activities on web like social networking, email exchanges, tweets it's desirable to study the temporal dynamics of human communications and impacts - like how does information spread on web, rate of communication and ratio of information diffusion. How do interaction patterns take shapes causing inclusion or exclusion both in a society and on web society. It's interesting to compare behaviours of both society on web and society in reality. Study of society in reality has greater importance than web based society for very nature of human behaviour and its longing for proximity. This raises importance in study of face-to-face interaction with 'sociometers' that measures physical proximity, location, movement, and other facets of individual behavior and collective interactions. Study of macro social network society and its temporal evolution is an interesting subject not only for netizens but also in reality. The impact due to mobility can be studied like how a pathogen like influenza spreads driven by physical proximity. Spread of rumours and political messages in social networking is now under intense study by governments. Individual profiles available on Internet from their interactions on web, provides immense information that help to understand individuals. This information can be made use for effective governance and even for business promotions. In short *Computational Social Science* has huge potential for application in understanding people for delivering services accordingly.

But the limitations the area of study faces include: Paradigm shifts, institutional obstacles, data availability and security, sustainability. Till now, social science study has been with one time collected data. On availability of huge data that changes with time, we need a paradigm shift to handle such data and interpret the patterns hidden. The study has another dimension - theorising social phenomena to understand their causes and subsequent impacts on nature as well as societal and governmental institutions. This study is fundamental in nature in understanding human, its habitat and its behaviour. This study is not new. Social scientists have put these questions before and have analysed emanating possible answers. Now, at the advent of computing technology attempts are being made at computational models that can be helpful to build a unified framework in explaining social phenomena.

Such studies face both academic and institutional obstacles to get us from traditional social science to computational social science. It's easy for biology to transit to computational biology but that is not so for social science. It needs looking at society afresh and to discover computability of its behaviours. Further, for the people engaged in this study are also required to be sensitive to social ethics and practices. This requires an institution level monitoring like say biological science research makes itself open to scrutiny of ethics. Sustainability of computational social science needs collaborative study of social scientists and computer scientists. In addition, cognitive science offers are also attractive to the development of computational social science. Now, let's see what system development is looking for and the types of systems we may have.

2   On Systems

In a seminal work on system categorization taking a lead from nature, Boulding [2] has proposed nine levels of design to depict both hard and soft facts of social systems. A complex natural system is composed of nine levels of complexity, as per Boulding's hypothesis. The taxonomy of these levels are:

1. *Frameworks* provide a static configuration of systems like we find in engineering diagrams.
2. *Clockworks* model dynamic behaviour of a system.
3. *Thermostats* achieves self-regulation of systems by externally specified criteria.
4. *Open Systems* desires self-maintenance based on resources available around.
5. *Blue-printed Growth Systems* intends to practice division of labour that reproduce not by duplication but by the production of seeds or eggs containing preprogrammed instructions for development, such as the acorn-oak system or the egg-chicken system.
6. *Internal Image Systems* can perceive its environment and make knowledge structures for further processing.
7. *Symbol Processing Systems* systems that use language and other symbols, are self-conscious, and can contemplate the past, present, and future. That mimics the level at which human works.

8. *Social Systems* have properties of symbol processing systems as well as obey social order. Ofcourse, in practice following social order is made as one's free will. But, usually these systems share a common social order and culture. Social organizations operate at this level.

9. *Transcendental Systems* are composed of 'unknowables'[2]. It is a system of higher order like a living system with the highest level complexity. These systems follow the theory of existentialism in space-time dimensions, depend on matter-energy for existence and demonstrate creativity. Ofcourse, it remains elusive to build such systems.

As per Boulding, a system of a given level incorporates all the features of its lower levels.

3   Society and Its Complexity

Society is always complex for its heterogeneity and so also are social systems. Social systems we are interested in, can recreate and respond to social phenomena. Before, doing that we need to understand what are the dimensions these systems should have more (than conventional information systems) to identify themselves as social systems. We will list some characteristics here, to emphasize on the complexity of social systems.

Information systems are designed to deliver services to people and to make those people friendly at best good user interfaces they aspire to have. But, had these systems been designed based on users' social behaviours than these systems could have more desirable uses and impacts. This requires understanding of social phenomena and is uses in design of systems. This general understanding of a society of people is mostly quantitative nature. Currently, for the purpose mainly statistical approaches are being followed. But this statistical understanding does not project exact social reality. The quest for realistic modelling now drives research on social phenomena modelling, and the result looks promising both for collaborative efforts of social and computational scientists and possible immense applications for social benefits. Understanding the importance we here will look at the complexities the domain has.

Heterogeneity is inherent in a society. For heterogeneity, society exhibits random non-linear behaviour. Events and their occurrences are unpredictable. Societal modelling should not only be qualitative but also take other issues like *emergence, phase transition* and *dissipation* into consideration. Discontinuity of prevailing order and emergence of new order occurs after a large number of repetitions; this phenomena of emergence can be specified by a mathematical function. Thus, model trajectories show appearances of emergent behaviours which can be explained as resultants for changes in rules that individuals or agencies apply in social interactions. These emergent behaviours bring in phase transition. A societal emergent behaviour is brought in by social *attractor*s. And the change initiated at some point in a society gradually gets dissipated all through it. And a rate of change is determined by constitution of the society. Usually, these changes are very slow and remain undetectable for quite sometime. That's the reason why social phenomena is to be studied for early detection of possible events for taking corrective measures if required.

Social systems sometimes behave linear but at other times behave non-linear too. This randomness makes such systems complex. Social realism is seen as a mix of philosophical expectations as well as scientific analysis in representing social behaviour. For modelling social phenomena, it takes into account of entities and their roles at different levels and situations. While basic entity is an individual, emerging collective form makes a society. Social phenomena can't be called as just aggregation of individual behaviour. But, it's rather complex, non-linear and unexpectedly different. A society at different times finds a system of knowledge, that is expected to be followed scrupulously for ensuring expected social order. In the march of knowledge evolution, time line is divided into three categories viz.. **i.** *modernism*, **ii.** *post-modernism* **iii.** *Post-Normal Science*. Modernist see phenomena in cause-and-effect paradigm. However, some phenomena are random, unexplainable and viewed as an emergent behaviour. Post modernist view- social phenomena either repetitive and stable, or random and non-linear. Non-linearity says- randomness and unpredictability can even build order, albeit a rather complex one. May be at very long run, one can find pattern in random behaviour. In post-normal science era, thinkers while admitting role of complexity theory, still find fault in identifying its inability in modelling role of pluralism in society. Also it intends to put social systems as self-organised adaptive systems where behaviours both at individual (micro) and societal (macro) levels can be explained and activated. When modernists follow de-constructive approach in analysing social phenomena the post-modernists took construction of reality and view a social phenomena in totality. Next we'll take on the methods, researchers at different times followed in modelling social phenomena.

3.1   Understanding Complexity

At different times researchers have viewed social phenomena from different angles and so have proposed many methods for modelling the phenomena. World of natural science is observable and quantifiable. Modernist have viewed social phenomena in cause-effect paradigm and been engaged in exploring rules that make formal models. Using these rule-based models and social observations, predictions are made and phenomena are explained. Post-modernist on taking up randomness and non-linearity took up chaos theory along with formal model to explain new aspects of phenomena. They contributed a notion of *dynamic order* i.e. deterministic chaos to find patterns in randomness. Evolution of patterns albeit a complex behaviour that were identified with quantitative approach e.g. by statistical functions. During evolution, there is discontinuity (of prevailing pattern) and emergence of new. Mathematical functions are designed to model discontinuity of old and emergence of new patterns. Theory of fractals is used to model these issues with non-linearity and feedback process. Post-modernists could predict some other expects of model behaviour like pseudo predictability, soft predictability and bifurcation points. Pseudo-predictability represents a set of alternatives but soft-predictability states conditionality of each alternative where as bifurcation point represents the state at which alternative trajectories take different paths. Complexity, that favours to place social systems at mid-way between stability and chaos, uses enormous observed data to make a social system evolving. It intends to put social systems as self-organised adaptive systems where behaviours both at individual (micro) and societal (macro) levels can be explained. Social scientists while favouring qualitative approach in modelling, find inability of mathematical approach (for representing breakdowns of reality). They proposed non-mathematical approach like production rules for the purpose. The thrust has been to identify mathematical analogy that can be considered as a tool to understand social phenomena.

Modelling individuals is essential as it makes a necessary part of a society. Individual's goals, beliefs, relations and dependencies guide one's social behaviour. More, its cognitive actions and reactions make it different than an artificial entity. Study on agents, intends to model individual behaviour in a habitat for a specified goal. Further, agents are ascribed with intelligence and memory; and are designed to act proactively for changes in habitats. This micro modelling of individuals as agents driven by software has been a promising area of research with a high expectation. Again study on multi-agents is offering a macro-model for simulating a society and its phenomena. Interaction and co-ordination among agents for distributed problem solving are currently of prime interest of researchers in this field. Though multi-agent framework is promising still many more issues are to be considered to bring realism to the framework. Research advances in object-oriented and artificial intelligence systems will contribute to modelling of individuals and their society.

Now, rapid socialisation on Internet has brought in a new kind of society-cyber society. For its both casual and social, political and business driven uses have given rise to interest among researchers to study social networking. Finding and forecasting emerging social phenomena on social networks are also of prime interest of study.

From the trend of developments of systems and methods used, we observe that the growing interest in this field tries to push boundaries in development of models adding more and more desirable features. Next section we will identify and list some of those features of social systems.

4   Desirable Features

In contemporary world, individual as well as society are of equally importance. Modelling of a society must imbibe the characteristics due to both. The essential features what a social system should have are identified and listed in [6]. These include *Identity and boundaries, Intentionality, Rational and Self Interest, Strategic Reflectivity , Collaboration, Sociality, Attractor, Dissipative, Consensus* and *Inclusiveness*. In describing these features we will touch upon three: information systems, agents (agent-in-software) and individuals (agent-in-world), to tell what these features mean and how these can be realised.

Identity and boundaries: In case of traditional software systems identity is not an issue. It does not play a role in system execution and behaviour. At the most, a software system, is identified by the logo of its producer (product logo) and that is used to enforce intellectual property right of the product. But, agent-based systems are different for each having identity with an agency. Agent's identity is carved out according to the well-defined agency. But, agents-in-world are still different with changing identities and boundaries. And these boundaries could be overlapping and inconsistent even. Thus, identity of an agent-in-world (in society) is a complex notion to define. Boundary of an agent can be thought of one's scope of social rights and responsibilities. These two obviously change according to the social dynamics. Other way round, the changes at individual bring in difference to social dynamics. Thus in modelling social phenomena it's important to model identities and boundaries of agents; and analyse the impacts of these changes to societies.

Intentionality: In case of software systems, objectives are specified in detail either following UML models or formal models. Here user requirements are not only specified but also achieved through well designed systems. But agent-in-software is one level higher, as agent considers intentions as some choices to perform. Agent based computing has proposed *BDI* : Belief Desire Intention model, a 3-tier architecture that programs agents activities in a domain [14]. Multi-agent systems works on global intention and works out on methods to realize it as joint efforts. Agents implementing intention into decision structure generate possible behaviours. It's realised implementation of proper data structures and internal states may make implementation of beliefs, desires and intentions of agents realisable . But, agent-in-world (an individual) is altogether different for not having pre-suppositions on its world. Rather, its world evolves from its habitat and its perceptions; so also its intentions. Incrementally, an agent-in-world makes strategy on achieving its intention. Again multi-agents-in-world work on global intention defining individuals' roles considering their locality. It may bring a trade-off between global and local issues on realization of intentions of an agent. They could be both competitive as well as co-operative - thus making issues interesting to investigate further.

Rational and Self Interest: Model languages used for specifying Software are not enough to specify rationality and self interest. Rather, designer puts its design specifications to meet user requirements as well as design decisions. Agents in world while acting on self-interest do intend to be rational. All agents are not self-centred; there are also altruistic ones. Rationality in a software agent can be designed for a defined scope taking its internal states and constraints into considerations. In contrast, for agents-in-world i.e. individuals are open to wider external context and this makes the design of rational and self interest agents difficult indeed. Further, the same issue is applicable for macro modelling to show how a society behaves rationally while keeping its group interests in mind.

Strategic Reflectivity is a rational behaviour that asks questions to self for explaining, to reason on run-time behaviour. On asking such questions a system evaluates choices available at the current state and makes a strategic decision to select and execute the choices. So, while specifying agents, these choices are to be explored and evaluated for the sake of stakeholders. This feature in software agents can be built thorough analysis; missing cases can be handled by default reasoning. But in reality, reflecting on one's own activities and taking decision are very very difficult to automate because of co-locality problem - of observed and observers. This is also true for a society to reflect upon its deeds and history. But, this is the challenge required to meet sooner or later in design of social systems.

Collaboration is a behaviour a society exhibits at times for personal gains, social causes as well as altruistic reasons. An agent collaborates with other in anticipation of returns. Thus an agent exhibits collaborative behaviour for a personal cause. A social being sometimes also offer unconditional collaboration for social causes. At times, these two may compete and bring out a trade-off that needs to be judged for judicious decision making for collaboration. This decision making may be a sacrifice or a self-gain leading to making of a personality. Another important issue for agents is initiation of actions, for example when an agent becomes conscious to initiate a collaboration. In case of software-agents, this initiation is triggered by external signals from external entities e.g system clock, remote calls. Ofcourse, an agent can seek collaboration on achieving a state. And that is to be specified. In contrast agents-in-world are capable of *self-initiation* of tasks to fulfil their objectives. Lastly, such systems evaluate self, asking how others get affected (positively or negatively) for their actions. This feature of a social system makes it socially responsive.

Sociality: is in nature with all the rational beings and so more with humans. Social systems need to be social for making its behaviour realistic. Mechanistic system, as we see now are designed for a desired output with respect to a specific given input. While designing a system, a designer considers a relationship among many that exist between a given sets of input and output. Thus, a mechanistic system unlike agents-in-world is exclusive for not considering the issues holistically also for not having contingency for future. Social systems need to be designed for implementing sociality into it.

Attractor: Social attractor is an entity that is able to generate resonance at members so that their states are synchronised to that of the attractor. Process of attraction goes through phases showing its growth, maintenance and decay. Identifying emergent views and persons that change course of society is an interesting problem to study. It reflects social dynamics. A society crosses individual boundary to visualise a new horizon led by an attractor. An attractor fades away and another emerges. Seems social attractor trajectory never repeats. Some time, there could be a void of an attractor in a society. Study of a society without an attractor and with of it is an interesting study.

Dissipation: Society possesses characteristics of dissipation such that external changes propagate among individuals without making any notable change to society. This phenomena is called *sand-piling*, as structure of a sand-pile remains the same in-spite of pouring more and more sands to the pile. That means mathematically, parameters of structure making are finalized not only by external factors but also, internal factors play a role. This shows roles of mathematics like fractals and chaos theory with high speed computations, in enabling social modellers following bottom-up approach, hither to unknown, in unfolding social realities by tweaking dependant variables differently. This helps not only to understand existing worlds but also to make varieties of possible worlds of interest.

Consensus is a problem studied much in distributed problem solving. It is a resultant global state obtained on synchronisation of local states. Further, the problem is as complex as Byzantine agreement with knowledge being local to individual. This feature has relevance in case of social decision making as for some cases wide agreement is required in mass. In case of social reality, while opting for consensus one has to be alert for not creating exclusiveness and looking for individuality respected. A social system should have feature for consensus and at the same time should judge trade-off with individualism.

Inclusiveness is the most wanted feature now for bridging growing disparities in society. For a given purpose the measures to be taken in a society to bring in inclusiveness is a matter of study. Further, one needs to be careful to assure that the measure does not bring in difference and exclusion in a round about way. In addition to these features, essential features like *trust* and *ethics* are also to be studied. Further, the roles of culture and spiritual belief in making of social phenomena are of interest in building social systems.

5   Current Research Trends

Considering the current fledgling state of social computing, we would like to cover its wider perspective showing the all around impacts it has on computing as well as users. If togetherness is a prime social feature, then computing has done with it in the name of parallel and distributed computing on juggling with the problems of parallelisation and synchronization. Again society as a collection of rational autonomous beings, has offered a paradigm for computing called multi-agent systems. These systems while trying to ascribe autonomy to computing have made efforts to implement social aspects like roles, dependency, trust, coalition and collaboration [1]. But then the research trends have taken different directions considering both the technical and social changes happening around. The former is due to overwhelming uses of Internet resulting large sizes of social networkings. And the later is for inquisitiveness of researchers to understand social phenomena and to provide means to overcome social problems. We will survey few recent works on both the aspects though our interest is with the later more.

Social networks, currently has been hot topics not only among netizens but also among researchers considering the changes technology has brought in social underpinnings. Small world, that's we all are connected by six degrees of separations, is no more a myth now. This now has been reality for social media like facebook, twitter etc. Users behaviour in a social media and data exchanged on it are to be studied to understand the impacts cyber society makes in current days. [8]

Tons of information available from social media users reflect emergent views and moods of a society. Further, finding out small but active groups is also an interesting problem. The kind of information flows in and the structures social networks make are useful to discover dynamically from social interactions. The problems are challenging for complexity as well as size. For example, an interesting problem of deriving domain ontology from annotated blog postings is studied in [16] . It also proposes deriving rules for interpreting blogs and forecasting emergent views from postings. Further who could be next to socialize, is a question with importance in making collaboration among business, political and social partners [5]. Gossiping, whispering and colluding are the phenomena need to be tracked for healthy development of society and effective governance. Organisations and individuals make networks for achieving their respective goals. And as time passes on, these networks may turn weak to appear as if these don't exist at all. For maintaining healthy practices and growth the $B2B$ and $B2G$ networks are to be reengineered to overcome weakness in networks [13].

A paper By Santos [15] sums up prospect of computational social systems in an elegant way telling the nascent state of the research in this area is looking forward to the flurry of investigations and developments in immediate future. The spurt of technological developments have aroused interests in understanding and simulating phenomena found in different branches of science including physical, chemical and biological sciences. Similarly, researchers make attempts in social science. Understanding social phenomena helps in developing several applications like modelling financial markets, understanding disease spread,determining the effects of catastrophes and crisis, uncovering covert activities, evaluating political stability, predicting elections, poverty elevation and making of inclusive society. The goal not only requires expertise in computing science but also in understanding and codifying theories scientists have already found in different faculties of social science like economics, sociology, law, political science and psychology. It's now required to have integrated study of society for better understanding and prescribing of curative measures.

Study of computational economics is useful to understand people behaviour in economic activities. Social consideration and personal choices guide a person to behave in its economic dealings. The real life economic activities are simulated in [9] following agent based computation that follows bottom-up approach in bringing up the model and making it adaptive to emerging situations. The paper identifies similarity and dissimilarity between real and simulated environment.

Social capital of an individual has been understood in terms of its social relationships. In [11] two new approaches are proposed to explore social capital. One is resource generator and the other is trait analysis. The first approach deals with collection of information on individual's ownership on possible resources available . A resource may be shared by a group of people. Positive correlation between two resource items indicates that while a person can access one resource than it can most likely access the other. Secondly, it proposes trait analysis following *item response theory* to model social capital as a collection of latent traits - showing how features in a population that describe individual attributes with values may change over time. Cumulatively, the emergent social capital is a resource that is shared by most in a population. So the paper proposes a new instrument *social resource generator* to measure social capital. It also proposes method to aggregate individual resource to measure social capital.

A fascinating work [12] demonstrates use of social networking in observing social behaviour. It uses data generated from multiplayer online games and analyses social behaviour of players. People engaged in such games generate a virtual income through economic activities to survive and are typically engaged in a multitude of social activities offered within the game. Researchers observe logs of these transactions and have discovered players making friend-, enemy- and communication networks. They have found striking differences in topological structure between positive (friend) and negative (enemy) tie networks. All networks confirm the recently observed phenomenon of network densification. They have proposed two approximate social laws in communication networks, the first expressing betweenness centrality as the inverse square of the overlap, the second relating communication strength to the cube of the overlap. These empirical laws provide strong quantitative evidence for the Weak ties hypothesis of Granovetter [7]. Thus online game offers a laboratory condition to study real life social phenomena.

Society with increasing use of computers in day to day activities needs these system to behave politely to bring in good will in cyber society. Till now human computer interaction has not considered *politeness* as a feature to implement in information systems. A social system needs to be polite implementing respect, openness, helpfulness, and social memory. In paper [3] researchers discuss on a proposal to implement these aspects and hope for further research in *polite computing*.

Most important in current times has been social movement like *Arab Spring, Jasmine walk, Occupy Wall Street* and *India Against Corruption* greatly facilitated by cyber society. From other angle it's important as well as challenging to visualise social phenomena using computational modelling techniques. This emerging area of research will remain hot in coming years.

6   Design Ideas

Presently, information systems mainly are being used to facilitate services for people. The design of these systems primarily aims to handle large data and to deliver service in time. Thus, issues like reducing time and managing data space are considered in designing. As we have discussed earlier, social system is different with its typical features and non-linearity. It is not only to worry about today's society but also needs to address future. When I say a society, I mean people, their habitats and external world. A social system should have micro worlds of individuals and a macro world that individuals project. Macro world is an emergent world that partly emerges from micro worlds. Further, in between two types of worlds there exists a composed world at the first level made from micro worlds and subsequently from evolving composed worlds. So, composed worlds could be different granularity and structures. These worlds make legislative, administrative and social organisations with some designated purposes. The composed worlds also contribute to making of macro world. Macro world is an abstract world pervading both micro and composed worlds. And this abstract world has impressive influence on people in making decision. As people differ in perceiving this world differently so their decisions differ. Composed world has structures like layered, hierarchical, graph-like and etc. having relevance to the purpose of compositions. Idea of this world abstraction, is to make a comprehensive view on which a social system operates and social phenomena are explained. We view working of a social system as interactions among entities of these worlds.

Individuals can be thought of as computational agents, each making a micro world in which agent is autonomous and rational in its behaviour [1]. In the paradigm of multi-agents there has been a lot of work on agent designs and implementation. Broadly, methods used for such design ranges from formal (logic) to structural (UML based). Already, some social issues like autonomy, trust and collaboration are designed into agent-based systems. Further these designs can be improved on to, simulate individuals' traits. The question is whether artificial intelligence techniques viz. reasoning, circumspection, learning, belief and etc. can be built into agent models for the purpose of building social systems - a question is to be investigated. Implementation and its practicality for domain specific usages are to be studied with rigour.

The agents of composed worlds of a social system can be thought of an organisation, nation state or any other in which individuals operate. How do individuals make this world? And how entities of this world interact with agents of micro worlds, is to be modelled in design of a social system. Viewing social systems as a system for executing services, system designer needs to automate actions of customers and service providers facilitating fair execution of service transactions. Ofcourse, these transactions are to follow domain rules and public policies. In addition, such a system needs to have some relevant social characteristics discussed earlier; and these required characteristics can be explored from the relations exist among types of entities found in three types of worlds viz. macro, composed and macro worlds.

In reality there could be several emergent views to construct competing or collaborating macro worlds. And macro worlds pervade entities of other two worlds and influence both structural and dynamic behaviour of service paradigms. Similarly, new kinds of services evolve from world dynamics. While micro world individuals exhibit free will (like choosing and availing / performing) to deal with services, macro world either promotes, demotes or remains indifferent in dealing with services. The world actions are rationalised for strategic decisions world entities make. But, again totally unexpected behaviours of entities take place for (influence of) attractors emergent views that impact (like, encouraging, discouraging, indifferent or introspective)on agents' actions. What is an emergent view? Is it rational to accept emergent views influencing social decision making? Ofcourse, dealing with these philosophical questions needs a higher order of system design that remains a challenge inviting researchers to deal with. Below, we present a process in design of social systems - designed to provide services to members of a society.

Social system design process includes the following steps:
- World perception,
- Defining world structures and dynamics,
- Service provisioning,
- Analysis and introspection.

For a given application, it's essential to find out the participating entities of the related worlds. The structures these entities make are vital to realize for success-ful implementation. More important, visualising macro world that emerges from micro and composed worlds. For example, people in a city and its municipality are the entities of micro and composed worlds respectively. But, the perception on the both, project a macro world that is a combination of emergent views due to people and municipality. The emergent views a macro world holds have a substantial bearing on world behaviour. Service provisioning, that traditional information system, is generally based on defined policies. Execution of policies gets affected by social power relations, culture and values that a macro world holds. Also system functioning gets galvanised by roles of social attractors. Basi-cally in second step, a stock has to be taken on the social features that a system in hand has to have. And also to decide on how these features influence a service provisioning. This makes social systems unique to information systems. Need of the hour is to make these social features computationally feasible. Below, we present a table showing possible use of techniques hitherto available.

Table 1. Techniques and Purpose

Chaos Theory	modelling butterfly effect in social dynamics.
Causality	represents *causal nexus* in social phenomena.
Field theory	generalisation, emergent view modelling.
Sociometry	measuring social relationships.
Information Theory	representing social perception, communication.
Game Theory	strategic decision making.
Catastrophe Theory	Studying Non-linear behaviour of society.
Fuzzy logic	reasoning with inexactness.
Agent-based computing	Autonomy and contract based service.
Soft-computing techniques	Approximation and optimisation.
Graph theory	Studying social structures.
Probability Theory	Prediction.
Artificial intelligence	Artificial society.
Internet technology	Social networking.
Datamining	Exploration of behavioural patterns.

At this discussion, we come to a point to make a recommendatory note on design of social systems. It includes:

- To (computationally) realise social characteristics
- and to integrate these in social system developments.

A broad outline of a process for social systems development is proposed here. In no means it's a final call rather a beginning with conclusive proposals in the next section.

7   Conclusion

In this paper, first on categorising levels of systems, we have focussed on social systems on listing the characteristics these systems need to have. Because, these not only help to understand social phenomena but also could be useful in design of information systems sensitizing those of social purpose, urgency and rationality. Recognising the flurry of research on social networking, it's reasoned that observations on netizens' Internet usages can help in understanding evolving social phenomena. For a digitally connected society study of netizens' behaviour is essential. However, in the context of developing countries, a mixed approach is required as a large part of population remain digitally divided for years to come in future. This scenario throws a research challenge to amalgamate both the requirements and to find a common design solution. I suggest the urgency of incremental approach in finding design solutions for domain specific social systems. And then generalize the approach to offer a grand design.

Success of social systems depends on implementing social phenomena in design, so to cater better services to people in a society [10]. Though the ability to model social phenomena holds the key to success of social systems; still, engineering of such systems is equally important.

References

1. Lacroix, B., Mathieu, P., Kemeny, A.: Formalizing the construction of populations in multi-agent simulations; Eng. Appl. Artif.Intel (2012),
   http://dx.doi.org/10.1016/j.engappai.2012.05.011
2. Boulding, K.E.: General systems theory - the skeleton of science E:CO Special Double Issue 6(1-2), 127–139 (2004)
3. Whitworth, B.: Politeness as a Social Software Requirement. IJVCSN 1(2), 65–84 (2009)
4. Lazer, D., et al.: Computational Social Science. Science 323, 721–723 (2009)
5. Liben-Nowell, D., Kleinberg, J.: The Link-Prediction Problem for Social Networks. In: Proceedings of the Twelfth Annual ACM International Conference on Information and Knowledge Management (CIKM 2003), pp. 556–559 (November 2003)
6. Yu, E.: Agent-Oriented Modelling: Software versus the World. In: Wooldridge, M.J., Weiß, G., Ciancarini, P. (eds.) AOSE 2001. LNCS, vol. 2222, pp. 206–225. Springer, Heidelberg (2002)
7. Granovetter, M.: The strength of weak ties. American Journal of Sociology 78(6), 1360–1380 (1973)
8. Liu, H., et al: Social Computing in the Blogosphere. IEEE Internet Computing, 12–14 (2010)
9. Tesfatsion, L.: Agent-Based Computational Economics: Growing Economies From the Bottom Up. Journal Artificial Life 8(1), 55–82 (2002)

10. Liua, L., Yu, E.: Designing information systems in social context: a goal and scenario modelling approach. Information Systems 29, 187–203 (2004)
11. Van Der Gaag, M., Snijders, T.A.B.: The Resource Generator: social capital quantification with concrete items. Social Networks 27, 1–29 (2005)
12. Szell, M., Thurner, S.: Measuring social dynamics in a massive multiplayer online game. Social Networks 32, 313–329 (2010)
13. Peng, M.W.: How Network Strategies and Institutional Transitions Evolve in Asia; Asia Pacific. Journal of Management 22, 321–336 (2005)
14. Rao, M.P.G.: BDI-agents: From Theory to Practice. In: Proceedings of the First International Conference on Multiagent Systems, ICMAS 1995 (1995)
15. Santos, E.E.: Computational Social Systems. Proceedings of the IEEE 100, 1271–1272 (2012)
16. Noh, T.-G.: Experience Search: Accessing the Emergent Knowledge from Annotated Blog Postings. In: International Conference on Computational Science and Engineering, pp. 639–644 (2009)

Localization Based on Two-Bound Reflected Signals in Wireless Sensor Networks

Kaushik Mondal[1,*], Arjun Talwar[2,**],
Partha Sarathi Mandal[1], and Bhabani P. Sinha[3]

[1] Indian Institute of Technology, Guwahati, India
[2] College of Engineering, Anna University, Chennai, India
[3] Indian Statistical Institute, Kolkata, India

Abstract. In absence of line-of-sight (LOS) signal, localization is a real challenge since multi-path effect takes place due to reflections and/or scattering of signals. In this paper we have assumed that there are few anchor nodes present in the network which broadcast ultrasonic and electromagnetic signals with their known positions. Based on receiving those ultrasonic signals and using received signal strength of the electromagnetic signals, a localization technique has been proposed for finding position of other sensor nodes. On the assumption that a signal may be reflected at most twice before reaching a node, our technique provides on an average 67% reduction of the area of the zone in which the sensor node will be bound to reside.

Keywords: LOS, NLOS, Obstacles, Localization, Wireless networks.

1   Introduction

Localization in absence of LOS signal is a challenging problem. For localization, usually distances and angles are measured by techniques like time of arrival (TOA) [1], angle of arrival (AOA) [2], time difference of arrival (TDoA) [2], received signal strength (RSS) [1], based on communication between anchors (nodes with known positions) and sensor nodes via beacons (ultrasonic or electromagnetic signals). Even if LOS signal is blocked by some obstacles, reflected or scattered signals may still reach the sensor nodes.

In this paper we use TOA, AOA, and RSS techniques for range estimation and try to find the position of sensor node in absence of LOS signal assuming that the signal is reflected at most two times before reaching the sensor node. A signal which reflects/scatters once before reaching to a sensor node is defined as *one-bound* signal in [8]. Similarly, a signal is said to be a *multiple-bound* signal if it reflects/scatters multiple times [9].

* The first author is thankful to the Council of Scientific and Industrial Research (CSIR), Govt. of India, for financial support during this work.
** The second author is thankful to the IASc-INSA-NASI Summer Research Fellowship in 2012, for financial support during this work.

C. Hota and P.K. Srimani (Eds.): ICDCIT 2013, LNCS 7753, pp. 334–346, 2013.
© Springer-Verlag Berlin Heidelberg 2013

Localization algorithms in WSNs, can be classified into *range-based* and *range free* methods. Accuracy of the range based algorithms [2] are higher than the range free [3] ones. Ebrahimian and Scholtz proposed a source localization scheme under a model which allows reflection [2] which uses sensor nodes those posses unidirectional antenna. To locate mobile users in urban area, Uchiyama *et al.* proposed UPL algorithm in [10]. Authors assumed that the position of the reflectors are known and got some certain degree of accuracy. Pahlavan *et al.* [7] proposed indoor geo-location under NLOS scenario. Another angle measurement method has been proposed by Oberholzer *et al.* called SpiderBat [6]. This is an ultrasonic-based sensor node platform that can provide accurate result. Seow *et al.* [8] proposed a localization algorithm where multiple-bound signals are present. The authors used a statistical proximity test for discarding multiple-bound signals with a high degree of accuracy. After that remaining LOS and one-bound signals they have used for node localization. Erroneous location estimation is possible in [8] as the discarding technique relays on statistical test.

1.1 Our Contribution

In this paper, we have proposed an Algorithm: LOCALIZENODE to find the position of a sensor node in presence of multi-path effects under the assumption that signals are received either directly or as one-bound (after one reflection) or as two-bound (after two reflections). The proposed technique calculates position of the sensor nodes accurately if the nodes receive either a LOS signal or a one-bound signal. In presence of only two-bound signals, the proposed technique calculates an area for the position of a node. To the best of our knowledge there is no work in the literature using multi-bound (reflected more than once) signals to locate the position of a node deterministically. Our achievements are the following:

- Our proposed technique distinguishes among LOS, one-bound and two-bound signals. It helps us to avoid misinterpretation of LOS or one-bound with two-bound signals and vice versa.
- In the situation, where only two-bound signals are available, the proposed algorithm can find an area where the node is located. Here the significance is the following. If a two-bound signal traverses d distance from an anchor then the possible location of the node is within a circle of radius d centering at the anchor. Our algorithm would eventually lead to substantial reduction of the area of the zone in which the sensor node will be bound to reside. Our simulation result shows that on an average, approximately 67% of the area will be reduced for locating the position of a sensor node compare to existing techniques.

2   Basic Idea

We have assumed sensor nodes with unique *ids* are deployed in a two dimensional plane such that more than one node is not located at the same point. Few reflectors and anchors are located on the same plane where the nodes are deployed. The position of the nodes are calculated based on a common coordinate system, using the known positions of the anchors. The anchor nodes are uniquely identified by their positions. An anchor node uses ultrasonic signal and electromagnetic signal to broadcast beacon along with its position. The sending signal strength S_s of the electromagnetic signal remain fixed. A sensor node receives the LOS signal if there is no obstacles or reflectors on the direct path, otherwise the node may receive Non-line-of-sight (NLOS) signal after at most two reflections according to our model. A node measures the (i) receiving angle of arrival (θ) of the beacon with the positive x−axis using directional antenna and (ii) RSS of the electromagnetic signal along with the phase shift. Then it transmits back the ultrasonic signal with the angle information, received signal strength S_r and phase shift along the same path using directional antenna. Anchor measures the angle of arrival (δ) of the beacon using directional antenna while receiving from the node. It calculates the distance (d) traversed by the beacon using round trip delay of arrival using TOA technique.

In the paper [5], the algorithm: FINDPOSITION detects position of a node, based on TOA and AOA measurements techniques under the model which allows up to one-bound signals which are insufficient in presence of two-bound signal. We can state the following result from the paper [5].

Result 1. *Under the model which allows up to one-bound signal, TOA and AOA measurement techniques are sufficient to distinguish LOS and one-bound signals.*

Theorem 1. *(Impossibility) Under the model which allows up to two-bound signal, the TOA and AOA measurement techniques are insufficient to locate a node in a specific position with the two-bound signals.*

Proof. We consider the case when a node Q receives two-bound signal from an anchor S. Total distance d (say) is calculated by the anchor S using TOA technique, which is actually the sum of the three distances, say, d_1, d_2, d_3, where d_1, d_2, d_3 are the distances from anchor S to first reflecting point P, first reflecting point to second reflecting point P' and second reflecting point to the node Q respectively. Using AOA technique, angles δ and θ are calculated at S and Q respectively with positive direction of x−axis in the counter clockwise direction.

Now, we want to prove that for any position of Q within the circle of radius d centering at S, there exist reflecting points P and P' satisfying TOA and AOA measurements. Look at the Fig. 1 for the proof.

Let Q' be an arbitrary position of Q such that $SQ' = r < d = ST$. SC_1 and $Q'C_2$ are two straight lines such that $\angle XSC_1 = \delta$ and $\angle C_2Q'X' = \theta$, where X, X' are the direction of the positive x-axis. We have to find two points P, P' on SC_1 and $Q'C_2$ respectively such that $SP + PP' + P'Q' = d$. From continuity, we can say there exist a point P such that $PQ' < d - SP$. Now our objective is to find a triangle $PP'Q'$ such that $PP' + P'Q' = d - SP$. Finding such an P' is straight forward from the definition of continuity. So, any point Q' within the circle of radius d is a possible position of Q. Hence it is possible to locate Q only somewhere within the circle of radius d; no further accuracy is possible.   □

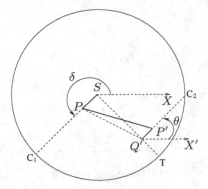

Fig. 1. Figure showing a two-bound signal received by node Q'

2.1 Distinguishing LOS, One-Bound and Two-Bound Signals

To reduce the area (the area within the circle of radius d centering at S, refer to the Theorem 1) of the possible positions of a node, additional measurement techniques are needed when a node receives only two-bound signals. So, first we need to identify the received signal whether it is LOS, one-bound or two-bound. In this work, to distinguish between LOS and two-bound signals, RSS technique has been used. We know that a signal experiences a phase shift of π per reflection from a surface having higher reflective index. Using this property it is possible to distinguish between one-bound and two-bound signals. RSS technique helps to reduce the area of the possible positions of a node if the node receives only two-bound signals.

Theorem 2. *An anchor node can distinguish among LOS, one-bound and two-bound signals from node, if the anchor measures TOA, AOA the phase shift and signal strength of the received electromagnetic signal.*

Proof. Let a node Q receive either the LOS signal or an one-bound signal (Fig. 2a) or a two-bound signal (Fig. 2b).

Let d be the total distance traveled by the signal which is measured using TOA technique, which can be expressed as follows.

$$d = \sum_{i \in \{1,2,3\}} d_i, \tag{1}$$

where i depends on the number of reflections. The value of i is equal to 1 for LOS signal, 1 and 2 for one-bound signal, and 1, 2 and 3 for two-bound signal.

The angles δ and θ are also known using AOA technique. For a LOS signal following eqn. 2 must be true.

$$\theta = \delta \pm \pi \tag{2}$$

But in the case of a two-bound signal as shown in Fig. 2c, eqn. 2 is satisfied. Fig. 2c is a specific configuration of Fig. 2b. So, the two-bound signal of Fig. 2c may

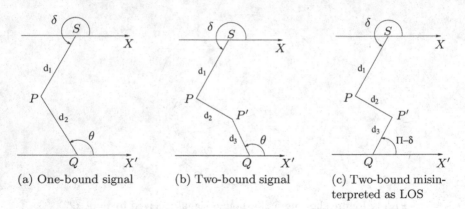

Fig. 2. Figures showing one-bound and two-bound signals reach to Q

be misinterpreted as a LOS signal. To distinguish between LOS and two-bound signals, the RSS technique is used. In case of LOS signal the Friis transmission equation [4] given below is used for RSS technique: $S_r = S_s \left(\frac{\lambda}{4\pi d}\right)^n$, where n is the path loss exponent, in case of multi-path effect the value of $n \in [2,6]$. In this paper, we take the value of n is equal to 2. But our algorithm will work for any specific n depending on the environment in which the sensor network is deployed. So, the equation for LOS signal is,

$$S_r = S_s \frac{c}{d_1^2} = S_s \frac{c}{d^2}, \tag{3}$$

where c is a known constant and S_r is the received signal strength.

In case of one-bound signal as shown in Fig. 2a, the signal travels from S to Q via the reflecting point P where $SP = d_1$ and $PQ = d_2$. We apply the Friis transmission equation on the path SP, then $S'_r = S_s \frac{c}{d_1^2}$ if S'_r is the signal strength at P. Let h percentage of the signal strength be decreased after reflection at P. Then Friis transmission equation for the remaining path PQ is $S_r = \frac{100-h}{100} S'_r \frac{c}{d_2^2} = \frac{100-h}{100} S_s \frac{c^2}{d_1^2 d_2^2}$, where S_r is the receiving signal strength at Q.

Finally, the Friis transmission equation in case of one-bound (eqn. 4) and two-bound (eqn. 5) signals are given below.

$$S_r = S_s \frac{c'^2}{d_1^2 d_2^2} \quad \text{where } c' = c\sqrt{\frac{100-h}{100}} \tag{4}$$

$$S_r = S_s \frac{c''^3}{d_1^2 d_2^2 d_3^2} \quad \text{where } c'' = c\left(\frac{100-h}{100}\right)^{\frac{2}{3}}, \tag{5}$$

where $\sum_{i \in \{1,2,3\}} d_i = d$. Now, LOS, one-bound and two-bound signals can be identified as follows:

If eqn. 2 is satisfied then the signal is either LOS or two-bound, otherwise the signal is either one-bound or two-bound.

LOS vs Two-bound: If eqn. 2 holds and the value of d from eqn. 1 also satisfies eqn. 3, then the receive signal is identified as a LOS signal. Otherwise, it is a two-bound signal.

There is another possibility that the values of d_1, d_2, d_3 are such that $S_s \frac{c}{d^2} = S_s \frac{c''^3}{d_1^2 d_2^2 d_3^2}$, where $d = d_1 + d_2 + d_3$. In this case the two-bound signal can be misinterpreted as a LOS signal. This happens if and only if $d_1 d_2 d_3 = c''d$. But, the conditional probability, $P((d_1 d_2 d_3 = c''d)|(d = d_1 + d_2 + d_3))$ almost equal to zero, since d_i for $i = 1$ to 3 can take any random value in $(0, d)$, so $d = d_1 + d_2 + d_3$ actually indicates all the points inside the triangle formed by the vertices, $(d, 0, 0)$, $(0, d, 0)$, and $(0, 0, d)$, which is a plane, again, $d_1 d_2 d_3 = c''d$ is the equation of a curve inside the triangular area. Hence, we disregard the possibility all together.

One-bound vs Two-bound: If eqn. 2 does not hold then it must be a one-bound or a two-bound signal. To identify this signal correctly, we use the phase shift property. The phase difference of the electromagnetic wave received by node Q due to traversal of distance d would be $2\pi d/\lambda = \phi$, where λ is the wavelength. Divide ϕ by 2 and find the remainder of the division. Call the remainder R. Now if the total phase difference is equal to R then the signal is a two-bound signal. On the other hand, if the total phase difference is equal to $R \pm 1$, then the signal is a one-bound signal.   □

2.2 Locating the Position of a Node

After identifying the signal according to the theorem 2 the value of $d_1 \times d_2$ is calculated from eqn. 4 in case of one-bound signal, the value $d_1 \times d_2 \times d_3$ is calculated from eqn. 5 in case of a two-bound signal. In the following discussion we are going to explain how to find location of a node Q after identifying different multiple-bound signals.

Case 1: If Q receives one LOS signal then it is sufficient to find the accurate position of the node Q and which is $\left(\pm\frac{d}{\sqrt{1+m^2}}, \pm\frac{md}{\sqrt{1+m^2}}\right)$ where d is the direct distance measured using TOA technique and $m = \tan\delta$ where δ is the receiving angle of the reply from Q at S with respect to the counter clockwise direction of x-axis as done in [5].

Case 2: If Q receives a one-bound signal then position of Q is calculated based on the values of δ, θ measured using AOA technique and the values of d_1 and d_2 are calculated from the following two equations:

$$d = d_1 + d_2 \text{ and } d_1 d_2 = \sqrt{c'^2 \frac{S_s}{S_r}} \qquad (6)$$

In this case position of Q is $\left(\pm\frac{d_1}{\sqrt{1+m_1^2}} \pm \frac{d_2}{\sqrt{1+m_2^2}}, \pm\frac{m_1 d_1}{\sqrt{1+m_1^2}} \pm \frac{m_2 d_2}{\sqrt{1+m_2^2}}\right)$

Although it represents four points, S can find the exact position by choosing the correct signs using known δ_i and θ_i.

Case 3: If Q receives a two-bound signal then exact position of Q is not possible to calculate, instead of that a bounded area can be calculated for the possible location of the node Q. We can rewrite eqn. 1 and eqn. 5 as follows:

$$d = d_1 + d_2 + d_3 \text{ and } d_1 d_2 d_3 = \sqrt{c''^3 \frac{S_s}{S_r}} \quad (= k, say) \qquad (7)$$

There is a possibility of infinitely many solutions of d_1, d_2, d_3 for the above two equations, which indicates that the possible solution of Q is not unique. The possible solution space of Q always lies within a circle of radius d with the center at the anchor S. Our objective is to reduce the solution space as much as possible compared to the whole circle. Eqn. 7 can be viewed as,

$$d_1 d_2 (d - d_1 - d_2) = k \text{ where } d_1, d_2 > 0 \qquad (8)$$

Each point on the curve 8 is a possible value of d_1 and d_2. We consider only the positive values of d_1 and d_2 as they are the distances. Eqn. 8 is symmetric with respect to d_1 and d_2 so, if (a, b) is a point satisfying eqn. 8, then so is (b, a).

For a particular solution of eqn. 8, say, d_1 and d_2, Q lies on the circle with radius $d - d_1 - d_2$ and center at $\left(\pm \frac{d_1}{\sqrt{(1+m_1^2)}} \pm \frac{d_2}{\sqrt{(1+m_2^2)}}, \pm \frac{m_1 d_1}{\sqrt{(1+m_1^2)}} \pm \frac{m_2 d_2}{\sqrt{(1+m_2^2)}} \right)$ as shown in the Fig. 3, where, $PP'' = P'Q$ and $P''Q = PP'$. Where $\tan \delta = m_1$ and $\tan \theta = m_2$. We can choose signs according the known angles.

Based on the above discussion, according to every point (d_1, d_2) on the curve (eqn. 8), we can find the center $(T_1(d_1, d_2), T_2(d_1, d_2))$ of the corresponding circle as shown in the Fig. 3 using the following linear transformations:

$$T_1(d_1, d_2) = \pm \frac{d_1}{\sqrt{(1 + m_1^2)}} \pm \frac{d_2}{\sqrt{(1 + m_2^2)}}$$

$$T_2(d_1, d_2) = \pm \frac{m_1 d_1}{\sqrt{(1 + m_1^2)}} \pm \frac{m_2 d_2}{\sqrt{(1 + m_2^2)}} \qquad (9)$$

It is easy to check that eqn. 8 is a continuous curve. Since the transformations of eqn. 9 are linear, so it maps the continuous curve of eqn. 8 to another continuous curve, which is the locus of the centers of all the circles. Hence, the curve consisting of the centers of all possible circles on which the node Q may lie is again a continuous curve. Now we look on the range of the radius of the circles. For the maximum radius we need to find the $\max(d - d_1 - d_2)$ among every point (d_1, d_2) on the curve (eqn. 8), which is same as to find the $\min(d_1 + d_2)$. Similarly, we can find the circle of minimum radius by finding $\min(d - d_1 - d_2)$.

We can find the points (d_1', d_2') and (d_1'', d_2'') corresponding to the minimum and maximum values of $(d_1 + d_2)$ for all (d_1, d_2) on the curve (eqn. 8), using Lagrange method of several variables or using some numerical scheme. Now the radius of the circles are varying from $(d - d_1'' - d_2'')$ to $(d - d_1' - d_2')$ continuously

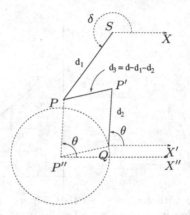

Fig. 3. The circle on which the node lies in case of the two-bound signals

over a continuous curve. The area covered by the circumferences of the all circles is the area where Q lies. The following theorem 3 helps to find the area.

Theorem 3. *Let* $C = (T_1(d_1, d_2), T_2(d_1, d_2))$ *and* $C' = (T_1(d'_1, d'_2), T_2(d'_1, d'_2))$ *be two points corresponding to points* (d_1, d_2) *and* (d'_1, d'_2) *respectively from eqn. 8. Then the circle with center* C *is contained in the circle with center* C' *if* $d_1 > d'_1, d_2 > d'_2$.

Proof. First we have to find the center corresponding to (d_1, d_2) and (d'_1, d'_2). There will be several cases.

Case 1: If $\delta \in (0, \pi/2) \cup (3\pi/2, 2\pi)$ and $\theta \in (0, \pi/2) \cup (3\pi/2, 2\pi)$ then

$$((T_1(d_1, d_2), T_2(d_1, d_2)) = \left(\frac{d_1}{\sqrt{(1+m_1^2)}} - \frac{d_2}{\sqrt{(1+m_2^2)}}, \frac{m_1 d_1}{\sqrt{(1+m_1^2)}} - \frac{m_2 d_2}{\sqrt{(1+m_2^2)}} \right) \text{ and}$$

$$((T_1(d'_1, d'_2), T_2(d'_1, d'_2)) = \left(\frac{d'_1}{\sqrt{(1+m_1^2)}} - \frac{d'_2}{\sqrt{(1+m_2^2)}}, \frac{m_1 d'_1}{\sqrt{(1+m_1^2)}} - \frac{m_2 d'_2}{\sqrt{(1+m_2^2)}} \right).$$

Let $C_r = d - d_1 - d_2$ and $C'_r = d - d'_1 - d'_2$ be the radius of the circles with centers C and C' respectively. $(CC')^2 \leq (d_1 - d'_1)^2 + (d_2 - d'_2)^2 + 2(d_1 - d'_1)(d_2 - d'_2)$ if $|\frac{(1+m_1 m_2)}{\sqrt{(1+m_1^2)(1+m_2^2)}}| < 1$ and $(d_1 - d'_1)(d_2 - d'_2) > 0$.

Assume that for some values of m_1 and m_2, $\left(\frac{(1+m_1 m_2)}{\sqrt{(1+m_1^2)(1+m_2^2)}} \right)^2 > 1$ holds. That implies $(m_1 - m_2)^2 < 0$, which is a contradiction. So, $(CC')^2 \leq \{(d_1 + d_2) - (d'_1 + d'_2)\}^2$ if $(d_1 - d'_1)(d_2 - d'_2) > 0$. Implies, $CC' + C_r \leq C'_r$ if $d_1 > d'_1, d_2 > d'_2$. Therefore, the circle with center at C is contained in the circle with center at C' as shown in the Fig. 4a, where $C'_r = C'G'$ and $C_r = CG$ are the radius of the circles with center at C', C respectively.

Case 2: $\delta \in (0, \pi/2) \cup (3\pi/2, 2\pi)$ and $\theta \in (\pi/2, 3\pi/2)$

Case 3: $\delta \in (\pi/2, 3\pi/2)$ and $\theta \in (0, \pi/2) \cup (3\pi/2, 2\pi)$

Case 4: $\delta \in (\pi/2, 3\pi/2)$ and $\theta \in (\pi/2, 3\pi/2)$

Similar proofs as Case 1.   □

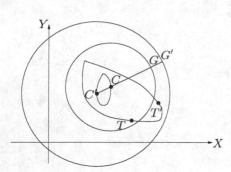

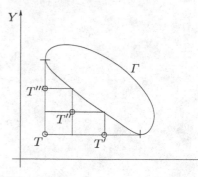

(a) Figure showing circle with center at C is lie within the circle with center at C', T and T' are the points on the curve (eqn. 8) and C and C' are the corresponding centers from eqn. 9

(b) Figure showing points $T = (x_m, y_m)$, $T' = (x_1, y_1)$, $T'' = (x_2, y_2)$, $T''' = (x_3, y_3)$ for the curve Γ (eqn. 8) and corresponding to the circles with center at C, C_1, C_2 and C_3 respectively

Fig. 4.

2.3   Area Calculation for a Node in Case of Two-Bound Signals

We use the above result of the theorem 3 to cover all the circles on which Q may lie. Using Lagrange multiplier for several variable or using some numerical techniques, we can find $y_m = min\{y\}$ and $x_m = min\{x\}$ on eqn. 8. Note that the values of x_m and y_m are same due to the symmetric nature of the curve (eqn. 8). Now, if we take the circle with center at $(T_1(x_m, y_m), T_2(x_m, y_m))$ and radius $d - x_m - y_m$ then by the above theorem 3, it includes all the circles (where Q may lie) corresponding to all other points on eqn. 8. So, the area bounded by the circle with center at $C = (T_1(x_m, y_m), T_2(x_m, y_m))$ and radius $R = d - x_m - y_m$ is the possible location of Q.

We can further reduce possible area of Q by choosing appropriate numbers of overlapping circles such that the area of the union of the circles is less compare to the circle with center at C and radius R. Let, we want to cover the the area by three circles. How to chose three circles (for example, in general p circles) instead of one circle for reducing the area is given below and corresponding illustration is given in the Fig. 4b. Let $C_1 = (T_1(x_1, y_1), T_2(x_1, y_1))$, $C_2 = (T_1(x_2, y_2), T_2(x_2, y_2))$ and $C_3 = (T_1(x_3, y_3), T_2(x_3, y_3))$ be centers and R_1, R_2 and R_3 be the radiuses of the three circles. Now, we have to find three set of center and radius for the circles. For which we can compute x_0 from eqn. 8 corresponding to y_m and the interval, $\frac{x_0 - x_m}{3} = u$ (say). Now $x_1 = x_0 - u$, $y_1 = y_m$ and $R_1 = d - x_1 - y_1$ specify the first circle. For second circle we have to compute $y_2 = y$ corresponding to x_1 from eqn. 8 and $x_2 = x_1 - u$ and radius $R_2 = d - x_2 - y_2$. Like second circle for the third circle we have to compute $y_3 = y$ corresponding to x_2 from eqn. 8 and $x_3 = x_2 - u$ which is same as x_m and radius $R_3 = d - x_3 - y_3$.

With reference to the Fig. 4b we can say that the three circles corresponding to the points T', T'' and T''' also covers all the circles as the circle corresponding to T does. For $p > 1$, we get lesser area than $p = 1$. It happens since the radius of the circle is the largest when $p = 1$. Since the radius of the circles decreases as p increases, the efficiency increases with p. Our simulation studies verified result for $p = 1, 2, 3$. If Q receives multiple number of two-bound signal from S then the intersection of the areas calculated using each of the two-bound signal as the possible position of Q in question. Then center of gravity of the intersected area can be considered as the approximate position of Q.

3 Proposed Localization Algorithm

System Model: All anchor nodes are equipped with an omnidirectional antenna for sending beacons and also a directional antenna for the measurement of AOA of a signal from other sensor nodes. Other sensor nodes are equipped with directional antennas to avoid collision when it receives more than one beacon from an anchor coming through different paths at different angles. An anchor is said to be a *neighbor* of another anchor if it is located within twice the transmission range of the second anchor. Anchor nodes are synchronized with some global clock (possibly through GPS) such that at a time only one anchor sends a beacon to avoid collision with the beacons from the neighboring anchors. This ensures that a receiving sensor node receives only one beacon at a time from a particular anchor.

The Algorithm: Based on the above discussions, Algorithm LOCALIZENODE given below finds the position of a sensor node Q using the beacon signals from an anchor S. Q may receive either the LOS signal from S and/or it may receive one or more reflected signals from S.

4 Simulation Results

We have simulated for the case of two-bound signals by randomly deployed nodes and reflectors over a square field. We have chosen the location of the anchor at a corner of the square which is considered as origin of the common coordinate system. If total distance traveled by a two-bound signal is d then possible position of the node is inside the circle of area πd^2, which is the red (largest) circle shown in the Fig. 5.

But we have found the possible area as $\pi(d - x_m - y_m)^2$ for Q which is the black (second largest) circle. The area surrounded by the black circle is much less than the red circle. Simulation results in Fig. 5 show that if we cover the area by two (pink-dotted) or three (blue-dotted) circles, then area of presence can be further reduced as discussed in the section 2.3. The union of infinitely many green circles in Fig. 5 (in the figure finitely many green circles are drawn where as theoretically there is infinitely many green circles) is the exact area of presence of the node which we try to cover by finite circles. For each run of our

---

Algorithm 1: LOCALIZENODE

1: Anchor S sends two beacons by omnidirectional antenna with *<anchor_id>* first, using electromagnetic signal and second, using ultrasonic signal.
2: **for** each sensor node Q who hears the beacons **do**
3:     Receives electromagnetic signal and measures receiving signal strength S_r and the phase shift ϕ of the electromagnetic signal.
4:     Measures the angles of arrival (θ) of the ultrasonic signal and transmits back *<node_id, θ, S_r, ϕ>* to S via the same path.
5: **end for**
6: S measures the angles of arrival (δ) while receiving the reply and computes the corresponding distances (d) traveled by the beacon by measuring the TOA.
7: S detect the signal as LOS, one-bound or two-bound using Theorem 2.
8: If the signal is LOS then position of Q is calculated accurately using δ and d (Ref. Case 1 of Sec 2.2).
9: If the signal is one-bound then using RSS method it gets another eqn. 4 and solves eqn. 6. Then using the angles δ and θ, it finds the position of Q accurately (Ref. Case 2 of Sec 2.2).
10: If the signal is two-bound then it calculate x_m from eqn. 8. Then it transforms the point (x_m, y_m) to $(T_1(x_m, y_m), T_2(x_m, y_m))$. The area surrounded by the circle with center at $(T_1(x_m, y_m), T_2(x_m, y_m))$ and radius $d - x_m - y_m$ is the possible location of Q. Lesser area is obtained using more than one circles (Ref. Sec 2.3).
11: If Q receives multiple number of two-bound signals the intersection of all such areas (calculated in the preceding step 10) is the position of Q.

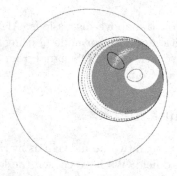

Fig. 5. In this figure a sensor node Q may lie on any one of the green circle, where internal green circles are inscribed in the union of three blue circles, the union of the blue circles is inscribed in the union of two pink circles and which is also inscribed in the larger black circle.

simulation 100 to 1000 two-bound signals are generated. The average reduced area is calculated for one circle, two circles and three circles, respectively as (explained in the section 2.3). The table 1 is showing the area reduced by our proposed algorithm for locating the position of a node with two-bound signals. On an average 63% area has reduced when one circle is used and 67% area has reduced when three circles are used to locate position of a node.

Table 1. % of average area reduced using one circle, two and three circles to locate position of a node with two bound signals

No of Runs →	1	2	3	4	5	6	7	8	9
% of average area reduced using (↓)									
one circle	63.80	63.39	62.91	63.74	64.01	63.44	63.57	63.18	64.12
two circles	65.56	65.12	64.92	65.11	65.78	65.37	65.91	64.89	66.07
three circles	66.71	66.39	65.98	66.34	67.17	66.85	66.48	66.13	67.82

5   Conclusions and Future Works

In this paper we have proposed a localization algorithm under a model where multiple-bound (up to two-bound) signals are allowed. The proposed algorithm distinguishes LOS, one-bound and two-bound signals. In case of LOS and one-bound, accurate positioning for a node is possible whereas in case of two-bound signal accurate positioning is not possible. Our proposed algorithm finds an area for the possible location of a node. Our simulation results show that our algorithm reduces 67% of the area calculated by any algorithm using AOA and ToA measurements to locate the position of the node.

In case of secure localization, if some malicious nodes report some faking position which lies outside of the area calculated by our algorithm as the possible area of presence of the node, then detection of such nodes are possible. In future we will try to solve the localization problem under a more practical model where we can allow more than two-bound signals.

References

1. Delaët, S., Mandal, P.S., Rokicki, M.A., Tixeuil, S.: Deterministic secure positioning in wireless sensor networks. Theoretical Computer Science 412(35), 4471–4481 (2011)
2. Ebrahimian, Z., Scholtz, R.A.: Source localization using reflection omission in the near-field. In: IEEE-ACES Conf. on Applied Comput. Electromagnetics (2005)
3. He, T., Huang, C., Blum, B.M., Stankovic, J.A., Abdelzaher, T.: Range-free localization schemes for large scale sensor networks. In: Proc. of 9th Annual Int. Conf. on Mobile Computing and Networking, MobiCom 2003, pp. 81–95. ACM, New York (2003)
4. Liu, C.H., Fang, D.J.: Propagation. in antenna handbook: Theory, applications, and design, ch. 29, pp. 1–56. Van Nostrand Reinhold (1988)
5. Mondal, K., Mandal, P.S., Sinha, B.P.: Localization in Presence of Multipath Effect in Wireless Sensor Networks. In: Koucheryavy, Y., Mamatas, L., Matta, I., Tsaoussidis, V. (eds.) WWIC 2012. LNCS, vol. 7277, pp. 138–149. Springer, Heidelberg (2012)
6. Oberholzer, G., Sommer, P., Wattenhofer, R.: SpiderBat: Augmenting wireless sensor networks with distance and angle information. In: IPSN, pp. 211–222 (2011)

7. Pahlavan, K., Akgul, F.O., Heidari, M., Hatami, A., Elwell, J.M., Tingley, R.D.: Indoor geolocation in the absence of direct path. IEEE Wireless Communications 13(6), 50–58 (2006)
8. Seow, C.K., Tan, S.Y.: Non-line-of-sight localization in multipath environments. IEEE Transactions on Mobile Computing 7, 647–660 (2008)
9. Sun, Q., Tan, S.Y., Teh, K.C.: Analytical formulae for path loss prediction in urban street grid microcellular environments. IEEE Trans. on Vehicular Technology 54(4), 1251–1258 (2005)
10. Uchiyama, A., Fujii, S., Maeda, K., Umedu, T., Yamaguchi, H., Higashino, T.: Ad-hoc localization in urban district. In: INFOCOM, pp. 2306–2310. IEEE (2007)

Trading of Grade Based Incentives
to Avoid Free Riding and Starvation in P2P Network

S. Moses Dian[1] and B. Ramadoss[2]

[1] Department of Computer Science and Engineering
National Institute of Technology, Tiruchirapalli-620015, Tamilnadu, India
mosesdian@gmail.Com
[2] Department of Computer Applications
National Institute of Technology, Tiruchirapalli-620015, Tamilnadu, India
brama@nitt.edu

Abstract. P2P networking has emerged as a successful Internet based computing paradigm, which can provide an inexpensive platform for distributed computing. The success of P2P network is directly affected by the selfish behaviours of the peers of the P2P network. To solve this issue, we propose a modified grade based incentive mechanism to reward the cooperating peers and to encourage the free rider to become a good contributor based on the peer contribution to network function. Further if the free rider continues to act against the principles of P2P network, it will lose its credit points and eventually it will be eliminated from the P2P network. It also addresses the issue of starvation and introduces the mechanism of trading of incentives to avoid starvation. We design a simulation to verify this approach and the results shows the improvement of fairness in resource sharing and robustness in P2P network.

Keywords: P2P, free-rider, fairness, Credit points, starvation, Grade

1 Introduction

Peer-To-Peer(P2P) systems are distributed systems which consist of thousands of interconnected heterogeneous nodes. These heterogeneous nodes can join or exit from P2P systems without any control. Main principles of P2P systems are self-organizing, and adapt to changing peer populations while providing services for content sharing and personal communications without requiring the support of centralized server or authority. Unlike Client/Server models, each node in a P2P system plays the role of a client as well as a server. These heterogeneous nodes share a part of their resources such as content, CPU cycles, storage and bandwidth etc[1].

P2P systems performance is plagued by many problems. One of which is the free-riding problem. A free rider is a peer that uses the file-sharing application to access content from others but does not contribute content to the same degree to the community of peers. Each node has a different character or has their own functions and also they belong to different organizations and individuals with different interests. Here an effective cooperative mechanism is lacking, and the nodes think of their own interests

C. Hota and P.K. Srimani (Eds.): ICDCIT 2013, LNCS 7753, pp. 347–360, 2013.

without doing anything for the benefit of P2P system which leads to the above said problem.

The rest of the paper is organized as follows. Section 2 explores some of the prior research works and related statistics. Section 3 describes the modified grading approach with the necessary and sufficient rules to promote fairness among peers in the P2P network. Section 4 shows the mathematical trace of the proposed system. In Section 5, principles behind trading of incentives are explained. In section 6 the simulation and modular diagram of the simulator along with the results are discussed and compared with the already available techniques to show the efficiency of the grading approach. The paper ends with conclusion and future work in section 7.

2   Previous Work and Related Statistics

An experimental evaluation on Gnutella [2] [3] indicates that 66% of users share no file. 47% of the entire download is from the top 1% of users. 99% of the download is from the top 25% of users. It is due to the absence of a mechanism to monitor the behaviour of any user in a P2P network which increases the possibility of free riding. Bit Torrent [4], a popular file sharing application, uses a variant of Tit-for-Tat strategy. Though it works well with peers having transaction history, it has serious limitations with newly entered peers. Newly entered peers have to produce some blocks initially to start the transaction. A free-rider who is not willing to share his blocks will cheat the newly entered peers by collecting the initial blocks they share. Also, if the newly entered peers at the beginning have no blocks to produce, then the peers will be put in a situation in which they cannot even participate in the transaction itself. This situation is called starvation [5]. It also fails to deal with zero-cost identity or white washing [6] which occurs when users change their identity and act as new comers or strangers in order to get away from the penalty imposed by the network. Asymmetric Transactions are not addressed by Tit-for-Tat strategy (i.e. how other peers have indirectly taken part in contributing to it).

In [7], an Adaptive Stranger policy is used to deal with zero cost identity. This policy works fully on suspicions and can fail to trust the strangers who are really good. In subjective reputation [8], a mechanism was designed to reduce the effect of Colluders who make a false representation of themselves in order to receive benefits from the network, by making each user to rate the other users transacted with it. Here the limitation is that it doesn't have a mechanism to detect the users who make a false rating of one another. In monetary payment scheme [9], the point-based mechanism is introduced. Peers receive points either with cash or by contributing to the network. But, the difficulty with this system is that a separate accounting system has to be maintained and it suffers from scalability issues. The incentive mechanism in [10] is based on user generosity to raise the cooperation among users. Some mechanisms try to prevent free riding by exchanging the bandwidth [11]. An experimental study of Bit Torrent [12] says, free riders are not penalized and high contributing peers are not honoured or encouraged.

3   Modified Grading Approach

In this paper, a modified grade based approach is proposed where the Peer Contribution to the Network determines the contribution of each peer to the entire network and based on the calculated PCN value, each peer is given a grade. The Grade determines the amount of Credit Points (CP) that the Peer has to receive or spend for each unit of data transfer. After uploading or downloading each unit of data, the PCN value is recalculated and the peer switches between different grades respectively. The peer is allowed to download only if it has sufficient CP with respect to its grade. peers should be motivated purely based on its contribution and no initial free credits points will be provided for newly entered peer to prevent free rider. Following subsection defines some keys to determine the credit points and grade, to be granted for peers and then explains the Grading approach.

3.1   Terminologies

The following terms are used in the modified Grading approach,

1) **Peer Contribution to Network (PCN):** The proposed PCN (Peer Contribution to Network) determines the contribution of the Peer to the entire network.

$$PCN = \frac{TotalUploaded}{TotalUploaded + TotalDownloaded}$$

2) **Grade:** The grade is allotted to the peer based on the calculated PCN value. It determines the amount of Credit Points (CP) that

- will be given to the peer for uploading 1 unit (e.g. 1MB) of data.
- will be deducted from the peer for downloading 1 unit of data.

3) **Credit Points (CP):** Based on the grade, the Credit Points are provided accordingly. The peer is allowed to trade only with this CP. Downloading the data will decrease the CP and uploading the data will increase the CP.

4) **Total Uploaded (TU):**   The Total Uploaded (TU) determines the total amount of data uploaded by the peer to all the peers connected globally, since the peer entered into the network.

5) **Total Downloaded (TD):**   The Total Downloaded (TD) determines the total amount of data downloaded by the peer from all the peers connected globally, since the peer entered into the network.

3.2   Steps to Determine Grade and Credit Points

The following steps are adopted to determine the grade of the peer. These calculations are repeated by the network every time after uploading or downloading 1 unit of data.

- Calculate the total uploaded (TU) amount and the total downloaded (TD) amount of the peer since the peer joined the network.

$$TU = \sum pu \qquad\qquad TD = \sum pd$$

Where $\sum pu$ denotes the total amount of data uploaded by the peer P and $\sum pd$ denotes the total amount of data downloaded by the peer P.

- Calculate the Peer Contribution to Network (PCN) of the peer.

$$P_{pcn} \quad = \quad \frac{\sum Pu}{\sum Pu + \sum Pd} = \frac{TU}{TU+TD}$$

where P_{pcn} denotes the contribution of the peer to the entire network.
Modified grade based approach follows the following principle

$$\begin{cases} P_{pcn} = 0; & \text{for TU} =0 \text{ and TD} \\ = 0 \\[2ex] P_{pcn} = \dfrac{TU}{TU+TD}; & \text{other-} \end{cases}$$
wise

- Allot the grade to the peer with respect to the calculated PCN value

$$P_g \quad = \quad \begin{cases} 1 & 1 \ge P_{pcn} > 0.75 \\ 2 & 0.75 \ge P_{pcn} > 0.5 \\ 3 & 0.5 \ge P_{pcn} > 0.25 \\ 4 & 0.25 \ge P_{pcn} > 0 \end{cases}$$

where Pg denotes the grade of the peer P based on the calculated P_{pcn}.
Fairness rule for any peer in P2P network is listed as follows.

- The peer's credit points (CP) should be increased when it shares or uploads data to the network.
- The peer's credit points (CP) should be decreased when it consumes or downloads data from the network.
- CU_g = Credit points rewarded for uploading 1 unit of data in Grade g where g = 1, 2, 3, 4 which takes the value as given below.

$$CUg = \begin{cases} 2 & g = 1 \\ 1.5 & g = 2 \\ 1 & g = 3 \\ 0.5 & g = 4. \end{cases}$$

The peer in the higher grade should get more credit points (CP) for uploading data than the peer in the lower grade i.e. Credit Points given for uploading in Grade g > Credit Points given for up loading in Grade g+1, where g =1, 2, 3,

4. Also, CD_g = Credit points detected for downloading in Grade g, where g = 1, 2, 3, 4 which takes the value as shown below.

$$CDg = \begin{cases} -0.5 & g = 1 \\ -1 & g = 2 \\ -1.5 & g = 3 \\ -2 & g = 4 \end{cases}$$

The peer in the lower grade should lose more credit points for downloading data than the peer in the higher grade. i.e. Credit Points deducted for downloading in Grade g < Credit Points deducted for downloading in Grade g+1, where   g =1, 2, 3, 4.

- Calculate the total credit points available (CP_{avail}) subsequently for uploading or downloading 1 unit of data.

For uploading one unit of data to the network, $CP_{avail} = CP_{avail} + CU_g$

For downloading one unit of data from the network, $CP_{avail} = CP_{avail} + CD_g$

3.3   Transaction Procedure

1.   Search for peers who have files the downloader needs.

    Let α be the size of the file (in units) to be downloaded and Dmax being the maximum units a peer can download from other peers. Then the size of the file to be downloaded should be between 0 and Dmax. i.e. $0 < \alpha < Dmax$

$$where, \quad D\max = \frac{CP_{avail}}{CD_g}$$

    Since   the CP_{avail} and grade will change after downloading each unit of data, we cannot exactly predict the value of α. However, the prediction of α helps the peer to understand the necessity of peer to stay in the higher grade.

2.   If the downloading peer has sufficient credit points (CP) to download each unit of data, with respect to its grade, then the requested unit of data can be downloaded from the selected peer.

3.   If the downloading peer has insufficient credit points (CP) to download a unit of data with respect to its grade (i.e. Dmax < 1), then the peer must upload some units of data which will yield the required Credit Points (CP) to continue downloading.

3.4   Starvation

Starvation is defined as a situation where a newly entered peer waits indefinitely due to unavailability of a file or data to upload to the P2P network, or as a result of initial zero credit point availability for newcomers. Starvation happens in two [15] instances.

- First instance occurs when a new peer joins the network with zero credit points, (i.e. TU = 0 and TD = 0) has no file of interest by any peer, thus unable to earn any credit points, eventually ending in starvation.
- Second instance occurs when an old peer acting against the principle of P2P network (i.e. downloading more data than uploading) quickly depletes all its credit points leading to starvation.

4   Mathematical Trace of the Proposed System

4.1   Transaction of a Newly Joined Peer

Assume that initial stage of a newly joined peer is in 4th grade, and a peer requires 2 CP to download 1 unit. Since his CP_{avail} is 0, he cannot download and can only upload. He has not yet uploaded as well as downloaded, so his TU is 0, TD is 0 and PCN is 0. In stage 2, the peer uploads 1 unit of data, he receives 0.5 CP. His TU increases to 1 and TD remains in 0. PCN is equal to 1 and his grade changes to 1st grade. His Dmax=1 i.e. he can download 1 unit of data. In stage 3, the peer uploads another 1 unit of data. He has 2.5 CP. With 2.5 CP, his Dmax=5 i.e. he can download

Table 1. Summary of the transaction of a newly joined peer

Stage No.	Comment	Total Upload(TU)	Total Download (TD)	PCN	Credit points (CP_{avail})	Grade
1	Initial stage of the peer	0	0	0	0	4
2	Uploads 1 unit of data	1	0	1	0.5	1
3	Uploads another 1unit of data	2	0	1	2.5	1
4	Downloads 1 unit of data	2	1	0.66	2	2
5	Downloads another 1 unit of data	2	2	0.5	1	3

5 units of data, since 1st grade requires just 0.5 CP to download 1 Unit. In stage 4, the peer now downloads 1 unit of data. He now loses 0.5 CP, since 1st grade demands 0.5 CP to download per unit of data. He has downloaded 1 unit of data, so his TD increases by 1. Now his PCN is recalculated which is 0.66. The peer degrades to 2nd grade. With 2CP, his Dmax=2 i.e. he can download 2 units of data, since 2nd grade demands just 1 CP to download 1 unit of data. In the beginning, it may seem that the peer hit 1st grade quickly with little effort. To retain the 1st grade, it should keep its PCN value greater than 0.75, which is possible only by maintaining his TU far greater than the TD. In stage 5, the peer downloads another 1 unit of data. His TD increases by 1. Now the PCN is recalculated which is 0.5. The Peer degrades to 3rd grade. With 1 CP, he cannot download even a single unit of data due to the insufficient amount of CP, since 3rd grade demands 1.5 CP to download 1 unit of data. All the above scenarios are shown in table 1.Thus the grading approach effectively keeps the free rider out of the P2P network and prevents the normal user from turning into a free-rider.

4.2   Transaction of a Good Contributor Peer

At some time t, since the peer is a good contributor let us assume that in initial stage, he is in 1st grade. Since he is a good contributor, he might have been in the 1st grade for a long duration, and so, for uploading each unit, he might have got 2 CPs. So let us assume that he has 5000 CP by uploading 2500 Units by remaining in the 1st grade. Let us assume that his TU is now 6,000 units. Let us also assume that his TD is now only 1,000 Units. Now his PCN is 0.86 . Since he is in 1st grade, with 5,000 CPs, his Dmax=10,000 units i.e. he can now download 10,000 units of data, unless his PCN falls below 0.75. In stage 2, the peer downloads 1 unit of data, so its TD now becomes 1001. He loses 0.5 CP, since 1st grade demands 0.5 CP to download 1 unit. Now his PCN is recalculated which is 0.857 that is greater than 0.75, so he retains his grade. His Dmax=9,999 units i.e. he can now download 9,999 units of data with the available 4999.5 CPs, since 1st grade demands 0.5 CP to download per unit. In stage 3, the peer downloads another 998 units of data. It can be clearly said that for each unit of data downloaded by the good contributor, his PCN decreases gradually only in

Table 2. Summary of a transaction of a good contributor peer

Stage No.	Comment	Total Upl-oad(TU)	Total Download (TD)	PCN	Credit points (CP_{avail})	Grade
1	Initial stage of the peer	6000	1000	0.86	5000	1
2	Downloads 1 unit of data	6000	1001	0.857	4999.5	1
3	Downloads another 998 units of data	6000	1999	0.7501	4500.5	1
4	Downloads another 1 unit of data	6000	2000	0.75	4500	2

fractions. He enjoys the benefits of the 1st grade for a very long time. It will be cut off only when his PCN value falls below 0.76. In stage 3, let us assume that the Good contributor has been downloading data and not been uploading any unit after since TU=6000. He now downloads 998 units of data, so his TD is now 1999. Now his PCN is recalculated which is 0.7501. The Peer is still in 1st grade, and he has 4500.5 CPs. So, he can download 9001 units of data, since, 1st grade requires just 0.5 CP to download 1 unit of data. In stage 4, he downloads another 1 unit of data and his TD increases by 1. Now his PCN is recalculated which is 0.75, and he drops to the 2nd grade. The peer is now in 2nd grade, and the he has 4500 CPs. With 4500, he can download only 4500 units of data, since 2nd grade demands 1 CP to download 1 Unit. All the above scenarios are clearly shown in table 2.

5   Trading Mechanism of the Proposed System

Starvation is defined as a situation where a newly entered peer waits indefinitely due to unavailability of a file or data to upload to the P2P network, or as a result of initial zero credit point availability for newcomers. To overcome starvation, it should use the following technique discussed below.

Let us assume that P_i is a newly entered peer trying to download its required file F_r. Since its $TU_{pi}=0$, $TD_{pi}= 0$ and $CP_{pi} = 0$ and P_i has no file to upload to earn credit points CP, starvation occurs for P_i.

Where TU_{pi} is the total number of units uploaded by peer P_i

TD_{pi} is the total number of units downloaded by peer Pi

and CP_{pi} is the total number of credit points earned   by peer Pi

Let C be the downloading peer and table 3 shows the list of all the uploading peers who have the file searched by peer C. From the table it is clear that, Peer D, peer G and peer Pi are in the last grade with different credit points. So C can choose among the peers in the last grade i.e. grade 4 with less credit points. So by making peer C to choose or give priority to peer Pi for downloading its required file Fr, (provided it has the required file) we can prevent starvation for any new comer like Pi. This approach can efficiently prevent starvation since the grades constantly change.

Table 3. Grades with credit points of uploading peers

Peer	Grade	Credit points
A	1	4000
B	2	3000
E	2	2800
F	3	1500
D	4	500
G	4	200
P_i	4	0

Consider a newly entered peer P_i is in urgent need of a file F_h due to some emergency situation. It can't wait for few minutes to earn credit points and download the required file. If the peer P_i is able to wait for some time, then it can allow the Peer P_i to download the incomplete version of the Hot File in the P2P network and earn credit points [16].

In order to give solution to this scenario, we propose an incentive trading mechanism. Using this trading mechanism a peer can effectively borrow credit points from another Peer. Using this borrowed credit point, the Peer can start downloading its required file F_r. Later, it can repay the borrowed CP to the Lender peer either with interest or by cash.

The reason why we choose grade based incentive mechanism among several available incentive mechanism because, to implement a credit point trading mechanism, the P2P network must be free of free-riders. Since a free rider may borrow some credit points from a lending peer & may disappear without repaying the borrowed credit points. No other incentive mechanism provides an effective solution like the grade based incentive mechanism, for keeping the P2P network free of free riders.

The existing grade based incentive mechanism [16] uses four grades: grade-1, grade-2, grade-3 & grade-4. However we can simplify this 4 grade mechanism into a three grade mechanism: grade-1 (NCR(Network Contribution Ratio) > 1), grade-2 (NCR=1) & grade-3 (NCR<1). But in this three grade mechanism, grade-2 is almost theoretical & cannot be practical. Because NCR will be equal to 1 only for a very fraction of time, since the total units uploaded (TU) is not always equal to total units downloaded (TD). Sometimes they may be equal, but only for a negligible amount of time. So grade-2 is meaningless and we can remove it from the three grade mechanism and we can convert it into a two grade mechanism with only grade-1 (NCR>1) &

Grade-2 (NCR=<1). But still there is a problem in this two grade mechanism. Since it does not differentiate a very good contributor from a good contributor. The four grade mechanism on the other hand provides clear separation of peers from excellent contributor to Bad Contributor. So use it for trading of incentives.

The following few changes should be made to make the four grade mechanism more effective. In the existing four grade mechanism, NCR is calculated using the formula NCR=TU/TD. Now we are changing it into PCN=TU/(TU+TD) for better grade allocation and accurate grade calculation. Since TU/(TU+TD) no longer mean a ratio, we are now changing the term Network contribution Ratio (NCR) to Peer's Contribution to the Network (PCN) therefore PCN=TU/(TU+TD).

The trading mechanism works when a Peer (Lp) is willing to sell its credit points to another peer who is in need of credit points. The lending peer first advertises the number of credit points it is willing to sell along with a fixed interest rate during repayment as shown in table 4.

Table 4. Credit point auction advertisement for all peers

Peer	Grade	Credit point	Interest
A	1	100	10 %
B	2	100	7.5 %
C	3	100	12 %
D	4	100	9 %

Those lending CP are then deducted from the lending peer's available CP. The deducted CP are converted according to the grade of the borrower Peer. The conversion table is shown in table 5.

Table 5. Credit point conversion chart

Lender \ Borrower	Grade 1	Grade 2	Grade 3	Grade 4
Grade 1	LCP x 1	LCP x 2	LCP x 3	LCP x 4
Grade 2	LCP x 1/2	LCP x 1	LCP x 3/2	LCP x 2
Grade 3	LCP x 1/3	LCP x 2/3	LCP x 1	LCP x 1/2
Grade 4	LCP x 1/4	LCP x 1/2	LCP x 3/4	LCP x 1

If a peer borrows CP from the same grade no conversion is required. If a peer borrows CP from another peer who is from a different grade, then the borrowed CP will be converted according to the value given in table 5 & then added up with the available credit points.For example if a Peer P_i which is in grade-4 borrows some credit points (LCP) from a peer P_j belonging to grade-1 then the $Pi_{avail} = Pi_{avail} + (LCP * 4)$ as shown in the table 5.

The trading mechanism effectively solves the starvation problem but however introduces a new breed of free riders into the P2P network whom may borrow credit points from the lender peer and may disappear. To avoid this kind of free riding, the borrowing peer B_p should pay a caution deposit to a third party mediator. If the borrower is not able to return the borrowed credit points along with the interest within the dead line, the caution deposit in the mediator should be transferred to the lending Peer L_p. To achieve this, every lender should advertise the credit points it is willing to lend along with the interest, dead line to repay, the debt & the safety deposit amount to be paid to the mediator. An example is shown table 6. The peers will trade the credit points. Newly entered peer can pay and purchase some credit points according to its need. Now the peer Pi can start downloading its required file immediately.

Table 6. Credit point auction advertisement for all peers

Peer	Grade	Credit point	Interest	Deadline	Safety Deposit
A	1	2000	10%	3 months	$ 100
B	2	1200	12%	4 months	$ 50
E	2	1000	8%	1 month	$ 40
F	3	500	15%	6 months	$ 20
D	4	300	9 %	1 month	$ 10
G	4	100	6%	15 days	$ 5

6   Simulation Results and Discussion

The proposed model was prototyped using C# in .net framework 4 environment. The model was setup in a 100 node setup. In this simulation, a peer P_i will perform 5 main events.

6.1   Simulator Events and Actions

1)   **Peer Identification**: In this event, a new comer Pi tries to join the P2P network. It advertises its availability by sending an "announce" message to all the peers in the multicast domain. Already existing peers add new comer P_i and acknowledge it by unicasting their details to P_i which helps the peer P_i to maintain a currently available peer list.

2)   **Peer Removal:**   In this event, a peer P_i which is already available in the P2P network tries to leave the P2P network. It achieves this action by sending a "de-announce" message to all the peers in the multicast domain so that the existing peers in the P2P network remove the peer P_i from their peer list.

3)   **File List Update:** This event helps the existing peers in the P2P network to update the shared file list of P_i. It is made possible by the peer P_i through re-announce message to all peers in the multicast domain.

4)   **Removing Obsolete Peers:** In P2P network, without any control a peer P_i may join or leave the network. To identify the current available peers in the network and removing the absolute peers, peer P_i sends a "prove" message once in every n seconds to all peers in its peer list. Peers available in the peer list and P2P network will respond by sending an acknowledge message to the peer P_i and the unacknowledged peer will be removed.

5)   **Peer Starves:** First the lending peer sends or broadcast a trade message to all peers in its peer list and the starving peers among receiving peers of the trade message will respond according to the incentive selling information. Then the borrowing peer chooses the best deal among received trade data and performs the trading with it. Finally the borrowing peer sends a locked message to all other peers in the peer list so that no other peer will try to purchase it. The borrowed peer must repay the credit point along with the interest or it will lose its safety deposit.

6.2   Modular Representation of the Simulator

After the P2P network got initialized and stabilized, a new peer P_i may want to join with zero credit point or an old peer P_j may rejoin with some amount of credit point. All the tasks mentioned above are dealt in the start up module shown in figure 1.The new peer P_i may face starvation if it has no file to share and unable to earn credit points. The starvation can be avoided by borrowing incentives from other peers which enables the starved peer to download the required file.After joining the P2P network, a peer may wish to download a required file. It checks the availability of the file in the P2P network by using the P2P network browser. As a result, it will get the list of peers having the required file. These tasks are performed in P2P network file browser module. Now the peer may start its download or upload which is dealt in the file transfer module. After every unit of download or upload, the TU and TD values are recalculated to audit the amount of data transfer in the accounting TU and TD module. Using these values, Peer Contribution to Network (PCN) value is calculated.

Based on PCN value, grade is allotted for every peer in the grade allotment module. Next credit points available (CP_{avail}) for a peer P_i are calculated followed by D_{max} calculation. Data transfer of the peer P_i is allowed or restricted based on D_{max} value. If more credit points are still available, the control will be flown back to start another unit of data transfer. This process will continue until the entire required file is downloaded or the peer's download gets denied due to insufficient credit points.

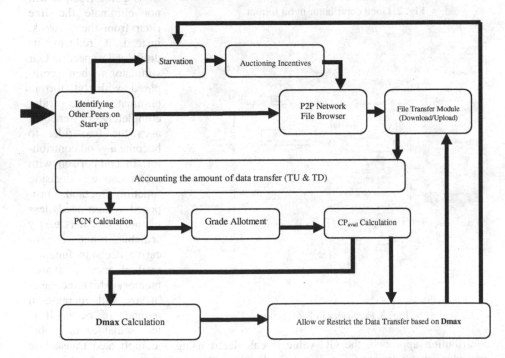

Fig. 1. Modular Diagram of the Simulator

6.3   Comparison with Available Approaches

The snapshot shown in figure 2 shows details of a day's download and upload by a peer in addition to total upload and download since its login into the P2P network.

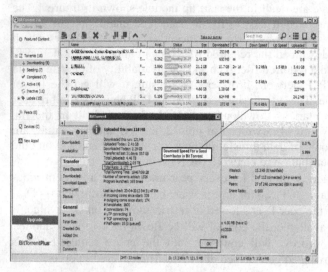

Fig. 2. Good contributor in bit torrent

Total ratio indicates the network contribution ratio. Here the total upload is more i.e. 4.46TB and the download amount is less i.e. 2.05TB. These values indicate that it is a good contributor. So bit torrent allows the peer to download at a faster rate. Figure 3 shows that bit torrent identifies the free rider when a peer's downloaded amount is more than its uploaded amount. If bit torrent finds a free rider, it will not eliminate the free rider from the network, instead it reduces its download speed. Our simulator when compared with bit torrent eliminates free rider completely or encourages the free rider to become a good contributor. In comparison with reciprocative decision function method, proposed system needs less memory and it is easily scalable. Since reciprocative decision function method uses a shared memory which increases in size with increase in number of peers, it is less scalable. In global

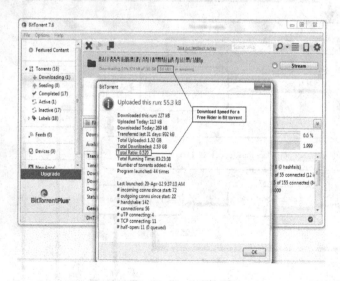

Fig. 3. Free rider in Bit torrent

contribution approach, the GC value is calculated using a complicated transaction procedure that estimate GC value with all other peers having the file and it is very difficult to implement whereas the proposed transaction procedure is very simple and easy to implement.

Consider a P2P sytem with peer A and peer B trying to upload unnecessary files to each other. By using this technique, they try to increase the contribution ratio and get benefitted from the network. This is possible in adaptive stranger policy and also it doubts good contributor.

On the other hand, grade based approach tackles this problem by increasing the CP when a peer uploads and decrease the CP when peer downloads i.e. if A's CP increases, B's CP decreases and vice versa. This will maintain fairness in the network and there is no need to trust or test good or bad strangers since it is shown by its credit points and its grade.

6.4 Advantages of the Proposed System over other Incentive Mechanism

1) Eliminates free rider
2) Transaction procedure is simple and easy to implement
3) It requires less memory
4) No faking of user is possible
5) Encourages free rider to become good contributor
6) Fairness is well maintained
7) Prevents starvation thoroughly.

7   Conclusion and Future Work

The proposed Grading approach, almost efficiently deals with free rider challenges faced by the P2P network. There are also some security problems to be considered which may completely retard the growth of the P2P network, and so an effective mechanism can be developed in the future to enhance the secure transmission of data. Also, the peers may upload some files which are of no use and may gain more CP. Though there are various rating mechanisms which rate the files, most approaches rate the file on the user's perspective. So the future work is to encourage the peers sharing the rarest or most important files which are not easily available. This grading mechanism does not function well for live streaming. Future work is to find an incentive mechanism for live streaming and merge with this grade based approach. The Grading approach, thus completely eliminates the free-riders by forcing them to share their resources and encourage the high contributed peers by making them stay in the top grade and thereby enjoying the benefits of it.

References

1. Tang, Y., Wang, H., Dou, W.: Trust based incentive in P2P network. In: Proceedings of IEEE International Conference on E-Commerce Technology for Dynamic E-Business(CEC-East 2004) (2004)
2. Adar, E., Huberman, B.A.: Free Riding on Gnutella. First Monday, pp. 134-139 (October 2000)

3. Hughes, D., Coulson, G., Walkerdine, J.: Free Riding on Gnutella Revisited: the Bell Tolls? IEEE Distributed Systems, 1–18
4. Li, M., Yu, J., Wu, J.: Free-Riding on BitTorrent-Like Peer-to-Peer File Sharing Systems: Modeling Analysis and Improvement. IEEE Transactions on Parallel and Distributed Systems 19(7), 954–966 (2008)
5. Ma, R.T.B., Lee, S.C.M., Lui, J.C.S., Yau, D.K.Y.: Incentive and Service Differentiation in P2P Networks: A Game Theoretic Approach. IEEE/ACM Transactions on Networking 14(5), 978–991 (2006)
6. Feldman, M., Papadimitriou, C., Chuang, J., Stoica, I.: Free- Riding and Whitewashing in Peer-to-Peer Systems. In: Proc. ACM SIGCOMM Workshop Practice and Theory of Incentives in Networked Systems, pp. 228–236 (2004)
7. Feldman, M., Lai, K., Stoica, I., Chuang, J.: Robust Incentive Techniques for Peer-to-Peer Networks. In: Proc. Fifth ACM Conference on Electronic Commerce, pp. 102–111 (May 2004)
8. Lai, K., Feldman, M., Stoica, I., Chuang, J.: Incentives for Cooperation in Peer-to-Peer Networks. In: Proc. Workshop Economics of Peer-to-Peer Systems (June 2003)
9. Feldman, M., Chuang, J.: Overcoming Free-Riding Behavior in Peer-to-Peer Systems. ACM SIGecom Exchanges 5(4), 41–50 (2005)
10. Golle, P., Leyton-Brown, K., Mironov, I.: Incentives for Sharing in Peer-to-Peer Networks. In: Proc. Third ACM Conf. Electronic Commerce, pp. 75–78 (2001)
11. Garbacki, P., Epema, D.H.J.: An Amortized Tit-For-Tat Protocol for Exchanging Bandwidth Instead of Content in P2P Networks. In: Proc. First Int'l Conf. Self-Adaptive and Self-Organizing Systems, pp. 119–228 (2007)
12. Jun, S., Ahamad, M.: Incentives in BitTorrent Induce Free Riding. In: SIGCOMM 2005 Workshops, Philadelphia, PA, USA, August 22-26 (2005)
13. Ham, M., Agha, G.: ARA: A Robust Audit to Prevent Free-Riding in P2P Networks. In: Proceedings of the Fifth IEEE International Conference on Peer-to-Peer Computing, P2P 2005 (2005)
14. Moses Dian, S., Ramadoss, B.: A Grade Based Incentive Mechanism for Peer to Peer Networks. American Journal of Applied Science and Engineering 5(3), 243–250 (2012)

Supporting Location Information Privacy
in Mobile Devices

Deveeshree Nayak[1], M. Venkata Swamy[2], and Srini Ramaswamy[3]

[1] KIIT University
Bhubaneswar, India
deveeshree@gmail.com
[2] University of Arkansas at Little Rock
AR, USA
vxmartha@ualr.edu
[3] Industrial Software Systems
ABB India Corporate Research Center
srini@ieee.org

Abstract. Social networking has evolved as a basic amenity in today's interconnected world. Users of social media tools do not always keep up with privacy policies and its adverse effects. It is very common that even experienced users are often
caught unaware of actions that happen behind the interface screens of their interconnection devices. Many-a-time mobile application developers take advantage of
such user complacency and leak location information from the device (and hence
information about the user) to other applications. Though there has been considerable alerts raised on the issue of location information leakage, there are situations
wherein applications sneak through these 'walls' and connect with devices / applications to extract / query desired information from the firmware. In this work, we
provide a in-depth review of literature on this emerging area of social interest, and
propose a four-layer context-based authentication framework (4-CBAF) to address
location privacy concerns. The 4-CBAF framework provides a facility for users to
share pertinent information only if the user specifically authorizes such information
sharing. The 4-CBAF is intelligent enough to reduce the number of human interventions that a user should attend to. The effectiveness of the proposed 4-CBAF is
also demonstrated for check-in application for Facebook using smart devices.

Keywords: Location, Privacy, multi-level authentication, Context, Mobile.

1   Introduction

Today's sophisticated mobile technologies makes modern civilization to realize the
world as a small and intensely interactive entity. An individual's geographical location at a point in time is thus by-and-large easily accessible. The major disadvantage
with the adoption of such technology is the unpredictable and inadvertent disclosure
of private information; in this work we are concerned with location disclosure.
Privacy leakage and discovery of personalized data poses a major threat to users by

C. Hota and P.K. Srimani (Eds.): ICDCIT 2013, LNCS 7753, pp. 361–372, 2013.

allowing the use of the referring mobile device as a location tracker. In [11], the authors identify thirteen major issues related to this technical approach. Location based tracking systems use various techniques to keep track of location information of users which in turn increases the risk on the misuse of private and secure information of individuals [12]. In addition to tracking individual location, estimation of location also may create severe privacy risks such that all comprehensive available records of location data produce nearly accurate predictions about the user [13]. There are techniques to assemble public information to produce private information though the private variable is not explicitly leaked to intruder. Information flow models attempted to address these issues in such cases.

Despite economic downturns, the advances and proliferation of mobile devices has continued to be on the rise, and is one of the most pervasive consumer electronic devices to expand unsurpassed global penetration during the past decade. Global Positioning System (GPS) have matured as a standard for smart mobile devices. Advances in mobile computing technology have enabled users to adopt location based services (LBSs) for routine activities. Individuals and organizations are leveraging location information for heuristics and investigative analysis [3]. LBSs through its accompanying suite of tools have attracted customers and hence become very popular within a short time. Some of the LBSs include Google Latitude, FindMyFriends, GeoMe, CouponApp, etc.

In general, LBS applications accumulate location information for an arbitrarily long time to provide attractive services to their users. However, they raise doubts in the user's mind about the exact nature and limitations of their individual privacy. It is not that every time a user may wish to divulge her/his location information to these applications or other individuals. The key problem hence is to provide support for occasional location information disclosure while also supporting contextual blocking of tracking users continuously [2]. These problems have led to several studies about privacy of location in mobile devices. Policies indicate that device manufacturers should design devices to support privacy-enabling and provide user-based control to individuals for selective sharing of location information. The study recommends mobile operating system providers to include necessary tools for privacy protection. Upon complaints from customers and legal recommendation from federal governments, all the mobile OSs allow users to select applications to access location data (eg. GPS). Selective access to applications is often sufficient in many instances. However, such technology is not yet clearly capable of contextual selection of access grants for applications that interact with these selective applications due to an open API structure for add-on applications development. In this paper, we propose a framework to incorporate a 4-layer context based authentication framework (4-CBAF) to address such elevated concerns in mobile environments.

The proposed 4-CBAF introduces a component that authenticates and authorizes requests from applications to access location information. The 4-CBAF component inherits properties from layered authentication proposed in [10]. The primary objective of the component is to authorize location information access. The layered approach distinguishes functionality of authentication, authorization and context based authorization in achieving the purpose. Each layer serves a distinct purpose and in all they verify "who are you, what you know, what you have, what is the purpose". The privacy components 4-CBAF not only verifies the requesting application validity but also verifies whether the application is legal to access location information at the given context. The decisions are based on policies devised in the component. The policies are dynamic and can be updated upon demand. This paper discusses the feasibility of the 4-CBAF framework in mobile devices. The outcomes of our exploratory study are the following:

- Identify privacy leakage of location information in mobile device applications
- Proposed a component architecture, 4-CBAF, to address the privacy issue
- Demonstrate that the improvements differ from current state-of-art technologies in accessing location information
- Discuss the feasibility of the proposed solution in real-time check-in application for Facebook in mobile devices.

The rest of the paper is organized as following. Related work is discussed in Section II. Existing location information privacy tools are discussed in Section III, and the proposed 4-CBAF component is illustrated in Section IV. Its feasibility in real-time application usage in presented in Section V, which is followed by conclusions and future work in Section 6.

2   Related Work

Several researchers have argued that when the collection of location information can cause a violation of privacy, suggested consent is necessary [30]. Users who share their location information often realize late that it may have impact on sensitivities within their culture and society [14]. There are tools to ease the sharing, such as GTWhois [15] and Visual Route [16], from where an intruder can collect users' location information such as IP address, email address and ISP. Although these variables cannot be used to derive accurate geographical location, one can predict the user's city and street. The US Privacy Act of 1974 [17] identifies an individual's right to privacy of her/his personal information. But location privacy is not included within this law. Several laws [18-21] have been passed to protect location privacy which necessitated a user's approval to broadcast his/her location data. It has been mentioned that a user's physical location cannot be disclosed publically because of privacy risks. Simultaneously, the European Union has approved a law - The Directive on privacy and electronic communications [22] – also known as the E-privacy Directive, which deals with the security, confidentiality and integrity of location information, user's opinion and user's personal information. Until now, however, there are no specific laws to check privacy leaks in applications utilizing location tracking system (LTS) [23]. The copious use of LTS applications in mobile devices has increased privacy risks for individuals. Research in [24-29] showed how a location tracking system is a threat to users in their day-to-day life. By monitoring the location of an individual, intruders integrate the recorded data to build his/her profile which violate fundamental rights of a user [29]. Motivated by these laws and studies, the objective of our work is to study and propose the development of a software check-pointing framework / mechanism to ensure privacy preservation while using location based services.

The increase in availability of information coupled with increased computing power in GPS-enabled smart devices makes it possible to deploy context sensitive services where the access of the resources is determined by a user's contextual need. The location of a user allows for establishing context and motive through data mining and hence poses an increasing threat to the individuals' privacy [31]. In LBSs, the requested resources are available to an individual only if the individual is at specified location [32]. LBSs are uncomplicated context based privacy implementations but pose a security threat by leaking individual's whereabouts without the users' explicit knowledge. The notion of privacy also diverges between countries and cultures [33-36]; for example between the US and India, where India is an example of a joint society and USA is an example of idiosyncratic civilization [37]. In India, while privacy concerns are relatively low compared to US [36], physical and societal threats by blatant privacy violations pose an immense threat; this is due to ignorance and unavailability of legal and structural recourse for such violations. Hence despite cultural differences, there are situations where privacy plays critical role in an individual's life. Therefore, LBS users have the right to take decision on their privacy while being served by LBSs. End users, irrespective of culture, often commonly find it objectionable for LBSs to advertise information about an individual [38]. Most individuals will strongly object to the leak of personal information without user's knowledge [39]. Literature asserts that a professed control, over revelation and subsequent use of personal information, plays an important role in a individuals' seclusion concerns and information disclosure performance [40]. Thus there is an urgent need for strong authentication and authorization techniques for privacy in LBSs [41].

GPS technology is often piggy backed with Navigation and Tracking services (NTs) to track and monitor a mobile user's geographical position. Ethical conflicts arise in tracking an individual who has right not to be monitored. There are unanswered questions by assumed consent – that attacks the core of an individuals' privacy [42].The work of Dobson and Fischer [44], Garfinkel et al. [44], Michael and Michael [45], Perusco and Michael [46], Kaupins and Minch [47], Perakslis and Wolk [48] and Stajano [49] have pointed out the need for a deeper understanding of moral principles in widespread use of LBSs. Tools such as Google Earth [50], NASA WorldWind [51], Microsoft VirtualEarth [52], and Skyline Globe [53], etc. generally provide GPS data of the user; which is often not desirable to end users who assume their privacy rights are protected. With the help of Google Earth like tools, an antagonist can pinpoint nearly the exact location of an individual by disregarding the privacy laws [54].

3   LBS Support Frameworks

3.1   Current State-of-Art

Until recently mobile operating systems did not have checks for authentication of applications for accessing location data. The mobile OSs now include a tool to allow/block an application to gain access to location data. A reference model for location privacy in mobile devices is LORE. LORE is an infrastructural design to support location aware applications. A method is proposed to publish a fake location to hide an individual's location information [4]. Dissemination of location information from identity protects one's privacy from dissuading monitoring of an individual by reconstructing path of an individual's track [5]. Identifying a range of queries and assigning an artificial id to protect privacy of an individual can address privacy in traffic monitoring systems [6]. A unified framework is developed using anonymity techniques, by hiding, often by obfuscation [8]. By taking various dimensions of attacks and location information into account, in [7] the authors developed a method to quantify location privacy.

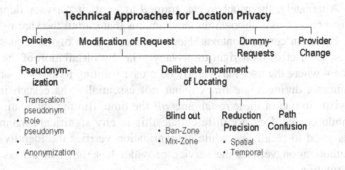

Fig. 1. CurrentTechnologies for Location Privacy [8]

As shown in Figure 1, most of the studies thus far have focused on techniques such as modification, faking, etc., but do not discuss policies to authenticate a request to grant access to location data selectively while providing privacy. Our work focuses on developing a framework based upon a multi-layered authentication mechanism using context based techniques (ex. is the request trustable), authentication techniques (who are you), and authorization techniques (what you want). In other words, our work attempts to address privacy issues by developing an appropriate encompassing framework to deploy privacy policies. The dearth of research in this area can be discerned by the 'policies' leaf in Figure 1; this area is currently critically ill-defined and often left to the mobile application developers and providers for interpretation.

3.2   Problem Definition

LBS have been evolving at a rapid pace to exploit location information availability so as to support effective customer services. However, as in every race in the market-driven world, that attempts to meet customer demand for information, often times, customers themselves are 'put' in a position of disadvantage by not knowing exactly how much privacy is being lost by such intrusive applications over time. Mobile application service providers retrieve location coordinates with the intent of providing value-added services. There are many instances where the service providers leak location information directly or indirectly using inferences. For example, in restaurant rating services, wherein a user rates a restaurant when she / he visits a restaurant is allowing for crowd sourcing to publish about food quality and ambience. The service provider is not publishing the location of the user directly but the application execution context could infer that the user was at the restaurant. If one assumes that employers of this user may monitor their employees' activities using third party services, and that the user may not want such information broadcast at all times, this could become an inadvertent privacy invasion scenario. Though there are tools to block a service provider access to location information, they do block the service provider themselves, as user are often left with an option to either share information all the time, or never at all. Such examples create the necessity for more fine-grained authorization of requests to location information besides authentication of service provider themselves. Alternately, the problem can framed as implicit "privacy depravation" - through a distinct lack of authorization mechanisms that curtail the sharing of private information based on certain contexts. Hence authentication of the requestor by default deprives the user of their right to privacy – i.e. by installation of the restaurant rating service – where the user may rightly be a user wanting to know / publish about 'good' restaurants during *some* times – but not essentially share such information about their visits to one of these restaurants *all* the time. But the application installed on their mobile device does not differentiate this in any significant manner. In this context, it is good to recall that while authentication verifies the identity of service provider, authorization verifies the service provider has rights to access to the requested information.

4   4-Layer Context Based Authentication Framework (4-CBAF)

Mobile operating systems are developed through a model driven engineering process. There are primarily three layers in these operating systems. One is the Core OS layer which interacts with the firmware, other is Core Services which talks to Core OS layer to provide services to higher layer, and the remaining layer is applications which includes media, touch, and third party applications. Figure 2 shows the architecture of one such mobile OS, the iOS.

Fig. 2. iOS Architecture

The Core Services layer implements location services by communicating with the Core OS API. In this paper we term location services as Navigation and Tracking Services (NT services); one of the core services in mobile operating systems. NT service components do not take privacy into account while providing services. The primary goal of NT services is to provide location based services to applications. Hence the current architecture of such systems is incapable of protecting users from privacy leakages. These limitations have motivated us to introduce a layered framework for authentication and authorization of service requests. The proposed layer for protecting privacy is presented in Figure 3. Partner and 3rd Party NT API and core NT API are shielded by a privacy protection layer called 4-layer Context Based Authentication Framework (4-CBAF) component. The 4-CBAF components analyses a given service request from third party application through a 4-level of authentication and authorization techniques. The component is illustrated in detail in the following.

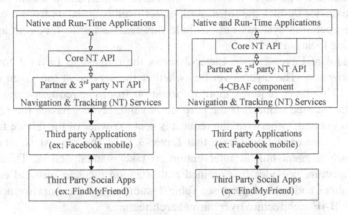

Fig. 3. Original and Proposed Mobile API architecture

The 4-CBAF component is developed from the lessons learned from our earlier work [10], which suggests that we need to employ a multi-layered approach to prevent one-stop defaults for authorization requests. Given the need for such authorization mechanisms by applications, we adapt a four-layer framework for authorization. Each of the 4-layers serves distinct actions to validate and authorize a request. The design of the four layers is presented in Figure 4.

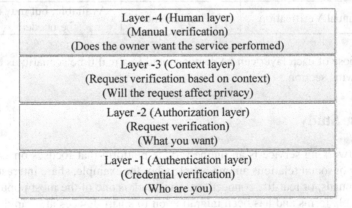

Fig. 4. Proposed 4-CBAF framework

Layer 1 is naïve which is simple authentication mechanism to identify a requestor. In simple words, the layer-1 authenticates the requestor irrespective of whether the requestor authorized for the requested service or not. Layer-1 could be password based authentication (PAP or CHAP) or key based. The primary purpose of layer-1 is to verify the requestor's credentials and to identify requestor i.e. who is the requestor. If Layer-1 passes the authentication check, then Layer-2 is invoked for the authorization of the requestor's request. Layer-2 verifies whether the requestor is legal to access the service. The layer-2 follows rule-based authorization technique and the owner of the device defines the rules. With effect from complaints from user community, mobile operating systems now include this feature i.e. to block an application from accessing location API.

If successful at Layer-2, then Layer-2 sends the request to Layer-3 for context-based authorization. The layer-3 verifies whether the service at the given context is legal or not. This layer requires more information from the requestor regarding the purpose of the service request. If the purpose is valid, layer-3 passes the request and the service is granted. Otherwise, the request is sent to owner of the device for manual verification. In the exceptional case that Layer-3 fails, the request is forwarded to Layer-4 which triggers human intervention to take manual action. This proposed layered architecture provides fine grained authorization mechanisms and each layers service a distinct and critical purpose. Table 1 summarizes the improvements of the proposed 4-CBAF architecture over current architecture.

Table 1. Improvements over current architecture

Layers	Current	4-CBAF
1. Authentication	Not implemented	PAP, CHAP, or key based
2. Authorization	Implemented	Rule based
3. Context Authorization	Not implemented	History, knowledge based
4. Manual Verification	Not implemented	Available, but may not be needed

The purpose of each layer can be demonstrated in a real time scenario as discussed in the following section.

5   Case Study

A social networking service is an online service platform that focuses on facilitating the building of social relations among people who, for example, share interests, activities, backgrounds, or real-life connections. Facebook is one of the most popular social networking platforms and has been migrating on to smart devices at a rapid acceleration. Facebook provides a platform called wall on which a user posts his/her announcements. There are many facebook applications and mobile applications that automate the posting for users' providing ease of access. These applications access device services to generate information for such posts. Smart devices include features such as GPS, gyroscope, etc. GPS is one of the most useful and controversial feature in smart devices. GPS locates the position of a device and mobile OSs provide core NT API to upper layers of the OS. To expose the privacy threats with the existing architecture, consider an application for check-in feature. The check-in application takes location information from device and friends' names that are with the user at the specific time and posts that information on the user's Facebook wall as a check-in message.

Now assume a user say 'A' and the set of users that are family and friends of 'A' is F(A). 'A' is visiting a restaurant with some his/her family and friends i.e. with a set of users R (A) <F(A). In this scenario, check-in application reads the location information from device which is the restaurant and list of users who are along with 'A' i.e. R(A) and posts a message on 'A's wall. This is visible to all the friends of 'A' that include F(A)-R(A). This kind of posts without user's consciousness, can cause social problems and originate unpleasant relationship issues. This might lead to break-ups at some point of time. Table 2 describes how the post is authorized in original OS architecture and in proposed 4-CBAF based architecture.

Table 2. Check-in application authorization

Layer	Current	4-CBAF
1. Application authentication	Not implemented	Successful
2. GPS service authorization	Successful	Successful
3. Context based authorization	Not implemented	Failed
4. Manual Verification	Not implemented	Implemented but not needed

From the Table 2, the check-in application generated message is posted on facebook wall upon authorization from GPs module for the application in original OS framework. In proposed 4-CBAF, the application is a legitimate requestor and legal to access GPS service but raise privacy concerns in given context and thus failed in layer-3. Therefore, the proposed architecture can address privacy issues in cases where current architecture does not support.

Another popular such social networking service such as micro-blogging activity is Twitter. Assume an application say tweetMyGeo which tweets all your geo-local positions time to time periodically. It is very usual that a mobile user, who downloads this application, relegates his/her twitter login credentials keeping trust on the application. There is a privacy check service neither on the twitter side nor in mobile device side. The 4-CBAF comes to rescue approach can support such users by providing a check point to such applications. The proposed models will blocks applications such as tweetMyGeo from obtaining GPS location of the mobile device through its 3rd Llayer-3. Context based authorization fails because it learned from history that the application broadcasts location information through twitter.

6　Conclusion

Social networking has been evolving as a basic amenity in today's world. Users of such social media tools do not always keep up with privacy policies and its adverse effects on its users. It is very common that users are caught unaware of the actions by applications installed on their devices. In this work, we have proposed and demonstrated the need and use of a four layer context-based authentication framework (4-CBAF) to address privacy concerns. The 4-CBAF framework provides facility to warn a user not to share sensitive information such as location and to share if the user insists to do so. The 4-CBAF is intelligent enough to reduce number of human interventions that a user should attend. Location information is a case and the 4-CBAF can be realized in privacy critical systems. The effectiveness of the proposed 4-CBAF is demonstrated for check-in application for Facebook in smart devices. Our next step is to implement the 4-CBAF in mobile devices.

References

1. Chen, Y., Liu, D.: Location-Aware Services and its Infrastructure Support. In: Enabling Technologies for Wireless E-Business, pp. 312–334. Springer, Heidelberg (2006)
2. Weiser, M.: Some Computer Science Issues in Ubiquitous Computing. Communications of the ACM 6(7), 75–84 (1993)
3. Harter, A., Hopper, A.: A distributed location system for the active office. IEEE Network 8(1), 62–70 (1994)
4. Chang, W., Wu, J., Tan, C.C.: Enhancing Mobile Social Network Privacy. In: IEEE Global Telecommunications Conference (GLOBECOM 2011), December 5-9, pp. 1–5 (2011)
5. Hoh, B., Gruteser, M., Xiong, H., Alrabady, A.: Enhancing Security and Privacy in Traffic-Monitoring Systems. IEEE Pervasive Computing 5(4), 38–46 (2006)
6. Xie, H., Kulik, L., Tanin, E.: Privacy-Aware Traffic Monitoring. IEEE Transactions on Intelligent Transportation Systems 11(1), 61–70 (2010)
7. Shokri, R., Theodorakopoulos, G., Le Boudec, J., Hubaux, J.: Quantifying Location Privacy. In: IEEE Security and Privacy (SP), May 22-25, pp. 247–262 (2011)
8. Shokri, R., Freudiger, J., Hubaux, J.-P.: A unified framework for location privacy. In: 3rd Hot Topics in Privacy Enhancing Technologies, HotPETs (2010)
9. Decker, M.: Location Privacy-An Overview. In: 7th International Conference on Mobile Business, ICMB 2008, pp.221–230, July 7-8 (2008)
10. Nayak, D., Ramaswamy, S.: A Multi-level Contextualization Framework for Authentication in Mobile Payment Applications. In: 11th International Conference on Wireless Networks (ICWN 2012), USA, July 16-19 (2012)
11. Minch, R.P.: Privacy Issues in Location –Aware mobile devices. In: 37th Hawaii International Conference on System Sciences, Big Island, HI, USA. IEEE Computer Society (2004) ISBN 0-7695-2056-1
12. Wang, J.I., Loui, M.C.: Privacy and Ethical issues in location–Based Tracking systems. In: Proc. of the 2009 IEEE International Symposium on Technology and Society, Wasington DC, USA (2009)
13. Bowen III, C.L., Martin, T.L.: A survey of Location privacy and an Approach for SolitaryUsers. In: 40th Hawaii Intnl. Conf. on System Sciences, Big Island, Hawaii (2007) ISBN 0-7695-2755-8

14. Zhu, C., Wat, K.K., et al.: Privacy and Social Effects in Location Sharing Services. In: Proceeding of 2012 IEEE First International Conference on Services Economics, Hawaii,USA, June 24-29 (2012)
15. GeekTools, "GTWhois," Centergate Research Group, LLC (2003)
16. VisualRoute, "VisualRoute 2006 Personal Edition," Visualware, Inc. (2006)
17. The Communications Act of 1934, 47 U.S.C(151-614), Public Law 416 (1934)
18. The Location Privacy Protection Act of 2001 (2001)
19. The Wireless Privacy Protection Act of 2003 (2003)
20. The Wireless Privacy Protection Act of 2005 (2005)
21. The Wireless 411 Privacy Act (2005)
22. European Union Directive on Privacy and Electronic Communications (2002)
23. Dowdell, E.M.: You are here! Mapping the boundaries of the Fourth Amendment with GPS technology. Rutgers Computer and Technology Law Journal 32(1), 109–139 (2005)
24. Lockton, V., Rosenberg, R.S.: RFID: the next serious threat to privacy. Ethics and Info. Tech. 7(4), 221–231 (2005)
25. Michael, M.G., Fusco, S.J., Michael, K.: A research note on ethics in the emerging age of uberveillance (überveillance). Computer Communications 31(6), 1192–1199 (2008)
26. Perusco, L., Michael, K.: Control, trust, privacy, and security: evaluating location-based services. IEEE Technologyand Society Magazine 26(1), 4–16 (2007)
27. Peslak, A.R.: An ethical exploration of privacy and radio frequency identification. Jour. of Business Ethics 59(4), 327–345 (2005)
28. Wasieleski, D.M., Gal-Or, M.: An enquiry into the ethical efficacy of the use of radio frequency identification technology. Ethics and Information Technology 10(1), 27–40 (2008)
29. Lin, D., Loui, M.C.: Taking the byte out of cookies: privacy, consent, and the Web. Computers and Society 28(2), 39–51 (1998)
30. Lin, D., Loui, M.C.: Taking the byte out of cookies: privacy, consent, and the Web. Computers and Society 28(2), 39–51 (1998)
31. Hengather, U., Steenkiste, P.: Avoiding privacy violation caused by context –sensitive services. In: Forth Annual IEEE International Conference on Pervasive Computing and Communications (PERCOM 2006), March 13-17, p. 233 (2006)
32. Myles, G., Friday, A., Davies, N.: Preserving Privacy in Environments with Location-Based Applications. IEEE Pervasive Computing 2(1), 56–64 (2003)
33. Xu, H., Gupta, S., et al.: Effectiveness of privacy Assurances Approaches In Location-Based Services:A Study of India and United States. In: Proceeding of Eighth International Conference on Mobile Business (2009)
34. Dinev, T., Bellotto, M., Hart, P., Russo, V., Serra, I., Colautti, C.: Internet users' privacy concerns and beliefs about governmentsurveillance: An exploratory study of differences between Italy and the United States. Journal of Global Information Management 14(4), 57–93 (2006)
35. Dinev, T., Bellotto, M., Hart, P., Russo, V., Serra, I., Colautti, C.: Privacy Calculus Model in E-commerce - a Study of Italy and the United States. European Journal of Information Systems 15(4), 389–402 (2006)
36. Kumaraguru, P., Cranor, L.: Privacy in India: Attitudes and Awareness. In: Danezis, G., Martin, D. (eds.) PET 2005. LNCS, vol. 3856, pp. 243–258. Springer, Heidelberg (2006)
37. Milberg, S.J.B., Smith, J.S.H.J., Kallman, A.E.: Values, Personal Information Privacy Concerns, and Regulatory Approaches. Comm. of the ACM 38(12), 65–74 (1995)
38. Nowak, G.J., Phelps, J.: Understanding Privacy Concerns: An Assessment of Consumers's Information-Related Knowledge and Beliefs. Journal of Direct Marketing 6(4), 28–39 (1992)

39. Wang, P.: Information-Systems Solutions for Transborder Data Flow Problems for Multinational Companies. International Journal of Information Management 13(1), 29–40 (1993)
40. Margulis, S.T.: On the Status and Contribution of Westin's and Altman's Theories of Privacy. Jour. of Social Issues 59(2), 411–429 (2003)
41. Bertino, E., Kirkpatrick, M.: Location-Aware Authentication and Access Control-Concepts and Issues. In: International Conference on Advanced Information Networking and Aplications(AINA), May 26-29. University of Bradford, Bradford, UK (2009)
42. Michael, K., McNamee, A., Michael, M.G.: The Emerging Ethics of Humancentric GPS Tracking and Monitoring. In: Proc. of the International Conference on Mobile Business (ICMB 2006), Copenhagen, Denmark, June 26-27. IEEE Computer Society (2006) ISBN 0-7695-2595-4
43. Dobson, J.E., Fisher, P.F.: Geoslavery. IEEE Technology and Society Magazine 22(1), 47–52 (2003)
44. Garfinkel, S.L., et al.: RFID Privacy: An Overview of Problem and Proposed Solutions. IEEE Securityand Privacy Mag. 3(3), 38–43 (2005)
45. Michael, K., Michael, M.G.: Microchipping People: the Rise of the Electrophorus. Quadrant, 22–33 (March 2005)
46. Perusco, L., Michael, K.: Humancentric Applications of Precise Location-Based Services. In: IEEE Conference on e-Business Engineering, pp. 409–418. IEEE Computer Society, Beijing (2005)
47. Kaupins, G., Minch, R.: Legal and Ethical Implications of Employee Location Monitoring. In: 38th Hawaii Intnl. Conf. on System Sciences (2005), http://csdl2.computer.org/comp/proceedings/hicss/2005/2268/05/22680133a.pdf
48. Perakslis, C., Wolk, R.: Social Acceptance of RFID as a Biometric Security Method. In: Proceedings of the IEEE Symposium on Technology and Society, pp. 79–87 (2005)
49. Stajano, F.: Viewpoint: RFID Is X-ray Vision. Communications of the ACM 48(9), 31–33 (2005)
50. Google Earth, http://earth.google.com/
51. NASA World Wind, http://worldwind.arc.nasa.gov/
52. Microsoft Virtual Earth, http://www.microsoft.com/virtualearth/
53. Skyline Globe, http://www.skylinesoft.com/
54. Fleet, G.J., Williamson, M.: Research data in Google Earth: how do we protect privacy and meet ethical obligations? In: Proceeding World Congress on Privacy, Delta Brunswick, Saint John, New Brunswick, Canada, August 25-27 (2009)

Adaptive Task Scheduling in Service Oriented Crowd Using SLURM

Vikram Nunia[1], Bhavesh Kakadiya[1], Chittaranjan Hota[1],
and Muttukrishnan Rajarajan[2]

[1] Dept. of Computer Science, BITS Pilani Hyderabad Campus, Hyderabad, India
{vikram,hota}@bits-hyderabad.ac.in, kakadiya91@gmail.com
[2] School of Engineering and Mathematical Sciences, City University London, UK
r.muttukrishnan@city.ac.uk

Abstract. Crowdsourcing is a distributed problem-solving paradigm. Service oriented crowdsourcing paradigm involves both consumers and service providers. A consumer requests for a service (task); a provider provides that service (does that task); and the providers are paid by consumers for the service as per their satisfaction. The challenge is to select a service provider from a list of providers which can provide maximum satisfaction to the consumer for that service. This work outlines an architectural model using SLURM tool for efficient management of crowd. At the center of this work, we proposed a novel idea of adaptive task scheduling which is based on the customer satisfaction feedbacks. Our approach improves efficiency, and decreases the cost of service to consumers. Experimental results demonstrate the viability of our approach.

Keywords: Crowdsourcing, Task scheduling, Simple Linux Utility Resource Management (SLURM).

1 Introduction

In 2006 Jeff Howe introduced the term *crowdsourcing* [1] which refers to "the act of taking a job traditionally performed by a designated agent (usually an employee) and outsourcing it to an undefined, generally large group of people in the form of an open call". The objective of crowdsourcing is to reduce the production costs. Crowdsourcing is used for numerous purposes like Microwork [7] is a crowdsourcing platform where users do small tasks for which computers lack aptitude for low amounts of money. In recent years, games with a purpose like the ESP game [4] and task markets like Amazon Mechanical Turk [12] have become successful crowd-based systems that attract crowd to perform a variety of tasks that are difficult for computers, yet solvable by humans.

A crowd platform dynamically provisions, configures, and de-provisions services as needed. The work done in this research will satisfy the needs of Service providers, Infrastructure providers and end-users. Large organizations need tremendous amount of computational resources in order to perform large number of tasks. Even though the computational capacity is larger than required, the inefficient resource mapping can lead to poor utilization and throughput. The resources can be unified by

C. Hota and P.K. Srimani (Eds.): ICDCIT 2013, LNCS 7753, pp. 373–385, 2013.

connecting individual resource units into crowd managed by resource manager such as SLURM [2]. A crowd consumer asks for a service, offers monitory reward, etc; and the service providers provide competitive deals to provide best solution. A consumer may select more than one service provider for a service but will pay to only one whose solution is selected as the best solution. Nowadays, crowd service providers offer recommendation systems [3], [5] and [6] attracting particular users on the Web. In these systems, each provider's service is ranked and shown to consumers.

In this paper we proposed an architectural model using SLURM tool for efficient crowd management. At the center of our work, we proposed adaptive task matching algorithm. In this paper consumers task is termed as a service. Whenever, consumer asks for a service, the crowd manager will recommend a set of service providers for that service. The consumer will select the service provider/s from this set to minimize the cost with acceptable service satisfaction. The recommendations will be based on consumer satisfaction levels expressed in terms of feedback. Thus, increasing efficiency of task completion and decreasing cost to consumers. Upon completion of any service, consumer will give feedback in the form of rating based on cost per service satisfaction which will help other consumers in future. Thus, our scheduling is adaptive, efficient and cost effective.

The rest of this paper is organized as follows: in Section 2 we review the related work and available crowd based tools. In Section 3, we describe crowd architecture model. Section 4 presents our task scheduling algorithm with an example case. We discuss implementation methodology and performance evaluation of our algorithm in Section 5 and finally, Section 6 concludes the work.

2   Related Work

In crowdsourcing, we can outsource the task to not only a small group of people, but also to tens of thousands of people. Haoqi Zhang *et al.* [8] discussed the interplay between algorithmic paradigms and human abilities, and illustrated through examples how members of a crowd can play diverse roles in an organized problem-solving process. That is the genuine advantage of the crowdsourcing, bringing in mass intelligence to solve problems of all kinds with affordable price. In crowd there are two groups: requesters and workers; but in our service oriented crowd we termed them as consumers and service providers. Consumers select service providers from the crowd and pay the offered amount.

Challenge in this type of crowd is to identify good service providers who provide right results and can work in the consumer's specified budget. One approach is select a number of service providers and take result of majority as right result and pay the best proposal. H. Psaier *et al.* [9] used concept of distinguished crowd members which act as responsible points of reference. These members mediate the crowd's workforce, settle agreements, organize activities, schedule tasks, and monitor behavior. But in this approach time spent on service provider selection, result selection, etc. are much greater than actual task execution time. M. C. Yuen *et al.* [5] proposed an approach for task matching in crowdsourcing to motivate workers; and the idea utilizes the past task preference and performance of a worker to produce a list of available tasks in the order of best matching with the worker during his task selection stage. V. C. Raykar *et al.* [10] used entropy score to rank annotators for crowdsourced labeling tasks. M. Hirth *et al.* [11] discussed that due to the anonymity of the workers, they are encouraged to cheat the employers in order to maximize their income. So, they presented two crowd-based approaches to validate the submitted work with different types of typical crowdsourcing tasks. Thus, task matching helps a consumer to quickly identify the right service provider thus, increases efficiency.

In this paper, our task scheduling algorithm helps consumers to get a list of service providers sorted by rank which is based on consumer's satisfaction feedback history and offered price range of a consumer.

To implement our algorithm we used Simple Linux Utility for Resource Manager (SLURM) [2], which is an open-source resource manager, used by many of the world's supercomputers and computer clusters. It provides three key functions. First, it allocates exclusive and/or non-exclusive access to resources (computer nodes) to users for some duration of time so they can perform their work. Second, it provides a framework for starting, executing, and monitoring work on a set of allocated nodes. Finally, it arbitrates contention for resources by managing a queue of pending jobs. Scheduler schedules tasks and uses SLURM as underlying tool for allocation of tasks as explained in the next section.

3   Architectural Model

SLURM consists of several components like 'slurmctld' daemon that controls system's core functionality. Slurmd is SLURM daemon that runs on every node in the system and carries out incoming orders. In our model we provided an user interface through which a consumer submits a task along with task properties to scheduler, selects service provider/s from the service providers list returned by the scheduler, sends satisfaction feedbacks; and a service provider defines specifications for each service like amount charged, etc. Scheduler stores the specifications specified by consumers and service providers for each service in its database named as scheduler DB as shown in Fig.1 for future scheduling purposes.

Crowd is divided into two categories (a) Consumers or service providers, and (b) Crowd managers. Consumers send service requests to the scheduler, consumer scheduler creates a service for that task and sends it to the crowd managers to give a list of service providers for that task. Crowd managers have the list of all service providers along with their ranking based on the feedback history. Crowd manager matches the task requirements with each service provider stored in their database and returns a list of service providers for that service back to the consumer scheduler along with their current state. In our model we have used slurm controller and slurm daemons as crowd managers. A crowd manager may be a consumer or a service provider. If slurm controller (crowd manager) is also a crowd user then, it will run slurm daemon as well. Scheduler executes the scheduling algorithm explained in the next section and interacts directly with slurm daemon or controller. Slurm controller also interacts directly to slurm daemons to get their current state. Slurm daemon executes tasks submitted by scheduler as shown in Fig.1.

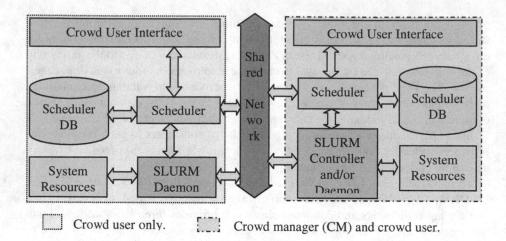

Crowd user only.   Crowd manager (CM) and crowd user.

Fig. 1. Architecture Model of Crowd using SLURM

4   Implementation and Algorithm

In this section we will define task properties, service provider's specifications, scheduling algorithm and then, we will explain our scheduling algorithm with an example.

A. Task Properties

Table 1. Task properties

Task Properties	Explanation
TASK_NAME	Name of task.
CONS_NAME	Name of consumer who submitted task.
TASK_TYPE	Type of task like execution, storage etc.
RES_REQ	Resources required for task completion.
EXP_RESP_TIME	Expected response time.
REWARD	Monetary reward offered by consumer for task.
OTHER_INFO	Any other information.

A consumer submits a task along with task properties to its scheduler. Task properties are given in Table 1. TASK_NAME is name of task, CONS_NAME is used by crowd managers or service providers to know who is consumer of task, TASK_TYPE defines what kind of service task is needed e.g., execution means task will use execution service. RES_REQ property means what resources a task needs for its successful completion, used by crowd managers to filter service providers who provide necessary resources and service providers use this property for allocation of resources. EXP_RESP_TIME is the expected response time of a task i.e. time in which the service provider responds back to consumer for that task. It is used by consumer scheduler for feedback calculation. REWARD is the price offered by a consumer to a service provider for any task. Also, REWARD can be within a range. OTHR_INFO contains extra information about the task e.g., it may contain variable information which is necessary for execution of the task, etc. These properties are submitted to scheduler in a special file as *{task_name}.conf* file.

B. Service Provider Specifications

Table 2. Service provider's (SP) specifications

SP Specifications	Explanation
SP_NAME	Name of service provider.
SP_MGR	Set if SP is crowd manager.
SP_LIST	List of services provided.
SP_CHARGE	Amount charged for each respective service.
SP_RESR	Resources provided.
SP_RANK	Rank of SP in each service in respective order.
SP_STATE	Last state recorded like up, down, idle and busy.
SP_TOT_CREDIT	Total amount earned by a SP.
SP_OTHER_INFO	Any other information.

When a user joins a crowd, it registers itself with specifications as explained in Table 2. SP_NAME is service provider's name. If any service provider wants to be a crowd manager, it will set SP_MGR flag and send this file to crowd controller. Crowd controller will store name of service provider into its database and will reset SP_MGR flag. In future if controller finds that some crowd manager is failed then, it will look into its database and select the top service providers who wanted to be crowd manager on the basis of their overall rank. SP_LIST contains the list of service provided by a service provider, used by crowd mangers to search service providers for requested services. Through SP_CHARGE field a service provider defines monitory charges of the service it provides. SP_RESR gives information about the resources a service provider is offering for all services set in SP_LIST field. SP_RANK defines current rating of any service provider; updated by crowd managers every time whenever satisfaction feedback is provided by any consumer. SP_STATE is current state of any service provider like up state means service provider is active in crowd, can be set by service provider or crowd managers. During shut down process service provider will send a down signal to crowd managers, and crowd managers will set its state as down. SP_TOT_CREDIT is sum of total amount earned by a service provider. OTHR_INFO is used to provide extra information about service provider. These specifications are stored on each crowd manager in a special file as *{SP_name}.conf* file.

C. Scheduling Algorithm

In this section we will explain our proposed adaptive scheduling algorithm. Once a consumer gets the submitted task executed, consumer will pay only to service provider (SP$_i$) whose result(α_i), it selected as the final result. But, consumer will send satisfaction feedback to each service provider whom it has sent that task.

Algorithm1. Adaptive Task Scheduling Algorithm

---

1   Submit task T(T.conf, CMGR_List);
2   {SP_List, OTHER_List} ← get_SP_List(T.conf,CMGR_List);
3   **if** SP_list == NULL **then**
         //If no SP is available for specified T.conf
4   **if** OTHER_List == NULL **then** return error(NO_SP_Available);
5   **else** return change_T_conf(OTHER_List);   //change T.conf
6   **else**
7   Sort(SP_List);   //Sort SP List
8   **if** SP_List.SP_NUM < N **then** N ← SP_List.SP_NUM;
                                                //Send T to N SPs
9   {TOT_RSLTS,RSLTS} ← send_T(T,T.conf,SP_List,N);
         //Select majority result returned by SPs
10   Final_RSLT ← Majority(RSLTS);
11   Pay_SP(Final_RSLT,T.conf);   //Pay to selected SP
         //calculate η and send to each SP
12   Calculate_send_feedback(TOT_RSLTS,CMGR_List);

In this section, we describe the formula used to calculate satisfaction feedback of each service provider (step 12 of Algorithm1).

$$
\eta_j = \begin{cases} \tau_{exp} > \tau_{resp_j} \text{ and } i \neq j \text{ and } \alpha_j = \alpha_i & \sigma - \left(\dfrac{\tau_{resp_j} - \tau_{resp_i}}{\tau_{exp} - \tau_{resp_j}} \right) \\[3mm] \tau_{exp} > \tau_{resp_j} \text{ and } i = j & \sigma \\[3mm] else & \begin{cases} \alpha_j \neq \alpha_i & 0 \\[2mm] else & \begin{cases} \dfrac{\sigma}{2} - \left(\dfrac{\tau_{resp_j} - \tau_{resp_i}}{\tau_{exp}} \right) & if > 0 \\[2mm] 0 & else \end{cases} \end{cases} \end{cases} \tag{1}
$$

Let the response time of SP$_i$ is τ_{resp_i}, response time for task 'T' of each service provider is τ_{resp_j}, α_j is result submitted by each service provider where $j \in \{1..N\}$, where N is the maximum number of service providers to whom task 'T' was sent, σ is maximum feedback score and τ_{exp} is the expected response time specified in '*T.conf*' then, satisfaction feedback (η) will be calculated for each SP_j as given in equation 1.

D. An Example Case

For example demonstration of our proposed architecture, let us consider 7 users C1, C2, C3, C4, C5, C6, and C7; C4 as slurm controller (slurmctld) and 2 users C4 and C5 are crowd managers as shown in Fig. 2. To explain the complete demonstration we divide our explanation into three parts (a) crowd setup, (b) task scheduling and (c) satisfaction feedback calculation.

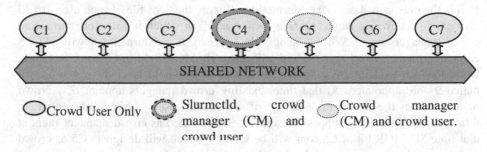

Fig. 2. Typical Crowd of 7 users

(a) Crowd setup

Initially every user will set its specification file as explained in service provider's specification section. If user wants to be a crowd manager in future it will set SP_MGR flag. A typical service provider specifications file (C5.conf) is as shown in Table 3.

Table 3. Service provider C5's specifications file (C5.conf)

C5 Specifications	Value
SP_NAME	C5
SP_MGR	1
SP_LIST	execution, storage
SP_CHARGE	0.10-sec-proc,0.25-hr-GB
SP_RESR	CPU-2,RAM-256,HDD-100
SP_RANK	0,0
SP_STATE	up-idle
SP_TOT_CREDIT	0.0
SP_OTHER_INFO	

In C5.conf file, SP_MGR flag is set to tell existing crowd managers that C5 also wants to become a crowd manager in future. Execution and storage are typical services provided by C5 i.e. it can execute some task, provide data storage. SP_STATE is set to up-idle which means C5 is available and is not busy. The other possible combinations which we used are up-busy and down. When a node is up-busy no task will be sent to it until it doesn't set itself to up-idle. This state can be used by any crowd user if he or she wants to be in crowd but not interested in providing any service. SP_CHARGE contains list of amount charged per unit for each service e.g., C5 will charge $0.10 per second per processor execution and $0.25 per hour per GB storage. SP_RANK will be set to 0 for each service. SP_RESR contains list of resources C5 is willing to share for services it provides. Each resource name is appended with resource instances for e.g. CPU-2(2 CPU), RAM-256 (256 MB RAM), HDD-100(100 GB HDD), etc.

Each user maintains a crowd manager list (CMGR_List). Initially slurm controller (slurmctld) acts as only crowd manager and hence, CMGR_List contains only slurmctld name. Every node will create their typical conf file and send it to slurmctld as it is the only crowd manager. Slurmctld will store the conf file of each user. It will also create a new file named "*future_crowd_mgr*" in which it will store the future crowd managers name. When C5.conf file is received by slurmctld it will add C5 entry into *future_crowd_mgr* file and will reset SP_MGR field in C5.conf. In future, when load on existing crowd managers exceed a threshold level then, new crowd managers are appointed. At that time, existing crowd mangers appoint new crowd managers on the basis of ranking of interested users (users list stored in *future_crowd_mgr* file). Suppose in future C5 is selected as crowd manager then, at that time SP_MGR bit of C5.conf will be set to 1 which will designate C5 as crowd manager and a message will be broadcasted in crowd that C5 is also a crowd manaeger so, every node will update their CMGR_List (crowd managers list).

Table 4. Task T1's Property file (T1.conf)

T1 Properties	Value
TASK_NAME	T1
CONS_NAME	C1
TASK_TYPE	execution
RES_REQ	CPU-1, RAM-250
EXP_RESP_TIME	20
REWARD	0.15-sec-proc
OTHER_INFO	

(b) Task scheduling

Once a user is connected to crowd, it can ask for any service. We have already considered C4 and C5 as crowd managers in our typical crowd. Suppose C1 submits a task 'T1' to its scheduler along with T1.conf which is shown in Table 4.

Now, C1 scheduler will create a query task 'QT1'for 'T1' (includes T1.conf in query). C1 will send QT1 to select randomly any of the crowd managers. The crowd managers have list of all service providers and their specifications. Crowd manger will search service providers who provide services queried by QT1. Crowd manager will filter the results to match the T1.conf properties like REWARD offered by T1 should be more than SP_CHARGE and RESR_REQ should meet with SP_RESR. Crowd manager will put filtered result in SP_List and remaining results (which are not in SP_List) in OTHR_List. So, SP_List contains service provider names who matches with T1's requirements and OTHR_List contains service provider names who provide service needed by T1 but don't match with T1's requirements. The crowd manager will return both lists i.e. SP_List and OTHR_List to C1. Typical, SP_List and OTHR_List returned by crowd manager (CM) are shown in Table 5 and Table 6 respectively. Now, C1 have SP_List who provides services needed by T1. If SP_List is null i.e. no service provider matches with T1's requirements then, C1 will check OTHR_List, and if OTHR_List is not null then, C1 scheduler will ask user to modify requirements else scheduler will return no service provider available for service you needed. If SP_List is not null then, C1 will sort SP_List in descending order of their rank and will select first N service providers from the sorted list and will send T1 to each service provider. For N=3, and if maximum score (σ) is 5 then, in our example C1 will send T1 to C5, C2 and C6 (from table 5).

Table 5. SP_List returned by CM

Name	Values		
SP_Name_List	C2	C6	C5
SP_Rank_List	4	3.4	5
SP_Num	3		

Table 6. OTHR_List returned by CM

Name	Values	
SP_Name_List	C3	C4
SP_CHARGE_List	0.25-sec-proc	0.20-sec-proc
SP_RESR_List	RAM-100	RAM-200

(c) Satisfaction feedback calculation

Now service providers C5, C2 and C6 will execute task T1 and return result back to C1 scheduler. Suppose response time and result returned of each service provider is given by Table 7 then, C1 will calculate majority of result.

Table 7. Result returned by service providers and satisfaction feedback calculated

Service Provider Name	Result Returned (α_j)	Response Time (τ_{resp_j})	Feedback calculated (η_j)
C5	16.52	18	3.5
C2	16.52	15	5
C6	16.52	35	1.5

From Table 7, majority of result (α_i) is 16.52. In majority we will select result submitted before expected response time of T1 and immediately return result to user. But if any response is coming after expected response time of T1 consumer won't consider it; but will return feedback to it. Once the majority result is identified then, the service provider who responded the same result in minimum time is selected for reward money. Form above table (Table 7) C2 will be rewarded with $2.25 (0.15*15).

Now, for each service provider satisfaction feedback is calculated according to equation 1 which is tabulated in Table 7. The calculated satisfaction feedback will be sent to each crowd manager. The crowd managers will calculate new average for each service provider returned by C1 and update respective conf file.

So, in this way our algorithm will work in the proposed architectural model using SLURM as underlying tool. We next describe the results.

5   Implementation Results

Table 8. Crowd setup details

Parameters	Value
Number of users	25
Crowd Managers	5
Services	execution, storage, compilation, convertor.
Charges	Randomly selected by each SP between 0 and 1.
Resources	CPU, RAM, HDD, compilers{ C, C++,etc}, converters { mp4 to mp3, .avi to .mp3, etc}.
#Tasks generated per user	1000
Maximum Score	10
Confidence Score	2
N	4

The crowd test bed setup details are given in Table 8. Tasks were generated with random time intervals on each consumer. Initially average score of each node was 0. Also, only 20 users were added to crowd. After simulating for 100 tasks we added 5 more nodes with initial score 0 to our already built in crowd. These 5 nodes will not be selected by any consumer till their score is less than a minimum score called *confidence score*. In this case, they will set the amount charged to minimal or will provide maximum resources with minimum charge till they get confidence score. In our simulation if any service provider's score is less than confidence score for any service, then respective SP_CHARGE field of that service provider was set to 0. When that service provider gained the confidence score for that service, respective SP_CHARGE was set back to its last value. After every random number of tasks serviced, a service provider returns wrong result for a task to introduce error rate in our simulation.

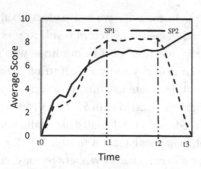

Fig. 3. Behavior of service providers (SP) in crowd using Adaptive Task Scheduling Algorithm (ATSA).

Fig.3 explains the behavior of our algorithm in crowd. In fig.3 we have shown the behavior of two service providers which provide same services with different specifications. Initially, at time 't0' both service providers start from the score zero; and later on at time 't1' they saturate to some score based on satisfaction feedbacks given by consumers. Suppose at time 't2' where t2>t1, due to some circumstances, one service provider starts to provide faulty responses then, average feedback score starts to fall down for faulty service provider and at time 't3' where t3>t2, its score reaches to zero while for non-faulty service provider average feedback score will move towards maximum score. Therefore, in our algorithm if any service provider provides faulty responses then after some time it will not be selected by any consumer while non-faulty service provider becomes more trust worthy with time thus, reduces error rates in crowd.

To evaluate performance of our approach, we compared our results with random algorithm (RA) [9]. In random algorithm a crowd consumer randomly polls 'M' where M>N, other service providers to match its requirements. Then sorts them in ascending order of charges and sends task T to N service providers. In our simulation, we used M as 9. Comparison is done on scheduling time, error rate, average response time error and average score of service provider. Scheduling time is the time needed to schedule task T on service providers, error rate is the ratio of error results to total results, response time error is the difference of response time of service provider and expected response time specified in task's properties file and average score is calculated by satisfaction feedbacks sent by consumers. The results are shown in Fig. 4 (a), 4(b), 4(c) and 4(d) respectively.

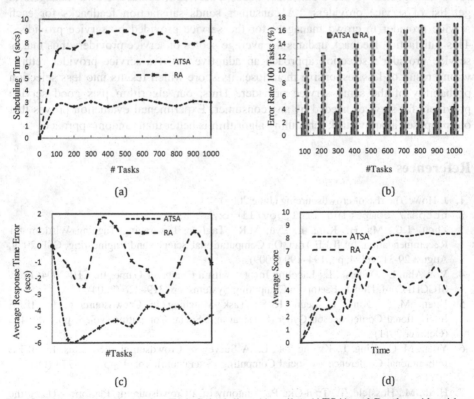

(a)

(b)

(c)

(d)

Fig. 4. Comparison of Adaptive Task Scheduling Algortihm (ATSA) and Random Algorithm (RA) on (a) Scheduling Time, (b) Error Rate, (c) Average Response Time Error, and (d) Average Score

In fig.4 (a), scheduling time is very less in our Adaptive Task Scheduling Algorithm (ATSA) as compared to Random Algorithm (RA). In random approach scheduling time is more because of polling, more number of packet transfers, etc. Fig. 4(b) shows that error rate is less in our ATSA algorithm than RA because of our adaptive algorithm. Negative response time error means that the service providers responded earlier than expected response time specified by task which is positive property of our algorithm as most of the responses have negative error in comparison to RA which is shown in Fig 4(c). In our algorithm average score of service provider tends to saturate towards maximum score with time while in RA it doesn't saturate because of error rate, non-linear delays, etc. as shown in fig 4(d).

6   Conclusion

In this paper we proposed adaptive scheduling algorithm which uses service scores (average scores change with each service served) to select service providers. Crowd managers maintain information about each service provider and also responsible for score management. When a consumer needs a service it contacts crowd managers to get list of service providers. A consumer sends satisfaction feedbacks for each service provider to crowd managers for the service provided by service providers. This satisfaction feedback updates the average scores of service providers thus makes service provider's selection approach an adaptive i.e. if a service provider returns wrong result or less responsive then, loses its score which results into less selection probability of the same service provider. Thus, our algorithm lists good service providers for services needed by any consumer. Experimental evaluation proves that our proposed adaptive task scheduling algorithm is better than random approach.

References

1. J. Howe The rise of crowdsourcing (June 2006)
2. https://computing.llnl.gov/linux/slurm/
3. Zhou, T.C., Ma, H., King, I., Lyu, M.R.: TagRec: Leveraging Tagging Wisdom for Recommendation. In: IEEE Tran. On Computational Science and Engineering, CSE 2009, August 29-31, vol. 4, pp. 194–199 (2009)
4. Von Ahn, L., Dabbish, L.: Labeling Images with a Computer Game. In: CHI 2004: Proc. SIGCHI Conf. Human Factors in Computing Systems, pp. 319–326 (2004)
5. Yuen, M.-C., King, I., Leun, K.-S.: Task Matching in Crowdsourcing. In: IEEE International Conference on Cyber, Physical and Social Computing, vol. 4, pp. 409–412 (October 2011)
6. Yuen, M.-C., King, I., Kwong-Sak, L.: A Survey of Crowdsourcing Systems. In: IEEE International Conference on Social Computing (Socialcom), vol. 3, pp. 766–773 (October 2011)
7. Hirth, M., Hossfeld, T., Tran-Gia, P.: Anatomy of a Crowdsourcing Platform - Using the Example of Microworkers.com. In: IEEE International Conference on Innovative Mobile and Internet Services in Ubiquitous Computing (IMIS), vol. 5, pp. 322–329 (June 2011)

8. Zhang, H., Horvitz, E., Miller, R.C., Parkes, D.C.: Crowdsourcing General Computation. In: ACM CHI 2011 Workshop on Crowdsourcing and Human Computation (January 2011)
9. Psaier, H., Skopik, F., Schall, D., Dustdar, S.: Resource and Agreement Management in Dynamic Crowdcomputing Environments. In: IEEE Enterprise Distributed Object Computing Conference (EDOC), vol. 15, pp. 193–202 (August 2011)
10. Raykar, V.C., Yu, S.: An Entropic Score to Rank Annotators for Crowdsourced Labeling Tasks. In: IEEE Conference on Computer Vision, Pattern Recognition, Image Processing and Graphics (NCVPRIPG), vol. 3, pp. 29–32 (December 2011)
11. Hirth, M., Hossfeld, T., Tran-Gia, P.: Cost-Optimal Validation Mechanisms and Cheat-Detection for Crowdsourcing Platforms. In: Workshop on Future Internet and Next Generation Networks, Seoul, Korea (June 2011)
12. Mturk website, http://www.mturk.com

An Efficient Method for Synchronizing Clocks of Networked ECUs in Automotive Systems[*]

Kumar Padmanabh, Amit Gupta, and Purnendu Sinha

Global General Motors R&D, India Science Lab
GM Tech Center (India), Bangalore 560066, India
padmanabh@ieee.org, amit.gupta@gm.com

Abstract. Advanced active-safety-critical automotive applications require close coordination of different activities including sensing, processing and actuations, typically performed by different Electronic Control Units (ECU) connected over a communication network. It is imperative that ECUs executing these tasks have a common reference of time. In a distributed system, a periodic resynchronization is a common approach to ensure this. In this paper, we have proposed a new protocol for clock synchronization keeping resource-constraints automotive systems. Our specific contributions include: (a) as compared to standard treatment of drift as a linear function of time, we use a realistic non-linear model of drift, and (b) in order to minimize communication overhead, we propose an algorithm to anticipate the time at which a specific ECU would go out of sync and participate only such identified ECUs for resynchronization instead of all ECUs, as traditionally done. Analytical results show that the proposed protocol incurs minimal communication as well computational load on the ECUs.

1 Introduction

Due to safety, comfort and connectivity related requirements, not only the number of ECUs is increasing in vehicles but the computational load on each ECU is also increasing. The number of new sensors and actuators are getting added to vehicles. The information required by various features of vehicles gets generated at different instants of time by these sensors located in different parts of the vehicle. Moreover, many ECUs host more than one feature and one particular ECU may require time critical information from other connected ECUs. Thus in this spatially and temporally distributed physical activities, it is important to streamline various processes on a common time scale by synchronizing all ECUs to a common clock so that processing of information happens in the same reference of time.

A typical clock synchronization protocol [1], [2], [3] and [4], has three distinct steps which get executed periodically whenever ECUs participate in resynchronization: (i) in the first step, time samples are collected from different nodes, (ii) in the second step, a convergence mechanism is used to converge all time values to a common agreeable

---

[*] This research work was conducted when Kumar Padmanabh and P. Sinha were with GM R&D, India Science Lab, Bangalore.

C. Hota and P.K. Srimani (Eds.): ICDCIT 2013, LNCS 7753, pp. 386–397, 2013.

value and (iii) in the third step, the deviations of individual clock from this common agreeable time is calculated so that all clocks would do the required correction respectively. Since all ECUs participate in the resynchronization process, most protocols use broadcast as an underlying communication technique to exchange clock values. We observe and claim the fact that all ECUs need not participate in resynchronization at the same time, as some of them would not have sufficiently drifted from the common reference time and thereby need not require any clock adjustment at the same moment of time.

Authors in [5] used reference broadcast method [RBS] which uses a "third party" for synchronization. Here instead of synchronizing the sender with a receiver (as in most of the previous work), their scheme synchronizes a set of receivers with one another. In RBS scheme, a node sends reference messages to their neighbors. A reference message does not include a timestamp, but instead, its time of arrival is used by receiving nodes as a reference point for comparing clocks. One of the limitations with these protocols is that they incur high overhead in message communication due to use of broadcasting, as the synchronization message needs to be sent out to all nodes instead of a selected few which would actually be going out of synchronization.

Most of the protocols in the literature considered drift as a constant or a linear function. However, drift is actually a non linear function of time [14] and it is responsible for deviation of the clocks. We have investigated further about the drift function and found that in most of the protocols [6], [8] and [10] time is modeled as $C_i(t) = a_i t + b_i$ where a_i is the drift, b_i is the offset and $C_i(t)$ is a time of ith clock in a network. It is to be noted that drift is considered as a constant and hence the deviation of the clock is assumed to be linear in nature.

Following our observations made earlier, we primarily focus on (a) using a non-linear model of drift and (b) developing a scheme which would avoid broadcasting of synchronization packets which imposes communication load even on those nodes which do not require synchronization. Towards this, we have developed a synchronization technique in which utilizing non-linear model of drift, we "anticipate" the chronological sequence in which ECUs would go out of sync and then we selectively synchronize them in the same sequence using point to point communication. This helps us in avoiding computation load due to synchronization on those nodes which do not require synchronization. Our analytical results show that the communication load is reduced to O(N) from $O(N^2)$.

Rest of this paper is organized as follows. In section-II we present the analytical model of time and the algorithm of our proposed time synchronization protocol. Section-III analyzes our protocol and in section-IV we discuss the analytical results.

2   System Modeling

2.1   Analytical Modeling of Time

We observe that the drift is non-linear in nature. The time function of the candidate clock is expressed in the terms of fundamental frequency as $C(t) = k \int_{t0}^{t} w(\tau) + C(t0)$.

The fundamental frequency of oscillators used in clocks which is ought to be constant all the time, is in fact a function of time. Since the drift of a clock is calculated as the rate of deviation of its time thus it can be expressed as $\gamma(\tau) = dw(\tau)/d\tau$. The frequency function can be expressed as: $w(\tau) = \int_0^\tau \gamma(\tau)d\tau$. Thus the time function can be represented in terms of drift function as following:

$$C(t) = k\int_{t_0}^{t}\int_0^{\tau}\gamma(\tau)d\tau dt + C(t_0)$$

The drift function is responsible for all major derivations and therefore we are considering it for all analysis. $C(t_0)$ is the time when the system was started. Since the entire system is initiated from beginning which corresponds to the time when the control system of the vehicle is powered on therefore the $C(t_0)$ will be zero.

2.2   Various Delays and Jitter in Communication Process

Let us assume that we have an intra-vehicular network of $N+1$ ECU including one master ECU. It is important to understand the time consumed by each individual processes of communication. We assume that the packet from a node to the master node always takes the same amount of time to travel. Thus propagation delay t_d is fixed between a node and the master node. When a node sends a response packet to the master node or vice versa, there are two distinct processes involved in it: (i) the packet processing which included physical reception of the packet, filtering, reordering and rendering information from the packet expressed as t_p and (ii) message preparation times which include packet formation and encapsulation, expressed as t_f.

Time Jitter: The various delays namely t_d, t_f and t_p will be different for different ECUs. Thus if the master ECU requests some information from other nodes due to variation in propagation, processing and message formation time, there will be a jitter introduced to the system. The jitter will increase with increasing number of nodes. Let us consider ξ is average jitter introduced by a single node and hence for N nodes jitter will be $N\xi$.

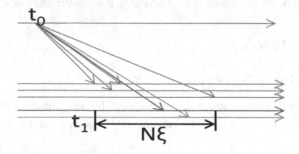

Fig. 1. Time Jitter in packet reception

3   Our Proposed Protocol

We are proposing a three stage protocol. In stage-1, the master ECU dictates its own time to other ECUs ensuring that error introduced due to propagation, processing and packet formation delay is adjusted. In the second stage, the master clock arranges to receive time-stamps of other nodes and compares them with its own time. Based on the variation, it finds the drift function of the clocks of the respective nodes. In this stage the master clock also predicts when a node would go out of sync and prepares a schedule of all such nodes in the network which would need to be synchronized. In the third stage, the master clock sends re-synchronization packet to the individual clock according to the schedule. The detailed steps of the algorithm are mentioned in Table-1.

3.1   Description of Proposed Algorithm

As stated earlier, the two key aspects of the proposed protocol are modeling of drift as a non-linear functional and avoiding broadcast of synchronization message to all ECUs.

Stage-1 of Protocol: Collection of Time Samples and Compensations for Delays
At the onset of starting the network, all ECUs would be having their own views of time and would be requiring synchronization. We assume that a designated master ECU is connected to the outside world and a mechanism exists to synchronize the master clock to an external clock. Once the master ECU gets powered on, after the initial boot up, it starts the synchronization process. It prepares a control message (in Ethernet it is a PCF message) and inserts a time stamp before sending it to the transmission queue.

The other ECUs receive the packet (control message) from the master ECU and immediately put their own time stamp. They process the packet and extract the time stamp sent by the master clock. They also register a time when processing of the packet is finished. Then they calculate the processing time which is the difference between the time of arrival and the time of completion of processing. All nodes then update their individual time with the time stamp of the master clock and adjust the processing time accordingly.   Each node also records its individual time and acknowledges the master

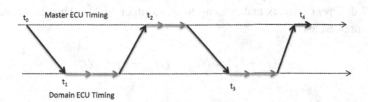

Fig. 2. Timing at different moment in stage-1 of the algorithms

ECU with its individual time stamp. The master ECU then calculates the propagation, processing and packet preparation delays, and then it sends the packet with the correction values to other ECUs.

It is to be noted that the master ECU uses broadcasting only in the stage-1. Subsequently point to point communication is used. The timing is mentioned in Table-1. Though every node will have the same process running, however due to EMC and network conditions, there will be a jitter introduced in receiving the packet at the master node. When a network of N nodes starts transmitting at a same time, the master node will receive all packets within $t_d + N\xi$ time interval, where $N\xi$ is the equivalent jitter for N nodes.

Theorem-1: If t_d be the uniform propagation delay between a node and the master ECU, t_p be the time required to process a received packet and extract relevant information out of it and if t_f is the time required to collect all required information and incorporate them into a packet then steps in stage-1 will be completed within a time limit of $2(N + 1)t_p(N + 2)t_f + 4(t_d + N\xi)$ where N is the number of nodes in the network and ξ is the average jitter.

Proof: As described in algorithm presented in table-1, for the simplicity let us express time interval $(t_4 - t_0)$ as following :

$$t_4 - t_0 = (t_4 - t_3) + (t_3 - t_2) + (t_2 - t_1) + (t_1 - t_0)$$

In the first part, in which the master ECU forms a packet and sends it to other ECUs, only propagation delay and associated jitter are involved. Thus the calculation for time required for this can be expressed as $t_1 - t_0 = t_d + N\xi$. In the second part ($t_2 - t_1$): there is an equivalent latency due to processing of packets involved in all other ECUs, packet formation and time required in propagation with jitter which could be further expressed as $(t_2 - t_1) = t_p + t_f + t_d + N\xi$. t_3 is an instant of time when the master ECU finishes the errors calculation, processes and sends them to other ECUs. It essentially requires processing of N numbers of packets and formation of N different packets and sending them to other ECUs. Thus this time duration can be expressed as:

$$(t_3 - t_2) = Nt_p + Nt_f + t_d + N\xi \tag{1}$$

Table 1. Algorithm for Synchronization

Stage-1:

At time t=t$_0$ {the Master ECU broadcasts its time stamp}

At time t=t$_1$ {

All other ECUs insert their own timestamps at following moments: (i) immediately after receiving the packet, (ii) after processing is done and (iii) after formation of acknowledgement packet (THIS IS NOT DISCUSSED EARLIER IN THE TEXT!!).

All other ECUs send the response packet to the master ECU.}

At time t=t$_2$ {the Master ECU receives the packets from participating ECUs, processes to find errors and sends the correction packets to other ECUs }

The Master ECU inserts its own time stamp (i) when the packets are received, (ii) when processing is done and (iii) jitter and placement of different information in the table is done.

The Master ECU sends the messages to respective ECUs with the error information.

At time t=t$_3$ {Domain ECUs receive correction packets from the Master ECU}   {

All other ECUs adjust their individual time with the error and send the updated time stamp to the Master ECUs. }

At time t=t$_4$ {the Master ECU receives the packet, update the respective table }

Stage-2:

All other ECUs keep sending the time stamp at regular interval.

The Master ECU keeps appending the time samples along with its own time stamp.

After receiving M such packets the Master ECU finds the individual drift function of the ECUs.

The Master ECU predicts the time when an individual ECU would require Synchronization.

The Master ECU prepares a list of the ECUs which will be synchronized at anticipated time instants.}

Stage-3:

 {According to the list, the master ECU sends the sync packet to the individual ECUs.

An individual ECU receives the packet and adjusts the delays in the received time stamp and updates its own clock.

Other ECUs send acknowledgement packet with its new time stamp.

the master ECU updates the entry of the table with new time. }

End

In the final step $(t_4 - t_3)$ there is a parallel processing happening at all ECUs which takes t_p time, then in parallel acknowledgement packet will be also formed which will take t_f time, propagation delay with associated jitter of $t_d + N\xi$ will be accounted for, then again there is a sequential processing of N packets accounting to Nt_p time before declaring the completion of stage-1. This can be further expressed as:

$$(t_4 - t_3) = t_p + t_f + t_d + N\xi + Nt_p \tag{2}$$

Therefore total time taken in this process of stage-1 is expressed:

$$(t_4 - t_0) = 2(N+1)t_p + (N+2)t_f + 4(t_d + N\xi) \tag{3}$$

This proves the theorem.

Stage-2 of Protocol: Estimation of the Drift Function

The master ECU receives multiple timestamps from individual ECUs. It calculates the value of drift and maintains a database of the same. Based on the sequential values of drift, it calculates the individual drift function using Lagrange's equation. Based on the drift function and various delays, the master ECU predicts the time when an individual ECU will go out of sync.

Let us consider that the non-linear characteristic function of the drift is an Mth order equation. In order to regenerate the equation we require exactly M numbers of samples of drift values. Thus the candidate ECUs for synchronization will send their individual timestamps consecutively for M times after adjusting with various delays, the master ECU will maintain a table of M entries.

Theorem-2: An ECU will require re-synchronization after a time t_1 if

$$K \int_{t_0}^{t_1} \int_0^t f(\tau)d\tau \geq \Delta t \text{ where } f_i(\tau) = \sum_{j=1}^{M} \left(\prod_{\substack{k=1 \\ k \neq j}}^{M} \frac{(\tau - f_i(t_k))}{(f_i(t_j) - f_i(t_k))} \right) \text{ in which } f_i(t_k)$$

are the collected time samples.

Proof: Let us consider that $f_i(\tau)$ is the characteristic drift function of ith ECU and the master ECU have the entries $f_i(t_j)$ at t_j^{th} moment of time where $j = 0 \ to \ M$

Based on these entries and using LaGrange's polynomial the drift function of the ith ECU can be expressed as:

$$f_i(\tau) = \sum_{j=1}^{M} \left(\prod_{\substack{k=1 \\ k \neq j}}^{M} \frac{(\tau - f_i(t_k))}{(f_i(t_j) - f_i(t_k))} \right) \tag{4}$$

By putting the various values of $f_i(t_j)$ one can calculate the drift function $f_i(\tau)$ from equation-4. The one set of data entry into the table require one message formation at the leaf ECU, one propagation time along with the jitter and N processing time at the master clock. Thus for one set of data it will require time span of $t_f + t_d + N\xi + Nt_p$ So total time required in stage-2 will be: $M(t_f + t_d + Nt_p) + N\xi$

Now let us assume that we have the tolerance of Δt. It means, if the master clock finds that the predicted time of the clock and its own time has a difference of Δt or more; then it will include that ECU in synchronization queue otherwise it will not.

Thus the time function of the clock $C(t)$ is calculated as: $C(t) = K \int_{t_0}^{t} w(\tau)d\tau$.

However, angular frequency function can be expressed as $w(\tau) = \int_{0}^{\tau} f(t)dt$.

Therefore, it can be expressed as:

$$C(t) = K \int_{t_0}^{t_1} \int_{0}^{t} f(\tau)d\tau dt \tag{5}$$

Putting the individual values of i, $f_i(t)$ is calculated from Lagrange's technique mentioned earlier. Moreover, since $C(t)$ cannot be more than Δt. This proves the theorem.

Stage-3 of Protocol: Resynchronization
Based on the data collected in previous stages, the master ECU prepares a list of ECUs which it anticipates to go out of sync in chronological sequence. Just before turn of the first ECU in the schedule, the master ECU sends a resynchronization packet to this ECU. Upon receiving the resynchronization packet master ECU resets its clock to the time stamp extracted from resynchronization packet and compensates the various delays calculated in first stage.

4   Analytical Results

In the previous section we have derived the time required to complete each stage of the algorithm. Summarily, the analysis of algorithm in concludes following:

1. Each stage of synchronization is completed within bounded time.
2. Resynchronization imposes a communication load on the network of the order of N, as compared to N^2 in other existing protocols.
3. The proposed protocol considers a realistic drift model as compared to idealistic linear model used in the existing literature.

These results are based on theoretical analysis of the proposed protocol. Though we have found that the protocol takes a bounded time to converge however, it is important to know the characteristics of these bounds. Especially, with increasing number of ECUs in the vehicle it is imperative to know whether this protocol is scalable.

Each oscillator would exhibit different form of non-linearity expressed as a unique mathematical function. We have assumed a parabolic drift function expressed as $(t) = K_1 t^2 + K_2 t$. We also assumed that M=4 is the number of samples required to reproduce the drift function by LagranGe's equation.   With typical length of cable of 1 meter we estimate that the typical propagation delay is 0.01. Similarly, with 100MHz processor of an ECU, processing delay for a 10 bytes packet would be $10\,\mu S$ and the time required to form a packet would also be $10\,\mu S$.

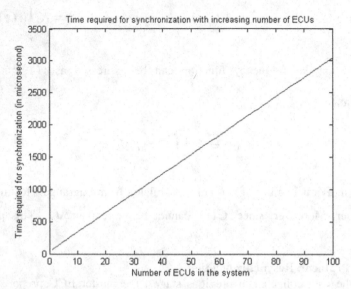

Fig. 3. Time required to synchronize with increasing number of nodes

We have plotted the equation-3 to understand how much time it requires to synchronize in the first stage. The results are shown in figure-3. With increasing number of nodes, we have calculated the time required to synchronize the first time when ECUs are powered on. It is evident that even for advanced vehicles having 30 ECUs the synchronization could be completed in microsecond. Resynchronization which involves point to point communication will only have processing and propagation delays of the order of 10 microseconds. Since these delays are known in advance and can be adjusted. It is the jitter which will be responsible for the residual deviation of a candidate clock for synchronization from the master clock. The jitter cannot be more than the time period of oscillator used in the clock.

While in the first plot (figure-3), our objective was to demonstrate the scalability of our proposed protocol. In the second plot we want to demonstrate feasibility of our proposed protocol. Precisely, we want to know if our mechanism of anticipation is working properly. As mentioned earlier, we assumed that drift function is parabolic in nature and can be expressed as $f(t) = K_1 t^2 + K_2 t$. Due to the drift, the candidate clocks will deviate from the reference clock. We have captured this deviation of the clock with increasing time. We also captured the deviation of clock using our anticipation mechanism and both of them are plotted on the same time scale. This is captured for 10 hours which is demonstrated in figure-4. We can notice that though due to parabolic function the deviation is more however we are able to predict it correctly. The difference in the actual offset and anticipated offset is always in the order of millisecond in the time horizon of 36000 seconds i.e., 10 hours.

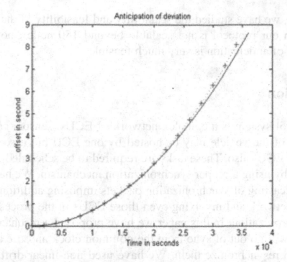

Fig. 4. The deviation of candidate clock from thereference clock and the anticipated deviation

In the third graph, (see figure-5), we have calculated the difference between the offsets. Even after 10 hours, this difference is not more than 450millisecond. When the offset is crossing the threshold, resynchronization can be initiated. Thus, the offset of 450 ms will not occur in reality as there will be numbers of re-synchronization performed within this time duration.

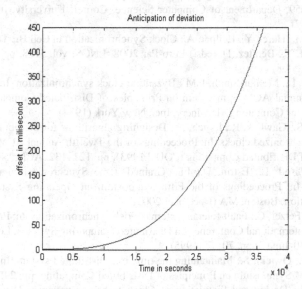

Fig. 5. Difference between the actual offset and anticipated offset with increasing time

In this section, we have studied the scalability and feasibility of the algorithm. We found that though our protocol is not scalable beyond 150 nodes, however the proposed mechanism of anticipation is very much feasible.

5   Conclusion

A vehicular control system is a complex network of ECUs, sensors and actuators. A particular feature of the vehicle may be hosted by one ECU but associated tasks are executed by other ECUs also. These tasks are required to be scheduled on the common global time scale by using a proper synchronization mechanism. We had two observations (i) the broadcasting of synchronization packets imposing additional communication load on the network and involving even those ECUs in the process which do not require any synchronization. In this paper we have proposed a mechanism to identify the ECUs which will go out of sync from the common clock and use a point to point communication to resynchronize them. We have used non-linear drift model and argued that it is more realistic. We have argued that with reduced communication and computation load, the performance of the microcontrollers of ECUs will increase and it could be possible that the existing ECUs would host more applications.

References

1. Schneider, F.B.: Understanding protocols for byzantine clock synchronization Research Report 87-859, Department of Computer Science, Cornell University, Ithaca, NY, USA (August 1987)
2. Biberstein, M., Harel, Y., Heilper, A.: Clock Synchronization in Cell BE Traces. In: Luque, E., Margalef, T., Benítez, D. (eds.) Euro-Par 2008. LNCS, vol. 5168, pp. 3–12. Springer, Heidelberg (2008)
3. Lamportand, L., Melliar-Smith, P.M.: Byzantine clock synchronization. In: Proceedings of the Third Annual ACM Symposium on Principles of Distributed Computing, pp. 68–74. Association for Computing Machinery, Inc., New York (1984)
4. Chaudhuri, S., Gawlick, R., Lynch, N.: Designing algorithms for distributed systems with partially synchronized clocks. In: Proceedings of the Twelfth Annual ACM Symposium on Principles of Distributed Computing (PODC 1993), pp. 121–132. ACM, New York (1993)
5. Elson, J., Girod, L., Estrin, D.: Fine-Grained Time Synchronization using Reference Broadcasts. In: Proceedings of the Fifth Symposium on Operating Systems Design and Implementation, Boston, MA (December 2002)
6. Cristian, F., Fetzer, C.: Fault-tolerant external clock synchronization. In: Proceedings of the 15th IEEE International Conference on Distributed Computing Systems, Los Alamitos, CA, USA, May 30-June 2, pp. 70–77 (1995)
7. Marzullo, K., Owicki, S.: Maintaining the time in a distributed system. In: Proceedings of the 2nd ACM Symposium on Principles of Distributed Computing, pp. 295–305 (1983)
8. Schedl, A.V.: Design and Simulation of Clock Synchronization in Distributed Systems. Doctoral thesis, Institut fur Technische Informatik, Technische Universität Wien, Treitlstr. 1-3/3/182-1, Vienna,Austria (April 1996)
9. Hanzlik, A.: A Case Study of Clock Synchronization in FlexRay, Technische Universitat Wien, Institut fur Technische Informatik", Research Report, 31/2006 (2006)

10. Lin, T.-H., Chang, K.-H., Tian, J.-B., Chu, H.-H., Huang, P.: Modeling and simulation comparison of two time synchronization protocols. In: Proceedings of the 3rd ACM Workshop on Performance Monitoring and Measurement of Heterogeneous Wireless and Wired Networks, pp. 117–123. ACM Press, New York (2008)
11. Romer, K.: Time Synchronization in Ad Hoc Networks. In: ACM Symposium on Mobile Ad Hoc Networking and Computing (MobiHoc 2001), Long Beach, CA (October 2001)
12. Claesson, V., Suri, N.: An Efficient TDMA Start-Up and Restart Synchronization Approach for Distributed Embedded Systems. IEEE Transaction on Parallel and Distributed Systems 15(7), 1–15 (2004)
13. Kopetz, H., Ademaj, A., Grillinger, P., Steinhammer, K.: The Time-Triggered Ethernet (TTE) Design. In: 8th IEEE International Symposium on Object-Oriented Real-Time Distributed Computing (ISORC 2005), pp. 22–33 (2005)
14. Zhang, L., Liu, Z., Xia, C.H.: Clock Synchronization Algorithms for Network Measurements. In: IEEE-Infocom 2002, pp. 160-169 (2002)

A Local Search Based Approximation Algorithm for Strong Minimum Energy Topology Problem in Wireless Sensor Networks

Bhawani S. Panda and D. Pushparaj Shetty

Computer Science and Applications Group
Department of Mathematics
Indian Institute of Technology Delhi, Hauz Khas
New Delhi 110016, India
{bspanda,prajshetty}@maths.iitd.ac.in

Abstract. Energy-aware network management is extremely important in wireless sensor networks as sensors in the network are powered by battery and it may not be possible to recharge the batteries of sensors after they are deployed. Topology control problem deals with the transmission power assignments to the nodes of a wireless sensor network so that the induced graph topology satisfies some specified properties. Given a set of sensors in the plane, the *Strong Minimum Energy Topology (SMET)* problem is to assign transmit power to each sensor such that the sum total of powers assigned to all the sensors is minimized subject to the constraint that the induced topology containing only bidirectional links is strongly connected. This will allow the sensors to communicate with each other, while conserving battery power as much as possible leading to increased network life time. So this problem is significant in both theory and application. However, the SMET problem is known to be NP-hard. Several heuristics have been proposed for SMET problem by various researchers. In this paper we propose a local search based heuristic for the SMET problem. We prove that our local search based heuristic is a 2-approximation algorithm. We compare our algorithm with several heuristic algorithms available in the literature. Simulation result shows that the local search based heuristic performs better than the existing heuristics.

Keywords: Wireless Sensor Networks, Topology Control Problem, Transmission Power Assignment, Heuristics, Local Search, Graph Theory, Minimum Spanning Tree.

1 Introduction

A wireless sensor network consists of a collection of battery powered sensors each of which is integrated in a single package with low power signal processing, computation, and a wireless transceiver. A survey paper by Akyildiz *et al.* [2] provides more details on wireless sensor networks. A sensor network consisting

C. Hota and P.K. Srimani (Eds.): ICDCIT 2013, LNCS 7753, pp. 398–409, 2013.

of n sensors $s_1, s_2, \ldots, s_n$ in the plane can be modeled as a weighted directed graph G by taking each sensor in the plane as a vertex and joining the vertices s_i and s_j and assigning $w(v_i v_j) = t.d^\alpha$, where d is the Euclidean distance between s_i and s_j, t is a threshold which is a function of signal-to-noise ratio at v_j, and α is a constant that is related to path loss and varies from two to four [14]. In ideal case we assume $t = 1$ and $\alpha = 2$. The graph so obtained is called a *communication graph*. The *Topology Control problem* in wireless sensor network can be considered as the following problem: Given a communication graph representing a sensor network, compute a subgraph with specific desired properties, such as connectivity, strong connectivity, short stretches, sparsity, low interference or low degree node. The main objective of topology control problem in WSNs is to increase the lifetime of the network by keeping the power assigned to each node at a minimum level and still maintain the desired connectivity.

The topology control problem is widely studied in [6,7,10,11,15,16]. The **strong minimum energy topology (SMET)problem** is one of the important topology control problems in sensor networks. Given a set of sensors in the plane, the *Strong Minimum Energy Topology (SMET)* problem is to assign transmission power to each sensor such that the sum total of powers assigned to all the sensors is minimized subject to the constraint that the induced topology containing only bidirectional links is strongly connected, i.e., there is a directed path between any two sensors in the network. This will allow the sensors to communicate with each other, while conserving battery power as much as possible leading to increased network life time. The SMET problem is shown be to NP-hard by Cheng *et al.* [5].

The first approximation algorithm for SMET problem is the Minimum Spanning Tree based algorithm [9]. Cheng *et al.* [5] gave a heuristic named Prim-incremental heuristic for SMET and showed by simulation results that Prim-incremental heuristic outperforms MST-based algorithm. Panda *et al.* [12] gave a Kruskal- incremental heuristic for the SMET problem and showed through extensive simulation that Kruskal-incremental heuristic outperforms both MST-based heuristic and Prim-incremental heuristic. The other known heuristic for SMET is the *valley-free* heuristic by Aneja *et al.* [3]. They showed that *valley-free* heuristic gives better results than both MST-based heuristic and Prim-incremental heuristics.

In this paper, we propose a local search based heuristic algorithm for the SMET problem. We compare our algorithm with several heuristic algorithms available in the literature. The simulation results show that the Local-search based heuristic gives better result than the existing heuristics. We also prove that the local search based algorithm is a 2-approximation algorithm.

The rest of the paper is organized as follows. In Section 2, we explain the graph theoretic model for wireless sensor networks and review four heuristic algorithms for the SMET problems, namely (*i*) MST based heuristic [9], (*ii*) Prim-incremental power greedy heuristic [5], (*iii*) Kruskal-incremental power greedy heuristic [12], and (*iv*) *valley-free* heuristic [3]. In section 3, we propose a local search based approximation algorithm for SMET problem. In Section 4, we compare our heuristic algorithm with the existing heuristic algorithms through extensive simulation. The paper concludes in Section 5.

2   Existing Heuristics for SMET Problem

In this section we first explain the graph theoretic model used to represent a wireless sensor network. Let $N = \{s_1, s_2, \ldots, s_n\}$ represents set of sensors on a plane. We model this as a weighted directed graph G, with each sensor in the plane is taken as vertex. A cost function $c : V \times V \to \Re^+ \cup \{\infty\}$ such that $c(u, v)$ is the power emission necessary for node u to send packet to node v. If $c(u, v) = \infty$, then node u cannot communicate to node v directly. A power assignment $r : V \to \Re^+$ induces a Communication Digraph $D_r = (V, A_r)$, where $(u, v) \in A_r$ if and only if $r(u) \geq c(u, v)$. The presence of the arc (u, v) guarantees that the transmission power of node u is sufficiently high so that node u can send a message to node v directly. The problem of assigning transmission range to the nodes such a way that the resulting communication graph D_r is strongly connected, is called Range Assignment problem and is studied in [9]. If both the arcs (u, v) and (v, u) are present in A_r, then these two arcs can be replaced by a *bidirectional arc uv*. Let $G_r = (V, E_r)$, where E_r is the set of all bidirectional arcs in D_r. Bidirectional links are preferred in wireless sensor networks because the messages sent over a link must be acknowledged by the receiver. Bidirectional network has a desirable property that the loss of any single link will not partition the network. It affords multiple path redundancy between every pair of nodes. Bidirectional links simplifies the routing protocol. Further, the current MAC layer protocols such as IEEE 802.11 and S-MAC only take bidirectional link into consideration [5,13]. The SMET problem is also called Symmetric Min-Power Connectivity Problem [4]. The power assignment is called symmetric because if a node u can directly communicate to node v, then node v also can directly communicate with node u.

Let $G = (V, E)$ be a graph. A subgraph $T = (V, E')$ of G is called a spanning tree if (i) there is a path in T between every pair of vertices in V, i.e., T is connected, and (ii) T has no cycle, i.e., T is acyclic. The cost of a spanning tree $T = (V, E')$ of a weighted graph $G = (V, E)$ with weight function w is $\sum_{e \in E'} w(e)$. A spanning tree of a weighted graph G is called a minimum spanning tree (MST) if T has the minimum cost among all spanning trees of G.

Two popular algorithms for finding an MST of a weighted graph are Prim's algorithm and Kruskal's algorithm (see [1,17]). Let $T = (V, E')$ be a spanning tree of a weighted graph $G = (V, E)$ having cost function w. Let $P_T(v) = \max\{w(uv)|uv \in E(G)\}$ and $P(T) = \sum_{v \in V} P_T(v)$. Here $P_T(v)$ is the transmission power assigned to each node v and $P(T)$ is the total transmission power of the tree T. The SMET problem now reduces to a problem of finding a spanning tree T of G such that $P(T)$ is minimum.

2.1 Minimum Spanning Tree Based Heuristic

The MST based algorithm was proposed in [9]. The details of the algorithm is described in Algorithm 1.

Algorithm 1. MST based heuristic

Input : $G = (V, E, w)$
Output: A feasible power range assignment P
1 Find a minimum spanning tree T of $G(V)$
2 Compute $P(u) = \max\{w(uv)|uv \in E(T)\}$
3 $P(T) = \sum_{v \in V} P(v)$
4 Output $P(T)$ and $P(u)$ for all $u \in V$

Theorem 1. [9] *Power assignment based on MST has a performance ratio of* 2

2.2 Prim-Incremental Power Greedy Heuristic

Cheng *et al.* [5] proposed the incremental power greedy which we call Prim-incremental heuristic as it is based on Prim's MST algorithm. The details of the algorithm is described in Algorithm 2.

Algorithm 2. Prim-incremental Power Greedy Heuristic

Input : $G = (V, E, w)$
Output: A feasible power range assignment P
1 **Initialization:** Let S be the set containing the subset of sensors considered so far during the execution of the heuristic. Let $T = (S, E')$. Let P be the total power of all the sensors in S, and $P(u)$ be the power expenditure in sensor u. Initially $P = 0, S = \{v_0\}$, where v_0 is any sensor, $P(v_0) = 0$, and $E' = \emptyset$.
2 Let $S' = V - S$. Find $u \in S$ and $v \in S'$ such that $\delta_T'(uv)$ is minimum among all $u \in S$ and $v \in V \setminus S$, i.e., connecting u and v needs minimum incremental power $\delta_T'(uv)$. Set $S = S \cup \{v\}, P = P + \delta_T'uv$.
3 **if** $S = V$ **then**
4 | output P and $P(v)$ for all $v \in V$, and stop;

5 **else**
6 | goto step 2

Though there is no performance guarantee for Prim-incremental power greedy heuristic, it has been shown by Cheng *et al.* [5] through extensive simulation that Prim-incremental power greedy heuristic outperforms MST- heuristic.

2.3 Kruskal-Incremental Heuristic

The Kruskal-based incremental heuristic is proposed by Panda *et al.* [12]. The demerits of Prim- incremental power greedy heuristic is that it enforces that the so far selected edges forms a connected component in addition to the constraint that these edges do not form any cycle. The connected component constraint forces the Prim- incremental power greedy heuristic to select an edge based on local minimum; secondly, the performance of Prim-incremental power greedy heuristic also heavily depends upon the initial vertex chosen. These two demerits are fixed in Kruskal-incremental heuristic. In the Kruskal-incremental power greedy heuristic, an edge xy is selected such that xy needs minimum incremental energy among all edges which are not selected so far subject to the condition that it does not form a cycle with the so far selected edges. $\delta'(xy)$ denotes the incremental energy needed to establish connection between the nodes x and y. For the nodes x and y under consideration $\delta(x)$ is the incremental energy required for node x and $\delta(x) = w(xy) - P_T(x)$, where $P_T(x)$ is the power assigned to node x. $\delta(y)$ is defined similarly. Now $\delta'(xy) = \delta(x) + \delta(y)$. The heuristic is described in Algorithm 3.

Algorithm 3. Kruskal-incremental Power Greedy Heuristic

Input : $G = (V, E, w)$
Output: A feasible power range assignment P
1 Initialization: $T = (V, E')$, where $E' = \emptyset$, $P = 0$, $P_T(u) = 0$ for all $u \in V$
2 Find an edge $xy \in E \setminus E'$ such that (i) $T = (V, E' \cup \{xy\})$ is acyclic and (ii) $\delta'_T(xy)$ is minimum.
3 $E' = E' \cup \{xy\}$, $P_T(x) = P_T(x) + \delta_T(x)$, $P_T(y) = P_T(y) + \delta_T(y)$, $P = P + \delta'_T(xy)$.
4 **if** $|E'| = n - 1$ **then**
5 | output $T = (V, E')$, P, and $P_T(v)$ for all $v \in V$ and stop;
6 **else**
7 | go to step 2

It is shown in [12] through simulation that Kruskal-incremental heuristic outperforms both MST based heuristics and Prim-incremental heuristics.

2.4 Valley-Free Heuristic

Aneja *et al.* [3] established a lower bound for the SMET problem. They provide a a necessary condition for the optimal value of SMET. The main results and few terminologies used in [3] are explained below.

Consider a simple path $v_0 v_1 \ldots v_p$ in $G(N, E)$ with cost sequence $c_{01}, c_{12}, \ldots, c_{p-1,p}$. Define this path to be of type Λ if minimum of the p numbers in this sequence is either c_{01} or $c_{p-1,p}$.

A tree T of G is defined to be *valley-free* if for every two nodes $u, v \in N$,the unique path between u and v in this tree is of type Λ.

The following theorem provides a lower bound for the SMET problem.

Lemma 1. [3] *Consider a spanning tree $T(N, E)$ of G. Then T is* valley-free *if and only if its associated total power is given by $\sum_{(i,j) \in E} c_{ij} + max_{(i,j) \in E} c_{ij}$.*

Lemma 2. [3] *A MST is an optimal solution for SMET if it is* valley-free

Based on the above results a simple *valley-free* heuristic was proposed in [3]. Let T be the minimum spanning tree of G and T' be the tree obtained by swapping a in-tree edge with an out-tree edge. If $P(T') < P(T)$ or T' is not *valley-free* then T' is considered as T_{imp}. The heuristic swaps in-tree edge with an out- tree edge and checks if T_{imp} exists, if so it retains the new tree. The valley-free heuristic is explained in Algorithm 4.

Algorithm 4. Valley-free Heuristic

   Input : $G = (V, E, w)$
   Output: A feasible power range assignment P
1 Let T be the minimum spanning tree of G.; $min = P(T)$;
2 **if** T *is* valley-free **then**
3   ⌊ Output T ;stop
4 **while** *there exist a T_{imp}* **do**
5   ⌊ $T = T_{imp}$
6 Output T and $P(T)$.

It has been shown by Aneja *et al.* [3] through simulation that valley-free heuristic performs better than Prim-incremental power greedy heuristic. In the next section we propose our local search based approximation algorithm for SMET problem.

3   Local Search Based Algorithm

In this section, we propose a local search based approximation algorithm for the SMET problem. Local search is an iterative Heuristic used to solve many optimization problems. Typically, a local search heuristic starts with any feasible solution, and improves the quality of the solution iteratively. At each step, it considers only local operations to get a better feasible solution, if possible, in the neighborhood of the feasible solution obtained in the previous iteration. The algorithm stops in the rth iteration if it fails to find a better solution in the neighborhood of the solution obtained in the $r - 1^{th}$ iteration. The details about local search can be found in [8]. Our algorithm performs local changes that improves the total energy. The local change includes swapping a tree edge with a non-tree edge. This notion can be extended to swapping many tree edges for an equal number of non tree edges. A local change operation involving at most k tree edges is termed a k-change. So k-change is costlier to implement than $(k-1)$-change. Algorithm using k-change generally performs better than an algorithm using $(k-1)$-change.

3.1 k-Locally Optimal Tree and k-Local Search Algorithm

Let $G = (V, E)$ be a complete graph with n vertices and let $w : E \to R^+$ be a weight function defined on E. Let T be a spanning tree of G. Note that a a a spanning tree T of G is a feasible solution to the SMET problem. Let $N_k(T) = \{T' | |E(T') \setminus E(T)| = k\}$. So each $T' \in N_k(T)$ can be obtained from T by removing k edges from T and adding suitable k edges from $E(G) \setminus E(T)$. Hence, $N_k(T)$ is the k- neighborhood of T. A spanning tree T admits a k-improvement if there exists a spanning tree $T' \in N_k(T)$ such that $P(T') < P(T)$.

A k-locally optimal tree, (k-LOT) of a given graph G, is a spanning tree of G that does not admit any k-improvement. Note that starting from an arbitrary spanning tree T, if we perform k-exchanges, then we may end up generating all the spanning trees of the input graph G. So the algorithm will be of exponential complexity as the number of spanning trees of a complete graph with n nodes is n^{n-2}. To get rid of this problem we do not delete the newly added edges. This ensures that we need to generate at most n trees and our algorithm will run in polynomial time. To describe our algorithm we need to introduce some more notations. Let $F \subset E(T)$. Let $N_k(T, F) = \{T' | |E(T') \setminus E(T)| = k$ and $(E(G) \setminus E(T)) \cap F = \emptyset\}$. So each $T' \in N_k(T, F)$ can be obtained from T by removing k edges from $E(T) \setminus F$ and adding k suitable edges from $E(G) \setminus E(T)$. The algorithm is explained in Algorithm 5.

Algorithm 5. k-Local Search Algorithm

   Input   : $G = (V, E, w)$ and an integer k
   Output: A feasible power assignment $P(T)$
1 Compute a minimum spanning tree T of G; $F = \emptyset$;
2 **while**   *there is a* $T' \in N_k(T, F)$ *with* $P(T') < P(T)$ **do**
3 | Find a tree $T' \in N_k(T, F)$ with $P(T') < P(T)$; $F = F \cup (E(T') \setminus E(T))$;
     | $T = T'$;
4 Output T and $P(T)$;

Theorem 2. *The running time of k-Local Search Algorithm is $O(n^{3k+2})$.*

Proof. The algorithm starts with a minimum spanning tree T which can be found in $O(n^2)$ time, where n is the number of nodes in G. Then it keeps applying k-*improvements* to the current spanning tree until it becomes a k-LOT. The number of distinct k-*changes* possible for a spanning tree is at most

$$\binom{\binom{n}{2} - (n-1)}{k} \binom{n-1}{k}$$

which is $O(n^{3k})$. Computing $P(T')$ from $P(T)$ would take at most $O(n)$ time. Since in each iteration at least k new edges are added and no newly added edges are deleted in future, the number of iterations required by while loop is at most $n - 1$. So the algorithm takes $O(n^{3k+2})$. This proves the lemma.   □

Figure 1(a) illustrates a spanning tree T_1 that admits a 1-improvement.The bold edges represent the edges of spanning tree. We denote local change operation on tree T by $T(in, out)$ where in is the set of edges which are swapped in from non-tree edges and out is the set of swapped out edges. The energy cost of T_1 is $P(T_1) = 6a + 2\epsilon$. After applying 1-improvement $T_1(\{23\}, \{26\})$, we get a spanning tree T_2 in Figure 1(b) having energy cost $P(T_2) = 6a$. We can observe that the tree T_2 does not admit any 1-improvement, but it has a 2-improvement. Figure 1(c) shows the tree T_3 after 2- improvement i.e $T_2(\{12, 54\}, \{23, 34\})$, where energy cost $P(T_3) = 5a + 6\epsilon$. Since ϵ is a small constant, it is evident that $P(T_3)$ is least among all the three trees, T_1, T_2 and T_3.

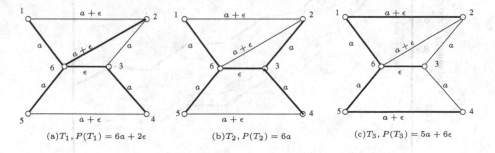

(a)$T_1, P(T_1) = 6a + 2\epsilon$ (b)$T_2, P(T_2) = 6a$ (c)$T_3, P(T_3) = 5a + 6\epsilon$

Fig. 1. Example of local change

Next we prove that k-Local Search Algorithm is a 2-approximation algorithm, i.e. k-Local Search Algorithm produces a spanning tree T such that $P(T) \le 2 \times OPT$.

Theorem 3. *The k-Local Search Algorithm has a performance ratio of 2.*

Proof. Let T be the MST constructed in Line 1 of k-Local Search Algorithm. Let $T_1, T_2, \dots, T_r$ be the trees obtained in the iteration 1 through iteration r. Clearly $P(T_r) < P(T_{r-1}) < \cdot, < P(T_1) < P(T)$. Since $P(T) \le 2 \times OPT$ [9], $P(T_r) \le 2 \times OPT$. Hence k-local search algorithm is a 2-approximation algorithm.   □

4   Experimental Results

In this section, we compare the existing heuristics, namely, (*i*) MST-heuristic, (*ii*) Prim-incremental heuristic, (*iii*)Kruskal-incremental power greedy heuristic and (*iv*) Valley-free heuristic with our proposed k-Local search algorithm with $k = 1$. The experimental set up contains n sensors distributed randomly over a

1000×1000 square. The power function used in the simulation study is $f(d) = t.d^{\alpha}$, where α is a constant between 2 and 4. We take $\alpha = 2$ in our simulation study, t is the threshold which is set to 1. For each n ranging from 10 to 100 in increments of 10, we run the heuristics 100 times with different seeds for random number generator. The average of the total powers is reported in Figure 2.The legend LocalSearch(MST) indicates the fact that we start with MST as an initial feasible solution.

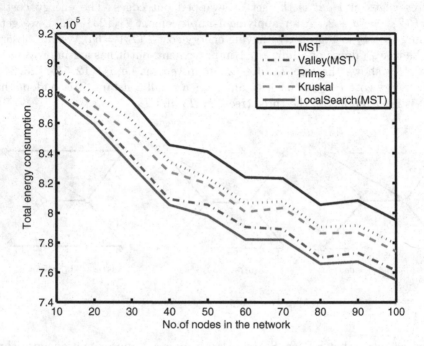

Fig. 2. Total Energy consumption

The Table 1 reports the total energy consumption for all the heuristics. This shows that the valley-free heuristic consumes 3.48 percent energy less than that of MST based algorithm on an average, whereas 1-Local search algorithm consumes 4.68 percent less energy than the MST based algorithm on an average. We find that total energy decreases with the increase in number of nodes. This is because when the sensors are densely located, it requires less energy to reach the neighbor and in sparse networks the energy consumption is higher as nodes are located far apart.

The maximum of total energy is reported in Figure 3. The variance of total energy is reported in Figure 4. Since we plot the average of 100 runs for each value of n, the comparison of maximum and variance is essential to test the

Table 1. Comparison of Total Energy consumption

No.of.Nodes	MST	Prim-incr	Valley-free	Krus-incr	LocalSearch
10	918190	881007	896209	895056	879460
20	896949	864862	879672	871256	858914
30	874986	837589	862112	852658	831583
40	845371	809327	834045	827487	805419
50	840927	805478	823525	819464	798170
60	823853	790591	806555	800733	782171
70	823187	789136	807685	803403	782086
80	805569	770070	790545	786438	765918
90	808373	773332	791634	786917	767351
100	795075	761235	779333	774190	754943

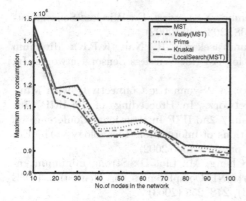

Fig. 3. Maximum Energy Consumption

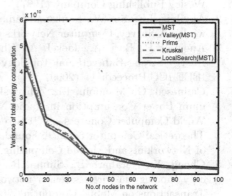

Fig. 4. Variance of Total energy

stability of the heuristic. The almost overlapping curves for the variance in Figure 4 indicates that k-local search heuristic is a stable algorithm. We find from simulation studies that the maximum energy in valley-free heuristic is 3.99 percent less than that of MST; and maximum energy in Local search is 5.38 percent less than that of MST. The variance is 9.61 and 12.52 percent less than that of MST in case of valley-free and Local search heuristic respectively. These studies indicate that the 1-Local search algorithm performs better than the existing heuristics.

We observe that both maximum transmit power and variance decrease as the number of nodes n increases. This can be explained as follows: If we put n sensors in a 1000×1000 square, then when n is small, nodes are dispersed far away and thus the maximum transmission power is higher. Also, in sparser networks, the total energy consumption depends more on the placement of the nodes. Thus the variance of the total energy consumption is larger.

5   Conclusion

In this paper we proposed a local search based algorithm, namely k-local search algorithm for the SMET problem. Our simulation results suggest that the 1-local search algorithm performs better than the valley-free heuristics. We also proved that the performance ratio of k-Local search heuristic is 2. Calinescu *et al.* [4] gave a practical but nontrivial approximation algorithm with improved performance ratio of 15/8. Careful theoretical analysis may result in better approximation ratio. Obtaining an algorithm with approximation ratio less than 15/8 for SMET problem is a challenging open problem.

References

1. Aho, A.V., Hopcroft, J.E., Ullman, J.D.: Data Structures and Algorithms. Addison-Wesley Publishing Company (1987)
2. Akyildiz, I.F., Su, W., Sankarsubramanian, Y., Cayirci, E.: Wireless Sensor Networks: A Survey. Computer Networks 38, 393–422 (2002)
3. Aneja, Y.P., Bari, A., Jaekel, A., Chandrasekaran, R., Nair, K.P.K.: Minimum Energy Strong Bidirectional Topology for Ad Hoc Wireless Sensor Networks. In: IEEE ICC Proceedings (2009)
4. Calinescu, G., Mandoiu, I.I., Zelikovsky, A.: Symmetric Connectivity with Minimum Power Consumption in Radio Networks. In: Proceedings of the IFIP 17th World Computer Congress - TC1 Stream / 2nd IFIP International Conference on Theoretical Computer Science: Foundations of Information Technology in the Era of Networking and Mobile Computing, pp. 119–130 (2002)
5. Cheng, X., Narahari, B., Simha, R., Cheng, M., Liu, D.: Strong minimum energy topology in wireless sensor networks:NP-Completeness and Heuristics. IEEE Transactions on Mobile Computing 2(3), 248–256 (2003)
6. Cheng, M.X., Cardei, M., Sun, J., Cheng, X., Wang, L., Xu, Y., Du, D.-Z.: Topology Control of Ad Hoc Wireless Networks for Energy Efficiency. IEEE Transactions on Computers 53(12), 1629–1635 (2004)
7. Gonzales, T. (ed.): Handbook of Approximation Algorithms and Metaheuristics, ch. 67. Chapman and Hall CRC (2007)
8. Lu, H.-I., Ravi, R.: The Power of Local Optimization: Approximation Algorithms for Maximum-leaf Spanning Tree. In: Proceedings Thirtieth Annual Allerton Conference on Communication, Control and Computing, pp. 533–542 (1996)
9. Kirousis, L.M., Kranakis, E., Krizane, D., Pele, A.: Power consumption in packet radio networks. Theoretical Computer Science 243, 289–305 (2000)
10. Labrador, M.A., Wightman, P.M.: Topology Control in Wireless Sensor Networks. Springer (2009)
11. Lloyd, E.L., Liu, R., Marathe, M.V., Ramanathan, R., Ravi, S.S.: Algorithmic aspects of topology control problems for Ad Hoc Networks, Mobile Networks and Applications 10, 19–34 (2005)
12. Panda, B.S., Pushparaj Shetty, D.: An Incremental Power Greedy Heuristic for Strong Minimum Energy Topology in Wireless Sensor Networks. In: Natarajan, R., Ojo, A. (eds.) ICDCIT 2011. LNCS, vol. 6536, pp. 187–196. Springer, Heidelberg (2011)
13. Ramanathan, R., Rosales-Hain, R.: Topology control of Multihop Wireless Networks using transmit power Adjustment. In: IEEE Infocom (2000)

14. Rappaport, T.S.: Wireless communications: Principle and Practice. Prentice Hall (1996)
15. Santi, P.: Topology Control in wireless ad hoc and sensor Networks. ACM Computing Surveys 37(2), 164–194 (2005)
16. Santi, P.: Topology Control in wireless ad hoc and sensor Networks. Wiley Inter Science (2005)
17. West, D.B.: Introduction to Graph Theory. PHI (2006)

MSSA: A M-Level Sufferage-Based Scheduling Algorithm in Grid Environment

Sanjaya Kumar Panda and Pabitra Mohan Khilar

Department of Computer Science and Engineering
National Institute of Technology, Rourkela, India
sanjayauce@gmail.com, pmkhilar@nitrkl.ac.in

Abstract. Scheduling is an emergent area in Grid Environment. It is essential to utilize the processors efficiently and minimize the schedule length. In Grid Environment, tasks are dependent on each other. We use Directed Acyclic Graph (DAG) to solve task scheduling problems. In this paper, we have proposed a new scheduling algorithm called M-Level Sufferage-based Scheduling Algorithm (MSSA) for minimizing the schedule length. It has two-phase process: m-level and sufferage value. M-level is used to calculate the earliest time. Sufferage is used to assign priority and select an optimal machine. MSSA always gives optimal or sub-optimal solution. Our result shows better results than other scheduling algorithms such as MET, MCT, Min-Min and Max-Min with respect to scheduling length and resource utilization.

Keywords: Scheduling algorithm, Grid environment, M-level, Sufferage, Directed acyclic graph, Makespan.

1 Introduction

Grid computing is a loosely coupled system and an innovative way to solve complex problems. In loosely coupled system, the inter-processor communication delay is large due to lack of coordination between systems. Each system in grid has different computation power, operating systems, peripherals and many more [4] [9]. It enables sharing in computational grid environment. Grid computing creates a structure to use the underutilized systems. A complex computation job can be divided into number of small partitions and it can be executed parallel in grid environment. So, we need a Grid Resource Broker (GRB) which divides the job into number of tasks [5]. GRB allocates task for a processor.

Scheduling is the way for allocation of the tasks. It depends on the criteria or requirements of tasks. The aim of scheduling are reducing Makespan (or scheduling length) and efficient utilization of the processors [10]. Scheduling is a NP-complete problem [6] [7]. Tasks are two types: dependent and independent task. Independent task can be scheduled in any order. Some of the algorithms are Min-Min, Max-Min, Minimum Completion Time (MCT), and Minimum Execution Time (MET). But, dependent task cannot be scheduled in any order. The dependency among tasks must

C. Hota and P.K. Srimani (Eds.): ICDCIT 2013, LNCS 7753, pp. 410–419, 2013.

be preserved. In order to represent it, task graph or Directed Acyclic Graph (DAG) is used. Some of the algorithms are Priority-based Task Scheduling (P-TSA) [3], Highest Level First with Estimated Times (HLFET) [12].

Parallelism in our approach is of two types: computation and communication. If a task is assigned to parent task processor then communication time is zero. Two tasks can share communication parallelism but cannot share computation parallelism. Let us assume that a task has two parents. The task has to wait until both parents complete its execution and communication between the parents to the given task is over. It is called as Strong dependency. If the task starts its execution partially before the parent task has finished, then it is called as Weak dependency [11].

Distributed system contains a huge number of workstations. They are connected through high speed buses. Nodes and interconnection are different from one environment to another environment [2]. For solving large scale complex problem, it is not possible to enhance the capability of a single computer. It is not only costly but also bulkier. But, in distributed system, the complex problem is divided to small chunks and it can be executed more efficiently. Idleness of CPU is reduced to greater extent.

The remaining part of this paper is organized as follows: related work is devoted in section 2. Section 3 elaborates preliminaries such as notations, assumptions, traditional scheduling algorithms. Section 4 proposes the M-Level Sufferage-based Scheduling Algorithm (MSSA). Section 5 discusses performance analysis with a suitable illustration. We conclude by summarizing the work in Section 6.

2   Related Works

There are numerous algorithms in the area of grid scheduling. Algorithm gives sub-optimal or optimal solution based on the criteria. We can say the algorithms are approximate solutions. If an algorithm gives optimum result for particular types of data set then it is a sub-optimum solution. Hemamalini compares different task scheduling algorithms in heterogeneous environment [5]. Bozdag et al. proposes a generic algorithm which preserves the Makespan by integrating processor schedules [8]. Sun et al. introduces a priority scheduling algorithm [3]. It calculates the task priority. Based on the priority, it groups the task into teams.

Scheduling may be centralized or decentralized. Pop et al. proposes a decentralized task scheduling using genetic algorithm [9]. Also, Navimipour et al. introduces a linear genetic representation for computational grid tasks. It uses different crossover operations. Genetic algorithm may not provide optimal solution [6]. But, it provides approximate solution. Priority among tasks and allocation of machine are two important steps of list scheduling. Hagras et al. introduces an approach for machine allocation which can be applied to list scheduling [13]. It can be applied to both insertion and non-insertion approach. If the task is scheduled without looking the hole, it is termed as non-insertion approach. But in insertion approach, task is filled to the first available hole [14]. Of course, insertion is a good approach then non-insertion one because idle time is reduced in some extent.

3   Preliminaries

3.1   Notations

MSSA: M-Level Sufferage-based Scheduling Algorithm
DAG: Directed Acyclic Graph
C_T: Computation Time
C_t: Communication Time
R_r: Ready Time
$C_t(T_i, T_j)$: Communication Time between task T_i and task T_j
SV: Sufferage Value
M-Level (T_i): M-Level of task T_i
P-TSA: Priority-based Task Scheduling
MET: Minimum Execution Time
MCT: Minimum Completion Time
FCFS: First Come First Served

3.2   The DAG Model

Task may be dependent or independent in real time environment. In banking system (or airline control system), each transaction has a sequential process. So, we cannot start in a random order. It is necessary to represent the task in a graph. Generally, DAG is used to represent the dependency among tasks. From DAG, we can schedule the task in an order.

Let us consider a DAG $D = (T, E)$, where T represents the number of tasks and E represents the number of edges. Each task requires some time to execute a set of instructions. The time is called Computational time. Two tasks are using a directed edge. This time is called Communicational time. In DAG, edges are unidirectional. So, it creates scheduling holes [14]. The task does not have parent task is known as Entry task. Similarly, the task does not have children task is known as Exit task. C_{Ts} of tasks are different in each processor because we are considering heterogeneous environment. It is very difficult to choose an optimal machine in grid environment. Finally, the problem statement is to find an optimal schedule in a heterogeneous environment.

3.3   Assumptions

Let us take a heterogeneous environment for results analysis. It contains systems with different architecture and different requirements. For our approach, C_T and C_t are provided before scheduling takes place. But, task can be added in between scheduling. C_t is ignored if and only if the task is assigned to parent processors. It is assumed that communication may overlap with each other.

3.4   Scheduling Algorithms

To get a close to optimal schedule, many traditional algorithms are developed. The algorithms are listed below.

3.4.1   P-TSA [3]

It computes task priority. For task priority, it considers depth of the task, estimated complete time, up link cost and down link cost. If two nodes are in the same depth, then they are in the same group. We calculate the priority value of each group tasks. Then, we will get a scheduling order.

3.4.2   MET

It focuses on minimum execution time. It schedules the tasks in FCFS sequence. Load balancing is not considered in this approach.

3.4.3   MCT

It focuses on minimum completion time. Like, it schedules the tasks in FCFS sequence. Completion time is the sum of execution time and ready time. Load imbalance is the demerit of this approach.

3.4.4   Min-Min

It selects small task before large task. It combines MET and MCT. First Min shows MET whereas second Min shows MCT. It works efficiently if and only if there are so many small tasks present in Grid. Otherwise, it will cause starvation to large tasks.

3.4.5   Max-Min

It is similar to Min-Min. But, it selects large task before small one. It is better than Min-Min algorithm. It causes starvation to small tasks.

4   Proposed Algorithm

4.1   Description

Our proposed algorithm MSSA contains two phases. In first phase, scheduler calculates m-level of each ready task. M-level is the sum of C_T, ready time and C_t between parent to given task. In second phase, scheduler calculates SV. It is the difference between two best or optimal machine. According to SV, tasks are sorted in descending order. The task having high SV will be given highest priority. We continue the above process until the ready list is empty.

4.2   Algorithm

1. Initially, ready list contains the entry task.
2. Assign the entry task to the processor.
3. Set C_T of entry task as R_T.
4. **Repeat**
    Calculate m-level for ready list tasks on each processor.
    M-Level $(T_i) = C_T + R_T + C_t (T_f, T_i)$
5. Calculate SV.
6. Sort the tasks in descending order of SV.
7. Select the task-processor pair which gives the earliest m-level time. Ties are broken randomly.

8. Assign the task to the respective processor.
9. Remove the task from ready list.
10. Update the R_T of each processor.
11. **if** (ready list is not empty)
12.   Go to Step 7.
13. **else**
14.   Repeat.
Until the ready list do not have any task.

5   Performance Analysis

5.1   Illustration

Let us consider a complex DAG (Figure 1) having seventeen tasks and three processors. Each node (or ellipse) in the DAG represents a task. The time required to execute the task is called C_T. It is shown in Table 1. We are considering a heterogeneous grid environment. So, the execution time is different in each processor. Connection between two tasks is called C_t. It is represented in rectangular box. Communication between task T_i and task T_j is represented as $C_t (T_i, T_j)$. A task can only execute if and only if its entire parent has been completed.

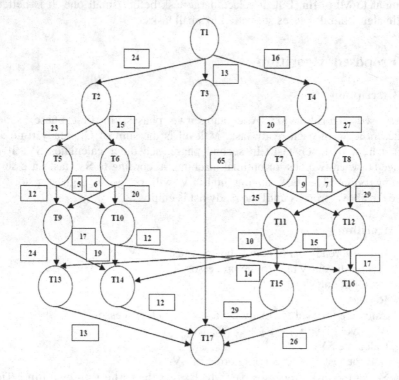

Fig. 1. A Complex DAG

Table 1. C_T of tasks

Task	P1	P2	P3
1	41	46	34
2	46	40	41
3	26	48	35
4	46	33	16
5	32	11	48
6	40	43	41
7	14	27	22
8	27	34	19
9	48	38	39
10	49	37	40
11	28	20	29
12	49	33	24
13	48	28	22
14	24	36	32
15	40	32	36
16	17	14	38
17	21	16	14

Here, T_1 is the start (or entry) task. So, ready list contains only one task T_1. Now, we assign the task to a processor which takes less time. For T_1, it is processor 3. All other processors are idle at the same time because T_1 is the parent of next level tasks. The C_T of T_1 is 34. Ready time (R_T) is initialized as 34.

After T_1 has successfully processed, the next level tasks are T_2, T_3 and T4. In order to assign the tasks to the processors, we have designed a two-phase process. At first phase, we calculate m-level of the tasks. M-Level of the task is the sum of C_T, ready time and C_t between parent tasks to the given task. The m-level of tasks are shown in Table 2. In second phase, we calculate SV of the tasks [1]. SV is the difference between the m-level of two best processors. It is shown in Table 3.

Table 2. M-Level of tasks

Task	Processor 1			Processor 2			Processor 3		
	C_T	R_T+C_t	M-level	C_T	R_T+C_t	M-level	C_T	R_T+C_t	M-level
2	46	58	104	40	58	98	41	34	75
3	26	47	73	48	47	95	35	34	69
4	46	50	96	33	50	83	16	34	50

Table 3. SV of tasks

	Processor 1	Processor 2	Processor 3	
Task	M-level	M-level	M-level	SV
2	104	98	75	23
3	73	95	69	4
4	96	83	50	33

Now, we sort the tasks in descending order of SV. Ready list is updated in the following sequence: T_4, T_2 and T_3. T_4 is assigned to processor 3. The R_T of processor 3 is modified to 50. The updated m-level is shown in Table 4. We need not calculate SV again.

Table 4. Updated SV of tasks

	Processor 1	Processor 2	Processor 3
Task	M-level	M-level	M-level
2	104	98	91
3	73	95	85

Again, T_2 is assigned to processor 3. The R_T of processor 3 is altered to 91. The updated m-level is shown in Table 5.

Table 5. Updated SV of tasks

	Processor 1	Processor 2	Processor 3
Task	M-level	M-level	M-level
3	73	95	126

Finally, T_3 is assigned to processor 1. After this, ready list is empty. So, we repeat the algorithm again and again until there is no task in the ready list. Final Gantt chart is shown in Figure 2. Dotted mark represents idle time and star mark represents communication delay time.

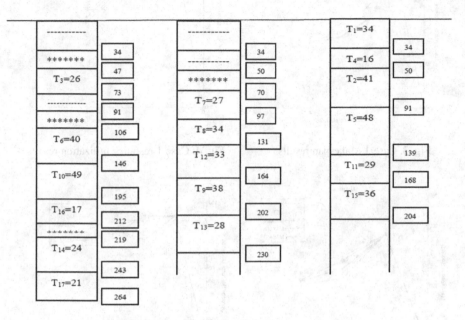

Fig. 2. Gantt chart

5.2   Results

The result shows that our proposed algorithm (MSSA) is better and efficient than the traditional scheduling algorithms. We have considered two performance measures to compare our proposed algorithm with other task scheduling algorithms. First, Makespan is used to calculate the scheduling length. It is the total time required to complete the task execution. Second, Resource utilization is the percentage of time a particular resource (or processor) is busy. We need maximum resource utilization as well as minimum scheduling length. We have taken two cases to evaluate the performance measure in all task scheduling algorithms. Performance metrics are shown in figure 3 (case 1), figure 4 (case 1), figure 5 (case 2) and figure 6 (case 2) respectively. Number of machines and tasks are varying in one case to another case. Each case has a complex DAG. In each case, we compare our results with the traditional algorithms results. X-axis denotes the number of machines and Y-axis denotes the Makespan (in figure 3 and 5), average resource utilization (in figure 4 and 6). If number of processor is restricted to one then the performance for all algorithms remains same.

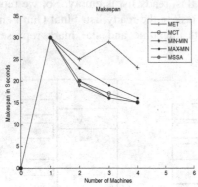

Fig. 3. Case 1 Makespan results

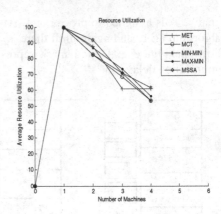

Fig. 4. Case 1 resource utilization results

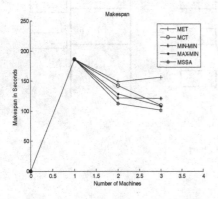

Fig. 5. Case 2 Makespan results

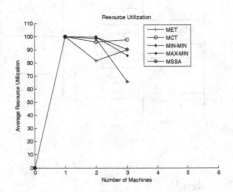

Fig. 6. Case 2 resource utilization results

6   Conclusion

MSSA scheduling introduces a new concept called m-level in which earliest time is calculated. By considering m-level value, SV is calculated. It provides priority among tasks. This scheduling has an improvement over all traditional algorithms in grid environment. Our result shows this. Makespan is reduced in greater extent. Resources are utilized efficiently in our algorithm. This proposed scheduling will help to faster execution in grid environment. Finally, it gives sub optimal or optimal solution.

In future work, we can further extend MSSA algorithm by using security, time constraints to the tasks and duplication of tasks. Communication between tasks and resources may be failed due to network problems, energy limitations and many more. It can be one of the best future works. It can be more realistic if all criteria are considered.

References

1. Maheswaran, M., Ali, S., Siegel, H.J., Hensgen, D., Freund, R.F.: Dynamic Mapping of a Class of Independent Tasks onto Heterogeneous Computing Systems. Journal of Parallel and Distributed Computing 59, 107–131 (1999)
2. Janakiram, D.: Grid Computing. Tata McGraw-Hill Publishing Company Limited (2005) ISBN 0-07-060096-1
3. Sun, W., Zhu, Y., Su, Z., Jiao, D., Li, M.: A Priority-based Task Scheduling Algorithm in Grid. In: IEEE Third International Symposium on Parallel Architectures, Algorithms and Programming, pp. 311–315 (2010)
4. Buyya, R.: High Performance Cluster Computing. Pearson Education (2008) ISBN 81-317-1693-7
5. Hemamalini, M.: Review on Grid Task Scheduling in Distributed Heterogeneous Environment. International Journal of Computer Applications 40(2), 24–30 (2012)
6. Navimipour, N.J., Khanli, L.M.: The LGR Method for Task Scheduling in Computational Grid. In: IEEE International Conference on Advanced Computer Theory and Engineering, pp. 1062–1066 (2008)
7. Zhang, Y., Koelbel, C., Kennedy, K.: Relative Performance of Scheduling Algorithms in Grid Environments. In: Seventh IEEE International Symposium on Cluster Computing and the Grid (2007)
8. Bozdag, D., Ozguner, F., Catalyurek, U.V.: Compaction of Schedules and a Two-Stage Approach for Duplication-Based DAG Scheduling. IEEE Transactions on Parallel and Distributed Systems 20(6), 857–871 (2009)
9. Pop, F., Dobre, C., Cristea, V.: Genetic Algorithm for DAG Scheduling in Grid Environments, pp. 299-305. IEEE (2009)
10. Yangyang, W., Hongfang, Y.: Considering the Utilization of Idle Time Slots for DAG Scheduling in Optical Grid Applications. In: International Conference on Information, Networking and Automation, pp. 303–307. IEEE (2010)
11. Ma, N., Xia, Y., Prasanna, V.K.: Exploring Weak Dependencies in DAG Scheduling. In: IEEE International Parallel & Distributed Processing Symposium, pp. 591–598 (2011)
12. Kwok, Y.K., Ahmed, I.: Static Scheduling Algorithms for Allocating Directed Task Graphs to Multiprocessors. ACM 31(4), 406–471 (1999)
13. Hagras, T., Janecek, J.: A Machine Assignment Mechanism For Compile Time List Scheduling Heuristics. Computing and Informatics 24, 341–350 (2005)
14. Simion, B., Leordeanu, C., Pop, F., Cristea, V.: A Hybrid Algorithm for Scheduling Workflow Applications in Grid Environments (ICPDP), pp. 1331–1348. Springer (2007)

Privacy Preserving Distributed K-Means Clustering in Malicious Model Using Zero Knowledge Proof

Sankita Patel[1], Viren Patel[2], and Devesh Jinwala[1]

[1] S.V. National Institute of Technology, Surat, Gujarat, India
[2] Government Engineering College, Dahod, Gujarat, India
{sankitapatel,virenjpatel,dcjinwala}@gmail.com

Abstract. Preserving Privacy is crucial in distributed environments wherein data mining becomes a collaborative task among participants. Solutions proposed on the lines of cryptography involve use of classical cryptographic constructs in data mining algorithms. Applicability of solutions proposed depends on the adversary model in which it is able to preserve privacy. Existing cryptography based solutions for privacy preserving clustering aim to achieve privacy in presence of semi honest adversary model. For the practical applicability of the solutions in real world settings, support of malicious adversary model is desirable. As per our literature survey, the existing research lacks any fool proof solution for privacy preserving distributed clustering in malicious adversary model. In this paper, we propose privacy preserving distributed K-Means clustering of horizontally partitioned data that supports privacy in malicious adversarial model. The basic construct involves use of secret sharing mechanism clubbed with code based zero knowledge identification scheme. We use secret sharing for privately sharing the information and code based identification scheme to add support against malicious adversaries.

Keywords: Privacy Preservation in Distributed Data Mining (PPDDM), Secure Multiparty Computation, Secret Sharing, Zero Knowledge Proof.

1 Introduction

Data mining research deals with the investigation of efficient techniques for the extraction of potentially useful information from large collections of data.Recent studies[1] have thrown light on some of the major challenges for data mining. One of the necessities identified is the increased user-friendliness of data mining results. This in turn, poses a threat to privacy concerns of individuals. Hence, there is a need to add privacy preserving mechanisms in data mining; yielding Privacy Preserving Data Mining (PPDM) [2].

In past one decade researchers have shown good interests in PPDM field. Soon after the field was introduced, many research groups started working on solutions for privacy preserving data mining (PPDM)[3][4]. The cryptographic approach is one of those directions [5] where researchers have come up incrementally with better and efficient results. The only drawback of cryptography based approach is its high overhead[6]. Hence, for this approach, one of the chief concerns is to minimize the over-heads incurred in implementing the protocols.

C. Hota and P.K. Srimani (Eds.): ICDCIT 2013, LNCS 7753, pp. 420–431, 2013.

However, there are other vital issues also associated with the existing solutions. In this paper, we concentrate on the clustering application of data mining and especially the K-Means clustering algorithm [7]. Existing solutions proposed for privacy preserving K-Means clustering are [2][8-14]. To the best of our knowledge, all of these solutions provide security in presence of the semi honest adversary model in which participating parties follow the prescribed protocol but try to infer private information using the messages they receive during protocol. Increased use of this model is also because of its less strict definition of security and privacy. Another model that can be considered is the malicious model in which parties arbitrarily deviate from the protocol run in order to infer private information. Although semi-honest model is realistic, solutions devised in malicious model provide higher security in real world settings [15].

In PPDM research, the assumption that no other party should be trusted is closest to reality, where individual never knows who to trust. More than that, even after the successful exchange of knowledge, an assurance about the integrity and trustworthiness of the shared information is required. Fulfillment of such conditions strengthens the protocol and can make it worthy of use in malicious models.

In literature, mechanisms to handle malicious environments are proposed [15-25]. Solutions for implementing basic building blocks in malicious model are proposed in [15-19][21][22][24]. [20][25] give solution for association rule mining in malicious model while [23] gives solution for k-nn classifier. As we further discuss in section 2.3, none of these mechanisms attempts to give solution for the data mining application like clustering. In this paper, we attempt to do so by adding malicious adversary support inthe privacy preserving distributed K-Means clustering algorithm proposed in [2].

1.1   Organization

The remainder of this paper is organized as follows: In section 2, we discuss background and related work. Section 3 describes our proposed approach. In section 4 and 5, we show theoretical and experimental analysis respectively.

2   Back Ground and Related Work

2.1   Zero Knowledge Proof Systems

In cryptography, a zero knowledge proof or zero knowledge protocol is an interactive method for one party to prove to another that a statement is true, without revealing anything other than the veracity of the statement. An effective definition of zero knowledge proofs of knowledge is given in [26] along with its relevance to identification scheme that we use in this paper.

2.2   Code Based Cryptography and Linear Codes

The identification scheme that we use in this paper is based on error-correcting code theory. We use definitions of linear codes and q-ary syndrome decoding problem from [27].

A linear code is an error-correcting code for which any linear combination of code words is also a code word. We can define it more precisely as:

"*A linear code of length n and rank k is a linear subspace C with dimension k of the vector space F_q where F_q is the finite field with q elements, q a prime power and k<n. Such a code is called q-ary code. The vectors in C are called code words. The size of the code is the number of code words and equals q_k.*"

The weight, ω, of a codeword is the number of its elements that are nonzero and the distance between two codewords is the hamming distance between them.

The distance d of a code is minimum weight of its nonzero codewords, or equivalently, the minimum distance between distinct codewords. The error-correcting capability of such a code is the maximum number of d errors that the code is able to decode. A linear code of length n, dimension k, and distance d is called an [n,k,d] code.

Q-ary Syndrome Decoding Problem

Given H $\in R$ q–ary(n, r), y $\in R$ F_q^n, and an integer $\omega > 0$, output a word x ϵ F_q^n, such that $w(s) <= \omega$; H.sT= y. This problem remains NP-complete [28].

2.3   Related Work

PPDM approaches are classified into two categories [6]: 1. *Randomization Based* and 2.*Cryptography Based*. The randomization based approach for privacy preserving clustering has been addressed in [29] and approaches in this category incur low computation and communication cost but compromise with the level of privacy. The cryptography based approaches provide high level of privacy but at the cost of high computation and communication cost [6]. In this category, the privacy preservation in clustering has been achieved using the Secure Multiparty Computation (SMC) [8-10], the Homomorphic encryption[10-12] and the secret sharing [2][13][14] based techniques.

However, to the best of our knowledge, all of the above privacy preserving clustering protocols were proven or claimed to be secure only in the semi-honest model. In [30], a systematic method is described for converting protocols that are secure in the semi-honest model to ones that are equally secure and privacy-preserving in the malicious model with the use of commitment schemes and zero-knowledge proofs. The first attempt towards adding malicious adversary support in distributed association rule mining in data grids is proposed in [20]. In [15], authors show several constructions on equality, dot product and set-intersection operations in malicious model for the first time. In [19], authors proposed efficient and secure dot product and set-intersection protocols in the malicious model while reducing the computational and communication complexity of the proof of knowledge of [15] drastically.Recently, [21] proposed efficient set operations against the malicious adversaries. They assume no trusted set up or trusted third party for the computation, thus increasing the communication overhead. In [22], authors propose private vector addition protocol using probabilistic zero-knowledge protocol. In [23], authors add malicious adversary support to already existing privacy-preserving secure scalar product for private distributed k-nn classifier. In [24], authors present an implementation of Yao's protocol with the cut-and-choose methodology, which is secure in the presence of malicious adversaries.

Relation between secret sharing and Zero knowledge proof has been discussed in [31]. Authors in [32] suggest verifiable secret sharing as one of the ways to add malicious adversary support. Authors in [25] proposed Peer for privacy(P4P) framework for privacy preserving data mining using Verifiable secret sharing to add malicious adversary support.

It is apparent however, that none of the paper gives solution for clustering in distributed environment in malicious model.

3   The Proposed Approach

3.1   Privacy Preserving Distributed K-Means Clustering Using Shamir's Secret Sharing Scheme [2]

In the distributed scenario, where data are located at different sites, the algorithm for K-Means clustering differs slightly. In distributed scenario, it is desirable to compute cluster means using union of data located at different parties. We use distributed Weighted Average Problem to compute intermediate cluster means in distributed scenario. To collaboratively compute cluster means, all parties need to send their local clusters to every other party. For example, if two parties want to jointly perform clustering, then each party needs to send its sum of samples and number of samples values (of each cluster) to other party. We shall denote (a_i, b_i) and (d_i, e_i) as sum of samples and number of samples pairs for party A and party B respectively. Joint computation of the clusters can be performed using $(a_i + d_i)/(b_i + e_i)$. If parties send (a_i, b_i) and (d_i, e_i) pairs in clear then there is a threat to privacy violations. In [2], authors proposed new and efficient privacy preserving computation of $(a_i + d_i)/(b_i + e_i)$ using Shamir's secret sharing scheme [33]. The approach is shown in figure 1.

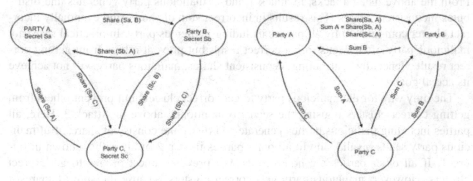

Step 1: Share generation and Distribution   Step 2: Sending sum of shares to each party

Fig. 1. Privacy Preserving Distributed K-Means clustering using Shamir's Secret Sharing scheme

As shown in figure 1, in step 1, each party generates and distributes the shares. In step 2, each party performs the addition of the shares it receives including its own share and sends the calculated sum back to every other party. By solving the linear equations corresponding to the received sums, parties are able to calculate the sum of the secret values of all parties using Lagrange's interpolation.

Taking an example of three party $\{P_1, P_2, P_3\}$ case where they share a public constants C = $\{3, 4, 2\}$ corresponding to each party and have private polynomials Q = $\{2x^2 + x + c, x^2 + 3x + c, 4x^2 + 3x + c\}$. The values they want to secretly share is let's say $\{3, 4, 3\}$ respectively. Let's take an example where each party generates share for every party including self. Now when party P_1 sends its share secretly to P_3, it uses equation $Q_1(C_3)$, i.e. it sends $2(2)^2 + 2 + 3 = 13$ to P_3, similarly P_2 sends 14 to P_3 and P_3 calculates its own share to be 25 by $Q_3(C_3)$. This way P_3 receives three quadratic equations including its own; their addition gives 52. Similarly P_1 and P_2 each will receive three values each and add up to get 94 and 150 respectively. These sums are called *sum of shares*.

3.2   Attacks in Malicious Adversary Model

In this paper, we concentrate on the malicious adversary attacks that are possible for the approach proposed in [2]. Some possibilities in malicious environment like a party aborting the protocol abruptly or sending blank messages cannot be avoided even while using standard zero knowledge proofs [22].These situations can easily be handled by programming. However, in practical scenario following attacks are possible for the approach proposed in [2]:

1. *Inconsistent shares, valid sum of shares*; (here inconsistent shares are the shares which when used for reconstruction of secret, don't reveal correct secret.)
2. *Inconsistent shares, invalid sum of shares*
3. *Consistent shares, invalid sum of shares*

From the above listed attacks, in attack 1 and 2, malicious party generates and distributes inconsistent shares. This results in incorrect sum of shares and eventually incorrect cluster computation by all parties including malicious party. In practical scenario, malicious party often wants to get correct result but prevent others from getting correct result. Hence, by distributing inconsistent shares, malicious party will not achieve its actual goal.

The only way for the malicious party to get correct clusters but prevent others from getting correct clusters is using the scenario mentioned above in Attack 3. Here, all parties including malicious parties generate and distribute consistent shares. But malicious party sends invalid sum to all other parties in step 2 of algorithm shown in figure 1. If all other parties are honest, this will prevent honest parties to get correct clusters. However, malicious party gets correct clusters because the sum of shares it receives from honest parties are valid. Hence, attack 3 is important to thwart against for the approach proposed in [2].

In this paper, we attempt to provide the solution to attack 3. At the point of sharing secret sums, we use zero knowledge proof identification scheme that identifies whether the secret sum calculated by sending party is actually the one received.

3.3   Verifying the Sum of Shares

A sum of shares received by one party P_1 is the sum calculated by P_3 as explained in section 3.1. In this case we consider, P_3 sends 52 as the sum of shares to P_1 and P_2. In case of P_1, its own share in 52 is 13. So the partial sum of shares that needs to be verified without P_1's own share will be 39.

In our verification scheme, we consider 39 as partial sum, the secret value that needs to be verified and should be proved by party sending it. For every such s, the prover (party P_3 in our case here) can generate a public (y, H, ω) such that y = H.s^T, H being a common random (r × n) q-ary parity matrix, and ω is the weight of code; where n is the size of the code, k is the dimension of q-ary parity matrix and r is equal to (n-k). Exactly following the zero knowledge identification scheme in [28], the sequence of messages between prover and verifier happens as shown in figure 2.

The scheme involves two parties; a Prover and a Verifier that communicate with each other in a five pass protocol. The Prover attempts to prove his knowledge of certain value that is known by Verifier but cannot be disclosed to him. The scheme utilizes q-ary codes over a finite field F, pseudo-random number generators and hash functions.

Once all parties verify their sum of shares from all other parties, they can solve a set of equations to get final sum of secret values of every party. If the sum of shares is not correctly verified by any party, then that party sends accusation to all other party and the protocol terminates.

P is prover and V is the verifier. Let us have q = 64, n = 6, r = 3;

H is r × n parity check matrix;

s is the integer value to be proved and verified; s is a liner code over F_q^n of weight ω,

α is randomly selected over F_q^n;

u is randomly selected over F_q^n;

γ is randomly selected q-ary code over F_q^{n*};

Σ is a permutation, $\Pi_{\gamma,\Sigma}$ is a permutation function and h is a hash function.

Step 1: P calculates $C_1 = h\, (\Sigma \,\|\, \gamma \,\|\, H.u^T)$ and $C_2 = h\, (\Pi_{\gamma,\Sigma(u)} \,\|\, \Pi_{\gamma,\Sigma(s)})$ and sends to   V

Step 2: V replies with α

Step 3: P calculates $\beta = \Pi_{\gamma,\Sigma(u + \alpha s)}$ and sends to V

Step 4: V randomly selects b from {0,1}

Step 5: If P receives b = 0, it sends Σ, γ to V,

                V verifies $C_1 = h\, (\Sigma \,\|\, \gamma \,\|\, H\, \Pi_{\gamma,\Sigma}^{-1}(\beta)^T - \alpha\, y)$

       If P receives b = 1, it sends $\Pi_{\gamma,\Sigma(s)}$ to V,

                V verifies $C_2 = h\, (\beta - \alpha\Pi_{\gamma,\Sigma(s)}, \Pi_{\gamma,\Sigma(s)})$ and wt $(\Pi_{\gamma,\Sigma(s)}) = \omega$

Fig. 2. Verification of integer value using Zero Knowledge Proof identification scheme [28]

The pseudo code of our proposed approach is shown in figure 3.As shown in figure 3, each party while sending the sum of shares, also prove the correctness of partial sum. Similarly, each party while receiving the sum of shares needs to verify with the party that has sent this sum too. If all sums are verified by all parties, then only the protocol can proceed. Upon getting the wrong/invalid sum by other party, party sends accusation to that party and protocol terminates.

4   Theoretical Analysis

In this section, we give security and overhead analysis of the subcomponent of our approach. We concentrate only on zero knowledge identification scheme which we use to add support of malicious adversary model.

4.1   Security Analysis

As explained in section 3, the construction we use to add the security against malicious adversary model is the zero knowledge interactive proof for $P(I, s)$ in the random oracle model; where I is the public construct consisting y, H and w. In identification scheme,

---

P: Set of parties $P_1, P_2, \ldots, P_n$

$v_{is} = (a_i, b_i)$: Secret value of party P_i, where a_i is sum of samples and b_i is no. of samples in cluster

X: A set of n publicly known random values $x_1, x_2, \ldots, x_n$

k: Degree of the random polynomial, here $k = n - 1$

c: no. of clusters

1:   do in parallel for each party $P_i \in \{1\ldots n\}$

      find $((a_i, b_i), \ldots, (a_c, b_c))$ using pseudo code described in Figure 2

2:      for each secret value $v_{is} \in \{a_i, b_i\}$

3:           Select a random polynomial $q_i(x) = a_{n-1}x_{n-1} + \ldots + a_1x_1 + v_{is}$

5:           for r = 1 to n do

6:                Compute share of party P_r, where $shr(v_{is}, P_r) = q_i(x_r)$

7:                send $shr(v_{is}, P_r)$ to party P_r

8:                receive the shares $shr(v_{rs}, P_i)$ from every party P_r.

9:           end for

10:         compute $S(x_i) = q_1(x_i) + q_2(x_i) + \ldots + q_n(x_i)$

11:         for r = 1 to n do

12:               Send $S(x_i)$ to party P_r

13:               Receive the sum $S(x_i)$ from every party P_r

14:               Provethe partial sum $S(x_i)- shr(v_{is}, P_r)$ to every party P_r

15:               Verify the partial sum $S(x_i)- shr(v_{is}, P_r)$ with every party P_r

16:               If (partial sum from party P_r not verified) then

17:                   Broadcast an accusation to Party P_r

18:                   Terminate the algorithm.

19:             endif

20:           end for

21:         Solve the set of equations using Lagrange's interpolation to find the

22:           sum of secret values

23:    end for

24: Recompute$\mu_i$using sumof samples/no. of samples

25: until termination criteria met

Fig. 3. Privacy preserving distributed K-means clustering in malicious adversary model using Zero Knowledge Proof

the secret key holder can prove his knowledge of s by using two blending factors: the transformation by means of permutation and a random vector. A dishonest prover not knowing s; can cheat the verifier with probability of $q/2(q-1)$; where q is the power of prime number (in our case 64). Thus the protocol has to be run several times to detect cheating prover. In our case, we run the protocol 16 times to re-duce the probability of cheating the verifier to 2^{-16}. Further, the security of the identification scheme relies on the properties of random linear q-ary codes.

4.2   Computational Cost

Adding support of malicious adversary in [2] adds extra computational cost. This includes the matrix vector multiplication and generation of pseudo-random numbers in the code based identification scheme. Apart from this, as the identification scheme requires parties to compute random on their own, this also adds up to computational overhead.

In order to find computation cost, we use following parameters from the identification scheme:

N: the number of bits needed to encode an element of F_q = 8 bits
ℓ_h: the output size of the hash function h = 160 bits
δ: the number of rounds = 16

The size of the matrix in bits would be $(r \times n) N = 144$ bits

As each party acts as a prover in our scheme, the computational complexity for ZKP over F_q for each party is given as:

$\delta((n^2)$multiplications + (n^2)additions $)$ i.e. $O(n^2)$

4.3   Communication Cost

In [2], the number of messages exchanged after single round of clustering algorithm for a single party is $O(akn)$ and for n parties it reaches to $O(akn^2)$; where a is the number of attributes in dataset, k is the numbers of cluster centers and n is the number of parties.

However, the ZKP scheme used to support the malicious behavior will also need some amount of message exchange among parties. The cost in bytes will depend on the size of q-ary codes used. Let N be the number of bits needed to encode an element of F_q, in our case q is 64, i.e. 2^6, our n is 6 in this case. Bits needed to represent each element of F_q will be thus 4. So N = 4. But in practical programming, we simply initialize a two-dimensional byte array for linear code and parity matrix. This will make our N = 8. The output size of our hash function is 160. Number of rounds δ is 16.

Size of hash: l_h = 160 bits
Size of α: l_α = 6•8 = 48 bits

Size of γ: l_γ = 6•8 = 48 bits
Size of β: l_β = 6•8 = 48 bits
Size of Σ: l_Σ = 6•8 = 48 bits

So the total number of bits exchanged per attribute:

$$=\delta(2 \bullet l_h + l_\alpha + l_\beta + 1 + (l_\gamma + l_\Sigma + nN)/2)$$
$$=16(2 \bullet 160 + 6\bullet 8 + 6\bullet 8 +1 + (6\bullet 8 + 6\bullet 8 + 6\bullet 8)/2)$$
$$=16 (320 + 48 + 48 + 1 + (48 + 48 + 48)/2)$$
$$=7824 \text{ bits} = 978 \text{ bytes}$$

Hence, the communication cost for verification of value by one party will be 0.98KB and for n parties it reaches to 0.98 × n × (n-1) KB and hence $O(n^2)$.

5   Experimental Results and Analysis

We implemented our algorithm in JAVA. The experiments are conducted on Intel Core 2 Duo CPU with 4GB RAM and 2.3GHz speed. The datasets are taken from UCI machine learning repository. We provide brief outline of datasets here, however interested readers may find details at UCI machine learning repository. Dataset1 is Mammal's Milk with 2KB size, dataset2 is the river dataset with 25KB size and dataset3 is a water treatment dataset with 82KB sizes. For our experiment, we select initial cluster centers randomly. To test the distributed application on real time data,we divided all the three datasets randomly into three sets. These three data sets were then placed on three different machines to perform real time distributed clustering. Our test application successfully shows fully functional distributed clustering over real network.

The Zero Knowledge Identification Scheme was simulated by creating Prover and Verifier programs communicating through java sockets for the verification of each "partial sum". As discussed in section 3, the Prover and Verifier follows 5-pass 16-round identification scheme. Thus for one attribute/iteration, number of messages exchanged will be (5· n· n-1) as Prover + (5·n·n-1) as Verifier through communication channel. i.e. 2·(5·n·n-1) messages.

A 16-round of zero knowledge identification protocol practically takes 185 milliseconds on local computer and 3011ms through LAN. The practical cost of this tunes out to be 2·185ms = 370ms between two parties and 370·(n·n-1)/2 for overall exchange over local computer and 2·3011 ms = 6022 ms between two parties making it 6022·(n·n-1)/2 through network communication channel.

Table 1 shows the percentage increase in overhead in terms of computational cost and communication cost for our approach. The observation differs here from those shown in [2] as in [2], the experiments were performed on local machine while in our experiment we show true distributed emulation of our algorithm.

Table 1. Comparison of Privacy Preserving Distributed K-Means clustering in presence of semi honest adversary and malicious adversary model

Test	Communication Overhead	Computation Overhead
	* Percentage increase in bytes attributes/iteration	*Percentage increase in time(ms) attributes/iteration
Mammal Dataset		
Privacy preserving K-Means Clustering in semi honest model	168%	77.26 %
Privacy preserving K-Means clustering in malicious model	19152%	9988.95%
River Dataset		
Privacy preserving K-Means Clustering in semi honest model	336%	226.23 %
Privacy preserving K-Means clustering in malicious model	19320 %	18462.68%
Water treatment Dataset		
Privacy preserving K-Means Clustering in semi honest model	504%	229.05%
Privacy preserving K-Means clustering in malicious model	19824%	27231.71%
*Percentage increased in resources is calculated with respect to distributed K-Means clustering algorithm without privacy preserving mechanism.		

6   Conclusion and Future Work

In this paper, we attempted to extend the approach proposed in [2] to add the support of malicious adversary model using code based zero knowledge identification scheme. We give theoretical and practical analysis of our proposed approach by considering 16 round ZKP scheme. In our proposed approach, the probability of cheating the verifier is 2^{-16} which is reasonably small. As we verify only integer values, the size of matrix used is small and it results in acceptable computation and communication cost. Experimental results show that adding malicious adversary support slows down the performance of the algorithm. But at the same time we achieve fair conduction of protocol in presence of malicious adversary model.

In future, we intend to consider the of inconsistent share distribution and provide the solution for the same. We also intend to reduce the overheads incurred by the algorithm.

References

1. Kriegel, H.P., Borgwardt, K.M., Kröger, P., Pryakhin, A., Schubert, M., Zimek, A.: Future trends in data mining. Data Mining and Knowledge Discovery 15(1), 87–97 (2007)

2. Patel, S., Garasia, S., Jinwala, D.: An Efficient Approach for Privacy Preserving Distributed K-Means Clustering Based on Shamir's Secret Sharing Scheme. In: Dimitrakos, T., Moona, R., Patel, D., McKnight, D.H. (eds.) Trust Management VI. IFIP AICT, vol. 374, pp. 129–141. Springer, Heidelberg (2012)

3. Agrawal, R., Srikant, R.: Privacy-preserving data mining. ACM SIGMOD 29(2), 439–450 (2000)

4. Lindell, Y.: Privacy Preserving Data Mining. J. Cryptology, IACR, 177–206 (2002)

5. Pinkas, B.: Cryptographic Techniques for Privacy Preserving Data Mining. SIGKDD Explorations 4(2), 12–19 (2002)

6. Wu, X., Chu, C.-H., Wang, Y., Liu, F., Yue, D.: Privacy Preserving Data Mining Research: Current Status and Key Issues. In: Shi, Y., van Albada, G.D., Dongarra, J., Sloot, P.M.A. (eds.) ICCS 2007, Part III. LNCS, vol. 4489, pp. 762–772. Springer, Heidelberg (2007)

7. Lloyd, S.P.: Least squares quantization in PCM. IEEE Transactions on Information Theory 28, 129–137 (1982)

8. Vaidya, J., Clifton, C.: Privacy-preserving k-means clustering over vertically partitioned data. In: Proc. 9th ACM SIGKDD International Conf. on Knowledge Discovery and Data Mining. ACM Press (2003)

9. Inan, A., Kaya, S.V., Saygin, Y., Savas, E., Hintoglu, A.A., Levi, A.: Privacy preserving clustering on horizontally partitioned data. Data Knowl. Eng., 646–666 (2007)

10. Jagannathan, G., Wright, R.N.: Privacy-preserving distributed k-means clustering over arbitrarily partitioned data. In: Proc. KDD, pp. 593–599 (2005)

11. Bunn, P., Ostrovsky, R.: Secure two-party k-means clustering. In: Proc. ACM Conference on Computer and Communications Security, pp. 486–497 (2007)

12. Jha, S., Kruger, L., McDaniel, P.: Privacy Preserving Clustering. In: de Capitani di Vimercati, S., Syverson, P.F., Gollmann, D. (eds.) ESORICS 2005. LNCS, vol. 3679, pp. 397–417. Springer, Heidelberg (2005)

13. Upmanyu, M., Namboodiri, A.M., Srinathan, K., Jawahar, C.V.: Efficient Privacy Preserving K-Means Clustering. In: Chen, H., Chau, M., Li, S.-h., Urs, S., Srinivasa, S., Wang, G.A. (eds.) PAISI 2010. LNCS, vol. 6122, pp. 154–166. Springer, Heidelberg (2010)

14. Doganay, M.C., Pedersen, T.B., Saygin, Y., Savas, E., Levi, A.: Distributed privacy preserving k-means clustering with additive secret sharing. In: Proc. 2008 International Workshop on Privacy and Anonymity in Information Society, Nantes, France, pp. 3–11 (2008)

15. Kantarcioglu, M., Kardes, O.: Privacy-preserving data mining in the malicious model. International Journal of Information and Computer Security 2(4), 353–375 (2008)

16. Lindell, Y., Pinkas, B.: An Efficient Protocol for Secure Two-Party Computation in the Presence of Malicious Adversaries. In: Naor, M. (ed.) EUROCRYPT 2007. LNCS, vol. 4515, pp. 52–78. Springer, Heidelberg (2007)

17. Lindell, Y., Pinkas, B., Smart, N.: Implementing Two-Party Computation Efficiently with Security Against Malicious Adversaries. In: Ostrovsky, R., De Prisco, R., Visconti, I. (eds.) SCN 2008. LNCS, vol. 5229, pp. 2–20. Springer, Heidelberg (2008)

18. Zhan, J., Chang, L., Matwin, S.: How to Prevent Private Data from being Disclosed to a Malicious Attacker, Learning. In: Lin, T.Y., Xie, Y., Wasilewska, A., Liau, C.-J. (eds.) Data Mining: Foundations and Practice. SCI, vol. 118, pp. 517–528. Springer, Heidelberg (2008)

19. Emura, K., Miyaji, A., Rahman, M.S.: Efficient Privacy-Preserving Data Mining in Malicious Model. In: Cao, L., Feng, Y., Zhong, J. (eds.) ADMA 2010, Part I. LNCS, vol. 6440, pp. 370–382. Springer, Heidelberg (2010)

20. Gilburd, B., Schuster, A., Wolff, R.: Privacy-preserving data mining on data grids in the presence of malicious participants. In: Proc. of HPDC 2004, Honolulu, Hawaii (June 2004)
21. Hazay, C., Nissim, K.: Efficient Set Operations in the Presence of Malicious Adversaries. In: Nguyen, P.Q., Pointcheval, D. (eds.) PKC 2010. LNCS, vol. 6056, pp. 312–331. Springer, Heidelberg (2010)
22. Duan, Y., Canny, J.: Practical private computation and zero-knowledge tools for privacy-preserving distributed data mining, In: SDM 2008 (2008)
23. Shah, D., Zhong, S.: Two methods for privacy preserving data mining with malicious participants. Information Sciences 177(23), 5468–5483 (2008)
24. Lindell, Y., Pinkas, B.: Secure Two-Party Computation via Cut-n-Choose Oblivious Transfer. International Association for Cryptologic Research (2011)
25. Duan, Y., Canny, J.F., Zhan, J.Z.: Efficient Privacy-Preserving Association Rule Mining: P4P Style. In: Proc. CIDM, pp. 654–660 (2007)
26. Feige, U., Fiat, A., Shamir, A.: Zero Knowledge Proofs of Identity. Computing, 210-217 (1987)
27. Bernstein, D.J., Buchman, J., Dahmen, E.: Post-Quantum Cryptography. Springer, Heidelberg (2008)
28. Cayrel, P.-L., Véron, P., El Yousfi Alaoui, S.M.: A Zero-Knowledge Identification Scheme Based on the q-ary Syndrome Decoding Problem. In: Biryukov, A., Gong, G., Stinson, D.R. (eds.) SAC 2010. LNCS, vol. 6544, pp. 171–186. Springer, Heidelberg (2011)
29. Oliveira, S.R.M.: Privacy preserving clustering by data transformation. In: Proc.18th Brazilian Symposium on Databases, pp. 304–318 (2003)
30. Goldreich, O.: Foundations of Cryptography. Cambridge University Press (2001)
31. De Santis, A., Di Crescenzo, G., Persiano, G.: Secret Sharing and Perfect Zero-Knowledge. In: Stinson, D.R. (ed.) CRYPTO 1993. LNCS, vol. 773, pp. 73–84. Springer, Heidelberg (1994)
32. Pedersen, T.B., Saygin, Y., Savas, E.: Secret sharing vs. encryption-based techniques for privacy preserving data mining. In: Proc. UNECE/Eurostat Work Session on SDC (2007)
33. Shamir, A.: How to share a secret. Communications of the ACM 22(11), 612–613 (1979)

Solving the 4QBF Problem in Polynomial Time by Using the Biological-Inspired Mobility

Bogdan Aman[1,2], Gabriel Ciobanu[1,2], and Shankara Narayanan Krishna[3]

[1] Romanian Academy, Institute of Computer Science
[2] "A.I.Cuza" University of Iaşi, Romania
[3] IIT Bombay, Powai, Mumbai, India 400 076
baman@iit.tuiasi.ro, gabriel@info.uaic.ro, krishnas@cse.iitb.ac.in

Abstract. Inspired by the cell motion expressed by endocytosis and exocytosis, we propose a class of membrane systems which uses elementary membrane division and mobility of membranes. We show that this class of mobile membranes using only elementary division and mobility can provide a semi-uniform polynomial solutions for the $4QBF$ problem, ascending to the fourth level in the polynomial hierarchy.

1 Introduction

Membrane computing [15] is a branch of natural computing abstracting the architecture and the functioning of living cells. Motivated from mathematical or computer science points of view, various classes of membrane systems (also called P systems) were defined. The model has several applications [7] being characterized by: (i) a membrane structure consisting of a hierarchy of membranes (either disjoint or included), (ii) multisets of objects associated to membranes, and (iii) rules for processing objects and membranes.

P systems with mobile membranes [11] are defined as a variant of P systems with active membranes [15]. New features are provided by mobility rules inspired by endocytosis (moving an elementary membrane, a membrane without any other membrane in, inside a neighbouring membrane) and exocytosis (moving an elementary membrane outside the membrane where it is placed) [1,9]. We consider a variant of enhanced mobile membranes which uses only elementary membrane division rules and mobility rules. There are two forms of mobility: (i) an elementary membrane while moving in/out of an adjacent membrane can replace an object in itself (*endocytosis/exocytosis* rules); (ii) an elementary membrane moves in/out of an adjacent membrane in the absence of some object(s) in the adjacent membrane, and no objects are replaced in either membrane (*inhibitive endocytosis/inhibitive exocytosis* rules). The power of mobility expressed in both process algebra and natural computing is treated in [4].

When membrane systems are considered as computing devices, two main research directions are usually considered: the computational power in comparison with the classical notion of Turing computability, and the efficiency in algorithmically solving hard problems in polynomial time. In this respect, the main

C. Hota and P.K. Srimani (Eds.): ICDCIT 2013, LNCS 7753, pp. 432–443, 2013.

results obtained so far show that membrane systems define classes of computing devices which are both powerful (mostly equivalent to Turing machines) and efficient. The computational power of various classes of mobile membrane systems was studied in [2,3,6] where it has been proven that mobile membrane systems with a small number of membranes can provide computational universality. Membrane system algorithms have been developed which provide efficient solutions to some NP-complete problems (e.g., SAT, Bin Packing, Knapsack).

In the context of active membranes, the complexity classes that have been studied are $\mathbf{P}, \mathbf{NP}, \mathbf{coNP}, \mathbf{L}, \mathbf{NL}, \mathbf{PP}, \mathbf{PSPACE}$. The reader can look at [14,8] for more details on these complexity classes. Characterizations of $\mathbf{P}$ have been obtained for P systems with active membranes without polarizations that do not make use of dissolution, as well as for P systems with active membranes which do not have membrane division [15]. The classes $\mathbf{L}, \mathbf{NL}$ have been characterized by polarizationless P systems with active membranes under tighter uniformity conditions (reductions computable in $\mathbf{AC^0}$ as opposed to $\mathbf{P}$) [15].

Starting from the complexity classes $\mathbf{P}$, $\mathbf{NP}$ and $\mathbf{coNP}$ new classes can be constructed, yielding classes of greater apparent complexity [12]. Thus is obtained the polynomial hierarchy, closely related to the arithmetical hierarchy. The classes in this hierarchy are denoted by Σ_k^P, Π_k^P, and Δ_k^P (where the superscript P is used solely to distinguish these from the analogous sets in the Kleene arithmetical hierarchy). It is known that the lowest level of the polynomial hierarchy is given by $\Sigma_0^P = \Pi_0^P = \Delta_0^P = \mathbf{P}$, while the classes $\mathbf{P}, \mathbf{NP}, \mathbf{coNP}$ are at level 1 of the polynomial hierarchy. The complexity classes in levels greater than 1 of the polynomial hierarchy have few characterizations : $\Delta_{i+1}^P = \mathbf{P}^{\Sigma_i^P}$, $\Sigma_{i+1}^P = \mathbf{NP}^{\Sigma_i^P}$ and $\Pi_{i+1}^P = \mathbf{coNP}^{\Sigma_i^P}$, $i \geq 0$.

In [15] it is stated that there is no known variant of P systems with active membranes that can solve NP-complete problems without using any of the features of polarizations, non-elementary division and dissolution. Likewise, the only variant of *polarizationless* P systems with active membranes that has gone beyond the first level of the polynomial hierarchy using only the operations of communication and elementary membrane division is the one in [10], where a problem in $\Sigma_2^P \cup \Pi_2^P$ (namely 2QBF) is solved.

In this paper we present a semi-uniform polynomial solutions for a Π_4^P problem (namely 4QBF) by using systems that can perform only elementary division and mobility, thereby going to the fourth level in the polynomial hierarchy. As far as we know, it does not exist in literature solutions of 4QBF problems in polynomial time (by some parallel/nondeterministic machine) that we can compare our solution to. The class NP (problems solvable by a nondeterministic Turing machine in polynomial time) lies on level 1 of the polynomial hierarchy, while 4QBF problem lies on level 4: in the form where existential quantifiers are the first block is an example of a problem complete for Σ_4^P, and where the first block is universal is an example of a problem complete for Π_4^P. The class Δ_5^P contains both Σ_4^P as well as Π_4^P. Our result is that the union of Σ_4^P and Π_4^P is contained in our class of P systems. We cannot say that our class of P systems is also a superset of Δ_5^P. However, both our membrane systems as well as Δ_5^P contain the union of Σ_4^P and Π_4^P. The comparison of these two classes is an open problem.

In order to find such a solution, the membrane systems are treated as confluent deciding devices that respect the conditions: (1) all computations halt, (2) two additional objects Y and N (successful and unsuccessful computation) are used, and (3) one of these objects appears in the halting configuration. Such membrane systems are called *recognizers*. $\mathcal{R}$ denotes an arbitrary class of recognizer P systems.

A decision problem, X, is a pair (I_X, θ_X) where I_X is a language over a finite alphabet (whose elements are called instances) and θ_X is a total boolean function (that is, a predicate) over I_X. Its solvability is defined through the recognition of the language associated with it. Let M be a Turing machine with alphabet Γ, L a language over Γ, and the result of any halting computation is Y or N. If M is a deterministic device, it recognizes or decides L whenever, for any string u over Γ, M accepts u iff $u \in L$ (the result on input u is Y); otherwise it rejects u (the result on input u is N). If M is a non-deterministic device, it recognizes or decides L if for any string u over Γ, $u \in L$, there exists a computation of M with input u such that the answer is Y.

2   Enhanced Mobile Membranes with Controlled Mobility

We assume the reader is familiar with membrane computing; for the state of the art, see [15]. The class of mobile membrane systems used is an extension of *P systems with mobile membranes and controlled mobility* [10], which is a construct $\Pi = (V, H, \mu, w_1, \ldots, w_n, R, i)$, where: $n \geq 1$ (the initial *degree* of the system); V is an alphabet (its elements are called *objects*); H is a finite set of *labels* for membranes; μ is a *membrane structure*, consisting of n membranes, labelled with elements of H (we distinguish the external membrane, usually called the "skin" membrane, and several internal membranes); $w_1, w_2, \ldots, w_n$ are strings from V^* (the free monoid generated by V under the operation of concatenation and the empty string denoted by λ, as unit element), describing the initial *multisets of objects* placed in the n membranes of μ, i is the output membrane of the system, and R is a finite set of *developmental rules* of the following forms, where membrane h is elementary and membrane m is not necessarily elementary:

(a) $[a]_h[\ ]_m \rightarrow [[w]_h]_m$, for $h, m \in H, a \in V, w \in V^*$ endocytosis
    a membrane labelled h enters the adjacent membrane labelled m under the control of object a; the labels h and m remain unchanged during this process; however, the object a is modified to w during the operation.

(b) $[[a]_h]_m \rightarrow [w]_h[\ ]_m$, for $h, m \in H, a \in V, w \in V^*$ exocytosis
    a membrane labelled h is sent out of a membrane labelled m under the control of object a; the labels of the two membranes remain unchanged; however the object a from membrane h is modified to w during this operation;

(c) $[\ ]_h[a]_m \rightarrow [[\ ]_h w]_m$, for $h, m \in H, a \in V, w \in V^*$ forced endocytosis
    a membrane labelled h enters the adjacent membrane labelled m under the

control of object a of m; the labels h and m remain unchanged during this process; however, the object a is modified to w during the operation.

(d) $[a[\ ]_h]_m \rightarrow [\ ]_h[w]_m$, for $h, m \in H, a \in V, w \in V^*$ **forced exocytosis**

a membrane labelled h is sent out of a membrane labelled m under the control of object a of m; the labels of the two membranes remain unchanged; however the object a of membrane m is modified to w during this operation.

(e) $[a]_h[\ ]_{m/\neg S} \rightarrow [[a]_h]_m$, for $h, m \in H, a \in V, S \subseteq V$ **inhibitive endocytosis**

a membrane labelled h containing a can enter m provided m does not contain any object from S; the object a and the labels h and m of the membranes also remain unchanged. The objects of S are *inhibitors* that prevent membrane h from entering membrane m whenever h contains the object a.

(f) $[[a]_h]_{m/\neg S} \rightarrow [\ ]_m[a]_h$, for $h, m \in H, a \in V, S \subseteq V$ **inhibitive exocytosis**

a membrane labelled h containing a can exit m provided m does not contain any object from S; the object a does not evolve in the process; the labels h and m of the membranes also remain unchanged.

(g) $[a]_h \rightarrow [u]_h[v]_h$, for $h \in H, a \in V, u, v \in V^*$ **elementary division**

in reaction with an object a, the membrane labelled h is divided into two membranes labelled h, with the object a replaced in the two new membranes by possibly new objects; the other objects remain unchanged.

The paper [10] did not consider the operations of forced endocytosis and forced exocytosis. The rules are applied according to the following principles:

1. The rules are applied in a maximal parallel manner (in each step we apply a multiset of rules such that no further rule can be added to the multiset, no further membranes and objects can evolve at the same time), nondeterministically choosing the rules, the membranes, and the objects.

2. Membrane m from the above rules is said to be *passive*, while membrane h is said to be *active*. In any step of a computation, any object and any active membrane can be involved in at most one rule, but the passive membranes are not considered involved in the use of rules (hence they can be used by several rules at the same time as passive membranes).

3. The evolution of objects and membranes takes place in a bottom-up manner. After having a (maximal) multiset of rules chosen, they are applied starting from the innermost membranes, level by level, up to the skin membrane (all these sub-steps form a unique evolution step, called a *transition* step).

4. When a membrane is moved across another membrane by rules (a)-(f), its whole contents (its objects) are moved.

5. All objects and membranes which do not evolve at a given step, are passed unchanged to the next configuration of the system.

By using the rules in this way, we get transitions among the configurations of the system. A sequence of transitions is a computation, and a computation is successful if it halts (it reaches a configuration where no rule can be applied). At the end of a halting computation, the number of objects from a special membrane called output membrane is considered as the result of the computation. A non-halting computation provides no output. The family of all sets of natural numbers $\mathbf{N}(\Pi)$ that are obtained as a result of a halting computation by a enhanced mobile membrane system Π of degree at most n using rules $\alpha \subseteq \{exo,$ $endo, fendo, fexo, iendo, iexo, div\}$, is denoted by $\mathbf{NEMCM}_n(\alpha)$. Here $endo$ and exo represent endocytosis and exocytosis, $fendo$ and $fexo$ represent forced endocytosis and forced exocytosis, $iendo, iexo$ represent inhibitive endocytosis and inhibitive exocytosis, while div represents elementary division. When the number of membranes is finite, and not fixed, we denote it as $*$.

In what follows we provide some examples that will clarify the semantics.

Example 1. 1. Consider the configuration
$$[[aabbcccccc]_1[uuv]_2[rrs]_3]_4, \text{ with rules}$$
(a) $[a]_1[\ ]_{2/\neg u} \rightarrow [[a]_1]_2$ $iendo$
(b) $[b]_1[\ ]_{2/\neg v} \rightarrow [[b]_1]_2$ $iendo$
(c) $[a]_1[\ ]_{3/\neg u} \rightarrow [[a]_1]_3$ $iendo$
(d) $[c]_1[\ ]_{3/\neg t} \rightarrow [[c]_1]_3$ $iendo$
(e) $[u]_2[\ ]_3 \rightarrow [[u']_2]_3$ $endo$

First we summarize the rules and their effects:

- Rules (a)-(d) are *iendo* rules for membrane 1. Membrane 1 has the distinct objects a, b, c. Membrane 1 cannot enter membrane 2 that contains the inhibitor u violating rule 1, and inhibitor v violating rule 2. However, membrane 1 can enter membrane 3 since there are no inhibitors in membrane 3 with respect to a, b, c in membrane 1.
- Rule 5 is an *endo* rule. Membrane 2 enters membrane 3.

The next configuration is
$$[[rrs[u'uv]_2[aabbcccccc]_1]_3]_4$$

2. Consider the configuration
$$[[pq[abc]_1\ [abb]_2\ [cde]_3\ [sr]_9\ ]_4\ [aa]_5\ [ef]_6\ [uv]_7\ ]_8, \text{ with rules}$$
(a) $[a]_2[\ ]_{3/\neg c} \rightarrow [[a]_2]_3$ $iendo$
(b) $[b]_2[\ ]_{3/\neg f} \rightarrow [[b]_2]_3$ $iendo$
(c) $[a]_2[\ ]_3 \rightarrow [[d]_2]_3$ $endo$
(d) $[a]_2[\ ]_{1/\neg t} \rightarrow [[a]_2]_1$ $iendo$
(e) $[a]_1[\ ]_{2/\neg n} \rightarrow [[a]_1]_2$ $iendo$
(f) $[a]_5 \rightarrow [b]_5[c]_5$ div
(g) $[e]_6[\ ]_5 \rightarrow [[f]_6]_5$ $endo$
(h) $[[r]_9]_{4/\neg s} \rightarrow [r]_9[\ ]_4$ $iexo$
(i) $[u]_7[\ ]_{4/\neg p} \rightarrow [[u]_7]_4$ $iendo$
(j) $[u]_7[\ ]_{4/\neg o} \rightarrow [[u]_7]_4$ $iendo$

First we summarize the rules and their effects:

- Membrane 2 cannot enter membrane 3 using *iendo* since rule (a) is violated. The distinct objects of membrane 2 are a, b, and there is an inhibitor in membrane 3 with respect to a. However, membrane 2 can enter membrane 3 using the endocytosis rule (c).
- Membrane 2 can enter membrane 1 using *iendo*, likewise, membrane 1 can enter membrane 2 using *iendo* - the relevant rules are (d),(e). However, exactly one of them can be used in a step.

- Membrane 5 divides. Membrane 6 has an *endo* rule to enter membrane 5 at the same step - it enters a copy of membrane 5 non-deterministically. The relevant rules are (f),(g).
- Membrane 9 can leave membrane 4 using *iexo* using rule (h).
- Membrane 7 cannot enter membrane 4 using *iendo*. Look at rules (i),(j). One of them says that membrane 7 containing u can enter membrane 4 provided membrane 4 does not have a copy of p, while the other says the same thing in the absence of o. Since these two rules have the same left hand side, we can club these two and write it as $[u]_7 [\ ]_{4/\neg o, \neg p} \rightarrow [[u]_7]_4$. Clearly, membrane 7 cannot enter membrane 4.

A possible next configuration using rules (c), (f),(g)and (h) is
$$[[pq[abc]_1 \ [cde[dbb]_2]_3 \ ]_4 \ [sr]_9 \ [ba]_5 \ [ca[ff]_6]_5 \ [uv]_7 \ ]_8$$
Another possible next configuration using rules (e), (f),(g) and (h) is
$$[[pq \ [abb[abc]_1]_2 \ [cde]_3 \ ]_4 \ [sr]_9 \ [ba]_5 \ [ca[ff]_6]_5 \ [uv]_7 \ ]_8$$
Another possible next configuration using rules (d), (f),(g)and (h) is
$$[[pq \ [abc[abb]_2]_1 \ [cde]_3 \ ]_4 \ [sr]_9 \ [ba]_5 \ [ca[ff]_6]_5 \ [uv]_7 \ ]_8$$

3 Solving the 4QBF Problem in Polynomial Time

Here we show that we can handle class of problems higher in the polynomial hierarchy; namely we give a solution for a Π_4^P complete problem. Our systems use only biologically inspired mobility and elementary membrane division. As stated in the introduction, we use mobile membrane systems as confluent deciding devices, in which all computation starting from the initial configuration agree on the result. A family $\mathbf{\Pi}$, of mobile membrane systems Π, solves a decision problem if for each instance of the problem there is a member of the family able to decide on the instance. In order to define the notion of semi-uniformity, some notations are necessary:

- for a suitable alphabet Σ, each instance of the decision problem is encoded as a string w over Σ;
- $\mathbf{\Pi}(w)$ - the member of $\mathbf{\Pi}$ which solves the instance w.

Inspired from [16], for mobile membrane systems we have:

Definition 1. *A decision problem X is a pair (I_X, θ_X) such that I_X is a language over a finite alphabet, whose elements are called instances, and θ_X is a total boolean function over I_X. Let $X = (I_X, \theta_X)$ be a decision problem, and $\mathbf{\Pi} = \{\mathbf{\Pi}(w) | w \in I_X\}$ be a family of mobile membrane systems.*

- $\mathbf{\Pi}$ *is said to be* polynomially uniform by Turing machines *if there exists a deterministic Turing machine working in polynomial time which constructs the system $\mathbf{\Pi}(w)$ from the instance $w \in I_X$.*
- $\mathbf{\Pi}$ *is said to be* sound *with respect to X if for each instance of the problem $w \in I_X$, if there exists an accepting computation of $\mathbf{\Pi}(w)$, then $\theta_X(w) = 1$.*
- $\mathbf{\Pi}$ *is said to be* complete *with respect to X if for each instance of the problem $w \in I_X$, if $\theta_X(w) = 1$, then every computation of $\mathbf{\Pi}(w)$ is an accepting one.*

Definition 2. *A decision problem X is solvable in* polynomial time *by a family of recognizer systems* $\Pi = \{\Pi(w) \mid w \in I_X\}$, *denoted by* $X \in \mathbf{PMC}^*_{\mathcal{R}}$ *if:*

- *The family Π is polynomially uniform by Turing machines.*
- *The family Π is polynomially bounded: there exists $k \in \mathbf{N}$ such that for each instance $w \in I_X$, every computation of $\Pi(w)$ performs at most $|w|^k$ steps.*
- *The family Π is sound and complete with respect to X.*

The family Π is said to provide a semi-uniform *solution to the problem X.*

As a direct consequence of working with recognizer membrane systems, these complexity classes are closed under complement and polynomial time reductions [16]. In this paper, since we are working with recognizer mobile membrane systems, we replace $\mathcal{R}$ with $\mathcal{MM}$. We are thus, interested in the class $\mathbf{PMC}^*_{\mathcal{MM}}$.

The following complexity result is presented in the style of membrane computing approach. We propose a polynomial time semi-uniform solution for solving satisfiability of 4QBF using the operations $rendo$, $rexo$, $rfendo$, $rfexo$, $iendo$ and $rdiv$. When we restrict $|w| = 1$ in rules (a) – (d) and (g) , we call the operations $rendo$, $rexo$, $rfendo$, $rfexo$ and $rdiv$ where r stands for "restricted".

A complete problem for Σ_k^{P} is satisfiability of quantified Boolean formulas with k alternations of quantifiers (abbreviated kQBF). This is the version of the boolean satisfiability problem for Σ_k^{P}. In this problem, we are given a Boolean formula φ with variables partitioned into k sets $X_1, ..., X_k$. We have to determine if it is true that $\exists X_1 \forall X_2 \exists X_3 \ldots \psi$, where ψ is in CNF. That is, is there an assignment of values to variables in X_1 such that, for all assignments of values in X_2, there exists an assignment of values to variables in $X_3 \ldots$, φ is true? The variant above is complete for Σ_k^{P}. The variant in which the first quantifier is $\forall$, the second is $\exists$, and so on is complete for Π_k^{P}.

We consider 4QBF with the Boolean formula $\varphi = \forall X_1 \exists X_2 \forall X_3 \exists X_4 \psi$ where $\psi = (C_1 \wedge C_2 \wedge \ldots \wedge C_m)$, $X_1 = \{x_1, .., x_k\}$, $X_2 = \{x_{k+1}, .., x_l\}$, $X_3 = \{x_{l+1}, .., x_r\}$ and $X_4 = \{x_{r+1}, .., x_n\}$. The sets X_j, $1 \leq j \leq n$ are pairwise disjoint, and each C_i is a clause (disjunction of literals x_i or $\neg x_i$). Construct the membrane structure

$$[\quad [\ldots[[\,[\ldots[[[\ldots[[[a_1 a_2 \ldots a_n]_0]_{1'}]_{2'} \ldots]_{n'} \,]_{1''}]_{2''} \ldots]_{n''} \,]_1]_2 \ldots]_m$$
$$[a_1 a_2 \ldots a_k]_{B_1} \; [a_1 a_2 \ldots a_k b_{k+1} \ldots b_l]_{B_2} \; [a_1 a_2 \ldots a_k b_{k+1} \ldots b_l c_{l+1} \ldots c_r]_{B_3}$$
$$[a_1 a_2 \ldots a_k d_0]_S \; [a_1 a_2 \ldots a_k]_{S'}$$
$$[\, [a_1 a_2 \ldots a_k b_{k+1} \ldots b_l e_0]_J \; [a_1 a_2 \ldots a_k b_{k+1} \ldots b_l e_0]_K \; [d_0]_L \; [d_0]_M \,]_E \quad [Y]_A]_O$$

1. The innermost membrane 0 consists of symbols corresponding to variables $x_1, \ldots, x_n$. This membrane divides to produce all combinations of $t_i, f_i, 1 \leq i \leq n$. Membranes i' and i'', $1 \leq i \leq n$ ensure that membranes 0 start moving out only after a_i has been replaced with t_i, f_i. The membranes $1, \ldots, m$ represent the m clauses; an assignment exit membrane j if it satisfies C_j.
2. The membranes B_j, $1 \leq j \leq 3$ represent the first 3 quantifier blocks. Membrane B_j has symbols a_i corresponding to variables in $\cup_{l=1}^{j} X_l$ and plays a major role in deciding if φ is true or not. The symbols a_i in all the B_j are replaced with t_i, f_i first; this is followed by membranes B_2, B_3 entering membranes B_1 such that the assignments for $a_1 \ldots a_k$ agree in B_1, B_2, B_3; then

the symbols b_i are replaced in B_2, B_3 with t_i, f_i. After this, membranes B_3 enter membranes B_2 such that the assignments for $a_1 \ldots, a_k, b_{k+1}, b_l$ agree in B_2, B_3; finally the symbols c_i in B_3 are replaced with t_i, f_i. This gives us the following structure: for every assignment of values to variables in X_1, we have a copy of B_1. Once in B_1, the variables in B_2, B_3 corresponding to X_2 are replaced. After B_3 enters B_2, the variables of X_3 get replaced in B_3.

3. The membranes J, K, L, M are used as auxiliary membranes in solving the problem. The membrane A holds the answer to the problem. It is initialized with 'Y' for yes; in case the formula is false, 'Y' is replaced with a 'N'.

The following are the rules:

1. $[a_i]_j \to [t_i]_j[f_i]_j$, for $j \in \{B_1, B_2, B_3, S, S', J, K\}, 1 \le i \le k$ $(rdiv)$,
   $[a_i]_0 \to [t_i]_0[f_i]_0$, for $1 \le i \le n$ $(rdiv)$,
   $[b_i]_j \to [t_i]_j[f_i]_j$, $j \in \{J, K\}$ for $k+1 \le i \le l$ $(rdiv)$,
   $[d_i]_j \to [d_{i+1}]_j[d_{i+1}]_j$, for $j \in \{L, M\}, 0 \le i \le l-1$, $(rdiv)$,
   (Generation of assignments corresponding to variables. Takes n steps in membranes 0, and l steps in membranes J, K, L, M)

2. $[t_i]_j[\ ]_{B_1 \ \neg\{f_i, a_i\}} \to [[t_i]_j]_{B_1}$, for $j \in \{B_2, B_3, S, S'\}, 1 \le i \le k$ $(iendo)$,
   $[f_i]_j[\ ]_{B_1 \ \neg\{t_i, a_i\}} \to [[f_i]_j]_{B_1}$, for $j \in \{B_2, B_3, S, S'\}, 1 \le i \le k$ $(iendo)$,
   $[\ ]_J[d_i]_L \to [d_{i+1}[\ ]_J]_L$, $l \le i \le (\lceil \frac{3n+m+4-l}{2} \rceil) + l$, $(rfendo)$,
   $[\ ]_K[d_i]_M \to [d_{i+1}[\ ]_K]_M$, $l \le i \le (\lceil \frac{3n+m+4-l}{2} \rceil) + l$, $(rfendo)$,
   (Membranes B_2, B_3, S, S' enter B_1 provided they agree on the assignment of values to variables in X. Membranes J, K enter membranes L, M from the $l+1$th step onward, each time the counter d_i is incremented)

3. $[[b_i]_j]_{B_1} \to [b'_i]_j[\ ]_{B_1}$, for $j \in \{B_2, B_3\}, k+1 \le i \le l$ $(rexo)$,
   $[b'_i]_j \to [t_i]_j[f_i]_j$, $j \in \{B_2, B_3\}$ for $k+1 \le i \le l$ (div),
   $[[c_i]_{B_3}]_{B_2} \to [c'_i]_{B_3}[\ ]_{B_2}$, for $l+1 \le i \le r$ $(rexo)$,
   $[c'_i]_{B_3} \to [t_i]_{B_3}[f_i]_{B_3}$, for $l+1 \le i \le r$ $(rdiv)$,
   $[[d_0]_S]_{B_1} \to [\ ]_{B_1}[d_1]_S$ $(rexo)$,
   $[[e_i]_J]_L \to [e_{i+1}]_J[\ ]_L$ for $0 \le i \le (\lfloor \frac{3n+m+4-l}{2} \rfloor - 1)$, $(rexo)$,
   $[[e_i]_K]_M \to [e_{i+1}]_K[\ ]_M$ for $0 \le i \le (\lfloor \frac{3n+m+4-l}{2} \rfloor - 1)$, $(rexo)$,
   $[[e_\beta]_J]_L \to [e]_J[\ ]_L$, for $\beta = (\lfloor \frac{3n+m+4-l}{2} \rfloor)$, $(rexo)$,
   $[[e_\beta]_K]_M \to [e]_K[\ ]_M$, for $\beta = (\lfloor \frac{3n+m+4-l}{2} \rfloor)$, $(rexo)$,
   (Membranes B_2, B_3 come out of B_1 $l-k$ times, each time replacing b_i with b'_i; on reentering, b'_i is replaced with t_i, f_i. Same reasoning for c_i. The membrane S comes out of B_1 and incrementing its counter to d_1)

4. $[t_i]_{B_3}[\ ]_{B_2 \ \neg\{f_i, b_i\}} \to [[t_i]_{B_3}]_{B_2}$, for $k+1 \le i \le l$ $(iendo)$,
   $[f_i]_{B_3}[\ ]_{B_2 \ \neg\{t_i, b_i\}} \to [[f_i]_{B_3}]_{B_2}$, for $k+1 \le i \le l$ $(iendo)$,
   $[d_i]_S[\ ]_{S'} \to [[d_{i+1}]_S]_{S'}$, $1 \le i \le 3n+m+10-k$ $(rendo)$,
   $[[d_i]_S]_{S'} \to [d_{i+1}]_S[\ ]_{S'}$, $1 \le i \le 3n+m+10-k$ $(rexo)$,
   $[d_{3n+m+11-k}]_S[\ ]_{S'} \to [[d_{3n+m+11-k}]_S]_{S'}$ $(rexo)$,
   $[[d_{3n+m+11-k}]_S]_{S'} \to [D]_S[\ ]_{S'}$, $(rexo)$,
   (Once division is completed in B_2, membrane B_3 enters B_2 provided assign-

ment of variables in blocks X, Y agree in both B_3, B_2. The membranes S, S' just keep incrementing the counter until a certain point of time)

5. $[[t_i]_0]_{i'} \to [t_i]_0[\ ]_{i''}, [[t_i]_0]_{i''} \to [t_i]_0[\ ]_{i'''}, 1 \le i \le n$, $\qquad$ (rexo),

   $[[f_i]_0]_{i'} \to [f_i]_0[\ ]_{i''}, [[f_i]_0]_{i''} \to [f_i]_0[\ ]_{i'''}, 1 \le i \le n$, $\qquad$ (rexo),

   (Once membranes 0 do not contain a_i, these come out of membranes i', i'')

6. $[[t_i]_0]_j \to [t_i]_0[\ ]_j, 1 \le i \le n, 1 \le j \le m$, if C_j has x_i, $\qquad$ (rexo),

   $[[f_i]_0]_j \to [f_i]_0[\ ]_j, 1 \le i \le n, 1 \le j \le m$, if C_j has $\neg x_i$, $\qquad$ (rexo),

   (Membranes 0 come out of membrane j provided the assignment of variables in them satisfy clause C_j)

7. $[t_i]_0[\ ]_{B_1 \neg\{f_i\}} \to [[t_i]_0]_{B_1}$, for $1 \le i \le k$, $\qquad$ (iendo),

   $[f_i]_0[\ ]_{B_1 \neg\{t_i\}} \to [[f_i]_0]_{B_1}$, for $1 \le i \le k$, $\qquad$ (iendo),

   $[t_i]_0[\ ]_{B_2 \neg\{f_i\}} \to [[t_i]_0]_{B_2}$, for $k+1 \le i \le l$, $\qquad$ (iendo),

   $[f_i]_0[\ ]_{B_2 \neg\{t_i\}} \to [[f_i]_0]_{B_2}$, for $k+1 \le i \le l$, $\qquad$ (iendo),

   $[t_i]_0[\ ]_{B_3 \neg\{f_i\}} \to [[t_i]_0]_{B_3}$, for $l+1 \le i \le r$, $\qquad$ (iendo),

   $[f_i]_0[\ ]_{B_3 \neg\{t_i\}} \to [[f_i]_0]_{B_3}$, for $l+1 \le i \le r$, $\qquad$ (iendo),

   (Membranes 0 coming out of membrane m enter membrane B_1 provided the assignments of variables in block X_1 match; this is followed by membranes 0 entering membranes B_2 and then B_3. If a membrane B_3 contains membranes 0, then the assignment of variables in blocks X_1, X_2, X_3 agree in both. If every membrane B_1 is such that, for all its children B_2, there is at least one elementary B_3, then it means that the condition $\forall X_1 \exists X_2 \forall X_3 \exists X_4$ is not met)

8. $[[e]_J]_E \to [e]_J[\ ]_E$, $\qquad$ (rexo),

   $[[e]_K]_E \to [e]_K[\ ]_E$, $\qquad$ (rexo),

   (When membranes 0 have reached membranes B_3, then J, K stop evolving the counters, and come out of membrane E)

9. $[t_i]_j[\ ]_{B_1 \neg\{f_i\}} \to [[t_i]_j]_{B_1}$, for $j \in \{J, K\}, 1 \le i \le k$ $\qquad$ (iendo),

   $[f_i]_j[\ ]_{B_1 \neg\{t_i\}} \to [[f_i]_j]_{B_1}$, for $j \in \{J, K\}, 1 \le i \le k$ $\qquad$ (iendo),

   $[t_i]_j[\ ]_{B_2 \neg\{f_i\}} \to [[t_i]_j]_{B_2}$, for $j \in \{J, K\}, k+1 \le i \le l$ $\qquad$ (iendo),

   $[f_i]_j[\ ]_{B_2 \neg\{t_i\}} \to [[f_i]_j]_{B_2}$, for $j \in \{J, K\}, k+1 \le i \le l$ $\qquad$ (iendo),

   (Membranes J, K enter membranes B_1 provided they agree on the assignment of values to variables in X_1; this is followed by membranes J, K entering membranes B_2 provided they agree on values of variables in X_1, X_2)

10. $[t_i]_{B_3}[\ ]_J \to [[t_i]_{B_3}]_J$, for $1 \le i \le l$, $\qquad$ (rendo),

    $[f_i]_{B_3}[\ ]_J \to [[f_i]_{B_3}]_J$, for $1 \le i \le l$, $\qquad$ (rendo),

    $[[e]_K]_{B_2} \to [g]_K[\ ]_{B_2}$, $\qquad$ (rexo),

    (Once J is inside B_2, it will detect if there is any B_3 which does not correspond to a solution of ψ: elementary B_3's, if any, enter J. In this step, K goes out of B_2)

11. $[\ ]_J[g]_K \to [h[\ ]_J]_K$, $\qquad$ (rfendo),

12. $[[e]_J]_K \to [C]_J[\ ]_K$, $\qquad$ (rexo),

13. $[[C]_J]_{B_2} \to [C]_J[\ ]_{B_2}$, $\qquad$ (rexo),

    (K returns to B_2 and then elementary J's, if any, enter K. If a membrane B_2

has J elementary, it means all its children B_3 are non-elementary. The elementary J, if any, comes out of K with a value C; then comes out of B_2)

14. $[C]_J[\ ]_{S \setminus \{d_\gamma, Y\}} \to [[C]_J]_S$, $\gamma = 3n + m + 11 - k$,   (*iendo*),

$[\ ]_{S'}[D]_S \to [D'[\ ]_{S'}]_S$,   (*rfendo*),

(The J then enters S; S' also enters S)

15. $[[t_i]_{S'}]_S \to [t_i]_{S'}[\ ]_S$,   (*rexo*),

$[[f_i]_{S'}]_S \to [f_i]_{S'}[\ ]_S$,   (*rexo*),

$[D'[\ ]_J]_S \to [\ ]_J[Y]_S$,   (*rfexo*),

(S' comes out of S; the J (if any), has entered S, comes out replacing D' with a Y. Essentially, when J replaces D' with Y, it is reporting that for a particular B_1 and a particular B_2, all B_3's are non-elementary. If at least one J in each B_1 does this, then that B_1 is considered fine - (the number of J's is equal to the number of B_2's). If there is a copy of B_1 such that every J corresponding to each of its B_2's is non-elementary, then the S in that copy of B_1 will retain the value D')

16. $[[D']_S]_{B_1} \to [D']_S[\ ]_{B_1}$,   (*rexo*),

$[Y[\ ]_J]_S \to [\ ]_J[Y]_S$,   (*rfexo*),

17. $[\ ]_S[Y]_A \to [N[\ ]_S]_A$,   (*rfendo*)

(Such an S will report the matter to membrane A; it will come out with D', and change Y in A to a N. Thus, if none of the S's come out, it means they all had Y in them; this is because there was at least one elementary J in each B_1; this means that for each B_1, there is at least one B_2 such that all its B_3's are nonelementary - this means the $\forall X_1 \exists X_2 \forall X_3$ condition is met. Of course, if S does not come out, the answer in A remains Y)

Analysis: Number of membranes in the initial configuration is $2n + m + 13$. Number of rules in the system: $7k + n + 2(l - k) + 2l$ rules of type-1; $8k + 2(\lceil \frac{3n+m+4-l}{2} \rceil + 1)$ rules of type-2; $2(r - k) + 1 + 2\lfloor \frac{3n+m+4-l}{2} \rfloor + 1)$ rules of type-3; $2(l - k) + 2(3n + m + 11 - k)$ rules of type-4; $2n$ rules of type-5; mn rules of type-6; $2r$ rules of type-7; 2 rules of type-8; $2l$ rules of type-9; $2l + 1$ rules of type-10; and 11 remaining rules. Thus, the total number of rules is polynomial wrt the size of the problem.

At the end of $3n + m + 3$ steps, membranes 0 if any, reach membranes B_3. It can be seen that at the end of the $3n + m + 4$th step, we have d_α where $\alpha = l + \lceil \frac{3n+m+4-l}{2} \rceil$ in membranes L, M and e_β where $\beta = \lfloor \frac{3n+m+4-l}{2} \rfloor$ in membranes J, K. The possibilities at this time are (i) $[[e_\beta]_J d_\alpha]_L$ that evolves into $[e]_J[d_\alpha]_L$. (ii) $[e_\beta]_J[d_\alpha]_L$, that evolves into $[[e_\beta]_J d_{\alpha+1}]_L$, followed by $[e]_J[d_{\alpha+1}]_L$. The maximum number of steps needed is $3n + m + 6$. This is followed by J, K coming out of E, entering B_1, and then B_2; elementary B_3 enter J and K comes out of B_2; K renters B_2; J enters K and exit with the value C out of K and B_2. The latest (assuming (ii)) J can be in B_1 at the end of step $3n + m + 14$, and the earliest (assuming (i)) J can be in B_1 at the end of step $3n + m + 13$. S started incrementing d_1 in step $k + 4$; thus, at the end of the $3n + m + 13$th step, we have $d_\gamma = d_{3n+m+11-k}$ in S. At the end of $3n + m + 13$th step we can have:

(a) $[d_\gamma]_S[\ ]_{S'}[C]_J$ in membrane B_1, that evolves to $[[d_\gamma]_S]_{S'}[C]_J$, followed by $[D]_S[\ ]_{S'}[C]_J$. Then S', J enter S, with S' replacing D with D', and S', J

leave S. When J leaves S, it replaces D' with Y. Potentially, we can have a maximum of l J's in B_1, that can enter/leave S. Assuming l J's enter/leave S, there are $3n+m+16+l$ steps. In case there are no J's, then S leaves B_1 with D', and enters A. Thus, the number of steps is $\leq max\{3n+m+16+l, 3n+m+19\}$.

(b) $[[d_\gamma]_S]_{S'}[C]_J$ and thus the number of steps is one less than the previous.

(c)$[d_\gamma]_S[\ ]_{S'}$ and no J sibling with and thus the number of steps is as in (a).

(d) $[[d_\gamma]_S]_{S'}$ and no J sibling with and thus the number of steps is as in (b).

It is straightforward that the construction is:

- semi-uniform;
- sound and complete: Π says Y iff the given problem has a solution.

This result, along with the fact that $\mathbf{PMC}^*_{MM}$ is closed under complements and polynomial time reductions, gives us the following result:

Theorem 1. $\Sigma_4^P \cup \Pi_4^P \subseteq \mathbf{PMC}^*_{\mathcal{MM}}$.

A natural question to ask is regarding the power of the operations used to solve this problem. Before presenting such results, we define the notations to be used: FIN, MAT and CS represent the set of finite languages, languages accepted by a matrix grammar without appearance checking and context sensitive languages respectively. It is known that $NCS, NMAT \subset NRE$, where NL represents the family of sets of numbers recognized by language L. The proofs of these results are presented in [5].

A context-free matrix grammar without appearance checking is a construct $G = (N, T, S, M)$ where N, T are disjoint alphabets of non-terminals and terminals, $S \in N$ is the axiom, and M is a finite set of matrices of the form $(A_1 \to x_1, \ldots, A_n \to x_n)$ of context-free rules. For a string w, a matrix $m : (r_1, \ldots, r_n)$ is executed by applying the productions $r_1, \ldots, r_n$ one after the another, following the order in which they appear in the matrix. We write $w \Rightarrow_m z$ if there is a matrix $m : (A_1 \to x_1, \ldots, A_n \to x_n)$ in M and the strings $w_1, \ldots, w_{n+1}$ in $(N \cup T)^*$ such that $w = w_1, w_{n+1} = z$, and for each $i = 1, 2, \ldots, n$ we have $w_i = w'_i A_i w''_i, w_{i+1} = w'_i x_i w''_i$. The language generated by G is $L(G) = \{x \in T^* \mid S \Rightarrow^* x\}$.

We have the following results:

Theorem 2. $- NEMCM_4(endo, exo, fendo, fexo) \subseteq NMAT$
$- NEMCM_*(rendo, rexo, rfendo, rfexo, iendo, iexo) \subseteq NFIN$
$- NEMCM_*(rdiv) \subseteq NCS$
$- NEMCM_*(rendo, rexo, rfendo, rfexo, iendo, iexo, rdiv) \subseteq NCS$

4   Conclusion

Membrane computing is part of natural computing, being a rule-based formalism inspired by biological cells. In this formalism, objects are represented using symbols from a given alphabet, and regions contain multisets of objects; rules are essentially multiset rewriting rules with some additional features.

The paper shows how a 4QBF problem can be solved in polynomial time by using a variant of mobile membranes. The proposed solution uses only the operation of elementary membrane division and the membranes mobility inspired by biological endocytosis and exocytosis. Size complexity aspects are also considered, by providing an explicit correspondence between the size parameters of the constructed membrane systems and the instances of the problem. Up to our knowledge, this is the first paper in the area of membrane computing that ascends to this level using only elementary division and no polarizations.

Acknowledgements. The work of Bogdan Aman and Gabriel Ciobanu was supported by a grant of the Romanian National Authority for Scientific Research CNCS-UEFISCDI, project number PN-II-ID-PCE-2011-3-0919.

References

1. Aman, B., Ciobanu, G.: Describing the Immune System Using Enhanced Mobile Membranes. Electronic Notes in Theoretical Computer Science 194, 5–18 (2008)
2. Aman, B., Ciobanu, G.: Turing Completeness Using Three Mobile Membranes. In: Calude, C.S., Costa, J.F., Dershowitz, N., Freire, E., Rozenberg, G. (eds.) UC 2009. LNCS, vol. 5715, pp. 42–55. Springer, Heidelberg (2009)
3. Aman, B., Ciobanu, G.: Simple, Enhanced and Mutual Mobile Membranes. In: Priami, C., Back, R.-J., Petre, I. (eds.) Transactions on Computational Systems Biology XI. LNCS, vol. 5750, pp. 26–44. Springer, Heidelberg (2009)
4. Aman, B., Ciobanu, G.: Mobility in Process Calculi and Natural Computing. Springer (2011)
5. Krishna, S.N., Aman, B., Ciobanu, G.: On the Computability Power of Membrane Systems with Controlled Mobility. In: Cooper, S.B., Dawar, A., Löwe, B. (eds.) CiE 2012. LNCS, vol. 7318, pp. 626–635. Springer, Heidelberg (2012)
6. Ciobanu, G., Krishna, S.N.: Enhanced Mobile Membranes: Computability Results. Theory of Computing Systems 48(3), 715–729 (2011)
7. Ciobanu, G., Păun, G., Pérez-Jiménez, M.J. (eds.): Applications of Membrane Computing. Springer (2006)
8. Garey, M., Johnson, D.: Computers and Intractability: A Guide to the Theory of NP-Completeness. W.H. Freeman (1979)
9. Krishna, S.N., Ciobanu, G.: On the Computational Power of Enhanced Mobile Membranes. In: Beckmann, A., Dimitracopoulos, C., Löwe, B. (eds.) CiE 2008. LNCS, vol. 5028, pp. 326–335. Springer, Heidelberg (2008)
10. Krishna, S.N., Ciobanu, G.: A $\Sigma_2^P \cup \Pi_2^P$ Lower Bound Using Mobile Membranes. In: Holzer, M., Kutrib, M., Pighizzini, G. (eds.) DCFS 2011. LNCS, vol. 6808, pp. 275–288. Springer, Heidelberg (2011)
11. Krishna, S.N., Păun, G.: P Systems with Mobile Membranes. Natural Computing 4, 255–274 (2005)
12. Meyer, A.R., Stockmeyer, L.J.: The Equivalence Problem for Regular Expressions With Squaring Requires Exponential Time. In: Proc. 13th Ann. Symp. on Switching and Automata Theory, pp. 125–129. IEEE Computer Society Press (1972)
13. Minsky, M.L.: Computation: Finite and Infinite Machines. Prentice-Hall (1967)
14. Papadimitriou, C.H.: Computational Complexity. Addison-Wesley, Reading (1994)
15. Păun, G., Rozenberg, G., Salomaa, A. (eds.): The Oxford Handbook of Membrane Computing. Oxford University Press (2010)
16. Pérez-Jiménez, M.J., Riscos-Núñez, A., Romero-Jiménez, A., Woods, D.: Complexity-Membrane Division, Membrane Creation. In: [15], 302–336

Slicing XML Documents
Using Dependence Graph

Madhusmita Sahu[1] and Durga Prasad Mohapatra[2]

[1] Department of MCA, C V Raman Computer Academy, Bhubaneswar-752054, India
madhu_sahu@yahoo.com
[2] Department of CSE, National Institute of Technology, Rourkela-769008, India
durga@nitrkl.ac.in

Abstract. Program Slicing is a popular technique that assists in various software maintenance activities like debugging, program comprehension and regression testing. It is a decomposition technique used for the extraction of program statements affecting the values computed at some point of interest. We propose a technique for computing slices of XML documents. Given a valid XML document, we produce a new XML document (a slice) containing the relevant information in the original XML document according to some criterion. We output a new DTD such that the computed slice is valid with respect to this DTD. Our technique first slices the associated DTD and the DTD slice is used as a slicing criterion in order to produce the associated XML slice.

Keywords: Tag dependence graph (TDG), Extensible Markup Language(XML), Document Type Definition (DTD).

1 Introduction

Program slicing [8] is a decomposition technique used for the extraction of program statements affecting the values computed at some point of interest. Weiser [5] was the pioneer to develop this technique. A program slice is constructed with respect to a slicing criterion. A slicing criterion is a tuple $< s, V >$, where s is a program point of interest and V is a subset of the program's variables used or defined at s. Program slicing technique is used in many application area of software engineering activities like program understanding, debugging, testing, maintenance, model checking and program comprehension etc.

Because of the quick development of Internet, more and more information are provided through the web pages and thus there is a need for the improvement of the quality of web pages and web applications. The increasing complexity of websites poses a great demand for tools which aid the web designers in their construction and maintenance. The Program Slicing technique can be used for easy understanding, testing and maintenance of web applications.

In this paper, we present a technique for computing slices of XML documents. The rest of the paper is organized as follows. In Section 2, we discuss some related works. Section 3 presents some introduction to XML. Section 4 presents the slicing technique. Section 5 concludes the paper.

C. Hota and P.K. Srimani (Eds.): ICDCIT 2013, LNCS 7753, pp. 444–454, 2013.
© Springer-Verlag Berlin Heidelberg 2013

2   Related Work

The slicing technique proposed by Weiser [5] to compute slice involves solving data flow equations and the slice is known as static backward slice. Ottenstein and Ottenstein [2] developed program dependence graph (PDG) for intraprocedural programs and computed the slice by traversing backward in the PDG. Horwitz et. al. [6] developed System Dependence Graph (SDG) to represent interprocedural programs. They proposed a two-phase algorithm to compute the slices. Larsen and Harrold [4] extended the work of Horwitz et. al. [6] to incorporate object-oriented features. For the first time, Zhao [3] developed the aspect-oriented system dependence graph (ASDG) to represent aspect-oriented programs. Silva [7] proposed a technique to slice XML documents. His technique involves computing the set of relevant elements with respect to the slicing criterion. The computed set is then modified in order to satisfy all the restrictions of the DTD including the attributes. The result is then used as a slicing criterion for the associated DTD and XML. He used the tree-like structure of XML documents and DTDs. In a tree-like structure of XML documents, it is difficult to show the tag values and tag attributes. We have used the graph representation for XML documents and tree representation for DTDs. In this graph representation, the tag values and tag attributes are shown clearly as vertices.

3   XML

The World Wide Web Consortium (W3C) was founded in 1994 to lead the Web by developing common WWW protocols like HTML, CSS and XML. An XML Working Group formed under W3C developed XML in 1996.

XML [1] stands for **EX**tensible **M**arkup **L**anguage. It is designed to describe data. XML tags are not prdefined. The user can define its own tags. XML tags are case sensitive. XML can be used to store and share data. The main building blocks of an XML document are "elements". An independent specification called *Document Type Definition* (DTD) is used to define the legal building blocks of an XML document. It defines the document structure with a list of legal elements. A DTD can be declared inline in the XML document or as an extrenal reference. In a DTD, XML elements are declared with a DTD *element* declaration. An XML document is said to be "well-formed" if it conforms to the standard XML syntax rules. A well-formed XML document is "valid" if it conforms to the rules of a DTD.

Fig 1 shows an example of XML document showing a CD catalog. Fig 2 is the external DTD document defining the elements of XML document given in Fig 1.

4   Slicing Technique

The program slicing technique is typically based on a data structure called Program Dependence Graph (PDG). We create a dependence graph called *Tag De-*

```
1   <CATALOG>
2     <CD>
3       <TITLE> Empire Burlesque </TITLE>
4       <ARTIST> Bob Dylan </ARTIST>
5       <COUNTRY> USA </COUNTRY>
6       <COMPANY> Columbia </COMPANY>
7       <PRICE> 10.90 </PRICE>
8       <YEAR> 1985 </YEAR>
      </CD>
9     <CD>
10      <TITLE> Hide Your Heart </TITLE>
11      <ARTIST> Bonnie Tyler </ARTIST>
12      <COUNTRY> UK </COUNTRY>
13      <COMPANY> CBS Records </COMPANY>
14      <PRICE> 9.90 </PRICE>
15      <YEAR> 1988 </YEAR>
      </CD>
16    <CD>
17      <TITLE> Greatest Hits </TITLE>
18      <ARTIST> Dolly Parton </ARTIST>
19      <COUNTRY> USA </COUNTRY>
20      <COMPANY> RCA </COMPANY>
21      <PRICE> 9.90 </PRICE>
22      <YEAR> 1982 </YEAR>
      </CD>
23    <CD>
24      <TITLE> Still Got The Blues </TITLE>
25      <ARTIST> Gary Moore </ARTIST>
26      <COUNTRY> UK </COUNTRY>
27      <COMPANY> Virgin Records </COMPANY>
28      <PRICE> 10.20 </PRICE>
29      <YEAR> 1990 </YEAR>
      </CD>
    </CATALOG>
```

Fig. 1. An XML document

```
<!ELEMENT CATALOG (CD+)>
<!ELEMENT CD (TITLE,ARTIST,COUNTRY,COMPANY, PRICE,YEAR)>
<!ELEMENT TITLE ANY>
<!ELEMENT ARTIST ANY>
<!ELEMENT COUNTRY ANY>
<!ELEMENT COMPANY ANY>
<!ELEMENT PRICE ANY>
<!ELEMENT YEAR ANY>
```

Fig. 2. A DTD defining XML document given in Fig 1

penedence Graph (TDG) to represent an XML document. We create a tree-like structure called *Document Type Definition Tree* (DTDT) for the DTD.

4.1 Construction of Tag Dependence Graph (TDG) and Document Type Definition Tree (DTDT)

The *Tag Dependence Graph* (TDG) is an arc-classified digraph (V, A), where V is the set of vertices that correspond to the tag elements, tag values and tag attributes of the XML documents and A is the set of arcs or edges between the vertices in V. The TDG for a XML document consists of following types of edges:

1. Value Dependence Edge (VDE): An edge from vertex i to vertex j is said to be *value dependence edge* if i is a vertex representing a tag element and j is a vertex representing the tag value that is displayed on the web page for that tag.

2. Control Dependence Edge (CDE): Let i and j are two vertices representing two tag elements. An edge from vertex i to vertex j is said to be *control dependence edge* if i is the parent element and j is the child element of i.

3. Attribute Dependence Edge (ADE): Let vertex i represents tag element and j is an attribute of that tag element. An edge from vertex i to veretx j is *attribute dependence edge* if i is a tag element and j is an attribute of that tag element.

The algorithm given in Fig 3 is used to construct TDG.

The *Document Type Definition Tree* (DTDT) is a tree (V, A) where V is a set of vertices and A is the set of edges. Each vertex in the tree represents a single element of the XML document of type 'ELEMENT' containing all its attributes. Edges represent aggregation relations between elements. The DTDT is constructed by taking root element in DTD as root of the tree. The child element of every element of type 'ELEMENT' is taken as child vertex.

The algorithm given in Fig 4 is used to construct DTDT.

The TDG and DTDT are shown in Fig 5 and Fig 6 respectively.

```
ConstructTDG()
  for each tag element
    if vertex is not present then
      create a vertex
    end if
  end for
  for each value of a tag element
    create a vertex
    add value dependence edge
  end for
  Let vertices A and B represent tag elements and vertex C represents an attribute of A
  if A is child element of B then
    add control dependence edge from B to A
  end if
  for each attribute C of A
    add attribute dependence edge from A to C
  end for
end ConstructTDG
```

Fig. 3. Algorithm to construct Tag Dependence Graph (TDG)

```
ConstructDTDT()
    for each tag element A
        if A contains a child tag element B then
            add an edge from A to B
        end if
        if A contains a tag attribute C then
            add an edge from A to C
        end if
    end for
end ConstructDTDT
```

Fig. 4. Algorithm to construct Document Type Definition Tree (DTDT)

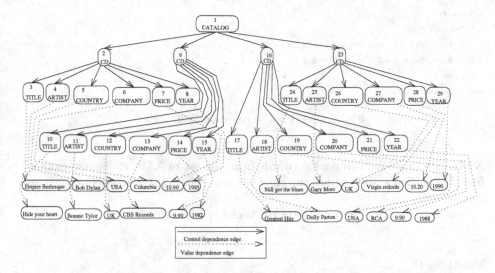

Fig. 5. Tag Dependence Graph (TDG) for the XML document given in Fig 1

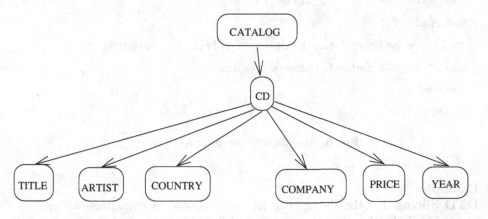

Fig. 6. Document Type Definition Tree (DTDT) for the DTD shown in Fig 2

4.2 Computing Slice

The slicing criterion consists of a set of elements from TDG or DTDT.

DTD Slicing: For a given set of elements from a DTD, we extract the elements from that DTD which are in the path from the root to any of the elements in the slicing criterion. The set of elements produced in the DTD slice is used as a slicing criterion to produce the associated XML slice.

The algorithm to compute the DTD slice is given in Fig 7.

```
DTDSlice()
  ConstructDTDT()
  Traverse backward the path in DTDT from the element in the slicing criterion to the root
  Let S be the set of these elements
  Return S
end DTDSlice
```

Fig. 7. Algorithm to compute DTD slice

XML Slicing: We traverse backwards from the set of XML elements obtained from DTD slicing and extract the elements from the XML document which are in that path.

The algorithm to compute the XML slice is given in Fig 8.

```
XMLSlice()
  ConstructTDG()
  Let s be the slicing criterion
  s=DTDSlice()
  Traverse backward the path in TDG from the element in s
  Let S be the set of these elements
  Return S
end XMLSlice
```

Fig. 8. Algorithm to compute XML slice

Example:
DTD Slicing: Let the slicing criterion consists of a set containing a single element "COUNTRY". The slices computed for the two documents are given in Fig 9 and Fig 10 respectively. Also the slices are shown as bold vertices in Fig 12 and Fig 13 respectively.

XML Slicing: Let the slicing criterion be the element "USA" of type "COUNTRY". We traverse backwards in TDG from the set of elements obtained from DTD slicing. The XML slice is shown in Fig 11 and as bold vertices in Fig 14.

4.3   Complexity

In the following we discuss the space and time complexity of our XML slicing algorithm.

```
1   <CATALOG>
2     <CD>
5       <COUNTRY> USA </COUNTRY>
      </CD>
9     <CD>
12      <COUNTRY> UK </COUNTRY>
      </CD>
16    <CD>
19      <COUNTRY> USA </COUNTRY>
      </CD>
23    <CD>
26      <COUNTRY> UK </COUNTRY>
      </CD>
    </CATALOG>
```

Fig. 9. Slice of XML document given Fig 1

```
<!ELEMENT CATALOG (CD+)>
<!ELEMENT CD (TITLE,ARTIST,COUNTRY,COMPANY, PRICE,YEAR)>
<!ELEMENT COUNTRY ANY>
```

Fig. 10. A slice of DTD given in Fig 2

```
1   <CATALOG>
2     <CD>
5       <COUNTRY> USA </COUNTRY>
      </CD>
16    <CD>
19      <COUNTRY> USA </COUNTRY>
      </CD>
    </CATALOG>
```

Fig. 11. An XML slice of XML document given in Fig 1

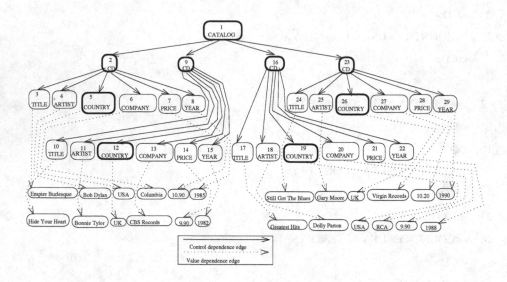

Fig. 12. Slice of XML document given Fig 1

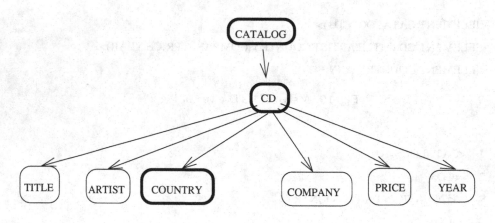

Fig. 13. A slice of DTD given in Fig 2

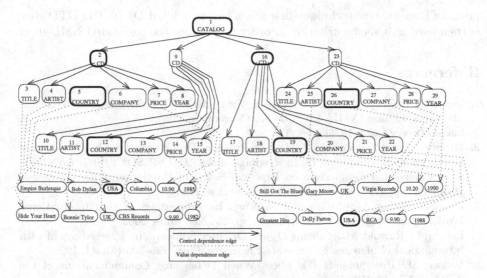

Fig. 14. An XML slice of XML document given in Fig 1

Space Complexity: Let P be a XML document having n statements in which there are statements corresponding to k types of tags. Let the number of times of occurrences of each tag be m and there are l number of tag attributes. The associated DTD contains statements corresponding to k tags and l tag attributes. The space requirement for storing TDG is $O((kml)^2)$ which is in turn $O(n^2)$. The space requirement for storing DTDT is $O(2^{kl})$. We require an additional space for storing DTD slice which is $O(kl)$ which is in turn $O(n)$. Also we require a space for storing XML slice which is $O(n)$. Thus our slicing algorithm requires $O(n^2)$ spaces where n is the number of statements in XML document.

Time Complexity: Let n be the number of statements in a XML document P. The time needed to compute the XML slice depends on the following factors:

(i) The time for constructing the TDG and DTDT which is $O(n^2)$.
(ii) The time for computing DTD slice by traversing the DTDT which is $O(n^2)$.
(iii) The time for computing XML slice by traversing the TDG and reaching at the specified node which is $O(n^2)$.

The total time requirement for computing slices is $O(n^2)$ where n is the number of statements in the XML document. The slices can also be extracted in $O(n^2)$ time.

5   Conclusion

In this paper, we propose a technique to compute slices of XML documents. First, we construct the TDG for XML document and DTDT for DTD. Then for a given slicing criterion, we traverse backwards in TDG and DTDT from the point of interest. Our technique first slices the associated DTD. The DTD slice is then used as a slicing criterion in order to produce the associated XML slice.

References

1. Bray, T., Paoli, J., Sperberg-McQueen, C.M., Maler, E., Yergeau, F.: Extensible Markup Language (XML) 1.0, 5th edn. (November 2008), http://www.w3.org/TR/RECu-xml
2. Ottenstein, K.J., Ottenstein, L.M.: The Program Dependence Graph in a Software Development Environment. In: Proceedings of the ACM SIGSOFT/SIGPLAN Software Engineering Symposium on Practical Software Development Environments, 19th edn., pp. 177–184. ACM SIGPLAN Notices (1984)
3. Zhao, J.: Slicing Aspect-Oriented Software. In: Proceedings of 10th International Workshop on Program Comprehension, pp. 251–260 (June 2002)
4. Larsen, L., Harrold, M.J.: Slicing Object-Oriented Software. In: Proceedings of 18th International Conference on Software Engineering, pp. 495–505 (March 1996)
5. Weiser, M.: Programmers Use Slices When Debugging. Communications of the ACM 25(7), 446–452 (1982)
6. Horwitz, S., Reps, T., Binkley, D.: Inter-Procedural Slicing Using Dependence Graphs. ACM Transactions on Programming Languages and Systems 12(1), 26–60 (1990)
7. Silva, J.: Slicing XML Documents. Electronic Notes in Theoretical Computer Science, pp. 187–192 (2006)
8. Binkley, D.W., Gallagher, K.B.: Program Slicing. Advances in Computers 43 (1996)

Effective Web-Service Discovery
Using K-Means Clustering

A. Santhana Vijayan[1] and S.R. Balasundaram[2]

[1] Department of Computer Science and Engineering,
National Institute of Technology, Tiruchirappalli – 620 015 Tamilnadu, India
vijayana@nitt.edu
[2] Department of Computer Applications,
National Institute of Technology, Tiruchirappalli – 620 015 Tamilnadu, India
blsundar@nitt.edu

Abstract. Web Services are proving to be a convenient way to integrate distributed software applications. As service-oriented architecture is getting popular, vast numbers of web services have been developed all over the world. But it is a challenging task to find the relevant or similar web services using web services registry such as UDDI. Current UDDI search uses keywords from web service and company information in its registry to retrieve web services. This information cannot fully capture user's needs and may miss out on potential matches. Underlying functionality and semantics of web services need to be considered. In this study, we explore the resemblance among web services using WSDL document features such as WSDL Content and Web Services name. We compute the similarity of web services and use this data to generate clusters using K-means clustering algorithm. This approach has really yielded good results and can be efficiently used by any web service search engine to retrieve similar or related web services.

Keywords: Web Service, WSDL document features, K-means Clustering, WV Tool.

1   Introduction

A Web service is a method of communication between two electronic devices over the web (internet). It is a software system designed to support interoperable machine-to-machine interaction over a network. It has an interface described in a machine-processable format (specifically Web Services Description Language, known by the acronym WSDL). The term Web-service describes a standardized way of integrating Web-based applications using the XML, SOAP, WSDL and UDDI open standards over an Internet protocol backbone [7]. XML is used to tag the data, SOAP is used to transfer the data (bind), WSDL is used for describing the services available (publish) and UDDI is used for listing what services are available (find). Fig.1. shows the web services triad that includes a broker, a service provider and a service requestor. Used primarily as a means for businesses to communicate with each other and with clients,

C. Hota and P.K. Srimani (Eds.): ICDCIT 2013, LNCS 7753, pp. 455–464, 2013.
© Springer-Verlag Berlin Heidelberg 2013

Web services allow organizations to communicate data without intimate knowledge of each other's IT systems behind the firewall.

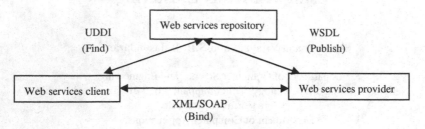

Fig. 1. The Web Services triad

1.1   Classes of Web Services

There are mainly two major classes of Web services, REST-compliant Web services, in which the primary purpose of the service is to manipulate XML representations of Web resources using a uniform set of "stateless" operations; and arbitrary Web services, in which the service may expose an arbitrary set of operations.

1.2   Problems Encountered in Retrieval of Non-semantic Web Services

There are so many problems encountered during the search for non-semantic web services. There is a difficulty in the discovery of non-semantic Web services through search engines as these engines do not recognize the Web service functionalities summarized in the WSDL file. Based on the Web service name, location and business defined in the WSDL file, the search engines partly relate the search terms entered by the user in order to retrieve the results back. Web service name is essential as a part of the search query in order to retrieve the exact service required. Hence, the user must take care in using the accurate keywords so that appropriate services can be obtained.

There is a possibility for the user to ignore services because of using alternate meanings for the keywords. For example, a service that includes "motorbike" in its name may not be retrieved from a query looking for "two wheeler". In order to effectively improve the service discovery process by tumbling the search space, clustering techniques can be used to group similar services based on their functionality which improves the search engine retrieval.

The rest of our paper is organized as follows. Section 2 gives a brief introduction on existing methods and related work. The structure of WSDL documents is described in Section 3. Our proposed clustering approach is introduced in Section 4. The feature extraction from WSDL documents is explained in Section 5. Section 6 describes the feature integration process in order to set up the relation between Web services. Section 7 includes the experiments and results. Finally, Section 8 concludes our paper and summarizes future research activities.

2   Existing Methods and Related Work

Nowadays, service discovery has become a recent research issue because of increasing use of web services by most of the web application developers. WSDL documents are used to describe the non-semantic Web services where as Web ontology languages (OWL-S) [2] or Web Service Modeling Ontology (WSMO) [3] are used to describe the semantic web services. Non-semantic Web services are becoming more popular because of the support obtained from both the industry and development tools. Based on the various Web services description techniques, the process of service discovery is somewhat different. By using various web service description methods, non-semantic web services can be discovered whereas semantic Web services can be discovered using web ontologies such as OWL-S [2] and WSMO [3]. In our approach, we focus on the discovery of non-semantic Web services. According to the approach proposed by Nayak [5], the discovery of web services can be improved using the Jaccard coefficient that determines the similarity between Web services. With respect to other users' experiences on similar queries, Nayak [5] give the users with associated search terms. In our approach, the search space is reduced by clustering the Web services based on their functionality. We extract two features such as WSDL content and web service name to compute the similarity between Web services. We modify the approach used by Kahlid Elgazzar et. al [1].

3   WSDL Document Structure

A WSDL document defines services as collections of network endpoints, or ports. In WSDL, the abstract definition of endpoints and messages is separated from their concrete network deployment or data format bindings[7]. This allows the reuse of abstract definitions: messages, which are abstract descriptions of the data being exchanged, and port types, which are abstract collections of operations. The concrete protocol and data format specifications for a particular port type constitutes a reusable binding.

A WSDL document uses the following elements in the definition of network services:

<Types> – a container for data type definitions using some type system (XSD).

<Message> – an abstract, typed definition of the data being communicated.

<Operation> – an abstract description of an action supported by the service.

<Port Type> –an abstract set of operations supported by one or more endpoints.

<Binding> – a concrete protocol and data format specification for particular port type.

<Port> – a single endpoint defined as a combination of binding and network address.

<Service> – a collection of related endpoints.

WSDL does not introduce a new type definition language. WSDL recognizes the need for rich type systems for describing message formats, and supports the XML Schemas specification (XSD) as its canonical type system [7].

4   Proposed Clustering Method

Our proposed method is based on the information available in WSDL documents. We find the WSDL documents in order to extract two features such as WSDL content and web service name which describe the semantic and behaviour of the Web service. The functionality of a Web service can be revealed from these features [5]. These features are then integrated together such that the web services can be clustered to form similar groups based on their functionally by using K-means clustering algorithm. A service search engine can use this step as a precursor in categorizing the Web services with users' requests.

5   Feature Extraction from WSDL Document

This section describes how the two proposed features such as WSDL Content and Web Service Name can be extracted from WSDL documents. Fig. 2. illustrates the steps involved in feature extraction process.

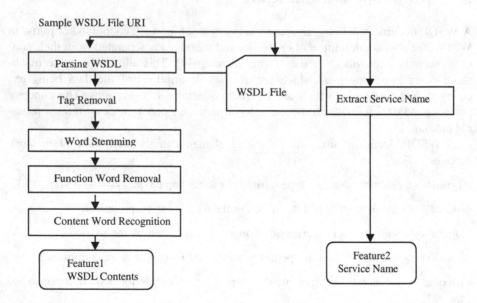

Fig. 2. Block diagram of feature extraction process

Feature 1: WSDL Content

The WSDL URI can be used to read the WSDL document contents. Let each f_i denote a WSDL document which describes a Web service s_i. A vector of meaningful content words for the given Web service s_i can be extracted by means of processing the WSDL document contents. In our approach, the vector can be constructed by using the following five steps.

1) Parsing WSDL: A vector of tokens T_i can be produced by parsing the given WSDL document contents with respect to white spaces.

2) Tag removal: In order to obtain a vector consisting only of valid content words, all tokens from T_i that are part of a XML tag are removed. As all XML tags specified in a given WSDL document are predefined, the process of removing XML tags from the tokenized vector is simple.

3) Word stemming: With the help of Porter stemmer algorithm [11], only the relevant words in T_i are reduced to their base words. Tokens among a common stem will generally have the similar meaning, for example, 'establish', 'established', 'establishing', and 'establishment' all have the same stem 'establish'. With respect to word deviations in the semantic of a Web service, using one or all of the tokens will not make a distinction. But, the words that appear frequently are more important when compared to others. The number of occurrences will be considered in the following steps.

4) Function word removal: Function words are said to be autonomous with respect to one another. With the help of Poisson distribution to model word occurrence in documents [6], function words can be differentiated from content words. Using this step all function words from the service word vector can be removed. By calculating the overestimation factor for all words in the word vector, we can decide which word is a function word as follows:

$$V_{ij} = \frac{f_{ij}}{f_{dj}} \tag{1}$$

f_{ij} is the number of occurrences of term 'i' in document j.
f_{dj} is the number of terms occurring in document j.

The overestimation factor [6] for all words in T_i and the average $avg[\wedge]$ of all overestimation factors can be calculated as follows. An overestimation factor threshold ($\wedge^{thre}$) is formulated as follows [6].

$$\wedge thre = \begin{cases} avg[\wedge] \text{ if } avg[\wedge] > 1 \\ \quad 1 \quad \text{ otherwise} \end{cases} \tag{2}$$

Any word is said to be a content word if it has an overestimation factor above the $\wedge^{thre}$. Otherwise the word is termed as a function word that should be removed from the vector T_i. By using this step, all function words from the service word vector can be removed.

5) Content word recognition: Certain general computing content words such as 'data','web','port', etc. are typically present in WSDL documents. We cannot distinguish between Web services based on these words as they appear in most WSDL files. The goal of this step is to eliminate words which do not correspond to the specific semantics of the Web service. The k-means clustering algorithm [8] with k = 2 on T_i is then applied to cluster the remaining words into two groups such that one group corresponds to the meaning of the Web service where as the other group is meant for general computing words. As the number of clusters is known earlier, K-means algorithm is used as it is simple, fast, and efficient. Normalized Google Distance (NGD) [9] is used as a featureless distance measure between two words x and y as follows.

$$NGD = \frac{max\{log\ f(x), log\ f(y)\} - log\ f(x,y)}{log\ M - min\{log\ f(x), log\ f(y)\}} \tag{3}$$

where M is the total number of web pages searched by Google; f(x) and f(y) are the number of hits for search terms x and y, respectively; and f(x, y) is the number of web pages on which both x and y occur. If the two search terms x and y never occur together on the same web page, but do occur separately, the normalized Google distance between them is infinite. If both terms always occur together, their NGD is zero, or equivalent to the coefficient between x squared and y squared.

Based on the similarity factor calculated using Equation (5), similar web services can be grouped for efficient service discovery.

Feature 2 : Web Service Name
The composite name such as 'ComputerArchitecture' can be split up into multiple names based on the assumption that a capital letter indicates the start of a new word. The similarity between services names can be then found using NGD as follows:

$$sim(sname_i, sname_j) = 1 - NGD(sname_i, sname_j) \tag{4}$$

where $sname_i$ and $sname_j$ are the names of the Web services s_i and s_j respectively.

6   Feature Integration

K- means clustering algorithm is used to cluster similar Web services based on the two similarity features presented above as it is computationally inexpensive. The similarity factor $\Theta(s_i, s_j)$ between two Web services s_i and s_j can be measured as follows:

$$\Theta(S_i, S_j) = 0.5S(T_i, T_j) + 0.5sim(sname_i, sname_j) \tag{5}$$

$\Theta(s_i, s_j)$ is equal to "1" if the two services are identical and
$\Theta(s_i, s_j)$ is equal to "0" if they are completely different.

We normalize $\Theta(s_i, s_j)$ by assigning weights of 0.5 to each of the two similarity features. We determined experimentally that these weights give reasonable results. In Equation (5), T_i and T_j are the content word vectors of services s_i, s_j respectively.

$S(T_i, T_j)$ is the average similarity between the content word vectors T_i, and T_j and is calculated with

$$S(T_i, T_j) = \frac{\Sigma a \, \varepsilon \, T_i \, \Sigma b \, \varepsilon \, T_j \, \text{sim}(a, b)}{|T_i| |T_j|}$$ (6)

where sim(a, b) is the featureless similarity factor computed between words a and b using NGD based on the word coexistence in Web pages. sim(a, b) is calculated using

$$\text{sim}(a, b) = 1 - NGD(a, b)$$ (7)

where a and b are the two most important content vector words belong to T_i and T_j respectively.

7   Experiments and Results

We use two criteria to evaluate the performance of our approach, namely Precision and Recall [10]. Precision and Recall have been often used to evaluate information retrieval schemes [4].We extend the use of these two measures to evaluate our approach as follows:

$$\text{Precision} = \frac{\Sigma_{i \in C} P_{c_i}}{\text{length}(C)} , \, P_{c_i} = \frac{\text{succ}(c_i)}{\text{succ}(c_i) + \text{mispl}(c_i)}$$ (8)

$$\text{recall} = \frac{\Sigma_{i \in C} R_{c_i}}{\text{length}(C)} , \, R_{c_i} = \frac{\text{succ}(c_i)}{\text{succ}(c_i) + \text{missed}(c_i)}$$ (9)

where c_i is the cluster i, P_{c_i} and R_{c_i} are precision and recall for cluster c_i respectively, succ(c_i) is the number of Web services successfully placed in the proper cluster c_i, mispl(c_i) is the number of Web services that are incorrectly clustered into c_i, missed(c_i) is the number of Web services that should be clustered into c_i but are incorrectly placed in other clusters, and length(C) is the number of clusters.

Our experiments are based on the WSDL files obtained from online Web service providers and brokers. The contents of the WSDL file can be directly obtained from the corresponding URI. Using K-means clustering algorithm, the WSDL documents are grouped together to form the following two categories such as "Computer Architecture" and "Weather".

The contents of the WSDL documents are parsed in order to produce the content word vector T_i. The next step is to obtain a vector consisting only of valid content words without the XML tags by using the java library word vector tool.

Using the Porter stemmer method, the vectors obtained in the previous step are reduced to their roots. Then the function words and content words can be differentiated by calculating the overestimation factor for all the words in each vector. The Term Frequency can be calculated using the WV Tool. The content words for the Web services can be then discovered by clustering each word vector into two groups using the k-means clustering algorithm, in which NGD is used as a featureless similarity measure between words.

We use Python as a scripting language for calculating the NGD and similarity factor. Feature extraction and integration is implemented using Java.

The word vectors and term frequencies generated as a result of feature extraction process for the sample web service categories such as 'weather' and 'computer architecture' are shown in Table. 1.

Table 1. Block Word vectors and Term frequencies generated for sample files

Term Frequency	Word Vector
0.760286	Computer
0.304114	technology
0.304115	year
0.076029	gener
0.152057	electron
0.076029	creat
0.076029	person
0.228086	perform
0.076029	memor
0.076029	stor
0.076029	rapid
0.076029	innov
0.152057	improvement
0.076029	emerg
0.076029	highes
0.152057	cost
0.076029	bus
0.228077	microprocessor

The clusters formed with respect to the sample service category files such as 'weather' and 'computer architecture' using K-means clustering algorithm with k=2 from content word recognition step are shown in Fig. 3.

The NGD and Similarity values obtained from feature integration process are tabulated in Table. 2.

The performance of our approach using recall and precision was compared with [1]'s approach and the results are tabulated in Table 3 and Table 4.

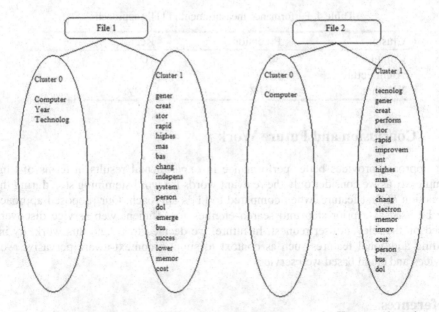

Fig. 3. Clusters generated from Content word recognition step by K-means clustering

Table 2. NGD and Similarity values generated by feature integration process

S.No	Word1	Word2	NGD	Similarity
1	computer	computer	0	1
2	computer	weather	0.52845	0.47154
3	computer	earth	0.39224	0.60775
4	computer	system	0.71737	0.28262
5	technology	computer	0.42513	0.57486
6	technology	weather	0.22959	0.77040
7	technology	earth	0.24365	0.75364
8	technology	system	0.26721	0.73278
9	weather	weather	0	1
10	weather	earth	0.34830	0.65169
11	computers	computer-architecture	0.21067	0.78932
12	computers	earth-weather	0.12563	0.87436

Table 3. Performance measurement of our approach

Cluster	Precision	Recall
Computer Architecture	100%	75.2%
Weather	75.1%	100%

Table 4. Performance measurement of [1]'s approach

Cluster	Precision	Recall
Computer Architecture	80.2%	100%
Weather	94.1%	100%

8　Conclusion and Future Work

Our approach provides better performance in experimental results in terms of time complexity as we consider only the relevant words for word stemming step during the extraction of first feature, when compared to [1]'s approach. Our proposed approach can be used as a prior step into search engines for efficient web service discovery based on the relevant user request. In future, we decided to extend this work, by including additional features such as context to support context-aware pervasive web services and cloud based web services.

References

1. Elgazzar, K., Hassan, A.E., Martin, P.: Clustering WSDL Documents to Bootstrap the Discovery of Web Services. In: 2010 IEEE International Conference on Web Services, vol. 1, pp. 287–294 (2010)
2. Burstein, M., Hobbs, J., Lassila, O., Mcdermott, D., Mcilraith, S., Narayanan, S., Paolucci, M., Parsia, B., Payne, T., Sirin, E., Srinivasan, N., Sycara, K., Martin, D.: OWL-S: Semantic Markup for Web Services. W3C Member Submission (2004)
3. Lausen, H., Polleres, A.: Web Service Modeling Ontology (WSMO). In: W3C Member Submission (2005)
4. Deng, S., Wu, Z., Wu, J., Li, Y., Yin, J.: An Efficient Service Discovery Method and its Application. International Journal of Web Services Research 6(4), 94–117 (2009)
5. Nayak, R.: Data mining in Web services discovery and monitoring. International Journal of Web Services Research 5(1), 63–81 (2008)
6. Liu, W., Wong, W.: Web service clustering using text mining techniques. International Journal of Agent Oriented Software Engineering 3(1), 6–26 (2009)
7. Coyle, F.P.: XML, Web Services and the Data Revolution. Pearson Education, South Asia (2002)
8. Jain, A.K., Dubes, R.C.: Algorithms for clustering data. Prentice-Hall, Englewood Cliffs (1988)
9. Cilibrasi, R.L., Vitnyi, P.M.B.: The Google similarity distance. IEEE Transactions on Knowledge and Data Engineering 19(3), 370–383 (2007)
10. Makhoul, J., Kubala, F., Schwartz, R., Weischedel, R.: Performance measures for information extraction. In: DARPA Broadcast News Workshop, Herdon VA (February 1999)
11. Porter, M.F.: An Algorithm for Suffix Stripping. Program 14(3), 130–137 (1980)

SPARSHA:
A Low Cost Refreshable Braille for Deaf-Blind People for Communication with Deaf-Blind and Non-disabled Persons

Ruman Sarkar[1], Smita Das[1], and Sharmistha Roy[2]

[1] Computer Science & Engineering Department, National Institute of Technology, Agartala
[2] School of Computer Engineering, KIIT University, Bhubaneswar
{ruman10k,smitadas.nita,sharmistharoy11}@gmail.com

Abstract. In the modern epoch, one of the most imperative issues is the nuisance of day-to-day survival of the physically disabled people. Recent development in science and technology has provided a helping hand towards those physically challenged people in the form of different hearing enhancement tools for deaf people, vision enhancement technology for blind people and different audio-vision combinational devices for deaf-blind people. But in true sense, assistive technologies, that too within budget for the lonely deaf-blind people has not been sufficient at all for many years. In our paper, we have tried to introduce SPARSHA which is a low cost refreshable Braille device for deaf-blind and blind people to communicate with other deaf-blind people, blind people and with the nondisabled people. SPARSHA is an electronic device which is connected with a computer and acquires the signal corresponding to alphabet, digit or special symbols and displays the corresponding Braille to represent those alphabet, digit or special symbols. There are six pin to represent the character equivalent to the Braille; similarly we have used six pins to represent SPARSHA. These pins are movable and they can be individually controlled .They can go downward or can go upward. From computer an equivalent signal representing alphabet, digit etc. is sent to the device and the corresponding character is displayed in Braille. Therefore, SPARSHA is a very cost effective and portable Braille display which may provide an affordable way to the blind or deaf-blind people who are facing trouble in communication with the other disabled or non disabled persons in their daily life.

Keywords: Deaf-blind people, Assistive Technology, Braille display, Tactile Display, Refreshable Braille Technology, Human Computer Interaction.

1 Introduction

World Health Organization has given a statistics that there are more than 314 million people in the world who are visually impaired among which around 45 million people are completely blind [6]. Tactile and auditory feelings are one of the most important

C. Hota and P.K. Srimani (Eds.): ICDCIT 2013, LNCS 7753, pp. 465–475, 2013.

forms of communication for blind people with the world [7]. A visual disfigurement forces a person to build up a strong aptitude to make functional use of other often-neglected sanity. As a consequence, the sense of touch can be developed to interpret stylish tactile patterns such as Braille and gather an amazing amount of information through delicate tactile cues such as the rubbing of a white cane against the ground. This awareness and appreciation for the sense of touch makes visually impaired persons innate users of excited technologies and invaluable allies in the progress of experimental interfaces that aspire to communicate information through this underused sense.

Tactile displays, which generate information by inspiring the sense of touch, depend on actuators to create spatial resolution in terms of three-dimensional contractions and movement. Tactile display is kind of refreshable Braille display that converts electronic text information from a computer to Braille dots for the blind to read [1]. Sophisticated tactile displays cannot be made available commonly, primarily due to their higher cost, large size and slow actuator's response etc. For the above mentioned limitations these are only be made available in the educational institutes, organizations for experimental purposes.

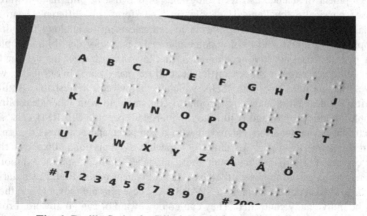

Fig. 1. Braille Script for Blind people for reading information

Refreshable Braille cell display permits the dots of the Braille character to be increased or decreased either mechanically or electronically or through any other mechanism. A fastidious transformation of dots in the up or down arrangement symbolizes a particular character or alphabet [8]. The refreshable Braille devices can fabricate one line displays with up to 80 characters per line. The refreshable Braille displays can rapidly change the lives of the visually impaired people by enabling them to capture assistance from the state of the art digital technology and many imminent computer controlled equipments. As sophisticated technology makes Braille easier to produce, the blind are faced with the unavoidable problem of high cost. It has been found that a Braille printers cost from $1,700 to $80,000 and refreshable Braille displays cost from $3,500 to $15,000 (usually around $5,000 per 40 cells). Unfortunately, most visually impaired people can't afford these prices and the available machines are limited mainly to business and educational uses.

2   Background of Braille

Braille is a recognizable system that contains few dots which enables visually impaired people to read and write through touch and feel as a alternative of vision [9]. Braille was devised in 1821 by Louis Braille, a Frenchman. Each Braille symbol consists of patterns of raised tangential dots arranged in groups of six in fix matrix called a cell [10]. The Braille system also includes several symbols to represent punctuation, mathematics and scientific characters, music, computer notation and foreign languages.

For the purpose of exchanging a few words with other people in everyday life, different kinds of devices have been developed to offer auditory and tactile information to the visually impaired people in modern days. These devices can be categorized into two different types namely: mechanical stimulating devices and electrical stimulating devices [11]. Electrical stimulating mechanism directly triggers nerve fibres inside the skin with electrical current from surface electrodes thus generating sensations of pressure or vibration [12]. Due to the invasive nature of the electrical stimulating device, more researchers focus on researching mechanical stimulating device which uses an array of pins as a graphic display or a Braille display. The pins usually are driven by piezoelectric actuators [13] or solenoid coils [14], [15].

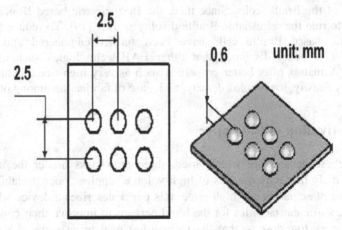

Fig. 2. International building standard for a Braille cell

3   Refreshable Braille Display

There is a sequence of dots or pins in a refreshable Braille cell display device which can be perpendicularly elevated or lowered mechanically or electronically using any other mechanism. A particular character is represented by the combination of dots in the elevated and slender position. The blind people can read these characters by touching the dots of their fingers. There are usually 40, 65, or 80 arrays (characters) per line of text [16]. A refreshable Braille display is typically coupled to a computer and it works in amalgamation with a screen reader. The users provide inputs to the computer with the assistance of a Braille keyboard and access the output in the Braille cells through a Braille displayer. The refreshable Braille displays are generally situated under the keyboards so that the users could easily access the Braille cells in connection with the keyboard [17].

The refreshable Braille displays have been modified a long way from the time of electromechanical actuator based displays based on solenoids, developed by Mr. Schaefer and marketed by Maryland Computer Services way back in the mid-1970s [18]. The Braille tip [19] was moved up or down on passing an electric current through a solenoid which caused the magnetic field to force the solenoid rod to pull an actuator. There were matters of higher power utilization associated with it. For avoidance of power consumption, the pins were permanently set aside in a raised position which implies that the readers would not be able to touch the display while it was refreshing. In the late 1970s, the idea of Braille displays based on the principle of piezoelectricity was introduced by Oleg Tretiakoff. Application of a potential difference between the opposite faces of the piezoelectric material led to a transformation in its shape and dimensions which was used to lift and lower the Braille tip. These Braille cells were less expensive and at the same time consumed less power for their working. In addition, the readers could touch the display while it was refreshing [19]. Questionably, this became one of the first commercially available refreshable Braille displays used by the visually impaired people. In 1980s, the Tieman Group pioneered the development of Braille cells improving the feel and the portability of the Braille cells. Since then, the Piezoelectric based Braille cells have continued to rule the refreshable Braille display market [19]. To reduce the cost, the piezoelectric based Braille cells have been further engineered and developed. However, it is being disagreed that other EAP technologies such as Dielectric Elastomer Actuators offer better properties such as very high linear actuation strain, high energy density, lower mass density, and, ease of fabrication among others [20].

4   Motivation of the Paper

Although these devices are widely used, three drawbacks hinder the use of these devices in daily life: requirements of high-voltage supplies, poor portability because of large size of actuators and high price, this paper describes a device which tries to provide the sufficient facilities for the blind persons to improve their communicating skills at a very low cost so that the technology may bring some changes in their communication with the World.

In this paper, tactile sensations synthesized using programmable pins to represent the standard six cells Braille to improve both the accessibility of textual content for visually impaired persons, and the understanding of this approach to computerized tactile stimulation. Braille has played a significant role in the empowerment of visually impaired persons by defining a tactile code that can not only be read but also written, and hence enabling literacy. Refreshable Braille displays, and more recently voice synthesis hardware and software, have for many years maintained the accessibility of written information as it migrated gradually to digital media. These solutions nevertheless present drawbacks. Refreshable Braille displays are limited to a single line by space and cost constraints yet generally more expensive that the personal computer they are used with. Voice synthesis, on the other hand, reduces control over the reading rate and provides an all Introduction 2 together different communication medium that hides individual characters and hence a crucial aspect of the written language. There is therefore much room for improvement and innovation in the delivery of textual information to visually impaired readers. The use of these technologies with screen readers has nevertheless provided an acceptable solution for access to computer interfaces and digital media until recently.

The increasingly pervasive use of visual content, however, threatens to severely limit the usability of digital interfaces and hence exclude the visually impaired community from some of the most exciting innovations. Graphical information is no longer restricted to isolated pictures and diagrams, and instead often provides the bulk of the content in applications such interactive mapping systems or a coherent structure for textual content in documents such as web pages.

5   Proposed System Architecture

The current paper is dedicated to make affordable Braille displays using innovative technology. The goal for this thesis was to create a greatly simplified in-line refreshable Braille display which is reliable and easy to use, using the fewest, most cost-efficient parts. The following are the desired features for the proposed display:

    a.   Standard Cell Size
    b.   Fast refresh rate
    c.   Low cost
    d.   Portable
    e.   Small size

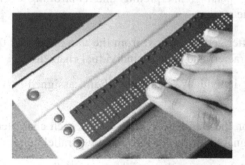

Fig. 3. Schematic view of a tactile display

Figure 3 show that a tactile display can translate electronic text information to the Blind people readable form.

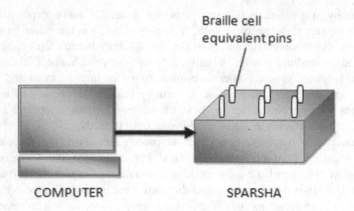

Fig. 4. SPARSHA: refreshable Braille display architecture

Figure 4 shows the block diagram of SPARSHA. The concept behind this Braille display is to represent the standard Braille code in the form of six pin which represent the six cell of Braille display technique. In this proposed model of Braille display the display device is connected to the computer system and gets the equivalent signals from the computer to display any particular character in Braille code. After getting the signal form the computer the device moves upward the particular pins for representing the particular character. for the next character the device gets refreshed and displays the next character in the similar way and so on until the text is displayed.

Inside the device there are six stepper motors which work as the actuator and they helps to move the pins upward and downward. The computer has an application program to take the text in English and the application program performs different language processing, parsing, interpreting and controlling operations to meet the desire objective of the system.

Text Processing: After getting the text from the non blind user the program split the text into array of characters and treats as individual character.

Interpreter: This individual character then assigned the standard Braille representation.

Controller: Based on the Braille representation of each character the program sends the corresponding signal to the device through the parallel port.

Inside the Device: After getting the signal corresponding to any particular character the signal is first amplified to level so that the signals can drive the stepper motors. The motor rotates and the mechanically attached particular pins move upward to represent the particular character.

In the proposed model of refreshable Braille display, the different components which are used as the part of the system are low cost. The six stepper motors used for moving the pins each of costs approximately $12. The other actuator parts required for representing each dot cost approximately $6.The total manufacturing cost of the refreshable Braille display may cost about $110.

6   Working Principle of SPARSHA

The working principle of the Control Program driven by the computer is depicted in the following figure 5 and the steps of the control program are as following:

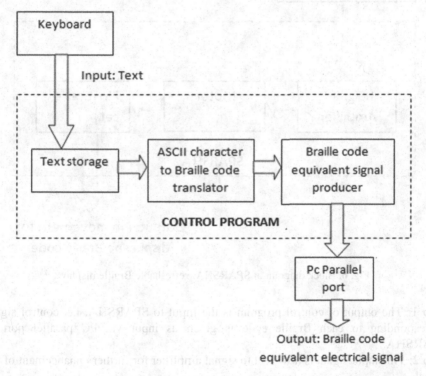

Fig. 5. Block diagram of the Control Program to control the display

Step 1: Text (alphabet, digit or special character) input is given through the keyboard by non disabled person.
Step 2: Given input is stored in the computer memory.
Step 3: Stored input is now split into array of characters.
Step 4: Each individual character is allocated to the standard Braille representations for translating each ASCII character to corresponding Braille code.
Step 5: Signal corresponding to each Braille code is generated and sent to electromechanical display device via the parallel port of computer.

The following figure 6 represents the SPARSHA device. The steps of working principle of SPARSHA are as following:

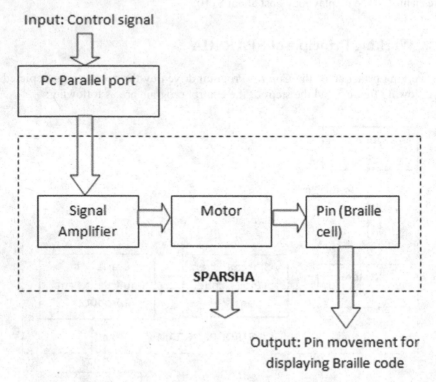

Fig. 6. Block diagram of SPARSHA: refreshable Braille display

Step 1: The output of control program is the input to SPARSHA, i.e. control signal corresponding to each Braille code is given as input via PC parallel port to SPARSHA.

Step 2: This input signal is now sent to signal amplifier for further enhancement of the signal.

Step 3: Amplified signal is used to drive the stepper motors.

Step 4: Mechanically connected Stepper motor, with one of the six pins of the Braille cell, rotates and forces the pin to move upward for representation of particular Braille character.

Step 5: To display the next Braille character refresh the display device and repeat Step 1 – Step 4.

7   Simulation of the Proposed Control Program

The simulation of the proposed control program of the SPARSHA device is shown below:

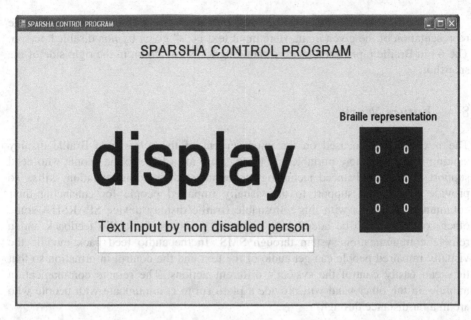

Fig. 7. Snapshot of SPARSHA control program

In figure 7, snapshot is taken from the main program which shows the GUI where text input (alphabet, digit or special characters) can be given by the non disabled person. As no input is yet given so corresponding Braille representation is empty.

The input text will be stored in the computer memory for further processing.

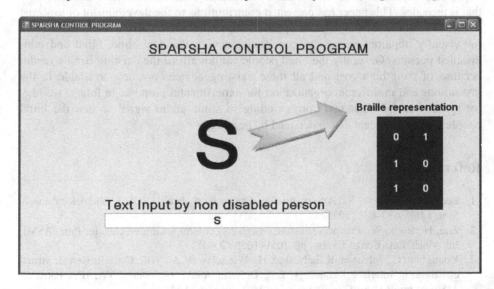

Fig. 8. Snapshot of Braille representation

In figure 8, snapshot is taken from the control program which shows the Braille representation of the given input. Here input text is "s" given by non disabled person. The 6 pin Braille representation corresponding to "s" is shown in the right side of the snapshot.

8   Future Work

The next work is focused on the improvement of the refreshable Braille display making it fast and more portable and more easily affordable to the people who need support from the advanced technology to enhance their communication skills. To provide a complete support to the visually impaired people for enhancing their communication skills with this refreshable Braille display device SPARSHA some other components to be added later as audio generator for audio feedback and a remote communication system through SMS. In the audio feed back module the visually impaired people can get audio of the text and the control information so that they can easily control the system's different actions. The remote communication module on the other hand will provide a platform to communicate with people who are in a far distance through.

9   Conclusions

Despite the growing popularity of voice synthesis for the accessibility of textual information, Braille remains a preferred or secondary medium for many visually impaired persons for the level of control over reading that it affords and granular view that it provides. This paper has presented contributions to the development of low cost refreshable Braille display and its applications to provide an affordable portable tool for visually impaired persons to communicate with the deaf-blind, blind and non-disabled persons. Generally the blind people cannot afford the existing Braille reader because of their high cost and all these existing devices are only available in the institutions and in different organization for experimental purpose. In future, we may try to convert the input text corresponding to some audio signal so that the blind people who are not deaf can understand by hearing.

References

1. Lee, J.S., Lucyszyn, S.: A micromachined refreshable Braille cell. J. Microelectromech. Syst. 14(4), 673–682 (2005)
2. Zhu, H., Book, W.: Practical structure design and control for digital clay. In: Proc. ASME Int. Mech. Eng. Congr. Expos., pp. 1051–1058 (2004)
3. Youngblut, C., Johnston, R.E., Nash, S.H., Wienclaw, R.A., Will, C.A.: Review of virtual environment interface technology, Inst. Defense Anal., Alexandria, VA, IDA Paper P-3186, http://handle.dtic.mil/100.2/ADA314134

4. Benali-Khoudja, M., Hafez, M., Alexandre, J.M., Kheddar, A.A.K.A., Moreau, V.A.M.V.: VITAL: A new low-cost vibro-tactile display system. In: Proc. IEEE Int. Conf. Robot. Autom., vol. 1, pp. 721–726 (2004)
5. Konyo, M., Todokoro, S.: Artificial tactile feel display using EAP actuator. Worldwide ElectroActive Polymers, Artificial Muscles 2(1), 1–16 (2000)
6. Bar-Cohen, Y.: Electroactive polymers for refreshable Braille displays, SPIE Newsroom (2009), DOI: 10.1117/2.1200909.1738
7. Koo, I.M., Jung, K., Koo, J.C., Nam, J.D., Lee, Y.K., Choi, H.R.: Development of Soft-Actuator- Based Wearable Tactile Display. IEEE Transactions on Robotics 24(3), 549–558 (2008)
8. Choi, H.R., Lee, S.W., Jung, K.M.: Tactile Display As A Braille Display For The Visually Disabled. Intelligent Robots and Systems, Proceedings 2, 1985–1990 (2004)
9. Abdallah, J., Abualkishik, M., Omar, K.: Quranic Braille System. International Journal of Humanities and Social Sciences, 313–319 (2009)
10. Mennens, J., van Tichelen, L., Francois, G., Engelen, J.J.: Optical Recognition of Braille Writing Using Standard Equipment. IEEE Transaction on Rehabilition Engineering 2, 207–212 (1994)
11. Chouvardas, V.G., Miliou, A.N., Hatalis, M.K.: Tactile display: Overview and recent advances. Displays 29(3), 185–194 (2008)
12. Kajimoto, H., Inami, M., Kawakami, N., Tachi, S.: Smarttouch - augmentation of skin sensation with electrocutaneous display. In: Proc. of 11th Symposium on Haptic Interfaces for Virtual Environment and Teleoperator Systems (HAPTICS 2003), Los Angeles, California, U.S.A, pp. 40–46 (2003)
13. Perkins, http://www.perkins.org/
14. Asamura, N., Shinohara, T., Tojo, Y., Koshida, N., Shinoda, H.: Necessary spatial resolution for realistic tactile feeling display. In: Proc. 2001 IEEE Int. Conf. on Robotics and Automation, Seoul, Korea, pp. 1851–1856 (2001)
15. Makino, Y., Asamura, N., Shinoda, H.: A whole palm tactile display using suction pressure. In: Proc. of 2004 IEEE Int. Conf. on Robotics and Automation, Barcelona, Spain, pp. 1524–1529 (2004)
16. http://www.kscitech.com/BC/D/Hinton.html
17. http://whatis.techtarget.com/definition/ 0,,sid9_gci823441,00.html
18. http://nfb.org/legacy/bm/bm00/bm0001/bm000110
19. http://www.kscitech.com/BC/D/Becker.html
20. Wingert, A., Lichter, M., Dubowsky, S., Hafez, M.: Hyper-Redundant Robot Manipulators Actuated by Optimized Binary Dielectric Polymers. In: Smart Structures and Materials Symposium 2002: Electroactive Polymer Actuators and Devices. Proc. SPIE, vol. 4695 (2002)

A New Approach to Design a Domain Specific Web Search Crawler Using Multilevel Domain Classifier

Sukanta Sinha[1,4], Rana Dattagupta[2], and Debajyoti Mukhopadhyay[3,4]

[1] Tata Consultancy Services Ltd., Victoria Park Building,
Salt Lake, Kolkata 700091, India
sukantasinha2003@gmail.com
[2] Computer Science Dept., Jadavpur University, Kolkata 700032, India
ranadattagupta@yahoo.com
[3] Information Technology Dept., Maharashtra Institute of Technology,
Pune 411038, India
debajyoti.mukhopadhyay@gmail.com
[4] WIDiCoReL Research Lab, Green Tower, C-9/1, Golf Green, Kolkata 700095, India

Abstract. Nowadays information published in the internet has become a common knack for all. As a result volume of information has become huge. To handle that huge volume information, Web researchers are introduced various types of search engines. Efficiently Web-page crawling and resource repository building mechanisms are an important part of a search engine. Currently, Web researchers are already introduced various types of Web search crawler mechanism for the various search engines. In this paper, we have introduced a new design and development mechanism of domain-specific Web search crawler, which uses multilevel domain classifiers and crawls multiple domain related Web-pages, uses parallel crawling, etc. Two domain classifiers used to identify domain-specific Web-pages. These two domain classifiers are used one after the other, i.e., two levels. That's why we are calling this Web search crawler is a multilevel domain-specific Web search crawler.

Keywords: Domain specific search, Multilevel classifier, Ontology, Ontology based search, Relevance value, Search engine.

1 Introduction

Keyword searching is a very popular mechanism for finding information from the Internet [1-2]. However, the Internet has become like an Ocean of various types of information. From this huge reservoir of information finding a relevant Web-page based on user given search query is not a matter of a joke. To overcome this situation Web researcher have introduced various types of search engines. Web-page crawling mechanism plays a big role to produce an efficient Web-page repository, which leads to produce better search result for a user given search query. There are various types of Web-page crawling mechanism already introduced by the Web researchers and they are focused crawler [3-5], domain-specific crawler [6], multi domain-specific crawler [7], hierarchical crawler [8], parallel crawler [9-12], etc.

C. Hota and P.K. Srimani (Eds.): ICDCIT 2013, LNCS 7753, pp. 476–487, 2013.

In our approach, we are introducing a new mechanism for the construction of a Web search crawler which follows the parallel crawling approach and supports multiple domains. To construct our prototype we have used two classifiers. These two classifiers are Web-page Content classifier and Web-page Uniform Resource Locator (URL) classifier. Based on these two classifiers we are customizing our crawler inputs and create a meta - domain, i.e., domain about domain. Web-page content classifier identifies relevant and irrelevant Web-pages, i.e., domain-specific Web-pages like Cricket, Football, Hockey, Computer Science, etc. and URL classifier classifies URL extension domains like .com, .edu, .net, .in, etc.

The paper is organized in the following way. In next section 2, the related work to the domain extraction as well as parallel crawling is discussed. The proposed architecture for domain-specific Web search crawler using multilevel domain classifier is given in section 3. All the component of our architecture is also discussed in the same section. Experimental analyses and conclusion of our paper is given in section 4 and 5 respectively.

2   Related Works

To find a geographical location in the Globe, we usually follow the geographical map. Same way to find a Web-page from the World Wide Web (WWW), we are usually using a Web search engine. Web crawler design is an important job to collect Web search engine resources from WWW [6, 8, 13-14]. A better Web search engine resource leads to achieve a better performance of the Web search engine. In this section, we describe a few related works.

Definition 2.1: Ontology –It is a set of domain related key information, which is kept in an organized way based on their importance.

Definition 2.2: Relevance Value –It is a numeric value for each Web-page, which is generated on the basis of the term Weight value, term Synonyms, number of occurrences of Ontology terms which are existing in that Web-page.

Definition 2.3: Seed URL –It is a set of base URL from where the crawler starts to crawl down the Web pages from the Internet.

Definition 2.4: Weight Table – This table has two columns, first column denotes Ontology terms and second column denotes weight value of that Ontology term. The ontology term weight value lies between '0' and '1'.

Definition 2.5: Syntable - This table has two columns, first column denotes Ontology terms and second column denotes synonym of that ontology term. For a particular ontology term, if more than one synonym exists, those are kept using comma (,) separator.

Definition 2.6: Relevance Limit –It is a predefined static relevance cut-off value to recognize whether a Web-page is domain specific or not.

2.1   Domain Extraction Based on URL Extension

Finding domains based on the URL extension was a faster approach, but the URL extension does not always return a perfect domain-specific Web-pages. In addition, we cannot tell the content of the Web-page from the Web-page URL. One of the most practical examples is that of a digital library, where many universities publish book lists with a link to online books like www.amazon.com. According to the URL extension, this Web-page belongs to commercial (.com) domain, but this URL is very popular to an educational (.edu) domain. To overcome this type of situation, we need to consider the content of the Web-page.

2.2   Domain Specific Parallel Crawling

In parallel crawling mechanism, at a time multiple Web-page crawl and download performs, because multiple crawler running simultaneously. Hence, it is a quick Web-page download approach. Using the parallel crawling mechanism we can download the Web-pages in a faster way, but we cannot tell whether the downloaded Web-pages belonging to our domains or not.

2.3   Domain Extraction Based on Web-Page Content

Finding domains based on the Web-page content was a great approach, but it is a time-consuming process as there was no such parallel crawling mechanism applied to downloading the Web-pages. For finding domains based on the Web-page content, first parsed the Web-page content and then extracted all the Ontology terms as well as syntable terms [15-18]. Then each distinct Ontology term was multiplied with their respective Ontology term weight value. Ontology term weight values are taken from weight table. In this approach, for any syntable term used corresponding Ontology term weight value. Finally, taken a summation of these individual terms weightage and this value is called relevance value of that Web-page. Now if this relevance value is greater than the predefined relevance limit of that domain, then that Web-page belongs to a predefined particular domain otherwise discard the Web-page, i.e., the Web-page didn't belong to our domain.

In Fig. 1 we have shown a mechanism to find a domain based on the Web-page content. Here, we consider 'computer science' Ontology, syntable and weight table of computer science Ontology for finding a Web-page belongs to the computer science domain or not. Suppose, the considered Web-page contains 'student' term 3 times, 'lecturer' term 2 times and 'associate professor' term 2 times and student, lecturer and associate professor weight values in the computer science domain are 0.4, 0.8 and 1.0 respectively. Then the relevance value becomes $(3*0.4 + 2*0.8 + 2*1.0) = 4.8$. Now, if 4.8 is greater than the relevance limit, then we called the considered Web-page belongs to the computer science domain otherwise we discard the Web-page.

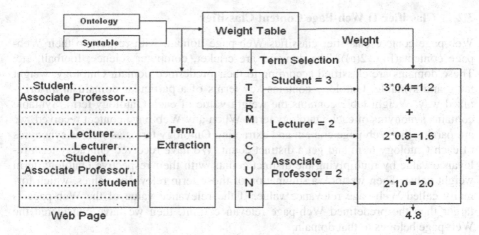

Fig. 1. Web-page Relevance Calculation Mechanism

3   Proposed Approach

In our approach, we have generated a new Web search crawler model which supports parallel crawling mechanisms as well as identifies the proper domain by using Web-page content classifier and Web-page URL classifier. In section 3.1 we have given basics of an Ontology. In section 3.2 and 3.3 we have described Web-page content classifier and Web-page URL classifier respectively. In section 3.4, we have explained our user interface and section 3.5 depicts the construction mechanism of our prototype. Finally, in section 3.6, we have given Web-page retrieval mechanism by using our prototype based on user given inputs.

3.1   Introduction to Ontology

The term Ontology is a data model that represents a set of concepts within a domain and the relationships between those concepts. It is used to reason about the objects within that domain. Ontologies are used in artificial intelligence, the Semantic Web, software engineering, biomedical informatics, Library Science, and information architecture as a form of knowledge representation about the world or some part of it. Ontology is a formal description of concepts and the relationships between them. Definitions associate the names of entities in the Ontology with human-readable text that describes what the names mean. Each domain can be represented by an Ontology and each Ontology contain a set of key information of that domain, which formally called Ontology term. We have assigned some weights to each Ontology term. The strategy of assigning weights is that, the more specific term will have more weight on it. And the terms which are common to more than one domain have less weight. The Ontology term weight value lies between '0' and '1'.

3.2   Classifier 1: Web-Page Content Classifier

Web-page content classifier classifies Web-page domain with respect to their Web-page content (Fig. 2(a)). The domains are cricket, computer science, football, etc. These domains are classified according to their predefined domain Ontology, weight table and syntable. Ontology contains key terms of a particular domain in an organized way. Weight table contains the weight value of each Ontology term. Syntable contains synonyms of each Ontology term. When any Web-page content received, we are parsing the Web-page content and extracting Ontology terms as well as synonyms of each Ontology term and get a distinct count. We have received Ontology term relevance value by multiplying the distinct counts with their respective Ontology term weight value. Then we took a summation of those term relevance values, which formally called Web-page relevance value. If the relevance value of the Web-page is larger than the predefined Web-page relevance limit, then we have considered the Web-page belongs to that domain.

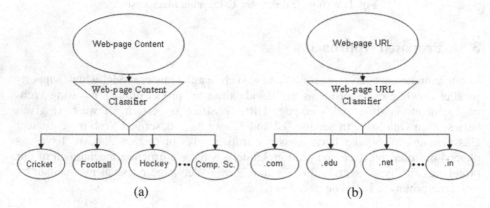

Fig. 2. (a) Web-page Content Classifier (b) Web-page URL Classifier

3.3   Classifier 2: Web-Page URL Classifier

Web-page URL classifier classifies Web-page URL domains like .com, .edu, .in, etc. (refer Fig. 2(b)). Web-crawler crawls down the Web-pages. We have extracted all the hyperlink URLs from already crawled Web-page content by doing a lexical analysis of keywords like 'href' and then sent those URLs into Web-page URL classifier. Web-page URL classifier parsed all the extracted Web-page URLs and classified according to their URL extension domain.

3.4   User Interface

In our proposed search engine, we have facilitated Web searchers to customize their search result by selecting classifier1 and classifier2 inputs. We have used radio buttons for classifier 1, i.e., at a time at most only one domain selection possible for Web-content classifier by the Web searchers (refer Fig. 3) and used check boxes for classifier2, i.e., Web searcher can select more than one Web-page URL extension domain. To get optimistic search results from our proposed search prototype, Web searchers have required some basic knowledge about the classifier2 inputs with respect to classifier1 selected input. Suppose, Web searcher has selected 'Computer Science' domain as classifier 1 input then classifier2 inputs should be .edu, .in or .net. We assume that .com is a commercial domain and no such Web-page exists, which belongs to 'Computer Science' domain. After providing required inputs, i.e., search string, classifier1 and classifier2 inputs, Web searcher have to click on "Go" button to get the search results. In addition, if we assume Web-searchers don't have the basic knowledge about the classifier 2 inputs and selects all the options, that time also our prototype produces the search result but it will take few extra seconds due to traversing more number of schema data (refer Fig. 4).

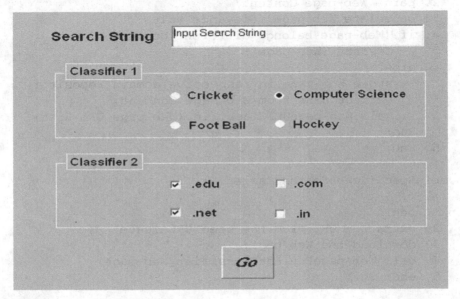

Fig. 3. A Part of User Interface

3.5   Proposed Algorithm

The proposed algorithm describes multilevel domain-specific Web search crawler construction in a brief. We have divided our algorithm into various modules. Module1 tells about Web-page URL classifier and module2 describes the Web-page content classifier. Module1 was invoked inside module2 and module2 invoked by the main domain specific Web-search crawler method.

Module1: Web-pageURLClassifier(Web-page URL List)

```
1. begin
2. while(Web-page URL List is not empty) do step 3-5
3. extract URL Extension;
```

```
4. find URL extension domain;
5. if (Web-page URL extension belongs different do-
   main)
       discard (URL);
   else
       pass URL to the respective crawler input;
6. end;
```

Module2: Web-pageContentClassifier(Web-page)

```
1. begin
2. parse Web-page Content;
3. calculate Web-page relevance value;
4. if (Web-page belongs different domain)
       discard (Web-page);
   else
       store Web-page in respective domain repository ;
       extract URLs from Web-page Content;
       call Web-pageURLClassifier(Web-page URL List);
   End;
5. End;
```

DomainSpecificWebSearchCrawler ()

```
1. begin
2. extract a URL from the seed URL queue;
3. download the Web-page;
4. call Web-pageContentClassifier(Web-page);
5. end;
```

A pictorial diagram of domain-specific Web search engine resource collector is shown in Fig. 4. In our approach, we have divided our data repository into multiple schemas based on the number of URL extension domains we are considering. To collect resources for each schema, we follow parallel crawling mechanism. For example, we have shown .net, .edu and .com crawlers and those crawlers expecting .net, .edu and .com seed URLs respectively. Each and every crawler runs individually, and all are connected with WWW. Initially based on first seed URL every crawler downloads the Web-page content and send it to the first level classifier, i.e., Web-page content classifier used for classifies Web-page domain and stores it in respective domain section, i.e., cricket, football, hockey, etc. In the second level of the Web-page content, we have extracted all the hyperlinks exists in the crawled Web-page content by doing a lexical analysis of keywords like 'href' and send all links to classifier2, i.e., Web-page URL classifier. After classification of all hyperlinks, send it to their respective crawler input. According to our approach classifier 1 identifies the Web-page domain and classifier 2 continuously supplying parallel crawler inputs.

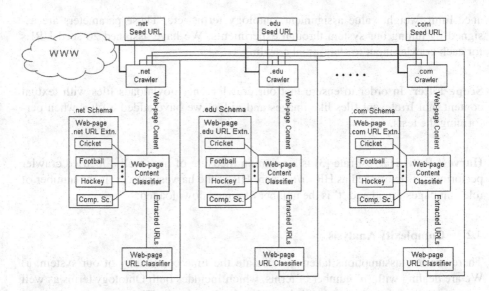

Fig. 4. Proposed architecture of Domain Specific Web Search Engine Resource Collector

3.6   Web-Page Retrieval Mechanism Based on the User Input

Web-page retrieval from Web search engine resources are an important role of a Web search engine. To retrieve Web-pages from our Web-page repository, we need to find the schema and domain based on the user given classifier1 and classifier2 inputs (refer Fig. 3). As discussed in section 3.4, at a time user can select only one classifier1 input and multiple numbers of classifier2 inputs. Classifier 1 input tells about user selected domain and classifier 2 inputs tell about the schema from where we are going to fetch the Web-pages. After identification of the domain and schema, we are taking the search string and parse it to find the Ontology terms. According to those Ontology terms, we have performed a Web-page search operation from identified resources based on classifier 1 and classifier 2 inputs.

4   Experimental Analyses

In this section, we have given some experimental study as well as discussed how to set up our system. Section 4.1 explains our experimental procedure, section 4.2 gives an overview of our prototype time complexity and section 4.3 shows the experimental results of our system.

4.1   Experiment Procedure

Performance of our system depends on various parameters, and those parameters need to be setup before running our system. The considered parameters are domain relevance limit, weight value assignment, ontology terms, etc. These parameters are assigned by tuning our system through experiments. We have assigned 20 seed URLs for each crawler input to start initial crawling.

Scope Filter. In order to ensure that our crawler only downloads files with textual content, not Irrelevant files like images and video, we have added a filter when performing the tests.

Harvest Rate. Harvest rate [3] is a common measure of how well a focused crawler performs. It is expressed as HR= r/t, where HR is the harvest rate, 'r' is the number of relevant pages found and 't' is the number of pages downloaded.

4.2   Complexity Analysis

There are few assumptions taken to calculate the time complexity of our system. a) We are dealing with 'n' number of terms, which includes both Ontology terms as well as synonyms of those terms. b)'d' time taken to download a Web-page because internet speed is a big factor to download a Web-page. c) We are dealing with 'm' number of URL extension domains. d) On an average we assumed we are receiving 'p' number of hyper link URLs in a Web-page content. e) Constant time complexity denoted by C_i where 'i' is a positive integer. We have given our prototype time complexity analysis in Fig.5.

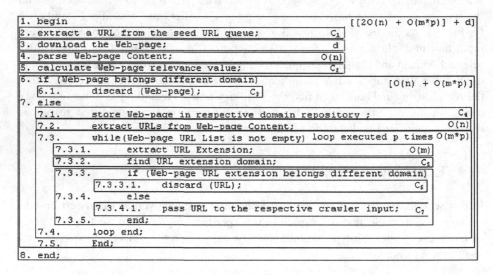

Fig. 5. Line by line complexity analysis

From the analysis we have found for a single crawler complexity becomes [2O(n)+ O(m*p)+d]. Now, we have found 'm*p' always << 'n', hence the final time complexity of a single crawler becomes [2O(n)+d]. In our approach we have used parallel crawler mechanism, so that if we used multiple crawlers then also our time complexity remains same.

4.3 Experimental Result

In this subsection, we have illustrated our proposed prototype accuracy testing results by using harvest rate and parallel crawling performance report.

Accuracy Testing of Our Prototype. To produce an accuracy report, we have used harvest rate. We have also given a comparative study with an existing unfocused crawler performance. In Fig.6. we have given a harvest rate plot for unfocused crawler. Unfocused crawler crawls a large number of Web-pages but found very few domain specific Web-pages.

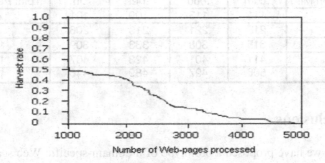

Fig. 6. Harvest rate for unfocused crawling

For a focused crawler harvest rate value monitored by the relevance limit of that domain and tolerance limit value. Relevance limit is a predefined static relevance cut-off value to recognize whether a Web-page is domain specific or not. On the other hand tolerance limit also a numeric value, which decrease the relevance limit value by doing a subtraction operation between relevance limit and tolerance limit. We have reached an optimal tolerance limit value by doing testing in various phases and achieved a satisfactory harvest rate. In Fig.7. we have shown the harvest rate of our domain specific crawler by taking relevance limit and tolerance limit are 12 and 5 respectively.

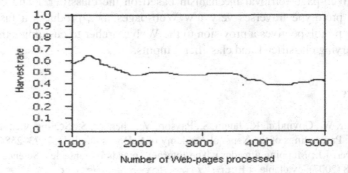

Fig. 7. Harvest rate for focused crawling

Parallel Crawling Performance Report. In table 1 we have given a performance report of our system. According to our seed URLs of each crawler, i.e., .com crawler, .edu crawler, etc., crawls Web-pages simultaneously. We have taken our statistic in various time intervals. Say after 10 minutes, we saw .com crawler crawls 111 Web-pages, .edu crawler crawls 113 Web-pages, .net and .in crawler crawls 109 and 101 Web-pages respectively. According to our strategy, all the crawler crawl Web-pages simultaneously, hence our system total performance after 10 minutes has become summation of all individual crawler output, i.e., 434 Web-pages. The same way we also consider other time intervals and measure our system performance.

Table 1. Performance Report of Our System

Time taken (in Min)	Number of Web-pages				
	.com	.edu	.net	.in	Total Performance
10	111	113	109	101	434
20	218	221	219	206	864
30	315	308	333	309	1265
40	411	401	423	407	1642
50	506	497	489	446	1938

5   Conclusions

In this paper, we have proposed a prototype of a domain-specific Web search crawler which supports multiple Ontologies. This prototype has used two classifiers, i.e., Web-page content classifier and Web-page URL classifier for identification of Web-page domains and URL extension regions more prominently. In addition, we have used the parallel crawling mechanism to download the Web-pages in a faster way. To perform searching operation, Web searcher must give a search string, classifier 1 and classifier 2 inputs. Based on the user given inputs, our prototype retrieves Web-pages from the Web-page repository. Our prototype supports multiple domains by using multiple Ontologies. This prototype is highly scalable. Suppose, we need to increase the supporting domains for our prototype, then we need to include the new domain Ontology and other details like weight table, syntable, etc. of that Ontology. According to the Web-page retrieval mechanism based on the classifier 1 and classifier 2 inputs, our prototype traverses very few Web-pages, i.e., produces a faster result. Finally, our prototype gives a provision to the Web searcher to customize their search result by varying classifier 1 and classifier 2 inputs.

References

1. Willinger, W., Govindan, R., Jamin, S., Paxson, V., Shenker, S.: Scaling phenomena in the Internet. Proceedings of the National Academy of Sciences (supl. 1), 2573–2580 (1999)
2. Rehmeyer, J.J.: Mapping a medusa: The Internet spreads its tentacles. Science News 171, 387–388 (2007), available at http://www.Sciencenews.org

3. Chakrabarti, S., Berg, M., Dom, B.E.: Focused Crawling: a New Approach to Topic-specific Web Resource Discovery. In: Proceedings of the 8th International World Wide Web Conference, pp. 545–562. Elsevier, Toronto (1999)
4. Bergmark, D., Lagoze, C., Sbityakov, A.: Focused Crawls, Tunneling, and Digital Libraries. In: Agosti, M., Thanos, C. (eds.) ECDL 2002. LNCS, vol. 2458, pp. 91–106. Springer, Heidelberg (2002)
5. Diligenti, M., Coetzee, F., Lawrence, S., Giles, C.L., Gori, M.: Focused crawling using context graphs. In: 26th International Conference on Very Large Data-bases, VLDB, pp. 527–534. Morgan Kaufmann, San Francisco (2000)
6. Mukhopadhyay, D., Biswas, A., Sinha, S.: A New Approach to Design Domain Specific Ontology Based Web Crawler. In: 10th International Conference on Information Technology, ICIT 2007, Rourkela, India, December 17-20, pp. 289–291. IEEE Computer Society Press, California (2007)
7. Mukhopadhyay, D., Sinha, S.: A New Approach to Design Graph Based Search Engine for Multiple Domains Using Different Ontologies. In: 11th International Conference on Information Technology, ICIT 2008, Orissa, India, December 18-20, pp. 267–272. IEEE Computer Society Press, USA (2008)
8. Kundu, A., Dutta, R., Mukhopadhyay, D., Kim, Y.C.: A Hierarchical Web Page Crawler for Crawling the Internet Faster. In: Proceedings of the International Conference on Electronics and Information Technology Convergence, Korea, pp. 61–67 (2006)
9. Yadav, D., Sharma, A.K., Gupta, J.P.: Parallel crawler architecture and web page change detection. W. Trans. on Comp. 7, 929–940 (2008)
10. Cho, J., Garcia-Molina, H.: Parallel Crawlers. In: WWW 2002, 11th International World Wide Web Conference (2002)
11. Lee, J.Y., Lee, S.H.: Scrawler: a Seed-by-Seed Parallel Web Crawler. School of Computing. Soongsil University, Seoul (2008)
12. Dong, S., Lu, X.-f., Zhang, L.: A Parallel Crawling Schema Using Dynamic Partition. In: Bubak, M., van Albada, G.D., Sloot, P.M.A., Dongarra, J. (eds.) ICCS 2004. LNCS, vol. 3036, pp. 287–294. Springer, Heidelberg (2004)
13. Burner, M.: Crawling towards Eternity: Building An Archive of The World Wide Web. Web Techniques Magazine 2(5), 37–40 (1997)
14. Cho, J., Molina, H.G., Page, L.: Efficient Crawling Through URL Ordering. In: 7th International Web Conference (WWW 1998), Brisbane, Australia, April 14-18 (1998)
15. Noy, N.F., McGuinness, D.L.: Ontology Development 101: A Guide to Creating Your First Ontology,
   http://www.ksl.stanford.edu/people/dlm/papers/ontology101/
   ontology101-noymcguinness.html (accessed May 2005)
16. Ehrig, M., Maedche, A.: Ontology-focused crawling of web documents. In: Proc. of the 2003 ACM Symposium on Applied Computing, Melbourne, Florida (2003)
17. Spyns, P., Meersman, R., Jarrar, M.: "Data modelling versus ontology engineering. SIGMOD, Record Special Issue 31(4), 12–17 (2002)
18. Spyns, P., Tang, Y., Meersman, R.: An ontology engineering methodology for DOGMA. Journal of Applied Ontology 5 (2008)

An Efficient and Dynamic Concept Hierarchy Generation for Data Anonymization

Sri Krishna Adusumalli, and V. Valli Kumari

Department of Computer Science and Systems Engineering, Andhra University
Visakhapatnam, Andhra Pradesh, India, 530 003
{srikrishna.au,vallikumari}@gmail.com

Abstract. Protecting individual sensitive specific information has become an area of concern over the past one decade. Several techniques like k-anonymity and l-diversity employing generalization/suppression based on concept hierarchies (CHTS) were proposed in literature. The anonymization effectiveness depends on the CHT chosen from the various CHTS possible for a given attribute. This paper proposes a model for constructing dynamic CHT for numerical attributes which can be: 1) generated on the fly for both generalization/suppression; 2) dynamically adjusted based on a given k. The anonymized data using our method yielded 12% better utility when compared to existing methods. The results obtained after experimentation support our claims and are discussed in the paper.

Keywords: privacy, data anonymization, Concept Hierarchy Tree (CHT), Dynamic Concept Hierarchy Tree (DCHT), information loss.

1   Introduction

Large amounts of data about individuals are being collected from various organizations like financial institutions and hospitals for organizational benefits or research purpose causing threat to privacy [1]. Though directly identifying attributes like SSN and Name are deleted in the published data, it is seen that certain combinations of the attributes still give information about the individual (linking attack) [2,9]. Several methods like k-anonymity [2], l-diversity [3],(α,k)–anonymity[4],t-closeness[5] etc., through anonymization using generalization/suppression [6] for achieving privacy. Generalization replaces the actual value with a less specific but a semantically consistent value. Suppression removes the value or totally suppresses the value.

Generalization was initially used for categorical attributes. Later it was extended for numerical attributes either by using pre-defined hierarchies which are constructed manually [7] or a hierarchy-free technique [8]. Hierarchy free generalization is performed based on determining small intervals/segments that include all initial values during anonymization process. For example, the age attribute values: 21, 24, 26 are generalized to the interval [21-26] and if subsequently 22, 24, 35 values occur again in the dataset they are generalized to [22-35]. This is because the hierarchy free

C. Hota and P.K. Srimani (Eds.): ICDCIT 2013, LNCS 7753, pp. 488–499, 2013.

generalization creates overlapping intervals for the attribute during generalization in anonymization process. Each of these two approaches has the following limitations. Creating predefined hierarchy for numerical attribute is complex, because its values are more diverse and may be continuous where as in categorical attributes the values are well established and discrete. A wrong classification or construction of predefined hierarchy will significantly impact the quality and usefulness of anonymized data. In hierarchy free generalization the attributes are divided into overlapping intervals that can be clumsy for the researcher when analyzing the published data. Most of the anonymization techniques require predefined hierarchies to anonymize the data. All these are overcome by creating dynamic hierarchies for numerical attributes.

This paper studies the problem of generalizing numerical attributes for data anonymization and has the following contributions: First, an approach for creating dynamic concept hierarchies in bottom up fashion for numerical attributes is defined. Second, a dynamic model for generating CHT's for both generalization using interval and generalization using suppression is defined. Third, the dynamic model is extended for generating CHT's based on k-anonymity principle. Finally, the results are compared with the approaches discussed in literature to demonstrate the efficacy of the approach.

Rest of the paper is organized as follows: Section 2 deals with related work. Section 3 discusses the dynamic generation of concept hierarchies and an analysis of the proposed algorithm. Section 4 shows the experimental results and comparative study with the published work and finally section 5 presents the conclusions.

2   Related Work

Most of the models proposed in literature use value based generalization hierarchies for numerical attributes. These hierarchies significantly impact the quality and usefulness of masked data during the anonymization process. Masked data can lose extra or little information depending on how well the hierarchy fits the distribution and the grouping of attribute values in the micro dataset. It also depends on the user's knowledge of the specific domain [7].

LeFevre [8] proposed a hierarchy free generalization model for numerical attributes. It provides flexible anonymization technique and it minimizes the information loss during the anonymization process. However, this technique is not suitable for an anonymity principle like k-anonymity which relies on generalization boundaries during the anonymization process. The generalization intervals that were being used during the anonymization process do not promise that those intervals are disjoint in nature. They cause difficulties during analysis of the anonymized microdata. This technique is also not suitable for personalized privacy [10]. In our approach, we overcome this ambiguity by creating the hierarchies dynamically.

Recently Alinaet.al [11] adopted the agglomerative hierarchical clustering [12] to build dynamic concept hierarchies for numerical attributes. The trees are created dynamically, but they are not suitable for privacy domain because they calculate the average distances between the clusters which are normalized to form groups.

However, during the anonymization process the information loss tends to increase thereby decreasing the utility considerably. Alina et.al [11] extended their work to improved On-the-Fly Generalization Hierarchies for Numerical Attributes (IOTF) [15].

Our approach overcomes these drawbacks by considering the normalized distance between the nodes in turn reducing the information loss during anonymization process when compared to [11, 15, 8, 7].

3   Dynamic Generation of Concept Hierarchy Tree(DCHT)

Manual construction of CHT requires expert domain knowledge and has the following limitations:

- Classification of data might be complex for continuous data.
- Maintenance of a CHT is a cumbersome task.
- Cost of creating a CHT and maintaining it requires a large amount of effort.
- Anonymizing the data using the manually constructed CHT is complex.

Dynamic Concept Hierarchy Tree (DCHT) framework is proposed (fig. 1) for creating concept hierarchy trees dynamically and addresses the above stated problems.

Table 1. Example Dataset

Age	Zipcode	Gender	Disease
20	521227	Male	Cancer
21	521228	Male	HIV
24	521229	Female	Flue
28	521239	Male	Cancer
30	521230	Female	HIV
38	521239	Male	Cancer
24	521227	Male	HIV
21	521230	Male	Flue
38	521228	Female	Flue
38	521227	Female	Cancer

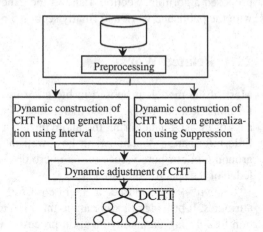

Fig. 1. Framework of DCHT

3.1   Preprocessing

To construct a DCHT for a given dataset, initially the required attributes are selected for example, age and zipcode in Table 1. The distinct values of each of the selected attributes and their respective frequencies are computed. The detailed process of construction of DCHT based on these is presented in the subsequent sections.

3.2   Initial CHT Construction

Step 1: For a given attribute N, node_set V is the set of distinct values $\{v_1, v_2, ..., v_m\}$. Each v_i in V is a leaf node of the CHT.

Step 2: The closest pair of nodes in V are determined using a distance matrix.

Step 3: The closest nodes are merged to form an intermediate node.

Step 4: Steps 2 and 3 are repeated until |V|=1 i.e., only one node is left in V is termed as the root of the CHT.

3.3   DCHT construction

DCHT is constructed based on generalization using one of the following two ways

i. *Interval:* All number type attributes like age use this method.

ii. *Suppression:* All number and String type attributes like zipcode[1] use this method.

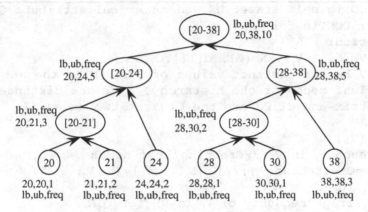

Fig. 2. Dynamic CHT for age

Generalization using interval.

Assume $\sum$ is a domain of the numerical attribute with ordered values. The domain is partitioned into ordered intervals $< I_1, I_2, ..., I_n >$ such that every value of a $\sum$ appears in some interval I_j. For instance, the age attribute of Table 1 is represented in terms of intervals as $< [20\text{-}21], [20\text{-}24], [28\text{-}30], [28\text{-}38], [20\text{-}38] >$. A node structure for root, intermediate and leaf node of the CHT is shown in Fig. 2. Here the nodes 20, 21, 24, 28, 30, 38 are leaf nodes, the nodes [20-21],[28-30],[20-34],[28-38] are intermediate nodes and [20-38] is the root of the CHT.

Definition 1(*node structure*). Every node in the tree is represented by $(lb, ub, freq)$ where *lb, ub* are the lower and upper bound values of the node and *freq* is the number of occurrences/frequency of that value in the dataset. The root of the tree has the same

---

[1]   In some countries zipcode is treated as both number and string type

node structure and the frequency represents the sum of the frequency of all nodes under this root node. For leaf nodes *lb* and *ub* are equal to the node value.

Definition 2 *(Distance between two nodes)*. The distance between two nodes N_i and N_j is determined as $dist(N_i, N_j) = |ub^j - lb^i|$ where lb^i and ub^j are the lower and upper bounds of the nodes N_i and N_j.

Definition 3 *(Closest pair of nodes)*. The pair of nodes having minimum distances and maximum frequency among all nodes in the node_set is called as the closest pair of nodes and is determined as follows.

$$closest\_pair(N) = \{argmin\{dist(N_i, N_j)\} \wedge argmax\{f_i + f_j\} \, \forall \, N_i, N_j \in N\}$$

Algorithm 1: DCHT construction based on Generalization using Interval

---

```
Input: Original dataset DS and numerical attribute QINₖ
Output: DCHT's for QINₖ
Assumption:
    V={V₁,V₂,..,Vₙ}, N={∅}, d[][],C₁,C₂;
    /* V be the distinct values of QINₖ, N be the set of
       leaf nodes of the hierarchy, d be the distance ma
       trix and C1,C2 are the Closest two nodes */
Begin
    Sort(V);
    For each Vᵢ in V  //Creating leaf nodes
        Nᵢ=CreateNode(Vᵢ);//(N₁,N₂,..,Nₙ)=(V₁,V₂,..,Vₙ)
        Nᵢ.lb= Nᵢ.ub=Vᵢ;
        Nᵢ.freq=frequency of Vᵢ in DS for QINₖ
    End for
    Repeat
        d[i][j]=dist(Nᵢ,Nⱼ)⊠ Nᵢ,Nⱼ∈N×N,i<j// definition 2
        (C₁,C₂)=closest_pair(N); //using definition 3
        //The merging of two nodes is based on definition 4
        Nₙₑw=CreateNode([C₁.lb-C₂.ub]);Nₙₑw.lb=C₁.lb;Nₙₑw.ub=C₂.ub;
        Nₙₑw.freq= C₁.freq + C₂.freq;C₁.parent= C₂.parent=Nₙₑw;
        N=N-{C₁,C₂}U{Nₙₑw}; /*the closest nodes are
        d[][]=∅;            deleted from N */
    Until(|N|=1);
End
```

Definition 4 *(Merging of nodes):* If two nodes N_i and N_j are determined as closest nodes then they are merged to create new node as $N_{new} = (lb_{new}, ub_{new}, freq_{new})$ where $lb_{new} = N_i.lb$, $ub_{new} = N_j.ub$ and $freq_{new} = N_i.freq + N_j.freq$.

The nodes N_i and N_j are descendants of the node N_{new}. These nodes are removed from V when merged. |V| is decreased by one when the nodes are merged. This process is repeated until |V|=1. The node that remains after the merging process is termed as root of the hierarchy. Its lb, ub are the lower and upper bound of the CHT and frequency is the total number of records in the dataset. The time complexity of the algorithm 1 is $O(n^2)$.

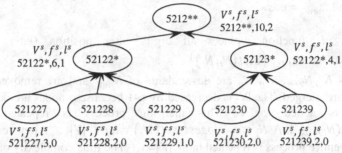

Fig. 3. Dynamic CHT for zipcode

Generalization using suppression.

In this approach, an original value is replaced by a less specific value, which is se-mantically intact with the original value. For example, the original ZIP codes {521227, 521228} can be generalized to 52122*, thereby stripping the rightmost digit and semantically representing a larger geographical area. In a classical relational da-tabase system, domains are used to describe the set of values that attributes assume. There might be a ZIP attribute, with a *number* domain and a *string* domain [6]. A node structure for root, intermediate and leaf nodes of the CHT in Fig. 3.

Definition 5 *(node structure).* Every node in the concept hierarchy is characterized by (V^s, f^s, l^s) where V^s is the value of the node, f^s be the number of occurrences of that value in the dataset and l^s be the number of suppressed digits in the value V^s. The root node of the hierarchy has same node structure and the frequency (f) represent the sum of the frequencies of all nodes under this root node. For all leaf nodes, V^s is equal to the initial value of the node.

Definition 6 *(distance between two nodes).* The distance between two nodes N_i and N_j is determined as $dist(N_i, N_j) = \mathrm{argmin}_{1 \le k \le p} r(k)$ where $r(k) = \begin{cases} k, & if\ N_i.V^s[k] \ne N_j.V^s[k] \\ \infty, & otherwise \end{cases}$. This function $r(k)$ is used to determine the position where the two node values differ. After finding this, $argmin$ returns the position of the most significant varying digit among the two node values.

Definition 7 *(Closest nodes).* The closest nodes are determined by finding closure or closest set of each node. The closest set of N_i is determined as

$$closest\_set(N_i) = \left\{ N_j \middle| d(N_i, N_j) = \left\{ \underset{x,y \leq |V|}{\mathrm{argmax}}\left(dist(N_x, N_y) \right) \right\}, \forall j < |V| \right\} \forall \ i < |V|$$

Definition 8 *(Merging of nodes)*. If the nodes $N_1, N_2, \ldots\ldots\ldots N_p$ are determined as closest nodes of N_i then they are merged to create new node as $N_{new}^s = (V_{new}^s, f_{new}^s, l_{new}^s)$ where $V_{new}^s = replace\_all(V_i^s, pos,'*')$, $f_{new}^s = N_j.f + \sum_{j=1}^{p} N_j.f$ and $l_{new}^s = pos$.

The *replace_all* function replaces all digits after position *(pos)* with '*' Where pos $= \mathrm{argmax}_{i,j \leq p}\left(dist(N_i, N_j) \right)$.

The nodes $N_1, N_2, \ldots\ldots\ldots N_p$ are descendants of N_{new}^s and are removed from V when nodes are merged. The |V| is decreased by p-1 because p nodes are deleted and one node is added to V. This merging process is repeated for all $|closest\_set(N_i)| \geq 1 \wedge N_i \not\subset closest\_set(N_j) \forall i, j \leq |V|$. After completing merging, the entire process is repeated until |V|=1. The time complexity of the algorithm 2 is $O(n^2)$.

Algorithm 2: DCHT construction based on Generalization using suppression

Input: Original dataset DS and attribute QIN$_k$
Output: DCHT for QIN$_k$
Assumption:
V={V$_1$,V$_2$,..,V$_n$},N={Ø}, TEMP={Ø}, C={Ø}; /* V be the distinct values of QIN$_k$, N be the leaf nodes of the hierarchy, TEMP is temporary set and C is the closet set*/
Begin
  Sort(V);
  For each V$_i$ in V //Creating leaf nodes
      N$_i$=CreateNode(V$_i$);// (N$_1$,N$_2$,..,N$_n$)=(V$_1$,V$_2$,..,V$_n$)
      N$_i$.freq=frequency of V$_i$ in DS for QIN$_k$
  End for
  Repeat
      d[i][j]=dist(N$_i$,N$_j$)▨N$_i$,N$_j$∈N×N,i<j//Using Definition 6
      TEMP=N;
      For each N$_i$ in TEMP
          C=*closest_set*(N$_i$) // Using Definition 7
          If(|C|>1) then
              V$_{new}^s$=*replace_all*(V$_i^s$,|C|,'*');N$_{new}^s$=CreateNode(V$_{new}^s$);
              N$_{new}^s$.f=N$_i$.f+$\sum_k^{|C|}$N$_k$.f ∀ N$_k$∈C
              N=N-C∪{N$_{new}^s$};TEMP=$\left(\text{TEMP-C}\right)$;
          End if
      End for
  Until(|N|=1)
End

3.4   Dynamic adjustment of CHT

Anonymity principles like *k-anonymity*, *l-diversity etc.*, use taxonomy tree or concept hierarchies for anonymizing the microdata. In *k-anonymity* each record is indistinguishable from other *k*-1 records in the dataset. For achieving this property each attribute value is generalized to any level from bottom to top in the concept hierarchy until it satisfies the *k-anonymity* principle. If the current node does not satisfy the *k-anonymity* principle the attribute value is generalized from current level to next level. If it does not satisfy, value is again generalized to upper level. This process is repeated until it satisfies the condition. So to generalize an attribute value, all intermediate levels from current level to the required anonymized level are traversed. During this process sometimes there can be unnecessary moves while anonymizing the data. To overcome these unnecessary moves or traveling through all intermediate levels we propose a new approach that dynamically adjusts the concept hierarchies to achieve *k-anonymity* property.

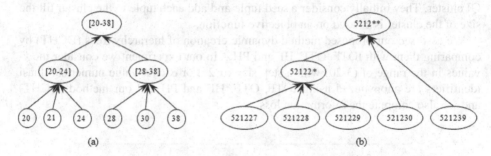

Fig. 4. Dynamically adjusted CHT for (a) age (b) zipcode

Dynamic adjustment of CHT is done by comparing support count of each intermediate level in the concept hierarchy to the *k value* of the *k-anonymity*. If it does not satisfy the condition the child nodes of the current node are assigned to the parent of the current node. This process is repeated for all intermediate nodes from leaf to root in the hierarchy. For instance, the dataset in Table 1 is anonymized based on the *k-anonymity* with *k*=5. The concept hierarchy trees for age and zipcode attributes are shown in Fig. 2 and Fig. 3 respectively. These trees when dynamically adjusted result in Fig. 4(a) and 4(b) based on the given *k value*.

4   Evaluation

4.1   Experimental Setup

We have done an extensive set of experiments on adult data set[14] to evaluate both the effectiveness and efficiency of our algorithms.

All the algorithms were implemented in java using Netbeans 7.0. The experiments are conducted in two phases. In the first phase, we compared our algorithm DCHT with improved on the fly hierarchies (IOTF) [15], on the fly hierarchies (OTF) [12], hierarchy free (HF) [8] and pre-defined hierarchies (PH) [7] on k-member clustering anonymization algorithm [13]. In phase II we conducted the same set of experiments as in phase I pertaining to Mondrian multi-dimensional algorithm [8]. In phase II we conducted comparison of discernibility measure (DM) [10] and average cluster size (CAVG) [8] for all 5 methods using k-member clustering anonymization algorithm [13] and Mondrian multi-dimensional algorithm [8]. The corresponding results are discussed in section 4.2.

4.2   Results

Phase I. In this phase we compare our proposed method DCHT with different methods present in the literature. For experimentation we adopted k-member clustering algorithm [13] for anonymization. In this method the clusters are created such that the size of the cluster must be at least k or more. These clusters are anonymized forming a QI cluster. They initially consider a seed tuple and add each tuple to the cluster till the size of the cluster is k based on an objective function.

We assessed our proposed method dynamic creation of hierarchy trees (DCHT) by comparing them with IOTF, OTF, HF and PH. In our experiment we consider the k-values in the range of (3-20) with a step size of 2. For each k value numerical quasi identifiers are anonymized using IOTF, OTF, HF and PH and our method (DCHT) and we also compute the information loss.

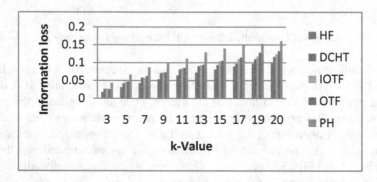

Fig. 5. Information Loss with k=3, 5...20 using DCHT, IOTF, OTF, HF, PH for k-member clustering technique

As expected, the predefined hierarchies (PH) give more information loss and perform worse because the generated hierarchies will lead to more interval ranges which are not in a binary fashion. In hierarchy free generalization the information loss is always less, however it is not applicable in all anonymization scenarios. When age, education and hours_per_week attributes are considered DCHT produces significantly low information loss when compared with OTF and PH.

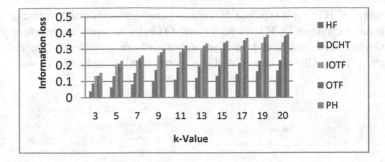

Fig. 6. Information Loss (IL) with k=3, 5…20 using DCHT, IOTF, OTF, HF, PH for Mondrian anonymization algorithm

Phase II. The setup for experiments conducted in phase II is similar to that of phase I. However the anonymization algorithm used is Mondrian [8]. In this method they modify the general anonymization technique into partitions. Their scheme of partition assumes a d-dimensional space, where d is the number of quasi-identifiers where each partition must have at least k tuples. Then they generalize the records in each partition such that a quasi-identifier group is formed. Fig. 6 shows information loss for DCHT, IOTF, OTF, HF and PH. When age, education and hours_per_week attributes our method results in above 12% less information loss than IOTF, OTF and PH.

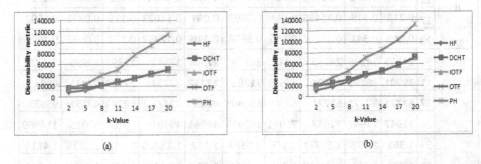

Fig. 7. Discernibility metric (DM) with k=2, 5…20 using DCHT, IOTF, OTF, HF, PH for (a) Mondrian anonymization algorithm and (b) k-member clustering algorithm

Phase III. This phase presents comparison of discernibility measure (DM) [10] and average cluster size (CAVG) [8] for all the 5 techniques, with k value ranging from 2 to 20 with a step size of 3. Discernibility metric is a measure for data quality. Data quality is measured based on the size of each equivalence class in this metric. Data quality diminishes as more records become indistinguishable with respect to each other, and DM effectively captures this effect of the k-anonymization process. As our approach mainly concentrates on the creating the smaller intervals based on the frequency of the values and not considering the size of the cluster created there is almost a tie between DCHT and IOTF. But of the 7 experiments conducted over discernibility metric our technique DCHT outperformed OTF by 4 times on an average when both k-member clustering and Mondrian techniques are considered. Same as is the case when Average Cluster size (CAVG) is considered. Graphs are shown in Fig. 7 and Fig. 8.

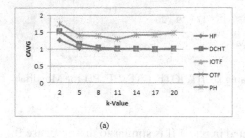 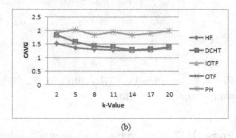

(a)   (b)

Fig. 8. Average cluster size with k=2, 5...20 using DCHT, IOTF, OTF, HF, PH for (a) Mondrian anonymization algorithm and (b) k-member clustering algorithm

Table 2. Comparison of various privacy metrics

Metrics	k	Mondrian anonymization algorithm					k-member clustering algorithm				
		DCHT	IOTF	OTF	HF	PH	**DCHT**	IOTF	OTF	HF	PH
IL	5	**0.132**	0.202	0.20899	0.063	0.2266	**0.042**	0.0454	0.047	0.0307	0.0665
	11	**0.184**	0.281	0.30184	0.11	0.3201	**0.081**	0.08381	0.085	0.0641	0.1117
	17	**0.213**	0.319	0.35436	0.144	0.3693	**0.097**	0.11023	0.115	0.0891	0.1502
	20	**0.229**	0.341	0.38148	0.166	0.3928	**0.116**	0.12332	0.132	0.0995	0.1603
DM	5	**24239**	24239	24239	18427	34309	**17347**	17347	17397	12995	23549
	11	**39801**	39801	39801	37919	71383	**27757**	27757	27757	27271	49843
	17	**57771**	57771	57771	57503	103801	**42435**	42435	42399	42351	95633
	20	**71947**	71947	71947	70971	132475	**49981**	49981	50169	50015	114969
CAVG	5	**1.361**	1.578	1.57771	1.578	2.0387	**1.152**	1.15209	1.157	1.0236	1.4114
	11	**1.279**	1.381	1.38148	1.381	1.9581	**1.01**	1.00978	1.01	1.0008	1.3016
	17	**1.289**	1.301	1.30095	1.301	1.8923	**1.005**	1.00487	1.005	1.0049	1.4285
	20	**1.361**	1.376	1.37611	1.376	1.9976	**1.007**	1.00691	1.007	1.0069	1.4922

4.3   Comparison of performance for different types of CHTS

We compared and evaluated different CHTS using metrics Information Loss (IL), Discernibility Measure (DM) and Average Cluster size (CAVG) using k-member clustering technique and Mondrian anonymization algorithm respectively. The results are shown in Table 2. Our proposed method DCHT outperformed IOTF, OFT and PH pertaining to IL metric for both k-member clustering and Mondrian anonymization algorithms whereas HF method gives slightly better results than DCHT. However, HF is not suitable for hierarchy based anonymization. Similarly we compared various CHTS using DM and CAVG metrics. The evaluations are shown in Table 2.

5   Conclusions

A method for constructing dynamic hierarchies for numerical quasi-identifier attributes capable of giving high quality and minimum information loss is proposed. The proposed method is dynamic and out performs when compared to IOTF, OTF and predefined hierarchies with respect to the information loss measures. The proposed method also gives similar results with IOTF with respect to the DM and CAVG measures.

Acknowledgments. This work was supported by Grant SR/S3/EECE/0040/2009 from Department of Science and Technology (DST), Government of India. We thank the anonymous reviewers for their insightful comments.

References

1. HIPAA: Health Insurance Portability and Accountability Act (2002), http://www.hhs.gov/ocr/hipaa
2. Sweeney, L.: k-anonymity: A Model for Protecting Privacy. International Journal on Uncertainty. Fuzziness and Knowledge-based Systems 10(5), 557–570 (2002)
3. Machanavajjhala, A., Gehrke, J., Kifer, D.: l-Diversity: Privacy beyond k-Anonymity. In: Proceedings of the IEEE ICDE, p. 24 (2006)
4. Wong, R.C., Li, J., Fu, A.W., Wang, K.: (α, k)-Anonymity: An Enhanced k-Anonymity Model for Privacy-Preserving Data Publishing. In: Proceedings of the SIGKDD (2006)
5. Li, N., Li, T., Venkatasubramanian, S.: t-Closeness: Privacy Beyond k-Anonymity and l-Diversity. In: Proceedings of the IEEE ICDE, pp. 106–115 (2007)
6. Sweeney, L.: Achieving k-Anonymity Privacy Protection Using Generalization and Suppression. International Journal on Uncertainty, Fuzziness, and Knowledge-based Systems 10(5), 571–588 (2002)
7. Iyengar, V.: Transforming Data to Satisfy Privacy Constraints. In: Proceedings of the ACM SIGKDD, pp. 279–288 (2002)
8. LeFevre, K., DeWitt, D., Ramakrishnan, R.: Mondrian Multidimensional k-Anonymity. In: Proceedings of the IEEE ICDE, Atlanta, Georgia (2006)
9. Samarati, P.: Protecting Respondents Identities in Microdata Release. IEEE Transactions on Knowledge and Data Engineering 13(6), 1010–1027 (2001)
10. Xiao, X., Tao, Y.: Personalized Privacy Preservation. In: SIGMOD (2006)
11. Campan, A., Cooper, N.: On-the-Fly Hierarchies for Numerical Attributes in Data Anonymization. In: Jonker, W., Petković, M. (eds.) SDM 2010. LNCS, vol. 6358, pp. 13–25. Springer, Heidelberg (2010)
12. Tan, P.-N., Steinbach, M., Kumar, V.: Introduction to Data Mining. Addison Wesley, Reading (2005)
13. Byun, J.W., Kamra, A., Bertino, E., Li, N.: Efficient k-Anonymity using Clustering Techniques. CERIAS Technical Report 2006-10 (2006)
14. UCI Repository of Machine Learning databases, http://archive.ics.uci.edu/ml/
15. Campan, A., Cooper, N., Truta, T.M.: On-the-Fly Generalization Hierarchies for Numerical Attributes Revisited. In: Jonker, W., Petković, M. (eds.) SDM 2011. LNCS, vol. 6933, pp. 18–32. Springer, Heidelberg (2011)

Wikipedia Articles Representation
with Matrix'u

Julian Szymański

Department of Computer Systems Architecture,
Faculty of Electronics, Telecommunications and Informatics,
Gdańsk University of Technology, Poland
julian.szymanski@eti.pg.gda.pl

Abstract. In the article we evaluate different text representation methods used for a task of Wikipedia articles categorization. We present the Matrix'u application used for creating computational datasets of Wikipedia articles. The representations have been evaluated with SVM classifiers used for reconstruction human made categories.

Keywords: text representation, documents classification, SVM, Wikipedia.

1 Introduction

Knowledge Representation (KR) can be defined as the application of logic and ontology to the task of constructing computable models of some domain [14]. KR defines the ways how the knowledge is stored and processed, thus it allows to operate on it eg. perform some inferences [6].

Analogically text representation defines the methods for machine-based processing of natural language given in the written form. Machine processing of the text is related to such domains as document categorization, translations or text recognition. In this paper we focused on the methods of text representation for documents categorization. The task of categorization involves computational intelligence methods used for automatic processing of the texts usually with their clustering and classification. These approaches find many practical applications: eg. classification is used for automatic organization of documents into existing systems of categories or for suggesting the most suitable categories to the moderator while a new documents arrives to the repository. Also classification can be used in antiplagiary systems where the thematic domain of the processed document needs to be calculated [18]. The unsupervised methods allow to organize documents sets into categories not defined earlier. These methods are used eg. in search engines where groups of similar web pages are automatically introduced. In information retrieval, clustering is also used for searching based on examples where it allows to find similar contents to the selected one.

There is a wide range of the computational methods which can be applied for text categorization. Mostly they are based on similarity measures which effective implementation is required to obtain good results. The term effective denotes here not only speed of the computations (which in case of large text repositories should be taken into consideration) but also relevance to the human users' interests. This second issue is especially

C. Hota and P.K. Srimani (Eds.): ICDCIT 2013, LNCS 7753, pp. 500–510, 2013.

hard to be achieved because humans understand the natural language and the machine can only interpret it. Thus to achieve good results it is crucial to construct such text representations that allow to compute the texts in the way similar to human understanding. The methods for creating computationable forms of a text are typically based on extracting from the processed documents features that will be descriptive and distinctive enough to process them by the machines. This approach employs so called vector space model where each of the documents is represented as a point in multidimensional space of features. As providing the proper features is a basis of achieving good categorization results in this paper we focus on a methods of extracting representative features from the text and evaluating them with machine learning task.

2   Text Representation Methods

The methods for text representation are based on two main approaches: text content and referential analysis.

In the first approach we extract features directly from the text content. The second one is based on the associations between documents and the representation of particular document (text) is constructed with relation to the others. Both approaches finally construct the matrix where columns are the features that represent the objects (texts) given in rows. This matrix is taken for further computations.

2.1   Words

The most intuitive approach to represent the text is to take words appearing in it. Thus the representation space is constructed by the dictionary of the size equal to all distinctive words in documents collection. As it can be very large typically methods for reducing dimensions on the preprocessing level are introduced:

- stop words filtering removes the most popular words such as: to, the, and, or that which do not bring much information. This kind of filtering allows considerably to reduce representation size (in our experiments even 35-45% of the original) but it can also remove some information eg. consider the text 'to be or not to be'.
- stemming and lemmatization allow to bring the word into its basic form. As words from a text may appear in different forms turning them into a core reduces representation space (in our experiments even 5-10% of the original).

The preprocessed words are called terms. They are not equally useful for machine learning thus some of their weightings are introduced. As the sophisticated weighting should be considered as post processing phase in the experiments presented here we use only the simplest weighting based on normalized term frequencies.

The method based on words breaks phrases into single words that may change the semantics of the text. Eg. processing in that way a phrase 'San Francisco' will produce features not really related to the name of the city. To capture such phrases in automatic way we test the approach for representation that use n successive words. In the experiments presented here we test $n = 2$.

2.2 N-Grams

The representation of the documents with mentioned above method based on words requires the application of natural language processing tools. As the machine can not understand the meaning of the utterances NLP methods have limited quality and they can bring noise to the representation. The second approach to constructing representations is based directly on the text content. This approach segments the text into fixed chunks of n letters. Introducing different n numbers considerably increases the representation size as well as allows to select required granularity of text representation. In the experiments presented in this article we evaluate the representation for $n = 4$ but it should be stressed that in other experiments [18] we use $n = 3 - 5$ that gave a little better results but the processing was much more time consuming. The n-grams representation is known to give good results in application for language identification [11] and spelling errors correction[9].

2.3 References

The text documents frequently have the references. If we consider books or scientific articles as the references their bibliographic notes can be used. As they are strongly related to the processed document they are very useful for determining its thematic domain. If web pages are considered their hyperlinks can be used that are known to produce compact and domain-centered representations.

The dimensionality of the feature space using references is much lower as in case of content-based representations. Typically it produces binary representations – where 0 denotes lack of reference and 1 denotes its existence. Also -1 can be used for description of back references while directed graphs are considered. The sparsity of the reference-based approaches may cause to form separated sub-regions of representation. To enrich them higher order references can be used providing additional references (usually introduced with lower weights) that come form the references from the document that was referenced directly. In our experiments we employ this approach for limited number of direct references.

The narrowing of references number has been performed for fixed n of the first links. If we consider as more descriptive the links appearing at the beginning of the document we can use only the selected number of them. This allows to reduce the representation size and should filter the noise. To focus this representation on highlighting the thematic domain we addition-

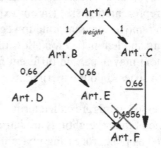

Fig. 1. Weighting with higher order references

ally introduce higher order references (*HOR*) that come form the beginnings of the referenced documents. The idea of this approach has been shown in Figure 1. The direct references obtain here weight 1, the higher order - proportionally smaller. To effectively calculate weights of HOR we use Floyd–Warshall algorithm [13].

2.4 ESA

The Explicit Semantic Analysis (ESA) [8] is the mixture of the approaches based on content and referential approach. The technique computes relatedness between the texts using context formed by providing referential set of documents. The semantic relatedness between texts is expressed with the cosine measure between the corresponding text vectors created with *TF-IDF* weighting and documents in referential set. In our experiments we randomly select the referential set from the articles that are to be represented augmented with the additional articles they reference to. In our case the referential set had cardinality of 60% of documents that are to be classified. It should be noticed here that providing the specified referential set of articles allows to distinguish source articles into predefined (with referential articles) directions.

2.5 Compression

The approach for computing representation of the text can also be based on algorithmic information [10]. The method introduce similarities that describe analyzed documents set as it is the referential approach but use different similarity measures than those based on links or referential set. The measure is introduced here with algorithmic information that may be estimated using standard file compression techniques.

The method is based on an assumption that similarity of two files containing the same information (that can approximate the content of text flies but not eg. graphic flies) can be estimated using the size of their compressions. The approach employs the fact that if two text files are similar, the sum of sizes of files compressed separately would significantly oversize the size of the file created with concatenated files. Analogically, if two files are different, the size of the file created after the compression of two files together will be similar to the value of the sum og two files sizes compressed separately. This observation is described with formula 1.

$$sim_{A,B} = 2\left(1 - \frac{size(A+B)_p}{size(A)_p + size(B)_p}\right) \tag{1}$$

where A and B denote text files, and the suffix p denotes the compression operation.

This measure of similarity implicitly takes into account strings of letters, collocations and longer phrases that are used to form a dictionary by the compression algorithm. Also it should be that noticed other applications of this approach in the domain of plagiarism detection, gene analysis, or chain letters analysis have been shown [1].

3   Feature Selection and Data Transformations

Methods presented in section 2 are the basis for further text categorization. Some improvements of the results can be achieved using their additional processing with usage of wide range of well known, general methods. As we are interested in evaluation of the representations as an entry point for machine text categorization, in the experiments their rough form is analyzed and the possible improvements are only briefly discussed.

3.1 Feature Selection

The weights introduced on the preprocessing level can considerably influence text representations. Eg. in the experiments we use only frequency weighting as a source for further modifications. The other weighting with usage of inverse document frequency, OKAPI BM25 [3], or confidence scoring [17] are used to improve the categorization results. It should be stressed that they relay on features frequencies and class distributions and they can be calculated secondarily. Also typical methods for feature selection used in machine learning can be added [2]. The comparative study [20] showed that the methods based on *information gain* and χ^2 *test* gave good results in comparison to their computation cost.

3.2 Transformations

The transformation of the data is a known technique for achieving better results in machine learning. Similarly as in case of feature selection it is second-order processing and as we are interested in evaluation of rough text representations, here we only briefly discuss some of them.

Principal Component Analysis [19] is well known method for finding linear combinations of original features and transforming them into space of artificial ones. The method employs eigenvectors analysis that finds many other applications eg. in spectral clustering [15] or in text context retrieval in Latent Semantic Indexing [7]. The method based on singular value decomposition allows to reduce original features space and to replace it with a smaller number of linear combination of original features which allows to extract the most usable features for machine processing. Also non linear methods such as Self Organising Maps and Multidimensional Scaling are used.

In our experiments [16] we got very good results while the original data have been transformed into metric space using cosine distance. This simple approach for data transformation employs cosine kernel that calculates distances between all objects in the dataset and further processing is performed on the object distances instead of on original features. For a comparative purpose in the experiments presented in this article we provide the results achieved after applying this transformation that shows considerable improvement of classification results.

4   Application for Generating Wikipedia Representation

The experiments presented in this article had been performed on the datasets created from one of the largest human knowledge repositories - Wikipedia. To allow to process the Wikipedia with the machine we create Matrix'u application that allows to select the categories and for the articles within them create particular representation. The articles

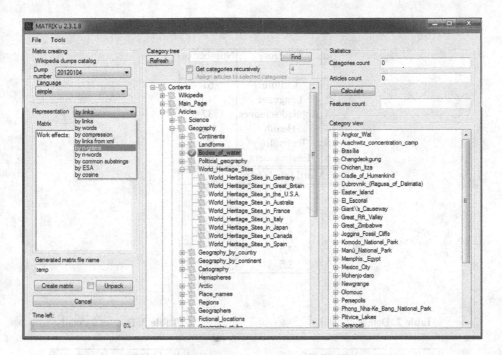

Fig. 2. Interface of Matrix'u application

representation is stored in the form of matrix of $m \times n$, where m denotes the number of the articles and n is the number of features used to represent them. The application allows also to apply particular NLP tools and see their effect directly on the processed text. Matrix'u can also be used as off-line Wikipedia viewer and as a tool for generating wide range of Wikipedia statistics. The screenshot of the application has been shown in Figure 2. The sources and compilations of the application are available online. They can be download form our project web page http://http://kask.eti.pg.gda.pl/CompWiki/ and are free for academic use.

5   Datasets and Results

To evaluate the representations we create three test datasets containing six categories from the same Wikipedia hierarchy level. In Tables 1-3 we provide the datasets details: the names of the used categories as well as the number of multi-label assignments and their sizes in the number of articles. These assignments to particular classes we describe with identifiers of the categories that form additional multi-label categories.

The test datasets allow us to evaluate the created articles representations in the classification task. In Table 4 we provide aggregated results of classifications qualities achieved for the datasets. The classification quality has been measured with averaged F-measure in stratified 10-fold cross-validation. As we deal with multi-class problem for each of the classes we construct separate classifier and train it in one-versus all model. For the classification we use our own implementation of Support

Table 1. Dataset 1 details

id	Category	Number of articles
1	Culture	61
2	Language	46
3	Applied sciences	37
4	Health	132
5	Technology	127
6	Environment	68
Multi labels ids		
3,4		3
3,5		2
1,2		2
6,4		2
4,5		2
2,5		5

Table 2. Dataset 2 details

id	Category	Number of articles
1	Agriculture	190
2	Arts	42
3	Business	115
4	Humanities	68
5	Life	19
6	History	34
Multi labels ids		
1,3		4
4,6		2
4,5		3

Table 3. Dataset 3 details

id	Category	Number of articles
1	Chronology	54
2	Law	91
3	Belief	48
4	Geography	90
5	Education	125
6	Politics	54
Multi labels ids		
5,2		2
5,6		2
3,6		3

Vectors Machines optimized for text classification. The library is available on line: http://kask.eti.pg.gda.pl/alphansvm.

To evaluate the representations on the larger scale we create a dataset selecting 118 categories from the Wikipedia category structure. The initial categories have been shown in Figure 3. From the categories marked with rounded rectangles we select recursively all sub-categories up to leaf nodes. For the categories marked with straight line we select only one level sub-categories. The results achieved for this dataset have been presented in Table 5.

Table 4. Average results for test datasets 1-3

Representation method	AVG representation data file size [MB]	STD size [MB]	AVG classification quality F-measure	STD [%]	AVG representation generation time	AVG classifier learning time
cosine kernel	5,54	0,08	**95,13%**	0,71	9min:21s	6min:39s
words	2,71	0,07	92,85%	0,95	2min:55s	**40s**
n–grams	14,64	0,35	92,67%	0,4	6min:16s	8min:41s
ESA	5,83	0,09	90,46%	5,27	12min:26s	17min:45s
links	0,49	0,09	90,21%	0,78	4min:50s	7min:53s
HOR	**0,01**	0,00	88,01%	0,56	**2min:28s**	4min:32s
compression	3,88	0,05	83,93%	1,15	2h:7min:6s	1h:30min:49s
n–words	1,72	0,28	83,32%	**0,07**	7min: 9s	15min:49s

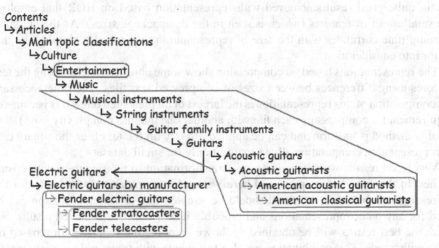

Contents
↳ Articles
 ↳ Main topic classifications
  ↳ Culture
   ↳ Entertainment
    ↳ Music
     ↳ Musical instruments
      ↳ String instruments
       ↳ Guitar family instruments
        ↳ Guitars
         ↳ Acoustic guitars
         ↳ Acoustic guitarists
   Electric guitars ←
   ↳ Electric guitars by manufacturer   ↳ American acoustic guitarists
    ↳ Fender electric guitars   ↳ American classical guitarists
     → Fender stratocasters
     ↳ Fender telecasters

Fig. 3. Wikipedia categories selected for a large scale dataset

Table 5. Results for large scale dataset created fro categories presented in Figure 3

Representation method	AVG representation data file size [MB]	AVG classification quality F-measure	STD [%]	AVG representation generation time	AVG classifier learning time
cosine kernel	67,3	**90,13%**	0,89	49min:32s	18min:09s
words	24,2	87,82%	0,99	12min:25s	**3min:39s**
n–grams	36,3	88,42%	1,1	14min:16s	19min:41s
ESA	42,7	88,72%	2,27	48min:23s	42min:19s
links	4,3	82,71%	0,81	9min:22s	19min:73s
HOR	**0,3**	83,11%	0,61	**4min:62s**	12min:34s
compression	29,2	78,42%	1,15	7h:2min:6s	3h:03min:32s
n–words	7,6	81,52%	**0,07**	27min:19s	35min:9s

6 Discussion and Future Work

The results presented in Tables 4 and 5 allow us to draw some conclusions on text representations used for Wikipedia articles.

Both approaches to representation as well as based on text content and with usage of referential methods gave quite good results. For the representation based on text content usage of words usually works better than others but the results achieved with n-grams are comparable. The comparative results (not included in the tables) show there are no significant differences in the classifications qualities while stemming is applied for representation based on words, but the size of features space is smaller. The n-words representations aiming at capturing phrases does not give expected improvement.

The referential approaches with usage of ESA gave the best results but it does not outperform the simpler representation based on links considerably. It should be noticed that ESA sometimes required considerably higher time to calculate classifier. We also obtain quite good results achieved with representation based on HOR that employs the smallest set of features (which is seen in the datapackage sizes). As the classifier learning time correlates with the size of representation thus we also should take this factor into consideration.

The representations based on compression show some abilities for extracting the text features using differences between sizes of compressed text files. The time necessary for computation of this representation is the largest of all presented ones. It is because of requirement for compressing each file with another one that has complexity $o(n^2) + n$. As this method is uniform and can be applied directly on the text files the square cost of representation computation allows to use it only for small datasets.

Very good results were achieved using transformation to metric space with cosine kernel. In the experiments presented here we apply this transformation only for the representations based on words. It should be stressed that this transformation can be used for any other representations and probably it will improve achieved results. We think the best results will be obtained while we combine the representation based on links with words. This combination we plan to achieve with transformation into metric spaces. The first experiments with cosine kernel show it is a good direction and now we plan to extend it with usage of cylindrical kernels [4].

What can be seen from the results the classification quality results are dependent on the dataset type and the number of classes. As more complicated cases are calculated the weaker results are obtained. But the degradation of quality comparing the datasets results given in Tables 4 and 5 is not shattering.

The applicability of approaches based on words are limited because of the lack of any semantics analysis eg. laptop and notebook will be treated as two different features. We made research to capture such similarities using WordNet dictionary and the first results are promising.

In the next iteration of Matrix'u development we plan to implement functionality for creating representation of any text based on Wikipedia articles [12]. The main idea is to map the text on the Wikipedia articles – in other words identify within provided text the concepts related to the articles. Effective implementation of that task should allow to represent the text on conceptual level. In that case conceptual representation is created by Wikipedia articles and their inner references and categories. Mapping the text into that space should allow to capture more sofisticated text similarities than those based on simple word co-occurrences.

The bag of features approach allows to efficiently use VSM to calculate similarity of the documents. As the elementary meaning of the utterances (eg. phrases) can not be captured in that way we plan to test alternative approaches. The main idea is to treat a text as a graph where nodes are the words and edges connect the neighboring words within one sentence. Additional edges added between nodes formed with sentences allow to capture changes of words alignment that is not possible while using VSM.

The experiments have been implemented on single computer, what limits the number of classes that can be used to create classifier. In future we plan to extent the implementation and create large scale classifier in our parallel framework in Beassy Cluster system [5].

Acknowledgments. The work has been supported by the Polish Ministry of Science and Higher Education under research grant N N 516 432338. The author would like also to thank Tomasz Pilarski and Jarosław Peć for their contribution to the application development.

References

1. Bennett, C., Li, M., Ma, B.: Chain letters and evolutionary histories. Scientific American 288(6), 76–81 (2003)
2. Biesiada, J., Duch, W.: Feature selection for high-dimensional data: A kolmogorov-smirnov correlation-based filter. Computer Recognition Systems, 95–103 (2005)
3. Büttcher, S., Clarke, C., Lushman, B.: Term proximity scoring for ad-hoc retrieval on very large text collections. In: Proceedings of the 29th Annual International ACM SIGIR Conference on Research and Development in Information Retrieval, pp. 621–622. ACM (2006)
4. Chevet, S.: Kernel associated with a cylindrical measure. Probability in Banach Spaces III, 51–84 (1981)
5. Czarnul, P.: Modeling, run-time optimization and execution of distributed workflow applications in the jee-based beesycluster environment. The Journal of Supercomputing, 1–26 (2010)
6. Davis, R., Shrobe, H., Szolovits, P.: What is a knowledge representation? AI magazine 14(1), 17 (1993)
7. Deerwester, S., Dumais, S., Furnas, G., Landauer, T., Harshman, R.: Indexing by latent semantic analysis. Journal of the American Society for Information Science 41(6), 391–407 (1990)
8. Gabrilovich, E., Markovitch, S.: Computing semantic relatedness using wikipedia-based explicit semantic analysis. In: Proceedings of the 20th International Joint Conference on Artificial Intelligence, vol. 6, p. 12. Morgan Kaufmann Publishers Inc. (2007)
9. Islam, A., Inkpen, D.: Real-word spelling correction using google web it 3-grams. In: Proceedings of the 2009 Conference on Empirical Methods in Natural Language Processing, vol. 3, pp. 1241–1249. Association for Computational Linguistics (2009)
10. Li, M., Vitányi, P.: An Introduction to Kolmogorov Complexity and its Applications, 3rd edn. Springer (2008)
11. Martins, B., Silva, M.: Language identification in web pages. In: Proceedings of the 2005 ACM Symposium on Applied Computing, pp. 764–768. ACM (2005)
12. Milne, D., Witten, I.: Learning to link with wikipedia. In: Proceedings of the 17th ACM Conference on Information and Knowledge Management, pp. 509–518. ACM (2008)

13. Papadimitriou, C., Sideri, M.: On the Floyd-Warshall algorithm for logic programs. Journal of Logic Programming 41(1), 129–137 (1999)
14. Sowa, J., et al.: Knowledge representation: logical, philosophical, and computational foundations, vol. 511. MIT Press (2000)
15. Szymański, J.: Categorization of Wikipedia Articles with Spectral Clustering. In: Yin, H., Wang, W., Rayward-Smith, V. (eds.) IDEAL 2011. LNCS, vol. 6936, pp. 108–115. Springer, Heidelberg (2011)
16. Szymański, J.: Self–Organizing Map Representation for Clustering Wikipedia Search Results. In: Nguyen, N.T., Kim, C.-G., Janiak, A. (eds.) ACIIDS 2011, Part II. LNCS, vol. 6592, pp. 140–149. Springer, Heidelberg (2011)
17. Wallach, H.: Topic modeling: beyond bag-of-words. In: Proceedings of the 23rd International Conference on Machine Learning, pp. 977–984. ACM (2006)
18. Westa, M., Szymański, J., Krawczyk, H.: Text Classifiers for Automatic Articles Categorization. In: Rutkowski, L., Korytkowski, M., Scherer, R., Tadeusiewicz, R., Zadeh, L.A., Zurada, J.M. (eds.) ICAISC 2012, Part II. LNCS, vol. 7268, pp. 196–204. Springer, Heidelberg (2012)
19. Wold, S., Esbensen, K., Geladi, P.: Principal component analysis. Chemometrics and Intelligent Laboratory Systems 2(1-3), 37–52 (1987)
20. Yang, Y., Pedersen, J.: A comparative study on feature selection in text categorization. In: International Conference on Machine Learning, pp. 412–420. Morgan Kaufmann Publishers, Inc. (1997)

Recovery Protocols for Flash File Systems

Ravi Tandon and Gautam Barua

Indian Institute of Technology Guwahati,
Department of Computer Science and Engineering,
Guwahati - 781039, Assam, India
r.tandon@alumni.iitg.ernet.in,
gb@iitg.ernet.in

Abstract. Supporting transactions within file systems entails very different issues than those in Databases, wherein the size of writes per transaction are smaller. Traditional file systems use a scheme similar to database management systems for supporting transactions resulting in suboptimal performance. Ext[6] based file systems either involve duplication of blocks, resulting in a reduced write throughput or provide only metadata consistency. The performance provided by a Log-structured file system on traditional hard disk drives is poor due to non-sequential reads that require movement of the read head.

This work presents an implementation of transaction support for log-structured file systems on flash drives. The technique makes use of the copy-on-write capabilities of the hitherto existing log- structured file systems. The major improvement is in the reduction in the overall write-backs to the disk. We provide protocols for recovery from transaction aborts and file system crash. The transaction support and recovery has been implemented in a flash file system[1].

Keywords: File Systems, Recovery, Transactions.

1   Introduction

A *transaction* can be defined as a unit of work that is executed in an *atomic, consistent, isolated and durable (ACID)* manner. With the advent of larger, more reliable and highly accessible systems, ensuring consistency of system data has become a necessity for modern user applications. DBMS (Database Management Systems) provide ACID properties to user applications through logging. However, databases do not provide uniform interfaces for supporting transactions. Support for transactions at the File System layer can provide a generic solution that can be used by any user level application.

Transaction support in file systems is provided through various logging techniques. Atomicity and durability are ensured by write-ahead logging, wherein updates are first made to the log. Each transaction has a start and a stop. Undo and redo based logging techniques are used to recover from a crash. Redo based recovery makes use of delayed writes, or the concept of aggregation of updates as in Ext3 [6]. Isolation and consistency are ensured by having concurrency control

C. Hota and P.K. Srimani (Eds.): ICDCIT 2013, LNCS 7753, pp. 511–522, 2013.

mechanisms used for ensuring serializability of schedules. Strict 2 phase locking scheme is widely used for ensuring consistency.

Logging schemes such as those used in Ext3 have two copies of data (one copy in the journal and the other copy in the actual file). This leads to a decrease in the bandwidth usage of the storage disk. Metadata logging schemes reduce the writes to the log, but fail to ensure complete transaction semantics can only be used to ensure consistency of a file system after a crash. Atomicity for instance might not be guaranteed by such a scheme. Other file systems such as the Log-structured file system have improved the write speed to the disk, by having sequential writes. Reads, however, are affected due to non-sequential storage of a files data. With the advent of new technology, such as Flash Devices, non-sequential write and read speeds have improved considerably. Also, the inherent *copy-on-write* nature of flash devices suits a log-structured file system well. Such a file system extends naturally to a transactional file system. Log-structured file systems provide easy crash recovery.

Our work focuses mainly on the recovery aspects in a log-structured file system designed for flash based storage devices. Our file system is based on client-server architecture. The client runs the user application program and the server runs the file system operations. We have designed protocols for recovery from crashes on the server side as well as transaction aborts on the client side. We also evaluate our design and provide a comparative study with a file system that uses a separate journal.

The rest of the paper is organized as follows: Section 2 throws light upon some of the existing works that have helped us understand and propose a design for the transactional file system for Log-structured file systems (LFS). Section 3 provides an overview of the underlying architecture on which transaction support for flash file system works. Section 4 describes the protocols used for recovery from client and server side aborts. Section 5 contains the experiments and the analysis of the results. Section 6 summarizes the work and proposes ideas for future work.

2   Related Work

Transaction support to user applications can be provided within user space or kernel space. The authors in [5] consider trade-offs between implementing transaction support within user space, on top of an existing file system, or in kernel space as part of a file sysem for a read or a write optimized file system. The dissertation shows that a careful implementation of a transaction support within the kernel in a write optimized file system can provide better performance than all other possible set of implementations, both for a CPU or I/O bound system. We, therefore, have implemented transaction support on a write-optimized file system within the file system. But our implementation of the file system is in user space due to time costraints. Other implementations such as Amino[8] have provided transaction support within user space. Implementations such as Sprite LFS [3], Ext3 [6], Transactional Flash[4] provide support for transactions in a generic manner.

Sprite LFS [3] is a prototype implementation of a log-structured file system. A log-structured file system writes all modifications to disk in a sequential manner similar to a log, thereby speeding up both write and recovery time. The log is the only structure on the disk, which contains the indexing information that is used to read files from the disk. The primary idea behind the design of Sprite LFS was to buffer writes in a memory cache and then to flush the writes to the disk in a sequential manner. This saves the time the read/write head spends in seeking to the accurate disk location for each random read/write. Sprite LFS essentially uses copy-on-write and therefore does not write data/metadata blocks in place. Traditional storage devices offer poor read performance for non-sequential reads. Solid state drives and flash file systems provide higher read performance and mitigate the effect of random reads.

Ext3 file system [6] provides faster recovery from crashes using metadata journaling on disk. A journal is a circular log stored in a dedicated area of the file system. Whenever updates are made to the disk, the corresponding metadata blocks are written to the journal before being flushed to the disk. The data blocks get updated to the disk first, and then the metadata blocks are written to the journal on disk. After the metadata blocks have been updated to the journal, the transaction is assumed to be committed. However, the journal cannot be erased unless and until the metadata blocks are synced back to the disk. Data blocks can also be written to the log, and if this is done, then a transactional file system can be implemented. However, the journal is mainly used only for metadata logging to provide easy recovery from crashes, as a transaction file system has not been implemented in Ext3 and there seems little point in incurring the extra overhead of data block writes to the log in the absence of such an interface.

Transactional Flash[4] is a write atomic interface implementation on a Solid State Device. It uses a cyclic commit protocol for ensuring atomicity of writes. The main aim of the commit protocol was to do away with the commit records that have to be written to the disk on each transaction commit operation. The authors of transactional flash have come up with a novel cyclic commit protocol, wherein they use page level tagging. The drawback of such a scheme is that each aborted transaction's writes to the disk must be erased from the disk, before a new version of the same page can be written to the disk. This induces a heavy erase penalty on the disk, as erase level granularity on flash disks is a block. To reduce the erase dependency, the authors develop another commit protocol BPCC. Each page points to the last committed version of the page. It, however, imposes certain restrictions on erase order, i.e. any page can be erased only after the pages that it marks aborted are erased. Our recovery protocol uses an idea that is similar to marking pages with some information (transaction identifier), and it does not impose any restrictions on the erase order.

3   Architecture

Our file system design uses a hybrid transaction management approach. Support for locking that provides isolation and consistency, has been implemented in user space[2]. The logging subsystem, that ensures atomicity and durability, has been implemented within the file system, currently also implemented in user space, although it can be easily moved to the kernel.

3.1   Top Level Architecture

A client-server architecture is built, wherein the client side runs the user application program and the server runs the file system (see Fig. 1). The transaction specific calls are implemented as a shared library. The user space is divided into two parts - transactional manager and YAFFS. The transaction manager implements locking, isolation and management of transaction state. The YAFFS file system implements the logging and recovery mechanism. Transaction manager consists of a transactional file system manager (TxFS Manager), update manager, a lock manager, a transaction management translation layer. The transactional manager was implemented in [2].

3.2   Implementation Details

The calls at the user level are traced using *LD_PRELOAD* runtime linker [7]. The system calls after being intercepted are sent to the server side using *Remote Procedure Calls*. The server handles the system call by creating a separate handler thread for each transaction. This thread acts as a dispatcher for all the system call requests on this connection. In the present architecture each client is a separate process. Each transaction begins with a txn_beg() and ends with a txn_end() or txn_commit(). The transaction reader (TxReader) listens to system calls from the user process. The transaction file system manager (TxFS Manager) interprets the system call. If the system call requests opening of a file, then the transaction file system manager sends a lock request to the Lock Manager. If the lock request is granted by the lock manager then the transaction file system manager sends a file open request to the translation layer. The translation layer forwards the request to the YAFFS. The YAFFS library handles the open (or close) request. On a read or a write system call, the transaction file system manager requests the update manager to handle them. The update manager checks whether the read or write system call is possible on the file (it checks whether the file has already been locked or not). Once the check is done, and the read or the write is allowed, then the update manager forwards the request to the translation layer (this is the part that has been implemented in this work). The translation layer converts the system calls for the Ext3 file system to those for YAFFS. These calls are then handled by the YAFFS system call library. In this work, we have replaced the Ext3 file system from the server side and we have used a log-structured file system (YAFFS Yet Another Flash File System [1]).

Top Level Architecture

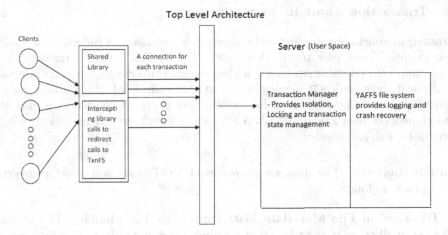

Fig. 1. Overview of the architecture of Transactional Flash File System

4 Recovery Protocols

Recovery protocols restore a file system to a consistent state by reconstructing the metadata and data of all the objects (files, directories, symbolic and hard links) that had been modified by aborted transactions. Transactions can fail due to two reasons. Firstly, there can be client side aborts. Secondly, there can be a server crash. Accordingly, the recovery protocols are divided into two broad categories viz. Transaction abort recovery protocol and Server crash recovery protocol.

4.1 Data Structures

YAFFS is a true log-structured file system. The log consists of blocks of chunks. The blocks correspond to segments in traditional Ext3 file system and chunks correspond to pages. Each chunk consists of an object identifier (inode number), chunk identifier (logical page number), byte count and sequence number. For the server crash recovery protocol, we have added a transaction identifier to each chunk. YAFFS maintains a node (called tnode) tree that maps each logical chunk in the file to a physical chunk on disk. We maintain a chunk map list (explained in subsection 4.2) that primarily stores a map that relates modified chunks of each file to their on disk location. For the transaction abort recovery protocol, we maintain a list of all the transactions that have modified any file, along with the file metadata (Transaction File Metadata List). Compression of transaction information maintained in the memory is not being performed as of now. For the server crash recovery protocol, a pair of bitmaps (in memory and on disk) is used in order to identify transaction status.

4.2   Transaction Abort Recovery Protocol

Transaction abort recovery protocol restores the metadata of objects that have been modified by a user transaction abort. Transaction recovery restores the chunk map tree (chunk map tree is a map which converts logical page indices to physical page indices), file size and the timestamps of objects that have been modified. A log-structured file system has previous consistent copies of data chunks (chunks are pages in YAFFS terminology) already on disk. Hence, rewrites to disk are avoided.

Data Structures. The data structures used for Transaction abort recovery protocol are as follows:

1. **Transaction File Metadata List:** Transaction File Metadata List stores a list of all those transactions that have modified any object. This list stores metadata of all the objects that have been modified by the transaction. The metadata is a snapshot of the previous state of the file before it was modified by the transaction. The recovery protocol switches the metadata state of objects to this consistent state once the transaction that modifies it aborts. The members of this list are as follows:
   - **Transaction Identifier:** Each element in the transaction file metadata list is uniquely identified by a transaction and an object identifier. The transaction identifier uniquely identifies a transaction.
   - **Object Identifier:** The object identifier is the inode identifier for a file (that has been modified by a transaction).
   - **File Length:** The length of each file that has been modified by a transaction is stored. During recovery, the file length is restored to the original file length (that was before a transaction modified it).
   - **Chunk Map List:** To restore a file the chunk map tree has to be restored in a log-structured file system. The chunk map list stores a map of pages that have been modified along with their previous consistent states on disk. The transaction file metadata list stores a pointer to a chunk map list.
2. **Chunk Map List:** Chunk map list stores a mapping from the logical space to the physical (on-disk) space for each chunk. Transaction abort recovery protocol is an undo based protocol. The physical identifier of a chunk in this list is the image of the chunk that was present before the transaction modified it. The list is an in-memory structure. Chunk map list consists of the following members:
   - **Logical Chunk Identifier:** The logical chunk identifier identifies a chunk (page) within a file. Only those chunks that have been modified by a transaction are stored within this list.
   - **Physical Chunk Identifier:** For each modified chunk the previous consistent image is stored in a physical chunk identifier. It translates to on-disk address of a chunk.

The Protocol. The transaction abort recovery protocol proceeds in three steps:

1. **Initialization:** The initialization phase initializes the transaction file metadata list by inserting the transaction identifier of each uncommitted transaction and the metadata of objects that each such transaction identifies.
2. **Update:** On a write call, since a copy-on-write takes place, data is written on to a new chunk. Whenever, a chunk is flushed to the disk (because of sync called by the user, use of write through mechanism, cache buffers become full), the logical chunk id to physical chunk id of each modified chunk is inserted in the chunk map list within the transaction file metadata list.
3. **Recovery/Rollback:** The recovery is an undo based rollback mechanism. The file length is updated. The chunk tree is restored to an earlier consistent state using the chunk map list in the transaction file metadata list.

4.3   Server Crash Recovery Protocol

The Server Crash Recovery Protocol is based on the concept of identification of the committed transactions through the on-disk inode (object header in YAFFS). Every time a commit takes place the file is closed and the inode is written to the disk. Each chunk written to the disk (both data and metadata chunk) has a tag field, which identifies the transaction that has written the chunk to the disk. Inodes written to the disk identify committed transactions.

Data Structures. The following data structures are maintained for the server crash recovery protocol:

- **In-Memory Transaction Bitmap:** It is an in-memory data structure that maintains the state of all the transactions. It stores the status of each transaction. Currently, the transaction state consists of a committed and an uncommitted state. The transaction identifiers are allocated by the file system itself, so there are no issues of collision of transaction identifiers (handled by keeping a pool of free transaction identifiers). The structure is a bitmap, storing binary information for each transaction identifier i.e. 1 for a committed transaction and 0 for an uncommitted transaction. Whenever a chunk is to be validated for commit or abort status, the transaction bitmap is looked up and the value provides the validity of the chunk.
- **On-Disk Transaction Bitmap:** On-disk transaction bitmaps are required to persist the status of transactions across reboots. Garbage collection in log-structured file systems may lead to intermediate inodes getting cleaned resulting in some data chunks becoming falsely uncommitted. The on-disk transaction bitmap stores the status of all transactions that have been committed. After every boot, a scan takes place that builds the in-memory data structures required by the file system. On encountering an inode-chunk the in-memory transaction bitmap is updated. On the completion of the scan process, the in-memory transaction bitmap is synced with the on-disk

transaction bitmap. If the on disk transaction bitmap is stale, we flush the in-memory transaction bitmap to the disk, thereby ensuring the consistency of all those transactions for which the mapping inode chunks have been invalidated due to a re-write of the inode chunk. It is implemented by allocating a set of chunks in a file (t_bmap).

The in-memory transaction bitmap gets flushed to the disk, only when the system restarts and the on-disk bitmap is not consistent with the in-memory transaction bitmap.

Protocol Implementation. The server crash recovery protocol consists of two stages, a scan stage and a sync stage.

1. **The Scan Stage:** The first stage in the recovery is the stage after the crash takes place and the file system boots. The file system scans the data and the metadata chunks in the opposite direction. This ensures that the inode chunks for each committed transaction are encountered first and followed by their respective data chunks . The in-memory transaction bitmap is initialized to all zeros - reflecting that as of now the file system does not know of any committed transaction. On a scan two categories of chunks are encountered:

    (a) **Metadata Chunks:** Each metadata chunk identifies a committed transaction. Therefore, the corresponding bit within the in-memory transaction bitmap is updated to reflect a committed transaction.

    (b) **Data Chunks:** There are basically two kinds of data chunks. They are:

        i. **Normal Data Chunk:** On encountering a normal files data chunk, the recovery protocol performs a validation check. The transaction identifier of the data chunk is checked against the in-memory transaction-bitmap. If the corresponding bit is set to one this data chunk becomes part of a committed transaction else the chunk is marked to be deleted.

        ii. **Bitmap Data Chunk:** On encountering the bitmap data chunk, the bitmap data is read in the t_bmap file as a normal file. This is later opened and read in the sync stage, so that the unmapped committed transactions persist across reboots.

2. **The Sync Stage:** After the scan completes, the t_bmap file is read and all the transactions that are marked committed in the on-disk bitmap are marked valid in the in-memory data chunk. This way the transactions for which the inode gets over-written persist across the reboots and the in-memory transaction-bitmap reflects a consistent view of the transaction-identifier space. The on-disk bitmap is checked for staleness. The on-disk bitmap becomes stale when there is at least a single committed transaction that has not been marked committed on the on-disk bitmap. This occurs when the transaction is committed after the last scan. The transaction bitmap is then written back to disk only if it was earlier found to be stale.

5   Evaluation

The primary objective of the experimental study was to measure the performance of our recovery protocols (implemented in YAFFS) with existing techniques. A file system that writes to a separate log file for journaling data (Separate Log FS) has been modeled. We have considered transaction aborts while measuring performance. Overheads due to data writes to files during the recovery process have been compared.

5.1   Experimental Setup

For the experimental study we have used client server (file server) architecture. The client sends request to the server through Remote Procedure Calls. The transaction aborts were communicated to the server by the client. Each transaction opens a file, writes data in the file and either aborts or commits. Finally the data is read by the last transaction. We have performed experiments on three sets of data writes per transaction. The sets have been divided according to the amount of data that is written to the disk per transaction. The three categories are:

1. **Small Data Per Transaction**
   For this category we have taken data of the order of 5-10 KB per transaction.
2. **Medium Data Per Transaction**
   For this category we have taken data of the order of 10-20 KB per transaction.
3. **Large Data Per Transaction**
   For this category we have taken data of the order of 20-50 KB per transaction.

For each of the above categories of data writes per transaction, we have simulated transaction aborts on the client side and measured the performance of our transaction abort recovery protocol. The parameter for performance measure is the overhead incurred during data writes to disk per transaction. Consistency of the data written by the client has also been checked. Each experiment consists of five different abort rates (0%, 20%, 32%, 70%, 77%). The results for each category (for a particular abort rate) have been obtained by taking an average over 1000 transactions. The numbers for abort frequency are taken at random intervals. We have tried to take low transaction abort rates (0%, 20%), moderate (30%) and high transaction abort rates (70%, 77%).

5.2   Separate Log File System

This file system uses a separate log to journal data writes. Recovery is done using undo operations that read consistent image of data from the journal. The earlier image of data blocks gets written to the log. On a transaction abort, all the data blocks that have been written by the aborted transaction are recovered from the log. On a transaction commit the inode block and all the data blocks are written to disk. The journal is a separate file. Unlike a log-structured file system, it supports writing in place. Only data blocks are persisted to the log to ensure consistency.

5.3   Results

In 1 each transaction writes about 7.5 KB of data to the disk and at very high abort rates the data written to the disk falls down to 1.5 KB (effective data written) per transaction. Some of the observations are:

1. The overhead ratio for the separate log scheme was almost 1.25 times more than that for YAFFS. This is because for each write to the disk the previous image of the data chunk is written to the disk. However, this is not close to two. For a sequential write model only a single page is written back to the disk per transaction.
2. YAFFS performs better than the separate log based journaling file system primarily because YAFFS does not write duplicate data to the disk. This reduces writes to the disk and the overall overhead is less.

Table 1. Comparison of Overheads: YAFFS VS Separate Log FS for small writes per transaction

Abort Rate (IN %)	Effective Data Written	Overhead Separate Log FS	Overhead YAFFS	Overhead Ratio Separate Log FS:YAFFS
0	7430	0.85	0.57	1.17
20	5922	1.33	0.91	1.21
32	4689	1.94	1.34	1.25
70	3001	3.56	2.48	1.31
77	1499	8.17	5.74	1.36

5.4   Comparison Across Writes

From Fig. 2a and Fig. 2b, the following observations can be made:

1. The overhead, when the abort rate is low, decreases as the size of data written per transaction increases. For each transaction commit inode is flushed to the disk. Therefore, if the amount of effective data that is written to the disk for each transaction is high, then the overhead cost that is incurred becomes low.
2. At higher abort rates, however the overhead for the large writes increases. This occurs because a large amount of data that belongs to aborted transactions is flushed to the disk. Thus, the overall writes to the disk increase.

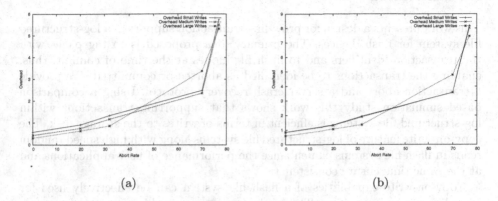

(a)   (b)

Fig. 2. Comparison of the overhead over different write sizes. (a) Shows the comparison of overheads for YAFFS across the three different write patterns. (b) Shows the comparison of overheads for Separate Log FS across the three different write patterns.

The experimental study performed conclusively shows that YAFFS outperforms file system with separate log, which incurs heavy overheads due to writes to the log. The overall data overhead for the file system with separate log was 1.25 to 1.40 to that of YAFFS. The overhead due to writes is affected by the size of data that gets written to the file per transaction and the abort rate. The overhead mainly occurs due to metadata writes, duplicate data writes (write on a partially written block involves rewriting some of the earlier data as the granularity of write is a block) and writes of aborted transactions. For a particular range of data writes per transaction (viz. small, medium, large) as the abort rate increased the overhead increased too. A comparison across write sizes reveals interesting results for a log-structured file system. At lower abort rates the overhead decreases as the writes per transaction increase. At a fixed abort rate variation in the overhead across different write sizes is observed due to metadata writes. As the amount of data written to disk per transaction increases the overhead decreases because the metadata written to the disk per transaction is independent of the data written to disk per transaction. As the abort rates increases a different effect is observed. The overhead due to aborted data became the dominating factor over the overhead due to the metadata write. This is because the metadata write is almost constant per transaction and the data written to disk per transaction increases. At 20% abort the overhead decreased from 0.91 (for small writes per transaction) to 0.64 (for large writes per transaction). At 70% abort rate the overhead was actually lesser for smaller writes (overhead $\approx$ 2.48) than that for large writes per transaction (overhead $\approx$ 3.37). This is because the overhead due to aborted writes becomes much larger as compared to the overhead due to metadata write per transaction.

6   Conclusion

This work presents a design for providing transaction support in a log-structured file system for flash devices. The primary idea proposed is to tag pages with the transaction identifiers and to flush file inodes at the time of commit, thus, enabling the transactions to be identified as aborted or committed. We provide a transaction abort and a server crash recovery protocol. Using a comparison based simulation study this work shows that supporting transactions within log-structured file systems is efficient in terms of writes to the storage disk. The copy-on-write feature of log-structured file systems along with high speed random reads in flash file systems can enhance the performance of user applications and at the same time ensure consistency.

Copy-on-write capabilities of a flash file system can be effectively used for an online versioning system. The versioning system would make use of transactional support from the file system. Applications such as an online backup of a transactional log-structured file system present scope for future research and development.

References

1. http://www.yaffs.net/
2. Deka, L.: Consistent Online Backup in Transactional File Systems. PhD thesis, Dept of Computer Science and Engineering, IIT Guwahati (April 2012)
3. Ousterhout, J.K., Rosenblum, M.: The design and implementation of a log-structured file system. In: Proceedings of the 13th ACM Symposium on Operating Systems Principles (February 1992)
4. Prabhakaran, V., Rodeheffer, T.L., Zhou, L.: Transactional flash. In: Proceedings of the 8th USENIX Conference on Operating Systems Design and Implementation, OSDI 2008, pp. 147–160. USENIX Association, Berkeley (2008)
5. Seltzer, M.I., Stonebraker, M.: Transaction support in read optimizied and write optimized file systems. In: Proceedings of the 16th International Conference on Very Large Data Bases, VLDB 1990, pp. 174–185. Morgan Kaufmann Publishers Inc., San Francisco (1990)
6. Tweedie, S.: Journaling the linux ext2fs filesystem (1998)
7. Wright, C.P., Spillane, R., Sivathanu, G., Zadok, E.: Extending acid semantics to the file system. Trans. Storage 2 (June 2007)
8. Wright, C.P.: Extending acid semantics to the file system via ptrace. PhD thesis, Stony Brook, NY, USA, AAI3238986 (2006)

Semantic Concurrency Control on Continuously Evolving OODBMS Using Access Control Lists

V. Geetha[1] and N. Sreenath[2]

[1] Dept. of Information Technology
[2] Dept. of Computer Science & Engg.
Pondicherry Engineering College
Puducherry – 605014
{vgeetha,nsreenath}@pec.edu

Abstract. Object oriented databases (OODBMS) are widely used for applications which require support of complex relationships on data. Transactions access the database for data or schema simultaneously. The runtime transactions read/modify the data. The design time transactions read/modify the schema. In a continuously evolving domain, more number of design time transactions is executed along with runtime transactions. Parallel execution of runtime and design time transactions affects the consistency of the database. Hence a concurrency control technique is needed to preserve the database consistency. Several concurrency control techniques using multi-granular lock models have been proposed in the literature. Multi-granular lock model provides better concurrency and is simple to implement. But high concurrency is provided to dynamic databases at the cost of heavy maintenance overhead. In this paper, a concurrency control scheme is proposed using access control lists to provide better concurrency, without the maintenance overhead. The performance of proposed scheme is compared with existing work. It is found that the proposed scheme gives better response time than the existing work and also eliminates the overhead of maintenance of access vectors.

Keywords: OODBMS, concurrency control, semantic locking, continuously evolving domains, access control lists.

1   Introduction

OODBMS are widely used for advanced applications like CAD, CAM etc., as they support representation of complex data and their complicated relationships. OODBMS is a collection of objects. The objects are of two types - classes and instances. A class object consists of attributes and methods. It defines the state (defined by attributes) and behaviour (defined by member functions) of an entity.

The clients can access the OODBMS in two modes - runtime mode and design time mode. In runtime mode, the domain data is mapped onto the attributes of instances and the associated member function operates on them to satisfy client transactions. The member function (also called as method) may read or modify the attribute values. Design time mode is used to read or modify the schema to reflect the changes in the domain. The design time operations can access attribute definitions,

C. Hota and P.K. Srimani (Eds.): ICDCIT 2013, LNCS 7753, pp. 523–534, 2013.
© Springer-Verlag Berlin Heidelberg 2013

method definitions, class definitions and class relationship definitions. In general, database access can be a read or write operation. The read operations can be executed in shared lock mode and write operations should be executed in exclusive lock mode. The client transactions can access the database in one of these granularities: - class lattice level, class level and instance level.

Usually, the clients send more runtime transactions to access the data. The design time transactions are few and are far in-between. But business domains require continuous updating of services. The continuous updating of domain requires continuous updating of schema. In the case of continuously evolving domains, the schema has to be changed frequently. It results in more number of design time transactions along with runtime transactions. This may affect the consistency of the database.

Among the three popular concurrency control mechanisms such as locking, optimistic concurrency control and time stamp ordering, locking is widely used due to its ease of implementation. Locking technique requires commutativity matrix as well as lock table for its efficient implementation.

Several lock based concurrency control mechanisms [2, 4, 5, 6, 7, 10] have been proposed in the literature. Multi-granular lock models are most favoured as they provide maximum concurrency. This is possible because the same data resource can be accessed by several transactions in parallel in small granularity sizes. As a result, deadlocks due to lock escalation are minimized. Concurrency control schemes using access vectors [8, 9, 11, 16] are introduced to further enhance the concurrency. They require access vectors in addition to commutativity matrix and lock table. They perform better in stable domains, where a large number of runtime transactions would arrive with very few design time transactions. But in the case of continuously evolving systems, the schema of the domain needs to be changed frequently to match the new changes in the domain. Then, the access vectors as well as lock table should be altered every time a schema change is made. Because of this, the maintenance overhead is more than the conventional locking technique. This introduced the need for a new concurrency control scheme to support evolving systems with less overhead.

In this paper, the author presents a concurrency control scheme using access control lists to provide maximum concurrency. The proposed scheme has these advantages. It is based on multi-granularity locking. The commutativity matrix defines the commutativity of various combinations of lock modes. It utilizes a rich set of lock modes defined in Geetha and Sreenath [11][16] that provide maximum concurrency possible using lock modes while ensuring semantic consistency. It uses access control lists only unlike using lock table as well as access control lists to improve concurrency. Further, it does not have any overhead of updating every time the schema is changed. The search time of lock status is also minimized. It does not need any prior knowledge of structure of objects. Further the proposed work allows more parallelism between design time transactions and runtime transactions.

The paper is organized as follows. In the next section, the related works are reviewed and their merits and demerits are discussed. In section 3, the scheme based on access control lists is proposed. In section 4, the performance evaluation of the proposed scheme is presented. The paper concludes in section 5.

2   Related Works

The various concurrency control schemes can be assessed based on the level of concurrency they provide for parallel execution of design time and runtime transactions without compromising on consistency. These two types of transactions induce three different types of conflicts among transactions to a class: conflicts among runtime transactions; conflicts among design time transactions and conflicts between runtime and design time transactions.

2.1   Conflicts among Run Time Transactions

The concurrency control schemes provide compatibility among transactions in two ways namely based on relationships and based on commutativity.

In Garza and Kim [1], Kim et al. [2], Lee and Liou[10], Geetha and Sreenath [3], Jun and Gruenwald [4], the concurrency control is based on object relationships. These algorithms offer smallest granularity of object level. So concurrency is limited. In class diagrams representing any business domain, the class relationships namely inheritance, aggregation and association exist in different combinations. These concurrency control schemes define lock modes for each relationship separately. They do not define lock modes for objects with combination of relationships. Hence they are not suitable for concurrency control of objects with complex relationships.

In the second group of concurrency control schemes, compatibility is defined based on commutativity. In Agrawal and Abbadi [5], the idea of right backward (RB) commutativity is introduced. However application programmers need to know all possible results of each method.

In Badrinath and Ramamritham [6], attribute is the smallest granularity supported. They state that any two methods can be executed in parallel if they do not share any attribute. But it requires knowledge of the structure of all methods in a class. In Badrinath and Ramamritham [7], the idea of recoverability is defined. i.e., the methods can be executed in any order. But the commit order is fixed. This also requires apriori knowledge of class structure.

In Malta and Martinez [8], the commutativity is automated by defining Direct Access Vector (DAV) for each method. A DAV is a vector whose field corresponds to each attribute defined in the class on which the method operates. Each value composing this vector denotes the most restricted access mode used by the method while accessing the corresponding attribute. Access mode of an attribute can have one of these values: null (N), read (R) and write (W) with N < R < W for their restrictiveness. DAV is constructed at compile time by extracting syntactic information from the source code. Then the commutativity table is constructed for each class based on the rule that two methods in a class commute, if their DAV commutes.

In Jun [9], concurrency is further improved by providing granularity smaller than attribute level up to break points. But this also requires prior knowledge of structure of objects. In all these schemes, whenever the signature or implementation of a method changes due to design time transaction, its DAV has to be updated.

In all the above schemes, the concurrency is improved by using DAV. The DAV requires prior knowledge of the structure of objects. This gives the best performance for stable domains in which the schema is modified very rarely. But the DAV for every method has to be updated whenever there is a schema change. During this time, other runtime transactions are not allowed. The runtime transactions are blocked whenever the schema is changed. So this locking scheme of commutativity and access vectors is not suitable for continuously evolving systems.

2.2   Conflicts among Design Time Transactions

In OODBMS, the schema is represented by a class diagram. The design time transactions can do changes to schema in two ways as specified in Kim et al. [13] and Bannerjee et al. [14]. They view the class diagram as directed acyclic graph. The classes are viewed as nodes and the relationship links connecting classes are viewed as edges. The schema changes are categorized into changes to node and changes to edges. In the node (class) changes, the following operations are allowed. The node can be changed or its contents can be changed. Node can be changed by adding/deleting a class, or changing the name of a class. A node typically contains instances, attributes and methods. Adding, deleting and changing these contents are the operations allowed in this category. Changes to edge include changing a class relationship or class position in class lattice.

In Lee and Liou [10], all the above operations are done using only one lock mode by locking the entire schema with Read Schema (RS) and Write Schema (WS). In Malta and Martinez [8], lock mode for changing the class definition (class contents) is provided by RD (Read Definition) and MD (Modify Definition) lock modes. They have omitted other types of schema changes. Agrawal and Abbadi [5] provided finer granularity by defining separate lock modes for attributes and methods (class contents). They also have not defined any lock mode for operations involving changes to nodes and edges.

In Jun [9], separate lock modes are defined for attributes, methods and class relationships. In this paper, lock table is represented as two access vector tables. Attribute Access Vector (AAV) and Method Access Vector (MAV) define the lock status of all attributes and methods. The lock status can be {Null, Read, Write}.The use of these access vectors provides fine granularity and thus brings maximum concurrency. But, operations involving class relationships, like changing class position and relationship are still serialized.

In Geetha and Sreenath [11], the granularity is further improved by defining lock modes for signature and implementation of method separately. They also ensure semantic consistency between classes where attributes and methods are defined and where they are used. This was overlooked in Jun [9]. Concurrency is further enhanced by defining Relationship Access Vector (RAV) which is used to lock only the related classes instead of locking the entire class diagram for operations involving node changes. RAV maintains a list of parent classes and child classes for every class. Parent classes are classes from which the class is derived. Child classes are classes which are derived from this class. RAV improved the performance further. In Geetha and Sreenath [16], separate lock modes have been defined to handle changes to nodes and edges. In these algorithms, fine granularity is provided with the help of commutativity matrix and access vectors. Access vectors can be omitted at the cost of limited concurrency. Hence there is a trade-off between limited concurrency and access vectors maintenance overhead. All the above schemes perform better for stable domains, but involve maintenance overhead of access vectors for continuously evolving domains.

2.3   Conflicts between Runtime Transactions and Design Time Transactions

During runtime transactions, the values of attributes are read or modified by executing the associated methods in a class. The attribute values are locked in read and write lock modes. In design time transactions, the attribute definitions are read or modified. Thus attribute has two facets and is chosen depending on the type of transaction.

Runtime transactions lock the methods in read mode as their contents are not modified by execution. Design time transactions read or modify the method definitions. When any attribute or method definition is modified, runtime transactions accessing them should not be allowed.

In the existing algorithms, concurrency control of runtime transaction is achieved using commutativity matrix and DAV of all classes in the class diagram. Concurrency control of design time transactions are achieved by commutativity matrix, AAV, MAV and RAV of all attributes, methods and classes. When runtime and design time transactions come in parallel, then all the above mentioned data structures are required to provide fine granularity. This involves search overhead as well as maintenance overhead of access vectors (DAV, AAV, MAV and RAV).

3   The Proposed Scheme

Though the use of Direct Access vector (DAV), Attribute Access Vector (AAV), Method Access Vector (MAV) and Relationship Access Vector (RAV) provide higher concurrency, they have the following limitations: 1. Prior knowledge of the structure of the class is required. 2. The access vectors are to be updated every time the schema is changed due to a design time transaction which involves maintenance overhead for continuously evolving domains. 3. The search overhead is also involved in searching the lock status of the data item requested by the transactions as it needs to search the entire list to read or update the lock status of a data item.

The proposed work uses the commutativity matrix defined in Geetha and Sreenath[11]. It defined lock modes for accessing the interface and implementation of methods separately. In object oriented programming, the attributes and methods are defined in a class and read by all classes related to this class by inheritance, aggregation and association. So, it is not enough if commutativity of locks is checked within the defined class for attributes and methods. It is also required to check the compatibility in the related classes that have adapted these attributes and methods. In Riehle and Berzuck [12], the methods defined in base class of inheritance hierarchy, are of two types namely template methods and hook methods. The signature and implementation of template methods are inherited as it is, in sub classes. This is called as implementation inheritance. So, they can be only read in sub classes. In the case of hook methods, only signature is inherited. The sub classes are allowed to have their own implementation. This is called interface inheritance. Then they should be treated differently and commutativity should be defined accordingly. Hence, another matrix is proposed between the transactions accessing the attributes and methods in classes, where they are defined and the transactions where they are used. All the design time transactions should check for compatibility in the defined class and adapted classes to maintain consistency. The concurrency is maximized in existing schemes as in table 1 and 2 with the help of DAV, AAV, MAV and RAV. So the existing works use commutativity matrix, lock table (represented as AAV, MAV and RAV) and DAV to provide maximum concurrency.

Table 1. Proposed commutativity matrix for design time transactions and runtime transactions with access vectors

	AA	RAA	RA	MA	DA	AM	RAMS	RMS	MMS	RAMI	RMI	MMI	DM	MAMI	RCD	MCD	RCR	MCR	IA
AA	Y	Y	Y	Y	Y	Y	Y	Y	Y	Y	Y	Y	Y	Y	Y	Δ	N	N	Y
RAA	Y	Y	Y	Y	Y	Y	Y	Y	Y	Y	Y	Y	Y	Y	Y	Δ	Y	N	Y
RA	Y	Y	Y	Δ	Δ	Y	Y	Y	Y	Y	Y	Y	Y	Y	Y	Δ	Y	N	Y
MA	Y	Y	Δ	Δ	Δ	Δ	Y	Y	Y	Y	Y	Y	Δ	Δ	Y	Δ	N	N	Δ
DA	Y	Y	Δ	Δ	Δ	Δ	Y	Δ	Δ	Y	Δ	Δ	Y	Δ	Δ	Δ	N	N	Δ
AM	Y	Y	Y	Δ	Δ	Y	Y	Y	Y	Y	Y	Y	Y	Y	Y	Δ	Δ	N	Y
RAMS	Y	Y	Y	Y	Y	Y	Y	Y	Y	Y	Y	Y	Y	Δ	Y	Δ	Y	N	Y
RMS	Y	Y	Y	Y	Δ	Y	Y	Y	Δ	Y	Y	Δ	Y	Δ	Y	Δ	Y	N	Y
MMS	Y	Y	Y	Y	Δ	Y	Y	Δ	Δ	Y	Δ	Δ	Δ	Y	Y	Δ	N	N	Δ
RAMI	Y	Y	Y	Y	Y	Y	Y	Y	Y	Y	Y	Y	Y	Δ	Y	Δ	Y	N	Y
RMI	Y	Y	Y	Y	Δ	Y	Y	Y	Δ	Y	Y	Δ	Y	Δ	Y	Δ	Y	N	Y
MMI	Y	Y	Y	Y	Δ	Y	Y	Y	Y	Y	Δ	Δ	Δ	Y	Y	Δ	N	N	Y
DM	Y	Y	Y	Δ	Y	Y	Y	Δ	Δ	Y	Δ	Δ	Y	Y	Δ	Δ	N	N	Δ
MAMI	Y	Y	Y	Δ	Δ	Y	Δ	Y	Y	Δ	Y	Y	Y	Δ	Δ	Δ	N	N	Y
RCD	Y	Y	Y	Y	Δ	Y	Y	Y	Δ	Y	Y	Δ	Δ	Y	Δ	Y	N	Y	Y
MCD	Δ	Δ	Δ	Δ	Δ	Δ	Δ	Δ	Δ	Δ	Δ	Δ	Δ	Δ	Δ	Δ	N	N	Δ
RCR	N	Y	Y	N	N	N	Y	Y	N	Y	Y	N	N	N	Y	N	Y	N	Y
MCR	N	N	N	N	N	N	N	N	N	N	N	N	N	N	N	N	N	N	Δ
IA	Y	Y	Y	Δ	Δ	Y	Y	Y	Δ	Y	Y	Y	Δ	Δ	Y	Δ	Y	Δ	Δ

Table 2. Commutativity matrix for defined class and adapted classes with access vectors

	RAA	RAMS	RAMI	RMI	MMI	MAMI
MA	Δ	Y	Y	Y	Y	Δ
MMS	Y	Δ	Δ	Δ	Δ	Δ
MMI	Y	Y	Δ	Y	Y	Y
DA	Δ	Δ	Δ	Δ	Δ	Δ
DM	Y	Δ	Δ	Y	Y	Δ

In Geetha and Sreenath [11] [16], the commutativity matrix for both runtime transactions and design time transactions is defined as in table 1 and table 2. The lock modes defined are as follows.

- AA – Add Attribute – New attributes with their names and domain names can be added to a class.
- DA – Delete Attribute – Existing attributes in a class can be deleted. Any attempt to use this attribute should raise error flag.

- AM- Add Method – New methods can be added by adding their signature and implementation using this   mode.
- RCD – Read Class Definition – This lock mode can be used for reading a class name, reading all its attributes and methods. .
- MCD –Modify Class Definition – This lock mode can be used to add a new class, delete an existing class and change a class name.
- RCR – Read Class Relationship – This lock mode is for reading the relationship with other classes in the class lattice.
- MCR– Modify Class Relationship – This lock mode is for changing the relationships between classes and changing the position of a class in class lattice.
- RAA – Read Adapted Attributes – Read attributes defined in base class and component class adapted in to this class
- RA – Read Attribute – Read attributes defined in this class.
- MA – Modify Attribute – Modify attributes defined in this class.
- RAMS – Read Adapted Method Signature – Read signature of template methods and hook methods adapted from other classes by inheritance and methods from component classes.
- RMS – Read Method Signature – Read signature of methods defined in this class.
- MMS– Modify Method Signature – Modify signature of methods defined in this class.
- DM- Delete Method-Any client transaction to a deleted method should raise error flag.
- RAMI – Read Adapted Method Implementation - Read implementation of methods adapted from other classes by inheritance and methods from component classes.
- MAMI – Modify Adapted Method Implementation - Modify implementation of hook methods adapted from base class by inheritance.
- RMI – Read Method Implementation - Read implementation of methods defined in this class.
- MMI – Modify Method Implementation - Modify implementation of methods defined in this class.
- IA – Instance Access – This mode is used for executing runtime transactions.

The proposed scheme provides the same level of higher concurrency as in table 1 and 2, without the limitations of access vectors, by splitting the lock table into three lists namely *Available, Shared and Exclusive* lists. This eliminates the need for maintaining DAV along with lock table. The maintenance overhead is minimized as access vectors are not needed. The search time is minimized as the lock table is split into three lists. Any request requires search of only one of these lists instead of all of them. This reduces the search overhead to roughly about one third. In *Available list*, the attributes and methods of each class that are currently available are included. In *Shared list*, the attributes and methods of each class that are currently in shared (read) lock mode are included. In *Exclusive list*, the attributes and methods of each class that are currently in exclusive (write) lock mode are included.

The format of *Available, Shared and Exclusive* lists are given in figures 1 and 2. The RType (resource type) can be attribute definition, attribute value or method definition. RType - attribute definition is used in design time transactions. RType - attribute value is accessed in runtime transactions. So, two entries are maintained for every attribute. The objective for maintaining two entries is to allow concurrent reading of attribute definition while attribute value is read or modified. Resource ID holds the name of the attribute or method. Class ID is used to distinguish attributes or methods whose names are used in more than one class. Shared list maintains one more field called Refcount to maintain the number of transactions sharing the resource.

Initially, the attributes and methods of all classes are included in the Available list. As the transactions arrive, they are checked for commutativity of locks in the commutativity matrix. If they are compatible, the requested resources are added to either Shared or Exclusive list, depending on the lock mode. Though all the resources are in Available list in the beginning, eventually they will be scattered to other lists depending on the lock type requested by transactions arrived. In order to save search time, list search policies given in figure 3 are used. Exclusive lock mode is allowed for a requested resource only if the resource is currently present in Available list.

Shared lock mode is possible, only if the resource is not in Exclusive list. It is allowed when the resource is in Available list or Shared list. Searching the resource in both lists is time consuming. So if it is not available in Exclusive list, grant message can be sent and resource can be accordingly updated from Available list or Shared list in the background. Several transactions can share a resource in read mode. Refcount field in Shared list is used to count the number of transactions that are currently sharing the resource. First grant message adds the resource to the Shared list and sets the count to 1. Every grant message after that, increments the count. Every release message decrements it. When the count is 0, the resource is removed and it is added to the Available list. Let us now see how the proposed scheme works for runtime and design time transactions.

3.1   Concurrency among Runtime Transactions

The runtime transactions request resources by giving the class ID and method ID. The attributes used along with their lock mode in every method can be documented using document tools like JavaDoc or C++Doc as given in [12]. From this, the attributes to be locked can be deduced by preprocessing. As mentioned in section 2.3, the methods are locked in read mode for runtime transactions. So the requested method ID is removed from Available list and added to Shared list. Several runtime transactions executing the same method can share the implementation. The value entries for the attribute IDs used in the methods are added to Shared list if they are input parameters, and to Exclusive list if they are not. In runtime transaction, only the attribute value is read or modified. So, entry with RType-attribute value is removed from Available list and added to Shared or Exclusive list. The granularity of runtime transaction is attribute level.

3.2   Concurrency among Design Time Transactions

The design time transactions usually read or modify the schema. As mentioned in section 2.2, the design time transactions can be one of these three types: Changes to node (class), class contents (attributes and methods) and changes to edges (relationships and position). The design time transactions are handled as below.

Class ID	RType	Resource ID	Ref count

Fig. 1. Format of Shared list

Class ID	RType	Resource ID

Fig. 2. Format of Available and Exclusive lists

Requested Lock mode	List to be checked
Exclusive (X)	Available list
Shared (S)	Exclusive list

Fig. 3. List search policies for S and X lock modes

The smallest granularity supported is the attribute. Attribute definitions can be read or modified. Runtime transaction on an attribute can be concurrently executed with read design transaction. RA lock mode uses RType – attribute definition entry. When RA and RAA are requested, corresponding attribute definition entry is added to Shared list based on the policy mentioned in section 3.

When MA lock mode is requested, parallel runtime transaction involving this attribute should not be allowed to maintain consistency. So, both definition entry and value entry of the attribute should be included in Exclusive list. If only definition entry is available, it implies that the attribute is currently being used in runtime transaction. Then, it has to wait until both entries are available in Available list.

When lock modes RAMS, RMS, MMS, RAMI, RMI, MMI, MAMI are requested on a method, the search policies as mentioned in section 3, are followed to update access control lists. When new attributes or methods are added in a class using lock modes AA, AM, they are added to the Available list. The arriving transactions can request for this attribute or method only after this. When existing attributes or methods are deleted using DA and DM lock modes, they can be removed only when they are in the Available list to preserve consistency. This is ensured in commutativity matrix in table 1and 2.Changes involving nodes and edges involve removing all the attributes and methods of the related classes from Available list and adding them to Exclusive list. They should be serialized to maintain the semantic consistency of the database.

4   Performance Evaluation

In order to evaluate the proposed technique in general environment, a simulation model is constructed and experiments are conducted. The simulation model is implemented using Java. It consists of transaction generator, transaction manager, scheduler, lock manager, deadlock manager. The transaction generator creates new transactions randomly. The transaction manager schedules the transactions. Lock manager is responsible for concurrency control. Deadlock manager is responsible for detecting cycles and resolving them. Transactions are restarted after deadlock resolution.

007 Benchmark by Carey [16] is well known for testing performance of OODBMS. It is used in Jun [9] for showing the performance of his proposal. But 007 benchmark defines the benchmark only for runtime transactions. It does not define any testing cases for design time transactions. So it cannot be fully adopted for the proposed scheme The database model and testing cases of runtime transactions are adopted. 007 benchmark classifies databases into small, medium and large, based on their size. Here, small size is chosen for simplicity. The design time transactions are framed to cover all three types of schema changes. Table 3 gives the simulation parameters.

Table 3. Simulation Parameters

Parameters	Default value(range)
Time to process one operation	0.00000625ms
Mean time to set lock by instant access	0.3301 ms
Mean time to set lock by class definition access transaction	0.3422ms
Mean time to release lock	0. 0015ms
Multiprogramming level	8 (5-15)
Prob. Of Traversal	0.25 (0-1)
Prob. Of Query	0.25 (0-1)
Prob. Of Schema change	0.5 (0-1)
Prob. Of Changes to nodes	0.15 (0-1)
Prob. Of Changes to edges	0.20(0-1)
Prob. Of changes to node contents	0.15(0-1)
Transaction inter-arrival time	500(100-1000)
Database model [16]	Small (small, medium, large)

Figure 4 shows the performance of the proposed scheme with access control list against Jun's scheme [9] and Geetha and Sreenath scheme (G&N scheme) with access vectors. The performance is tested by varying the design time transaction to runtime transaction ratio. Jun scheme requires highest response time. This is because only three lock modes have been defined for design time transactions namely modify attribute (MA), modify method (MM) and modify class relationship (MCR). MCR covers all the schema changes involving changes to contents and changes to nodes. It does not support changes to edges. In G & N scheme, separate lock modes like AA, DA, AM, DM, MCD and MCR to support changes to nodes and edges. Concurrency is improved in changes to node contents by defining more lock modes like RAMS,

RMS, MMS, RAMI, RMI, MMI and MAMI. However, fine concurrency is possible only with access vectors. Access vectors involve maintenance overhead for continuously evolving domains.

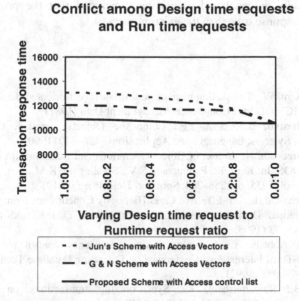

Fig. 4. Performance varying Design time transaction to Runtime transaction ratio

The results in fig 4 show that the performances of all the schemes are approximately same for stable domains where 100% of transactions are runtime transactions. But as the ratio of design time transactions increase (implies evolving domains), the performance of Jun scheme and G & N scheme deteriorates. The reason is that, as the ratio of design time transaction increases, the time taken to update the access vectors increase. As a result, response time increases for the schemes. In the proposed scheme, it can be observed that the response time is relatively constant because there is no need for updating access control lists. The proposed scheme gives almost the same response time for all combinations of design time transactions and runtime transactions. Further it does not need any apriori knowledge of object structure. Thus, the proposed scheme performs the best.

5   Conclusion

Concurrency control schemes for OODBMS are tedious, because of their complex modeling and long duration transactions. In this paper, a concurrency control scheme is proposed to meet out the above requirements and support continuously evolving domains with no overhead. The existing algorithms require maintenance of multiple data structures for providing maximum concurrency. Though the existing algorithms perform well for stable domains, their performance deteriorates in continuously evolving domains. In the proposed work, the same level of concurrency is provided with minimal data structures that require less searching overhead and maintenance overhead. The performances of the existing works are compared with proposed scheme and results are analyzed. It can be concluded that the proposed scheme provides better response time than the existing works.

References

1. Garza, J.F., Kim, W.: Transaction management in an object oriented database system. In: Proc. ACM SIGMOD Int'l Conference, Management Data (1987)
2. Kim, W., Bertino, E., Garza, J.F.: Composite Objects revisited. Object Oriented Programming, Systems, Languages and Applications, 327–340 (1990)
3. Geetha, V., Sreenath, N.: Impact of Object Operations and Relationships on Concurrency Control in DOOS. In: Kant, K., Pemmaraju, S.V., Sivalingam, K.M., Wu, J. (eds.) ICDCN 2010. LNCS, vol. 5935, pp. 258–264. Springer, Heidelberg (2010)
4. Jun, W., Gruenwald, L.: An Effective Class Hierarchy Concurrency Control Technique in Object – Oriented Database Systems. Elsevier Journal of Information and Software Technology, 45–53 (1998)
5. Agrawal, D., Abbadi, A.: A non-restrictive concurrency control for object-oriented databases. In: Third International Conference on Extending Database Technology, Vienna, Austria, pp. 469–482 (1992)
6. Badrinath, B., Ramamirtham, K.: Synchronizing transactions on objects. IEEE Transactions on Computers 37(5), 541–547 (1988)
7. Badrinath, B., Ramamritham, K.: Semantic- based concurrency control: beyond commutativity. ACM Transactions of Database Systems 17(1), 163–199 (1992)
8. Malta, C., Martinez, J.: Automating Fine Concurrency Control in Object Oriented Databases. In: 9th IEEE Conference on Data Engineering, Austria, pp. 253–260 (1993)
9. Jun, W.: A multi-granularity locking-based concurrency control in object oriented database system. Elsevier Journal of Systems and Software, 201–217 (2000)
10. Lee, S.Y., Liou, R.Y.: A Multi-Granularity Locking model for concurrency control in Object – Oriented Database Systems. IEEE Transactions on Knowledge and Data Engineering 8(1) (1996)
11. Geetha, V., Sreenath, N.: A Multi–Granular Lock Model for Distributed Object Oriented Databases Using Semantics. In: Natarajan, R., Ojo, A. (eds.) ICDCIT 2011. LNCS, vol. 6536, pp. 138–149. Springer, Heidelberg (2011)
12. Riehle, D., Berczuk, S.P.: Properties of Member Functions in C++. Report (2000)
13. Kim, W.: Introduction to Object Oriented Databases. MIT Press, Cambridge
14. Banerjee, J., Kim, W., Kim, H.J., Korth, H.F.: Semantics and Implementation of Schema evolution in Object–Oriented Databases. In: Proc. ACM SIGMOD Conference (1987)
15. Carey, M., Dewitt, D., Naughton, J.: 007 Benchmark. In: Proceedings of ACM SIGMOD Conference in Management of Data, Washington, USA (1993)
16. Geetha, V., Sreenath, N.: Semantic Based Concurrency Control in OODBMS. In: Proceedings in IEEE Computer Society International Conference on Recent Trends in Information Technology, Chennai, India, June 3-5 (2011)

Querying a Service from Repository of SMaps

Supriya Vaddi and Hrushikesha Mohanty

Department of CIS, University of Hyderabad
supriyavaddi@gmail.com, hmcs_hcu@yahoo.com

Abstract. Recent advances in Internet technologies have populated web with large number of services. For effective retrieval of services we have proposed SMap [10] specification that enables service provider to describe a service concealing its business logic. The details of a service includes its constituents, promotion and associated conditions. Here we propose a scheme to store SMaps in a relational database. For service retrieval a query processing system is also proposed. Retrieved services are ranked based on a score computed from structural characteristics of services.

Keywords: webservice, RDBMS, Service Search.

1 Introduction

With increase in number of on-line services, a consumer has a large number of choices at hand. Selecting a service from a large number of services is a tough task. Several researchers have addressed the problems on service discovery and have proposed different approaches for search based on IOPE, function name, ontology and semantics. Input and Output based search though precise still limits the choices of a match for fixing a rigid boundary around search space. This is due to hard matching of words in inputs and outputs of matching services. Further, annotating IO with precondition has still narrowed down the search.

Use of ontology to web service matching has introduced soft matching that widens scope of match resulting to choices to a search result. Search strategies including IO, IOPE and ontology are based only on the matching of exposed service to a query. Service composition does not reveal more information about a service like the way it is designed, promoted and restricted itself for use of consumers. For enhanced service description Service Map (SMap)[10] was proposed. SMap is a specification for web services to detail design of a service with different service items and the way these items are packaged to cater to different needs of users. With SMap, a service provider describes a service and also promotions and conditions associated to it.

Further for a service consumer, we propose a query syntax that is expressive to accommodate consumer choices. Processing of such queries results in qualitative search results with alternatives, promotion and conditions associated to each match. Further scalability of the proposed approach is achieved using RDBMS for storage and retrieval of web services.

Here, we would like to point out the fact that SMap specification lies in between OWLS [6] and WSMO [4]. It overcomes the rigidity in OWLS by allowing

C. Hota and P.K. Srimani (Eds.): ICDCIT 2013, LNCS 7753, pp. 535–546, 2013.

providers to specify the way a service is packaged not restricting only to inputs outputs and message sequences. SMap specification has avoided complexity not being ambitious of proposing a genric specification like WSMO. Thus SMap while being leaner remain enough expressive for advantage of both service provider as well as consumers.

The remainder of the paper is organized as follows Section 2 gives an overview of the existing search techniques for web services and motivation of our work, Section 3 briefly gives specification details and syntax for describing service in SMap, Section 4 details on extracting and storing SMap in relational database, section 5 proposes an algorithm for processing an SMap query, Section 6 gives a framework and Section 7 concludes with summary and future work.

2   Related Work

Service discovery has received a lot of attention from researchers with large number of available services. To discover a service it is searched for in a registry by matchmaking, the process of identifying an appropriate service meeting a consumer requirement. As the service is exposed in terms of interface most of the research works in discovering a service focus on matching Input, Output and their data types very few works consider service structure and the way service is packaged. This section gives an overview of service matching approaches categorised into *similarity based* and *pattern based* where the former approach determines the similarity of inputs or outputs based on distance metrics while the later one is based on structure of a service.

In SOA architecture search in UDDI registry was keyword based [7], but this approach was found to be insufficient [2] as user queries may be more precise than by keywords and cannot be captured in very small text fragments in web services. [2] proposed Woogle that supports service discovery for service operations following clustering approach. Matchmaking of input (or output) is determined on obtaining similarity with clustered group of semantically similar parameter names of registered web-service operations. Later ontologies were introduced, [9] proposed a method to compute semantic similarity between services described in OWL-S [6] and request resulting into four degrees of match exact, plug-in, subsumes and fail. This is performed by determining the minimal distance between concepts in the taxonomy tree of its ontology.

To narrow down the search, conditions are specified over IO in OWL-S profiles using SWRL [1]. Here, Input, Output, Precondition and Effect (IOPE) are matched using subsumption, semantic distance and WordNet based scoring, the obtained scores between request and advertisement pairings are used as weights in bipartite graph matching for service discovery.

While a set of services having same IO may differ in their functionalities also certain information services may not have precondition and effect [8] addressed this issue by describing service functionality as a pair of its action and the object of the action. For efficiency and scalability [5] stores service IO information in RDBMS, it pre-computes solutions for web service composition by generating a composition graph from published services and ontology information. For a query specified in IO, semantic web service composition is achieved by performing join operation on tables containing composition graph.

Under *pattern matching* classification [3] proposes a matching approach based on the internal process of services. Where both service internal process and request is modeled as FSM, when two services accept the same language they are said to be matched. For this all possible sequences of both FSM's are obtained as strings and each string of request is compared with all sequences of service. Based on certain distance metrics viz common process count (CPC), longest common substring (LCStr), longest common subsequence (LCSeq) and edit distance (ED) the structural similarity is calculated.

Both IO and function name based searches do not view structural details as well as business options as means to specify services. So that matching a query can be qualitatively rich. For example a restaurant service is packaged with several service items like family dining, party dining and casual dining etc. Along with say party dining it provides additional service items like wifi and music services. Say for family dining it offers promotions of 20% discount with a condition on the minimum number of diners to be booked. In this paper we propose a scheme SMap for specifying services; have shown how services with such specifications can be stored in a RDBMS and can be queried on for a qualitative match to a query of user interests. It's to be noted that service items are to be considered as service-lets but not as service instances. And readers are also urged to consider the SMap specification presented here encompasses only structural details of a service. In our ongoing work we are taking up behavioural specifications of services into SMap. Next section presents proposed SMap specification.

3   Specifying Service in SMAP

The SMap syntax to specify a service is given below in BNF notation, Table. 1 gives details of acronyms used in stated syntax

$WSMap := < ServName > < Asscn > <ItemNd>*$
$<ItemNd> := <ItemD> [< Asscn > | < Op ><ItemNd>]*$
$<ItemD> := <ItemN>[has<FeatureName>[with <FeatureValue>]]$
$< Asscn > := <Func> | < Causal >$
$<Func> := "inc" | "akf"$
$< Causal > := "lst" <PromoCond>$
$< Op > := "and" | "or"$

SMap provides the ways items of a service are sequenced to deliver a service in different ways. Each service item is connected to the other using associations viz.includes(inc), a-kind-of (akf), leads-To (lst) and has-with (hw). We find these associations useful to describe a web service, each SMap is specified by a service provider and is stored in a relational database. For the sake of completeness we will have a brief introduction to SMap [10].

Constructs used for the purpose are characterized to association and combination operators as listed below.

Association Operators

- **Includes(inc):** is an association operator that specifies containments of a service item. i.e the components it has.
- **Is A kind Of (akf):** A service that is similar to a given service.

Table 1. Acronym with their meanings used in BNF notation

Term	Meaning
WSMap	Webservice Service Map
ServName	ServiceName
ItemNd	ItemNode
ItemD	ItemDetail
ItemN	ItemName
Asscn	Association
Func	Function
Op	Operation

- **LeadsTo(lst):** specifies business promotions attached to a service. Availing the service leads to availing some extra services.
- **Has-With(hw):** specifies attributes detailing both functional and qualitative aspects of a service.

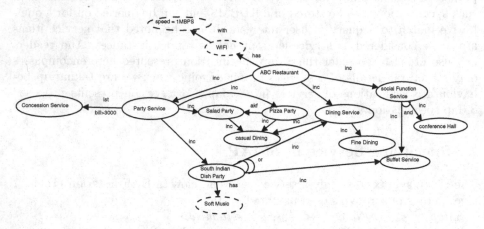

Fig. 1. Concept Map of an ABC Restaurant Service

Combination Operators

- **and :** The items that can be availed collectively but not individually are combined with *and* operator. Sometimes these items become *conditional* to consumer when other service items in combination are not anticipated.
- **or :** An alternative to a given service item is defined by this operator.

An use of these operators in specifying a webservice is stated here. A restaurant offers services packaged with party service, dining service and social function service. Each one of these items is composed of several items in different combinations. It provides WIFI as complimentary and gives discount offers for certain items Figure. 1 presents an SMap of this service with details that are self explanatory.

3.1 Score Assignment

Once a service provider publishes a service as a SMap it is processed to compute preference score (PS). This score aims at guiding the query processor to select a service from a set of possible matches for a given query. A score of a service reflects the richness its SMap contains as alternatives, similarities, to constituent items and limitation as well as promotions defined on them. The score is of importance for variety of reasons, a service with extra features are preferred over services. For example, while a service with similar features and promotions are preferred the ones with limitations are not. The metric PS computes service preference with additive factors P- no. of promotions, A- no. of alternatives and F- no. of features and negative factor C - conditions a service has. Thus PS with respect to total size of SMap N- The number of nodes exist is:

$$PS = \text{P+A+F-C} \; / \; \text{N}$$

PS always results in a rational number between -1 and 1. When number of promotions,alternatives and features are greater than number of conditions it implies service has an advantage of additional characteristics for a service requisite. Else a service with PS<0 has more limitations than opportunities and so is less preferable. During query processing for enhanced result an SMap with the maximum score is selected and processed to identify the requested items. In case not found a service with the next availability of highest PS score is selected for further search. The search continues till a service with all the requested items are found.

4 RDBMS for SMAP

Previous section has discussed service constructs and the specification detail using SMap. This section gives an overview of SMap storage and processing. The SMap is specified diagrammatically using an editor SMapEditor which saves an SMap in xmi(Xml Metadata Interchange) format. This data is processed to identify the relations that exist in a SMap. An ER diagram Figure. 2 presents the types of relations that exist among the SMap entities and their uses in Table. 2 followed by the derived schema of tables.

The major entities in ER diagram for SMapStorage are *SMap* and *ServiceItem*, SMap score is dependent on existence of SMap hence is a weak entity. A service item can include more than one service items, this is shown in the figure as 1 to n *includes* relation from a service item back to itself, schema for Includes table has IncludedItems column that is multivalued similarly AlternativeItem and PromoItem. The number of alternatives, promotions, conditions and features are calculated during xmi conversion and populated in table *SMapScore*.

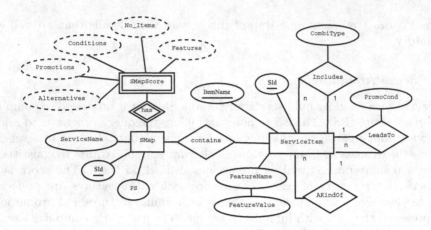

Fig. 2. ER Diagram for SMap Storage

Table 2. Acronym with their meanings used in BNF notation

Symbol	Used For
SId	Unique Identification of a service
ServiceItem	A basic entity of SMap
LeadsTo	Indicates relationship with a promotional item
PromoCond	Condition on a Promotional item
AKindOf	Relationship with an alternative item
Includes	Relates all included items in an item
CombiType	Type of Combination among included Items
FeatureName	An additional attribute of the service
FeatureValue	Quantitative detail of the attribute
PromoItem	An Item offered as a promotion
NO_Items	Number of Items in an SMap
PS	Preference Score
SMapScore	A weak entity containing all derived values(A,P,F,C) from SMap

The schema derived out of ER Diagram is as follows:

ServiceItemDetail :: (<u>SId</u>, <u>ItemName</u>, FeatureName, FeatureValue)

Includes :: (SId, ItemName, IncludedItems, CombiType)

LeadsTo :: (<u>SId</u>, ItemName, PromoItem, PromoCond)

AKindOf :: (<u>SId</u>, ItemName, AlternativeItem)

SMap :: (<u>SId</u>, ServiceName, PS)

SMapScore :: (<u>SId</u>, Alternatives, Promotions, Conditions, No_Items, Features)

5   Querying SMap

A service that is well described but having constraints on syntax in framing a query would limit the results to very few services. This is one of the disadvantages with existing IO search techniques where a consumer has to specify a query in terms of input and output. A naive consumer does not understand and cannot predict input and output, but a service can be described with expected service items. Even if few items are queried for by the user query processing result should direct consumer by revealing more information about a service. For this as stated in introduction an expressive and unbound query syntax based on a predefined structure is proposed for SMap that allows consumer to request for any number of service items following the specified structure and syntax.

GetS withSitem {(<servItem> |(<servItem> **has** <servFeat>)| (<servItem> **has** <servFeat> **with** <featValue>) | **and**|**or**)}
[**withItemDetail** {(<servItem> inc {<servItem>})}]
[**withPromo** {(<promo> **on** <servItem> **with** <servCond>)}]
[**withAltTo**{<servItem>}]

A generic syntax for querying SMap repository is shown above, the advantage of this type of query syntax is it makes search faster and directed as the same associations used in specification are used to connect service items in query.

Also query gives flexibility to consumer in asking for details other than just service constituents by querying withPromo and withAltTo clause. When consumer's choice is inclined towards various promotions offered on a service query '*WithPromo*' is used. If promo item name is known then it is given in <promo>, In order to query for a service with maximum promotions *withPromo maximum* is used. When a queried service is not available a consumer may query for a similar or alternative service this is specified 'withAltTo' keyword.

Format of Resultant Output

On query processing, output of a search query would result in either an atomic or composite service. An atomic service would contain all or some (sub set)of the requested service items in a single SMap and the expected output will be of the format stated below.

Result :=<Serial.NO> <ServName>*"matched"* <matched-items >*"It also contains"* <IncludedItems>*" provides"* <PromotionN> *"offer"* [*on* <promo-cond>] *"with"* <Condition> *"Conditions having"* <Features> [*"has"* [<Alternative-Item>]* *"as an alternative "*]*
<**Alternative-Item**> := <Result>
<**IncludedItems**> := [<ItemN> |"," >]*

For a composite service the requested functionality is achieved on composing the resultant services each matching some of total requested items. Each combination of composed services has a CompositionID thus allowing consumer to select one of them. Obtaining different service compositions would be our future work. The output syntax for composite service is as follows:

Result :=<CompositionID>*"The Service is composed of"* [<ServName> *"service containing"* <IncludedItems>*" providing"* <PromotionN> *offer* [*on* <promo-cond>] *"with"* <Condition> *"Conditions having"* <Features>]*
<**Alternative-Item**> := <Result>
<**IncludedItems**> := [<ItemN> |"," >]*

6   Query Processing

Query processing is an important step in service search and selection. SMap query syntax and processing approach gives enough flexibility to the user to specify requirements in various combinations targeting different goals. A consumer in need of a service has a general idea of what is expected of the service and these are the service items that constitute a service. A consumer specifies a query with required service items following the syntax discussed in Section 5. Initially the query is checked for syntax correctness in preprocessing stage, later query processor executes the query following the steps in algorithm discussed below

Steps in Processing a Query

The following are stages in processing a query initially query is preprocessed for syntax correctness, then query plan is generated and the resultant output is processed for acceptability of user.

1. *Preprocessing:* In this stage the query is parsed and checked for syntax correctness. The query is validated to check if the requested query items are valid in a particular service, later query plan is generated.

2. *Algorithm:*

   The core of algorithm is to identify service paths to reach a service item in a table, path is obtained by performing join operation on a table.

   An SMap query processing algorithm takes consumer query, domain of the query and SMapRepository tables as input and generates an output that gives details of all matched services and the service items they contain along with alternatives, promotions and conditions. Steps followed during query processing are

   Step1 : SMap Selection
   Step2 : Search Service Items
   Step3 : Service Detail:Path identification
   Step4 : Finding Associated Info

   Step1 : SMap Selection
   The algorithm starts with obtaining query items from Query Q. Then selecting an SMap (Step 1) for query processing based on preference and domain using *getSMap(Domain,pref)* which returns SMapID. Here *pref* with least value is most preferred service hence *pref* is initialised to 1 later when the requested items are not found, an SMap with next *pref* value is chosen.

   Step2 : Search Service Items
   The service items and root are obtained using SMapID on creating a view over ServiceItemsDetail table and then the query items are searched in ItemName's column to initialize foundItems array shown in lines:8-10.

   Step3 : Service Detail:Path identification
   When found items are not null then the algorithm proceeds to generate Service Map Table (SMT) joining all the details with includes, akf and leadsto this table SMT contains all the attributes and features of a service item.

Algorithm 1. SMap Query Processing

1: **Input:** ConsumerQuery Q,Domain, SMapRepository (ServiceItemDetail, Includes, LeadsTo, AKindOf, SMapScore);
2: **Output:** ServiceID, MatchedItems, IncludedItems, Alternatives, Promotions and Conditions
3: Array QI[],SD[], matched[]; {QI - Query Items}
4: INT pref=1; String SMapID,CombiItem,root;
5: Table SMT; {SMT - Service Map Table}
6: QI[] = getQueryItems(Q); {Get SMap with maximum PS}
7: SMapID ← getSMap(Domain,pref);   - - - - *STEP 1*
8: root = getRoot(SMapID)
9: SD = getServiceItems(SMapID);
10: foundItems[] = SearchInItems(SD,QI)   - - - - *STEP 2*
11: **if** matched is NULL **then**
12:     Pref ← Pref + 1
13:     Go To Line7
14: **end if**
15: SMT ← ServiceItemDetail $\bowtie_{C1}$ Includes $\bowtie_{C2}$ AKindOf $\bowtie_{C3}$ LeadsTo
    where SId = SMapId   - - - - *STEP 3*
16: Create Tables SP1, SP2 similar to SMT
17: **repeat**
18:     SP2 = SP1 $\bowtie_{SP1.SrcItem=SMT.DestItem}$ SMT   - - - - *STEP 4*
        {computing join result}
19:     where Path ←— SP1.DestItem → SP1.SrcItem → SP2.SrcItem
20:     **if** SP1.CombiType like %and% **then**
21:         CombiItem ← getOtherItem(SP1.SrcItem,and)
22:         **if** If CombiItem not in QI **then**
23:             CombiType ← concat(SP1.DestItem,and,CombiItem)
24:         **else**
25:             Update CombiType traversing along CombiItem
26:         **end if**
27:     **end if**
28:     **if** SP1.CombiType like %or% **then**
29:         CombiItem ← getOtherItem(SP1.SrcItem,or)
30:         **if** CombiItem in QI **then**
31:             CombiType ← concat(SP1.DestItem,or,CombiItem)
32:         **end if**
33:     **end if**
34:     **if** SP1.AltItem ≠ null **then**
35:         AltItem ← concat(SP1.SrcItem,alt,AltItem)
36:     **end if**
37:     **if** SMT.AltItem ≠ null **then**
38:         AltItem ← concat(SMT.SrcItem,alt,AltItem)
39:     **end if**
40:     **if** SMT.FeatureAtt ≠ null **then**
41:         FeatureAttr ← (SMT.FeatureAttr,SP1.FeatureAttr)
42:     **end if**
43:     SP1 ← SP2
44: **until** SP2.SrcItem = root
45: **for** Each item in foundItems[] **do**
46:     search for the item in obtained ServiceDetail
47:     Display Associated info
48: **end for**

This table can also be saved in uddi to reduce query processing time. Next back tracking approach is followed to compute different paths to the root from each destination item of SMap. This is obtained on joining a copy of table SMT (SP1) with SMT the partial result is stored in SP2 temporarily and then copied to SP1 to continue path identification from joined partial result.

Step4 : Finding Associated Info

Various operations that need to be performed during join are listed from line 20- 43. The conditional items are checked and appended to the CombiType attribute of result line 21 -34. Alternative items if exists in path from source to destination path is updated with these items. Additional features if any are added to the result line 41-43. Later SP1 is replaced with SP2 the joined result of tables and then it repeats till the root node is reached. In the next stage output is processed to show consumer with all the matched items along with the segregated details in each path.

7   Framework and Architecture

A framework to process SMap is discussed in this section giving details of modules in architecture and uses of the proposed architecture. The existing UDDI

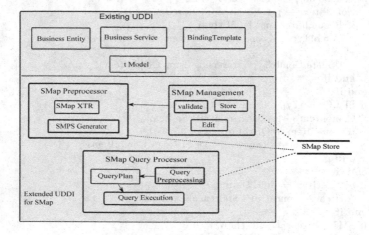

Fig. 3. Architecture Diagram for Publishing and Querying SMap

contains BusinessEntity, BusinessService, BindingTemplate, t-Model to capture the details of service provider and technical details of service. The proposed architecture shown in Figure. 3 is an extension to existing uddi supporting SMap processing. The major components of the architecture are SMapPreprocessor, SMapManagement and SMapQueryProcessor.

We would explain the architecture for publishing and querying SMap using sequence diagram shown in Figure. 4 giving interactions between service provider and SMap Editor, consumer and SMapQueryProcessor. A service provider with service details would create an SMap using Edit module of SMapManagement. It contains modules for creating, editing and storing SMaps. Once service provider creates and publishes an SMap, It is validated by validate module. A valid SMap

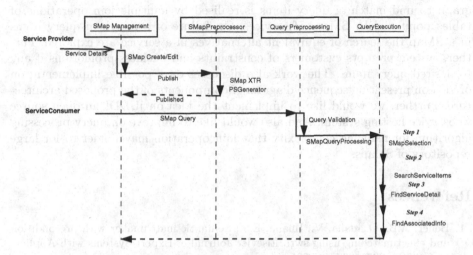

Fig. 4. Sequence Diagram for Publishing and Querying SMap

is in xmi format, SMapXTR component of SMapPreprocessor extracts service details from xmi and populates them in SMapStore of RDBMS. In this process preference score is calculated using PSGenerator module of SMapProcessor, on publishing the control returns back to provider with successfully published message. When a consumer queries with a service requirement, query is preprocessed by QueryPreProcessing module to check for syntax correctness and query type determination. Later control is given to QueryExecution module, which follows the steps discussed in algorithm. For executing a query, initially an SMap is selected for query processing (Step 1) based on PS, In step 2 the service items are searched in the selected SMap for query items if items are found FindServiceDetail is called in step 3, In step 4 associated information of service items are tracked using FindAssociatedInfo. Obtained service results along with details are shown to the consumer for service selection.

8 Conclusion

Webservices, traditionally, are being hosted with reference to their inputs and outputs, further service protocols were also included both for user reference as well as service compositions. The aspects we find missing in present form is of two kinds i.e. inability of a provider in telling about a service that could be useful to customers; and similarly, possibility of users to specify bit more of its requirement. The work reported here specifies a service as SMap that essentially presents structural description of a service placing its constituents, alternatives and promotions at places in a specification in form of a graph. It also presents a means useful to customers to specify queries expressing one's interest. For making the proposal workable as well as scalable we have advocated use of well proven relational database technology for SMap repository. Traversal of a SMap graph to find match of query items is realised by multiple join operations of tables populated by SMaps of services. On failure of a match of query items in a SMap the search of equivalent alternatives in a service are explored. Further, system prompts customers of constraints and business promotions if any to desired query items. The work also discusses on a possible implementation of idea on presenting sequence diagram of components of the proposed architecture. Further, we would like to implement the idea on jUDDI an open source webservice hosting system. And also would like to improve on query processing algorithm for reducing complexity that join operation may render to for large repository of SMaps.

References

1. Bener, A.B., Ozadalia, V., Ilhana, E.S.: Semantic matchmaker with precondition and effect matching using swrl. Elsevier Journal of Expert Systems with Applications 36(5), 9371–9377 (2009)
2. Dong, X., Halevy, A., Madhavan, J., Nemes, E., Zhang, J.: Similarity search for web services. In: Proceedings of the Thirtieth International Conference on Very Large Data Bases, VLDB 2004, vol. 30, pp. 372–383. VLDB Endowment (2004)
3. Günay, A., Yolum, P.: Structural and Semantic Similarity Metrics for Web Service Matchmaking. In: Psaila, G., Wagner, R. (eds.) EC-Web 2007. LNCS, vol. 4655, pp. 129–138. Springer, Heidelberg (2007)
4. D. F. M. H. U. K. e. a. Jos de Bruijn, John Domingue.: Web service modeling ontology, wsmo (June 3, 2005)
5. Lee, D., Kwon, J., Lee, S., Park, S., Hong, B.: Scalable and efficient web services composition based on a relational database. Journal of Systems and Software 84(12), 2139–2155 (2011)
6. B.M.H.J., Martin, D.: Owl-s: Semantic markup for web services (November 22, 2004)
7. U. V. OASIS Uddi spec technical committee draft. Organization for the Advancement of Structured Information Standards, OASIS (2004)
8. Shin, D.-H., Lee, K.-H., Suda, T.: Automated generation of composite web services based on functional semantics. Web Semantics: Science, Services and Agents on the World Wide Web 7(4), 332–343 (2009)
9. Srinivasan, N., Paolucci, M., Sycara, K.: Adding owl-s to uddi, implementation and throughput. In: Proc. 1st Intl. Workshop on Semantic Web Services and Web Process Composition (SWSWPC 2004), pp. 6–9 (2004)
10. Vaddi, S., Mohanty, H., Shyamasundar, R.: Service maps in xml. In: CUBE Conference, pp. 635–640. ACM (2012)

Faster Query Execution for Partitioned RDF Data

Sandeep Vasani[1], Mohit Pandey[2], Minal Bhise[2], and Trupti Padiya[2]

[1] University College London, Grower Street Campus, London, UK
[2] Dhirubhai Ambani Institute of Information and Communication Technology,
Near Indroda Circle, Gandhinagar, Gujarat, India
{sandeep.vasani,mohitpandey31,trupti4u}@gmail.com,
minal_bhise@daiict.ac.in

Abstract. This work demonstrates use of Materialized Views to enhance query performance for partitioned RDF data. Given a query, our system determines which views or combinations thereof can be used to answer it. Break- even analysis for the proposed system has been done based on view materialization and refreshment costs. The system performance was evaluated for 7 query types, 3 having Sub-Obj joins. It shows that our approach reduces query response time by an average of 26% for all query types w.r.t response time using just vertical partitioning. Specifically, for queries with Sub-Obj joins, the average reduction is by 37%. On scaling data up 8 times, the reduction changed from 37% to 79% for queries with Sub-Obj joins, and from 26% to 51% on an average for all query types. With the proposed technique, Semantic Web Applications shall be more interactive since queries having Sub-Obj. joins are expected for them.

Keywords: Materialized Views, Query Execution, RDF Data, Semantic Web Data, Vertical Partitioning.

1 Introduction

The Semantic Web is an effort by the W3C to enable integration and sharing of data across different applications and organizations [2]. Due to its increased application in real world, a tremendous growth in semantic web data is being seen. To maintain this growth and for realizing the semantic web vision, efficient data storage and low query execution time is desired. The Semantic Web data is stored using Resource Description Framework (RDF).

RDF represents data as statements about resources using a graph connecting resource nodes and their property values with labeled arcs representing properties. Syntactically, this graph can be represented using XML syntax (RDF/XML).This is typically the format for RDF data exchange. RDF data is queried using SPARQL. In SPARQL, querying documents is based on tree traversal and simple pattern matching. Structurally, the RDF graph can be parsed into a series of triples, each representing a statement of the form<subject, property, object>. These triples can then be stored in a relational database with a three-column schema. This technique is known as Triple Store. Trend of using RDBMS for storing RDF data has gained momentum [2]. This is because query processing, optimization, and transaction management technologies are well developed for RDBMS.

C. Hota and P.K. Srimani (Eds.): ICDCIT 2013, LNCS 7753, pp. 547–560, 2013.

Triple store representation is simple and flexible but it suffers with performance issue. As there is only a single triple table to store the entire data, complex queries will need multiple joins and will result in poor query execution time. To overcome the issue of triple store, data partitioning technique is used. The two major techniques used are Property Table [7] and Vertical Partitioning [1], [2]. The property table technique de- normalizes RDF tables by physically storing them in a wider, flattened representation more similar to traditional relational schemas. The flattening is based on finding sets of properties that tend to be defined together. In Vertical Partitioning technique, we create a two-column table for each unique property in the RDF dataset. The first column contains subjects that define the property and the second column contains the object values for those subjects. Our system uses the technique of vertical partitioning. To enhance system performance further, we have used materialized views on top of vertical partitioning.

Views are virtual relations that can be used to speed up query processing. To do this, we can pre-compute the view definition and store the result. When the query is posed on the materialized view, the equivalent query is executed directly on the pre-computed result. This approach, called View Materialization is likely to make queries faster.

The main contributions of this paper are: 1) Use of materialized views to further improve query execution time for partitioned data. 2) Analysis of query execution times and data scaling for different query types. 3) Determination of feasibility of the system based on break-even analysis.

This paper is organized as follows. The related work in this area is presented in section 2. In section 3, preliminaries are discussed, followed by section 4 describing the system architecture and experimental setup. Section 5 and 6 contain the result, analysis, and conclusion.

2   Related Work

Techniques of data partitioning and improvements due to them are discussed by D. Abadi [2] and T. Padiya [1]. The property table and vertical partitioning approaches both perform a factor of 2-3 times faster than the triple-store approach [2]. But the limitations of property table like inability to store multi-valued attributes and wastage of storage space due to existence of large number of nulls makes vertical partitioning approach more popular. Halevy discusses the different ways of answering queries using views in [3]. In his work he discusses two techniques for query optimizing: System R approach and Transformational approach. The technique we have used is a hybrid of the two. S. Chaudhuri has worked on using materialized views for optimizing query performance for traditional RDMS [5]. Use of materialized views for semantic web data is not explored yet by others. In our work we have extended S. Chaudhuri's work for Semantic web data.

3 Preliminaries

Inference queries like "suggest friend of a friend" are very common on Semantic Web data. Consider a table called "Triples" which has data regarding friends of a subject. In "suggest friend of a friend" query, we first need to find friends of the subject from the table, and then join this data with the table again to get friend of friend. In general, these queries (e.g., if X is a part of Y and Y is a part of Z then X is a part of Z), are evaluated using Sub–Obj joins. The process can be accelerated by storing the result beforehand in the form of materialized views which avoids self-joins. The main reduction in time by using materialized view based query is because fewer number of tuples need to be traversed and fewer number of join operations need to be performed at runtime. As views have fewer tuples than the base table because they are formed by imposing condition(s) on base table. Also in the views we can store beforehand the join outputs in the form of an attribute.

The proposed system takes input as conjunctive queries. A logical conjunctive query [5] has the form: $Q(X) : R1(X1), \ldots , Rn(Xn)$

Where $Q(X)$ is query's output and R1 . . . Rn are relation names. The atoms $R1(X1) , \ldots , R(Xn)$ are the sub-goals in the body of the query. The atom $Q(X)$ is called the head of the query, and refers to the answer we require. The tuples X, X1, . . . ,Xn contain either variables or constants. Also the system takes as input set of views which are materialized beforehand.

A materialized View V shall be re-written as: $V(X) \rightarrow L(X,Y), I(X)$

Where $L(X,Y)$ is the conjunctive query that defines the view and $I(X)$ is the conjunction of inequality constraints [5]. These one level rules are generated from SQL definition of the views. All materialized views shall be defined as one-level rules.

4 System Architecture

Our system takes in a user query, finds equivalent rewritings for the query, determines the most optimal rewriting, and executes the same. The system architecture is shown in Fig. 1.

There are two inputs to system: RDF data and Query. Section 4.3 discusses the FOAF dataset that we have used. As shown in Fig. 1, first we need to convert the dataset into triple store and then to Vertically Partitioned Data. We need to execute the query for this data. There are two major phases in converting vertically partitioned data based query to equivalent materialized view based query. First, we create equivalent re- writings of the query using materialized views. For this we identify possible ways in which one or more one-level rules can be substituted in place of the query's sub-goals. We have materialized set of views based on the frequent queries that social networks get; view materialization process is further described in Section 4.3. In the second phase, we find the optimal re-writing based on the cost. The cost that we have considered here is total execution time for a rewriting.

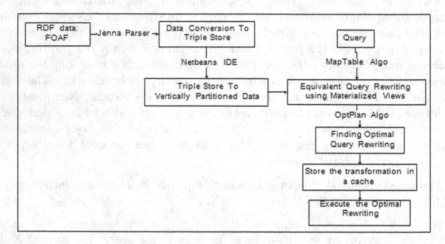

Fig. 1. System Architecture

4.1   Query Re-writing

Using one-level rules we want to derive queries that are equivalent to the given query in the presence of materialized views. The algorithm mentioned in [5] is extended for our system. In [5] the authors have considered dangling inequality selection condition arising due to substitution of materialized view. This is not required in our case. Thus algorithm needs to be modified slightly for partitioned RDF data. In our case the substitution algorithm becomes simpler. Also we have considered the case when no subgoal that syntactically matches the view definition but materialized view substitution is possible.

```
Algorithm MapTable (Q, R) [5]:
Begin
Initialize MapTable
For each rewrite rule r:  V -> L in R do
        For each substitution σ from r to Q do
                MapTable: = MapTable U [L, V, σ]
        EndFor
EndFor
End
```

Fig. 2. Algorithm used for query re-writing

Each substitution results in a new query, equivalent to the given one. We encode the equivalent queries by storing the information about substitutions in the MapTable. MapTable is a table with three columns; Deletelist, Addliteral and Renaming. We record the information about substitution V(X) -> L(X,Y), I(X) as a triple [L, V, σ] stored in the MapTable. The first component "L" denotes the delete-list, list of sub- goals to be deleted from the query. The second component "V" denotes the add-literal, the name of the view to be added in the query. The third component "σ" denotes the re- writing rule used for the substitution. The algorithm to generate the MapTable is given in Fig.2.

The rewritings that we get here are equivalent to the original query as both returns same bag of tuples, when executed over the database. To make the process more efficient, we have associated unique literal-ids with each literal (Relations and Views) and we separately maintain a literal table. Thus the table contains literal-id and not literal as such. The complexity of this algorithm is $O(n^2)$.

To understand the working of our algorithm, consider the following query: "Find the names of friends having email id and homepage". The logical conjunctive query representation is: Query(k,m,h) : Knows("xyz",k) Mbox(k,m) Homepage(k,h) *[here 'k' stands for 'knows', 'm' stands for 'e-mail id' and 'h' stands for 'homepage'.]*

Table 1. Table of Mapping

1	Knows ("xyz", k)
2	Mbox (k, m)
3	Homepage (k ,h)
4	View1(s,k,m,h) -> Knows(s,k) Mbox(k,m) Homepage (k,h)
5	View3(s,k) -> Knows (s,k)
6	View11(s,k,m) -> Knows(s,k) Mbox (k,m)
7	View12(s,k,h) -> Knows(s,k) Homepage(k,h)

Table 2. MapTable

Deletelist	AddLitera	Renaming
1,2,3	4	s = "xyz"
1	5	s = "xyz"
1,2	6	s = "xyz"
1,3	7	s = "xyz"

There are 4 possible equivalent query rewritngs:-
Query"(k,m,h): View1("xyz",k,m,h)
        : View3("xyz",k), Homepage(k,h), Mbox(k,m)
        : View11("xyz",k,m), Homepage(k,h)
        : View12("xyz",k,h), Mbox(k,m)

Now the task is to find the optimal rewritten query.

4.2   Finding the Optimal Re-writing

After getting the equivalent rewritings we need to select the optimal one. Now if there are "n" entries in the MapTable, then there will be "n" rewritings. We consider the optimal rewriting as the one with the least execution time. For finding the optimal rewriting we make use of the bottom-up approach used by traditional Query Optimizer (like System R). The bottom up approach is dynamic programming based. We first find the optimal plan for the single literal in the query and then store its cost. Next optimal plans for possible single join are evaluated and the cost is stored. Then, optimal plans for possible two joins are evaluated by joining literal with single join plan and the cost is stored. Similarly the process is continued for 3 joins, 4 joins and so on. The algorithm that we have used is given in Fig. 3.In the algorithm, "qi" is one of the literals in the query. The complexity for this algorithm is $O(n2^{n-1})$.

```
Algorithm OptPlan (Q) [5]
Begin
If existOptimal (Q) then
        Return CostTable (Q);
bestplan: = a dummy plan with infinite cost
For each qi ε Q
        Let Pi: = Q - qi;
        Temp: = OptPlan (Pi);
        p := Plan for Q from Temp and qi
        If cost(p) < cost(bestplan) then
                bestplan := p
Endfor
CostTable [Q]: = bestplan
Return (bestPlan)
End
```

Fig. 3. Algorithm used for finding optimal re-writing

The system maintains a cache of query transformation (from query for Vertically Partitioned Database to equivalent rewritten query using Materialized Views) so as to make the query processing faster. By this we can avoid the time required to translate the query into equivalent rewriting.

4.3   Experimental Setup

NetBeans IDE, java 1.6 and Postgres 9.1.3 were used as software tools in a system with 2 GB of RAM. Java NetBeans was used to populate data in Postgres. All algorithms were implemented in Java. We chose Postgres as the row-store to experiment with because Beckmann [4] experimentally showed that it was by far more efficient dealing with sparse data than commercial database products. This is because Postgres does not waste space storing NULL data.

DataSet: FOAF [6] dataset from University of Maryland was used as a benchmark for experiment. It contains 406540 triples, 550 distinct predicates and 234 unique properties.

QuerySet: We wanted to check system performance for different query types. Thus we have evaluated query execution time for 7 different types of queries. For each type, we have considered 3 queries making a total of 21 queries. The 7 types of queries are: 1) No Join Queries, 2) Single Join Queries, 3) Multiple Join Queries, 4) Aggregate Queries, 5) Union Queries, 6) Intersection Queries and 7) Nested Queries. Our system explicitly converts Union, Intersection and Nested queries into conjunctive query. Appendix has SQL definition for all the queries that we have used. The queries that we have considered are the one which are frequent for social network.

Vertical Partitioning: FOAF data is in RDF triples format. It was then partitioned vertically. This was done by considering the different properties of the data. Thus, if the data has n distinct properties, the vertically partitioned data will have n number of tables, each table having two columns: Subject and its corresponding Object. In FOAF data, there are 234 unique properties hence we made 234 vertically partitioned tables.

Materializing Views: For view materialization we have created three PL/pgSQL functions: createView, dropView and refreshView. The function createView will see if a materialized view with that name is already created. If so, it raises an exception. Otherwise, it creates a new table from the view. The function dropView destroys the materialized view and function refreshView is called to refresh the materialized views so that the data does not become completely stale. This function only needs the name of the materialized view. It uses a brute-force algorithm that will delete all the rows and reinsert them from the view.

5   Results and Discussion

Hot and Cold runs were taken for query evaluation. For our system, hot run denotes query execution when the query transformation cache has a transformation for the query. Cold run denotes query execution when the cache is empty. Each run was taken multiple times for all the queries, and then the Geometric Mean of the run for each query was considered as its final execution time. We have considered vertically partitioned data's hot run as it is the best performance for vertically partitioned data. We want to compare this best performance with our approaches performances. We have also evaluated query performance for scaled data, i.e. for 813080 triple, 1626160 triple and 3252320 triple.

5.1   Query Execution Time and Analysis

Fig. 4 shows query performance of all the queries for vertically partitioned data's hot run and Materialized view based query's hot and cold run. Fig.4 clearly indicates that in all queries the performance is enhanced when we use materialized views over partitioned data.

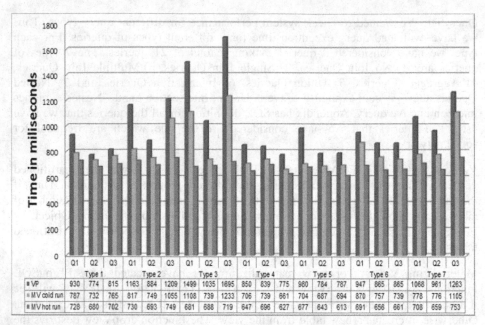

Fig. 4. Query Performance Comparison

Fig. 5 shows the relative gain when materialized views are used in addition to vertical partitioning for all the queries. Fig. 5 clearly indicates that we get an average gain of 15% in case of cold run of Materialized View based query and we get an average gain of 26% in case of hot run of Materialized View based query. We get more gain in case of hot run because of the query transformation cache. Hence the time spent in converting the query is saved.

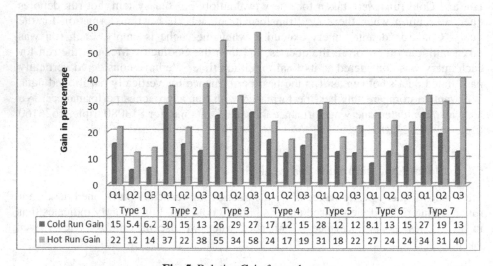

Fig. 5. Relative Gain for each query

Fig. 6 shows the geometric mean of relative gain for each type of queries that we have considered. Fig. 6 clearly indicates that in case of queries without Sub-Obj joins (Type1, 4, 5, 6) relative gain is low. The gain that we get in these queries is because of the fact that by using materialized views we were able to reduce the number of tuples needed to be searched to get the output.

5.2   Breakeven Analysis

The break-even analysis depends on materialized view creation time and total refreshment time which in turn depend on the number of tuples in the relations inferred by the query and the number of join operations needed to be performed. For break-even analysis, we have considered two cases: 1) Hot Run 2) Cold Run. For both these cases, we need to consider the frequency of database updating. Now consider break-even analysis for a query "Suggest a friend of a friend" as follows:-Table 3 mentions the costs involved for break-even analysis for this query.

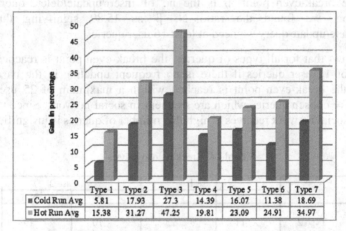

	Type 1	Type 2	Type 3	Type 4	Type 5	Type 6	Type 7
■ Cold Run Avg	5.81	17.93	27.3	14.39	16.07	11.38	18.69
■ Hot Run Avg	15.38	31.27	47.25	19.81	23.09	24.91	34.97

Fig. 6. Relative Gain for each query type

Table 3. Costs for "Suggests Friend of a Friend" query

Materialized View Creation Time (MC)= 2356ms
Materialized View Refreshment Time (MR)=6864ms
Query exec. time for Vertically Partitioned DB (v) = 1163.33ms
Query exec. time for MV based query hot run (h) = 729.62ms
Query exec. Time for MV based query cold run (c) = 817.6ms

Case 1 (Cold Run). In this case the query transformation cache is not maintained.

a) The base tables are not updated frequently: This means that the view creation time can be considered as the biggest cost. The break-even point will be reached when N*v = MC + N*c. Here N is the no. of user queries to be executed to reach the break-even point. Using the values from table 3, the value of N we get is 6.85.

b) The base tables are updated frequently: Here the system will take more time to reach the break-even point as the view refreshment will have to be done frequently and this is costly. The break-even point will be reached when $N*v = \beta*MR + N*c$. Here N is the no. of user queries to be executed to reach the break-even point. β is the no of insert/update/delete queries. After calculation, we found the ratio N: β as 19.96 signifying that for 1 insert/delete/update query we need at least 20 user queries.

Case 2 (Hot Run). In this case the query transformation cache is maintained.

a) The base tables are not updated frequently: The break-even point will be reached when $N*v = MC + N*h$. Here N is the no. of user queries to be executed to reach the break-even point. After calculation, the value of N as 5.45

b) The base tables are updated frequently: The break-even point will be reached when $N*v = \beta*MR + N*h$. Here N is the no. of user queries to be executed to reach the break-even point. β is the no of insert/update/delete queries. After calculation, we found the ratio N: β as 15.89 signifying that for 1 insert/delete/update query we need at least 16 user queries.

Table 4 shows that for all types of queries, the break-even point is reached within a maximum of 11 user queries if there is no frequent updating in the base table(s). Otherwise the break-even point is reached within a maximum of 25 user queries. Now we have chosen queries which are frequent in social network. Since the kind of traffic that social network receives is high this number of queries is insignificant.

Table 4. Breakeven Analysis

	Case 1		Case 2	
	N	N:β	N	N:β
Type 1	11	14	6	7
Type 2	11	25	10	19
Type 3	11	6	6	4
Type 4	9	18	6	13
Type 5	7	16	5	11
Type 6	6	6	4	6
Type 7	13	11	7	5

5.3   Data Scaling

As mentioned earlier, we had scaled the data up to a factor of 8 times in steps of 2. Thereafter we ran the same queries and their execution times were recorded. After that analysis similar to the one as for the un-scaled data were carried out. Fig. 7 shows the gain trend for Materialized Views. In Fig. 7, Voaf4, Vfoaf8, Vfoaf16, Vfoaf32 implies there are 4lac triples, 8lac triples, 16lac triples, and 32lac triples in the database respectively. From the figure we see that on scaling gain increases. It is expected that this trend will continue on further scaling.

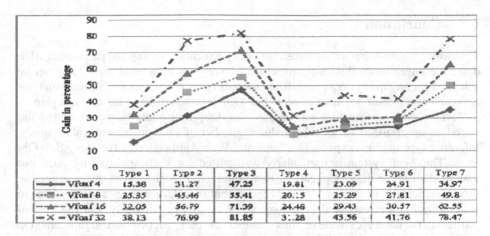

Fig. 7. Gain trends for MV when data is scaled

In particular, we were interested in performance of queries with Sub-Obj joins upon scaling. Fig. 8 shows that for the same increase in data size, gain increases more rapidly for queries with Sub-Obj joins. The gain changed from 37% to 79% for queries with Sub-Obj joins. Thus gain changes by a factor of 2.1 times when data is scaled 8 times. On the other hand, the gain changed from 21% to 33% for queries without Sub-Obj joins. Thus, in this case gain changes by a factor of 1.5 times when data is scaled 8 times.

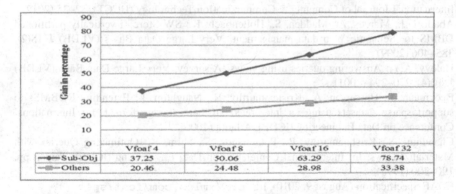

Fig. 8. Gain trends for queries with and without Sub-Obj join upon scaling

In our work, we have considered data scaling only. In our experimentation, Postgres row-store RDBMS was used. In row-stores, complete record needs to be fetched even if a single attribute is required for query answering. This will be slower in comparison to column-stores [8]. In column-stores, each attribute is stored as an individual file. Hence, only a particular file needs to be fetched to answer a query and not the complete record. In future, we would like to extend our experiment using column stores such as MonetDB [9].

6   Conclusion

This work demonstrates enhancement of query execution timing for partitioned RDF data. We have shown that using materialized views, a gain of at least 12% can be achieved for any query. We considered different types of queries and showed that our approach works best for queries with Sub-Obj join which have an average gain of 37%. The better performance was because Sub-Obj joins could be pre-computed and stored as materialized views. This reduces number of joins in the equivalent query. Inference type queries, expected for Semantic Web Applications have many Sub-Obj joins. Thus, our system is particularly well suited for such applications. Also our system shall make these applications more interactive as it reduces query execution time significantly. Break-even analysis shows that the additional costs incurred due to materialization are recovered in an average of 10 user queries only. For the kind of traffic social databases receive, this number of user queries is insignificant. On scaling the data by a factor of 8 times, the gain changes from 37% to 79% over using Vertical Partitioning for queries with Sub-Obj joins. The average change in gain for all queries was from 26% to 51%. Thus, it can be expected that the system shall have excellent results when it is scaled for Big Data. Query performance can further be improved by using column–oriented DBMS such as MonetDB.

References

1. Padiya, T., Ahir, M., Bhise, M., Chaudhary, S.: Data Partitioning for Semantic Web. International Journal of Computer & Communication Technology (IJCCT), 32–35 (2012)
2. Abadi, D.J., Marcus, A., Madden, S., Hollenbach, K.: SW-Store: a vertically partitioned DBMS for Semantic Web data management. Very Large Data Bases (VLDB) J. 18(2), 385–406 (2009)
3. Halevy, A.Y.: Answering queries using views: A survey. Very Large Data Bases(VLDB) J. 10(4), 270–294 (2001)
4. Beckmann, J., Halverson, A., Krishnamurthy, R., Naughton, J.: Extending RDBMSs to support sparse datasets using an interpreted attribute storage format. In: International Conference on Data Engineering (ICDE), Atlanta (2006)
5. Chaudhuri, S., Krishnamurthy, R., Potamianos, S., Shim, K.: Optimizing Queries with Materialized ews. In: International Conference on Data Engineering (ICDE), Taipei, pp. 190–200 (1995)
6. FOAF Specification (August 9, 2010), http://xmlns.com/foaf/spec/
7. Wilkinson, K., Sayers, C., Kuno, H., Reynolds, D.: Efficient RDF storage and retrieval in Jena2. In: Semantic Web Databases (SWDB), Berlin, pp. 131–150 (2003)
8. Abadi, D.J., Madden, S., Hachem, N.: Column-stores vs. row-stores: how different are they really? In: SIGMOD Conference, Vancouver, pp. 967–980 (2008)
9. Monetdb (May 10, 2012), http://www.monetdb.org/Home

Appendix

This is the list of 21(3 queries for each 7 types) queries used for experimentation. The sql syntax for all the queries for vertically partitioned data is given below. "xyz" indicates query fired for that particular subject. Query types are as follow: Type-1 [*No join query*], Type-2 [*Single join query*], Type-3 [*Multiple joins query*], Type-4 [*Aggregate queries*], Type-5 [*Union queries*], Type-6 [*Intersect queries*] and Type-7 [*Nested queries*].

Type 1 (a):find friends of 'xyz'
SELECT k.knows
FROM knows k
WHERE s.subject='xyz'

Type 1 (b): find spouse of 'xyz'
SELECT s.spouseof
FROM spouseof s
WHERE s.subject='xyz'

Type 1 (c): find hobbies of 'xyz'
SELECT i.interest
FROM interest i
WHERE s.subject='xyz'

Type 2 (a):suggest friend of a friend of 'xyz'
SELECT distinct k.subject, k.knows as knows, m.knows as foaf
FROM knows k, knows m

WHERE k.knows=m.subject and k.subject='xyz'

Type 2 (b): find friends of 'xyz' having photos in jpg
SELECT distinct d.subject, d.depiction
FROM knows k, depiction d
WHERE d.subject=k.knows and k.subject='xyz' and d.depiction like '%.jpg'

Type 2 (c): find people having mailbox as 'xyz'
SELECT k.subject, k.knows, m.mbox_sha1sum
FROM knows k, mbox_sha1sum
WHERE k.knows=m.subject and m.mbox_sha1sum = 'xyz'

Type 3 (a): find friends of 'xyz' having e-mail id and homepage
SELECT k.knows, m.mbox_shasum, h.homepage
FROM knows k, mbox_shasum m,homepage
WHERE k.subject='xyz'and k.knows=m.subject and k.knows=h.subject

Type 3 (b): find friends of 'xyz' whose spouse has a homepage
SELECT distinct k.subject, k.knows, s.spouseof, h.homepage
FROM spouseof s, homepage h, knows k
WHERE s.subject=k.knows and h.subject=s.spouseof and k.subject='xyz'

Type 3 (c): find homepage of friend of a friend of 'xyz'
SELECT distinct k knows as friend, m.knows as foaf, h.homepage
FROM knows k, knows m, homepage h
WHERE k.subject='xyz' and k.knows=m.subject and m.knows=h.subject

Type 4 (a): find total number of friends of 'xyz'
SELECT k.subject, count(k.subject) as TotalFriends
 FROM knows k
WHERE k.subject='xyz'
GROUP BY k.subject

Type 4 (b): find the total no. of homepages of 'xyz'
SELECT h.subject, count(h.subject) as HP_count
FROM knhomepage h
WHERE h.subject='xyz'
GROUP BY h.subject

Type 4 (c): find the no. of people having hobby 'xyz'
SELECT i.interest, count(i.interest) as People
FROM interest i
WHERE i.interest='xyz'
GROUP BY i.interest

Type 5 (a): find all friends of 'xyz' and 'abc'
SELECT k.knows
FROM knows k
WHERE s.subject='xyz'
UNION
SELECT k.knows
FROM knows k
WHERE s.subject='abc'

Type 5 (b): find all hobbies of 'xyz' and 'abc'
SELECT i.interest
FROM interest i
WHERE i.subject='xyz'
UNION
SELECT i.interest
FROM interest i
WHERE i.subject='abc'

Type 5 (c): find all homepage of 'xyz' & 'abc'
SELECT h.homepage
FROM homepage h
WHERE h.subject='xyz'
UNION
SELECT h.homepage
FROM homepage h
WHERE h.subject='abc'

Type 6 (a):find mutual friends b/w 'xyz' and'abc'
SELECT k.knows
FROM knows k
WHERE s.subject='xyz'
INTERSECT
SELECT k.knows
FROM knows k
WHERE s.subject='abc'

Type 6 (b): find common interest in one's circle
SELECT i.interest
FROM interest i
WHERE i.subject='xyz'
INTERSECT
SELECT distinct i.interest
FROM interest i, knows k
WHERE i.subject=k.knows and k.subject='abc'

Type 6 (c): find friends who share your birthdate.
SELECT d.dateofbirth
FROM dateofbirth d
WHERE d.subject='xyz'
INTERSECT
SELECT d.dateofbirth
FROM dateofbirth d,knows k
WHERE k.subject='abc' and d.subject=k.knows

Type 7 (a):suggest friend of a friend of 'xyz'

SELECT distinct k.knows
FROM knows k
WHERE k.subject IN
(SELECT m.knows
 FROM knows m
WHERE m.subject ='xyz')

Type 7 (b): find friends of 'xyz' whose spouse has a homepage
SELECT distinct h.homepage
FROM homepage h
WHERE h.subject IN (SELECT s.spouseof
 FROM spouseof s
WHERE s.subject IN
(SELECT k.knows
 FROM knows k
WHERE k.subject='xyz'))

Type 7 (c): find homepage of friend of a friend of 'xyz'

SELECT distinct h.homepage
FROM homepage h
WHERE h.subject IN
(SELECT m.knows
 FROM knows k, knows m
WHERE k.subject='xyz')

A Selection Algorithm for Focused Crawlers Incorporating Semantic Metadata

Saurabh Wadwekar* and Debajyoti Mukhopadhyay

WiDiCoReL Research Lab
Department of Information Technology
Maharashtra Institute of Technology
S. No. 124, Paud Road, Kothrud
Pune 411038, India
{sw.saurabhw,debajyoti.mukhopadhyay}@gmail.com

Abstract. The search results offered currently by majority of search portals are horizontal by nature. This denotes that these search engines intend to index as much web pages as possible and present search results based on these web pages. These results often offer generalized results. Focused Crawlers were built to download web pages relevant only to a pre-specified topic. Searching on these kinds of pages is called as Vertical Search, as it attempts to drill down on a single topic, rather than exploring a plethora of other pages on web which are related to search query in one way or another. In this paper, we propose an algorithm which helps a focused crawler decide whether a web page should be downloaded on not. The selection algorithm proposed in this paper makes use of semantic properties of the content to arrive at a decision.

Keywords: Semantic web, focused crawling, web mining, information retrieval, document vector, ontological domains.

1 Introduction

Crawlers are programs that download web pages from a network (mostly World Wide Web) and index the information present in them for future searches. Crawlers are instrumental in downloading the web page before the search query is fired and keeping the information available at the time of query. In the early stages of WWW, traditional crawlers were able to cover a vast amount of web pages present on the World Wide Web. But now, with exponentially and ever increasing web, it is difficult for crawlers to visit every web page. Also, the numbers of power users who know exactly what they want to search have also increased significantly. Users are aware of the domain in which they want their search results, and want to filter out the results from other unnecessary domains. For providing such kind of search results, a focused crawler is used. A focused crawler downloads only pages which fall within the purview of a pre-defined topic. It reduces the overhead incurred by the crawler to

---

* Corresponding author.

C. Hota and P.K. Srimani (Eds.): ICDCIT 2013, LNCS 7753, pp. 561–572, 2013.

download the pages of domains which are not of current interest. Indexing and searching on web pages indexed by focused crawler is called as vertical search. Traditional focused crawlers have created class taxonomy for defining the classes under which the indexing should be performed. The web pages present in these classes are thus downloaded for future use. In this paper, we have employed semantic metadata as the parameter for evaluating the relevance of a web page. The proposed algorithm decides the inclusion or exclusion of a web page for indexing on the basis of vectors constructed out of semantic metadata.

2   Related Work

Focused crawling has been researched extensively regarding their crawl efficiency, harvest rate and network bandwidth usage. Giles and Tsioutsiouliklis [1] studied the different strategies of focused crawling, and came up with an evolving algorithm which finds links having good authority on the topic. They calculated hubs and authorities, and set the crawl directions based on these pages. Chakrabarti, Van den Berg and Dom[2] designed a focused crawler consisting of a classifier, distiller and a crawler module. The classifier categorizes the web page according to a category taxonomy created beforehand by the system. Relevance of a page is calculated on the basis of hypertext classifier, which induces a hierarchical partition of data set. This often results in categorizing the content in a single taxonomy structure, whereas the content might have information pertaining to different subjects. Ehrig and Maedche[3] went on to use a pre-defined ontology to classify the web-page. This crawler has better harvest rate than taxonomy based crawlers, but relied heavily on the given ontology for analyzing content. Guilherme et al[4] used genres of topics in implementing focused crawl. They analyzed the content of the page, compared it against a single domain, and selected the page if it matched with the specified domain. It had the limitation of defining a topic genre beforehand, and each new crawl needed creation of genres of the topics. An interesting novel approach was used by Almpanidis, Kotropoulos and Pitas [5], where content- and link-based techniques were used for both the classifier and the distiller, resulting in efficient crawls. Pattern matching was successfully employed by Kozanidis [6] in training the crawler to download the web pages having semantic correlation with the pattern. In this paper, we have tried to base the focused crawl based on the semantic data present in the content. Semantic metadata is used for arriving at selection criteria, instead of taxonomy tables and keyword parameters.

3   Problem Description

An algorithm is to be developed which could be easily embedded into the classifier of a focused crawler. The algorithm should clearly demarcate the relevant and irrelevant web-pages from the perspective of the current crawl conditions. The algorithm should work with various combinations of seed URLs to generate uniformly accurate results.

It should also provide leeway for the developer to specify the degree of similarity between the seed URLs and the visited web pages.

4   Proposed System

4.1   Requirements

A system is proposed which uses a basic web crawler implementing the newly developed algorithm. The algorithm used to create semantic vector is developed by Mukhopadhyay and Wadwekar[7], in their ranking algorithm. These vectors represent the multi-dimensional topics present in a document in a clear and concise manner. Any generic document vector is created in following manner -

Generic Semantic Vector Equation

The vectors are constructed on the basis of semantic metadata present in the content of the given web page. All the major domains and the topics present in the document are extracted and are correspondingly converted into vector form, so that they can be used in future for calculations. Any content/text can be logically said to contain these two entities -

1. Ontological Domain - This includes the broad topic in which the content falls. (For eg – Technology, Business Finance, Entertainment etc.). Any document/web-page would contain information of one domain, or at the most two domains.
2. Social Contexts/Topics – These are the main topics which are covered in the content. These topics summarize the crux of the web-page. The terms which are extracted under this head are the actual subject areas which are mentioned in the page.

For extracting these entities from any page/document, the content of the document is first parsed from the web-page, and is sent to a web service (OpenCalais) for semantic metadata extraction. The web service uses natural language processing and machine learning to extract rich semantic metadata from the submitted content. The data from the web service can be retrieved in different formats – RDF or JSON. For example, when an article of 'Abraham Lincoln' is submitted for semantic metadata extraction, the results returned are (Table 1) -

Table 1. Semantic information extracted from a web-page containing article of 'Abraham Lincoln' -

Type	Term
Domain	Politics
Domain	Social Issues
Topic	History of United States
Topic	19th Century in United States

The major ontological domains which were present in the above article were of 'Politics' and 'Social Issues'. These are broad areas which were present in the content. Various topics which must have been mentioned are of 'American Civil War', 'United States Presidential Election', etc.

The vector of any document is represented in the form of:

$$\vec{V} = (a.\vec{d1} + b.\vec{d2} + ... + n.\vec{dn}) + (p.\vec{t1} + q.\vec{t2} + ... + z.\vec{t3})$$
$$= \vec{D} + \vec{T}$$

Where $\vec{d1}, \vec{d2}, \vec{dn}$ are unit vectors of ontological domains and a, b, c are the weights associated with them. $\vec{t1}, \vec{t2}, \vec{tn}$ are unit vectors of topics, and p, q, z are their respective weights. $\vec{D}$ and $\vec{T}$ are simplified generic vectors representing the ontological domain and topic of the concerned document. For example, according to the semantic information extracted in the above table, the semantic vector of the document would be–

$$\vec{D1} = (a.\vec{d1} + b.\vec{d2}) + (p.\vec{t1} + q.\vec{t2} + r.\vec{t3} + s.\vec{t4} + u.\vec{t5} + v.\vec{t6})$$

Where $\vec{d1}$ is unit vector of domain 'Politics', $\vec{d2}$ is unit vector for domain 'Social Issues', $\vec{t1}$ is unit vector for topic 'History of United States' and so on.

The proximity or nearness between any two documents can be calculated by taking the dot product of two documents' vectors:

$$\vec{D1}.\vec{D2}$$

Since any vector has two different entities present in them – domains and topics, the dot product would also yield the result of 'Domain' vector and Topic' vector separately.

$$a.\vec{Domain} + b.\vec{Topic}$$

Domain/Topic Coefficient Calculation

The value of weight coefficient associated with any domain/topic can be calculated using different methods. One method of calculating topic weights is described below. For example,

$$\vec{D1} = (a.\vec{d1} + b.\vec{d2} + ... + n.\vec{dn}) + (s.\vec{t1} + q.\vec{t2} + ... + z.\vec{t3})$$

The value of coefficient 's' can be calculated as:

$$s = \sum (\text{Keywords found in the content which can grouped under } \vec{t1})$$

This type of weight assignment required natural language processing, since the assigning keyword under a particular topic is subjective process, and depends on the context in which the said keyword is used. A keyword, for example 'apple' can be grouped under 'fruit' or 'corporation' depending upon its relative usage in the document.

The weight of a domain coefficient can be calculated as –

$$b= \sum (\text{Topics of } \overrightarrow{d2})$$

Every topic which is extracted from a piece of information can be grouped under a broader ontological domain. The weight of any domain found in a document can simply be calculated by adding the number of that specific domain's topics present in the document. One more way to determine the domain weights can be:

$$a= \sum (\text{Topics coefficients})/ \text{Number of Topics}$$

In above formula, the topics considered are the only ones which fall in the domain, and the topic coefficients are the weights calculated in the previous section. This formula will tend to accurately depict the domain coefficient in cases where the content is heavily based on a single domain. In the simulation described below, the value of coefficients is set as 1 by default.

The weight of topic coefficients can be derived by interpreting the significance of the topic in context to the particular document. This can be determined while semantic metadata extraction is performed.

Centroid and Crawl Radius Creation

Focused crawler requires initial web URLs to initiate the crawl. These URLs are called as seed URLs, and are fed into the crawler manually. These URLs reflect the nature of content the user wants to download from the focused crawler. Focused Crawlers then visit these pages, download their content, and then proceeds to download the web pages from the links found in these seed URLs. In a traditional crawler, the harvest rate of a crawler drops after few thousand visits, as the links contained in these web-pages do not content similar to seed URLs. Also, even if the meaning of the content is similar, the classifier of the focused crawler is not able to recognize it due to lack in keyword matches. Thus, even web-pages with high degree of content match get filtered due to mismatch between the keywords or classes of seed URLs and the web page visited. In this paper, a new algorithm is proposed which compares the semantic meaning of the web-page against a centroid vector constructed from the seed URLs. The centroid construction and crawl radius derivation process is described as follows –

- The crawler will visit the web pages mentioned in the seed URLs and download their content.
- Semantic metadata is extracted from the content of all the seed URLs.
- Domain vectors for all the seed URLs are constructed based on the extracted data.
- Centroid vector of URL vectors is calculated as –

$$\vec{Vc} = f\,(\,\vec{V1},\vec{V2} + \ldots,\vec{VN})$$

where
$f\,(\,\vec{V1},\vec{V2})$ can be simplified as –

$$\left(\tfrac{a+b}{2}\right)\vec{d1} + \left(\tfrac{c+d}{2}\right)\vec{d2} + \ldots + \left(\tfrac{m+n}{2}\right)\vec{dn} + \ldots + \left(\tfrac{y+z}{2}\right)\vec{tn},$$

$$\vec{V1} = (a.\vec{d1} + c.\vec{d2} + \cdots + m.\vec{dn}) + (s.\vec{t1} + q.\vec{t2} + \ldots + y.\vec{tn})$$
$$\text{and,}\;\; \vec{V2} = (b.\vec{d1} + d.\vec{d2} + \cdots + n.\vec{dn}) + (u.\vec{t1} + v.\vec{t2} + \ldots + z.\vec{tn})$$

- Similarly, centroid vector of multiple seed URLs is calculated using the below formula –

$$\vec{Vc} = \left(\tfrac{a1+a2+\cdots+an}{n}\right)\vec{d1} + \ldots + \left(\tfrac{m1+m2+\cdots+mn}{n}\right)\vec{dn} +$$

$$\left(\tfrac{b1+b2+\cdots+bn}{n}\right)\vec{t1} + \ldots + \left(\tfrac{n1+n2+\cdots+n}{n}\right)\vec{tn}$$

where $\vec{d1}$, $\vec{dn}$ are different domains found in the content of seed URLs, and $\vec{t1}$, $\vec{tn}$ are different topics. a1, a2 are the respective domain weight coefficients of domains in their respective vectors.

- If any domain or topic is present in one vector and not present in another vector, then the weight coefficient of vector in which it is absent is taken to be 0.
- This centroid vector, $\vec{Vc}$, is the accurate description of nature of the content present in web pages of all seed URLs.
- For calculating the crawl radius, the distances of the above considered domain vectors are calculated with respect to the newly constructed centroid vector. The distance between any two vector is given by taking their dot products –

$$\text{Dist}\,(\vec{V1},\vec{V2}) = \vec{V1}.\vec{V2}$$

- This would compute a higher degree of proximity for vectors having similar content.
- In the above said manner, distance of all the vectors (constructed from seed URLs) is calculated. Let these distances be (dist)1, (dist)2 ,…., (dist)n.
- Crawl radius is derived from these distances as –

$$\text{Cr} = (\text{dist})\text{max} + \text{Af}$$

where Cr is the crawl radius,
(dist)max is the maximum distance present in the above calculated distance,
Af = Adjustment Factor

- Adjustment factor is initially a user decided value, manually entered in the system, which states the maximum allowed divergence in the selection criteria.
- The crawl radius can be depicted as (Figure 1) –

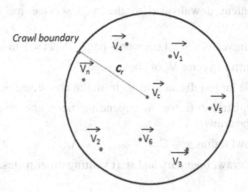

Fig. 1. Crawl radius diagram

Selection Criteria for Downloading a Web Page

The selection criteria for download a web page can be given as –

$$Selection(URLi) = \begin{cases} 1, & dist(Vi, Vc) \leq Cr \\ 0, & dist(Vi, Vc) > Cr \end{cases}$$

Where V_i = Domain vector of content present on URL_i
V_c = Centroid Vector, and
C_r = Crawl Radius

The above formula states that if the distance between the current web page's vector and centroid vector lies within the crawl radius, then the web page is passed on for downloading and indexing. In other words, the crawl radius defines the boundary of focused crawler. All the content lying within the confines of it is selected, and the content present outside it is rejected. This equation, when applied to a focused crawler, finds only the web pages having extreme proximity to seed URLs. This process is analogous to finding a needle in a haystack, eliminating all the irrelevant content to filter out the desired piece of information.

4.2   Theoretical Foundation of Implemented System

A system is designed comprising of the enhanced focused crawler having connectivity with a database. The focused crawler is fed manually with the seed URLs and the crawl is initiated. Crawl radius and centroid vector for the initial set of seed URLs are created, and the rest of the pages present in the links of these pages are visited. The content present in these web pages is then analyzed by creating their vectors, and then comparing its distance with the centroid vector. If the distance falls in the crawl boundary, the web-page URL is selected to be downloaded and indexed. The process employed in the system can be described summarily as –

a.   Feed the seed URLs. - array(URL_i), i = 1 to n, where n is the last seed URL.

b.   Visit and download the content present in each URLs.

   c.   Pass the content downloaded to the web service for domain and topic extraction.

   d.   Create domain vectors of all the web – pages. V_i, i = 1 to n.

   e.   Calculate centroid vector V_c of above vectors.

   f.   Determine the largest distance of V_c from the above vectors – $dist_{(largest)}$

   g.   Compute adjustment factor A_f depending upon the rigidity of proximity required in the crawl

   h.   Calculate crawl radius as – $C_r = dist_{(largest)} + A_f$

   i.   Establish the crawl boundary and start visiting other pages.

5   Experimental Results

The developed algorithm is implemented and run with two different set of URLs, and result generated is analyzed. As mentioned earlier, the crawl is restricted to Wikipedia web pages, due to their well-structured nature (making it easier to extract metadata). The seed URLs for the first crawl are pages having content related to computer programming. The seed URLs are articles having content of following topics (Table 2) -

Table 2. Seed URLs – Set 1

Seed URL article headings
AMOS (Programming language)
Computer programming
B (Programming language)
Fourth generation programming languages

The centroid vector of the above mentioned seed URLs is the mean of all the vectors of their contents. Some of the unit vectors in the centroid for this particular case (Table 3) –

Table 3. Some unit vectors present in centroid vector

Type	Unit Vector
Domain	Technology Internet
Topic	Curly bracket programming languages
Topic	Programming paradigms
Topic	Procedural programming languages

For the above centroid vector and the seed URLs, crawl radius is computed and crawl boundary is computed. The adjustment factor, A_f, for the current scenario is very less, to the keep the crawl rigidly in intended domains. Around 15000 web pages are crawled, and the links are searched which fall under crawl boundary. The number of results returned after the crawl are 40 web links. As the adjustment factor was set extremely less, the algorithm selected only 40 web pages out of 15000 web pages. These 40 web pages are extremely similar in content to the initial seed URL content. Topics of some of the links selected are –

Table 4. Pages selected by focused crawler – Set 1

Seed URL article headings
BASIC
BCPL
Computing
Computer program
Computer science

These topics have been selected after algorithm is implemented on a focused crawler for given set of seed URLs. It can be observed that links containing content about programming languages such as BASIC and BCPL were selected as the seed URLs covered content of many programming languages. Also, Turbo Pascal was selected, which is an IDE for Pascal. The number of pages selected by the focused crawler versus number of pages visited is skewed in nature. The graph, when plotted is as (Figure 3) –

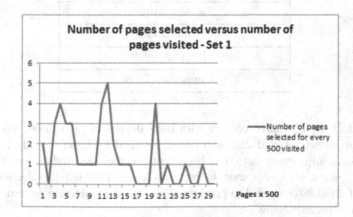

Fig. 2. Set 1 graph - Graph of pages selected vs. pages visited

The graph shows that the crawler picked up pages in skewed manner. It initially picked up around 4 pages per 500 visited, then its rate dropped to around 1 page per 500 visited.

To demonstrate that the algorithm works well with all set of seed URLs, a different set was selected to be fed into the crawler. Second set of seed URLs consisted were –

Table 5. Seed URLs - Set 2

Seed URL article headings
Religion and mythology
Sermon on the mount
Last supper
Bible

This set of seed URLs was purposefully selected to be different from previous set, which was related to technology. The crawl is initiated with these seed URLs, and the Adjustment Factor, A_f, in crawl radius is made large to allow flexibility during crawl. This would allow the crawl the focused crawler to digress a little from the centroid vector, and select pages with greater distances as well. The pages selected by the focused crawler from this set of seed URLs are –

Table 6. Pages selected by focused crawler - Set 2

Seed URL article headings
Afterlife
Abraham
Ambrosians
Book of Jonah
Council of Trent

The selected pages have content with high degree of proximity with the initial URLs. This crawl selected 255 web pages for seed URL set relating to 'religion' domain. Since adjustment factor had been kept lax, the crawl radius computed in this case was greater than computed in previous case. This led to selection of more number of articles (compared to previous 40). The page selection pattern by focused crawler in this scenario was –

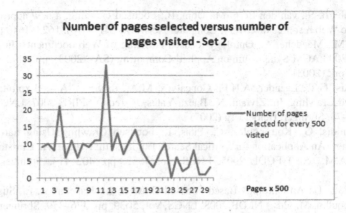

Fig. 3. Set 2 graph - Graph of pages selected vs. pages visited

6   Conclusion

In this paper, we have designed an algorithm which would evaluate the relevance of a web page visited by a focused web crawler. The selection criterion returns a measure which could be used to decide whether the content of web page is worth downloading in context to seed URLs. Crawls are performed using different sets of seed URLs, and it is observed that pages with extremely high relevance are selected. The algorithm has the ability to locate resources with exact level of desired similarity. It can be effortlessly integrated into the classifier of a focused crawler to yield perfect results. In future work, we intend to include web pages from various URL domains, apart from Wikipedia pages. A tunneling focused crawling strategy [8] can be implemented which evaluates the current crawl direction dynamically and prunes specific paths from time to time. The algorithm can also be modified to search only for SWD (Semantic Web documents), which would lead to better semantic metadata extraction. This approach was explored in project Swoogle, by Ding et al [9]. Finally, semantic metadata extraction works best when a comprehensive semantic ontology is present. Hence, efforts can carried out to keep the ontology ever evolving to yield accurate results with changing time. [10]

Acknowledgements. We would like to thank the OpenCalais Web Service for providing the web service for semantic metadata extraction. Also, we are thankful to Crawler4j, an open source focused crawler on which the algorithm was implemented. We also extend our gratitude to WIDiCoReL research lab for providing the required support.

References

1. Johnson, J., Tsioutsiouliklis, K., Giles, C.L.: Evolving Strategies for Focused Web Crawling. In: Machine Learning–International Conference, vol. 20, Part 1, pp. 298–305 (2003)

2. Chakrabarti, S., van den Berg, M., Dom, B.: Focused crawling: a new approach to topic-specific Web resource discovery. Computer Networks 31(11-16), 1623–1640 (1999)
3. Ehrig, M., Maedche, A.: Ontology-focused crawling of Web documents. In: Proceedings of the 2003 ACM Symposium on Applied Computing (SAC 2003), pp. 1174–1178. ACM, New York (2003)
4. de Assis, G.T., Laender, A.H.F., Gonçalves, M.A., da Silva, A.S.: Exploiting Genre in Focused Crawling. In: Ziviani, N., Baeza-Yates, R. (eds.) SPIRE 2007. LNCS, vol. 4726, pp. 62–73. Springer, Heidelberg (2007)
5. Almpanidis, G., Kotropoulos, C., Pitas, I.: Focused Crawling Using Latent Semantic Indexing - An Application for Vertical Search Engines. In: Rauber, A., Christodoulakis, S., Tjoa, A.M. (eds.) ECDL 2005. LNCS, vol. 3652, pp. 402–413. Springer, Heidelberg (2005)
6. Kozanidis, L.: An Ontology-Based Focused Crawler. In: Kapetanios, E., Sugumaran, V., Spiliopoulou, M. (eds.) NLDB 2008. LNCS, vol. 5039, pp. 376–379. Springer, Heidelberg (2008)
7. Wadwekar, S., Mukhopadhyay, D.: A Ranking Algorithm integrating Vector Space Model with Semantic Metadata. In: CUBE 2012 Proceedings, Pune, India, September 3-5, pp. 623–628. ACM Digital Library, USA (2012)
8. Bergmark, D., Lagoze, C., Sbityakov, A.: Focused Crawls, Tunneling, and Digital Libraries. In: Agosti, M., Thanos, C. (eds.) ECDL 2002. LNCS, vol. 2458, pp. 91–106. Springer, Heidelberg (2002)
9. Ding, L., Finin, T., Joshi, A., Pan, R., Scott Cost, R., Peng, Y., Reddivari, P., Doshi, V., Sachs, J.: Swoogle: a search and metadata engine for the semantic web. In: Proceedings of the Thirteenth ACM International Conference on Information and Knowledge Management (CIKM 2004), pp. 652–659. ACM, New York (2004)
10. Flouris, G., Plexousakis, D., Antoniou, G.: Evolving Ontology Evolution. In: Wiedermann, J., Tel, G., Pokorný, J., Bieliková, M., Štuller, J. (eds.) SOFSEM 2006. LNCS, vol. 3831, pp. 14–29. Springer, Heidelberg (2006)

Author Index

Adusumalli, Sri Krishna   488
Agrawal, Pragya   92
Aman, Bogdan   432
Arasanal, Rajashekhar M.   115
Asrar Ahmed, Mohammed   103

Balasundaram, S.R.   455
Barua, Gautam   511
Basu, Prasenjit   126
Behera, Ajit Kumar   183
Bhatta, Bijaya Kishor   137
Bhattacharya, Suman   126
Bhise, Minal   547
Borah, Himangshu Ranjan   145
Bordoloi, Himkalyan   145

Chaki, Nabendu   255
Ciobanu, Gabriel   432
Cortesi, Agostino   157

Daca, Bartłomiej   278
Das, Gautam K.   92
Das, Rajib K.   232
Das, Smita   465
Dash, Ch. Sanjeev Kumar   183
Datta, Anwitaman   47
Datta, Suparno   195
Datta Banik, Abhijit   208
Dattagupta, Rana   476
De, Suddhasil   220
Dehuri, Satchidananda   183
Dian, S. Moses   347
D'Souza, Meenakshi   171
Dutta, Anushua   232
Dutta, Ayan   195

Fahrnberger, Günter   244
Feinerman, Ofer   1

Gan Chaudhuri, Sruti   195
Geetha, V.   523
Ghosh, Ammlan   255
Goswami, Diganta   220
Gupta, Amit   386
Gupta, Suneet K.   267

Halder, Raju   157
Hota, Chittaranjan   373

Jaiswal, Dibyanshu   290
Jana, Prasanta K.   267
Jetley, Raoul   69
Jinwala, Devesh   420

Kakadiya, Bhavesh   373
Kanhere, Salil S.   19
Khan, Khaleel Ur Rahman   103
Khatua, Sunirmal   232
Khilar, Pabitra Mohan   410
Knapik, Teodor   171
Korman, Amos   1
Krawczyk, Henryk   278
Krishna, Shankara Narayanan   432
Kuila, Pratyay   267

Mandal, Partha Sarathi   334
Mistry, Sujoy   290
Mohanty, Hrushikesha   302, 319, 535
Mohapatra, Durga Prasad   444
Mondal, Kaushik   334
Mukherjee, Arijit   290
Mukherjee, Nandini   290
Mukhopadhyay, Debajyoti   476, 561
Mukhopadhyaya, Krishnendu   195

Nandi, Sukumar   220
Nayak, Deveeshree   361
Nunia, Vikram   373
Nurminen, Jukka K.   27

Oggier, Frédérique   47

Padiya, Trupti   547
Padmanabh, Kumar   386
Pamies-Juarez, Lluis   47
Panda, Bhawani S.   398
Panda, Sanjaya Kumar   410
Pandey, Mohit   547
Pandia, Manoj Kumar   183
Patel, Sankita   420
Patel, Viren   420
Proficz, Jerzy   278

Rajarajan, Muttukrishnan   373
Ramadoss, B.   347
Ramaswamy, Srini   69, 361
Roy, Samir   126
Roy, Sharmistha   465
Rumani, Daanish U.   115

Sahu, Madhusmita   444
Samanta, Sujit K.   208
Sampath, R.   69
Sarkar, Ruman   465
Shetty, D. Pushparaj   137, 398
Sinha, Bhabani P.   334
Sinha, Purnendu   386
Sinha, Sukanta   476
Sreenath, N.   523

Sudarsan, Sithu   69
Swamy, M. Venkata   361
Szymański, Julian   500

Talwar, Arjun   334
Tandon, Ravi   511
Thakkar, Kunjal   232

Vaddi, Supriya   535
Valli Kumari, V.   488
Vasani, Sandeep   547
Vijayan, A. Santhana   455
Virani, Sagar   290

Wadwekar, Saurabh   561